By the Hills Embraced:

A Social And Cultural History Of Hangzhou, China

Stephen L. Koss

China Books, Inc.
San Franciso

Published in the United States of America by
Sinomedia International Group
China Books
360 Swift Ave., Suite 48
South San Francisco, CA 94080
www.chinabooks.com

-CR-

ISBN 978-0-8351-0321-3

Printed in the USA

10 987654321

Book design: Beijing Weinuo Studio
Cover art: Yang Mingyi, *On the West Lake*

There is no scenic site
Like Hangzhou in the world;
The city embraced by green hills
And the country dreams with lovely lake;
The dwellings surrounded by
Endless lotus blooming; and
A city by the pine forest
Half hidden from the eye! [1]

– Bai Juyi 白居易 (772- 846)

It is better to appreciate West Lake on rainy days than on sunny days, on moonlit nights than on rainy days, and on snowy days than on moonlit nights. [2]

– Wang Keyu 汪砢玉 (b. 1587)

I am sure that the proud citizens of this province would say that Peking is the head of China, but Hangchow is the heart of China. [3]

– Formal toast offered by
President Richard Nixon at
a State Dinner in Hangzhou,
February 26, 1972

CONTENTS

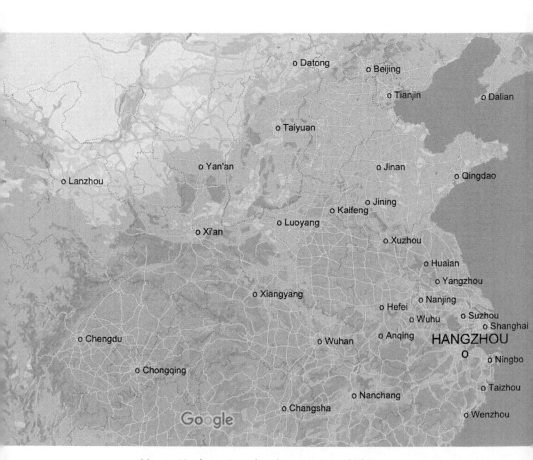

Map 1 – Northern, Central, and Eastern-Coastal China

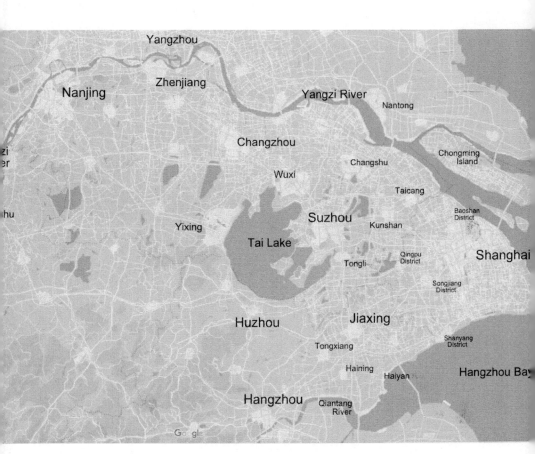

Map 2 – Jiangnan (primarily lower Jiangsu Province and upper Zhejiang Province, between the Yangzi and Qiantang Rivers)

Huzhou o   o Nanxun

o Jiaxing

o Anji   o Tongxiang o Zhapu
          o Deqing   o Haiyan   Hang
                    o Haining   Ba
Hangzhou

o
o Lin'an   o Xiaoshan   o Cixi

o Fuyang   o   o Yuyao
          Shaoxing

o Tonglu
          o Zhuji   Ning
o Huangshan
City
(Anhui Province)

o Jiande   o Pujiang

          o Yiwu

o Lanxi

o Jinhua

Quzhou o   Google
          o Yongkang

Map data ©2021   10 mi

Map 3 – Greater Hangzhou region

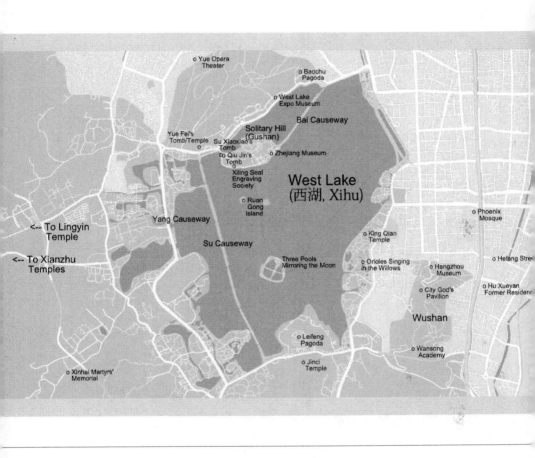

Map 4 – Greater West Lake area

INTRODUCTION

Hangzhou without West Lake is like a man without eyebrows and eyes.
How could a man be without them? [1]

Su Shi (1037 – 1101)

When Chairman Mao Zedong welcomed President Richard Nixon to China in February 1972 to cement formal diplomatic ties between their two nations, the Americans arrived in Beijing and departed a week later from Shanghai. In between, a scheduled "day off" for sightseeing called for the President and First Lady to join Premier Zhou Enlai in the city of Hangzhou. As part of the opening diplomatic move toward rapprochement between two of the world's great powers, Hangzhou was presented to Nixon, and to the accompanying American press, as China's cultural and scenic centerpiece. In a speech that same evening, Nixon described Beijing and Hangzhou, respectively, as the "head" and the "heart" of China (see full quote in the Epigram).

This elevated esteem for Hangzhou was hardly new.

- When barbarian invaders overran northern China and its capital (at that time, Kaifeng) in 1127, the only surviving member of the Song imperial family reestablished the Dynasty further south—and chose Hangzhou as the site of a "temporary" new capital for the next 150 years.

- After returning to Venice in the 1290s, Marco Polo described Hangzhou as "beyond dispute, the finest and the noblest city in the world." [2] It was almost certainly the richest and most populous city in the world at that time.

- When the Kangxi Emperor began his series of grand Southern Inspection Tours, he extended his journeys to include Hangzhou as his southernmost stop in the last five of his expeditions after failing to do so on his first one.

10

- When Kangxi's grandson, the Qianlong Emperor, conducted his own series of inspection tours between 1750 and 1785, he made Hangzhou the last southbound stop in all six of his southern sojourns. Shanghai at this relatively late date was still little more than a flourishing market town, not even the capital of its own district.[3]

- When in 1929 post-imperial China first sought to display its domestic industry and welcome foreign businessmen via industrial exhibition, Hangzhou was selected to host the nation's first such international event, known as the West Lake Exposition.

- After Mao Zedong as Chairman of the People's Republic first visited Hangzhou in late 1953 for a one-month stop that became a three-month stay, he returned to the city dozens of times and declared it his third home.

- When China was chosen to host its first-ever G20 Meeting in 2016, Hangzhou served as the host city for representatives of the world's great industrial economies.

- Hangzhou was chosen as China's host city for the 2022 Asian Games.

Hangzhou occupies its own special place in Chinese history and culture, yet the city remains largely unknown or underappreciated in the West. Among the Chinese people themselves, however, Hangzhou persists to the present day as one of the nation's most cherished cities and among its most popular tourist destinations.[4] The twenty-one chapters following this Introduction explain why. In addition, they provide valuable background for visitors, residents, and those interested in understanding China to appreciate one of the world's great cities and its vital place in Chinese history and culture.

Where Is Hangzhou?

To begin with, "Hangzhou" in Chinese looks like this:

杭州

and it is sounds phonetically like this:

hǒng-jōe.

In the modern version of the English transliteration system known as *pinyin*, the city name is spelled Hangzhou, as opposed to the pre-1980s spelling Hangchow. To achieve the correct Mandarin Chinese pronunciation, one would follow the pronunciation tones in the following *pinyin* representation (rising tone, then level high tone):

The city of Hangzhou is located near the east-central coast of China, at a latitude (30.27° N) roughly equivalent to that of Chengdu (Sichuan Province), Basrah (Iraq), Cairo (Egypt), or in the United States, Jacksonville, Baton Rouge, and Austin. The city is easily located on a map of China's eastern coast, positioned beyond the narrow, curving, inner end of the funnel-shaped bay (Hangzhou Bay) formed by the Shanghai peninsula to the north and the Ningbo peninsula on the south.

Hangzhou also serves as the lower vertex of a lopsided, east-leaning triangle formed with it by the cities of Suzhou (about seventy-five miles north-northeast) and Shanghai (105 – 110 miles northeast). Extending this triangular area eastward to the Pacific coast, northward to the Yangzi River, and northwestward beyond Lake Tai as far as Nanjing encompasses the area commonly referred to as Jiangnan 江南. Translated simply as "south (南 *nan*) of the [Yangzi] river (江 *jiang*)," Jiangnan includes most of the Yangzi River Delta plain: all of the southern section of Jiangsu Province, Shanghai Municipality, and most of Zhejiang Province north of the Qiantang River.[5]

During much of the later imperial era, Jiangnan was the national center of agricultural productivity, wealth, commerce, scholarship, fashion, fine crafts, and the arts. The region was hailed as "the land of rice and fish" and celebrated by the adage "Up above there is Heaven; here below there are Suzhou and Hangzhou" (上有天堂,下有苏杭, *Shang you tiantang, xia you Su Hang.*)

For the last thousand years, Hangzhou has been the capital of Zhejiang Province, the name taken from Zhe Jiang (浙江, "crooked river"), the former name of today's Qiantang River. Zhejiang is bordered on the north by the Yangzi Delta plain of southern Jiangsu Province, on the south by Fujian Province, and on the west by Anhui and Jiangxi Provinces. Encompassing only 39,300 square miles, Zhejiang is one of the geographically smallest provinces in China, roughly equal in size to the state of Kentucky (40,409 square miles) in the United States.[6] Yet where Kentucky had a 2020 reported population of 4.5 million, Zhejiang's population that same year was more than an order of magnitude greater, 64.6 million. In fact, Hangzhou's 2019 urban district population alone, 5.36 million, exceeded by nearly a million that of the entire state of Kentucky.

Although seventy percent of its land area is mountainous, Zhejiang is nevertheless a modern economic powerhouse. For the past two decades, the province has ranked fourth in China in Gross Domestic Product.[7] Zhejiang's GDP in 2020 of 6.46 trillion RMB, or one trillion US dollars, was only exceeded by the GDPs of California, Texas, New York, and Florida among American states.[8] Hangzhou City's GDP in 2020 ranked eighth among all Chinese cities with full-year GDP of 1.611 trillion Chinese RMB (about $245 billion US dollars),[9] exceeding by itself the comparable figure for twenty-four American states.[10]

Zhejiang Province extends modestly north beyond Hangzhou into the richly fertile Yangzi delta plain, with the cities of Jiaxing and Huzhou serving as (sub-provincial) prefectural capitals in their respective areas. Across the Qiantang River to the southeast is the prefectural capital Shaoxing, while the cities of Jinhua and Quzhou occupy similar administrative positions to the southwest through the Qiantang River tributary network. Collectively, these cities and their sub-districts have for centuries formed a satellite network with Hangzhou as their gravitational center. Along with the cities of Ningbo, Wenzhou, and Taizhou along the eastern coast, they represent the majority of Zhejiang Province's population and economic activity.

Hangzhou's urban/suburban footprint has expanded substantially since 1995 and now includes districts that were once separate cities and counties on either side of the Qiantang River. The central urban area now consists of four districts:

- Shangcheng, which includes the area once circumscribed by the ancient city walls;
- Gongshu, to the north of the ancient city;
- Xihu, to the west and southwest; and
- Binjiang, across the Qiantang River to the south.

In addition, Hangzhou's direct administrative (prefectural) area currently includes six suburban districts (Xiaoshan, Yuhang, Linping, Qiantang, Fuyang, and Lin'an) as well as two more distant counties to the southwest (Tonglu and Jiande) and a county-level city district (Jiande).

West Lake

When we speak of the city of Hangzhou, we speak, explicitly or otherwise, of West Lake. In Chinese, 西湖 Xihu, pronounced "shee-hoo." The city and its lake are inextricably bound to one another in physical fact, historical evolution, and poetic imagination, like Paris with the Seine, London with the Thames, or Venice with its canals. And when we speak of West Lake, we speak of many things: scenic beauty, cultural mythology, Buddhist temples and pagodas, classical poems and paintings, traditional literati culture, historical events, and famous persons from emperors to military and revolutionary heroes to extraordinary commoners. A traditional Chinese saying, likely no longer geographically accurate, declares: "There are thirty-six West Lakes in China." Practically speaking, there is only one West Lake, and a number of other lakes that happen to have the same name.[11]

By world geographic standards, West Lake is little more than a pond. Occupying 1,580 acres, or about 6.4 square kilometers (2.47 square miles), West Lake would have to be multiplied nearly seven hundred times over to match the physical extent of Lake Poyang, China's largest freshwater lake, or more than nine thousand times to match Lake Michigan. Nor at an average depth of 7.4 feet (2.27 meters) does the lake particularly impress by its carrying capacity. West Lake has never been celebrated for its physical measurements, however. Rather, the aura of West Lake emanates from its embodiment of a harmonious relationship between Man and Nature, amplified and valorized by centuries of artistic and literary imagination.

Modern visitors to West Lake perceive the Man/Nature interaction in the immediately and readily visible: the dikes, bridges, roadways, temples, pagodas, and even the artificial mid-lake islands. Less obvious and rarely understood is the fact that the lake itself is effectively man-made. Without constant human intervention, most especially dredging and reclamation of poached land, West Lake would likely have disappeared multiple centuries ago. Nature formed the lagoon that became the lake, but only the water-dependent presence of Hangzhou city and repeated restoration and preservation projects prevented Nature from taking it back. The precariousness of West Lake's pre-modern existence should become clear in the chapters to follow.

Hangzhou without West Lake and its enfolding hills nevertheless seems inconceivable. It would be an entirely different city, and it would occupy an entirely different (and certainly lesser) place in the minds and hearts of the Chinese people. The history of West Lake is deeply intertwined with the history of the city, and together they occupy a significant place in China's history, both imperial and modern. One can safely say that it is impossible to understand the scenic and cultural allure of Hangzhou to the Chinese people without knowing the story of West Lake.

The reverse is true as well. Appreciating fully the significance of West Lake requires some awareness of Hangzhou's (and China's) history. As a way of emphasizing their duality, each of this book's twenty-one chapters begins with an ancient poem or short prose piece, the majority of them literary celebrations of West Lake over the ages.

Contents of the Book

While *By the Hills Embraced* encompasses some seven thousand years of Chinese history and proceeds chronologically, it is by design not a history in the classical sense. Interspersed with historical events emanating from or relevant to the Hangzhou area are the stories of individual persons—some renowned, others perhaps little known— each of whom contributed in some way to significant events or to the development and evolution of Chinese culture. It is their work and their lives, whether remembered, little known, or forgotten, that is celebrated by the millions of Chinese people who visit Hangzhou and West Lake every year.

The story of Hangzhou has, from earliest time, been heavily influenced by lake, river, and tide. **Chapter 1 – The Age of Water** begins with the story of Yu the Great, the semi-mythical king who "tamed the waters" for the Chinese nation. The discussion then proceeds chronologically backwards to the Liangzhu and Hemudu Neolithic cultures that developed in northern Zhejiang 5,000 – 7,000 years ago. Their discoveries in the mid-20th Century prompted radical scholarly revisions concerning the ancient sources of Chinese civilization. Chapter 1 closes by introducing the two bodies of water that have dominated Hangzhou's and the region's history—the Qiantang River and West Lake—along with the world-famous tidal bore that for centuries ravaged the Hangzhou Bay and Qiantang River shorelines, simultaneously fascinating and terrifying observers and occasionally inundating the nearby towns and countryside.

The 6th Century BCE saw the emergence of two powerful new southeastern coastal states, Wu and Yue, who contended for power with each other and with the already well-established feudal states in the north. **Chapter 2 – Southern States Emerge** traces the Wu-Yue conflict, some of it apocryphal but nearly all of it integral in the development of local cultural identity and the associated mythologies of heroes and villains, warriors and beauties. To the present day, vestiges of the Wu (in Jiangsu Province) and Yue (in Zhejiang) identities remain relevant in many cultural arenas and are a common source of historical reference and allusion. Names like Goujian, Fan Li, Xi Shi, Helü, Fuchai, and Wu Zixu are as familiar among Chinese people as are Caesar, Brutus, Marc Antony, and Cleopatra to Westerners.

Hangzhou was little more than a riverside village settlement in the first five centuries of the Common Era. For most of that time, the city's present-day location remained submerged beneath the flows and tides of the Qiantang River. Consequently, **Chapter 3 – Union and Disunion** focuses primarily on persons and events in the Shaoxing area, center of the earlier Yue State. The poor but persevering woodcutter Zhu Maichen loses a wife, rises to a governorship, and creates a moralistic legend. A local government official (Hua Xin) attempts to tame the Qiantang River tidal bore, and the filial daughter Cao E sacrifices her life to recover her father's drowned body. The fictional young couple Liang Shanbo and Zhu Yingtai, separated by social custom, can only see their love requited by death and transformation into a pair of butterflies. A traveling monk named Huili brings Buddhism (and a monkey) to the shores of West Lake and founds Hangzhou's most famous temple. Chapter 3 closes with two literary introductions: the poetess Su Xiaoxiao and the story of China's arguably greatest single work of calligraphy at the hand (and brush) of Wang Xizhi, the "Father of Chinese Calligraphy."

The city of Hangzhou makes its first substantive appearance in **Chapter 4 – Wells, Walls, and Water for Tea**, beginning with establishment of its first defensive walls in 591 and the decisions of Sui Emperors Wendi and Yangdi to create a great canal network linking Hangzhou in the south to the capital of Kaifeng in the north. Water plays a significant role in this chapter, from construction of the Grand Canal and directing fresh water into the city's Six Wells to Bai Juyi's preservation and management of West Lake and Lu Yu's classic codification of tea culture. Through the first seventy years of the 10th Century, three generations of the Qian family guided Hangzhou and the rest of Jiangnan safely through the politically precarious period between the fall of the Tang Dynasty and the founding of the Song Dynasty. The Qian rulers also left enduring marks on the scenery and culture of West Lake.

Chapter 5 – Song of the North and **Chapter 6 – Song of the South** encompass the Song Dynasty, divided in the text as it was in reality into the nationally unified Northern Song era (960 – 1127) and the dispossessed Southern Song era (1127 – 1279). Hangzhou in the 11th Century matured into a populous and prosperous commercial center, described for posterity in the diaries of the Japanese monk Jojin. The city's wealth fostered the emergence of educated elites such as the literatus-recluse Lin Bu and the remarkable polymath Shen Gua. New demands and pressures upon West Lake due to the city's growth required aggressive preservation measures led by far-sighted poet-officials such as Su Shi. As invaders gathered along the northern borders, marauding rebels like Fang La in the south dramatically weakened the Song government and forced an alliance with the Jurchen Jin, who soon became northern China's conquerors.

Chapter 6 – Song of the South begins with the close escape of Prince Zhao Gou from the grasp of the Jurchen Jin invaders, his ascension to the Song throne as Emperor Gaozong, and the establishment of Hangzhou, renamed Lin'an, as the new "temporary capital" of the remaining Han Chinese empire. Lin'an/Hangzhou would remain the dynasty's capital for a decidedly un-temporary 146 years, from 1133 to 1279. Those who fled the Jurchen-controlled north flooded into Hangzhou and the surrounding area, with Li Qingzhao, arguably China's greatest poetess, among them. The city thrived, an urban refuge from the war-torn north, accommodating such memorable figures as the "Mad Monk" Ji Gong, the star-crossed lovers from Shen Garden, Lu You and Tang Wan, and the mysterious poetess Zhu Shuzhen, who rivaled Li Qingzhao but who was believed by many in later centuries never perhaps to have existed. On another front, this chapter charts the rise of the revered military general and patriot Yue Fei and his political nemesis, the forever-reviled Qin Hui.

The contents of **Chapter 7 – The Mongols Conquer China** are fully reflected in its title. Likely the world's richest and most populous city of the time and the jewel of Khubilai Khan's new kingdom, Hangzhou was largely preserved intact. Marco Polo sang the city's praises, but the Confucian principle of filiality as applied to dynastic loyalty tested the consciences of men like Zhou Mi and Zhao Mengfu, both from Huzhou. Meanwhile, foreign traders from across the Mongol empire poured into Hangzhou: Nestorian Christians, Jews, and Moslems. Zhao Mengfu, a direct descendant of the Song royal family, eventually broke from the Song loyalist ranks and submitted himself to official service under the Mongol Yuan dynasty, broadening his horizons in a way that later enabled him to revolutionize Chinese painting and immortalize his relationship with his equally talented spouse, Guan Daosheng.

Chapter 8 – The Prosperous Ming encompasses the 276-year reign of the Ming Dynasty (1368 – 1644), the last imperial rulership by Han Chinese over their own nation. When the Mongol Yuan Dynasty rapidly but inevitably weakened its hold over the massive territory it had conquered, Hangzhou was drawn into Zhang Shicheng's losing side of the dynastic succession battle. The city fared badly under Hongwu, the first Ming Emperor, but expansionist policies and the massive public works projects of his son, the Yongle Emperor, helped reverse the city's fortunes.

By the mid-15th-Century, Hangzhou was truly an earthly paradise for the Chinese people. West Lake became a favored site for memorializing national military heroes like Yue Fei and Yu Qian as well as officials who acted locally to preserve and enhance the lake and its environs. The ghost of a new local worthy mysteriously claimed his rightful place in the City God's Temple on Wushan Hill. Literature and the arts flourished as Zhejiang's literati elite increasingly dictated aesthetic standards of elegance and vulgarity. The city's merchants prospered economically, its young scholars prospered academically, and West Lake prospered as a bustling tourist venue and Buddhist pilgrimage locale. Clouds appeared for a time in the form of coastal pirates, but they were eventually dispersed by strong military leadership. A different form of invasion arose in the late 1500s in the form of Jesuit missionaries from Europe. With the assistance of three local scholar-official converts ("the Three Great Pillars"), Hangzhou formed one of their strongest bases of Chinese Catholicism and became the site of a cathedral still in operation today.

The Ming Dynasty weakened in the late 1500s and early 1600s before facing serious threats from northern invaders and rebels in the 1640s. **Chapter 9 – Transition: The Southern Ming** traces the fall of the Ming Dynasty and the capture of Hangzhou by the Manchus. In China's last great transition between imperial dynasties, past, current, and aspiring Ming officials faced crushing personal dilemmas of dynastic loyalty: whether and how to actively resist, quietly withdraw from service, commit honorable suicide, or betray their principles to join the new Qing Dynasty. Chapter 9 presents the varying responses to their dynasty's fall from several Ming loyalists from Shaoxing—Qi Biaojia, Wang Siren, Chen Hongshou, and Zhang Dai—along with Qian Qianyi (from Changshu, near Suzhou) and his famous wife from Jiaxing, Liu Rushi. As Chapter 9 ends, West Lake's condition had deteriorated significantly, described by one observer in 1649 as "a desolated marsh."

The two-and-a half century reign of the Qing Dynasty (1644 – 1911) was a period of immense struggle, suffering, and change for the Chinese nation. **Chapter 10 – Qing Dynasty: The First Century** (1644 to 1735) begins with the Hangzhou area's difficult transition from Han Chinese rule under the Ming to the "foreign" Manchu rule of the Qing. Manchu imposition of new dress and hair styles tore at individual loyalties throughout Jiangnan. In Hangzhou, construction of a large, Manchu-only military garrison inside the city walls caused further resentment as well as massive dislocation of Han Chinese families.

Hangzhou nevertheless moved forward. Prose literature flourished and women's literary groups like the Banana Garden Poetry Club found new outlets for producing, sharing, and publishing collections of their work. However, the new Manchu rulers took singular and violent exception in 1660 to an effort by Ming loyalists in Huzhou to write a history of their recently past dynasty when they discovered that it was sprinkled with decidedly anti-Qing overtones.

In 1661, the Kangxi Emperor took the throne at the age of eight. Over the next sixty years, his five Southern Inspection Tour visits re-established Hangzhou with West Lake and its "Ten Views" as among the empire's most favored places. Meanwhile, the playwright and theatrical performer Li Yu broke new literary ground, and the widely-read writings of the Hangzhou-based Jesuit missionary Martino Martini brought new and eagerly sought knowledge of Chinese geography, cartography, and history to Europe.

The next hundred years occupy **Chapter 11 – Qing Dynasty: The Second Century**, much of it under the rule of Kangxi's grandson, the Qianlong Emperor. Retracing his grandfather's majestic sojourns to the south, Qianlong visited Hangzhou on all six of his imperial inspection tours, further reinforcing Hangzhou's reputation as a special place.

His discovery of two sets of Song-era illustrations of rice growing and silk producing (riziculture and sericulture, respectively) in the Hangzhou region led Qianlong to canonize a series of four-hundred-year-old illustrations from Jinhua as idealized representations of model peasant life across the empire.

The Hangzhou area also figured significantly in the creation of Emperor Qianlong's great literary compilation, the *Four Treasuries*, but a literary inquisition that grew out of that project also swept away other valuable works in its path. Women's writing advanced further into prose, and leading male literati like Yuan Mei and Chen Wenshu began taking up the cause of female education. West Lake remained an esteemed national treasure and was further modified by reclamation and preservation efforts. By the early 1840s, the scourge of opium led to naval conflicts around Canton and the southeast coast. In 1842, the contest escalated northward to Zhoushan Island and Ningbo, culminating with British boots on the ground at Zhapu (Hangzhou's traditional downriver port on Hangzhou Bay) and China's first-ever ground-war battle with European troops.

The 1850s witnessed a peasant-inspired, pseudo-religious, anti-Manchu rebellion that swept through the southern half of China, devastating Jiangnan and most of Zhejiang Province in the first half of the 1860s. **Chapter 12 – The Taiping Rebellion** describes how Taiping commander Li Xiucheng twice captured Hangzhou and how Qing General Zuo Zongtang recovered the city and drove the rebels out of Zhejiang Province, with some timely assistance from the mixed, Franco-Chinese Ever-Triumphant Army.

Following the rebellion, the Hangzhou area in 1864 began a painful but still hopeful recovery. **Chapter 13 – Recovery and Opening** describes how provincial officials, gentry, and literati scholars led much of this effort, accelerating the already shifting relationship between the imperial center and the provinces. Charitable and civic organizations formed throughout the Hangzhou area to bury the dead, renovate and restart schools and temples, feed the starving, restore urban businesses and rural agriculture, and even repair such damaged historical treasures as Hangzhou's copy of Qianlong's great *Four Treasuries*. Most important, the Hangzhou region's silk industry recovered, at first slowly and then spectacularly when European silk production collapsed from disease and infestations in the 1860s. Renewed economic growth brought opportunities for wealth, none more spectacular in its rise and fall than that of Hangzhou's Hu Xueyan.

The end of the Taiping conflict also opened the doors—not always legally—to Western missionaries, most of whom firmly believed they were bringing both salvation and civilization to China. They soon discovered that they were not always welcomed with open arms. **Chapter 14 – Good Intentions, Unsought** addresses the fitful arrival of the early Christian missionaries into Hangzhou and the conflicts that arose from their unsought presence. Four of the most well-intentioned and socially beneficial of those individuals receive special attention: Mary Aldersey (the ghost-talker of Ningbo), Dr. David Duncan Main (famously known in Hangzhou as Dr. Apricot), and the teachers Mary Vaughan and Louise H. Barnes (respectively, founder and founding principal of Hangzhou's first high school for girls).

Chapter 15 – The Imperial Age Ends addresses one of the most crucial periods in China's modern history, the years from 1895 to 1911. Despite concerted efforts at military and naval self-strengthening, a crushing defeat in the 1895 – 1896 Sino-Japanese conflict created a national crisis of confidence in the Qing government. The resulting postwar treaty also forced Hangzhou to open fully to Japanese and European businesses and Christian missionaries. Calls for new educational institutions and massive governmental and educational reforms led to the formation of new schools in Hangzhou, including the Qiushi Academy and a number of boys' and girls' primary and early secondary schools established by Western missionary organizations. Women like the Manchu garrison widow Huixing advocated dramatically for female education; others like Shan Shili began to travel outside China and publish accounts of what they saw and learned. Foreign visitors like young Sidney Gamble (in 1908) discovered Hangzhou and West Lake and began educating the Western world about Chinese life and culture by publishing the results of their detailed socioeconomic and anthropological field work.

In the opening years of the 20th Century, the contest to determine who would build and control China's incipient rail network caused local officials, gentry, and business leaders in Zhejiang to adamantly oppose British (and central government) interests and successfully recover those development rights. At the same time, growing perception that the imperial form of government could not meet the demands of the modern world spawned thoughts of revolution. In the case of Qiu Jin, a radical female revolutionary from Shaoxing, those thoughts were transformed into a failed action that nevertheless made her a revered national hero, albeit a sometimes controversial one. In 1911, revolution came to Hangzhou as it did elsewhere throughout the empire, and the Qing Dynasty was overthrown.

In Hangzhou, one of the most immediate consequences of the 1911 Revolution was destruction of the city's reviled military garrison and eviction of its Manchu inhabitants. **Chapter 16 – Troubled Transition Years**, acknowledges the hardships suffered by the near-instantaneous creation within the city of a class of dispossessed refugees, but with these actions came critical decisions about the future of both the city and the lake alongside which it rested. Removal of the garrison walls and western sections of the ancient city wall opened the garrison land for development of a New Business District that repurposed the West Lake shore area from military parade ground to recreational lakefront and tourist zone. As Hangzhou people said, "West Lake entered the city."

The 1910s proved to be a turbulent era of shifting national priorities and perceptions, reflected for example in the story of the repeated disinterment and reburial of Qiu Jin's body. Two Huzhou natives, Chen Qimei and Zhang Jingjiang, were instrumental in supporting Sun Yat-sen's early Republican government; Zhang would be equally important in the government under Chiang Kai-shek. Educational reform continued, led nationally by Shaoxing native Cai Yuanpei, and cultural ferment sprang from new magazines and newspapers. Traditional arts like seal carving found safe haven at West Lake's Solitary Island, while painters like Hangzhou's Wu Changshuo sought expressive forms that adapted traditional styles to the new era. Chapter 16 closes with the European-American betrayal of China by the 1919 Treaty of Versailles that propelled Chinese students' anti-imperialist activism, forever memorialized as the May Fourth Movement.

19

The political revolution of 1911, the educational reform movement spearheaded by Cai Yuanpei, and the student-led activism of the May Fourth Movement provided more than sufficient impetus for a new kind of cultural movement in the 1920s, surveyed in **Chapter 17 – A "New Culture" Rises**. A student magazine in Hangzhou, the *Zhejiang New Tide*, published an influential essay bitterly critical of filial piety, an age-old pillar of Confucian culture. Around the same time, an unknown writer from Shaoxing named Zhou Shuren published a groundbreaking short story under the pseudonym Lu Xun that was equally critical of the "social cannibalism" he perceived in traditional Chinese culture. Yu Dafu, a native of Fuyang (just southwest of Hangzhou), published stories of psychological despair over personal and national weakness, and a little-known artist-illustrator from Jiaxing named Feng Zikai combined Japanese manga with excerpts from classical Chinese poetry to create a new form of artistic presentation. In the world of Chinese opera, a new style with origins in the peasant culture of rural Shaoxing found surprising popularity in urbane Shanghai.

Chapter 18 – The Nationalist Era and **Chapter 19 – The Japanese War in Zhejiang** cover the conflict-riddled period from 1927 – 1949, beginning with the rise of Chiang Kai-shek and the struggle to end the warlord era and culminating with the establishment of the People's Republic in 1949. Sandwiched between, of course, was the War of Resistance Against Japanese Aggression, from its early sparks in 1932 Shanghai to the full-fledged conflict from 1937 – 1945. The Hangzhou area was impacted directly from all of these events: collapse of the Leifeng Pagoda (1924), capture of Hangzhou by the Republican National Army (1927), staging of China's first international exposition (1929), creation of the Chinese Aviation School (1932), capture of the major cities in northern Zhejiang by the Japanese invaders (1937), demolition of the Qiantang River Bridge (1937), and Japanese retaliation with biological warfare for the Doolittle Raid on Tokyo (1942).

Yet those same years witnessed more than just conflict. In **Chapter 18**, the young revolutionary Mao Zedong makes his first visit to West Lake. Hangzhou native Lin Huiyin and her husband Liang Sicheng begin their meteoric rise in the world of Chinese architecture. West Lake represents China to the world with the nation's first international exhibition in 1929, the West Lake Expo. The West learns more about China through the popular literary works of two women authors with Hangzhou connections, Pearl Buck and Alice Tisdale Hobart. Qiu Jin's daughter, Wang Canzhi, helps further immortalize her mother and also becomes one of China's first senior aviation experts, while Jiaxing's Mao Dun makes his first breakthrough appearances as Lu Xun's literary successor.

While the wartime events in Hangzhou and northern Zhejiang from 1937 – 1945 are the main focus of **Chapter 19**, this chapter also relates the story of Zhejiang's University's heroic preservation of the last remaining "southern copy" of the Qianlong Emperor's *Four Treasuries*. Feng Zikai's artwork evolves during the anti-Japanese conflict, era, as does the literary work of Yu Dafu, while the wartime propaganda effort refines the work of another, soon-to-be-famous illustrator from Shaoxing named Zhang Leping.

In **Chapter 20 – Another Recovery, and a People's Republic**, Zhang Leping's cartoon orphan boy, San Mao, lightens the national mood after more than two decades of political and military conflict. Mao Zedong becomes the founding Chairman of the People's Republic and famously bids farewell to America's presence in China in the person of Leighton Stuart, a Westerner with deep family roots in Hangzhou. Chairman Mao's repeated visits and extended stays at his "third home" of West Lake helps set the modern course of Hangzhou's future as a city of scenic beauty for the people's leisurely enjoyment, necessitating renewed focus on historical and cultural preservation.

Lin Huiyin and Liang Sicheng cement their esteemed places in Chinese architectural history, the Grand Canal is restored as part of national industrial redevelopment, and "ping pong diplomacy" brings an American President to Hangzhou. Feng Zikai, Zhang Leping, and Mao Dun cap off their respective careers, and Lu Xun achieves posthumously an exalted place in the People's Republic. A variety of social and physical scientists from Hangzhou and Shaoxing—Zhu Kezhen, Ma Yinchu, Qian Sanqiang, and Qian Xuesen—also make their mark on Chinese science and society.

The present period, beginning with Deng Xiaoping's "opening" of the economy after 1978, has seen arguably the greatest socioeconomic transformation in China's long history. **Chapter 21 – Into the New Millennium**, offers several ways to view the magnitude and scope of these changes upon the cities of Hangzhou, Shaoxing, Huzhou, and Jiaxing. This chapter discusses the continued development of West Lake as both scenic tourism venue and exhibition center, introduces a unique adaptation of modern life to the Qiantang River tidal bore, and describes how Qiu Jin's peripatetic corpse reached its final place of rest and honor.

Readers are also introduced to two more Hangzhou-area cities that have experienced transformative changes of their own: formal recognition of Quzhou as a major site of Confucian heritage and family lineage, and creation of a world economic powerhouse at Yiwu, an ancient and formerly tiny city of wandering traders and now "the city of a million small things." The main text closes with a brief look at two post-millennium public buildings (an opera theater and a sports center) that demonstrate Hangzhou's efforts to construct strikingly modern architecture while simultaneously and successfully integrating its history and traditional culture.

Appendix A – "Ten Views of West Lake" provides a more detailed discussion of the traditionally premier experience of a West Lake visit – observing the famous, imperially certified Ten Views. Each of the original views is presented with more background and specifics, followed by a similar explanation for the "New Ten Views of West Lake," created with public survey input in 1984.

Hangzhou, Shaoxing, Jiaxing, Huzhou, and their surrounding areas provide an enormous array of sightseeing options. More a starting point than a travel guide, **Appendix B – Selected Historical/Cultural Places to Visit** nevertheless lists a number of tourist sites, grouped by geography to the extent possible, with brief discussion of each.

Author's Note

Suzhou and Hangzhou, two hugely historical, near-coastal cities located only one hundred miles apart in east central China, have for centuries been paired together by Chinese people as "heaven on earth." Belgian Sinologist Pierre Ryckmans (1935 – 2014), writing under the name Simon Leys, once paired them in a less ethereal way, writing in 1977 that "Suzhou is an exquisite town in commonplace surroundings, Hangzhou a commonplace town in exquisite surroundings."[1] One could easily contest both uses of the word "commonplace" as wildly outdated today, but my personal experience in both cases wholly supports both uses of the word "exquisite."

To have visited China, and especially to have visited nearby Shanghai and not seen either or both of these cities is hardly to have visited China at all. Shanghai is *sui generis*, unique unto itself, the New York City of China. Suzhou and Hangzhou are cultural and historical centers, more the Paris, Kyoto, Florence, or Venice of China. To experience Suzhou or Hangzhou is to experience at least some of the essence of Chinese history and life; there is good reason why both cities consistently hold top ranks among Chinese people as domestic tourism destinations.

Although it is extensively researched, footnoted, and sourced, *By the Hills Embraced* was neither conceived nor is it intended as a purely academic work. It draws upon a surprisingly vast body of past and recent work: books, journal articles, literary translations, dissertations, newspaper articles, published diaries, and the like. I wrote it, as I did my earlier book about the city of Suzhou, *Beautiful Su*, for a general readership audience who may have little or no knowledge of Hangzhou and perhaps even little familiarity with China or its history.

Both books seek to view the long course of Chinese history and cultural development through a specific urban lens, in this instance Hangzhou and its nearby satellite cities. This localized history mirrors national events but illustrates the effects of those larger events on the people and culture of a specific city region and, in turn, their impact on the nation. In my view, this approach makes for a more personalized, human-centered view of history and even serves as an aid for readers' prospective sightseeing visits.

Having lived in Suzhou on and off for almost twenty years and visited Hangzhou multiple times, I firmly believe that anyone who becomes well informed about the combined history and culture of these two cities will have taken a sizable first step in understanding the complexities of Chinese history and appreciating the beauties and achievements of a rich, varied, and long-lived culture.

Nevertheless, no reading experience can be better than visiting and walking the streets and lanes of these cities (and the cities, towns, and villages that surround them) at first hand. Even for an old hand, they never cease to surprise and delight. My fondest wish is that my books will inspire readers to discover and explore Hangzhou (and Suzhou) for themselves. I can state with absolute confidence that the intrepid reader-visitor will not be disappointed.

About the Text

Chinese words and phrases, including person and place names, are anglicized as often as possible in *Hanyu pinyin*, the modern-day system for converting Chinese characters into their English-sounding equivalents. In three instances where the Mandarin names and associated *pinyin* transliterations would not be easily recognizable to Western readers, their better-known traditional (Wade-Giles) forms have been retained: Sun Wu rather than Sunzi, Sun Yat-sen instead of Sun Zhongshan or Sun Yixian, and Chiang Kai-shek instead of Jiang Jieshi. In addition, the Yangzi River is presented in the form generally recognized in the West (instead of Changjiang, the common name in China), and the historical name Canton is used until the post-Mao years, when the modern name Guangzhou is adopted in its place. Where displayed, Chinese characters are rendered in their modern, simplified forms.

The *pinyin* forms of common vocabulary words and phrases are italicized, but Chinese place names (cities, towns, streets, bridges, and gardens) and personal names presented in *pinyin* form retain normal typeface. Names of individuals are written exclusively in Chinese form, family name followed by given name. Wherever possible, person names are accompanied at their first appearance by the corresponding Chinese characters and birth-death years (or reign years in the case of emperors).

Because the names of so many cities changed over time, Chinese city names can be particularly problematic for Western readers. Early or ancient names provide an evolutionary historical context, but they can also create confusion due to unfamiliarity. In general, I have introduced historical names in their appropriate eras with parenthetic reference to their modern counterparts before continuing with their modern names for the sake of clarity and ease of identification on modern maps. In the cases of Hangzhou and Shaoxing, I have used their historical and modern names somewhat more interchangeably according to the era in which they were used: Qiantang and Lin'an for Hangzhou, Kuaiji, Shangyu, and Yuezhou for Shaoxing. Beijing is similarly identified interchangeably with the historical names Yanjing and Dadu.

Chapter 1

THE AGE OF WATER

(5000 – 1600 BCE)

In order to decide about defending the tidal bores, I inspected the sea walls,
Terrified, I had a glimpse of the startling tides;
The huge tidal bores were the biggest on the third day of the third month,
As if they were awaiting my arrival;
Riding on my horse, [I] headed eastward to [Haining],
I saw a strand of silver thread approaching from the horizon;
In a second they arrived, rolling up the river and stirring up the sea,
[As if] they welcome the [Imperial] Boat;
I heard their sound before I could even see them,
Roaring, blowing, and crashing, they sprawled over;
I stopped, then walked slowly, watching their shapes,
Grand and spectacular, what can compete with them?[1]

– *Qianlong Emperor (1762)*

In the Beginning

In the beginning, there were Three Sovereigns and Five Kings (三皇五帝, *Sanhuang wudi*). Or at least, that is the myth.

The Three Sovereigns were demigods who created the foundational knowledge base of Chinese civilization. Fuxi 伏羲 invented the skills of domestic life: hunting, fishing, cooking, and writing.[2] Shennong 神農 invented the tools and knowledge of agriculture, created the calendar, and discovered the efficacious use of herbs for traditional Chinese medicine. Huangdi 神農 (the Yellow Emperor) taught the people how to domesticate animals, build houses and boats, and make clothing. He also invented mathematics and the basics of

24

astronomy. His wife Leizu 西陵氏 is said to have invented sericulture (silkworm rearing and silk production) in about the year 2700 BCE.

The reign of the Five Kings began, according to tradition, in around 2600 BCE with Shaohao 少昊, followed by Zhuanxu 颛顼, Emperor Ku 帝喾 (*Di Ku*, c. 2436 – 2366 BCE), Emperor Yao 帝尧 (*Di Yao*, c. 2356 – 2255 BCE), and Emperor Shun 帝舜 (*Di Shun*, c. 2294 – 2184 BCE). Although their historicity has been subject to debate, these kings and emperors served as the mythical founders of Chinese civilization. They also buttressed the millennia-long belief that the origins of that civilization were exclusive to North China, particularly along the Yellow River valley. Archaeological discoveries near Hangzhou beginning in the 1930s would overturn that thesis.

During the time of Emperor Yao, when great floods plagued the nation, a seventh-generation descendant of Zhuanxu named Gun 鲧 was commissioned to control the waters. Gun built dikes and dams on the rivers over a period of nine years, but his embankments ultimately overflowed and collapsed. Before Gun's death, he commanded his son Yu 禹 to complete the task at which he had failed. Yao's successor, Emperor Shun, reluctantly but wisely agreed to this nepotistic assignment at the behest of his advisors.

Yu traveled to the sites of his father's unsuccessful projects, analyzed the reasons for their failures, and consulted at length with the experienced men who had worked with his father. He gradually realized that Gun's approach to controlling the great rivers had been misguided; such waters should not be caged but allowed to run. The solution was to manage *where* they ran by devising a network of dredged channels and canals that also provided a controlled flow for irrigation.

Although he had recently married and his new bride was pregnant, Yu understood the emergency nature of the situation. He set out immediately to oversee construction of a new water management network, a task that took the next thirteen years of his life. According to legend, he passed his own home three times during those years but was so devoted to his assignment, he declined to visit his wife and growing son. Nearly twenty years later, when Emperor Shun was nearing death, he chose Yu over his own son to succeed him, thereby instituting a line of leadership descent from Zhuanxu. Yu's brilliance and perseverance in taming the waters earned him the name Da Yu 大禹, or Yu the Great.

Down through the ages, it has been said of Yu the Great that he "tamed the waters" of China and made the land habitable. One of China's earliest works of history, *The Commentary of Zuo* (左傳, *Zuo zhuan*, c. 4th Century BCE), contains a bit of Chinese punning that honors Yu's achievements. In "Book X – Duke Zhao," Duke Ding of Liu compliments his diplomatic counterpart Zhao Wenzi of Jin, comparing the beneficial consequences of the latter's peace efforts to the water control work of Yu the Great. "If not for Yu 禹," Duke Ding jokingly declares, "we would all just be *yu* 鱼." That is, fish.[3]

Da Yu ruled over a confederation of tribal groups for more than forty years, during which time he organized their territories into nine separate prefectures (洲, *zhou*) or provinces. The early histories describe Yu as dying at Tushan,[4] a mountain southwest of present-day

Shaoxing, from an illness contracted during an eastern inspection tour or hunting trip. Yu's son Qi 啟 chose to bury his father on Tushan, and because his father had once convened a meeting of the area's tribal leaders there, the mountain was renamed Guiji 貴集, (貴 *gui*, lords or nobles, 集 *ji*, gather together) in remembrance.[5]

Prior to Da Yu, the emperor had been chosen for merit and not by hereditary succession; no son had ever assumed his father's position among the previous leaders. This time, however, the chiefs chose Yu's son Qi by acclamation, thus initiating China's first dynasty, the Xia 夏 (c. 2070 – 1600 BCE), with Yu the Great as its founder. Da Yu's tomb would become the site of official visits and sacrifices down through the dynastic ages and would influence the futures of both Shaoxing and Hangzhou.

Before the Beginning

In May 1935, early excavation work for a new cemetery at the foot of Laohe Hill (老和山, Laohe shan), just northwest of West Lake, was interrupted by the discovery of some ancient stoneware and potsherds. The news of this archaeological find caught the attention of He Tianxing 何天行 (1913 – 1986), a Hangzhou native studying at Shanghai's Fudan University. After He's preliminary investigations uncovered evidence of similar pieces in local antiquities markets, he returned to Laohe Hill the following summer to conduct additional field studies. Those explorations took him even further northwest into the towns of Pingyao 瓶窯 and Liangzhu 梁渚.

In each area, He Tianxing found more pottery and stone objects of the same type and style, leading to his first conjectures of a previously unknown ancient culture. Additional study and discussions with other archaeologists reassured him enough to write one of China's earliest archaeology reports, *Stone Objects and Black Pottery of Liangzhu Town, Hang County*, in April 1937. Twenty-four-year-old He Tianxing had unknowingly put Liangzhu on the archaeological map, made himself "the Father of Liangzhu Culture," and paved the way for a revolution in historians' views of the development of Chinese civilization.

Around the same time, Shi Xingeng 葹昕更 (1912 – 1939) used the work of He Tianxing and others to begin investigating his hometown of Liangzhu. Although lacking He Tianxing's high-level education and formal training, Shi Xingeng's employment with the West Lake Museum had expanded his knowledge base and sharpened his investigative and analytical skills. While participating in the archaeological dig at Laohe Hill, he observed relics and pottery that bore striking similarity to pieces he had often seen around Liangzhu.

From December 1936 through March 1937, Shi conducted excavations around Liangzhu and Pingyao, identifying more than a dozen distinct sites containing black pottery, stoneware, and jade objects. His findings spurred outside investigations under the Museum's sponsorship that confirmed his results, which he outlined in technical detail in *Liangzhu: A Tentative Report on the Black Pottery Culture in the Second District of Hang County*. Shi continued his research through 1938 and published several additional papers that year. Sadly, a promising career ended in 1939 when he died from illness at age 27. He likely never imagined the sheer magnitude of what he had uncovered.

Prior to He Tianxing and Shi Xingeng, national archaeological interest in the Yangzi River Delta had been nearly nonexistent. Chinese historians and anthropologists had long adhered to the traditional belief that Chinese civilization originated in the north and west and had focused their research efforts accordingly. When artifacts of potential interest occasionally surfaced in the Yangzi Delta, confirmation bias[6] helped explain away those "anomalies" as having migrated from other regions through population movements or from the travels of antiquities merchants and collectors.

He Tianxing's and Shi Xingeng's work in the Liangzhu Town vicinity sparked enthusiastic new archaeological interest in the Yangzi Delta. Through the 1950s and 1960s, field researchers discovered site after site in the Hangzhou-Huzhou-Jiaxing plain, the Lake Tai area, and beyond. Even more significant, their respective artifacts demonstrated so much similarity that in 1959 archaeologists began referring to them collectively as relics of a newly-discovered "Liangzhu Culture."

In addition to a sizable concentration of sites in the northern Zhejiang area,[7] other excavations whose relics qualified them as Liangzhu Culture ranged as far southeast as the Shaoxing-Ningbo plain and as far northwest as Zhenjiang and Nanjing. To the north, the modern-day areas of Suzhou and Shanghai each contained multiple settlements, with still others located north of the Yangzi River into the upper reaches of Jiangsu Province and the Huai River.[8]

Continued research, supplemented by carbon-dating technology, placed Liangzhu Culture in the period from around 3300 to 2300 BCE, making it more than 5,000 years old. Further excavation around the original Liangzhu Town site in 2007 gradually revealed a grand royal city, complete with both inner and outer city walls. The outermost walls measured seven kilometers (four miles) in circumference with at least six water gates, dating to around 2500 BCE,[9] identifying Liangzhu as the capital of that eponymous civilization. Between 1936 and 2007, at least 135 related sites were discovered in Jiangsu and Zhejiang provinces, with the greatest concentration in the Hangzhou – Huzhou – Jiaxing triangle. Over 9,300 jade objects of Liangzhu origin had also been recovered by 2009.[10]

Liangzhu was gradually revealed as a rice-cultivating culture characterized by black pottery and lacquerware, fine jade carving and ornamentation, wine brewing, and silk weaving. Liangzhu people's lives were marked by a social hierarchy capped by a wealthy class, monotheistic worship of a mixed human-animal god (human torso, bird feet), and formal funerary rites. Their living quarters rose above the ground on wooden pilings, with construction that reflected advanced woodworking skills. One crucial difference from other Chinese civilizations of the same era was Liangzhu culture's lack of bronze metalwork for tools or weapons.

More intensive archaeological exploration in the Yangzi Delta eventually led to further discoveries of cultures even more ancient. In 1973, excavations near the village of Hemudu 河姆渡 in Yuyao City (located midway between Shaoxing and Ningbo) uncovered thousands of relics, spread over an area of 40,000 square meters, that gave evidence of a still more primitive culture dating back 6,000 to 7,000 years (estimated 5050 – 3050 BCE).

Multiple sites containing similar relics were subsequently found in the Ningbo – Shaoxing plain, prompting their group classification under the name Hemudu Culture. Several dozen Hemudu excavation sites have since been discovered, ranging from Shangyu (Shaoxing) to eastern Yuyao, south as far as Taizhou, and in the Zhoushan Islands off the Zhejiang Province coast.

This early civilization was characterized by cultivated rice agriculture, domestication of dogs, pigs and buffalo, use of bone and wood spades, cloth made from woven fibers, production of black pottery, carved jade, and carved ivory, and use of colored lacquers for decoration. Rice husks found at the Hemudu site provide the earliest evidence to date of rice cultivation in China, around 5000 – 4750 BCE. A red lacquer bowl, also dating back 7,000 years, is regarded as among the earliest examples of Chinese lacquerware. A square water well supported with a complex internal frame of joined wood is similarly believed to be one of China's earliest wells and also demonstrates technical sophistication in design and construction.

Yet another distinctive feature of Hemudu culture was the existence of longhouses built on wood pilings or stilts to elevate living spaces over the husbanded animals and above periodic flood waters. Sun Guoping 孙国平 in 2013 described the Hemudu excavations as "widely regarded as one of the most significant archaeological finds in China during the 20th Century."[11]

Other identifiably distinct cultures evolved in the Yangzi Delta in early times.[12] The Shangshan 上山 (9050 – 6550 BCE) and Kuahuqiao 跨湖桥 (6050 – 5050 BCE) cultures pre-dated the Hemudu and have been found in archaeological layers directly beneath Hemudu sites. The Kuahuqiao culture was only formally identified and archaeologically excavated in 1990 (and again in 2001 – 2002) in the Xiang Lake areas of Hangzhou's Xiaoshan district, located directly across the Qiantang River from Hangzhou's ancient city site. Carbon-dating of pottery, tools, and other relics (including a 7,500-year-old wooden canoe) suggested a foraging, hunting, and fishing culture seven-to-eight thousand years old with early signs of rice cultivation.[13]

The Majiabang 馬家浜 (5050 – 3850 BCE) culture in northern Zhejiang and southern Jiangsu existed more or less contemporaneously with the Hemudu. The Qingliangang 青蓮崗 (4500 – 3000 BCE) culture succeeded the Hemudu, while the Songze 崧泽 (3750 – 3350 BCE) succeeded the Majiabang. The Liangzhu culture grew out of or assimilated influences from each of these various earlier cultures.

In the past fifty years, Chinese archaeologists have come to regard the Hemudu and Liangzhu cultures of particular importance for several reasons. First, the mere existence of such sophisticated early cultures forced a major reassessment of where and how Chinese civili-

28

zation arose, generating recognition that the Yellow River basin was not its sole source.

> In traditional Chinese historical studies and in the early decades of Chinese archaeology, it was long believed that the Yellow River region was seen as the cradle of the Chinese civilization...while the Yangtze River region (the Jiangnan region) was disparaged as being the territory of various 'barbarian' groups....The discovery of an "advanced" Liangzhu Culture forced archaeologists to rethink this traditional understanding and recognize the importance of Liangzhu in early Chinese history.[14]

> The discovery and recognition of Liangzhu and other cultures that preceded it have...fundamentally alter[ed] the diffusionist theory that treated the Yellow River valley as the sole center of all prehistoric cultures and prompted scholars to consider a multitude of regional cultures as contributors to the formation of Chinese civilization.[15]

> Radio-carbon dating [of Yangzi Delta relics] fundamentally altered the traditional perspective that regarded the Yellow River valley as the center of prehistoric China. From this time onward Chinese archaeologists began to consider seriously Neolithic cultures in other parts of China and to reflect upon the formation of Chinese civilization.[16]

Second, the Hemudu and Liangzhu cultures together formed the basis for the region's later Wu and Yue cultures that have characterized Jiangsu and Zhejiang provinces since at least the first millennium BCE.

> The Liangzhu Culture engendered the subsequent Maqiao, Haochuan and Hushu Cultures, which were the last echoes of the Liangzhu Culture and in turn gave birth to the Yue Culture and Wu Culture....The discovery of [the Liangzhu] culture site not only proves that the culture of Zhejiang dates back to the distant ancient times but also traces the origins of Wu and Yue cultures to a time thousands of years earlier.[17]

> The cultural system of the Lake Tai area originated with the Majiabang culture of 7000 B.P. [years before present] and the Liangzhu culture of 4000 to 5000 B.P. and extended down to the Wuyue culture of 3000 B.P., a period of four to five thousand years....Thus the Wuyue culture, which eventually became strong enough to compete with the cultures of the North China Plain during the Eastern Zhou period, had a long period of individual development.[18]

Third, some Chinese archaeologists proposed the notion that the main Liangzhu culture site, at Liangzhu Town, was itself the first and most ancient iteration of modern-day Hangzhou.

> According to Wang [Wang Zunguo 汪遵國, from the Nanjing Museum]... the Liangzhu Site was where Hangzhou started; today's downtown and

the West Lake came into being later. Su Bingqi [苏秉琦, (1909 – 1997)] agreed that the Liangzhu Site was where the ancient Hangzhou was.[19]

To the extent that the Liangzhu civilization could be classified as a full-fledged state defined by royalty or central control, a capital city, and satellite cities or settlements who took direction from the center—admittedly, a debatable proposition—Liangzhu / Hangzhou could perhaps have been the earliest capital city in China.[20] Former curator of Beijing's Palace Museum, Zhang Zhongpei 張忠培 (1934–2017), went even a step further, stating that Liangzhu deserves to be called "the first and foremost city of China."[21]

Historians have speculated over the possible causes for the rise and fall of these various Neolithic cultures and their complete disappearance around four thousand years ago: military conflict, climate catastrophe, sea level rise, temperature change, famine, disease epidemics, or floods. Studies of sediment layers have suggested flooding as a contributing factor, but a recently published study[22] strongly indicates that climate change cycles may have resulted in alternating periods of large-scale flooding followed by mega-droughts that led to abandonment of the area.

In the present day, continuing archaeological research has been accompanied for the Hemudu and Liangzhu cultures by museums describing their civilizing achievements and exhibiting some of their remarkable relics. The Museum of Hemudu Cultural Ruins was opened in 1994, located about halfway between Yuyao and Ningbo in Hemudu Town. The Liangzhu Museum, opened in 2008, is located in Liangzhu Town, about 10 miles northwest of Hangzhou. On July 6, 2019, the Liangzhu archaeological site was designated by UNESCO as a World Heritage site.

Before the Before – The Qiantang River

Before Da Yu, before Liangzhu or Hemudu, before human settlement, there was water. Streams poured into rivers, and rivers flowed into oceans, leaving behind alluvial deposits that built up new land. Lakes formed from springs, while rivers formed bays and lagoons became lakes.

Hangzhou was gifted by Nature with plentiful water, and man-made canals later tamed the land and brought transport, commerce, and agricultural bounty. However, two of the city's Nature-given water elements, the Qiantang River 钱塘江 and West Lake (西湖, Xihu)—and certain quirks in their existence—have played such a continuous and outsized role in the city's 2,000-year history as to be essential context for everything that followed. Both will play recurring roles throughout Hangzhou's history.

Like so many of the world's major cities, Hangzhou is a river city. For all but the most recent decades of its existence, it was situated entirely on the northern bank of the Qiantang River. In earlier times, the river was called the Zhe Jiang 浙江, or "Crooked River," the name by which the entire province is known today. The name Qiantang came into use by the time of the Han Dynasty (206 BCE – 220 CE), when the entire area was called Qiantang County.

As the half-mile-wide Qiantang snakes past Hangzhou in a more or less northeasterly direction, it gradually widens into a winding, long-necked funnel. A short distance downriver at Haining, the Qiantang reaches a width of about two miles. At Ganpu, it widens to about twelve miles, and at Haiyan, the river broadens to about twenty miles and effectively disappears into the broad-mouthed Hangzhou Bay. The bay's southern side, north and east of Ningbo, is dotted with a range of small islands and one larger one, Zhoushan 舟山, from which the whole island group gets its name. At its easternmost extent, the bay opens to about sixty-five miles' width at land's end.

The Hangzhou Tidal Bore

On paper, Hangzhou's location on the banks of the Qiantang River with nearby access to the East China Sea makes it appear well-suited to be a major port city. However, Hangzhou Bay's relatively shallow depth of less than fifteen meters has largely prevented this in modern times. In earlier times, a unique natural phenomenon further minimized Hangzhou's feasibility as a major port: the lowest reach of the Qiantang River is the site of one of the world's greatest tidal bores.

Tidal bores only occur under specific geographic, topographic, and astronomical conditions. A bore can form wherever a shallow, narrow-channeled river opens into a large, shallow, flat-bottomed bay that empties into an ocean. When the ocean's tidal force is great enough, the waters of the incoming tide overpower the outflowing river water and create a sort of backflow, forcing the river water backward against its own current. The result has the look, sound, appearance, and force of a tidal wave as the reverse flow of water rushes up the river channel until its tide-infused energy finally dissipates.

Although ocean tides oscillate from high to low twice daily, they do not always create a bore every day at every location where bores occur.[23] Lunar tidal effects are strongest when the moon is closest to the earth (at new moons and full moons), and they are further amplified the more the sun falls into direct alignment with the earth and moon. Consequently, tidal bores reach their greatest magnitude on the several days around the new moon and full moon each month. In general, the first to fifth and fifteenth to twentieth days of each lunar month, corresponding respectively to new moon and full moon occurrences, are the best times to view a tidal bore.

Tidal bores can be found in about sixty locations throughout the world, but by most measures, the bore as seen today on the Qiantang River is the largest anywhere. Human interventions at the mouth of the Yangzi River about three thousand years ago initiated major and rapid growth of the delta from sedimentation deposits.[24] This eastward expansion formed that land upon which Shanghai now stands, but to the south, the new coastline also created the elongated funnel shape and shallow bottom of Hangzhou Bay. The result focused an increased volume of tidal flow toward the Qiantang River's mouth and magnified the effect into a more violent bore.

For centuries, the incoming bore followed a southern passage, poetically known by locals as Heaven's Gate, between the Zheshan 赭山 and Kanshan 龕山 Mountains west of

31

Haining. Around the year 1695, shifting sand bars and silting caused the bore to reroute itself onto a northern passage, above Zheshan. After that time, the bore twice found a third, middle passage for periods of twelve to fifteen years, but since the mid-1750s, the tidal flows have remained along the north passage. All of these changes occurred well downriver from Hangzhou City.

While the Qiantang experiences bores of varying sizes twice daily year-round,[25] the tidal bore on the eighteenth day of the eighth lunar month (Tide-Viewing Festival day) has for centuries been one of China's "must see" events for everyone from emperors and officials to literati poets, artists, and of course, commoners. At its grandest, depending on water temperatures, ocean current strengths, and wind conditions, the autumnal tidal bore has generated waves on the Qiantang River as high as thirty feet, moving upriver at twenty-five miles per hour. The effect is both awe-inspiring and terrifying, as witnessed below by just a few of the many descriptions over the ages:

> When it begins to arise far away at Ocean Gate, it appears but a silver thread; but, as it gradually approaches, it becomes a wall of jade, a snow-laden ridge, bordering the sky on its way. Its gigantic roar is like thunder as it convulses, shakes, dashes, and shoots forth, swallowing up the sky and inundating the sun, for its force is supremely vigorous.[26] [Zhou Mi 周密 (1232 – 1298)]

> As it drew closer, we could make out the white crests, like a flock of tens of millions of goslings being herded towards us, their wings flapping as if about to take off in panicked flight. Nearer still and the bore began to billow foam and ice flakes flew in all directions, like a million snow lions descending upon the river, whipped forward by the thunder; ten thousand heads stretching up and none daring to fall behind. Nearer still it advanced towards us, as if driven by a typhoon, with a force that seemed as though it would crash against the banks and surge over them....It was only after sitting down for some considerable time did I manage to regain my composure.[27] [Zhang Dai 張岱 (1597- 1689?)]

> We could see the Bore approaching, miles away to the east, at first not much more than a dark line, brokenly occasionally with streaks of white. Nearer it came and more distinct, its roaring heard miles away, a seething, boiling furious wave. Suddenly it had struck the sea-wall some two miles to the east of us, and the rebound from this was in some respects the grandest sight of all. It resulted in a huge wave, apparently some twenty feet high, riding on the back but diagonally across the main wave, with which, however, it soon merged so that when it passed where we were standing it was simply a straight line extending right across the river—a sloping wall of water, perhaps 15 feet high, coming with the speed of a race horse, and with a fury and impetuosity simply indescribable—a sight once seen, never to be forgotten.[28] [Rev. George F. Fitch, 1894]

Suddenly at 1 p.m. a white streak is seen near the horizon off to the East on

the north side of the river which is several miles broad in that section....The streak comes nearer and nearer and we can see the water dashing up wildly into the air. Still it comes and then above the din of voices the roar of the water is heard; higher and higher it banks up, toppling over the receding tide which is still running down swiftly....the wave is now from twelve to fifteen feet high, the top curling over. In a moment, the solid wall of water passes us, boiling, seething and churning up the mud, and running at a terrific speed.[29]
[William R. Kahler, 1905]

The Lake West of the City

According to legend, Jade Dragon and Golden Phoenix ruled the heavens together in ancient times. One day, they happened to spy a beautiful crystal, the likes of which they had never before seen. For hundreds of years, they worked together to carve and polish the crystal into a shining orb, a pearl so perfectly formed it emanated other-worldly radiance. When the Queen Mother of the Western Heavens learned of the pearl's magnificence, she stole the precious jewel for herself one day while the two great creatures were asleep.

Believing they could not bear to live without their pearl, Jade Dragon and Golden Phoenix stormed the Queen Mother's heavenly palace. In their struggle to retrieve the jewel, it fell from the sky over Hangzhou and transformed into a beautiful lake. Rather than live on forever grieving their loss, Dragon and Phoenix chose to reside for eternity beside the lake formed by their fabulous pearl. They transformed themselves into Jade Dragon Mountain and Golden Phoenix Mountain where they remain to this day, still protecting the lake that was once their pearl.

Nothing in Hangzhou is more integral to the city's history and to its very identity than the lake that borders it to the west, a fresh-water body still in its infancy as measured in geologic time. Several hundred million years ago, the area was covered by ocean; there was no lake, nor were there any surrounding hills. Between 250 and 100 million years ago, movement of the Indo-China tectonic plate set the formation of the Tianmu Mountain chain in motion. Combined with the erosive effects of weather, the hills that today seem to embrace the lake began to take shape. At their foot, a broad valley formed and became gravel-covered from mountain erosion.

In more recent geologic time, perhaps seventy-five million years ago, a saltwater bay formed around the present lake site. As recently as 7,000 – 10,000 years ago,[30] natural climate warming caused much of the land east of Hangzhou to be covered by a shallow sea. During the period that followed, about six thousand years past, the West Lake area was inundated by seawater that reached the base of Lingyin Hill and transformed the Baoshishan and Wushan hills into waterside landings.

As sea levels fell during the period from about 2400 BCE to 500 BCE, the northern Zhejiang plain (Jiaxing – Huzhou -Hangzhou area) began to emerge as the seawater retreated. Notably, the area that is now occupied by Hangzhou remained underwater during that time, but the basin that contains West Lake today began to form as a lagoon due to silt build-up from the Qiantang River outflows and mud from the tidal bore. Finally, around the beginning of the Common Era two thousand years ago, West Lake was well-established as a lagoon and the land to its east dried out enough to begin accommodating human habitation.

Underground springs and fresh water runoff from the nearby hills gradually desalinated the lagoon and transformed it into a freshwater lake. That same runoff from the hills also brought a continuous supply of silt that threatened always to convert the lake into a swamp. Dredging would become essential to the lake's healthy existence, and the dredged silt would play an integral role in shaping West Lake as it appears in the modern era.

Records are unclear as to when the water was officially regarded as a lake. No mention of the lake occurs in any records as late as the Jin Dynasty era (265 – 420 CE) despite detailed descriptions of the nearby Wulin Mountains, site of the famous Lingyin Temple.[31] Another commentator extends the time frame even further, into the early 7th Century: "There are no records of a freshwater lake until the Tang period…, at the time when Hangzhou first became well known for its scenery."[32] The lake remained relatively shallow, with an average depth of about 2.5 meters (about eight feet), and a circumference of around fifteen kilometers (nine miles).

During the Han Dynasty (202 BCE – 220 CE), claims of a golden ox mysteriously rising out of the lagoon waters—read as a positive omen for the reigning emperor—resulted in the lake being called *Jinniu Hu* 金牛湖, Golden Ox Lake.[33] In the more permanent, fresh-water form achieved by around the time of the Sui Dynasty (581 – 618), the lake became officially known as Qiantang Lake 钱塘湖, after the original name of Hangzhou. During the Tang Dynasty, the people gradually adopted a new, locally informal name, neither particularly imaginative nor distinctive: Xihu 西湖, or West Lake.

The river, the tidal bore, the lake, and the surrounding hills—together, a natural archetype of the Chinese concept of *shanshui* 山水 (landscape, literally "mountains and water")—would play vital roles in Hangzhou's history, culture, development, and identity in the 1,500 years of the city's formal existence. Before that story begins, however, it must first give way to the story of nearby Shaoxing, the region's dominant city for a thousand years before Hangzhou built its first walls.

34

Chapter 2

SOUTHERN STATES EMERGE

(514 – 465 BCE)

Drinking Above the Lake in Clear Weather Followed by Rain[1]

The water's brightness, vast and rippling, looks best in clear weather;
The mountains' color, vague and misty, stands out even in the rain.
West Lake is like West Maid [Xi Shi]:
Whether the makeup's light or heavy, it always looks just right.

— *Su Shi (1037 – 1101)*

Wu and Yue

Shortly after imperial China's longest-lasting dynasty, the Zhou (c. 1046 – 256 BCE), first succeeded the Shang (c. 1600 – c. 1046 BCE), the Duke of Zhou (uncle to the adolescent King Cheng) established a new governmental structure to control the vast empire. His *fengjian* 封建 system established a confederation of vassal states enfeoffed by and subject to the central rule of a hereditary king who held the Mandate of Heaven. Over time, the vassal states became semi-independent powers in their own right, acknowledging the Zhou king as their nominal leader but less directly beholden to central rule.

These early independent states, located exclusively in north-central China, forged alliances and battled one another interminably for power, influence, and territory. By around 771 BCE, the vassal states had effectively overthrown the central control aspect of the *fengjian* system. Instead, the major states met together in regular conferences to make policy decisions and choose from among themselves an overlord (霸, *ba*) or hegemon.

As growing predator states conquered and absorbed smaller, prey states, five dominant kingdoms emerged north of the Yangzi River: Qin 秦, Jin 晋, Qi 齊, Song 宋, and

35

Chu 楚. Less noticed along the eastern coast, in an area south of the Yangzi River long regarded by northerners as barbarian wilderness land, two more states emerged: Wu 吳 and Yue 越. Both states benefitted from their frontier location on the southeastern fringe of the Zhou empire since, as they developed, they were largely excluded from the interstate rivalries and endless political machinations taking place among the powerful northern states.

The State of Wu (吳國, Wuguo) more or less corresponded to Shanghai and today's Jiangsu Province, with its capital established at Suzhou[2] in 514 BCE. The State of Yue occupied most of today's Zhejiang Province south of the Qiantang River as well as northern sections of modern Fujian Province. Yue's capital city was called Kuaiji 会稽, centuries later to become part of Shaoxing. The area south of Yue was populated by various indigenous tribes called the Baiyue 百越, or Hundred Yue, extending all the way into northern areas of present-day Vietnam. In fact, "Viet" is simply the pronunciation of "Yue" in the Vietnamese language.

Conflict in Jiangnan

The 6th-Century BCE states of Wu and Yue shared much more than a border. As inheritors of the earlier Liangzhu and Hemudu cultures, they shared water-rich territory so bountiful it was called "the land of rice and fish." Both states also embodied entirely distinct cultural roots from the northern states: different dialects, different foods based on rice rather than wheat or millet, and different clothing, hairstyles (cut short), and personal decoration (tooth blackening, body tattooing). They also developed uniquely fine skill at fashioning bronze swords. Perhaps because of their distant location from the traditional power centers, their growing demographic, military, and naval strength went relatively unnoticed and unchallenged for the first five hundred years of the Zhou Dynasty.

One area where Wu and Yue regrettably demonstrated an all-too-human similarity with their northern state contemporaries was lust for territory and power and a corresponding thirst for revenge. In 514 BCE, Wu King Helü 王阖闾 constructed a grand new capital, a walled and moated city (present-day Suzhou) located on the water-laden, rice-growing plain about fifteen miles east of Tai Lake (太湖, Taihu). Four years later, Wu forces attacked Yue in an effort to gain control of additional rice-growing land, but they failed to overthrow Yue or supplant its ruler, King Yunchang 王允常 (d. 497 BCE). Helü's unsuccessful invasion nevertheless initiated a series of intermittent conflicts between Wu and Yue that would last thirty-seven years and elevate some of its principals to near-mythological status. Theirs would be the founding stories of the Wu and Yue cultures, recalled as models for good or ill and celebrated to the present day.

Yue King Yunchang's first attempt to exact revenge came in 505 BCE. The year before, Helü had turned his sights westward and launched a successful assault on the State of Chu, even managing to capture the Chu capital city of Ying. A feared warrior himself, Helü was further aided by the wise counsel and military leadership of two generals: Wu Zixu 伍员 (526 – 484 BCE) and Sun Wu 孫武 (544 – 496 BCE), neither of whom were

36

Wu natives. According to legend, Wu Zixu, a native of Chu, was the architect of Helü's grand capital city, having chosen the capital's site and engineered its design. Sun Wu, a native of Qi, is widely known as the author of *The Art of War* (孙子兵法, *Sunzi bingfa*) and is commonly regarded as one of history's great military strategists and tacticians.

The Yue attack on Wu's rear guard in 505 BCE caused King Helü to lose his hold on the Chu State and nearly cost him his throne to an attempted usurpation by his brother, Fugai 夫概. Enraged by Yue's assault, the Wu King nevertheless bade his time. When Yunchang died from natural causes in 497 BCE, Helü moved almost immediately to exact his revenge on Yue while its young new king, Yunchang's son Goujian 勾践 (r. 496 - 465 BCE), was still observing the prescribed period of ritual mourning.

The Wu and Yue armies faced off at Zuili 檇李, near present-day Jiaxing.[3] Early records of the battle include a shocking, perhaps apocryphal account[4] of how the battle began. As the two forces faced one another, King Goujian sent forward thirty Yue men who advanced a short way toward the enemy, shouted as they withdrew their knives, and cut their own throats in unison. As they fell, Goujian sent forth another thirty men who repeated this ruthlessly suicidal maneuver, and after them, yet another thirty.

The Wu soldiers froze in place, so stunned by the exhibition that they failed to notice the Yue attack advancing upon them from another direction. They could not have known in the moment that the ninety dead men were in fact convicted criminals to whom Goujian had promised ample rewards to their families in return for their self-sacrifice. The battle was bitterly fought before the Yue force managed to fend off the Wu incursion. More than that, however, they also inflicted on King Helü a wound, possibly an Achillean spear to the foot,[5] that caused his death and halted the Wu invasion.

On his death bed, Helü made Fuchai 夫差 (d. 473 BCE), his son and heir to the Wu throne, swear revenge against Yue and King Goujian. In short order, Fuchai gathered together his advisors Wu Zixu, Sun Wu, and Bo Pi 伯嚭 (d. 473 BCE) to plan a counterattack on Yue. When Goujian learned of Fuchai's efforts to strengthen and prepare the Wu armies for a retaliatory campaign, he proposed a pre-emptive counterstrike of his own. He, too, had capable and loyal counsel in the persons of Fan Li 范蠡 (536 – 488 BCE) and Wen Zhong 文种 (d. 472 BCE).

Not much is known about either Fan Li or Wen Zhong, and most alleged details about them relate to their connection with King Goujian. Fan Li is said to have been born to a peasant family in the present-day area of Nanyang 南阳, Henan Province, in what was then part of the Chu State. After he met and befriended his district's governor, Wen Zhong, the two men decided to emigrate together to the Yue State. They offered their service to King Goujian, who elevated them to ministerial rank.

When Goujian consulted Fan and Wen about striking at Fuchai and the heart of Wu, both advisors counseled strongly against the move, recommending that the King bide his time. It was one thing to continue defending the homeland successfully, they argued, but Yue was not yet adequately equipped to invade, conquer, and hold a state as large and powerful as Wu. As Fan Li counseled the young king:

> Think again. I have heard that arms are unlucky, war an evil force, and that disputes are minor affairs. If you plot with an evil force, by unlucky means, risking your life over a minor affair, you will be flouting Heaven's will and your campaign will not prosper.[6]

Unfortunately, the youthful king was not dissuaded by his more judicious elders. Goujian launched an invasion into Wu territory in 494 BCE, but his army suffered a devastating defeat at Fujiao 夫椒.[7] When Goujian retreated, the Wu army pressed its victory aggressively. Fuchai refused to relent in his pursuit, bent on fulfilling his promise of revenge at his father's deathbed. At the last, King Goujian, his advisors, and the remnants of their army, about 5,000 men, were surrounded at Kuaiji Mountain, upon which stood the tomb and temple of Yu the Great. Perhaps Goujian explicitly sought out this place for his last stand, since he and his lineage ancestors had claimed a multi-generational connection to Yu.

King Goujian's impetuosity had cost him dearly. As he was preparing to kill his queen and commit suicide in what would surely be his final battle, Fan Li and Wen Zhong came before him. Fearful that a Wu conquest and disappearance of the royal line would mark the extinction of the Yue State, the two counselors proposed a surrender strategy. Goujian and Fan Li would stand before Fuchai, abase themselves, and swear fealty as vassals of the Wu State. To convince Fuchai of their submission, Goujian, his wife, and Fan Li would also submit to being prisoners and willingly placed in whatever service to the Wu State that Fuchai decided for them. Wen Zhong would remain behind to shepherd the people and quietly rebuild Yue's strength. Only by enduring this humiliation, his advisors contended, could King Goujian preserve Yue and protect his subjects.

Goujian reluctantly consented. When he was finally brought before Fuchai, he presented himself humbly, offering lavish gifts and praising the Wu king effusively for his wisdom, valor, and mercy. Goujian's promise of servitude doubtless appealed to Fuchai's vanity and desire for revenge even more than would his opponent's death, since Fuchai could now spend pleasurable years observing his royal counterpart's bitter subjugation.

Fuchai's advisor Wu Zixu immediately saw through Fan Li's plan and erupted in opposition. Yue would never stand to be a subject of Wu, he exclaimed. The only sensible finish to this bitter conflict was execution of Goujian and his queen and senior officials and complete eradication of the Yue State. Why should King Fuchai allow one of his most threatening enemies to live, Wu Zixu continued. Only harm could come from such a decision. But nothing the loyal advisor could say was enough to convince Fuchai, who only saw in Fan Li's plan the sadistic satisfaction of watching the enemy king and queen forced to live and work like the lowliest peasants.

When Goujian's captivity began in 492 BCE, Fuchai assigned his new captives to a humble cottage and ordered them to take care of the royal horses and clean the royal stables. The Yue king accepted his fate, committing himself to suffer humiliation and degradation as punishment for failing his subjects. The trio of prisoners performed their duties diligently for months under the occasional but bemused eye of King Fuchai. In fact, the Wu king was so impressed with their sacrifice and dedication on behalf of the Yue people, he began to feel sympathy for his captives' plight.

When Fuchai openly suggested after a time that he should perhaps show mercy and allow them to return home, Wu Zixu was aghast. He argued vehemently that the three prisoners should be put to death. The venal, greedy, and obsequious Bo Pi sided with the Wu king, offering the opinion that such a kindness would only inspire gratitude and more loyalty in return. King Fuchai failed to perceive Bo Pi's motives: to discredit and supplant Wu Zixu on the one hand, and to continue receiving generous bribes from Yue on the other. In the end, Fuchai allowed his prisoners to return to their Yue homes. Wu Zixu was apoplectic, proclaiming to his king that Goujian "will end up eating the great king's heart…[and] devouring the great king's liver."[8]

Goujian received a warm welcome upon his return to Kuaiji in 490 BCE. He admitted his errors and promised the people he would work tirelessly to restore Yue to its former glory. His advisors counseled that Yue should self-strengthen as quietly as possible. Meanwhile, they exploited the rift between Wu Zixu and Bo Pi and plied Fuchai with fine gifts and tribute that appealed to his vanity and hedonistic weaknesses.

The Yue leaders also took actions that reinforced the impression of vassalage and submission. For example, when Goujian ordered Fan Li to build a new Yue capital city at Kuaiji in 490 BCE,[9] his advisor cleverly left the northwestern section of the wall open as a signal of Yue's continuing subservience to Wu. The new Yue capital was a walled city, about 8.4 kilometers (about five miles) around, punctuated by three land gates and three water gates. Goujian's palace was surrounded by its own wall, more than one kilometer in circumference, with four land gates and a single water gate.[10]

Through the years following Goujian's return to Yue, he is said to have eaten common foods and foregone the usual royal pleasures. The most famous legend of his commitment holds that the Yue king licked a hanging gallbladder in his room every time he passed by as a bitter reminder of the suffering his mistakes had inflicted on his subjects. He also slept on a bed of sticks every night for the same reason. In later times, the phrase *woxin changdan* 卧薪尝胆 ("sleeping on brushwood and tasting gall") came to symbolize a great leader's patience, commitment, and self-sacrifice in overcoming defeat and humiliation.

Xi Shi, the Greatest Beauty of All[11]

So far, Fan Li's surrender plan had succeeded admirably, requiring only a few tolerable years of subservience. The Yue leaders also reaped another, perhaps unanticipated, benefit: they now fully understood the incautious profligacy of Fuchai, the dangerous wisdom of Wu Zixu, and the profound corruptibility of Bo Pi. All this information was now employed to sap Wu's strength while rebuilding their own.

Fan Li and Wen Zhong mapped out a strategy of strengthening Yue's economy, building up its grain reserves, and expanding and training its armies. On the diplomatic side, they sought opportunities to flatter and distract Fuchai with expensive gifts and encourage him in wasteful projects. Furthermore, they continued currying Bo Pi's favorable leanings toward Yue by bribery while creating opportunities to undercut Wu Zixu's influence with Fuchai.

Having seen at close hand Fuchai's hedonism and sexual debauchery, Fan and Wen devised a radical plan to create the ultimate gift for the Wu king. They initiated a search for the most beautiful young women of Yue, from among whom they would select the two most irresistible and present them as further tribute to the Wu State. Those two maidens would be charged with winning Fuchai's heart and creating as many distractions and as much wasteful extravagance as possible. They were the Yue State's "Trojan horses," weakening the Wu State with captivating feminine charms rather than hidden soldiers.

The search for eligible maidens ran high and low through Yue territory until two young peasant women were chosen from among the eligible candidates: Shi Yiguang 施夷光 and Zheng Dan 鄭旦. The two maidens were friends, and both were natives of Zhuji 諸暨, a small town about twenty-five miles southwest of modern Shaoxing. Because Shi Yiguang lived with her parents on the west side of Zhuji, she was also known as Xi Shi 西施 ("Shi from the west").

Both Xi Shi and Zheng Dan were stunningly beautiful. They were also uneducated and uncultured, utterly unsuited for the Wu king. For three years, they were groomed under Fan Li's watchful eye in courtly speech, dress, and movement, how to apply make-up and dress their hair, and how to be demure yet clever in conversation. In addition, they received rigorous instruction in the finest of womanly arts: singing, dancing, reciting poetry, and playing stringed instruments. Xi Shi in particular was described as being so enticing that when she washed silk in a stream or stood by a garden pool, the fish would forget to swim and sink to the bottom.[12]

When Fan Li felt that the two young women were ready, he presented them to King Fuchai as gifts of loyalty. Wu Zixu easily guessed his adversaries' motives and counseled adamantly against accepting the two beautiful maidens, but Fuchai was instantly smitten. He rejected his advisor's counsel out of hand.

Although Zheng Dan is said to have died in her first year at Fuchai's court, Xi Shi played her subversive role to perfection. She asked for rare and expensive dishes, encouraged Fuchai to shower her with extravagant gifts, and enticed him into long nights of drinking and love-making. To curry Xi Shi's favors, the Wu king built the magnificent Guanwa Palace (館娃宮, Guanwa gong) atop Lingyan Mountain (灵岩山, Lingyan shan) in Suzhou's western hills. Because Xi Shi and her maidens enjoyed playing music out of doors at Guanwa, Fuchai ordered construction of a raised wooden platform covered with a layer of earth. When Xi Shi and her maidens walked on the platform or danced to music, their footsteps resounded like a drum.

40

On the still more distant Xishan 西山, an island in Tai Lake, Fuchai is said to have taken his Yue paramour to a smooth natural stone formation at the foot of Shigong Mountain (石公山, Shigong shan) to view the moon together. To the present day, this place is still called Mingyuewan (明月湾, Bright Moon Slope). On the same island, local legend also tells of Fuchai building a long dock extending into Tai Lake in a southeasterly direction so that Xi Shi could admire the night skies while looking in the direction of her native home.

The renowned Tang Dynasty poet Li Bai 李白 (701 – 762) later versified in a haunting and joyless voice on Xi Shi's life with Fuchai:

> Above the Gusu Tower as the crows come to roost,
> Inside the palace of the king of Wu, Xi Shi gets drunk.
> Before the performance of Wu song and Chu dance is over,
> The verdant mountains are about to swallow half the sun.
> As the silver arrow sinks within the gold clepsydra, many moments drip away,
> They arise to see the autumn moon sinking into the river's waves.
> As [the sun] gradually rises in the east, where will they seek pleasure next?[13]

and

> The wind stirs the water-lilies filling the palace with their perfume,
> The king of Wu banquets at the top of Gusu Tower.
> Xi Shi dances drunkenly, charmingly weak from exertion,
> Smiling, she reclines against a white jade couch in front of the eastern window.[14]

The Conflict Concludes

As Yue's strength waxed, Wu's waned. Despite the two states' past enmity toward one another, Fuchai refused to see Goujian's growing threat to his south. More interested in playing the dynastic power game, the Wu king elected instead to launch an attack northward into the Qi State (present-day Shandong Province) in 484 BCE. Bo Pi supported Fuchai's plan while Wu Zixu opposed it, arguing that the King should focus on the Yue threat.

Fuchai went ahead with his plans with a good measure of success. Having proved to his own satisfaction that Wu Zixu's counsel was no longer useful, Fuchai had a sword delivered to his advisor, a symbolic but unmistakable royal order that Wu should commit suicide. Loyal to the end, Wu Zixu complied, but not before having the last word. In an angry and ill-omened message intended for Fuchai, Wu Zixu declared: "Pluck out my eyes and set them over the East Gate, so that I can watch the men of Yue march into Wu."[15]

Meanwhile, during the dozen years since Goujian's return to Kuaiji, the Yue king had grown increasingly emboldened by the progress in his state's recovery. Because a number of his ploys had succeeded in weakening Wu, Goujian was also growing impatient to exact revenge and deliver a conquest to his people. Having learned from his impetuosity a decade earlier, he grudgingly heeded Fan Li's and Wen Zhong's counsel to wait until the

41

time was right. In 482 BCE, the right time arrived.

In the spring of that year, Fuchai traveled north for a convocation of the confederated Zhou states, among whom Wu was now one of the most powerful members.[16] While the Wu king was basking in the glory of being chosen as the overlord (*ba*), Goujian launched his assault on Wu. This time, the Yue armies took the Wu capital city, burned the Guanwa Palace to the ground, and executed Fuchai's son and heir apparent.

Fuchai rushed back to defend his lands and gained a truce with Yue that lasted another six years, but the die had been cast. When conflict resumed, a series of bloody battles ended with Fuchai and the remnants of his army surrounded at Gusu Mountain (姑苏山, Gusu shan) in 473 BCE. With his situation hopeless, Fuchai sent emissaries to Goujian asking to be spared and reminding the Yue king of the merciful treatment he had received at Kuaiji Mountain so many years before. Fan Li counseled for Fuchai's capture and execution, but before that could take place, Fuchai chose suicide over imprisonment. In the end, Goujian graced his enemy counterpart with an honorable burial.

In 1986, an interesting pre-historical connection was added to the stories of the Wu - Yue conflict when an ancient tomb was discovered at Yanshan 嚴山 (in Jiangsu Province).[17] The burial site, believed associated with King Fuchai of Wu, contained a large quantity of fine jade objects, some of which were identifiable as works of the Liang-zhu Culture. Their presence suggests not only ancient recovery of Liangzhu relics but enough respect for their quality and historicity in the Wu-Yue period to include them among the high-quality objects reserved for the afterlife of an important personage.

In the following months, Goujian assumed control over the entire Wu State, partitioning some areas and returning them to the states from which Fuchai had seized them. In recognition of Yue's power and in gratitude for his generosity in dividing the territorial spoils of his conquest, the Zhou confederation leaders proclaimed King Goujian of Yue as the new *ba*. He had reached the apex of his power and influence by snatching it from Fuchai just as the Wu king had reached the peak of his.

Goujian ruled over the expanded Yue State until his death in 465 BCE, after which his sons and descendants continued that reign from the new Yue capital Goujian established farther north at Langya 琅琊 (modern Huangdao District 黄岛区 in Shandong Province). In the 4th Century BCE, the Chu State counterattacked Yue and killed the Yue king, but evidence suggests[18] that the Yue State maintained its independence up to the final decades of the 3rd Century BCE when the Qin Dynasty finally united the nation by conquest. Among all the various kingdoms, only the State of Qi survived longer than Yue before falling to the first Qin Emperor, Shihuangdi 始皇帝 (259 – 210 BCE).

The two states of Wu and Yue may have ceased to exist more than two millennia in the past, but their stories persisted, variously embellished for moral education or romanticized for entertainment. The events and participants evolved into examples of conquest and revenge, loyalty and obsequiousness, debauchery and impetuosity, humiliation and patience, deceit and trickery.

The earliest extant histories of the Wu – Yue conflict were not recorded until more than five hundred years after the events they described.[19] By that time, the reality was so colored by myth as to be unrecoverable. Perhaps it no longer mattered. As oral tradition, those accounts had served their own didactic purposes, object lessons in right and wrong behaviors and their consequences. For the people of Wu and Yue, however, these stories *were* their history and cultural identity, factual or not, and the individual participants, real or mythical, were alternately honored, reviled, or worshipped for their roles. Whoever the real people were and whatever their true stories, they have lived on in Chinese culture for the past 2,500 years. The names Yue and Wu would persist through the ages.

The Legends Live On

No individual from the Wu-Yue story achieved greater renown than Xi Shi, the great *femme fatale* of Chinese history. She became the subject of poems, stories, and operas, many of which added their own new elements to her story. West Lake itself, so often regaled for its natural beauty, came to be seen as Nature's physical embodiment or reincarnation of Xi Shi, as can be seen in the poem that opens this chapter. In fact, poets and local people sometimes referred to the lake by the name Xizi 西子, meaning "Lady Xi [Shi]." Yet, as Olivia Milburn points out, "Her story was a relatively late addition to the history of the conflict between the kingdoms of Wu and Yue."[20]

Beyond the specifics of Xi Shi's role in the fall of King Fuchai and the Wu State, her story gelled into a common tale with varied endings. In one version, the beautiful but unpolished silk-washing peasant girl from Zhuji and the esteemed court official Fan Li fell deeply in love. However, they honored their obligations to their king and kingdom, sacrificing their relationship in the most painfully personal of ways in order to bring about Fuchai's demise. In some tellings, Fan Li and Xi Shi renewed their love after Wu's defeat and were last seen sailing away together across Tai Lake. Other tales have Xi Shi executed at Fan Li's or Goujian's hand, since a woman of such distracting beauty was an equally potential threat to the future welfare and continuity of the Yue State.

The earliest extant opera featuring Xi Shi appeared in the Ming Dynasty. Liang Chenyu's 梁辰鱼 (1520 – 1592) groundbreaking play, *The Girl Washing Silk* (浣纱记, *Huanshaji*) was the founding work of what became one of China's premier theatrical forms, Kunqu Opera. Liang's play told Xi Shi's story largely along traditional lines but added a fascinating wrinkle to Fan Li's relationship with the great beauty. After Wu is vanquished, Fan Li departs Yue with Xi Shi by his side, sailing into the unknown not only for love, but also for loyalty to Goujian. Having seen the behavioral damage Xi Shi was capable of inflicting on Fuchai, Fan Li realizes she could do likewise to Goujian. Fan Li's safest course for preserving Yue was to spirit her far away, where the couple lived out their lives together, never again seen in Kuaiji.

Fan Li's legendary Wu-Yue afterlife also took some interesting twists over the centuries. Some stories have Goujian's loyal advisor realizing after the conquest of Wu that he may have outlived his usefulness to the king and might even be perceived as a threat. As Wu Zixu had reputedly observed to Fuchai, "When the clever hares have been caught, the hound is thrown into the kettle to boil."[21] In these tales, Fan Li leaves Yue, with or without Xi Shi, and pursues a second career as a wealthy businessman selling traditional Chinese medicine. Through the ages, Fan Li was said to have written a book of rules for business success and has sometimes been regarded as a god of wealth or "the father of business." He also became associated with the practice of fish farming, including alleged authorship of the earliest known treatise on that subject.[22]

Before departing Yue, Fan Li advised Wen Zhong that he, too, should leave Goujian's service for the same reasons. Loyalty to his king, coupled with Fan's departure, led Wen to stay on as an advisor. Within a year, Goujian indeed called Wen to the court and presented him with a sword by which to commit suicide. The king had indeed thrown at least one hound into the boiling kettle.

Although Wu Zixu served loyally as the most senior advisor to the Wu State, his legendary afterlife took a rather strange turn into the Yue State. After he committed suicide at Fuchai's order, his body was said to have been unceremoniously dumped into a river. The *Spring and Autumn Annals of Wu and Yue* (吳越春秋, *Wuyue chunqiu*) outlines a myth that lasted ten or more centuries, at least into the Song Dynasty era.

According to that ancient history, a massive, roaring wave appeared shortly after Wu Zixu's dead body entered the river, sweeping the corpse away. The next year, the "water immortal" Wu Zixu emerged from the ocean, carved a channel under the mountain where Wen Zhang was buried, and carried his interred body away.[23] The connection between the two was simple: both upright and loyal advisors had been forced to commit suicide by unappreciative kings. The two water spirits were said to return regularly from the ocean to wreak their eternal revenge in the wild, angry waters of the Qiantang tidal bore, Wu Zixu in the lead, Wen Zhong following behind.[24]

Another historical record from the 1st Century CE indicates that temples to Wu Zixu were constructed along the Qiantang River as far upstream as Hangzhou "for the purpose of appeasing his anger and stopping the wild waves."[25] A local, fifth-century gazetteer also identifies a Wu Zixu temple built near Hangzhou after people saw the water god appear "riding the crest of the Hangzhou tidal bore in a white carriage drawn by white horses."[26]

The Sword Maiden of Yue

One more character of interest, also likely mythical, emerged out of the various tellings and retellings of the Wu-Yue conflict. In order to better prepare the Yue soldiers for their eventual assault on Wu, Fan Li suggested to Goujian that the men should receive additional sword training. He advised the Yue king about a young woman in the mountainous area of southern Yue who had developed impressive new sword skills. If her swordsmanship proved indeed of such quality, she might be persuaded to convey her skills to Goujian's armies.

Goujian agreed to the idea, however unconventional, and sent his envoys south to find this sword-wielding young lady. Standing before King Goujian, she explained that she had not been properly educated in the remote area where she lived. Lacking that opportunity, she had developed an interest in archery and swordsmanship that grew into passions. Despite being self-taught, she had cultivated some simple but powerful techniques that could be readily mastered with practice.

The sword maiden's methods relied on control of one's emotions while strengthening one's spirit, as well as applying *yin* 阴 and *yang* 阳 principles, which she compared to opening and closing doors and windows. She then demonstrated her skills with such proficiency that Goujian crowned her "Maiden of Yue" (越女, Yue Nü) and ordered that she teach her methods to all of his senior military officers and most proficient soldiers. They, in turn, were commanded to instruct the men in the lower ranks.

The Maiden of Yue never achieved the subsequent acclaim of Xi Shi. However, the notion of a woman of ancient times achieving such proficiency in a masculine art as to instruct male warriors established her as one of the earliest models of female knight-errantry. Her story would inspire Zhejiangese women of later centuries who sought entrée into the cultural, civic, and even military arenas traditionally dominated in Chinese society by men.

Chapter 3

UNION AND DISUNION

(221 BCE – 618 CE)

Noise of Breakers in the Eighth Month[1]

In the Eighth Month the noise of breakers comes roaring through the land,
The head a dozen yards high butts the hill and turns.
An instant, and it bends round to enter Sea Gate,
Rolling back heaps of sand like heaps of snow.

– Liu Yuxi (772 – 842)

Union

After the Chu State overran Yue in 306 BCE, the Hangzhou-Kuaiji region became a military outpost and was renamed Qiantang County. A little less than a century later, Qin Shihuang 秦始皇 (259 – 210 BCE)[2] swept ruthlessly across the land beginning in 230 BCE, subjugating the independent states and areas as far south as present-day Guangdong Province by military conquest. In 223 BCE, the powerful Chu State fell before him, and with it went the territories formerly known as Wu and Yue. Two years later, after conquering the Qi State, he declared himself the first emperor (秦始皇帝, Qin Shihuangdi) of the Qin Dynasty 秦朝 (221 – 207 BCE) and a unified China.

Qin Shihuangdi's administrative and structural achievements were rightfully legendary: building a grand capital at Xianyang 咸阳 (Xi'an, Shaanxi Province), initiating construction of the Great Wall (万里长城, *Wanli changcheng*), creating a national administrative structure of thirty-six districts, instituting an inter-territorial road network, and standardizing weight measures, currency, and basic script-writing. His rule was harsh, however, characterized by brutal military conflict, anti-intellectual literary inquisitions and book burnings,

46

cruel punishments and executions of scholars, paranoid fear of assassination, and boundless obsession with personal immortality.

During a tour of his eastern realm, Qin Shihuangdi traveled to Kuaiji Mountain to pay homage at Yu the Great's tomb. At this time, Hangzhou was at best a small riverbank settlement or fishing village along the Zhe (Qiantang) River. According to traditional belief, China's first emperor moored his ship to a large stone at the base of Precious Stone Hill (宝石山, Baoshi Shan), now one of the northern hills bordering West Lake. This "Rock on Which the King of Qin Anchored His Boat" (秦王拦船石, *Qin wang lan chuan shi*) was allegedly carved in around 1120 into a massive, gold-decorated Buddha head for the Temple of the Big Stone Buddha at West Lake.[3] Qin Shihuangdi was the first emperor of China to visit Yu's tomb and temple, but others would follow and conduct rituals, leave inscriptions, or compose poetry.

Qin Shihuangdi's reign, and that of his dynasty, was unusually brief, lasting barely fifteen years: eleven years under his rule, and just four years under his hapless, eunuch-dominated son, Qin Er Shi 秦二世 (r. 210 – 207 BCE). Ironically, unified China's briefest reign was followed by its longest, that of the Han 汉朝 (207 BCE – 220 CE). Beginning with the stabilizing efforts of Emperor Gaozu 汉高祖 (r. 206 – 195 BCE), the Han Dynasty ruled from its capital at Chang'an 长安 (close by Qin Shihuangdi's destroyed capital of Xianyang). The early Han emperors Wendi 汉文帝 (r. 180 – 157 BCE) and Jingdi 汉景帝 (157 – 141 BCE) established Confucianism as the foundation of the empire's governing principles and made demonstrated knowledge of the Confucian texts the basis for acceptance into government service.

Despite opening the Silk Road for trade, extending the imperial court's domestic control as far south as Guangdong Province and northern Vietnam, and turning back incursions from Xiongnu 匈奴 tribesmen in the northwest, the fifty-four-year reign of Han Emperor Wudi 汉武帝 (r. 141 – 87 BCE) ended in economic and political chaos. The dynastic decline ended in 23 CE with a two-year civil war and relocation of the capital from Chang'an, now in ruins, to Luoyang 洛阳, causing the dynasty to be subdivided by modern historians into Western Han and Eastern Han eras.

What began well enough in Luoyang with the first three Eastern Han emperors (Guangwu 光武, r. 25 – 57, Xiaoming 孝明, r. 57 – 75, and Xiaozhang 孝章, r. 75 – 88) fell into another downward spiral in 88 CE, starting with the nine-year-old Emperor Hedi and passing through an uninterrupted succession of child emperors who were mostly overseen by unscrupulous Regents. Their ages at the time of accession to the throne are sufficient to tell the story:

- Hedi 汉和帝, age 9, (r. 88 – 106)
- Shangdi 汉殇帝, age 1 (r. 106 – 106)
- Andi 汉安帝, age 12 (r. 106 - 125)
- Shundi 汉顺帝, age 10 (r. 125 – 144)
- Chongdi 汉冲帝, age 1 (r. 144 – 145)
- Zhidi 汉质帝, age 7 (r. 145 – 146)

47

- Huandi 汉桓帝, age 14 (r. 146 – 168)
- Lingdi 汉灵帝, age 12 (r. 168 – 189)
- Xiandi 汉献帝, age 8 (r. 189 – 220)

Spilled Water

The *History of the Former Han* (汉书, *Han shu*), published in 111 CE,[4] tells the uplifting but ultimately tragic personal story of a self-taught, rags-to-riches official named Zhu Maichen 朱买臣 (d. 115 BCE) who served as Prefect of Kuaiji early in the 2nd Century CE. Zhu Maichen was a native of nearby Jiangsu Province ("a man of Wu"), born to a life of poverty but sufficiently educated to be literate. Although he earned a meager living cutting and selling firewood, he dreamed of becoming an important official. Consequently, he was never without a book at hand, even as he walked to or through the woods or stopped work long enough to eat a midday meal.

Zhu's wife chastised him ceaselessly for his bookishness. She argued that Zhu would never be accepted as an official, so he should devote himself entirely to earning a passable living. The woodcutter disagreed, assuring his frustrated wife that he would succeed. He advised her to be patient, that he knew with certainty from a fortune-teller that he would achieve wealth and success at age fifty.

After enduring year after year of hardship and seeing no hope of anything better, Zhu's exasperated wife finally did the socially and morally unthinkable: she asked her husband to divorce her. After she repeatedly rejected her husband's confident entreaties to bear with him until he reached the heights of his true fate, he gave in and wrote a paper of divorce. Not long after, his ex-wife remarried to a craftsman or laborer from Kuaiji, a poor man but at least one with a steady income.

Zhu's readings in the classic works gradually educated him as though he had the formal training of a scholar. One day, he met an old friend named Yan Zhu (d. 122 BCE) who promised to recommend the woodcutter for an official position. Maichen then traveled to the capital at the court's invitation, where he favorably impressed Emperor Wudi with his self-acquired knowledge, plain-spokenness, and honesty. According to the abbreviated account in the *Han shu*, the Emperor appointed him Prefect of Kuaiji.

Prior to Zhu Maichen's arrival as Kuaiji's new governor, city officials organized a project to repair the roadway on which he would travel. Passing along the road where the laborers were working, Zhu spied his ex-wife and her new husband among them. "He ordered his carriage stopped, and commanded his former wife and her husband to be transported in a carriage at the back of the cortege." The couple remained in residence at the government compound (衙门, *yamen*) for a month until Zhu's former wife hanged herself out of shame she could no longer bear.[5]

The late-blooming Zhu Maichen went on from his position in Kuaiji to gain multiple promotions and a largely successful record. Sadly, his career and life ended abruptly in execution after he promoted false accusations against a political foe that resulted in the latter's suicide. He would likely have been forgotten to history if not for his marital dissolution and the unusual circumstance of his wife having demanded the divorce. Her resulting regret and suicide-inducing shame became repeatable Confucian object lessons on the perils of female immorality.

In the Tang Dynasty, the *Han shu* version of Zhu Maichen's biography first received fictionalized treatment that filled in some elements, added others, and invariably focused on the cautionary tale of women seeking divorce. Zhu's former wife was identified with the name Cui Shi 崔氏, her feelings of shame were more explicitly expressed, and a new and highly theatrical confrontation was introduced.

In those later retellings, Cui Shi appears before her former husband, now a high official in Kuaiji, in a public setting. She begs Zhu Maichen to take her back, apologizing for having ever doubted him. Her former husband listens passively, then orders a bucket of water to be placed before him. With a sharp, swift kick, he spills the bucket's contents everywhere around him. When Cui Shi has gathered up all that spilled water and replaced it in the bucket, Zhu declares, he will take her back. Shamed and driven half-mad, Cui Shi finds her only escape in suicide. This theatrical scene forever popularized the Chinese adage, 泼水难收 (*Po shui nan shou*). A reasonably literal translation is "Spilled water can't be retrieved." The adage's more idiomatic Western parallel might be, "Don't cry over spilled milk."

Zhu Maichen's heroic rise by persistent study and unflagging effort, and Cui Shi's dramatic fall for lack of persistence in the matrimonial bond, proved an irresistible dramatic framework from the Tang Dynasty era onward. Poems, short stories, radio plays, and theatrical adaptations[6] all became commonplace, culminating in the celebrated Kunqu Opera *Lanke Mountain* (烂柯山, *Lanke shan*).

Taming the Bore

From the earliest days of settlement along the Qiantang River, proximity to the river meant exposure to the tidal bore. While the bore itself was predictable enough, its magnitude and severity were less so due to ocean storms, wind direction, solar and lunar alignments, and even hidden shifts in the sand shoals and sea bed beneath Hangzhou Bay. By at least the Han Dynasty era, officials in bayside and riverside towns began efforts to control the bore and mitigate the impact of its worst torrents as they rushed upstream toward the early settlements that grew to be Hangzhou and the riverside towns to its east.

One of the earliest known officials to tackle the river embankment problem is reported to have been a Han governor named Hua Xin 华信. According to legend, Hua undertook a project in around 85 CE to build one of the first river embankments using mud and stone. He let it be known all around the area that he would pay a thousand cash to each person who brought a load of soil and rock to the riverside. Within a short time, people arrived "in clouds" and received their payment. At a certain point as the construction progressed, however, Hua announced that he had regrettably run out of money. Those present threw down their loads and stormed off in anger. From the materials they left behind, he was able to complete the work as planned with the limited funds he had available.[7]

Unfortunately, Hua's mud and stone wall did not survive the worst rages of the tidal bore for long. It would be more than eight hundred years before the earliest successful barriers could be designed and constructed. In the meantime, there was little recourse other than sacrificing and praying to the god of the tides.[8]

An Exemplar of Filial Piety

In July of 143 CE, a singer and shaman named Cao Xu 曹盱 from Shangyu (modern Shaoxing) stood on the banks of the Shun River 舜江.[9] As was his custom, he had come to the riverside to meet the tidal bore and conduct a performance to appease Wu Zixu, the Tide God. Standing alongside the churning, silt-loaded waves whose thundering roar literally swallowed his chants, Cao Xu was unexpectedly swept into the water and drowned.

Cao Xu's thirteen-year-old daughter, Cao E 曹娥, was devastated by her father's death and cried inconsolably. She stayed by the riverside for days, determined to retrieve her father's body from the water and give him an honorable burial. Day after day for more than two weeks she watched and waited in vain as the passing river refused to yield her father's corpse. After seventeen days, Cao E yielded to her grief, walked to the water's edge, and threw herself into the river. For several days, no sign of either body was observed by her family or the local people who watched hopefully for some sign of the drowned maiden.

On the fifth day after Cao E's death, a body was seen in the river. As it was being pulled from the water, the people realized that there were actually two figures: Cao E's body, with her arms wrapped around her father's corpse. Such was the young maiden's filial piety that the Tide God was moved to release her father's body back to her, at the cost of her life.

Eight years later, in 151 CE, Cao E was formally honored for her filiality. An inscribed stele in Cao E's honor was erected, "enumerating the good deeds of the dead [maiden]… as a model of morality" and "serving an educational purpose through the ages within the family and even in the community." The local magistrate conducted a ritual sacrifice and read an elegy:

> As for the filial girl,
> Graceful and gorgeous was she,
> Swaying as if dancing.
> Her fine bearing and decorous character
> Made her a lovely, comely lady.
> Her dimples appeared with her ravishing smile;
> Would that she should enjoy her wedded life at her [future husband's] home
> On the south bank of the Qia River [where there was a marriage made in Heaven],
> She was ready for the wedding ceremony.
> Alas, she [suddenly] lost her loving father.
> Oh, azure heavens, what was your intent?
> "Without my father, upon whom can I rely?"
> She then appealed to the gods expressing her grievance.

She then went towards the river wailing all along.
Regarding death as a "return."
Thereupon she lightly left her life far behind,
Jumping into mud and sand.
The filial girl, shifting and drifting,
Now floating, now sinking,
At times approaching islets and holms,
At times in mid-stream,
At times rushed along with the torrent and currents,
At times returning on waves and ripples.
Ten thousand men lost their voices;
A myriad agonized in condolence.
Onlookers packed the roads,
Gathering like clouds filling up passages,
All bursting into tears,
Startling and saddening the imperial capital.

The elegy closes with praise for a low-class maiden whose filial behavior outshone that of fine ladies who also had suffered loss, lamenting that the common people must stand strong and upright without support:

How sad this stern uprightness.
For a thousand years it will remain unchanged.
Alas, how sad.[10]

A temple was built in Shangyu to further honor Cao E's filial piety, and the Shun River was renamed by the people as the Cao E (often written as Cao'e), down to the present day.

One measure of the strength and persistence of Cao E's legacy occurred more than seventeen centuries after the young maiden's legendary sacrifice for her father's repose. In 1882, Shaoxing city officials released an updated version of the *Temple Gazetteer of the Filial Daughter of the Cao River* (曹江孝女廟之, *Caojiang xiaonü miaozhi*) that included forty-two images of the filial young maiden. The gazetteer's preface reiterated Cao E's importance as a model of filial piety and her spiritual protection of those who fished or traveled the Cao'e River. The gazetteer even acknowledged the local people's belief that she had been in some way instrumental in delivering Shangyu from the Taiping rebels.[11]

Cao E's temple, and reputedly her tomb at the temple site, can still be seen in present-day Shangyu, located (naturally) in the Cao'e Scenic Area of (naturally) the city's Cao'e subdistrict.

Disunion

Despite the relatively longer reign periods of the last three Han emperors,[12] their era was marked by earthquakes, floods, locust plagues, famine, official corruption, nearly unfettered eunuch control and nepotism in the imperial court, and mass departures of honest officials.

By Emperor Lingdi's reign, regional warlords had effectively taken over the empire. Three of those warlords in particular—Cao Cao 曹操 (c. 155 – 220), Liu Bei 刘备 (161 – 223), and Sun Quan 孙权 (182 – 252), and their immediate descendants—partitioned the nation for the next sixty years into the Three Kingdoms of (respectively) Wei 魏, Shu Han 蜀汉, and Wu 吴.[13]

During this conflict-filled period, whatever village-like settlement had formed in Qiantang County and the West Lake vicinity was part of the Kuaiji commandery, beholden to Sun Quan. However, there is little historical indication of any substantive settlement at Hangzhou's modern site alongside West Lake until the 4th Century. Geil's 1911 treatment of China's eighteen capitals dismissively asserted that there is "no record of anything before 326"[14] other than perhaps some fishermen's or peasant farmers' settlements. Even then, according to Giles, it would still be "nearly three hundred years before anyone thought it worthwhile to erect any walls."[15]

The Wu Kingdom, with its capital at Jiankang 建康 (modern Nanjing), ranged west from the southeastern coast, encompassing not only present-day Zhejiang Province but also Fujian, Guangdong, Anhui, Hunan, Guangxi, and the southern half of Jiangsu as well as most of northern Vietnam. Sun Quan maintained relative stability from Kuaiji, with a strong enough military to hold the Wei and Shu Han states at bay and deflect much of the fighting well to the west and north. Sun also welcomed Buddhism into his domain, helping establish and support temple construction in the Zhejiang and Jiangsu areas.

The end of the Wu State in 280 marked the beginning of a three-hundred-year span known as the Period of Disunion. Northern China first experienced a period of 135 years whose name alone, the Sixteen Kingdoms (304 – 439), indicates the level of instability and chaos after being overrun by nomadic peoples from the northern steppes. The Northern Wei Dynasty (386 – 535) established a degree of stability, after which the northern dynasties fractured into the Eastern Wei (535 – 550) and Northern Qi (550 – 577) on the one hand and the Western Wei (535 – 557) and Northern Zhou (557 – 581) on the other.

The southern kingdoms, with their capital on the south bank of the Yangzi River at Jiankang, fared somewhat better but still suffered the instability of six different dynasties who collectively averaged reign periods of only fifty-four years: Western Jin 西晋朝 (265 - 316), Eastern Jin 东晋朝 (265 - 316), Liu Song 刘宋朝 (420 - 479), Qi 齐朝 (479 - 501), Liang 梁朝 (502 - 556), and Chen 陈朝 (557 - 589). The last three of these dynasties—Qi, Liang, and Chen—ruled for only a combined 110 years and managed to enthrone a destabilizing total of fifteen emperors.

Despite the governmental chaos of multiple regime changes, life in and around Shaoxing moved along under its own impetus. During these early centuries, the formerly "barbarian" lands of the Yangzi Delta grew in wealth and power as the Chinese population began a substantial migration from the war-plagued north.

Shaoxing and the Hangzhou vicinity benefitted once again by their southeasterly locations, well away from most of the intra- and inter-dynastic conflict. Population grew, agricultural technology and productivity advanced, and the seeds of intellectual and cultural development were sown and cultivated. Kuaiji, with its capital at Shangyu, continued to be an important location along the Qiantang River. Visitors from the north saw a rich and fertile land that inspired effusive praise, such as this florid description by the painter Gu Kaizhi 顾恺之 (344- 406):

> The landscape of Kuaiji consists of a thousand rival precipices overhanging ten thousand ravines and gushing torrents, crowned by trees and luxuriant vegetation that appear like variously colored clouds.[16]

Gu Kaizhi's was the type of hyperbole that helped elevate the reputation of Hangzhou and Suzhou to "heaven on earth" status, encapsulated in the oft-repeated ancient phrase, "In the sky there is heaven, but on earth there are Suzhou and Hangzhou" (想有天堂下有苏杭, "*Xiang you tian tang, xia you Su Hong*").

A Spring Outing that Lived on Forever

For aspiring literati throughout imperial times, proficiency with the Confucian classics was a pre-condition for admission to the scholarly caste. However, being conversant with the Four Books and Five Classics[17] was far from sufficient if one sought recognition as a true literatus. The highest-level scholars, those honored and regaled through the ages, demonstrated mastery of the "three perfections" (三绝, *sanjue*): poetry (诗, *shi*), painting (绘画, *huihua*), and painting's close cousin, calligraphy (书法, *shufa*).[18]

For the Chinese scholar, these three arts were valued as windows into the soul, indicators of the creator's true spirit and state of mind at the moment of creation. That such might be the case for poetry and painting seems universally evident across cultures, Eastern and Western. But regard for written script as an art, more than simply the collectible memorabilia of famous persons, has long been a uniquely important part of Chinese culture and aesthetics.

In 353 CE, on the third day of the third lunar month (三月三 *sanyuesan*, or "Double Third"), a convocation of forty-two scholars gathered together at Lanting 兰亭 ("Orchid Pavilion"), Kuaiji Prefecture, to celebrate the symbolic purification rituals traditionally observed each year on that date. On a fine, early-Spring day, this esteemed group picnicked outdoors alongside a clear, gently running stream, drinking wine and plucking orchids at the invitation of the prefectural governor, Wang Xizhi 王羲之 (303–361).

Wang was already well known to his fellow revelers as a masterful calligrapher, highly proficient in several script forms. A native of Shandong Province, Wang's aristocratic family had moved south after the Western Jin Dynasty (266 – 316) capital of Chang'an fell to the nomadic Xiongnu tribesmen in 316. Despite high-level family connections, Wang had served with only lackluster results in minor official positions. His final post, as a military commander, took him to Kuaiji, where he retired in 355 and lived out the remainder of his life.

Among the group's entertainments that spring day, Wang and his family and scholarly friends played a literati drinking game. From a spot slightly upstream from where they all sat, servants placed small cups of wine in the racing water. If a cup stopped before one of the guests, he either composed a poem extemporaneously to celebrate the day's outing or drank the wine. Or perhaps both.

By game's end, the mildly inebriated group had produced thirty-seven poems, authored by twenty-six of the guests. As host, and perhaps a bit influenced by the wine, Wang Xizhi spontaneously recorded a preface to this collection, known as the "Lanting Xu" 蘭亭序, the "Preface to the Poems Collected at the Orchid Pavilion." Written in a free-flowing calligraphic style called running script (行書, *xingshu*), Wang's *Preface* begins by describing the events of the day with an air of serenity and high spirits:

> Young and old congregated, and there was a throng of men of distinction. Surrounding the pavilion were high hills and lofty peaks, luxuriant woods and tall bamboos. There was, moreover, a swirling, splashing stream, wonderfully clear, which curved round it like a ribbon, and we seated ourselves along it in a drinking game, in which cups of wine were set afloat and drifted to those who sat downstream....The day was fine, the air clear, and a gentle breeze regaled us, so that on looking up we responded to the vastness of the universe, and on bending down were struck by the manifold riches of the earth. And as our eyes wandered from object to object, so our hearts, too, rumbled with them. Indeed, for the eye as well as the ear, it was pure delight! What perfect bliss!

About halfway through the *Preface*, Wang reverts to a wistful and melancholic contemplation of life's transience:

> But when eventually [men] tire of what had so engrossed them, their feelings will have altered with their circumstances, and, of a sudden, complacency gives way to regret. What previously had gratified them is now a thing of the past, which itself is cause for lament. Besides, although the span of men's lives may be longer or shorter, all must end in death. And, as has been said by the ancients, birth and death are momentous events. What an agonizing thought!

> .... For men of a later age will look upon our time as we look upon earlier ages—a chastening reflection. And so I have listed those present on this occasion and transcribed their verses. Even when circumstances have changed and men inhabit a different world, it will still be the same causes that induce a mood of melancholy attendant upon poetical composition. Perhaps some reader of the future will be moved by the sentiments expressed in this preface.[19]

Wang's spontaneous expression of joy in life's pleasures and resignation over its transience made his *Preface* worthy of preservation, but likely not enough for such unconstrained adulation across seventeen centuries. What elevated *Lanting Xu* to a Chinese masterpiece was the combination of its content with the form of its presentation. In 324 characters, aligned vertically in twenty-eight columns read right-to-left, Wang Xizhi's calligraphy exhibited such mastery of form, spacing, exuberance, and dynamic expression of individual characters that it rose to the unrivaled apex of Chinese calligraphic achievement to the present day.

Wang Xizhi's calligraphic reputation advanced over the ages along with that of his *Lanting xu* preface. He came to be regarded as the Sage of Calligraphy, one of the greatest, if not *the* greatest, calligrapher in history. Legends formed and grew as well. It was said, for example, that Wang's reputed love of geese arose from and perhaps even informed his calligraphic style, the shape and movement of their necks inspiring the way he held and manipulated his ink brush.[20] Many centuries later, literati painters would depict him with geese or admiring them from a nearby pavilion.

As one might study the brushstrokes of a Van Gogh, Wang's brushstrokes in the *Preface* have long been examined and admired by critics and aficionados for their seemingly unrestricted flow from his heart at the moment of creation. Some have noted that characters used more than once in the *Preface* were written in different forms each time, a rather remarkable accomplishment when considering that the character 之 (*zhi*) appears more than twenty times yet is never written the same way twice. Wang himself was so pleased the next day with his calligraphy in the *Preface* that he tried to reproduce an equal presentation. After hundreds of attempts,[21] he surrendered, simply unable to generate the free-flowing spirit and appearance he had managed the day before.

Early in the 8th Century, a Tang Dynasty scholar named He Yanzhi 何延之(fl. late 8th Century) would write a fictionalized account of the fate of Wang Xizhi's famous calligraphic Preface.[22] According to He's retelling in "Record of the Lanting Pavilion" (蘭亭记, Lanting ji), for which he even supplied a feasible oral source, the *Lanting Xu* manuscript passed quietly from generation to generation within Wang's descendants' families until Tang Emperor Taizong 唐太宗 (r. 626 – 649) learned the whereabouts of the original scroll. A Buddhist monk named Zhi Yong 智永, a seventh-generation descendant of Wang Xizhi's, possessed the *Lanting Xu* and had passed it to a trusted disciple named Bian Cai 辨才 before his death.[23]

Emperor Taizong had spent years obsessively pursuing every known work from Wang Xizhi's brush—more than two thousand scrolls and pieces—but Wang's greatest masterwork had so far escaped his clutches. Three times he sent emissaries to Bian Cai demanding that the scroll be handed over for the imperial library, but each time the monk rebuffed them by claiming that the scroll had tragically been lost. In He Yanzhi's account, Taizong finally acquired the scroll by trickery. He dispatched Xiao Yi 蕭翼, a knowledgeable Investigating Censor, to travel incognito to Hangzhou and develop a friendship with Bian Cai based on a mutual interest in fine calligraphy. The Emperor's envoy eventually induced Bian Cai to bring out the *Lanting Xu* to share with a fellow admirer. Taizong's emissary quickly grabbed the scroll, revealed his identity, and hurried off to deliver the prized calligraphy to the Emperor.

Taizong ordered multiple copies to be produced by tracing and hand copying, then inscribed faithfully in stone and reproduced as rubbings. His passion for copying *Lanting Xu* was ironically fortunate, since the original manuscript was never seen again after his death. The Emperor's obsession with Wang Xizhi's calligraphy apparently knew no bounds, since he ordered the *Lanting Xu* to be buried with him upon his death. Many believe that this command was indeed carried out according to Taizong's wishes.

Copies of Wang's *Preface* proliferated over the ages, with rubbings from engravings begetting more copies, yielding still more engravings. *Lanting xu* versions appeared in an endless cycle of "authentic" copies that obscured the lost original and created an entire cottage industry of collectors, connoisseurs, authenticators, treatise writers, and guidebook authors by the 11th Century and beyond. *Preface* collectors in the 12th and 13th Centuries would accumulate a hundred or more copies and revel in their mastery of each copy's provenance and the minute differences among them. Song Emperor Lizong (r. 1224 – 1264), for example,[24] reportedly compiled a collection of 117 rubbings of Wang Xizhi's famous essay.

To the present day, experts still revere *Lanting xu* as the *ne plus ultra* of Chinese calligraphy and regard Wang Xizhi as the great Sage of Calligraphy. He was a dedicated practitioner, applying himself so rigorously during his years in Kuaiji that he is said to have turned the waters black in the small pond near his home where he washed his brushes. Wang Xizhi's former residence has been transformed into a museum, complete with a nearby "Ink Pond." The famous Double Third picnic is now memorialized by the Orchid Pavilion Park at Lanting Town, located a few miles southwest of today's Shaoxing City. More recently, a forty-episode Chinese drama series entitled *Sage of Calligraphy Wang Xizhi* (书圣王羲之, *Shusheng Wang Xizhi*) was produced in 2015.

Fly Away Together: A Butterfly Tale

Once upon a time during the Eastern Jin Dynasty (317 – 420), there lived a wealthy and respected family in Shangyu (Shaoxing) named Zhu 祝. The Zhu's had only one daughter, a beautiful and intelligent maiden named Yingtai 英台 who displayed what for her time was a decidedly unfeminine thirst for learning. Comeliness and being an only daughter worked to Yingtai's advantage with her father, who allowed her to pursue her intellectual interests at home.

The time eventually came when the young girl recognized that her learning could no longer progress without attending school. Such notions were impermissible in her day, nor would any school accept a female student even if her father allowed her to attend. Determined as ever, Yingtai devised a plan: to disguise herself with the dress and appearance of a young male scholar. After day upon day of persistent begging and cajoling, her wearied father yielded to his daughter's wishes to enroll in the prestigious Wansong Academy (万松书院, Wansong shuyuan) in Hangzhou.

On her way across the Qiantang River to Hangzhou, Zhu Yingtai met a poor young student named Liang Shanbo 梁山伯, also from the Shangyu area. Like Zhu Yingtai, Liang was traveling to Wansong Academy to begin his studies. The two novice scholars chatted amiably along their way, slowly realizing they enjoyed one another's company. By the time they reached Hangzhou, they had formed a friendship secured by an oath of fraternity.

During the three years that the two young scholars studied together and enjoyed academic success, Zhu Yingtai developed a deep romantic attachment to Liang Shanbo. She could not reveal her true identity and feelings, however, and Shanbo was too upright and studious to suspect Yingtai's effeminate behavior. Yingtai believed she had no option except to continue posing in her false identity for as long as they both continued attending Wansong Academy.

Everything changed one day when a messenger delivered a letter to Yingtai from her father, instructing her to return home promptly. Heartbroken but resolute in her filiality, she prepared to leave Wansong by revealing her female identity to the surprised wife of the school's headmaster. As Liang Shanbo escorted her along the route to the river crossing, Yingtai tried desperately to hint at who she was, comparing their long friendship to a pair of mandarin ducks who by their nature mated for life. Although the allusion should have been obvious, the guileless Shanbo failed to grasp Yingtai's meaning. Finally, Yingtai invited Shanbo to visit her home in Shangyu so she could introduce him to her "sister."

Back home in Shangyu, Yingtai's father informed her that he had arranged a marriage for her with Ma Wencai 马文才, son of the wealthy governor of Shangyu. When Liang Shanbo visited his fellow student a few months later, Yingtai surprised him by revealing that she herself was the "sister" the young scholar was supposed to meet. Despite the couple's love for one another and vows never to part, the reality of Yingtai's arranged marriage was an insurmountable barrier to their happiness. Shanbo departed, deeply dejected, but tried to move on with his life. The pain of lost love was too great, however. His health deteriorated unchecked until he passed away and was buried.

On the day of Zhu Yingtai's marriage to Ma Wencai, the wedding procession route happened to pass near the site of Liang Shanbo's grave. As the procession arrived at that place, a strong whirlwind rose and obstructed them from moving forward. Yingtai, despairing of a marriage she did not desire and the loss of the one she might have had, descended from her palanquin to pay her final respects to Liang Shanbo. Standing over Shanbo's grave and grieving his death, Yingtai begged to join her true love forever. With a thunderous roar, the grave suddenly opened and Yingtai threw herself inside before it closed again over her. The stunned members of the wedding procession could only watch as a pair of butterflies took to the air above the grave, never again to be seen and never again parted.

The story of the "Butterfly Lovers," called *Zhu Yingtai and Liang Shanbo* 梁山伯与祝英台 or simply *Liang Zhu* 梁祝, emerged by at least the Song Dynasty[25] and grew to be acclaimed as one of Chinese culture's most widely-celebrated love stories. This romantic tale evolved into its modern form during the Ming Dynasty, when the dead couple's departing souls were consistently represented as butterflies and their earlier school studies were situated at Wansong Academy, which was not founded until 1498.

Flying Mountain with Monkeys

According to legend, a Buddhist monk from India named Huili 慧理 (fl. 320s) arrived at West Lake around the year 318, accompanied in some tellings by a pet monkey. Charmed by the quiet lagoon waters and gently surrounding hills, Huili decided that the area would serve wonderfully as the site of a temple for contemplation and reclusion. He chose a location near the northwestern corner of the future West Lake and christened his new religious institution Lingyin Si 灵隐寺, Temple of the Soul's Retreat.

Lingyin Temple served as the anchor of a full community of Buddhist temples that gradually appeared in the hills around West Lake. In due time, Hangzhou would grow into one of the most important pilgrimage sites in Jiangnan for Buddhist adherents, hosting more than three hundred temples in the Tang Dynasty (618 - 907) and nearly a thousand during the Southern Song (1127 – 1279).[26] Their manifold presence would influence for centuries the manner in which West Lake was viewed and the businesses which developed around it. In addition, Lingyin Temple would become the nexus for a fascinating array of legends and inhabitants, including Huili himself.

After settling on the location for his temple, Huili noticed the craggy peaks of a nearby hill towering over his monastery. Unusual among a range of more gently contoured hilltops, those rocky outcroppings reminded the monk of one of India's most sacred mountains, one in fact where the Buddha had once resided. Huili's conviction on this account was so strong, he named the adjacent mountain Feilai feng 飞来峰, meaning "the peak that flew here."

Huili's choice of names not only conferred upon his temple a deeply religious connection to the Buddha, it also provided an explanation for the numerous monkeys in the vicinity as having been carried from India to China on the flying peak. Some writers have further suggested that the story of a traveling Buddhist monk accompanied by a subservient monkey and a panoply of lesser monkeys parallels the story of monk Xuanzang and his magical monkey disciple in China's great classical novel, *Journey to the West* (西遊記, *Xiyou ji*). By this interpretation, Huili's monkey would have been the artistic inspiration for the infamous trickster of traditional Chinese literature, the Monkey King. Regardless, the hills around Lingyin Temple became famous for their live monkey population that lasted well into the 1800s.

Huili may have inadvertently designated the site for another temple complex that followed his more than two centuries later. In 585, Buddhist monks transformed the site of a nearby shrine erected by Huili into the Tianzhu Monastery.[27] Over time, three different temples arose south of Lingyin Temple. During one of Qing Emperor Qianlong's 乾隆帝 (r. 1735 – 1796) visits to Hangzhou, he named them Faxi Temple (法喜寺), Fajing Temple (法净寺), and Fajing Temple (法镜寺), but today they are simply known, respectively, as Upper (上, Shang), Middle (中, Zhong), and Lower (下, Xia) Tianzhu 天竺. Of the three monasteries, Lower Tianzhu Temple was the first one constructed, while Upper Tianzhu is the youngest, built in the 10th Century.

Little Su

As the town of Qiantang grew, the people of Jiangnan (and beyond) took increasing notice of that riverine market town surrounded by fruitful lands and nestled alongside a picturesque, hill-bordered lake. They also perceived in such a romantic setting the parallel prospect of human romance, whether triumphant or tragically lost. The region gained a reputation, sometimes embellished to near-mythic levels, for feminine beauty and grace unparalleled throughout the empire. In such a place, great tales of romance were born and flourished, as later were stories of talented and intelligent courtesans who fought for their dignity and right to control their own fate.

In the closing decades of the 5th Century, a young woman of extraordinary beauty reputedly graced the Qiantang environs. She was popularly known by the diminutive Su Xiaoxiao 蘇小小 (d. c. 501), that is, "Little Little Su" or preferably in English, "Petite Su." Trained in the fine courtesan arts of her day, the beautiful young girl excelled at singing and clever conversation, but she was best remembered for her poetry.

To the Tune of "Butterflies Adore Flowers"

I live by the Qiantang River.
Flowers fall, bloom again, but I don't care about flowing years.
Swallows have carried the spring off in their beaks.
A few yellow plum blossoms shower my gauze window.

With a slant unicorn comb in my half-loosened hair
I gently play my hardwood clappers
and sing about gold thread,
about my dream interrupted, colorful clouds nowhere to be found,
a bright moon deep in the night emerging over the south river mouth.

And:

Emotions on Being Apart

Thousands of miles off, behind countless mountain passes,
you make me grieve.
Do you even know that?
Since you left
I've counted the leftover days in winter, waited out spring.
Still not one word.
All the flowers have bloomed
and you are still gone.[28]

Yet among all her surviving work, an eerily prophetic love poem of just four lines became her greatest literary legacy. In one common version of her story, Su Xiaoxiao met a handsome young scholar at West Lake by the name of Ruan Yu. Their acquaintance was a case of love at first sight, but her social station precluded any chance that they might somehow marry. Societal and family pressures left Ruan with no other recourse than to forswear his heart's desire. Su Xiaoxiao's poem lamenting her lost love is known by the name "Song of Su Xiaoxiao" or "Song of Xiling Lake."

I ride in a red painted carriage.	妾乘油壁车
You pass me on a blue dappled horse.	郎跨青骢马
Where shall we bind our hearts in a love knot?	何处结同心
Along Xiling Lake under the cypress tree.[29]	西陵松柏下

"Xiling Lake" is a sort of double reference to both West Lake and the Xiling Bridge that connects West Lake's Solitary Island (孤山, Gushan) to the lake's north shore. At such a lovely setting, Su Xiaoxiao wishes in her poem that she and her lover could one day be entombed together under the shadowing trees and thus be bound forever in a "heart knot." When she fell ill and died of a metaphorical broken heart at age 19, those to whom she had so endeared herself built her tomb alongside Xiling Bridge, where poets, literati, and romantics visited, sighed, and were inspired for the next 1,500 years.

Although Su Xiaoxiao's tomb suffered damage in the 1960s, it was restored at Xiling Bridge beneath the new Mucai ("Admiring Talent") Pavilion (慕才亭, Mucai ting) in 2004. Her yellow-domed tomb, resting beneath a six-pillared pavilion each of whose four-square columns is poetically inscribed on all sides, recalls the tragic early death of a great and talented beauty and remains one of West Lake's most popular tourist sites.

The South Emerges

Oddly, the three-century period of imperial roulette, from 280 – 581 CE, benefitted the Jiangnan area. Numerous imperial family members, court officials, wealthy landowners, and educated elites who survived the incessant conflicts in the north headed south to the fertile lands below the Yangzi. Southern China blossomed as population migration by the aristocratic and educated elites triggered a North-South role reversal. Now it was North China filled with invading barbarians, while the once-barbaric south preserved and advanced Han Chinese civilization. Jiankang, formerly the capital of Sun Quan's Wu State, was reincarnated as a cosmopolitan capital (hereafter called Nanjing), with trade flourishing and poets, painters, artisans, and builders filling the city.

Buddhism, brought down from the North where it had been officially sanctioned, was accepted by southerners as something of a psychic complement to Confucianism. Where the latter focused on the practice of worldly affairs, the former provided pathways to contemplate the mysteries of life beyond life. It was during this troubled era that monk Huili (in 318) established Lingyin Temple at West Lake and Wang Xizhi (in 353) brushed his solemn musings on life's transience at Orchid Pavilion.

It was also during this period, from 399 – 412, that monk Faxian 法显 (337 – c. 422) traveled on foot to India to learn Buddhist principles and practices. After enduring a perilous trip home by sea, Faxian brought numerous Buddhist books and scriptures to Jiankang and translated them into Chinese.[30] His remarkable trek and the scriptures he acquired paved the way for the more famous religious pilgrimage to India and back (629 – 645) by monk Xuanzang 玄奘 (fl. 602 – 664), memorialized fictionally in *Journey to the West*.

Chapter 4

WELLS, WALLS, AND WATER FOR TEA

(581 – 978)

Composed on the Lake in Spring[1]

Spring arrives at the lake, like a painting,
Jutting peaks wind around its calm face.
Pines line the hillsides, a thousand layers of jade-blue;
The moon touches its rippled heart, a bright pearl.
Early rice sprouts stick up, loose threads on an azure carpet;
New rushes spread across the lake, belts on a green gauze dress.
Unable to leave Hangzhou behind;
What makes me linger is this lake.

– Bai Juyi (772 – 846)

Reunification, Politically and Physically

Yang Jiang 杨坚 (541 – 604) was a military aristocrat, son of a military noble, and heir to a privileged lineage that stood in service to the northern dynasties for more than two centuries. Born in a Buddhist temple in Shaanxi Province and raised by a Buddhist nun, Yang nevertheless received early training in military arts and horsemanship. During the two decades following his first military posting at age 14, he rose rapidly in military rank and political influence, culminating with high-level command. He was honored still further when his daughter was chosen by Northern Zhou Emperor Wudi北周武帝 (543–578, r. 561 – 578) as the first wife of the heir apparent.

In 578, Yang's son-in-law, now Northern Zhou Emperor Xuandi 北周宣帝 (559–580, r. 579 – 580), elevated Yang Jiang to Minister of Defense. Two years later, as he was preparing to launch a military campaign to bring down the southern Chen Dynasty in Nanjing, Emperor Xuan fell gravely ill and soon passed away. Yang engineered his appointment as Regent to Xuan's six-year-old heir, Emperor Jingdi (北周靜帝, 573 – 581), but by the spring of 581, he had successfully forced the young boy to abdicate. Yang Jiang then declared himself Emperor Wendi 隋文帝 (r. 581 – 604) of the new Sui Dynasty. The dynastic name Sui (隋) came from the Yang family's fiefdom, where his father's title (and his, by inheritance) had been Duke of Sui.

In short order, Emperor Wendi consolidated his power in the capital, not only having the boy-emperor murdered but conducting a vicious campaign to eliminate the entire ruling family clan. He then launched the planned assault on the southern Chen Dynasty and enjoyed early success, but in an act of monarchical chivalry, he withdrew his forces when he learned of the Chen Emperor's death. From 582 through 587, Wendi confined his efforts to his northern domain, strengthening his hold over the various fiefdoms and kingdoms that had fractured the northern half of China for the past two centuries.

Near Chang'an, Wendi built a colossal new capital called Daxing 大兴, a rectangular walled city measuring five or six miles on each side. His choice was partially made for defensive reasons, but it also carried strong historical connotations and an unmistakable signal of his intentions. The last dynasty to rule a unified China, the Han, had built their original (western) capital at the same location, alongside the Wei River. Before them, the first great unifier, Qin Shihuangdi, had constructed his capital city of Xianyang there as well.

Finally, in 589, Emperor Wendi felt secure enough in the north to turn his unification intentions back southward. Sui forces landed east and west of Nanjing, while another force under General Yang Su 杨素 (544–606) advanced along the Yangzi River. Nanjing, the Chen Dynasty, and the southern territories all fell in short order.[2] By the end of the year, Sui Wendi ruled all of China, the empire's first effective reunification in 300 years.

Emperor Wendi proved himself a capable and indefatigable administrator and ruler. He began his reign by retiring as many soldiers from the former competing states as possible, forcing the troops to surrender their weapons and giving them land to farm in return. What military he left in place he put under tight central control. Similarly, in order to rein in the power and influence of the great aristocratic families of northern China, Wendi eliminated access to government positions by family recommendation and affiliation. Government appointments were now made through a new, centralized Board of Civil Office, many of whose decisions the tireless ruler personally reviewed.

In the more public realm, Emperor Wendi introduced major land and tax reforms and improved the empire's northern defenses by repairing the Great Wall and creating military outposts with self-supporting agricultural lands. Consistent with his early-childhood upbringing, the Emperor actively supported the spread of Buddhism throughout his realm. By one count, his reign saw the addition of four thousand new temples and more than one hundred thousand carved figures.[3]

In the earliest days of the new dynasty's administration, the prefecture established for the Hangzhou area was designated as Hang. This name reflected the historical fact that, in addition to Qiantang County, the region had also been known as Yuhang 余杭, taking on the name of the first known settlement (which legend had proudly but incorrectly associated with Yu the Great). Since the Sui administrators also chose to make the city by the lake the prefectural capital (the 州 *zhou*) of Hang, the Sui renamed Qiantang as Hangzhou 杭州.[4]

In 591, as he was completing his assignment to put down residual anti-Sui rebellions and bandit groups, General Yang Su (now crowned the Duke of Yue) petitioned the Court to erect a defensive wall around Hang prefecture's new capital. Hangzhou's first such wall stood "36 li, 90 paces" (about 20.2 km, or 12.1 miles) in circumference. Inside those walls, the city was subdivided into 108 walled wards,[5] of which two were designated as markets. The decisions to elevate Hangzhou to prefectural capital status and encircle it with fortifications signaled that the young city on the Qiantang River was finally maturing, growing in size and administrative importance in its region.

The Great Transport River[6]

Emperor Wendi's pre-imperial experiences dealing with the nomadic tribes from the north and west had well informed him of the need for improved defenses in those regions. Stationing more soldiers along the northern frontier posed difficult logistical problems, however, particularly with providing adequate food supplies. Creating agricultural colonies at military outposts was a start, but with the conquest of the water-rich south, the dynasty now had access to seemingly unlimited rice production. Such bountiful supplies could also help insulate the northern regions from food shortages caused by insect plagues, droughts, and river floods. The course of action was clear: improve the empire's water transport system.

In 587, Emperor Wendi ordered reconstruction of the Shanyang Canal 山阳渎, connecting the Yangzi River city of Yangzhou northward to the Huai River. The restored canal largely followed the route of the ancient Hangou 邗沟 (Han Conduit) Canal built by King Fuchai of Wu in the late 5th Century BCE to facilitate troop and supply movements. Wendi's actions in 587 were similarly motivated, taken in preparation for his assault on the Chen Dynasty lands south of the Yangzi. Wendi's canal-restoring initiatives not only paved the way for even greater plans, they also suggested that construction of the Grand Canal in the Sui era actually represented the culmination of a more fragmented project that began almost 1,200 years earlier.

Wendi's reign came to an uncertain end in 604, perhaps from illness but possibly under criminal or even patricidal circumstances.[7] He was succeeded by the second of his five sons, Yang Guang 杨广 (569 – 618), under the reign name Sui Yangdi 隋炀帝 (r. 604 – 618).

Yang Guang grew up a privileged northern prince, handsome and with a strong intellect. His official career began with an assignment away from the capital at the tender age of 11. Yang's arranged marriage to the daughter of a high-ranking southern family took place only a year later, followed by promotions and new civil and military postings.

In 589, at age 20, Yang Guang led the Sui army conquest of the Chen Dynasty that re-unified China. Following the downfall of the Chen capital at Nanjing, Yang Guang returned in triumph to Daxing, heading a military procession to deliver to his father the defeated Chen Emperor.

His marriage to Lady Xiao 萧皇后 (c. 566 – 648) had introduced Yang Guang to southern Chinese culture, but his next assignment made him an adopted son of the South. Barely a year after his victory celebration over the Chen, Wendi ordered his favored son to take over control of the southern territories after another son, Yang Jun 杨俊 (571 – 600), proved utterly incapable in that position.

For the next decade, Yang Guang and Lady Xiao resided in the South, where the future emperor grew increasingly enamored of the lifestyle, the literary culture, the architecture, and even the local language. Yang Guang would be the rare emperor who mastered with fluency the mellifluous Wu dialect native to the region (and still in common use today). His ten years in southern China undoubtedly also contributed later to his vision for the renowned north-south canal network whose construction he would soon oversee.[8]

Upon Emperor Wendi's death in 604, Yang Guang (now Sui Emperor Yangdi) seized immediate control of his father's throne. After securing it against the usurpation threat of another brother (Yang Liang 杨谅, c. 575 – 605),[9] Yangdi set out in December 604 with the first of the financially profligate measures that would ultimately cause his downfall: constructing a spectacular new palace at the old Eastern Capital of Luoyang. By employing as many as two million laborers per month under the corvée system (a State-imposed tax paid by mandatory labor service), the regenerated Eastern Capital was ready for occupancy at the beginning of 606. However, the human costs were reportedly staggering. As many as 40 – 50% of the laborers died in the process.[10]

Even as the massive Luoyang project was underway, Yangdi ordered construction of the Tongji Canal by still more conscripted labor, likely at least a million men and women. This new inland waterway linked Luoyang to the Yellow and Huai Rivers. The new Emperor also renovated and further broadened and deepened the ancient Hangou Canal, running from the Huai River south to the Yangzi. Those two canal projects strengthened his reign's north-south connections and ensured access by Luoyang to the south's agricultural cornucopia.

As if these projects were not already stressing the Sui treasury, Yangdi embarked on still more costly initiatives. Planning for an active personal presence in his domain, he authorized creation of a network of palaces to accommodate his travels. Furthermore, since his travels would require the use of waterways, an imperial fleet was necessary, headed by two truly awe-inspiring dragon ships, one for himself and a lesser one for the Empress. Each dragon ship was a floating, four-decked palace, 35 to 40 feet high. Yangdi's first southern tour began in October 605 and ended eight months later. According to some reports, the massive entourage that followed, with ships numbering into the thousands, stretched out along the waterways for up to 100 kilometers (62 miles).[11]

In 607, the Emperor committed another million laborers to build additional sections of the Great Wall, followed in 608 by yet another major Great Wall project and a new canal. The Yongji Canal ran northeast from Luoyang, connecting the Sui Eastern Capital with Jicheng 薊城, part of modern-day Beijing. Yangdi's purpose was primarily military, to support troop and supply movements northeastward for a planned assault on the Korean kingdom of Goguryeo (高句麗, Gaogouli).

Finally, in 610, Emperor Yangdi initiated construction of the Jiangnan Canal, starting on the south side of the Yangzi at Jingkou (modern Zhenjiang) and ending at Hangzhou. He also ordered dredging and restoration of the ancient Xiling Canal,[12] connecting Xiaoshan on the south bank of the Qiantang River with Yuezhou (Shaoxing) to its east. Much of this work consisted of dredging and restoring ancient canal sections dating variously to the ancient Wu and Yue States of Fuchai and Goujian as well as the Qin and Han Dynasties. Table 4.1 below summarizes the names and terminal points of the Grand Canal's different sections and their lengths, including the Xiling Canal running south of the Qiantang River toward present-day Ningbo.

Canal Section	Location Start/End	Construction Start/End	Length (km/miles)	Canal Name
Tongji	Luoyang/Shanyang	605 – 611	728 / 452	Tongji
Hangou	Shanyang/Yangzhou	605 - 605	204 / 127	Huaiyang
Yongji	Luoyang/Beijing	608 - 611	1,018 / 633	Wei
Jiangnan	Zhenjiang/Hangzhou	610 - 610	407 / 253	Jiangnan
TOTAL	Beijing/Hangzhou		2,357 / 1,465	Yunhe/ Grand Canal
Xiling	Xiaoshan/Shaoxing[13]	610 - 610	239 / 149	Zhedong

Table 4.1. Original Grand Canal Sections, Construction Periods, and Section Lengths

In just seven years, Sui Emperor Yangdi shifted China's political and economic centers of gravity eastward and southward and altered the future course of the nation's history. In the zero-sum game of relative importance and influence, cities like Xi'an, Kaifeng, and even Luoyang would gradually fade as the more easterly (and mostly southerly) Beijing, Nanjing, Yangzhou, Suzhou, and Hangzhou would rise from this time forward.

Together in their entirety, Yangdi's various canal segments formed a water-borne, Y-shaped, superhighway, the Grand Canal (大運河, Da Yunhe, literally "great transport river"). This "sideways-Y"-shaped network of lakes, stretches of river, and excavated channels connected the militaristic north with the more agricultural south and linked China's four great east-west rivers—the Yellow, Huai, Yangzi, and Qiantang—into a national transport network that would become known as the *caoyun* 漕运, the imperially-controlled tribute grain transport system.

The price exacted by one of history's greatest public works projects was a steep one, however. As many as nine million laborers are estimated to have died in Yangdi's canal-building projects, sparking rebellion and turning the common people against him. Coupled with the Emperor's extravagant spending and three failed military ventures (in 612, 613, and 614) directed at the Goguryeo territories in Manchuria and North Korea, the Sui Dynasty's survival was at stake.

As Sui soldiers deserted in increasing numbers and turned to acts of rebellion, Yangdi abandoned his capital at Luoyang for Jiangdu (Yangzhou). Li Yuan 李渊 (566 – 635), former governor of Shanxi Province, rose against Yangdi in 617, seized control of Daxing, and installed Yangdi's grandson, Yang You 楊侑 (605 – 619, r. 617 – 618) as a child emperor. By the end of the year, Li deposed the child and declared himself Emperor Gaozu 高祖帝 (r. 618 – 626), ruler of a new dynasty, the Tang 唐. The Sui Dynasty had lasted just 37 years.

With the loss of his hold over the northern realm, Emperor Yangdi turned inward to a life of hedonism in Yangzhou. In the spring of 618, his own hand-picked elite guards mutinied and strangled him, executing most of his family members as well.[14] Yangdi left behind a disunified realm, weakened by his failed military campaigns and reckless spending. He may be judged by history as a failed leader for the human costs of his reign and the ruin of his dynasty, but he also left behind in the Grand Canal a vision for how to unify the nation both politically and economically.

Six Wells for the City

In the few centuries of its existence, the city of Hangzhou had necessarily restricted its physical expansion to conform with the natural water resources that surrounded it: the Qiantang River to the south and east and a hill-bounded lake to the west. Only to the north and northeast could the city expand, causing it to take on a rather misshapen rectangular form.

With the completion of the Grand Canal, Hangzhou would now have to accommodate the pressures of being the southern terminus of a 1,500-mile-long supply line. Almost anything produced or grown in points south and southwest, or delivered to southerly ports by foreign traders, would converge on Hangzhou for transport northward. Prefectural governors and city leaders faced entirely new challenges in handling the demographic, trade, and transport traffic growth.

Ironically for a city surrounded by water, providing fresh water inside the city walls represented one of the first such challenges. From its earliest times, water management in Hangzhou had meant constructing a modest urban canal network, but residents' potable water tended to be brackish, salty, and bitter. Finally, as the city grew in population and commercial activity, a Tang official named Li Bi 李泌 (722 – 789) took action.

In 781, during the first year of his two-year term as Governor of Hang Prefecture, Li Bi oversaw construction of six lake-fed wells inside the city walls. Lakeshore ponds with wooden gates fed water through bamboo tubes into the wells. Grasses of various kinds were added to the bamboo pipes as natural water filters. The new wells were positioned north to south, more or less linearly, inside the city's western (lake-side) wall. The Six Wells,[15] as they were known, continued in active use well into the Song Dynasty (960 – 1279).

The Master of Tea

Among the many reasons why clean, potable water was important to the citizens of Hangzhou, one of the less obvious was the Tang era's immense growth in the consumption of tea. The main proponent of this movement in Hangzhou and throughout the Jiangnan region was Lu Yu 陆羽 (733 – 804), China's most famous tea aficionado, long-time resident of Huzhou, and author of the first and still most famous treatise on tea, *The Classic of Tea* (茶经, *Cha Jing*).

Tea already had a long and unusual history in China by Lu Yu's time.[16] According to Chinese tradition, tea was first discovered by the great sovereign Shennong—perhaps by leaves accidently falling into his boiling cooking water—during his legendary researches for medicinal plants in around 2750 BCE. Depending on the version, he was either saved from poisoning by tea's reputed curative powers or simply impressed by its physical effects on his body.[17]

Whatever the case, tea first took its place in Chinese culture as a medicine. Fresh tea leaves were boiled in water to produce a foamy broth with a pleasing aroma that settled the stomach and refreshed body and mind. Early practitioners of herbal medicine proclaimed tea's myriad health benefits, everything from alleviating insomnia and preventing heat strokes to curing fatigue, ulcers, and poor eyesight to recovering from too much drink and contributing to a longer life. The herb itself had no name of its own, initially referred to simply as *tu* 茶, a bitter thistle plant common to North China. As tea grew in popularity, one stroke in the center of the *tu* character was removed in about the seventh century, and the new herb was christened *cha* 茶.[18]

Over time, practitioners discovered that both the taste and medicinal properties of tea could be enhanced by first steaming the leaves and pounding them into small pieces before boiling them. The heated liquid was then whipped into a frothy, soup-like mixture and consumed from a bowl, leaves and all. Continued experimentation in the last centuries BCE determined still more effective ways to age and store the leaves to improve the mixture's taste.

In its earliest days, tea consumption served mostly ritual purposes at the most rarified levels of Chinese society. The next boost to its popularity came in the Han Dynasty era (206 BCE – 220 CE) when Buddhist monks and Confucian scholars "prized it for the mental clarity, emotional calm, and inspirational insight it provided."[19] By the 4th Century CE, tea was sufficiently known and appreciated in the capital that it became an imperial tribute item to be remitted by the peasants and officials in areas where it was grown, including Hubei, Sichuan, Yunnan, and Zhejiang Provinces.

By Lu Yu's time, in the second half of the 8th Century, tea had become a commonplace in the daily life of the Chinese people, from the lowliest peasants and traveling traders to Buddhist and Daoist monks, scholar elites, and courtiers and emperors. Tea in that era was produced in brick form,[20] wherein the picked leaves were first spread on mats to dry, after which they were steamed, pounded, and shaped into bricks. The pressed tea was then dried in a shed by burning wood and charcoal in a firepit dug into the shed floor, after which the dried bricks were packaged.

The types and qualities of different teas marked one's status, and the literati elite fashioned increasingly complex standards and rituals consistent with their self-claimed status as arbiters of tea drinking as high art. Not just the variety of tea mattered to the literati. Equally important were the season and time of day when the leaves were picked and even who picked them, as were the water source, the bowls and implements used for preparation, and the drinking cups.

Lu Yu was more than just a practitioner of the high art of tea. He was an aficionado extraordinaire, a dedicated student and researcher. Born in or near Jingling 竟陵 (modern Tianmen 天门) in Hubei Province in 733, Lu Yu was given his name by the Zen Buddhist monk Zhiji 智积 (active 735 – 768),[21] who found him as an abandoned infant along a riverbank. The orphaned boy was raised in a Buddhist monastery, but despite repeated punishments from his master, he openly rebelled against his training as a monk. He preferred poetry and the Confucian classics to Buddhist scriptures, and his thirst for knowledge seemed insatiable. In his audacious "Autobiography of Imperial Instructor Lu," he described how, lacking paper and ink, he practiced writing by tracing characters with a bamboo stick onto the backs of the cattle he tended.[22] The monks' tea culture was one of the few elements of temple life in which the boy developed notable interest.

Monk Zhiji ultimately conceded that his adopted protégé would never be monk material and secured for him the rudiments of a secular education. But for Lu Yu, temple life would never suffice. At age 12, he abruptly joined a traveling band of entertainers for whom he wrote humorous skits and participated as an actor. By his own account, he was befriended by Li Qiwu 李齐物 (d. 762), Jingling Prefecture's governor and a member of the Tang dynastic family. Li appreciated Lu Yu's talents and personal charms and introduced him to official life in Jingling. Li also arranged for Lu to undertake several years of additional studies under a retired scholar.

Upon returning home after five years with his tutor, Lu Yu discovered that Jingling had a new governor, Cui Goufu 崔国辅 (c. 678 – c. 755), with whom he soon became friendly. Their shared interest in tea and tea culture inspired Lu in 754 to propose a "tea quest" southwestward into the Bashan Mountain area of Sichuan Province, believed at the time to have been the locale of tea's original discovery. Cui supported Lu's proposal and outfitted him for what turned out to be two years of water tasting, tea tasting, sample collecting, and note taking.

Back home again in Jingling, Lu Yu's work to organize his research findings was interrupted by a devastating anti-Tang rebellion led by the warlord general An Lushan 安禄山 (c. 703 - 757). Like so many others, Lu's response to that conflict involved crossing south over the Yangzi River in 756. His travels during his escape to safety led him into Zhejiang

Province, where he finally resettled in Huzhou and lived out most of the rest of his life.

Lu could hardly have made a more propitious choice. Not only had he chosen an area where he could continue exploring tea plant cultivation, harvesting, and processing, he also met and befriended the great Buddhist poet Jiaoran 皎然 (730 – 799) at the Miaoxi Monastery. Intimate knowledge of tea meant appreciation of its preparation as well as how it was grown, picked, and processed for sale, and Jiaoren, thirteen years Lu's senior, was among the greatest of "tea monks." Two years after they first met, the two men traveled together to Xixia Monastery near Nanjing, where Lu began organizing his samples and notes for his treatise on tea.

In 760, Lu Yu returned to the Huzhou area and took up residence in another secluded mountain area. It was here that he began his manuscript while rebellion raged on in the north. Five or six years later, he completed the first draft of his study of tea and tea culture. The manuscript was circulated among a small group of friends and associates, but Lu Yu was not yet satisfied.

Returning to Huzhou again in 773, Lu was invited to join a government-sponsored library project as a senior editor. Access to a wide-ranging collection of historical books and records, some of which addressed tea production and processing, provided Lu with information he could never have seen any other way. For the next seven years, he not only refined his tea manuscript, he produced works ranging from genealogies and biographical dictionaries to a local history of Huzhou Prefecture, and even a treatise on the interpretation of dreams. In 780, after twenty-six years of research and writing, he finally published his three-volume *Cha Jing*, the *Classic of Tea*.[23]

Unlike any work before Lu's time, *Cha Jing* presented a comprehensive, ten-chapter treatment on tea: tree cultivation, harvesting and processing of leaves into tea cakes, brewing utensils, tea preparation, tea drinking, stories and historical records about tea, comparison of tea-growing areas, and what could best be described as "tips" for enjoying tea outdoors or in less refined environments.

Similar such guides and sequels would follow, but Lu Yu's treatise stands as the original, and he stands alone as China's "Sage of Tea" or "Tea Saint." His *Cha Jing* formalized Chinese tea culture and was highly regarded even in its own time. A Tang-era story asserted, for example, that a barbarian tribal king was willing to deliver a thousand war horses in exchange for just one copy of Lu Yu's treatise.[24]

Tea and tea rituals would take an esteemed place in literati culture, and tea production would play unexpected roles in China's history for the next thousand years. In the immediate Hangzhou area, Dragon Well tea (龙井茶, *Longjing cha*), harvested in and around Dragon Well Village (龙井村, *Longjingcun*) a few miles west of the city, would eventually be celebrated as among the nation's finest into the modern era.

The final twenty-five years of Lu Yu's life were consumed with writing, traveling, enjoying tea and water tastings, and even writing another tea book in which he ranked and carefully graded different water sources he had sampled. He twice received invitations in the 780s for attractive official posts, both of which he managed to turn down without incurring the imperial wrath. He passed away in 804 at his home in Huzhou.

Lu Yu's *Classic of Tea* completed the transformation of tea from a medicinal potion "no different from slurping vegetable soup"[25] to a widely accepted drink that evolved into an elitist, ritualized art and the subject of poetic praise from literati scholars. Three of the most memorable tea poems came from Tang Dynasty poets Lu Tong and Yüan Zhen and from Ming poet Xu Cishu in his *Treatise on Tea* (茶疏, *Cha Shu*).

Seven Cups of Tea (Lu Tong 卢仝, 795 – 835)[26]

> The first bowl moistens my lips and throat.
> The second bowl banishes my loneliness and melancholy.
> The third bowl penetrates my withered entrails,
> Finding nothing there except five thousand scrolls of writing.
> The fourth bowl raises a light perspiration,
> As all the inequities I have suffered in my life
> Are flushed out through my pores.
> The fifth bowl purifies my flesh and bones.
> The sixth bowl allows me to communicate with immortals.
> The seventh bowl I need not drink,
> I am only aware of a pure wind rising beneath my two arms.
> The mountains of Penglai,[27] what is this place?
> I, Master of the Jade Stream, ride this pure wind and wish to return home.

Tea: A Pagoda Poem (Yüan Zhen 元稹, 799 – 831)[28]

> Tea
> Fragrant leaves, tender buds
> The desire of poets, the love of monks
> Ground in carved white jade, sifted through red gauze
> Cauldron brewed to the color of gold, bowl aswirl in floral foam
> At night it welcomes the bright moon, at daybreak it dispels dawn's rosy mists
> Past and present, drinkers are refreshed and tireless, praisefully aware it quells drunkenness.

Times for Drinking Tea (Xu Cishu 许次纾, 1549 – 1604)[29]

> In idle moments
> When bored with poetry
> Thoughts confused
> Beating time to songs
> When music stops
> Living in seclusion
> Enjoying scholarly pastimes
> Conversing late at night

Studying on a sunny day
In the bridal chamber
Detaining favored guests
Playing host to scholars or pretty girls
Visiting friends returned from far away
In perfect weather
When skies are overcast
Watching boats glide past on the canal
Midst trees and bamboos
When flowers bud and birds chatter
On hot days by a lotus pond
Burning incense in the courtyard
After tipsy guests have left
When the youngsters have gone out
On visits to secluded temples
When viewing springs and scenic rocks.

Hangzhou native Xu Cishu, author of the poem immediately above and an aficionado of tea and oddly shaped rocks, published his own *Treatise on Tea* in 1607. Concise but comprehensive in scope, his tea commentary "addresses practically all aspects of the production and consumption of tea in a systematic way, and is the first to discuss some of the important innovations in tea-drinking" in the Ming era. Xu's *Treatise on Tea* is considered one of the most important and representative texts on tea in the Ming period."[30]

Naming the Lake

Bai Juyi 白居易 (772 – 846) is a difficult man to categorize: a prolific and esteemed poet, a scholar, and an honest and accomplished official, but hardly a revolutionary one. To his detriment, he was an obstinate politician in a politically difficult time, born after the greatest glories of the Tang Dynasty but fortunate not to live in the worst of the dynasty's declining years. Yet despite relatively short official assignments in Hangzhou and Suzhou, he left behind achievements for which the people of his day celebrated him and which are still honored in the 21st Century.[31]

Although Bai Juyi was born nine years after the An Lushan Rebellion, China north of the Yangzi River was still suffering the chaotic after-effects of the conflict. He lived his earliest childhood years in Zhengyang 正阳 (Henan Province) but experienced his adolescent years as a refugee in the Xuzhou area of northern Jiangsu Province. As the son of a minor official, he received a formal education, but the family struggled financially when his father died in 794.

Five years later, Bai secured his provincial (举人, *juren*) degree, and the metropolitan (进士, *jinshi*) degree followed just one year later in 800. Lacking placement in an official post, the newly-crowned scholar submitted to a special placement exam and earned an assignment at the Palace Library in the Tang capital of Chang'an. Joining him that same year was fellow graduate Yüan Zhen, author of the pagoda-shaped tea poem cited earlier.

Bai and Yuan would form a mostly epistolary relationship, interspersed with occasional in-person visits, that would stand as one of the great friendships in Chinese history.

During Bai's time in Chang-an, he demonstrated his unique intellectual and literary insights by crafting a literary encyclopedia consisting of collected and categorized literary quotations in the manner of *Bartlett's Familiar Quotations*. In 806, even amid his developing official career, he composed arguably his most renowned poetic work, a ballad of the An Lushan Rebellion titled "Song of Everlasting Sorrow" (長恨歌, "Chang hen ge"). His poem told the tragic tale of Tang Emperor Xuanzong and the forced execution of his favorite concubine Yang Guifei 楊玉環 (719 – 756).[32] Bai describes the death scene, and summarizes in his closing:

> The six armies of imperial guards all refuse to move on
> Till the beauty with long moth-eyebrows twists and dies before their horses.
> Her jewelry is scattered on the ground and no one picks up
> Her hairpieces of emerald, gold, and jade.
> The emperor cannot save her. He just covers his face.
> When he turns to look, tears and blood streak down together
> And yellow dust spills everywhere in whistling wind.
> …..
> Though heaven and earth are long, they will cease at last,
> But this regret stretches on and on forever.[33]

Back in Chang-an after completing one or two early official posts, Bai Juyi asked for a higher-level position in the provinces, in part to escape court politics. In 822, he was named Governor of Hangzhou. He appears to have felt both relief and an upbeat laxity toward his new assignment, writing in a poem: "There are plenty of wise people at Court to look after the affairs of the nation. I for my part have turned my face to the lakes of Hangzhou, where my only business will be poetry and wine for two or three years."[34]

Arthur Waley (1889 – 1966), author of a classic 1949 biography of Bai Juyi, mentions that among Bai's gubernatorial challenges were summer droughts in 822 and 823 and repeated fatal attacks by man-eating tigers in the nearby villages. In the latter case, Bai's official appeal to the god-spirit of wild animals to rein in the tigers reads as deferential yet subtly iconoclastic, reminding the governing spirit to recognize that every tiger victim represents one less human who can worship and sacrifice to him.[35]

It was on the water management front, however, where Bai earned his lasting fame in Hangzhou. To address problems with the fresh water supply inside the city walls, he ordered that Li Bi's deteriorated Six Wells be excavated and restored to their original condition. He also understood that the effects on local agriculture of the recent two years' droughts had been compounded by past failures to maintain the city's western-side lake as a reserve water supply for crop irrigation. Much of this problem arose from the collapse of the older and unrestored White Sands Dike (白沙堤, Bai sha di) that had apportioned a northern section of the lake as a reservoir. These lapses in maintenance were further magnified by insufficient dredging of the lake itself, so that the accumulated silt had lowered the lake's depth and reduced its carrying capacity.

Bai memorialized the throne for his project to dredge Hangzhou's lake, using the recovered silt to rebuild and raise the level of the former dike. His plans met with some local resistance over the fish and water-plant crops that would suffer during the project, but Bai countered those objections by arguing for the welfare of the people over that of the fish.[36] The restored dike succeeded in its water management objectives, providing a reservoir for summer crop irrigation between Hangzhou and Haining to the east. At the project's completion, Bai wrote an essay describing the need to relieve the suffering of the people during droughts and providing instructions for operating, maintaining, and preserving the dike. He then had a stone stele with an engraved copy of his essay, "The Story of the Qiantang Dam," erected on the new dike. [37]

The resulting causeway, running parallel to the northern lakeshore for almost a thousand meters to connect with Gushan (Solitary Hill) Island, unexpectedly enhanced the lake's natural beauty. The people of Hangzhou were so pleased, they honored their Governor by renaming White Sands Dike as Master Bai's Embankment (白公堤, Bai gong di), the name by which the causeway is still known today.

Bai Juyi the poet gave one more gift to Hangzhou before his departure in 824. He loved visiting Qiantang Lake (as West Lake was still formally known) and wrote some two hundred verses about it. Two poems in particular had long-lasting resonance: "On the Boat Returning to Hangzhou" (杭州回舫, "Hangzhou hui fang") and "Returning in the Evening from West Lake, Looking Back at Solitary Hill in the Distance" (西湖晚歸回望孤山寺贈諸客, "Xihu wan gui huiwang gushan si zeng zhu ke"). Both poems mark the earliest known literary references to West Lake (西湖, Xihu), the name which gradually overtook Qiantang Lake in common usage.

At his departure in 824, Governor Bai wrote a fond and self-effacing farewell:

Good-bye to the People of Hangzhou

Elders and officers line the returning road;
Wine and soup load the parting table.
I have not ruled you with the wisdom of Shao Gong;
What is the reason your tears should fall so fast?
My taxes were heavy, though many of the people were poor;
The farmers were hungry, for often their fields were dry.
All I did was to dam the water of the Lake
And help a little in a year when things were bad.[38]

Years later, Bai reminisced in verse about his years as Governor of Hangzhou (822 – 824):

To the Tune: "Memories of the South," A Reminiscence

The beauty of the South!

Once I was familiar with all its sights and sounds.
At sunrise, river flowers redder than flame,
In spring, river waters the blue of indigo.
Can I help remembering the South?

Memories of the South!
Most fondly I remember Hangzhou.
Visiting temples in the hills in quest of cassia seeds dropped from the moon;
Watching the Tidal Bore from my pillow in the pavilion of my office.
When shall I ever revisit Hangzhou?[39]

Bai Juyi enjoyed thirteen years of peaceful retirement in the Luoyang area, spending much of his time collecting and organizing his life's work. He passed away in 846 after years of declining health, leaving behind an oeuvre of more than three thousand poems. He continues in modern times to be celebrated as one of the Tang Dynasty's greatest poets.

A Leader Emerges from Lin'an County

Although the Tang Dynasty survived An Lushan's attempted usurpation of the imperial throne, the ruling family's Mandate of Heaven began gradually slipping away. The rebellion (755 – 763) had shattered the empire, leaving an estimated 20 – 30 million dead from war, famine, and disease. Census records, perhaps negatively influenced by the chaotic dispersion of northerners during those years, nevertheless told the inarguable story: a census count of fifty-three million one year before the rebellion began, reduced to seventeen million one year after the rebellion ended.[40]

Equally significant, devastating conflict in the north once again propelled those who could escape—the wealthy, the educated, current and former officials—to migrate south across the Yangzi River. The population center of gravity was shifting more and more eastward and southward. The Yangzi River Delta, for so long seen as wild and barbaric, was steadily transforming into a major seat of arts, culture, and scholarship.

The final 112 years of the Tang, from 795 – 907, saw the reign of twelve emperors who were, variously: induced to place the military under eunuch control (Dezong 唐德宗, r. 779 - 805), murdered by eunuchs (Xianzong 唐憲宗, r. 805 – 820), fatally injured in a polo accident after a reign of just four years (Muzong 唐穆宗, r. 820 – 824), again murdered by eunuchs (the teenage Jingzong 唐敬宗, r. 824 - 827), chosen by eunuchs after murdering other candidates and their mothers and later self-poisoned at age 33 by consumption of immortality elixirs (Wuzong 唐文宗, r. 840 – 846), and another poisoned after a thirteen-year reign by an immortality potion (Xuanzong 唐宣宗, r. 846 - 859).

By the time Xuanzong's wasteful and capricious son 14-year-old, the Yizong Emperor (唐懿宗, r. 859 – 873) died in 873, the court was riven by factional and eunuch-official infighting under the gaze of a 12-year-old emperor, Xizong (唐僖宗, r. 873 – 888), followed by his even younger brother, Zhaozong (唐昭宗, r. 888 – 904). Meanwhile, the common people were being driven from their land by over-taxation even as famine reigned, and roving bandits (and wealthy landlords) further victimized the powerless. Local outbreaks and rebellions presaged worse to come.

Finally, in 875, a military officer named Wang Ying sparked a rebellion in the Yangzi Delta area that resulted in the seizure of Changzhou and Suzhou. Wang's uprising spread across the Jiangsu plain and along the Zhejiang coast as far south as Wenzhou. After some delay, the 13-year-old Emperor Xizong's court issued a three-pronged response: sending troops from nearby Hunan Province, ordering a naval response from the provinces themselves, and authorizing local officials to form their own militias.

In the Hangzhou area, a local warlord named Dong Chang 董昌 (d. 896) answered the call by forming a militia from the surrounding counties. Among those who responded was a charismatic young man from the Hangzhou area (Lin'an County) named Qian Liu 钱镠 (852 – 932), who brought with him a group of capable followers. Qian was born into the small village life of poor peasants who fished and farmed. Legends portray him in boyhood perched on a high rock under a village tree, overseeing his youthful followers in "war games" in which they dared not ignore his directions.

A natural if intimidating leader, Qian developed a fondness for chivalry (任侠, *renxia*) and cultivated excellent skills with bow and lance. He disdained the life of his family and community, opting instead to lead a gang that dabbled in salt smuggling and undertook other "assignments" of a dubiously legitimate nature.[41]

Dong Chang recognized Qian Liu's leadership qualities and successfully petitioned to place the fearless young man as his second in command. Together, they surrounded and killed Wang Ying in 877. Yet even as minor rebel leaders like Wang were successively put down, word rose about the much larger and more threatening approach of a force led by Huang Chao 黄巢 (835 – 884). Under Dong Chang's command, the eight counties comprising Hangzhou Prefecture each created a thousand-man militia with local leadership; the combined force soon became known as the Eight Battalions of Hangzhou. Second in command was Qian Liu.

Huang Chao was a salt-smuggler-turned-rebel-leader from Shandong Province. His followers were starving peasants resentful of the tax burden inflicted by the wastefulness and opulence of the Tang court. Huang's uprising began as early as 874, and his early battlefield successes demonstrated instinctive abilities as a military tactician. By 878, his growing army, numbering at its peak as many as 600,000, moved south into the area of modern-day Anhui Province and threatened to advance eastward toward Hangzhou.

According to Ouyang Xiu's classical account, Qian Liu selected a small group of the Eight Battalions' best soldiers and organized an ambush of several hundred rebels. Qian's guerrilla-style defense killed the troop's commander and smashed the advance force, reputedly influencing Huang Chao's decision to bypass Hangzhou Prefecture.[42] Instead, the entire rebel force crossed the Qiantang River, attacked Yue Prefecture (Yuezhou 越州), and continued south, devastating Fujian Province on their march into Guangdong Province.

Huang Chao laid siege to the trading port city of Canton in 878. Historical Arab sources have long asserted that after capturing that city, the rebels massacred as many as 120,000 Muslims, Jews, Zoroastrians, and Christians, rich traders and merchants who Huang saw as contributors to the failings of the Tang Dynasty. In just five years, Huang Chao had cut a bloody, north-south swath through eastern China, from Shandong Province to the southernmost coast. He was not finished yet.

Meanwhile, Dong Chang's and Qian Liu's success in deflecting Huang's rebel armies away from Hangzhou earned them prestige and official promotions: Dong Chang as Prefect of Hangzhou and Qian Liu as commander of the Eight Battalions. Through the years 879 – 881, Dong and Qian maintained local order in the Hangzhou area as the nation suffered the chaos of another march through China by Huang Chao's rebel army. This time, Huang advanced westward from ravaged Canton to Guilin, then northward and eastward in a rambling, warlike advance that ended, unbelievably, with the capture of the Tang capital of Chang'an in January 881. Huang Chao declared himself emperor of the new state of Qi, residing in Chang'an until driven out in 883 and finally killed in July 884. It would take almost twenty-five more years, but the Tang Dynasty effectively ended with Huang Chao's rebellion.

Hangzhou had once again escaped direct assault from Huang Chao's rebels, but the conflict created administrative instability that gave rise to bandits and warlords. Qian Liu put down those outbreaks in the northern Zhejiang and lower Jiangsu regions, gaining more promotions along the way. In the last two decades of the 9th Century, he advanced from military commander to Prefect of Hangzhou and then Governor of the prefecture.

By 896, after seizing Yuezhou from an increasingly megalomaniacal Dong Chang in accordance with an imperial edict, Qian Liu was granted military control on both sides of the Qiantang River. In the century's final years, he also captured Hu Prefecture (Huzhou) and Su Prefecture (Suzhou). Meanwhile, Tang Emperor Zhaozong 唐昭宗 (r. 888 – 904) in Chang-an had been reduced to little more than a bystander as various military commanders like Qian Liu vied for territory and dismantled the unified nation.

In 902, as the Tang Dynasty neared collapse, Qian was elevated by the court to Prince of Yue and, two years later, Prince of Wu. With the fall of the Tang in 907 and the ascent of Taizu 太祖 (r. 907 – 912) as first emperor of the Later Liang 后梁 Dynasty, the period known as the Five Dynasties and Ten Kingdoms began. The Chinese empire devolved once again into a loose confederation of semi-independent states with a nominal emperor at its head. The political game had changed into one of state-to-state realpolitik, and Qian Liu and his descendants, controlling the immense wealth of the Yue and Wu territories, were about to prove themselves masters of that art. The benefits to Zhejiang and lower Jiangsu, and especially to Hangzhou, would be inestimable, as much for what they avoided as for what they accomplished.

Wu + Yue = Wuyue

In 907, Later Liang Emperor Taizu granted the title Prince of Wuyue to Qian Liu after the latter astutely chose to support the dynastic change. In return, Taizu openly acknowledged Qian's vassal-like control over nearly all of present-day Zhejiang Province and most of Jiangsu Province south of the Yangzi River. The State of Min (roughly Fujian Province today) bordered Wuyue on the south, while the State of Wu (roughly the northern half of Jiangsu plus Anhui and Jiangxi Provinces, twice Wuyue's territorial size), bordered both Wuyue and Min to their west. More distant in that direction were the States of Chu and Former Shu, while the Southern Han controlled the far southeastern and southern coastal territories. All five of these states, as well as Wuyue, operated as independent kingdoms in 907 or shortly after; five more independent states would form over the next five decades as some states rose and others fell.

Five consecutive dynasties would hold sway and control sizable territories in the north between 907 and 960: in order, the Later Liang (907 – 923), Later Tang (923 – 935), Later Jin (936 – 947), Later Han (947 – 951), and Later Zhou (951 – 960). Combined, they would see eleven claimants to their various thrones in just those fifty-three years. The years from 907 to 960 were thus a period of enormous instability and constant conflict, one where military strength was necessary but hardly sufficient for survival. At a time when alliances of almost any two states could fatally weaken or destroy any third state standing alone, only the most Machiavellian could successfully maneuver this game of lesser thrones unscathed.

With Hangzhou as his capital, Qian Liu went to work as a civil administrator as well as military commander. His kingdom consisted initially of twelve prefectures: Hangzhou, Yuezhou, Huzhou, Wenzhou, Taizhou, Mingzhou (Ningbo), Chuzhou (Lishui), Quzhou, Wuzhou (Jinhua), Muzhou (northwestern Zhejiang), Xiuzhou (Shanghai-Jiaxing), and Suzhou. Fuzhou would be added later, in 947.

Around 909, Qian Liu initiated two major infrastructure initiatives by following in the footsteps of his ancient predecessors. Like Sui Dynasty Governor Yang Su, he built walls, enlarging his capital city's enclosed area by extending the walls southward toward the Qiantang River to encapsulate fully both Wushan and Fenghuangshan. And like Da Yu, he "tamed the waters" by dredging the lakes and waterways, adding seawalls, and constructing history's first successful embankment against the Qiantang River's tidal bore. Qian installed a series of bamboo gabions (cages or cylinders) filled with rocks, anchored to wooden pilings and tied with heavy iron chains.[43]

According to the legendary story "King Qian Shoots the Tide" (錢王射潮, Qian wang she chao), Qian Liu at one point grew annoyed at the lack of progress on the new seawalls. Twice every day, the tidal bore roared up the river and undid the work just completed. In order to quell the spirit that animated the rushing waters, Qian arrayed five hundred of his finest archers to halt the tide's progress by firing three thousand arrows into the oncoming bore so that more work could be completed.[44] Closer to his own capital city, he constructed catchment basins outside the city walls to eliminate repeated instances of flooding through the city gates. To the north, particularly around the south and east of Tai Lake, Qian also established a bureau of 7,000 - 8,000 men responsible for waterways, dikes, and agricultural water management.[45]

On the diplomatic front, Qian began in 916 a Wuyue tradition of sending lavish tributes to the reigning dynasty in the north. His actions demonstrated the generous obeisance of a vassal state, maintaining relationships with a powerful ally who would deter other states from attacking his kingdom. At the same time, Qian consistently managed to leave the dynasty of the moment with just enough uncertainty regarding possible Wuyue alliances with other powerful states that they had to appease him as well. He also arranged some of his children's marriages[46] in order to build or strengthen alliances.

In 923, the Later Liang Emperor granted the title King of Wuyue to Qian Liu, cementing his kingdom's position as an independent vassal state. By the time of his death in 932, Qian had restored order to his kingdom, expanded its agricultural productivity, established a flourishing commercial and handicrafts trade both intrastate and interstate, and positioned Wuyue as a formidable player in the dynastic realpolitik. His advice to his sons during his last days summed up his political insight: protect and manage the kingdom you have and do not attempt to establish a new dynasty.[47]

By consent among his sons, Qian Liu's throne and titles were assumed by his seventh son, Qian Yuanguan 钱元瓘 (887 – 941, r. 932 – 941). In 937, Later Jin Emperor Gaozu granted him the same title his father had held, King of Wuyue. Aside from a military misadventure in the State of Min, Yuanguan's reign was relatively uneventful until a dreadful fire broke out in Hangzhou in 941. Much of the palace and treasury were destroyed, but the damage to the physically-unharmed king's mental health was apparently far worse. Unexpectedly, Yuanguan's physical wellness deteriorated rapidly. He died before the year was out and was succeeded by his 13-year-old son, Qian Hongzuo 钱弘佐 (928 – 947, r. 941 – 947).

Accession to leadership by a barely teenaged adolescent offered all the marks of a clan rule at risk. Fortunately, Hongzuo was level-headed and intelligent, applying himself diligently to learning the ins and outs of civil and military administration. His reign's main accomplishment came in 947. After several years of civil war in the State of Min, the Southern Tang state intervened and took control of Min altogether. Appeals for assistance by the head of Fuzhou Prefecture led Hongzuo to send ground and naval forces in response. Wuyue troops landed on the coast and decisively defeated the Southern Tang army, which then withdrew from the northern half of Min. Hongzuo left his troops to occupy Fuzhou, thus ending the State of Min and incorporating Fuzhou Prefecture into Wuyue.[48]

After Qian Hongzuo died suddenly in 947 at age 18, his younger brother, Qian Hongzong 钱弘倧 (928 – 971, r. 947 – 948) ascended the kingship of Wuyue. His reign was brief, troubled by difficulties in controlling several generals who had been abusing their power. One of those generals, Hu Jinsi 胡进思 (d. 948), fearing imprisonment or execution, placed Hongzong under house arrest. He then proposed Hongzong's overthrow to the king's younger half-brother, Qian Hongchu, who accepted on condition that Hongzong's life be spared. Such was the case, and Hongzong lived out the last twenty years of his life at a garden-filled palace in Yuezhou Prefecture.

By the time of Qian Hongchu's 钱弘俶 (929 – 978, r. 948 – 978) ascension in 948 as the fifth (and final) occupant of the Wuyue throne, the northern kingdom was witnessing the start of its fourth dynasty and eighth reign in the same period. Like his grandfather, Hongchu would play the diplomatic game to near perfection, delivering his subjects and lands peacefully into a new era and leaving behind major physical markers of his reign.

As had been the case for the past forty years, Qian Chu (as he was later called)[49] submitted himself as vassal to Emperor Gaozu of the Later Han Dynasty. He continued this practice in the early 950s when the Later Zhou Dynasty began, and again in 960 when the Song Dynasty began. Wuyue, from Suzhou to Huzhou and Hangzhou, and on to Ningbo and Fuzhou along the eastern coast, prospered during Chu's reign. Commerce and trade flourished, not just domestically but across the sea with the Korean states. As a coastal state, Wuyue naturally maintained a naval trade orientation.

The State's dependence on ocean-borne trade might seem strange for the terminal city on the Grand Canal, but the great inland waterway had suffered from disuse during the rebellion-filled years of the Tang Dynasty and the conflict-riddled, multistate years of the Five Dynasties. Not only was the canal not well-maintained, travel through one state and into the next was fraught with risk. Wuyue's lavish program of tribute gifts to the successive northern dynasties, for example, had to find a combination of sea-river-land routes to transport safely to the capital its valuable cargoes of gold, silver, silks, gold- and silver-plated dinnerware, high-quality ceramics,[50] and other desirable objects.

As early as 935, Qian Yuanguan had initiated contacts with Japan that continued into Qian Chu's reign, although these never developed into full-fledged diplomatic or commercial relations. Exchange of a rather different nature did take place with Japan (and also Korea), however. Qian Liu and Qian Chu, grandfather and grandson, were devout practitioners of Buddhism.[51] Qian Liu actively supported Buddhist temples and religious worship, particularly through the person of his wife, Lady Zhuangmu of Wuyue 吴越莊穆夫人 (858 - 919). However, Qian Liu's efforts in regard to religious practice paled in comparison to those of Qian Chu, who transformed Hangzhou into a major center of Tiantai 天台 Buddhist practice and worship.[52]

Numerous Japanese and Korean monks dwelled at Tiantai Mountain for extended periods during the Qian family's reign over Wuyue. In return, Wuyue monks traveled to Japan and Korea to spread their faith, establishing Hangzhou for other East Asian peoples as an important site for Buddhist study. Religious exchanges and commercial trade (with Korea) made Wuyue one of the most outward-looking of the Ten Kingdoms.

Temples and Pagodas Rise...

Where Qian Liu had focused his efforts on short-term matters of survival and stabilization of the new Wuyue State, Qian Chu enjoyed the luxury of building upon his grandfather's solid foundation. And build he did, particularly in the final decade of his reign. In 954, Qian Chu built the Jingci Temple[53] 净慈寺 on the southern shore of

West Lake, at the foot of Nanping Hill 南屏山. Second only to Lingyin Temple, Jingci's most renowned occupant was the monk Yongming Yanshou 永明延壽 (904 - 975), a Hangzhou native whose fame attracted numerous monks from Korea and even royal gifts from the Korean king.

In 959, work began on the Yunyan Pagoda atop Suzhou's Tiger Hill, the historic site of Wu King Helü's tomb. Completed two years later, Yunyan Pagoda soared over Suzhou from a little more than a mile outside the city walls. Like the renowned tower in Pisa, Italy, Yunyan Pagoda became known for its very noticeable lean toward the northeast, almost four degrees from vertical. Although historians typically position Suzhou's landmark pagoda as a work of the Song Dynasty (960 – 1279), there is no doubt that Suzhou Prefecture was fully under Qian Chu's control in 959 – 961 and remained so for another fifteen years or more.

In 963, Qian Chu traveled to Kaifeng at the order of the powerful Song Emperor Taizu 宋太祖 (r. 960 – 976). Such trips had been commonplace for the Wuyue kings, personally submitting themselves to the constantly-changing string of dynasties and emperors that characterized the period. On this occasion, the Qian ruling clan not only prayed for Qian Chu's safety but authorized construction of a nine-story pagoda on the peak of Precious Stone Hill (宝石山, Baoshi shan). They named the structure Baochu Pagoda (保俶塔, Baochu ta), or "Protecting Chu Pagoda." The Wuyue king returned safely to Hangzhou and continued his reign.

Just four years later, in 967, Qian Chu built another temple, this time opposite the Jingci Temple at the northeastern corner of West Lake, about halfway between the Qiantang and Wulin Gates and more or less beneath the Baochu Pagoda. Originally called the Bodhi Temple, Song Emperor Taizong 宋太宗 (r. 976 – 997) changed its name in around 980 to Zhaoqing Temple 昭庆寺. Located outside the city gates and alongside the lake, the temple complex suffered repeated bouts of destruction and reconstruction from wars and fires over the ensuing centuries.

In the Ming Dynasty (1368 – 1644), Zhaoqing Temple was the equal of Lingyin and Jingci Temples in size and popularity for such religious observances as incense burning or releasing life (returning live animals back to Nature). The temple's convenience to the walled city also made it a prime locale for spring festivals and a prosperous everyday market for selling toys, books, jewelry, art and antiques, local products, and household items. In the later imperial era, Zhaoqing Temple was commonly regarded as one of Hangzhou's four great Buddhist temples, along with Lingyin, Jingci, and Haichao Temples.[54]

After the 1911 Revolution, construction of roadways around West Lake for a growing city necessitated the removal of Zhaoqing's temple buildings in the early 1920s. Only Daxiong Hall remained until that building, too, was destroyed by fire in 1929.[55] Today's restored Daxiong Hall stands amid the Hangzhou Children's Palace[56] as a reminder of the great but nearly forgotten temple that served as an integral part of the people's daily lives in earlier times. In 1994, twenty-three (mostly) bronze temple artifacts were discovered in an ancient well at the site and turned over to the Hangzhou Museum.

Two more famous pagodas were erected in Hangzhou before the State of Wuyue disappeared. In 970, Qian Chu ordered construction of the magnificent Liuhe ("Six Harmonies") Pagoda (六和塔) along the northern shore of the Qiantang River. In addition to creating a navigational marker, Qian sought to reinforce his grandfather's efforts to appease the spirit of the tidal bore and calm the bore's destructiveness.

In 975, he ordered construction of yet another pagoda, an octagonal, five-story structure rising from the south shore of West Lake. The new brick and wood pagoda rose in five years against the backdrop of the lake's southern hills and stood in direct counterpoise to the needle-like, hill-topping Baochu Pagoda directly opposite. Qian Chu's purpose for building Leifeng (雷峰, Thunder Peak) Pagoda was apparently much more than aesthetic and much less civic-minded than the previous structures, however. The traditional explanation for the pagoda was solely to honor the king's favorite concubine, Consort Huang (黄妃, Huangfei), after the birth of a son.[57] This story is likely inaccurate for several reasons; a more plausible explanation would be Qian's wish to honor his wife Sun Taizhen 孫太真, who died a few years later in 976 or early 977.[58]

Leifeng Pagoda also harbored a secret that would remain unknown until the 20th Century. Qian Chu installed an inscription in which he described the pagoda's original conception, identifying the builder (himself) as a Buddhist layman who "never stops reciting and poring over Buddhist sutras in the little spare time between ten thousand administrative affairs."[59] To reinforce this claim of religious piety, he ordered that the pagoda's floor tiles each be manufactured with a hollow cylindrical core into which was inserted a single sutra, carefully secured with blue brocade, covered in yellow silk, and protected in a sutra bag. On each copy, Qian Chu included a preface announcing that, "The Great General of the Army under Heaven, King of Wu-yue, Qian [Chu], had made 84,000 copies of this sutra and interred them in the brick pagoda…as eternal offerings."[60]

One final and often overlooked architectural remnant of the Qian family's commitment to Buddhism still stands today near the south foot of Phoenix Hill. On the shores of the Qiantang River, the Qian family erected a navigation marker in the form of a pagoda.[61] Built of white stone in the Tibetan Buddhist style, this octagonal structure survives to the present day in White Pagoda Park (白塔公园, Baita gongyuan) near Zhakou, an ancient port town just southwest of Hangzhou's formerly walled city area. The pagoda consists of nine tapering levels and stands about ten meters high.

Altogether, in a period of less than twenty-five years, Qian Chu had radically altered West Lake's scenic environs—for the better, by nearly all accounts to the present day.

…but Wuyue Falls

The advent in the north of the expansionist Later Zhou Dynasty in 951 marked a new diplomatic era for Qian Chu and all the leaders of the southern kingdoms. In 956, Zhou Emperor Shizong 世宗帝 (r. 954 – 959) overthrew the delicate balance of power in the south by attacking the largest among those states, the Southern Tang, and winning

81

control of that state's lands north of the Yangzi River. As part of his attack plan, Shizong had pressed Wuyue to apply military pressure from the south while his forces advanced on Southern Tang from the north.

Qian Chu complied somewhat half-heartedly in attacking his powerful neighboring state until 958, when Zhou's victory seemed assured. In the final months of the conflict, Qian pressed Southern Tang aggressively and committed a large naval force to the conflict. Southern Tang was not eliminated, but it was mortally wounded. Wuyue gained from seeing its neighbor weakened, but it lost by now having the larger and more powerful Zhou State directly on its northern borders in place of the buffer formerly provided by Southern Tang.

Unfortunately, the immediate diplomatic benefits to Qian Chu were somewhat limited. Zhou Emperor Shizong fell ill and died in the final months of 959. His seven-year-old son ascended the throne, placing the Empress Dowager in the position of Regent. This arrangement proved unacceptable to the military leaders, who threw their support behind one of their leading generals, Zhao Kuangyin 赵匡胤 (927 – 976). In 960, Zhao usurped the throne and declared the beginning of the new Song Dynasty, with himself as Emperor Taizu 宋太祖 (r. 960 – 976).

In short order, Qian Chu aligned himself with the new dynasty by dramatically increasing the frequency and generosity of his tribute missions, many of which "were headed by one of Qian Chu's sons or other family members. In return, the Song often sent gifts of sheep, horses, and camels…and honored Qian Chu on the anniversaries of his birth."[62]

The reasons for such mutual and respectful exchange were simple. For Wuyue, the alliance offered protection and survival. For Song, retaining Wuyue as an ally held the remainder of the Southern Tang state in check while Taizu attended to other conquest matters: the States of Nanping (also known as Jingnan) and Chu in 863, Shu in 865, and Southern Han in 971. Finally, in 976, Wuyue joined in the Song's final attack on the Southern Tang, with Qian Chu personally leading two assaults on Changzhou and joining the seizure of Jinling (Nanjing).[63] Before the end of 976, Song Taizu had reunified much of the empire, with Wuyue remaining as the last major power to be addressed.

Following the conquest of Southern Tang, Emperor Taizu invited Qian Chu to visit the Song capital at Kaifeng. Qian obliged, bringing his wife and heir apparent along with him. Taizu received his Wuyue guests regally, but the implications were clear. Taizu's death in the same year interrupted arrangements, but his successor, the Taizong Emperor 宋太宗, (r. 976 – 997), invited Qian for a second audience in 978. This time, Qian offered concessions that would leave Wuyue as an independent vassal state. His suggestion was politely but firmly declined.

Later that year, Wuyue formally surrendered and accepted full incorporation into the Song empire. Qian Chu and his family members thereby received multiple titles, ranks, and positions from the new dynasty. In return, he and three thousand members of his family and household relocated to Kaifeng to assure the Song emperor of their loyalty.

Qian Chu maintained an amiable relationship with Taizong, although his sudden death on the celebration of his 60th birthday in 988 may have been the result of poisoning.

Like a master airline pilot in the modern day, Qian Chu had navigated the diplomatic storms and crosswinds of his time and delivered his craft of state virtually unscathed into the grand new era of the Song Dynasty. That the Wuyue region was so well-positioned to reach new heights of prosperity, cultural achievement, and political importance in the next several centuries can be attributed in great part to the Qian family rulers of the Ten Kingdoms period, especially the founder Qian Liu and the last king, Qian Chu.

Wuyue's capital of Hangzhou, a city whose existence barely registered before the year 600, was now an increasingly important player in the imperial realm. Already by 1057, Northern Song Emperor Renzong 宋仁宗 (r. 1022 – 1063) would write that Hangzhou "has lakes and mountains that are beautiful" and that the city could be regarded as "the number one prefecture in the Southeast."[64]

Chapter 5

SONG OF THE NORTH

(960 – 1127)

Drinking by the Lake: Clear Sky at First, then Rain[1]

The shimmer of light on the water is the play of sunny skies,
The blur of color across the hills is richer still in the rain.
If you wish to compare the lake in the west to the Lady of the West,
Lightly powdered or thickly smeared the fancy is just as apt.

— Su Shi (1037 – 1101)

Although the Song Dynasty was far from perfect, particularly in its defense of the homeland, it nevertheless served as a vital period of imperial stability and maturation in civil administration. The military operated under civil control, population expanded, agricultural production increased, and arts and culture reached new heights.

Despite losing half the empire to northern tribesmen and being forced to relocate the court to a new southern capital, the imperial line of the reigning Zhao family demonstrated remarkable longevity. Of the eighteen men who held the Song throne for a combined 319 years, ten reigned for at least fifteen years, and eight of those lasted more than twenty years. Of the remaining eight reigns, four were cut short due to the chaos of barbarian invasion; in fact, three of those four lasted no more than a year each. This chapter covers the first half of the Song Dynasty, from 960 – 1127, when Bianjing 汴京 (modern Kaifeng) in north China was the imperial capital. In history, this period would be known as the Northern Song era.

Plum Trees and Cranes

Perhaps no individual in the first decades of the Song Dynasty more singularly represented the national shift in cultural primacy from sword to brush, and better modeled the fully-realized lifestyle aspirations of so many Chinese scholar elites through much of the next eight centuries, than Lin Bu 林逋 (967 – 1028).

Born in Hangzhou and well-educated in the classics, Lin Bu renounced a life of government service in favor of traveling, contemplating Nature, and discussing Buddhist principles. His classical training prepared him well as a poet, and his work drew sufficiently widespread attention to attract offers for official positions. Lin rejected them all, preferring the eremitic life he made for himself composing poetic verse on the West Lake island known as Solitary Hill (孤山, Gushan) Island and boating on the lake's quiet waters.

With a poet's sensibility, Lin Bu developed an unusual affinity for the winter-flowering tree *prunus mume*, often referred to as winter plum. In the dreary, daylight-shortened months of January and February, winter plums burst forth with fragrant white and red flowers to enliven the colorless depths of the winter cold. Their vibrancy symbolized perseverance and hope, and Lin found great pleasure in planting and cultivating dozens of those trees. He also wrote lovingly about them:

Small Plum Tree in a Garden in the Hills [2]

> When all the other flowers have fallen, it alone shows warmth and beauty,
> Taking charge of all romantic feeling in the small garden.
> Spare shadows slant across waters that are clear and shallow,
> Hidden fragrance hangs and drifts under a moon hazy and dim.
> The frosty bird wants to alight but steals a glance first,
> If powder-dabbed butterflies knew of it, their hearts would break.
> Luckily, chanting poetic lines softly I'm able to befriend it,
> No need for the singing girl's clappers or a golden goblet of wine.

In addition to his *prunus mume*, Lin Bu also kept a pair of cranes on Gushan. In Chinese culture, cranes symbolize longevity and nobility of character. Because the birds mate with a single partner for life, they also represent everlasting love and faithfulness in marriage. One legend asserts that because Lin enjoyed boating excursions on West Lake, his servants would release the cranes into flight to alert their master when visitors arrived.

Lin famously countered criticisms of his solitary existence by saying that the winter plums were the wife for whom he cared and the cranes were his children. He passed away at 61 years of age and was buried on Gushan, where his tomb can still be found today alongside the Releasing Cranes Pavilion (放鶴亭, Fanghe Ting). Posthumously, he was renamed Lin Hejing 林和靖, where "Hejing" suggests a meaning like "tranquil harmony." His poetry achieved long-lasting popularity not only in China but in Japan, where he came to be regarded as a poetic immortal. He also became the subject of numerous paintings down through the centuries, often shown with one or two cranes nearby.

85

A Foreign Visitor

Over the first century of the Song Dynasty (960 – 1060), Hangzhou regained and then surpassed its Tang-era place in the commercial life of the Chinese empire. Population continued to expand with immigrants from the north in the decades following the An Lushan Rebellion and the six or seven decades of political instability after the fall of the Tang Dynasty. Hangzhou's silk and brocade production helped propel it to a major source of tax revenue for the new Song Dynasty. The city also evolved as a national center of book publishing and related woodblock and movable type printing[3] and paper-making technologies. Foreign trade in handicrafts, porcelains, and silks grew as well, not only with Japan and Korea but also with Southeast Asia and Persia. Hangzhou was becoming a first-rate city of wealth, culture, international flair, natural beauty, and comfort.

In 1073, an aging Japanese monk in Ningbo[4] packed up a collection of Buddhist scriptures he and his small entourage had accumulated over nearly sixteen months of travel in China. He ordered five of his disciples to accompany these invaluable documents on their journey back to Japan and to make sure, after safe arrival, that they were translated, copied, and distributed across his home country. In addition, he gave his followers one additional item to transport home: the travel diary he had kept since arriving in Hangzhou the prior year. Thus, it is through his thousand-year-old personal account, *The Record of a Pilgrimage to the Tiantai and Wutai Mountains* (*San Tendai Godai san ki*), that we know of the monk Jojin 成尋 (1011 – 1081).

By all accounts, Jojin was born into great prospects.[5] His father came from a politically powerful lineage, and his mother was the granddaughter of a former emperor. However, those prospects dimmed significantly when his father died while Jojin was still a young boy. Given the circumstances, his mother placed him and his brother in a Buddhist temple, intending that they become monks. In around 1042, Jojin was elevated to abbot of a monastery near the capital. His sect, Tiantai 天台, was associated with the dominant group of Buddhists in Hangzhou and the Zhejiang Province area. They also had a history of pilgrimage travel to China dating back more than two hundred years. In fact, the Japanese school of Tiantai Buddhism, known at Tendai, was founded by the monk Saichō after visiting the Guoqing Temple 国清寺 at Tiantai Mountain (天台山, Tiantai shan) in 804.[6]

In 1070, the 60-year-old Jojin began arranging his own pilgrimage to the sacred Tiantai and Wutai 五台 Mountains, apparently planning never to return to Japan. Unable to secure the required travel documents after months of waiting, he found a Chinese merchant who agreed to provide a less official passage. With seven disciples in his party, Jojin set sail from Kyushu in the early summer of 1072.

Their ship docked at Hangzhou a little more than a week later, avoiding the normal disembarkation at Mingzhou (Ningbo) because of their lack of proper documentation. Jojin wrote in his diary upon arrival at Hangzhou that the city's closely-packed houses all had thatched tile roofs, "constructed in an impressive manner," and that "there were countless big ships."[7] Fortunately, they managed to obtain permission from Hangzhou's customs office to enter the city and secure an interpreter. Jojin wrote in his diary of visiting the city's night market with what, for him, was unusual detail:

> During the dog hours, I set out...to go sightseeing in the city. It was as magnificent as hundreds of thousands of the seven precious jewels. A single place had perhaps two or three hundred lanterns. Glass lamps hung in line with flames burning within....

> There was a large number of musical entertainers, unimaginable. In addition, there were various puppets made to dance with the water, beat drums, and rise out of the water. Two were twirling like magicians. From two puppets' mouths, they spurt out water as high as four or five feet. Two issued water from their elbows rising five feet high. Two were galloping on horses. In all, there were over a hundred puppets atop the elevated constructed stage....

> The market area was over thirty blocks to the east and the west. North and south, it was over thirty blocks. Each block had major and minor roads. I cannot even say how many numerous vendors there were. Bystanders packed the streets and filled the buildings. With a silver tea utensil, everyone drank tea and paid out one coin....I fear I did not see everything as I returned to our lodging.[8]

Their party soon departed Hangzhou for Tiantai Mountain, near Taizhou in southern coastal Zhejiang Province. Jojin spent five months at Tiantai, during which time he petitioned the court for permission to visit Wutai Mountain in Shanxi Province. What he received in reply was an unexpected invitation for an audience with Song Emperor Shenzong 宋神宗 (1048 – 1085, r. 1067 – 1085) in Kaifeng. After traveling the inland waterways for sixty-five days, Jojin and his seven-monk entourage were cordially received at the capital. Shenzong granted them gifts, arranged a magnificent vegetarian banquet in their honor, and granted them imperial permission to continue on to Wutai Mountain.

Jojin was able to collect more Buddhist scriptures and materials on his return trip through Kaifeng in 1073. He stayed at the capital for three more months, during which time he received the title of Dashi 大师, Great Master, from the Emperor. Shenzong also granted Jojin's request to return once again to Tiantai for further study. Their party traveled with an official escort back to Hangzhou via the Grand Canal, and then on to Ningbo where he parted company with his disciples and thus ended his diary. All told, Jojin had collected over six hundred volumes of Buddhist sutras, along with various paintings, poems, calendars, silks, and other materials;[9] all were transported safely back to Japan and further advanced the practice of Buddhism there.

Jojin's last diary entry, on the twelfth day of the sixth lunar month, contained one last surprise. Among the items bound for Japan was a letter for the Japanese emperor, written by the hand of Emperor Shenzong—a diplomatic initiative, unconventionally conveyed via traveling Buddhist monks.

87

Little is known of Jojin's final years, but he is thought to have died in Kaifeng in around 1081. As for Hangzhou, Jojin had even more firmly established Zhejiang Province, from Tiantai Mountain in Taizhou to Yuezhou and Hangzhou, as a vitally important locale for Japanese Buddhists to visit, worship, and study.

A Great Worthy of West Lake

Born in Sichuan Province, began official life in the Song capital of Kaifeng, held government offices in multiple cities, banished twice to far-off locales, and twice resided in Hangzhou for a combined total of only about five years. Yet for the past thousand years, Su Shi 苏轼 (1037 – 1101) has been revered in Hangzhou as much as any native son for his contributions to the preservation of West Lake and his poetic celebration of the city and its scenic environment.

Su Shi and his brother Su Zhe 苏辙 (1039 – 1112) seemed destined for stellar official careers when they achieved their *jinshi* degrees together in 1057 Kaifeng. Su Zhe was just 18 years old, a remarkable accomplishment at such a young age. Su Shi, two years older, nevertheless outdid his younger brother by finishing second in the examination candidate rankings. Unfortunately, their nascent official lives were interrupted almost immediately by the three-year mourning period for their mother's death, and again in 1066 for their father's passing.

When Su Shi finally returned to Kaifeng in 1068, Emperor Shenzong had recently ascended the throne and adopted new budgetary reforms espoused by Wang Anshi 王安石 (1021 – 1086). Su was strongly opposed to Wang's program and deeply frustrated that his views carried no weight, so he asked for a posting away from the capital. In 1071, at age 34, he was granted his first position as an assistant magistrate in Hangzhou. He and his family settled into their official residence on Phoenix Hill, where they could look down upon the Qiantang River to the south and the pleasure-boat-filled waters of what was still formally known as Qiantang Lake to the west.

Su Shi's responsibilities as an assistant magistrate—hearing and adjudicating court cases— were important but not onerous. Left with ample time to enjoy the temperate climate, he hiked in the surrounding hills, visited monks at their temples, boated on the lake with friends or family, and enjoyed life away from the politically fractious capital. He partook of wine and women, although neither recklessly so, and wrote poems with regularity. Many of Su's poems celebrated the natural beauty of the area, but he was also cognizant of the people's lives and hardships. In addition, he wrote verses and songs describing the Qiantang River bore and the daring surf riders who challenged the strongest tides, only identified amid the raging, ravenous waves by the colored flags they held aloft.

Su particularly indulged in a relatively new and popular form of poetry called *ci* 詞, in which verses were set to one of a number of established tones and meters from song tunes. Upon his departure from Hangzhou at the end of his three-year term, Su wrote an "advisory" poem to an incoming commissioner that summarized his own experience of the city:

The landscape of West Lake tops the world,
Tourists of all classes, intelligent and otherwise,
Find and appreciate each what he wants.
But who is there that can comprehend the whole?
Alas, in my stupid honesty,
I have long been left behind by the world.
I gave myself completely to the joys of hills and water—
Is it not all determined by God's Will?
Around the three hundred sixty temples,
I roamed throughout the year.
I knew the beauty of each particular spot,
Felt it in my heart but could not say it in my mouth.
Even now in my sweet sleep,
Its charm and beauty remain in my eyes and ears.
Now you come as a commissioner;
Your official pomp will insult the clouds and haze.
How can the clear streams and the purple cliffs
Reveal their beauties to you?
Why not dismiss your retinue
And borrow a couch from the monk,
Read the poems I inscribed on the rocks,
And let the cool mountain air soothe your troubled soul?
Carry a cane and go where you like,
And stop wherever seems to you best.
You'll find some ancient fishermen
Somewhere among the reeds. Talk with them,
And if they say wise things to you,
Buy fish from them and argue not about the price.[10]

Aside from a handful of worthy poems, Su Shi's work in Hangzhou from 1071 – 1074 seemed competent but unremarkable. However, he carried away impressions and appreciations for Hangzhou and Qiantang Lake, for life south of the Yangzi River, and for the importance of water management. In the latter case, he took special note of a project initiated in 1071 by the governor at the time, Chen Xiang陈襄 (1017 – 1080), to repair Li Bi's Six Wells inside the city walls.

After additional postings in Minzhou (Shandong Province, 1074 – 1077) and Xuzhou (Jiangsu Province, 1078 – 1079), Su must have been delighted to receive a transfer to Huzhou, a mere forty miles northwest of Hangzhou. Yet somehow, intentionally or otherwise, he managed in a letter of gratitude addressed to Emperor Shenzong to insult the coterie of court officials aligned with Wang Anshi's reform program, effectively calling them out as unqualified "young upstarts." His entire poetic oeuvre quickly fell under close review by those same "upstarts," looking for—and finding—phrasings whose interpretations could be twisted to suggest that their author was impugning the government, or even the Emperor himself.

Su was soon relieved of his Huzhou post, imprisoned, and put on trial for nearly two months in what became known as the Crow Terrace Poetry Case (烏臺詩案, Wutai shi'an).[11] After the hearings ended, he languished in prison as his case was summarized for the Emperor and then further delayed when the Empress Dowager passed away. Su's enemies wanted him executed, but Shenzong had no intention of losing a valuable subject. Instead, the Emperor quietly sent an observer into Su Shi's jail cell late one night, only barely rousing the sleeping prisoner who went right back to sleep. The observer disappeared early the next morning and reported that Su had slept soundly all night, albeit "snoring like thunder." Shenzong had the evidence he wanted: "I know that Su Shi's conscience is clear!"[12]

Su Shi was released with consequences. Sent out of the capital in 1080, he received a low-ranking position in moderately distant Huangzhou 晃州, not far from present-day Wuhan. Duly chastened, he took up farming in addition to serving his official post, tilling the soil on a hillside east of the city known as Eastern Slope (東坡, Dongpo) and referring to himself as "the Recluse of the Eastern Slope." From that time onward, he was as often called Su Dongpo as Su Shi. It was perhaps during his jobless days in Huangzhou that he popularized a method of stewing roast pork that bears his name to the present time: Dongpo Pork. He also wrote a sarcastic, two-line poem at the birth of a son in 1083 that showed his continued disdain for Song court officials in Kaifeng:

> May you, my son, grow up dumb and stupid,
> And, free from calamities, end up as a premier.[13]

Further assignments followed, but it was Shenzong's death in 1085 that catapulted Su Shi back into favor. The new emperor, Zhezong 宋哲宗 (1077 - 1100, r. 1085 -1100) was only eight years old, so the Dowager Empress acted as Regent. She immediately dismissed many of Wang Anshi's followers from the court and reversed most of the policies Su Shi had opposed. Su was recalled to the capital, given a dizzying succession of advancing ranks between 1085 and 1088, and sent back to Hangzhou in 1089 as the military commander of Western Zhejiang Province, including the city of Hangzhou. He was now 52 years old and at his intellectual and administrative prime.

Water management had long been a major civic challenge for Hangzhou, and Su Shi discovered that the situation had only worsened since his first posting there eighteen years earlier. The city's main transport canal, open to the Qiantang River and known as the Salt Canal, was clogged and required frequent dredging, and the drinking water in the Six Wells was salty. Even worse, the lake was seriously overgrown with floating islands of water plants that were causing the lake bed to rise. Su wrote plaintively in a memorial to the throne that if nothing were done to address the lake's condition, the lake itself might not exist in another twenty years.

To deal with the Salt Canal, Su oversaw a plan to install locks at the river entrance and use subsidiary canals in the city to allow the silt to settle before the water entered the main line. For the Six Wells, Su sought out the only monk still alive from the 1071 project to oversee major renovation of the fresh water system. The monk and his associates repaired the holding reservoirs in the lake and replaced the entire underground system of bamboo water lines with clay pipes, reinforced and protected by flagstones. Within several months of taking office, Su had already addressed two of the city's pressing water problems, but the most urgent, and the most complex, was the lake itself.[14]

In a memorial to the throne, Su Shi laid out a comprehensive rehabilitation and water management plan. The request itself made some history of its own, since its very name—"Request for Dredging West Lake"—may well be the first reference to Qiantang Lake as "West Lake" in any official Chinese document. In his memorial, Su presented a five-point argument for West Lake's importance to Hangzhou: "serving as a 'life-releasing pond' that accumulated merit for the State, providing drinking water for Hangzhou residents, offering irrigation for nearby farmlands, supporting the canals that ran through the city…, and accruing profit for the government by providing water used to brew rice wine."[15]

In order to remove the masses of floating paddies and excavate the heavily silted lake, Su managed to secure financing for as many as 200,000 laborers, half of the money coming from the capital. The mud and sludge they excavated was dumped along a north-south line toward the west side of the lake, connecting the south shore at Nanping Hill with the north shore near Xiling Bridge. The resulting dike stretched approximately 2.8 kilometers (about 1.7 miles), along the length of which Su planted willow and peach trees whose roots would help hold the soil in place. The solid embankment was interrupted by six bridges, allowing boats to pass from the main lake area into the newly-created inner lake on the far west side of West Lake.

As part of the same restoration project, Su Shi also instituted new controls over agricultural production in the lake. He ordered three stone pagodas installed in the lake bed to demarcate the areas where planting within diked paddies would still be permitted. In addition, he reserved several other areas for harvesting water chestnuts, with the taxes from all planted areas reserved for future maintenance of the lake.

In just eighteen months, Su Shi had effectively remade West Lake as well as the city's fresh water system. The tree-lined dike, positioned in aesthetic (and perpendicular) counterpoise to Bai Juyi's, was christened Su Causeway (苏堤, Su di) by the people of Hangzhou, and the three stone pagodas would become one of the most cherished of the many famous sites at West Lake. In later times, those modest pagodas would be celebrated by the view they created, called "Three Pools Mirroring the Moon" (三潭印月, Santanyinyue), the same name by which the lake island adjacent to them is known today.[16]

Remarkably, Su's West Lake and water management projects were far from his only contributions to the people of Hangzhou. During his brief tenure, he oversaw repair of the city gates, *yamen* offices, and granaries. He "single-handedly and passionately worked for famine relief against the colossal indifference of officials at the court and in the neighboring provinces."[17] In response to a famine and out of concern that crowded conditions made Hangzhou prone to epidemics, he also ordered (and personally contributed toward) construction of the city's first public infirmary in 1089.

He certainly knew that a little more than a decade earlier, in 1075 – 1076, a famine and epidemic had killed up to a half-million in the Hangzhou area and as many as one-half of those residing in Yuezhou.[18]

Su Shi's life after Hangzhou was a difficult one. Outspoken to a fault and rather intolerant of the political obeisance game at court, Su Shi made an easy target for those who disagreed with him or were jealous of him. His enemies at court hounded him relentlessly, scouring his poems and writings for any phrasing whose interpretation could be twisted into something seditious. They were regrettably all too successful.

With the death of the Empress Dowager in 1093, Wang Anshi's reform-minded followers regained control of the court and engineered Su Shi's banishment to a minor post in Huizhou, Guangdong Province. Still not satisfied, they successfully engineered another exile on even more remote Hainan Island in 1097. Finally allowed after four years to return to his mainland residence, Su arrived in Nanjing in May 1101 and passed away just three months later at his home in Changzhou.

In addition to his achievements as a public official, he left behind a corpus of nearly 3,000 poems, works that are studied and admired to the present day. Su Shi also had a little-known connection to Hangzhou's renowned tea culture. During his term as Governor of Hangzhou, he occasionally met and conversed over tea with a local Zen Buddhist monk named Biancai Yuanjing 辨才元淨 (1011-1091). In 1079, Biancai transplanted some tea trees at the site of the ancient Dragon Well (龙井, Longjing) in the western hills.[19] Tea plantations subsequently spread across the nearby hills around Meijiawu Village, known today for producing one of China's most famous varietals, Dragon Well Tea (龙井茶, Longjing cha).

A Great Hangzhou Polymath

Although Su Shi (1037 – 1101) was not a native of Hangzhou, another remarkable individual in Chinese history was born there six years before Su's birth. Their respective intellectual pursuits and career paths differed, but the two men led remarkably parallel lives, including deaths that also came separated by the same six-year difference.

Shen Gua 沈括 (1031 – 1095) was the son of Shen Zhou 沈周 (978–1052), a mid-level official whose career postings ranged from coastal Fujian Province to inland Sichuan Province, including a judicial posting in the capital at Kaifeng. Shen's great-grandfather, grandfather, and uncle had all experienced successful if modest official careers, and his nephew Shen Gou 沈遘 (1025 – 1067) had been the family's first to reach the higher ranks. His Suzhounese mother guided her son's early Confucian studies with expectations of an official career, but the family's travels from one side of the empire to the other were also activating the young man's capacious intellectual curiosity about the natural world.

After passing the lower level examinations and observing a three-year mourning period for his father's death in late 1051, Shen Gua occupied several low-level posts from 1054 to 1062. These opportunities came about through the traditional "protection privilege"

(荫, *yin*), under which educated young men from official families were granted the privilege of minor positions while still studying for their highest academic degree.[20]

In 1063, Shen was among the highest scorers in the imperial (*jinshi*) examinations, and his early official career in a minor posting at Yangzhou showed great promise. He excelled as a practical problem-solver, earning recommendations for more responsible positions and a fast-rising career track in the capital. In Kaifeng, his first assignment placed him at the Imperial Libraries, where he rose from intern to an editor in short order. At the court's direction, he performed studies on a variety of administrative issues, from grain storage and disaster relief to water conservancy, canal dredging, and land reclamation. In 1072, his six-year project to upgrade the astronomical observatory and institute a new calendar[21] earned him a position as Director of the Astronomy Bureau, where he planned a program of systematic astronomical observations.

An anecdote[22] from Shen Gua's assignment concerning water management of the critically important Bian Canal, the transport link between Kaifeng and both the Yellow and Huai Rivers, demonstrates the clarity and cleverness of his problem-solving thought processes. The court wished to investigate connecting the Luo River into the Bian Canal by means of a long-distance, artificial channel. As part of this project, Shen was charged with measuring the difference in altitude between a city gate at Kaifeng and a point on the Huai River about 250 miles away, with uneven terrain in between.

Surveyors already used relatively primitive water-level instruments to measure altitude differences, but these required a clear line of sight between two observers, thus limiting the distance they could be apart. Surveying the route, Shen noticed that a number of open ditches ran perpendicular to the canal, left over when soil was taken from them to build up the embankments. By filling each ditch with water and constructing dikes to contain it, he was able to measure the rise or fall in altitude between successive pairs of these ad hoc mini-reservoirs along the entire, 250-mile canal segment.

By adding all the rise and fall measurements together, Shen Gua determined the net difference in altitude between the two distant endpoints. In what may have been the first topographical measurement in Chinese history, he found that the Kaifeng city gate stood about 60.5 meters (198.5 feet) higher than the southern endpoint in Anhui Province.[23]

Shen was eventually elevated to a more diplomatic and military role, first as an envoy to the northern Khitan Liao kingdom in 1075 and then (in 1080) as a military officer participating in the defense of Yanzhou (modern Yan'an) against the Western Xia kingdom. When he was improperly blamed in 1082 for the actions of an incompetent military commander that resulted in sixty thousand soldiers killed, his official career effectively ended. After several years of forced solitary confinement in a Buddhist monastery in northern Hubei Province and the death of Emperor Shenzong, he was released and allowed to live where he chose.

Remarkably, his not-insignificant accomplishments as a government office-holder pale alongside his "free time" activities and observations in the natural sciences. In addition to his water conservancy work and oversight of projects that recovered thousands of acres of swamp land for agricultural use, Shen Guo identified, described, and categorized hundreds of plants and animals, produced a series of twenty-three maps of the Chinese empire at a uniform scale of 1:900,000, created topographic (raised-relief) maps using a mixture of sawdust, beeswax, and wheat paste ("among the most celebrated specimens of Chinese cartography")[24] and made numerous improvements to the devices used for astronomical observation.

By 1088, Shen had settled into retirement at a garden residence in Zhenjiang, Jiangsu Province that he had purchased, sight unseen, a decade earlier. He lived out the rest of his life there, at a property so closely matched to a dreamscape he claimed to have "visited" multiple times in his sleep that he named it Dream Brook (梦溪, *Mengxi*).

Sometime between 1088 and 1095, Shen published his most famous work, the *Dream Brook Brush Talks* (梦溪笔谈, *Mengxi bitan*), "by any reckoning one of the most remarkable documents of early science and technology."[25] *Brush Talks* and its short sequels consisted of about six hundred brief essays and observations that summarized his life's work, both conceptual and practical, in the exploration of natural phenomena. He explained his book's title:

> When I retired under the trees, I dwelt in deep seclusion and cut off all intercourse. Then I would think of the discussions I had had with guests in the past, and from time to time I would note down one thing or another with my brush. It was as if I had someone to converse with, and I would quietly pass the days that way. Since my interlocutors were no more than my brush and ink-slab, I called them "Brush Talks."[26]

The wide range and scientific insight of his short essays nearly defy belief for a man of the late 11th Century. Over the course of his life's work and writings, including many found in the pages of *Dream Brook Brush Talks*, Shen Gua:

- Hypothesized on the geomorphic formation of mountains and the processes of erosion and silting in forming land masses long before Western geologists developed these notions;
- Developed three-dimensional topographic maps more than six hundred years before the first such map was created in the Western world;
- Proposed the use of petroleum, which he called 石油 *shiyou* (literally, "rock oil," using the same etymological roots as the word "petroleum"),[27] as a substitute for industrial wood-burning;
- Suggested a link between the composition of meteorites and the element iron;[28]
- Described the workings of the magnetic needle compass;
- Explained the difference between true north and magnetic north and how to determine their declination;
- Determined the distance between the pole star and true north;

- Provided scientific explanations for the apparent retrograde motion of the planets;
- Explained the formation of rainbows as a product of light refraction through rain and asserted the principle of astronomical refraction, which disguises the true astronomical position of the sun and stars as observed from earth;
- Speculated on gradual past climate changes based on his finding of petrified bamboo too far north to have grown there in his times;
- Expressed concern over the environmental impact of deforestation resulting from iron production and ink-making and developed a new type of ink from pine soot;
- Described the forging of cast iron using blasts of cold air, prefiguring the modern-era Bessemer process for steel production;
- Explained the geometric and physical properties of focal points in the *camera obscura*;
- Described in detail the new technology of movable type printing, invented by Bi Sheng 毕昇 (990 – 1051);
- Presented details on the recent technological developments of drydock ship repair and pound locks for improved canal transport;
- Wrote about the control of invasive and destructive pest populations by using natural predator insects;
- Provided observational justification for the belief that the Sun and planets were spherical;
- Documented repeated occurrences around Yangzhou of a mysterious, unidentified flying object that allegedly emitted a brilliant light when its door opened.

Shen Gua passed away in Zhenjiang in 1095 and was buried in his native town of Hangzhou, in a tomb at the base of Taiping Hill in Anxi, Yuhang District, Hangzhou City. Lost for centuries, his tomb site was finally located in 1983, placed under government protection in 1986, and restored in 2001.[29] His Dream Brook residence in Zhenjiang has also been preserved as an exhibition hall and museum. In 1964, the Purple Mountain Observatory in Nanjing discovered an asteroid that the Chinese Academy of Sciences named in Shen Gua's honor in 1979 on the international Small-Body Database.[30]

Some historians of science have faulted Shen Gua as merely a dabbler who failed to develop any general theory of the natural sciences, but this criticism might as easily apply to da Vinci for lacking a theory of fluid dynamics or to Edison for not pointing the way toward atomic theory or quantum mechanics. Not surprisingly, other historians have disagreed, seeing in Shen the extraordinary curiosity and intellectual range of a polymath, capable of reaching keen insights well out of step with the beliefs and prejudices of his time.

Nathan Sivin suggests that despite Shen's mind being "shaped for the civil service...by an early education centered in moral philosophy and letters" to be a generalist, he rose above those constraints through "open curiosity, mental independence,...[and] sympathy for the unconventional."[31] Joseph Needham (1900 – 1995), arguably the premier Western scholar and writer on the history of Chinese science, described Shen simply as "one of the greatest scientific minds in Chinese history."[32]

Had he been able to devote his life's work entirely to the natural and physical sciences without the burdens of official office and court politics, Shen Gua might well have joined the pantheon of such ancient and Renaissance figures as Aristotle, Copernicus, Galileo, Bacon, and da Vinci. Yet one can also make the case that he saw well beyond those famous individuals and anticipated scientific theories and issues of the present day: biological pest control, climate change, plate tectonics, deforestation, and petroleum as an "inexhaustible" energy source. Shen was less a pure theoretician, perhaps, than simply a 12th-Century man with a 20th-Century mind.

Rebels in the South (1121 – 1122)

The year before Su Shi passed away, Emperor Zhezong died from illness at the age of just 23. With no living sons, he was succeeded by a half-brother, the 18-year-old Emperor Huizong. The new emperor was a remarkable man of his time, an aesthete accomplished in music, painting, calligraphy, and poetry. What Huizong was not, unfortunately, was an effective leader. In fact, he had relatively little interest in matters of civil administration or military preparedness. He preferred simply to defer to the advice of others at court, thereby allowing him to attend to his vast collection of art and calligraphy, institute a music academy, and design gardens.

Song China had been beset for years by border tribe incursions in the north and west, particularly the powerful Khitan Liao who occupied much of present-day northeastern China, the Mongolian plain, and a substantial portion of Siberia. At a time when the empire was spending as much as seventy-five percent of its shrinking budget on military defense and the common people were burdened by heavy taxes, Huizong lived luxuriously and spent extravagantly on grand new palaces in Bianjing (Kaifeng).

In 1102, just two years into his reign, Huizong established Fashioning and Manufacturing Bureaus (遭作局, Zaozuoju) in Suzhou and Hangzhou to furnish his palaces with the empire's finest embroidered silks and handicrafts. These operations were initially overseen by the eunuch Tong Guan 童貫 (1054 – 1126), but when Tong was granted a military position in 1105, a Suzhou man named Zhu Mian 朱勔 (1075 – 1126) took his place managing the flow of fine goods and tribute items to the capital.

At first, Huizong's demands for unusual and exotic items were relatively modest, including a growing fascination with exotic plants and strangely-shaped rocks for his imperial gardens. Zhu Mian would therefore send a few items two or three times a year to Kaifeng in addition to the manufactured goods. Everything changed, however, when the Emperor conceived a grand new imperial park to be built more or less abutting the northeast boundaries of Kaifeng's city walls.[33] Genyue 艮岳 (variously translated as "Impregnable Mountain" or "Northeast Marchmount") would extend a little over three miles in circumference and feature "ranges, cliffs, deep gullies, escarpments and chasms. In some places the structure rose two hundred and twenty-five feet above the surrounding countryside, and in others it fell away, through foothills of excavated earth and rubble, to ponds and streams and thickly planted orchards of plum and apricot."[34]

Incredibly, Huizong was ordering construction from scratch of a mammoth, man-made mountain park. The costs in labor and treasury were astronomical. The Emperor authorized formation of an entirely new bureau, the Flower and Rock Network (花石綱, Huashigang), to scour the southern provinces, especially Jiangsu and Zhejiang, looking for exotic plants and flowers and the most beguiling of the multiform, convoluted rocks carved from the limestone bedrock of Taihu Lake. Leading this effort, and granted virtually unlimited authority for confiscation on Huizong's behalf, was Zhu Mian.

Furnishing exotic flora and strange rocks for a new, man-made mountain required more than the few occasional items Zhu previously shipped to Kaifeng. Genyue would need a small army of "harvesters" scouring northern Zhejiang and lower Jiangsu to gather thousands of suitable items, regardless where they were or who owned them. No one could deny the objects Zhu claimed on the Emperor's behalf. Even worse, the owner was responsible for the cost of transporting the item by canal boat to Kaifeng. Complicating matters still further, Zhu commandeered whatever boats or barges he needed, including rice barges, sometimes stringing twenty or thirty together in a caravan that received first priority in the shipping lanes and locks.

By 1122, Huizong had his imperial mountain park at Kaifeng. His "impregnable mountain" owed more of its existence to the Hangzhou region than just provision of the rarities confiscated by Zhu Mian, however. According to James Hargett, this man-made mountain was modeled after Phoenix Mountain at Hangzhou's West Lake, and the stone masons who fashioned its rockeries were conscripted artisans from Huzhou, well-versed in designing gardens using Taihu stones.[35]

During the four years required for more than 100,000 laborers to construct Genyue, the people of the Yangzi Delta reached their existential tipping point. Burdened with ever-increasing taxes and corvée labor demands to prop up a wasteful emperor and his equally corrupt and profligate court, they were a cause without a leader. In 1121, that leader finally appeared in a remote border area between Zhejiang and Anhui Provinces.

Fang La 方腊 (d. 1121) owned a lacquer plantation in Muzhou Prefecture, a forested mountain area in present-day Jiande, located about eighty-four miles southwest of Hangzhou along the route of the Fuchun and Xin'an Rivers. Zhu Mian's confiscatory predations in this relatively remote area provided the springboard for Fang La's uprising, and he quickly formed a thousand-man following.

Initially, Fang La's rebels occupied a multi-tunneled cave network in Muzhou. From this hideout, they conducted local raids to burn and pillage the residences of local gentry and tax officials and kill those on whom they could get their hands. When Fang La refused the remonstrances of prefectural officials to back down and the government began preparing for military action, his following expanded into the tens of thousands. In the early months of 1121, his rebel army defeated a government force of about 5,000 men and took control of the prefectural capital. By also declaring a new year-title, he effectively declared himself a rival emperor to Huizong.

Spurred on by the taste of revenge and the adrenaline of victory, Fang La led his growing army northeast, a peasant-borne spear that quickly pierced Tonglu and Fuyang, heading straight for Hangzhou. Just days before the Lunar New Year of 1121, the Prefect of Hangzhou abandoned his city; it fell all too easily. As they marched triumphantly through the provincial capital, the rebels reportedly chanted in unison, "Kill Zhu Mian!"[36] The avenging peasant army killed the government officials they could catch, then set about burning and looting the city. As one ancient source stated, "The bandits set fires in the city for six days; three out of ten officials and civilians perished."[37] In a remarkably short period of about two months, Fang La's generals took control of territories as far north as the Yangzi River, southeast as far as Taizhou and the ocean coast, and southwest as far as Quzhou.[38]

Once the court in Kaifeng realized the extent of Fang La's early successes, Huizong ordered redeployment of 150,000 imperial troops from the northern borders to the Zhejiang-Anhui region. While necessary, this troop withdrawal weakened the Khitan Liao border region in the north, disrupted a planned attack to recover Yanjing (present-day Beijing, then serving as the Liao southern capital), and compromised relations with the Jurchen Jin who bordered the Liao.

Emperor Huizong assigned command of the anti-rebel force to the eunuch Tong Guan, who moved immediately (with the court's permission) to dismantle the Flower and Rock Network. He then deployed forces both east and west, driving Fang La out of his new base at Jiaxing in the east and retaking Quzhou in the southwest. Both well-trained forces advanced rapidly against the rebels, retaking Hangzhou and moving southwest to close the pincer movement. By the early summer of 1121, Fang La had been cornered in the mountain caves of the Jiande region where his rebellion had begun.

After scouring the hills in their search, imperial troops under a young general named Han Shizhong 韓世忠 (1089 – 1151) located and captured the rebel leader and his family, all of whom were subsequently transported to Kaifeng and executed about a month after their arrival at the capital. Four hundred thousand of Fang La's followers were permitted to return to their former homes and professions.[39]

Short-lived though it was, the Fang La Rebellion devastated one of the richest regions of the empire at a time when tax revenues were weak and the Emperor was spending with abandon. The human costs were extraordinary as well, seeming out of all proportion for a rebellion carried out by poorly-armed peasants. Estimates of the casualties have ranged as high as 3,000,000, one-third of those being combatants and two-thirds civilians.[40]

The Fang La Rebellion in the south and the Sung Chiang Uprising in the northeast, also occurring from 1119 – 1121, should have raised alarms in Kaifeng about the health of the empire and dynasty. Unfortunately, they only marked the beginning of much worse difficulties.

Invaders in the North: The Enemy of My Enemy?

Although Emperor Huizong's withdrawal of 150,000 of the dynasty's best troops from the northern border area to address the southern rebellions was undoubtedly appropriate, his decision had unfortunate consequences for the empire as a whole and for Hangzhou in particular. On its face, the troop reallocation appeared only to set back temporarily the secret Song plans to retake Yanjing from the Khitan Liao, at least until the troops could return to the northern border. In reality, the entire situation became far more complicated—and ultimately fatal—because of the expansionist actions of the Liao's tribal neighbors to the north and east, the Jurchen Jin.

Since the 11th Century, the Jurchen tribes had occupied the area of far northeastern China roughly equivalent to Jilin, Heilongjiang, and the Yalu River region. Although they had occasionally switched allegiances between the Goryeo (of northern Korea) and the Khitan Liao, they operated in the early 1100s as a vassal state of the Liao. Everything changed, however, with the rise of a Jurchen tribal leader named Wanyan Aguda (1068 – 1123). In 1114, Aguda first attacked a Liao border area with a probing action. Although his forces were heavily outnumbered, he nevertheless achieved a far easier victory than he expected.

Emboldened by his assessment of Khitan Liao's weakness, Aguda rapidly moved ahead. After declaring his own dynasty, the Jin (金, "gold") in 1115, he advanced into Liao territory, winning victory after victory and adding Khitan defectors and members of other "wild" tribes to his growing army. Jin forces captured the Liao Eastern Capital in 1116 and their Northern Capital in 1120.

By 1118, word of Aguda's successful forays into Liao territory had reached Emperor Huizong in Kaifeng. For the first time, the Emperor sent envoys to Jin in hopes of meeting with Aguda and establishing a relationship. Meanwhile, the eunuch military general Tong Guan proposed to Huizong that the time might be ripe for the Song to retake former Han Chinese territories lost to the Khitans at the close of the Tang Dynasty, memorialized as the "Sixteen Prefectures" (燕云十六州, Yanyun shiliu zhou).[41] These were primarily located in Shanxi and Hebei provinces and included the Khitan's Southern Capital of Yanjing and the modern city of Datong. Loss of these territories had haunted the Song Emperors since the founding of their dynasty.

Envoys traveled in both directions between Huizong and Aguda, and somewhat protracted negotiations ensued. Aguda quickly conceded that the Sixteen Prefectures would be Song territories once again on two conditions: that Song participate militarily in the recapture of Yanjing and that they make annual tribute payments of gold and silk to Jin in an amount that approximated the payments Huizong had already been making to Liao. At the time (mid-year 1120), Aguda left as ambiguous his views on the ultimate disposition of Datong and other of the Sixteen Prefectures. By year's end 1120, the two parties had an agreement in writing, and Tong Guan began preparing Song's northern troops for an assault on Yanjing.

Then came Fang La and several other rebel bands, requiring Tong Guan and 150,000 troops to leave the northern borders and not return to their former northern posts until the early months of 1122. While they were gone, Aguda's Jin armies raged through Liao, taking the Khitan Central and Western Capitals and several prefectures just east of Yanjing. Aguda's plans to retain rather than return those territories to Song likely solidified as he realized the weakness of the Song military. He remained committed, however, to allowing Yanjing and a few adjacent prefectures to return to Song control as long as they participated in the assault on that city.

Early in 1122, the Song army finally and belatedly organized its 100,000-man assault on Yanjing.[42] The city was certainly not the largest in the empire at that time, but its thirty-foot-high walls stretching twelve miles around still presented a formidable challenge. Tong Guan first attempted alternate methods of conquest, including promises of amnesty and fomenting internal insurrection within the city. These efforts failed to take root, and a Liao counterassault in June against the Song forces actually caused an embarrassing retreat.

Huizong doubled the size of his attacking force and had some successes in recovering outlying territories south of the city, but Yanjing remained defiantly in Khitan hands. A scheme to take the city by subterfuge in the final days of October 1122 achieved initial success, but when support troops failed to arrive, fresh Khitan troops drove the Song force into another hasty and disorderly retreat. An exasperated Aguda finally decided in early December to move on Yanjing without Song participation. He won the city's surrender without fighting when the Khitan military commanders refused to resist the Jin assault.

Aguda kept his word and returned Yanjing and nearby prefectures to Song control, but only at the additional price of annual payments to Jin equal to the tax revenues of the entire Yan region. Having no meaningful negotiating leverage, Emperor Huizong reluctantly agreed to the Jin-dictated treaty terms in 1123.

The Song empire had to forfeit treasure but nevertheless regained in Yanjing one of its major territorial recovery objectives with minor loss of military forces. The true and ultimately fatal cost of the Song-Jin alliance against the Khitan, however, was not measured in gold or soldiers. Rather, Huizong had inadvertently exposed the weaknesses of the Song military. Aguda and the Jin leadership took the measure of their wealthy ally, recognized that the Song were merely superfluous in the Liao conquest, and judged them vulnerable.

The End of the Song Dynasty – Almost

Aguda, as the founding Emperor Taizu 太祖 of the Jin Dynasty, passed away in 1123. He was succeeded by his younger brother Wuqimai (1075 – 1135), crowned Jin Taizong 金太宗 (r. 1123 – 1135). Distrust continued to dominate the Song-Jin relationship, and reports by Song envoys clearly indicated that the Jin were massing at the border for an invasion. In December 1125, their armies entered Song territory and set siege on Taiyuan, in Shanxi Province. Further east that same month, a second Jin force recaptured Yanjing; Song's hold on the city had not even lasted three years.

Meanwhile, panic reigned at the imperial palace in Kaifeng. Declining to relocate the capital west to Chang'an, Huizong chose instead to abdicate the throne to his son and heir apparent, declaring himself "Emperor in retirement" (太上皇, *Taishang Huang*). The unlucky and unwilling[43] ascendant to the throne, Huizong's oldest son Zhao Huan 赵桓 (1100 – 1161), became Emperor Qinzong in January 1126. His "retiring" father departed Kaifeng not long after, heading for safer lands south of the Yangzi River.

Kaifeng stood formidably in Wuqimai's conquest path, well-provisioned and defended by high walls and 100,000 soldiers. On January 7, Jin army troops commanded by one of Aguda's sons, Wolibu 斡离不 (d. 1127), arrived outside the city walls. Rather than defend against a siege, Emperor Qinzong offered to negotiate a settlement. The Jin responded by demanding five million ounces of gold, fifty million ounces of silver, two million bolts of silk, and three Song prefectures. By mid-January, both sides signed the treaty, and Song officials began desperately scouring the imperial palace, the temples, and the homes of Kaifeng's citizens, rich and poor, for gold and silver. Remarkably, the palace and wealthy citizens of the city managed by February 10 to satisfy the Jin demands for treasure; shortly after, Wolibu's army decamped and the city breathed a collective sigh of relief.[44]

During the spring of 1126, Qinzong sent multiple requests asking his father to return to Kaifeng. Retired Emperor Huizong had actually crossed the Yangzi River and reached Zhenjiang, a little east of Nanjing, but his son's entreaties convinced him to rejoin his family in the Song capital in mid-summer. In the next several months, the second of Jin's two invading armies completed a 260-day siege of Taiyuan and moved on to join Wolibu, who had returned outside the Kaifeng city walls in November. Their combined force now exceeded 100,000 men.

In the final months of 1126, the Jin armies began their second siege of Kaifeng. The Song forces concentrated on defending the city walls and seldom sent out sorties to disrupt their attackers. The outer walls fell, leading to the usual consequences: mass panic and flight, suicides (especially by women), fires, and looting (by soldiers of both sides). Now that the Jurchens controlled the city walls, they withdrew their troops outside the city and offered Qinzong a form of cease-fire. If the Song court agreed to Jin demands, they would not set their soldiers loose to rape, pillage, and plunder the city. Qinzong personally traveled to the Jin encampment, signed a formal surrender agreement, and accepted the terms of the cease-fire.

In the next two or three months, the Jin closed Kaifeng's gates and issued multiple outrageous demands in return for not giving their soldiers free rein to seize whatever spoils they desired. Their settlement demands skyrocketed to impossible levels: ten million bolts each of silk and satin; two hundred fifty million ounces of gold; five hundred million ounces of silver; ten thousand horses; all the city's weapons, wine, books, documents, calligraphy, lanterns, Buddhist temple paraphernalia, musical instruments, and medicines; and a variety of craftsmen, musicians, and other persons of special talent. All of these demands were issued under time pressures and with repeated threats of wholesale pillage of the city if not fulfilled.[45]

Kaifeng in early 1127 thus experienced an extraordinary, piecemeal self-ransacking, a drawn-out form of economic extortion and cultural humiliation. The Jin further compounded Song humiliation by offering to allow their impossible demands for gold and silver to be satisfied by delivery of "acceptable" women at fixed conversion rates depending on the social status of each woman, from princess to prostitute. Over eleven thousand women[46] were delivered to the Jin as substitutes for bars of gold and silver.

By March 1127, the Jin had satisfied themselves that there was little left to extract from Kaifeng. They installed a puppet leader and declared him the emperor of a new dynasty, the Great Chu (大楚, Da Chu). Jin soldiers descended from the city walls and prepared to march back to their northern homeland. Other troops helped gather up Emperors Qinzong and Huizong along with their wives, consorts, and children, thousands of imperial family clansmen, and several thousand more individuals whose skills the Jin valued. Some fifteen thousand people formed seven separate prisoner convoys. After four months in Yanjing, the two former Song emperors were moved north to present-day Harbin and ultimately even further northeast into today's Heilongjiang Province.

Qinzong, the last Song Emperor to live in Kaifeng, remained in the distant northeast until his death in 1161. His father Huizong died in 1135. The Song Dynasty had seemingly been terminated by barbarian horsemen from the north, but such was not the case. One individual spark of hope remained, and his survival would change Hangzhou forever.

Chapter 6

SONG OF THE SOUTH

(1127 – 1279)

At an Inn in Hangzhou[1]

Beyond the hills, blue hills; beyond the mansions, mansions—
To song and dance on the West Lake when will there be an end?
Idlers fuddled on the fumes of the warm breeze
Will turn Hangzhou that rises into Kaifeng that fell.

– Lin Sheng (c. 1180)

A New Emperor Flees South

Early in 1126 Kaifeng, Song Emperor Qinzong sent his 19-year-old half-brother Zhao Gou 赵构 (1107 - 1187) on a negotiating mission to the Jin invaders. When the encamped Jurchens doubted Zhao's legitimacy as a member of the imperial family, they sent him back to Kaifeng and demanded a new envoy in his place. Later the same year, having acquired better knowledge of the Song royal family, the Jin asked that Zhao Gou, since crowned Prince Kang, return north to renew negotiations. They allowed him to leave the now surrounded capital under little or no guard, a fateful decision. Along his way, Zhao was intercepted by Song loyalists who convinced him instead to become part of the resistance.

In the early months of the following year, as the conquering Jin swept thousands of members of the Zhao clan into Kaifeng, Zhao Gou remained at large. He shifted his headquarters frequently among the northeastern provinces of Henan, Hebei, and Shandong and managed to evade the Jin troops intent on his capture. When the Jurchens left Kaifeng in May 1127 and returned north to their homelands, they were laden down with mountains of treasure and thousands of imperial clan members, but Zhao Gou was still not among their captives.

Among the Jin prisoners were not only Gou's elder brother (Emperor Qinzong) and father (retired Emperor Huizong), but as well several (half-)brothers whose claim to the throne would normally precede Gou's. Yet despite the possible continued survival of so many rightful claimants, the thousands of Song loyalists surrounding the young prince insisted he accept the throne in lieu of the captives. Better no doubt an emperor in the hand than a half-dozen or more in the metaphorical bushes of the far northern plains.

Reluctantly or not, on the run or not, Zhao Gou and his advisors still found an appropriately symbolic opportunity for him to ascend to the Song throne on June 12, 1127. The coronation site was Shangqiu 商丘 (Henan Province), first capital of the ancient Shang Dynasty (c. 1600 – c. 1046 BCE) and the city where the Song Dynasty's founding emperor Taizu had served as a military governor. Shangqiu's history lent a touch of legitimacy to the enthronement of the man who would become known as Emperor Gaozong 宋高宗 (r. 1127 - 1162), first emperor of the Southern Song Dynasty.

Close Calls

As the sole living and non-captive son of Huizong, Emperor Gaozong could only guarantee preservation of the imperial lineage by remaining alive and free from the Jurchens. Even as loyal Song troops coalesced around him in Shangqiu, pressure from advancing Jin troops forced Gaozong in late 1127 to relocate the now-mobile Song capital to Yangzhou. Remaining north of the Yangzi may have been a symbolic statement that Gaozong had not abandoned north China or the true emperor (Qinzong) and the rest of the imperial family, but it was daringly temporary. In the latter half of February 1129, the Jurchens were advancing rapidly and in force. There was no more time for symbolic statements of loyalty, filiality, or good intentions.

In a state of panic-induced chaos, Song loyalists and commoners alike fled Yangzhou by the tens of thousands, most of them seeking passage across the Yangzi River. Gaozong's infant son and household crossed the Yangzi on February 21 and headed for Hangzhou, 140 miles further south. Two days later, the new Emperor crossed as well, spending the night sleeping on the floor of the Zhenjiang prefectural office. A sizable advance corps of Jurchen horsemen arrived at Yangzhou the same day Gaozong departed. They headed at full gallop for the riverside, only to discover that they had missed capturing the last direct heir to the Song throne by just hours.[2]

Gaozong had hoped to install his court in Nanjing, a city well suited by size and geomantic features to serve as an imperial capital. Because the Jurchen threat and their continued advances made this choice untenable, the Emperor opted for Hangzhou, perhaps recognizing the value of the Qiantang River and the nearby ocean as an escape route. Traditionalists in the court were hardly pleased, however. One referred to Hangzhou as "narrow, overcrowded, and noisy,…a mean little place, lost in a corner of the empire and most unworthy of becoming a capital." Another wrote, "Being in [Hangzhou] is like going to the side-room of a house and sitting; when you look out what you see outside is utterly without symmetry."[3] Fortunately, preservation of the dynasty and the

104

royal family prevailed over such petty aesthetic considerations.

Although Gaozong finally made it safely to Hangzhou, the year 1129 would prove to be the most treacherous of his life. Chased from Yangzhou in February, he was forced by a group of dissatisfied court officials in Hangzhou to abdicate in favor of his infant son and a Regency. Around April 20, loyal troops came to the Emperor's aid and dismantled the attempted coup, but his first-born son died of illness not long after his father returned to the throne. Through the summer and fall, the Jurchen Jin crossed the Yangzi River further to the west, raiding Hunan and Jiangxi cities and towns with abandon.

Gaozong was still struggling to assemble a functioning government in Hangzhou when more bad news arrived late in the year: the Jurchen armies had turned toward Hangzhou. As the Jin advanced eastward, the Emperor and his court did likewise, taking up another temporary residence closer to the Zhejiang seacoast and assembling a fleet of ships in preparation for a hasty sea escape. On January 26, 1130, the Jurchens seized Hangzhou. That same day, the acting Song Emperor set sail for Zhoushan Island, not far off the coast from Ningbo. The relentless Jin continued their pursuit and forced Gaozong and his waterborne court to retreat as far south as Wenzhou before the enemy abandoned their imperial hunt. By May, the Jurchens had withdrawn entirely from the south, re-crossing the Yangzi River and heading back into north China. All in all, it had been a rough start for Qinzong's brotherly successor.

Gaozong and his household returned to Zhoushan Island as the Jin withdrew, but Hangzhou, until recently occupied by the Jurchens and never planned as an imperial capital, was in no condition yet to serve in that capacity. Efforts began immediately to restore the city, construct an imperial palace on Phoenix Hill[4] (凤凰山, Fenghuangshan) inside the city walls, and build appropriate government offices (*yamen*).

In the meantime, the imperial family and court remained on the south side of the Qiantang River in Yuezhou, within easy reach of the coast but nevertheless an auspicious omen. It was here that the persevering and ultimately resurgent King Goujian had built Kuaiji, the capital of the Yue State, in the 6th Century BCE. In 1131, having achieved a renewed if still cautious sense of dynastic security, Emperor Gaozong declared the opening of the new, optimistically-named Shaoxing 绍兴 ("Continued flourishing" or "Continued ascendancy") reign era (1131 – 1163). The name represented a short-form version of 绍祚中兴 *shaozuo zhongxing*, or "continuing the imperial throne and leading the restoration."[5]

The people of Yuezhou reinforced the Emperor's vision, petitioning him to permit the name of their city to be changed accordingly. Gaozong consented, and Yuezhou became Shaoxing. This name change marked a cultural and psychic transition point, when an important and historic city in southern China shed its Yue-name primacy (Yue State, Wuyue, Yuezhou) for formal identification with the relocated northern Song emperor. The empire may have sundered for the moment, but the South seemed more closely linked with the North, and with the empire's collective fortunes, than ever before.[6]

A New Name for a New Imperial Capital

As Gaozong forged southward in Jiangnan to escape the Jin clutches, he was followed by massive numbers of former officials, courtiers, military commanders, literati, and commoners, all seeking refuge from the invaders. Everything must have felt new to them – the summer heat and nearly insufferable humidity of Jiangnan, the water-rich topography that privileged boats over horses and canals over roads, the swampy rice and water-vegetable paddies, the unintelligible Wu and Yue dialects of the local people. Oddly, their curiosity but lack of familiarity with the region's most famous natural wonder, the Qiantang tidal bore, may even have led to disaster when "several hundred spectators were swept to their death in the surf when the tide unexpectedly destroyed their viewing place"[7] in the autumn of 1132.

All, or at least enough, was finally ready in early 1133 for Emperor Gaozong and his court to move into their new capital and imperial palace complex. The city they entered was now more than just a prefectural capital. It was an imperial one that deserved an appropriate name, but one that clearly signified (at least politically) the intent to recapture lost land and return the capital north to Kaifeng. Hangzhou would be treated as merely a safe waystation on the route to a fully restored empire. Hence, the city was renamed Lin'an 临安, meaning "Temporary Peace."

Northern capitals had always been built according to certain geomantic guidelines from the Confucian classics: square shape,[8] symmetrical, oriented to the cardinal directions (N, S, E, W), with an imperial palace located northerly or centrally and facing south. Hangzhou's West Lake and Qiantang River surroundings and the hills contained within its walls made much of this impossible or impractical, but accommodations could be made. After all, Lin'an was only intended as 行在 *xingzai*, a "temporary stop" or "temporary residence," and never as a true capital. In fact, it was not until five years later, in 1138, that Gaozong pronounced Lin'an to be the official capital.

In this provisional capital, the desired square shape yielded to a misshapen rectangle, elongated south to north (about 5 kilometers end-to-end) and unevenly compressed (barely one kilometer at its narrowest) east to west. Lin'an's compass orientation loosely satisfied the demands of geomancy, but the location of Gaozong's palace completely reversed the Confucian order. The capital complex rose from the south end of the walled city at the foot of Phoenix Hill, the site of the former Wuyue Palace of Qian Liu and Qian Chu. In keeping with tradition, however, most of the palace buildings faced south, with the Qiantang River before them and the entire city of Lin'an now behind them.

The imperial city spread out over Phoenix Hill, its multiple palaces, pavilions, and towers surrounded by an "inner" wall with four gates. Lizhengmen 丽正门, the southernmost gate, served as the "south-facing" palace's main entrance, even though it was farthest from the rest of the city. The northern gate, Heningmen 和宁门, exited into the city's urban area but was effectively the palace's "back door." Two side gates, Donghuamen 東華门 and Dongbianmen 東便么门, provided additional entrances and exits.

During its first three decades of existence, the imperial palace complex grew and expanded, adding grand halls, palace residences, multiple pavilions, exotic gardens and rockeries, and even a "little West Lake." The Imperial Court by 1160 rivaled or even surpassed its predecessor palace complex in Kaifeng.

A grandly paved, fifty-foot-wide Imperial Way stretched four kilometers northward from the palace's Heningmen gate toward the city's north wall, following the line of an ancient street and dividing the urban area into two unequal halves. An imperial procession along this "heavenly street" (天街, *tian jie*) would pass by the government offices and a magnificent new Temple of the Imperial Ancestors before reaching the ceremonial Heaven's Gate, Chaotianmen 朝天门. In this area between Heningmen and Chaotianmen could be found the mansions of many royal family members and senior court officials.[9]

Continuing north before turning toward West Lake, the great road narrowed somewhat. The procession could stop to observe the imperial examination halls before ending at the Jingling Palace, "an imperial shrine where the clothes and hats of imperial ancestors were enshrined from 1131 to 1162. The shrine was later expanded on a grand scale that…provided proper buildings for the statues of the preceding emperors, empresses, and important loyal officials."[10] Four times a year, at the beginning of each season, an imperial procession would travel the reverse path, starting at Jingling Palace 景灵宫, stopping at the great ancestral temple, and ending south of the palace in an open area at the south foot of Yuhuang (Jade Emperor) Hill (玉皇山, Yuhuang shan). Here, the Emperor performed ritual sacrifices for the coming harvest at the sacrificial altar called Baguatian (八卦田, Eight Trigrams Field).

By the time of Gaozong's reign, Song Dynasty Hangzhou had already evolved into an important commercial city. The ward system still existed for administrative purposes, but these districts were no longer walled and gated as they had been during the Tang Dynasty era. The city was much more open, with bustling stores lining either side of the Imperial Way. Many of these stores offered the finest wares: "pearls and jewels, treasures and rarities, fresh flowers and fruits, seafood and wild food, marvelous implements and utensils, all the unique commodities of the world are assembled here."[11] Proceeding further north within the walled city, one passed through the main entertainment quarter into an area of tightly packed residences. To be sure, Lin'an was not Kaifeng, but the city on the lake still had merits worthy of an emperor.

By 1158, Lin'an's walls had been expanded southward toward the Qiantang River. There were now thirteen land gates and five water gates.[12] Six of the land gates punctuated the eastern wall, along with one on the south, four on the West Lake side, and one each on the northeastern and northwestern corners. Across the river, the once sleepy Xiaoshan area suddenly achieved a new level of strategic importance as the southern protector of the Emperor and his imperial capital. Four new garrisons were established along the Qiantang's southern shores, including one at Xixing 西兴, in the present day a residential sub-district of Hangzhou's Binjiang District.[13]

A Shaoxing Rhapsody

The Southern Song court may have been biding time in the "temporary capital" of Lin'an until the north could be recovered, but even emperors cannot suspend the flight of time's arrow. With the passage of time inevitably comes death, and imperial passings required imperial burials in imperial tombs.

The first such instance occurred in 1131. While Emperor Gaozong waited in Shaoxing for completion of the palace complex in Lin'an, Empress Dowager Longyou 隆祐皇太后 (1073 – 1131)[14] passed away from illness. Baoshan Mountain, southeast of Shaoxing,[15] was chosen as the site for her entombment. A dozen years later, when the bodies of Emperor Huizong and his princesses were finally recovered from the Jin, they too were buried at Baoshan. Thus began the tradition by which six Southern Song emperors,[16] some of their empresses, and several high-ranking ministers were all buried outside Shaoxing at what became known as Imperial Mountain.

In 1158, the Shaoxing area's rich history—Da Yu's tomb, capital (as Kuaiji) of King Goujian of the Yue State, Xi Shi's birthplace, Gaozong's renaming of the city from Yuezhou to Shaoxing and recognizing it as an auxiliary capital to Lin'an, site of imperial tombs— prompted the scholar-official Wang Shipeng 王十朋 (1112 – 1171) to celebrate the city with three prose-poems known as *Three Rhapsodies on Kuaiji* (会稽三賦, *Kuaiji sanfu*). Although born in Wenzhou along the southern Zhejiang coast, Wang Shipeng had spent more than eleven years (1145 – 1156) studying at the Imperial Academy in Lin'an. He kept a low profile during those years, but his spectacular third-try success in the civil service examinations (where he unexpectedly finished first) opened the way to expressing countervailing views on policy.

As a new official appointee in Shaoxing, Wang chose to celebrate its history and customs in a daringly dramatic way. By long tradition, the *fu* 賦 or rhapsody form had been employed to praise and ennoble the imperial capital, but not lesser cities. To create a rhapsody for a city explicitly named to suggest a purely transitory capital, hardly seemed justified and might even have conveyed a politicized position in favor of not recovering the north. Yet creating a rhapsody for a lesser city, even the *de facto* "auxiliary capital" of Shaoxing, would appear to have been equally politically fraught, if not more so.

Aside from its veneration of Shaoxing's past, Wang's *Three Rhapsodies* can therefore be best viewed as an indirect rejection of Lin'an as imperial capital and a call for recovery of the former capital, Kaifeng, from the Jin. Early in his rhapsodic trilogy, Wang even contested Lin'an as the chosen capital site by referring to Kuaiji as "truly the great prefectural capital of the southeast."[17]

Whatever their political impact, Wang Shipeng's three rhapsodies nevertheless recalled for the Southern Song court the glories of Yue, the area's great persons, and its traditions. Referring to the city as Kuaiji instead of Shaoxing or even Yuezhou, his *Rhapsody on Land and People* (風俗賦, *Fengsu fu*) described Kuaiji's geography, local products and customs, common fruits and animals, silkworm raising, and eminent persons.[18]

The *Rhapsody on the Hall of Official Affairs* (民事堂賦, *Minshitang fu*) presented the history of Kuaiji, and the *Rhapsody on the Hall of Paradise* (蓬萊閣賦, *Penglaige fu*) described government officials in the city.

Shocking by its absence is Lin'an; Wang Shipeng's rhapsodies eschewed any mention of the capital and barely included the emperor as a presence. "In so doing,...Wang turned the geo-political orientation of the rhapsody on its head" in "a discourse...that criticized both the exaggerated empty rhetoric of the [local gazetteer] genre and its monocentric spatial hierarchy."[19] By omission, Wang's *Three Rhapsodies* on Shaoxing added his poetic voice to the issue that polarized the Southern Song Dynasty to the end: whether to risk military defeat and obliteration by attempting to retake the north and restore the empire.

A Blossom Like No Other[20]

Uneasy peace settled over Lin'an in the 1130s, but the continuing threat of a Jin return led Emperor Gaozong to reach a humiliating settlement with the Jurchens in 1141. The Song accepted vassal status under which they were required to submit annual tribute. Throughout this period, loyalists poured across the Yangzi River into the restored Song empire under Gaozong's rule. Many of the wealthy and educated elite brought their money and services to the temporary capital of Lin'an. Others arrived under financial or physical duress, seeking familiar intellectual environs and a safe harbor in which to restart their lives.

Among this latter group in 1132 came a childless, 48-year-old poetess and widow from Shandong Province, traveling with what little remained of her assets after repeated abandonments and thefts during her flight south. She would live out the last twenty years of her life in Lin'an and its environs, adding more works to an already existing oeuvre that have marked her for the past nine hundred years as arguably the greatest female poet in Chinese history.

Li Qingzhao 李清照 (1084 – c. 1155) was the undeniable beneficiary of a fortunate birth. She was born and raised in Shandong Province into a family of scholars and high-ranking officials on her father's side and well-educated individuals on her mother's side. Li herself was an enthusiastic learner who demonstrated unusual poetry-writing skills from a young age. She particularly favored *ci* poetry,[21] a genre that began in the Sui Dynasty and became immensely popular in the Song era and afterward.

Little is known of Li Qingzhao's early life until her marriage at age eighteen to Zhao Mingcheng 赵明诚 (1081 – 1129), son of a former prime minister[22] in the Northern Song court. The young couple fell into a happy marital relationship in Kaifeng, characterized by a shared passion for antiquities, ranging from calligraphy and paintings to bronze and stone inscriptions. One of Li's poems, written on a silk kerchief, touchingly expressed her deep feelings toward her husband while he was away on official business:

Sorrow of Departure to the Tune of "Cutting a Flowering Plum Branch"

> Red lotus incense fades on
> The jeweled curtain. Autumn

Comes again. Gently I open
My silk dress and float alone
On the orchid boat. Who can
Take a letter beyond the clouds?
Only the wild geese come back
And write their ideograms
On the sky under the full
Moon that floods the Western Chamber.
Flowers, after their kind, flutter
And scatter. Water, after
Its nature, when spilt, at last
Gathers again in one place.
Creatures of the same species
Long for each other. But we
Are far apart and I have
Grown learned in sorrow.
Nothing can make it dissolve
And go away. One moment,
It is on my eyebrows.
The next, it weighs on my heart. [23]

After seven years in Kaifeng, adverse political winds and the death of Zhao Mingcheng's influential father forced them to return to Shandong. Li Qingzhao wrote poems while Zhao served as a magistrate in Laizhou and then in Qingzhou (both in Shandong Province). By her own account, the couple passed their time together in a sort of academic bliss, sharing their intellectual preoccupations:

> We often spent beyond what we could afford for our collections. Whenever we got a book, a painting or an engraved sacrificial vessel, together we would examine and edit the book, observe or fondle the article, or attempt to detect its blemishes, making it a rule to work in the evening until a candle had burned out. Gradually our collection became the finest and the most complete of the time....I was good at forcing myself to memorize things. After dinner, we would often prepare tea in our Kuei-Lai Hall....Then I would point at our huge piles of books and suggest teasingly that we play a guessing game. Whoever succeeded in naming the right book, the right page and line where a certain event could be found, would be the winner and would have the honor of drinking the tea first. Often by the time I had the tea cup in my hand, I was so excited and laughed so hard that the tea spilled all over my lap. So happy were we that we would have been contented to live there forever... [24]

The couple's surpassing preoccupation with inscribed bronzes and stones reflected more than just a peculiar obsession. Rather, their interest was spurred by Zhao Mingcheng's lifelong passion project, an encyclopedic study of ancient stone and bronze inscriptions that would ultimately be published in thirty volumes as *Record of Inscriptions on Bronze and Stone* (金石錄, *Jin shi lu*).

As the Jin advanced into northern China, Li's and Zhao's idyllic lives were summarily uprooted. Zhao Mingcheng left his post as governor of Zizhou (modern Zibo, Shandong Province) in the early months of 1127 when he learned of his mother's death in Nanjing. Li Qingzhao stayed behind, packing up their household goods and lovingly curated collection of antiquities into a fifteen-cart caravan. She left an almost equal quantity of collected materials behind. Most important, she carried Zhao's working copy and notes for his treatise on inscriptions.

By early 1128, the couple were together again in Jiankang (Nanjing), where Zhao Mingcheng had been appointed governor. He was removed from that position after only a few months and felt compelled to leave the city, heading west in disgrace. In mid-1129, Emperor Gaozong recalled him to Nanjing for a personal audience and appointment to the governorship of Huzhou. Zhao never made the meeting, falling ill while traveling and passing away in late 1129. He was just 49 years old.

Li Qingzhao was devastated, but there was no time for sorrow as the Jurchens pressed southward in pursuit of Gaozong, the only royal family member not yet captured. As the Emperor and court officials gathered themselves to flee south toward Hangzhou, Li took the best available option and followed in their path with as much of the couple's collection as she could manage. Her tearful trail passed through Hangzhou, but like Emperor Gaozong, she headed south and east when the Jin advance threatened that city. Ultimately, she ended up on the same floating, ocean-borne caravan as the Emperor until the Jin withdrew.

Like the court, Li Qingzhao resided in Shaoxing in 1131 and followed the Emperor's return to Lin'an in 1133. Her life in the capital was an unsettled one: flights to safety in Jinhua to escape threatened Jin attacks, loss of most of her collected antiquities to theft, and a reputed marriage that was brief and allegedly abusive to a man who fraudulently misrepresented himself and his position. Through all her struggles in Lin'an, Li never wavered in her commitment to Zhao Mingcheng's treatise on inscriptions, and she continued producing extraordinary—if sometimes tragically sorrowful—poetry.

Included in these works was a poem of astonishing power and creativity, the type of stylistic breakthrough modern readers might associate with Cummings or Ginsberg. All the more remarkable that such a work should come from a female poet at a time when most female poetry was kept hidden in women's "inner chambers," never to be published and often burnt by the writers themselves out of fear of being publicly shamed.

To the Tune "Note after Note, Long Song (声声慢)"[25]

Search. Search. Seek. Seek.	寻寻觅觅
Cold. Cold. Clear. Clear.	冷冷清清
Sorrow. Sorrow. Pain. Pain.	凄惨凄惨戚戚
Hot flashes. Sudden chills.	乍暖还寒时候
Stabbing pains. Slow agonies. I can find no peace.	最难将息

I drink two cups, then three bowls	三杯两盏淡酒
Of clear wine until I can't	怎敌他
Stand up against a gust of wind.	晚来风急
Wild geese fly overhead.	雁过也
They wrench my heart.	正伤心
They were our friends in the old days.	却是旧时相识
Gold chrysanthemums litter	满地黄花堆积
The ground, pile up, faded, dead.	憔悴损
This season I could not bear to pick them.	如今有谁堪摘
All alone, motionless at my window,	守着窗儿
I watch the gathering shadows.	独自怎生得黑
Fine rain sifts through the wutong trees,	梧桐更兼细雨
And drips, drop by drop, through the dusk.	点点滴滴
What can I ever do now?	这次第
How can I drive off this word—hopelessness? [26]	怎一个、
	愁字了得?

During her years in Shaoxing and Lin'an, Li Qingzhao finally completed the work that had always remained near and dear to her heart, the one remnant of her former life on which she and Zhao Mengjing had collaborated and that had never left her side: Zhao's encyclopedia of stone and bronze inscriptions. In its final form, the 30-volume *Jin shi lu* contained detailed historical and epigraphic analysis and commentaries on two thousand inscriptions, ranging from the ancient Xia Dynasty (2070 – 1600 BCE) to the more recent Five Dynasties and Ten Kingdoms period (907 – 960).

Li Qingzhao later added an unusually personal Postscript[27] describing how she and Zhao had scrimped and saved to purchase the pieces they studied, how they enjoyed collaborating in their analyses, and how the book itself came into existence. She closed her reminiscences with a succinct, lessons-learned commentary on the vagaries of life: "In order to have, one must be prepared also to lose; if one wants to be united, one must also reckon with separation. This is the way of the world."[28]

In addition to publishing *Jin shi lu*, Li continued in Lin'an with one of her most productive periods of poetry writing. However, in her changed circumstances (and the dynasty's), her poems "took on a melancholy air of gloom and nostalgia":

To the Tune "Spring in Wuling"

The gentle breeze has died down.
The perfumed dust has settled.
It is the end of the time
Of flowers. Evening falls
And all day I have been too
Lazy to comb my hair.

112

Our furniture is just the same.
He no longer exists.
All effort would be wasted.
Before I can speak,
My tears choke me.
I hear that Spring at Two Rivers
Is still beautiful.
I had hoped to take a boat there,
But I know so fragile a vessel
Won't bear such a weight of sorrow.[29]

The last years of Li Qingzhao's life are shrouded by the mists of time. It is commonly believed she resided in and around Lin'an until her death, variously thought to have occurred in the first half of the 1150s. According to the official history of the Song Dynasty (宋史, *Song shi*), she produced six volumes of poetry and seven volumes of essays in her lifetime, but much of this work was tragically lost. Wang Jiaosheng notes in his 1989 study of Li's *ci* poems that only about seventy-eight of her poems are extant, "of which forty-three are believed to be from her pen, the remaining thirty-five, though generally attributed to her, are still of doubtful authorship."[30]

Li Qingzhao's biography is at once idyllic and ill-fated, poetically ascendant yet marked by loss and shrouded in gaps and uncertainties. Nevertheless, she lived a remarkable life in difficult times, one that appears by her own brush to have been matrimonially companionate, intellectually stimulating, poetically accomplished, and far from forgotten.

"Serve the Dynasty with Unswerving Loyalty"

Once Gaozong and his court had settled into Lin'an in 1133, they faced several pressing issues. On the most fundamental level, the Jurchens still represented an existential threat to the Song Dynasty's survival. Second, and irrespective of the first, the Emperor had an obligation not only to recover the lands lost to the invaders but also to rescue the still-living Emperors Huizong and Qinzong and the rest of his imperial clansmen. On this second matter, Gaozong likely experienced mixed feelings about recovering the north and freeing his elder brother from captivity, since it would mean yielding back the throne.

Rival factions formed in court and argued aggressively: one side for immediate offensive action to recover the north, the other side to pursue a treaty settlement. Meanwhile, conflicts with the Jin continued through the early 1130s, a situation further complicated by the rise of bandit groups in the middle Yangzi Valley. When a young general named Yue Fei 岳飞 (1103 – 1142) was dispatched west from Lin'an to restore order in 1134, he regained control of the important Han River fortress of Xiangyang 襄阳 (in Hubei Province) and suppressed the banditry. He returned to Lin'an a hero, now one of the Southern Song's most esteemed military commanders. He also made no secret of his wish to march north, retake Kaifeng, and drive the Jurchens out of Han Chinese lands.

113

Yue Fei was born into a farming family in Tangyin, Henan Province, near the Liao State border. He received a passable education but was more enthused by things military than the prospect of farming. The young man was solidly built, taller and stronger than average, forceful and respected in the way of those who are quietly resolute. He adapted easily to the ways of military training and demonstrated great proficiency with weaponry, especially in archery.

In 1122, Yue eagerly answered the Song call for young warriors to defend the empire against the Liao and proved himself a daring and capable fighter in skirmishes against roving bandit troops. He returned home for the next three years to fulfill the requisite mourning period for his father's death in 1123, but he volunteered for military service again in 1126.

When the Jin first abandoned Kaifeng and headed back to their homelands in May 1127, Yue Fei was among those who re-entered the city and took up its defense. Meanwhile, the newly-crowned Gaozong had taken up residence in Yangzhou. After Gaozong crossed the river and headed for Hangzhou, Yue Fei remained among those who resolved to defend Nanjing. His troops, fiercely loyal to their commander, persistently resisted and harassed the Jurchen forces during their foray into Jiangnan until the invaders eventually gave up their pursuit of Gaozong in 1130 and withdrew north of the Yangzi.

Yue Fei's stature and reputation for daring victories swelled during those troubled years. In 1133, the resettled Emperor called him to Lin'an for an audience and placed the young general, now only 30 years old, in charge of military operations and defense in the central region of the Yangzi River, well west of the capital. For the next several years, Yue achieved multiple successes in his new post. He drove back several Jin advances in the west and recaptured a number of strategic military posts in addition to Xiangyang.

In 1135, Yue Fei also suppressed a violent rebellion in the western region led by Yang Yao 楊幺 (1108 – 1135), who had built up a large, river-borne fleet of highly maneuverable armored ships. Following Yang's defeat and execution, tens of thousands of the rebels were added to Yue's force. Equally if not more important, the remnants of Yang Yao's fleet came under his command and constituted the basis of the Song's new inland navy.

Yue Fei was not the only military leader who openly espoused recovery of the north, but his was now one of the most powerful voices. He presented his views aggressively to the Emperor, who had little political choice but to agree, at least outwardly. Meanwhile, Yue was creating enemies jealous of his success and influence, making himself the prime target of the court's peace faction, led by Chancellor Qin Hui 秦桧 (1090 – 1155).

In May 1140, a Jin force in the central plains advanced south once again. Yue's troops marched out to meet them and won tremendous victories at Yancheng and then, with his adopted son Yue Yun 岳云 (1119 – 1142) in command, at Yingchang (both in Henan Province). From there, his forces recaptured both Zhengzhou and Luoyang and moved further northeastward until they were just twenty miles south of Kaifeng. In the minds of Yue Fei, Han Shizhong, and the other generals at the front, the moment had arrived to recover the north and drive the Jurchens out of China.

Back in Lin'an, Qin Hui and his peace faction exerted maximum pressure on Emperor Gaozong, arguing against inflaming the Jin any further and for using the strength of the current Song advance as a negotiating lever. After all, hadn't the Jin sought a settlement of the conflict, albeit on unfavorable terms for Song, just three years earlier?[31] This time, the Emperor would be in a much stronger bargaining position. Furthermore, there was always the possibility that Song recapture of Kaifeng would prompt the Jin to release Emperor Qinzong from captivity, threatening Gaozong's rule as well as the positions of Qin Hui and everyone else in the Lin'an court.

Gaozong ultimately relented and agreed to negotiations, sending orders to Yue Fei and the other generals to withdraw. Knowing Yue's independent streak, the Emperor sent his pull-back command twelve times for emphasis, each directive issued as a golden plate or plaque. An exasperated Yue Fei reluctantly complied. Qin Hui remained unsatisfied, however, certain that Yue Fei would never relent in his views and would be a formidable enemy who would continue to have the Emperor's ear. To remove this influential opponent, Qin arranged for both Yue Fei and Yue Yun to be arrested on spurious charges on their return to Lin'an.

After two months of imprisonment and torture, neither father nor son had confessed to any criminal wrongdoing. According to legend, when Qin Hui was asked whether Yue Fei was truly guilty of the crimes of which he was accused, the Chancellor answered with a phrase equivalent to: "Could be," or more cynically, "He might as well be" (莫须有, *Mo xu you*). As public pressure mounted for Yue Fei's release, Qin Hui's wife Lady Wang conceived a scheme involving a false execution order that resulted in both prisoners' deaths in January 1142 and confiscation of all their family property.

Public outcry was nearly instantaneous, and stories about Yue Fei sprang from every corner. In one version, Yue Fei removed his shirt while being tortured to reveal a four-character tattoo on his back, purportedly inscribed there by his mother: 精忠报国 ("*Jing zhong bao guo*"), that is, "Serve the dynasty with unswerving loyalty." Another legend declares that such was the common people's anger that a street vendor in Hangzhou began forming dough into the figures of Qin Hui and Lady Wang and throwing them into hot oil for frying. Gradually the dough was elongated into two intertwined strips and was said to be the origin of the classic Chinese breakfast cruller known today as 油條 *youtiao*.

In 1161, the aging Emperor Gaozong granted posthumous pardons to Yue Fei, Yue Yun, and others from the military who had been falsely accused in 1141–1142. For the Yue family, these pardons not only meant restoration of their ancestors' titles and ranks but return of their confiscated properties. The following summer, Gaozong abdicated the throne in favor of his stepson, the Emperor Xiaozong 宋孝宗 (r. 1162–1189), who fully supported the official rehabilitation of Yue Fei. In his first year on the throne, Xiaozong proposed construction of a grand tomb and temple on the northern shore of West Lake in honor of the great war hero of the Southern Song era.

Fortunately, a sympathetic prison official had quietly removed Yue Fei's body after his execution twenty years earlier and buried it away from the city, out of harm's way from Qin Hui and his supporters. He included rings and other of Yue's personal effects in the grave to verify the identity of the corpse and planted two orange trees as markers. Later, he informed his son of Yue Fei's burial site in anticipation of a more honorable burial someday. That day arrived in 1162, and the prison official's son came forward with the necessary information to relocate Yue's remains to its final West Lake resting place.[32] Yue Yun was entombed alongside his adoptive father.

Star-Crossed Lovers in the Garden

Following Emperor Gaozong's 1141 treaty with the Jin, the Jurchens retained control of the north and the Song the south, with the Yangzi River as a rough dividing line between the two. In eastern China, the Jin generally stayed north of the Huai River and the Song south of the Yangzi; the land in between, today's northern section of Jiangsu Province, more or less provided a buffer between the two. The Song accepted an inferior position relative to the Jin, agreeing to pay annual tributes and tolerating ceremonial treatment typically accorded to a vassal state by a ruling one.[33]

Life in Lin'an under Emperor Xiaozong's reign gradually achieved a sense of administrative normalcy and civil stability. Inside the imperial palace and among the literati and official classes, fierce dissension still reigned between those who preferred submission with peace and those who viewed the treaty arrangements as a humiliating stain that only military aggression could erase. Outside the palace, however, the city teemed with commerce and culture. Immigrants from the north continued to flood into the temporary capital to escape the Jin. Others settled closer to the Yangzi River in Nanjing, Changzhou, or Suzhou, or opted to cross the Qiantang River to Xiaoshan or Shaoxing, putting even more distance (and another river) between themselves and the Jurchens.

One of the migrant families who chose Shaoxing was that of Lu You 陆游 (1125 – 1210), sometimes transcribed as Lu Yu). Lu was born aboard a river boat in the final months of the Northern Song as his father Lu Zai 陆宰 (1088 – 1148) was transporting the family to a new government assignment. The next year, as Kaifeng fell, the Lu family fled south to the safety of Shaoxing.

Lu You was raised in Shanyin (Shaoxing Prefecture) with a family heritage of distinguished officials and *jinshi* degree holders as far back as his great-great-grandfather Lu Zhen 陆轸 (*jinshi* 1018). In his youth, he studied in preparation for the civil service examinations as had so many of his recent ancestors. He also developed excellent writing skills and showed early promise as a poet. Lu's early efforts on the examinations at age 19 were disappointing, however, so he returned to his studies. Back again in Shanyin, he remained close to his childhood sweetheart, his cousin Tang Wan 唐琬 (1130 – 1156). The two gradually fell in love and married happily, but Lu You's dissatisfied mother demanded in the first year of their marriage that her son divorce Tang Wan while they were still childless.

116

Trapped between personal love and the dictates of filial piety, Lu You sadly respected his mother's wishes and petitioned for a divorce. Time moved on, and the couple went regretfully their respective ways. Lu You married again in closer accord to his mother's wishes. Tang Wan remarried as well, to an aristocrat named Zhao Shicheng 趙士程.

Lu You resumed his studies and, after three years of mourning his father's death in 1148, he traveled to Lin'an in 1153 for another attempt in the examinations. This time, he finished with the highest score and was invited to participate in the palace examination at the capital. As it happened, Lu had unknowingly outscored Qin Hui's grandson, and Grandfather Qin was having none of it. Lu You's examination fate was sealed: the vengeful Chancellor pre-arranged the young man's failure in the palace exam.[34] Lu You had no choice but to return to Shaoxing, where fate dealt him the hand that made him a Chinese romantic legend.

On a spring day in 1155, Lu You was enjoying a quiet stroll through Shen Garden 沈园 when he saw Tang Wan from across the grounds, accompanied by her husband. She spied him as well and, after a brief hesitation, asked her husband if they could send a small snack and a cup of wine to her cousin. By some accounts, the refreshments were delivered by a servant, but other accounts have them delivered by Tang Wan's hand. Regardless, both realized that their love together, no longer possible, had never ended.

Out of frustration, Lu You wrote a tragic love poem afterward on the garden wall:

To the Tune of "Phoenix Hairpin"

Her pink and creamy hands,
Some yellow-label sealed wine,
A city full of spring and willows by palace walls.
The east wind is evil,
Our happiness short.
A cup of sorrow,
Many years apart.
Wrong! Wrong! Wrong!

The spring is the same,
Someone wastes away in vain,
Her handkerchief of mermaid silk is soaked with tears and rouge.
Peach blossoms fall on
An abandoned pool and pavilion.
Our vows are still mountain strong
Yet it's hard to send even cryptic messages.
No! No! No![35]

Sometime later, Tang Wan saw the poem inscribed on the garden wall and responded with her own, written to the same tune:

Human relationships are short.
Human intentions are evil.
When rain accompanies evening, flowers fall easily,
But morning wind is dry.
Tearstains remain.
I want to write you my feelings
But I only whisper to myself, leaning against the bannister.
Hard! Hard! Hard!

We are separate.
Today is not yesterday.
My sick soul moves like a swing between us.
A cold blast from a horn.
The night is late.
Afraid of questions,
I swallow my tears and smile.
Hide! Hide! Hide![36]

Tang Wan died, tragically, just a year later, but Lu You lived on for another fifty-five productive years.[37] He received his first official posting in 1158 to Fujian Province, followed by others in Zhenjiang (Jiangsu Province), Longxing (Jiangxi Province), and (from 1169 - 1177) Sichuan Province. He recorded his observations traveling to and from Sichuan in a diary which is celebrated as an early model of fine travel writing.[38]

His official career was marked by more downs than ups, partly due to his adamantly vocal support for war to recover north China and partly because of his own dissolute behavior in office. Nevertheless, his innate abilities earned him continuous new postings: Fujian (1178), Shanyin (1181), and Yanzhou (1186), where he published a collection of 2,500 of his poems in 1187. Back in Lin'an, he was temporarily elevated as a director in the Ministry of Rites but resigned after more accusations of improper behavior. He returned to Shanyin for more than a decade, only to be called upon in 1202, at age 78, to help record the official histories of the reigns of Emperors Xiaozong and Guangzong 宋光宗 (r. 1189 – 1194). After that honorable assignment, he returned to Shanyin in permanent retirement.

Throughout the latter half of his life, Lu You produced between nine thousand and twelve thousand poems.[39] One such piece, written in 1199, recalled his too-brief contact with Tang Wan in Shen's Garden forty-four years earlier:

The Shen Garden

1.
A military horn sounds sad on the city wall in the setting sun.
The old landscape of the Shen Garden doesn't seem the same.
The green spring waves under the bridge hurt my heart—

They once reflected her shadow coming like a startled swan goose.

2.
For forty years a dream and fragrance—interrupted.
Willows in the Shen Garden are too old to blow catkins.
My body is going to turn into Qi Mountain soil soon,
And yet mourning over the old traces I'm all tears.[40]

Lu You never relented in his belief that the Song court was duty- and honor-bound to recover the north. In his dying days, as he still despaired over this Song failure, he wrote a brief memorial as a reminder to his family:

Shown to My Children

When I depart in death, I know that all matters become empty,
But I grieve that I did not see the Nine Regions united.
On the day the imperial troops go north to pacify the central plain,
In the family rites, do not forget to inform your father.[41]

Lu You passed away in January 1210, age 85, fortunate perhaps not to have lived long enough to witness even worse to come a few decades hence.

The Mad Monk

In its temporary role as the Song Dynasty's southern capital, Lin'an grew and prospered from the court's presence and the continuing influx of northern landowners and scholar elites. The city also became increasingly a major Buddhist pilgrimage site, thanks in part to the proliferation of temples within the city walls as well as those generously sprinkled through the surrounding hills. While none exceeded the prestige of Lingyin Temple, other monasteries came to enjoy fame and adherents of their own: Jingci Temple 净慈寺, the three Tianzhu Temples 天竺寺, Zhaoqing Temple 昭庆寺, and Hupao Temple 虎跑寺, among others.

Life as a truly observant Buddhist monk or nun demanded strict adherence to religious practices, dietary laws, and civil behavior, and Lin'an was populated with thousands of them, albeit variously observant. The setting was perfect for a memorable iconoclast, and in around 1166 such a monk made his first appearance. He would go on to achieve a status few men reach in any field: honored with statues and worshipped in temples constructed in his name, regaled in paintings and poems, and made the modern-day subject of numerous movies and television series.[42] His legend grew to mythic proportions, ascribing to him feats that were certainly well beyond the realm of human achievement.

His birth name was Li Xiuyuan 李修缘 (1130 – c. 1207),[43] but he is universally remembered by his Buddhist name, Ji Gong 济公. An additional moniker is frequently attached to his popular name, often transcribed as Crazy Ji or Mad Monk Ji Gong. Much loved by the common people, the nickname is meant far more affectionately than it sounds.

119

Little is known about the early life of Li Xiuyuan beyond his birth in Tiantai, Zhejiang Province. One common legend asserts that at the boy's birth, the statue of a Buddhist saint (*arhat*) toppled over unassisted, "proof" that the infant was the reincarnation of a former holy man, the Taming Dragon Arhat (降龙罗汉, Xianglong luohan). When his parents both passed away in the boy's eighteenth year, the young man headed for Lin'an, where he entered the monkhood at the famed Lingyin Temple. He was given the temple name Daoji 道济.

However well-intentioned, the young monk quickly tired of the temple's strictures and openly flaunted them. He ate meat when he cared to, and he imbibed wine with such enthusiasm that he was often seen drunk in public, disheveled and unwashed. When the temple monks raged at his behavior, he replied that meat and wine merely passed through his body, but the Buddha remained forever in his heart.[44] The common people grew to love him for his wit, his empathy, and his seeming knack for medicinal cures and other aids to the problems of their lives. He was one of them, and it was they who dubbed him Ji Gong, the Living Buddha (济公活佛, Jigong huofo).

When his mentor at Lingyin Temple died and the monks expelled him, Ji Gong simply walked to the south side of West Lake and submitted himself to another famous monastery, Jingci Temple. During his stay there, a fire destroyed the temple's main hall. The abbot wished to begin repairs as soon as possible, but securing the massive logs necessary for the reconstruction would take months, perhaps longer. According to legend, Ji Gong informed the abbot not to worry, they would soon have all the wood they needed.

The next day, Ji Gong called the other monks to join him alongside a temple well. After waving a palm leaf over the well and uttering some mysterious phrases, he stepped back as a massive log erupted from the well. As fast as the monks could remove it, another followed, and another, and another. Finally, when sufficient wood was at hand, he yelled "Enough!" and the timber flow stopped. One final log had been rising in the well, however, and it was left as it was, jammed in the well pit as ostensible evidence of this spectacular event for many years thereafter.

Another story tells of Ji Gong's premonition that a flying mountain peak would soon descend on a nearby village and kill all the residents. Naturally, no one in the village believed the monk's outrageous story. The next day, Ji Gong burst into a wedding ceremony, grabbed the bride, and ran off with her. Everyone in the village gave chase as the mad monk fled with his captive into the countryside. Behind the angry crowd, a huge flying boulder crashed into the village and destroyed all their empty homes.

Ji Gong died while living as an ordained monk at Hupao (Tiger Spring) Temple in the West Lake area and is said to have been buried there. He showed that one could be poor and imperfect, enjoy life's small pleasures, and still battle injustice, treat the sick, aid the impoverished, and render help to those in need.

In the 1890s, Guo Xiaoting 郭小亭 compiled many of the Ji Gong legends from theatrical performances and street storytellers. He recorded them as a pseudo-biography of the Mad Monk under the title *The Complete Tales of Lord Ji*. Guo's work has since been translated into English by John Robert Shaw.[45]

In the present day, a large memorial hall in Ji Gong's honor at Lingyin Temple[46] displays twelve large, folding screen panels depicting the main events and legends from his life. Hupao Temple maintains a Ji Gong Pavilion, while one of the wells at Jingci Temple is still named Shenmu 神木 (Legendary Wood). Statues and paintings of the Mad Monk can be found throughout China. He is typically depicted wearing a crumpled hat and torn robe, a broken palm leaf fan in one hand and a wine gourd in the other. And almost always with a big smile on his face.

The Poetess of Heartbreak

By an odd quirk of fate, the woman whom some scholars and critics contend was Li Qingzhao's nearest rival for the honorific "greatest female poet in Chinese history" might have been six years old when Li passed away in 1141. "Might have been" is the relevant expression in this case, since scholars have struggled for nine centuries to create a more complete biography of Zhu Shuzhen 朱淑真. Although more than three hundred of her works are extant, she is not mentioned in the Song Dynasty's official history, nor in any similar materials from the Ming or Qing Dynasties. So little is known about her life, in fact, that some scholars have suggested she may never have existed.

The standard scholarly conjecture holds Zhu Shuzhen's dates as (c. 1135 – c. 1180). She is thought to have been a native of Hangzhou, but others have argued for a birthplace in Haining, Huzhou, or even Anhui Province. The various versions of her life story include an unhappy marriage in Hangzhou to a corrupt and vulgar merchant or to an official with no interest in her writing, as well as possibly an adulterous affair with a more appreciative reader of literature, and perhaps even a suicide.

The one "fact" that does seem consistent across these uncertain biographies is that upon Zhu's death, her disgraced parents burned her entire poetic oeuvre. Fortunately, Wei Zhonggong 魏仲恭 (fl. 1121 – 1182, *jinshi* 1121) published a collection of 369 of Zhu's poetic works[47] in 1182, recovered from various copies he was able to locate. It was also Wei Zhonggong who put a title to his compilation of her work: *A Collection of Heartbreaking Poetry* (断肠集, *Duanchang ji*). Not highly celebrated during her own lifetime, Zhu remained "undiscovered" until Ming Dynasty anthologists began including her poems in their works.

Where Li Qingzhao's poetic voice was filled with the pleasures of an intellectually companionate marriage and relative freedom of movement and activity, Zhu's works reflect the more typical life of talented women in Song-era Hangzhou households. Domestic affairs bounded most of her subject matter, reducing her poetic focus to flowers and trees, rain and snow, changes of the four seasons, ancient heroes and myths, and the tribulations of married life.

The general tone of Zhu's poems is one of sadness and loneliness, reflective of her marital unhappiness. The very category names into which her poems have been grouped reflect the nature of their content: "Describing Still Lifes," "Describing Scenery," "Grieving for an Unhappy Marriage," and "The Longing for Love." By one analysis, the poems in Zhu's *Duanchang ji* contain the character 愁 (*chou*, "to worry," as in 哀愁 *aichou*, "sorrow" or "sadness," and 愁绪 *chouxu*, "melancholy") nearly eighty times, the character 恨 (*hen*, "regret") twenty times, and the phrase (断肠, *duanchang*, "heartbreak") twelve times.[48]

Spring Poem[49]

By the house are teasing willows and cawing spring crows,
In the light breeze behind the curtain, swallows slant their wings.
By fragrant grass and pond my dreams have just been disturbed,
Flowering apples in the garden have their sorrows extreme.
Sounds of sweet and delicate orioles' cries,
Several clusters of frail and slender apricot blossoms.
I lean against the dressing window, weary of making myself up,
Only regretting that my golden youth is going to waste.

Melancholy[50]

Rain falls, spills, soughs,
    Dusk falls in the courtyard.
Alone I face a solitary lamp,
    Resentment high.
Heartbroken, I
    Take up needlework listlessly.
The wind's knife cuts leaf after leaf
    From the parasol trees.

Autumn rain falls with heavy drops,
    Drip, drop all night long.
Dreams won't come,
    I grow restless, lonely, cold.
On banana leaves,
    In parasol trees,
Dian, dian, sheng, sheng—
    The sounds of heartbreak.

Yet for all the sadness captured by Zhu's verses, elements of rebellion against the strictures of a patriarchal society also emerge. Not only do her poems complain openly about marital unhappiness and hint at a secret love affair, they sometimes break out in surprisingly sharp sarcasm about the societal rules and standards that constrained her and, by extension, suppressed others.

Self-Reproving

It is truly a great guilt for women to dabble in writing,

Let alone chant the breezes and even hymn the moonlight.
To rub through the inkstone is not for us to handle,
How more creditable it is to embroider till breaking the needle!

Moved by Hearing Farmers' Words in Bitter Heat[51]

Burning the vast sky with rolling fire is the sun,
In the sixth month it is now the hottest season.
A thousand layers of arid clouds, barren and with no rain,
Earth cracked, rivers dried up, clouds of dust in the wind.
The farmers are afraid that the crops will die in farmland,
The water wheels rescue the land with no time for rest.
During the long day throats are thirsty and parched,
To whom can they speak of their diligent blood and sweat?
Significant are the efforts to sow, seed, and weed,
Worried that even in late autumn there is still no harvest.
In vain for them to work hard if no rain clouds come,
Regret that they cannot raise heads and cry to Heaven.
I must say to the frivolous fops of wealthy clans,
What can you do with silk scarf and feather fans?
Green paddies in the farms wither and turn into yellow,
Sitting comfortably in the high hall, about these do you know?

While not considered the literary equal of Li Qingzhao, Zhu Shuzhen's poetry was well-noted in the Ming and Qing eras. Indeed, at least one scholar[52] has conjectured that the two women together were purposely "canonized" in the late Ming in order to "form a reference point, a benchmark for Chinese women's poetry" against which contemporary female poets of the time could be measured. Zhu Shuzhen may not have started a feminist rebellion, but her open frustrations with an unhappy marriage and the restricted life of the inner chambers doubtless inspired Jiangnan's talented women (才女, *cainü*) and gentlewomen (闺秀, *guixiu*) of later times to carry forward her torch of personal isolation and social liberation.

On the Eve

In 1263, Lin'an celebrated its 125th anniversary as the Song Dynasty's official "temporary capital." In many ways, palace and court life remained unchanged from earlier times: luxurious, isolated, and filled with factionalism, jealous rivalries, political intrigue, eunuch maneuvering, and the almost inevitable scramble for succession. But if life inside the palace walls went on as always, the city outside those walls had radically changed, if only out of sheer necessity.

Hangzhou's peculiar geography had never really permitted easy organic growth. Bounded as tightly as it was by West Lake and the partially enfolding Qiantang River, options for physical expansion were limited: a modest suburban area to the east, and a northern corridor that reached toward the terminal point of the Grand Canal. These areas would, of course, be outside the fortified city walls, less safe from the Jurchen Jin should they attack again.

Despite these physical constraints, migration from the lost north and designation as the imperial capital placed enormous population pressures on Lin'an. Fudan University's Dr. Wu Songdi 吴松弟 (1954 –), a historian and population researcher, estimated that as many as five million people migrated southward (below the Huai River) between 1126 and 1141 and that perhaps six or seven hundred thousand of them relocated in either Suzhou or Hangzhou.[53]

Jacques Gernet (1921 – 2018) cited historical Chinese records to estimate a population approaching 500,000 in around 1170. In the 1240s, Lin'an's population easily exceeded the half-million mark, and by 1270, that figure had expanded to about 900,000. Since these figures did not include visitors and may not have included soldiers quartered in the city, Gernet suggested that the Lin'an urban area and near suburbs probably hosted a combined figure of over one million residents.[54] In all likelihood, Lin'an in 1263 was the world's most populous city. London in the same era had an estimated population of 80,000 – 100,000, Paris around 200,000, and Venice around 150,000.[55]

Lin'an adapted both organically and administratively in order to accommodate such massive population growth and residential density.[56] As idle land inside the walled city disappeared, there was only one direction left: upward. The northern section of Lin'an's walled city was mostly residential, and it was here that the alleys and lanes narrowed like hallways. In these cramped districts, houses of wood and bamboo soared three, four, even five stories above the ground; some astonished visitors described residential buildings towering ten levels above the streets, although this was probably exaggerated. Others claimed that neighbors on either side of the lanes could reach out and touch one another.

Not surprisingly, these overcrowded quarters invited problems. The city's roads were everywhere paved, but Hangzhou's heavy summer humidity left the narrow lanes close and damp. Sewage and sanitation were challenging problems, but the true danger came from fire. Lacking the broad byways designed into China's past capital cities, small fires in Lin'an threatened quickly to become mass conflagrations. Far too often, they did.

Emperor Gaozong had no sooner settled into the palace residence in 1132 when a fire broke out that destroyed 13,000 of the city's houses, traveling two miles within the first hour. That incident was only the worst of the four serious fires of 1132. The next year, five more fires endangered the city, and in 1137, flames destroyed 10,000 more buildings.[57]

With safe habitation so precarious, city administrators responded with a comprehensive fire plan. The prefectural governor divided the city into fire districts, both inside and outside the walls, and provisioned those districts with over three thousand trained and well-equipped fire-fighting soldiers. Critically, officials also erected a number of fire towers and positioned them strategically around the city. Spotters manned those lookouts day and night, communicating smoke sightings with flags in the daytime and with lanterns at night.

Despite these precautions, major fires periodically ravaged the city throughout the Song era. In April 1208, a massive fire destroyed nearly 60,000 houses and government offices, lasting four days and nights and resulting in numerous deaths. Other major fires raged through the city in 1229, 1237, and 1275. The fire threat to high-value commercial products, book and art collections, and precious antiquities prompted a fascinating free-market solution: fire-secure warehouses. Privately-built edifices arose in Lin'an's northeastern sector, surrounded by water and protected by guards.[58] A small pamphlet dating to 1235 described the setting:

> And inside the walls…wealthy houses have built in the water a series of *t'a fang*, between ten and twenty of which form buildings of over a thousand divisions, while even the smaller ones have several hundred divisions or more—in which to store the goods of the shops in the metropolis and of the merchants from other places. They are surrounded with water which both serves as a protection against storm and fire and saves them from burglars. These are a great convenience to the rich houses of the metropolis.[59]

Lin'an's other major challenge concerned supplying food and water, the fundamental necessities of daily life, to half a million to a million people. Markets and shops inside the walls catered to the most basic staples: rice by the ton, delivered by barges to the wholesale markets on the north side of the city, and pork butchered and sold in a more central market. Shops proliferated near the palace's north gate and all along the Imperial Way, purveying everything from household wares to luxury items. Additional markets operated outside the gates, each specializing in a particular type of goods: vegetables, fresh fish, crabs, cloth, flowers, medicines, pearls, and books.

Barges and sailboats also delivered other essential materials to the city outskirts for distribution by canal boats, pack-mules, or porters: bricks, wood, salt, and coal. As a common saying went, "Vegetables from the east, water from the west, wood from the south, rice from the north."[60] Transport of all these items into and through the city to the multitude of markets and shops depended largely on the city's canals, as did the efficient collection and transport of night soil and garbage out of the city. These waterways, so vital to Lin'an's existence, were consequently protected by sluice gates to reduce silting, and regular dredging was considered an administrative priority.

Similarly, maintenance of the city's potable water warranted regular attention to West Lake and the Six Wells. As early as 1137, officials responsible for the city's water supply began adding soldiers to the West Lake dredging corps and reinforcing restrictions on encroachment by cultivated paddies. Historical records indicate lake dredging and repair of the Six Wells in 1148, reconstruction of the wells again in 1169, and repair of the wells and water gates in 1189. These types of maintenance continued into the 13th Century, including major dredging and well repair work in 1247.[61]

This last initiative, conducted in 1247 under the leadership of Governor Zhao Yuchou 赵與疇 (fl. early 13th Century), led to the creation of another causeway that provided a water-land connection between the lake and the Lingyin and Tianzhu temples in the western hills.[62] Known as the Zhaogong Causeway (赵公堤, Zhaogongdi), evidence of its existence can be seen today in the similarly named roadway (赵公堤路, Zhaogongdi lu) running westward from the lake's western shore (near the north end of Yanggongdi) to Lingyin Road.

Throughout the decades, officials were compelled to fight against persistent efforts by individuals to encroach on West Lake's borders when water levels fell or to cultivate fish or water vegetables in the lake's waters. Successful water management in the Southern Song capital was one measure of each Prefect's governance and provided singular opportunity for career advancement.

For all the population, space limitation, and water management challenges, Hangzhou in the Southern Song succeeded admirably as the Song Dynasty's "temporary" capital. Trade boomed, goods were plentiful, teahouses and street entertainments proliferated, and arts and culture blossomed. Publishers, bookstores, and book stalls on temple grounds proliferated; "book boats," many originating in Huzhou, plied the Zhejiang waterways, broadening knowledge by selling and trading their wares to readers and collectors in towns and villages.[63]

Now that Lin'an had hosted thousands of the empire's "best and brightest" over more than a century for the triennial imperial examinations, those elite visitors had made commonplace—by verse, painting, or word of mouth—the notion of West Lake as a place of unrivaled scenic beauty. Home to as many as five hundred temples during the Song era, Hangzhou also became a major center of Buddhist practice in southern China. Countless numbers of religious pilgrims visited every year, and they spread the city's and the lake's fame even further.

But danger loomed once again in the north. History was about to repeat itself, and lessons unlearned would prove fatal.

Chapter 7

THE MONGOLS CONQUER CHINA

(1271 – 1368)

On Visiting the Former Imperial Palace at Xingzai
(after the Mongol Conquest)[1]

Like an ancient ruin, the grass grows high; gone are the guards and the gatekeepers.
Fallen towers and crumbling palaces desolate my soul.
Under the eaves of the long-ago hall fly in and out the swallows
But within: Silence. The chatter of cock and hen and parrots is heard no more.
                                                                    – Xie Ao (1249 – 1295)

A t the turn of the 13th Century, the Southern Song shared northeastern Asia with four other nation-states. The Jurchen Jin still retained the northern half of the former Song empire. To their west were the lands of the Tanguts, known as the Xi Xia empire. To Xi Xia's south, and Southern Song's west, was the Kingdom of Dali 大理国 (937 – 1253), occupying the area of today's Yunnan Province and northern Laos. Finally, to the north of the Jin and Xi Xia were the Mongols, newly risen and unified under the leadership of Temüjin (1158 – 1227), the man who would soon and forever after be known as Genghis (or Chinggis) Khan. Well before the 13th Century ended, his empire would rule them all.

The Enemy of My Enemy, Again

In 1195 Lin'an, a man with no examination credentials but connections by marriage to Emperor Ningzong 宋宁宗 (r. 1194 – 1224) ascended to the kind of dangerous political power last seen at court in the person of Qin Hui. When Han Tuozhou 韩侂胄 (1152 – 1207) gained a position as head of the imperial bodyguard, he achieved proximity to the

Emperor that other court officials could only accomplish in their daydreams. By 1205, thanks to Ningzong's general passivity and disengagement, Han Tuozhou and his followers had seized the civil, military, and financial levers of Song governance.

As a fierce advocate for recovery of northern China from the Jin, Han managed to persuade the Emperor that the Jurchens had softened since Yue Fei's time. He believed an attack across the Huai River could retake Kaifeng and eviscerate the Jin state. After an initial but minor victory on his first incursion into Jin territory, an overconfident Han Tuozhou launched a full-scale thrust in 1206. The Jurchens responded quickly, dealing such crushing defeats to the Song forces that retreat and humiliating peace negotiations were the only options. As part of the settlement, Han Tuozhou was secretly decapitated and his head delivered to the Jin capital.

Whatever taste for military engagement might still have existed in Lin'an, the 1206 defeat left the military confidence of the palace badly shaken. It was therefore with a sense of relief and even hope[2] that the Song court learned in 1211 of the Mongol advance into Jurchen territory. In those first actions, Chinggis Khan began a series of probing attacks on the still-powerful Jin state. The Mongol force consisted primarily of mounted archers, perhaps 50,000 under Chinggis' command, and a second, similar force led by his three sons. As they moved into Jin territory, they incorporated Khitans and Jurchens unhappy with Jin rule, along with increasing numbers of Han Chinese. They also picked up badly needed military knowledge, since horse-riding warriors from the open plains had limited experience attacking heavily fortified walled cities where lightning cavalry strikes were mostly useless.

The Jurchens proved still to be a fearsome opponent. By 1215, the Mongols had captured the Jin Western Capital (Datong, 1211) and, with great difficulty, the Central Capital (modern day Beijing, 1215). For the next eight years, as Chinggis's horde roamed further west for conquests in Persia and India, the remaining Mongol forces roamed almost at will through both the Jin and Xi Xia realms, seizing territory, creating chaos and devastation, and worrying little about civil administration of the lands they had conquered.

In 1226, Chinggis initiated a new assault against Xi Xia, whose leaders had formed an anti-Mongol alliance with the Jin. By the fall of 1227, the Xia had surrendered; their ruling family were executed *en masse* to eradicate the royal blood line. It was the Great Khan's final conquest; he died of uncertain causes in August, during the capture of the Xi Xia capital.

In 1229, Chinggis' successors launched a full-scale assault on the Jurchens, who by now had moved the Jin imperial court to their Southern Capital at Kaifeng. The Jurchens fought stubbornly and valiantly, but they realized the outcome was inevitable. In desperation, they offered settlement terms that the Mongol leaders refused. As a last option, the Jurchens appealed to Song Emperor Lizong 宋理宗 (r. 1224 - 1264) in Lin'an to join them in resisting the Mongols. Whether or not a mutual defense arrangement might have changed the future course of events, Song hatred of the Jurchens made such an alliance unthinkable.

In the spring of 1233, Kaifeng fell to the Mongols, and in February 1234, the last Jin emperor committed suicide.[3] It remained to be seen how the Mongols would reign over their newly-seized lands and where their territorial advances would stop. However, by remaining neutral in the conflict, Lin'an had effectively aligned itself with their new Mongol neighbors, the enemy of their enemy, as they had done with the Jin against the Khitan Liao a century before, in 1120. Things had not ended well that time.

Choke Point

Most likely to the relief of everyone in Lin'an, the Mongol's southward advance stopped at the Jin border in 1234. Although the Mongols executed some probing actions along the Song western border in Sichuan from 1232 – 1234, their main military thrust was directed westward. Over the course of the next thirty years, Mongol cavalry cut a swath across the steppe plains to sack Moscow, Kiev, Cracow, and Budapest and advanced through Persia to capture the cities of Baghdad, Aleppo, and Damascus. Lin'an had peace. Song Emperor Lizong appeared to have chosen wisely in not coming to the aid of the Jurchens.

In September 1253, however, the first dark cloud reappeared on the Song horizon when a young Mongol commander named Khubilai from the Khan's family set out from Gansu Province for an attack on the independent Dali Kingdom. With Dali's surrender the following year, the Mongols established a base in Yunnan, the southwesternmost province of today's China.

Four years later, the Mongols initiated a two-pronged campaign against the Southern Song. One army advanced south through Sichuan, while Khubilai moved eastward down the Yangzi River toward Wuchang (today's Wuhan), where the two armies would join together on their march toward Lin'an. The early months of their plan progressed as expected, but everything stopped in the summer of 1259. The Khan, Khubilai's older brother, had died.

During this same period of the 1250s, three very different Song leaders emerged whose actions would determine the future of the their dynasty: on the military side, generals Lü Wende 呂文德 (d. 1269) and Liu Zheng 刘整 (1212 – 1275), and on the civilian side, Jia Sidao 賈似道 (1213 - 1275). A native of Anhui Province, Lü Wende experienced a meteoric rise through the Song military due to his multiple successes in defending against and defeating the Mongols in the 1230s and 1240s. In 1254, he was promoted to one of the three military commissioner posts in Southern Song China. Two of his brothers, two of his sons, a son-in-law, and several of his extended family[4] also gained important military or prefectural posts, as did others of his military followers.

Jia Sidao rose to civil power in a rather different manner. A native of Taizhou in Zhejiang Province and a *jinshi* degree holder, Jia had the good fortune to be the brother of Emperor Lizong's favorite concubine. He held moderately high positions before his sister's death in 1247, but during the 1250s he ascended the official ranks to become Prime Minister in 1259. Known to history for his concupiscence, general hedonism, and self-serving profligacy if not outright theft at government expense, Jia has been described as a person who "elevated occasional leisure to an art of perpetual sensuality. Whether on yachts on the lake or villas on surrounding hills, he demanded entertainment of decadent sumptuousness."[5] He was a talented political manipulator and survivor at court whose official actions were not always ill-conceived: "he eliminated the influence of eunuchs, curbed the political ambitions of imperial clan members and of the empresses' families, and generally tried to keep protectionism at a minimum."[6]

The Mongols' 1258 march into Sichuan Province had been met by Song forces under Lü Wende, who sailed up the Yangzi to oppose the invaders' advance at Chongqing. At the same time, Lü's younger brother Wenhuan 吕文焕 (d. 1286) was preparing to defend Hanyang, one of the three river towns that comprise modern Wuhan, against the down-river assault from Khubilai's army. A second Song force under the command of Jia Sidao took up a defensive position at Wuchang, on the south bank of the Yangzi, opposite Hanyang.

Khubilai laid siege to Wuchang despite his brother's death and the arrival of Lü Wende's reinforcements. However, the rapidly evolving Mongolian leadership struggles forced him to break off the attack in 1259 and return to his homeland. He left behind a small force to continue the siege at Wuchang, but Jia Sidao was able to defeat what amounted to token opposition. Whatever Jia knew about the truth of Khubilai's withdrawal, Emperor Lizong and the court learned only that Jia had achieved a great and easy victory at Wuchang and forced the Mongols to flee homeward. His misrepresentations were rewarded with promotion to Prime Minister. They also caused the Southern Song court to misread disastrously the Mongols' military strength and intentions.

In 1260 and 1261, Emperor Lizong rejected two Mongol offers for a treaty settlement that would have formalized southern China as a vassal state but with the Song court left intact. Meanwhile, Lü Wende leveled unfounded accusations of misappropriation of military funds against his fellow general Liu Zheng, causing Liu to turn against Lin'an and surrender his army wholesale to the Mongols. Of all the mistakes made by the Song court in the 1260s, provoking Liu's defection would prove to be among the worst.

Liu Zheng suggested to Khubilai that the traditional Mongol use of two or three separate, fast-moving forces attacking simultaneously at different points of enemy territory would not be effective south of the Yangzi. The land was filled with lakes, rivers, canals, and marshes, and populations were concentrated in well-defended walled cities that likely could only be defeated by long, drawn out sieges. Instead, Liu recommended that Khubilai concentrate his forces on a single strategic objective. Capturing that target might take time, but the place of attack would be of Khubilai's choosing and defended from counterattack by the size of his concentrated force. Meanwhile, Song forces would still need to maintain defensive positions against potential Mongol attacks elsewhere. Once the first objective was achieved, it would serve as the launchpad for further advances toward Lin'an.

As it happened, the Song military had actually invested heavily in creating a strategic defense point at Xiangyang 襄阳, the heavily fortified city on the Han River (in present-day Hubei Province) that Yue Fei had fought valiantly to recover from the Jin in 1134. Xiangyang and its sister city of Fancheng 樊城 (situated directly across the Han River) served as a critical choke point for access to the Yangzi River and were regarded as vital to the Song Dynasty's survival. Liu Zheng's knowledge of Song defenses reassured Khubilai that taking Xiangyang would open conquest of the Yangzi all the way to Nanjing, and from there by land and water past Suzhou and on south to Lin'an.

Khubilai's departure from Wuchang in 1259 began a battle for succession against another of his brothers that lasted four years By 1264, Khubilai had elevated to Great Khan, begun consolidating his power base, and initiated construction of his grand new capital at Dadu 大都 (present-day Beijing), not fully completed until 1293. With insight and strategic advice from Song defectors like Liu Zheng, he began developing his plans for conquest and rule over the entire Chinese empire.

Finally, in late 1268, he sent his forces south under General Bayan 伯顔 (1236 – 1295)[7] to surround both Xiangyang and Fancheng. Lü Wende recognized the danger and planned a counter-assault, but he died in 1270 before the relief force could be organized. Rather than permit Lü Wende's brother Lü Wenhuan or another military official to take charge of Song defense, however, Jia Sidao appointed an official named Li Tingzhi 李庭芝 (1219 – 1276) as civil military commissioner.

For Lü Wenhuan, now under siege in Xiangyang, Li's appointment simply reinforced his view that the Song court distrusted his family's loyalty.[8] In fact, Khubilai had made several very enticing offers for Wenhuan to join the Mongol force, but the Song general had resisted each one. Now, however, his political situation vis-à-vis Jia Sidao was increasingly reminiscent of Yue Fei's with Qin Hui, a similarity whose grievous outcome likely bore heavily on Wenhuan's thinking.[9]

Li Tingzhi's attempts to raise the siege achieved only limited success, and only at repeatedly high costs in lives and ships lost. The two cities and their protective river navy had been weakened by the Mongols, but they nevertheless remained stubbornly untaken until Khubilai introduced new weaponry in 1272. Thanks to the Mongols' connections to Persia, the Great Khan was able to call upon two Persian military engineers, Ismail and Ala al-Din, for assistance. The two men demonstrated a powerful new counterweight trebuchet capable of hurling massive stones, five hundred pounds or more each, against city walls and gates with surprising range and accuracy. Those new catapults, which the Chinese called "Moslem cannons" (回回炮, hui-hui pao), could also hurl huge explosives over the city walls. General Bayan had twenty or more of these devices built and put into immediate and devastating use.

With the addition of the hui-hui pao, Khubilai and Bayan made a tactical decision to mass their entire force, including Liu Zheng's, for an assault on Fancheng alone. They were convinced that the fall of the smaller city would lead to the fall of the larger one. After a fearsome struggle, the Mongols finally breached Fancheng's walls on February 2, 1273, unleashing a horrific massacre of everyone who had not already committed suicide. To weaken Song morale in neighboring Xiangyang, they stacked as many as 20,000 dead bodies[10] outside Fancheng's walls, in plain view across the river, to a height said to have exceeded that of the walls themselves.

A little over a month later, with no apparent political support and no hope of reinforcements from Lin'an, Lü Wenhuan accepted the inevitable and surrendered Xiangyang on March 14, ending a siege that had lasted five years. Like Liu Zheng several years earlier, he reacted to the perceived loss of Lin'an's trust and failure to provide adequate reinforcements by allying with the Mongols. The Lü family's influence within the ranks of the Song military was now fatally weaponized against Song Emperor Duzong 宋度宗 (r. 1265 – 1274) and his dynasty.

The End of Lin'an

With the fall of Xiangyang, Bayan moved his forces down the Han River toward its juncture with the Yangzi. Fighting continued along the Mongol route, but Khubilai also used this period to send thousands of reinforcements and further enhance Bayan's naval and weapons strength. In Lin'an, meanwhile, Emperor Duzong died unexpectedly from a chronic infection, leaving behind his son Zhao Xian to succeed him as Emperor Gongdi 宋恭帝 (r. 1274 – 1276). Since the new Emperor was only four years old, power reverted to his Regent, the Dowager Empress Xie 謝皇太后 (1210 – 1283), widow of Emperor Lizong.

As the Mongols moved eastward along the Yangzi River, they put Lü Wenhuan in charge of one of their armies; Liu Zheng was already in command of another force. Cities fell or surrendered before the Mongol advance, with numerous Chinese troops joining the Mongol side. In part, these defections resulted from Lü Wenhuan's encouragement within his clan's military network. In January 1275, they finally reached Hanyang and Erzhou (modern-day Wuhan), where they made heavy use of their "Moslem cannons" to crush a massed Song fleet.

In 1274, the Song court martialed its still substantial ground and naval resources under Jia Sidao, planning what amounted to a last-ditch attempt to halt Bayan's advance in the vicinity of Wuhu, only 55 miles west of Nanjing. The two opposing forces met in a titanic naval clash in early 1275 at Tongling, a river city between Wuhu and Anqing. Once again, the cavalry-oriented Mongols defeated the riverine Song navy on their own waterways, capturing countless more ships and driving the remnants of the Song fleet back eastward to Yangzhou.

These repeated naval victories reflected Khubilai's astute plan of co-optation. By sini-cizing his dynasty and promising critical reforms, he transformed his army through voluntary enlistment and by forced impressment into a majority Han Chinese inva-sion force. Only about one in five of Bayan's troops were Mongols; most of the rest were Han Chinese, including badly needed engineers, boat builders, and river sailors. Mongol cavalry still struck with speed and dreadful efficiency along both banks of the Yangzi River, while the Han Chinese carried out Bayan's naval strategy.

Jia Sidao, his credibility destroyed, could do little more in Yangzhou than memorialize the throne to abandon Lin'an and relocate the Song Court to coastal Ningbo. Empress Dowager Xie rejected Jia's advice and sent a peace offer to the Mongol force conditioned on their withdrawal. General Bayan in turn rejected her proposal out of hand. Jia Sidao would not live out the year, assassinated by the commander of the troop charged with escorting him into exile.

The Mongol invasion force swept virtually unchallenged past Nanjing in April 1275 and seized Yangzhou, the famously wealthy center of the government salt monopoly. Now that the Mongols had arrived within striking distance of Lin'an, however, Song loyalism and resistance strengthened. Dowager Empress Xie issued a modestly successful "succor the Emperor" (勤王, *qinwang*) call for volunteers to defend the dynasty and the capital, following which the Mongols were subjected to frequent small-scale, harassing attacks. After Bayan was recalled north for consultations with Khubilai during the summer of 1275, Yangzhou and a few other cities were actually retaken by Song troops.

Bayan returned in the winter and massed his troops at Nanjing for the final assault on Lin'an. He fortified his hold on Nanjing, recaptured Yangzhou, and took Zhenjiang with little resistance. The next push eastward along the Yangzi was Changzhou, and here Bayan made a fateful decision. He issued his usual ultimatum to Changzhou's officials and citizens: surrender and live, or face total annihilation. When the loyal residents of that river city chose maximum defensive effort over surrender, Bayan took their loyalism as stubbornly annoying resistance. Once Changzhou's walls were breached, the Mongol general authorized a horrific slaughter that killed ten thousand or more of the city's men, women, and children.

The massacre in Fancheng had not been forgotten, but it had occurred far away in Hubei Province at a time when the Mongols were a much more distant threat. The devastating assault on Changzhou occurred when Khubilai's ascendance to the Chinese throne appeared inevitable. More important, such bloodthirsty behavior stood in stark and violent contrast to the more benevolent and sinicized image Khubilai had labored so carefully to project.

In the short run, Changzhou undoubtedly eased Bayan's march on Lin'an, cowing other Jiangnan cities like Wuxi, Suzhou, and ultimately even Lin'an into almost total acquiescence to the Mongol advance. In the longer run, however, Bayan inadvertently spawned a long-lasting Song loyalism that would never accept the Mongols as the rightful holders of Heaven's Mandate.

Bayan's army marched down the Grand Canal in mid-January 1276 and camped about fifteen miles north of Lin'an. Another force under Liu Zheng was positioned south of the Song capital, and a massed naval force patrolled the eastern coast and Hangzhou Bay. Khubilai was explicit that he wanted Lin'an preserved: no pillaging or looting and no destructive fires. Lin'an in 1276 was one of the world's greatest cities, and even if it was not destined to be the seat of Khubilai's Yuan Dynasty,[11] it could still be a shining star in his kingdom.

Bayan worked patiently with Dowager Empress Xie on the terms and conditions of a peaceful surrender. Selected contingents of Mongol officials began entering the city after February 10 to secure documents, libraries, government seals, and the treasury. Bayan briefly toured the city that day, then visited the Qiantang River to observe the tidal bore before returning to his encampment at recently fallen Huzhou.[12] Bayan ordered the libraries of the Southern Song Historiography Institute and the Court of Rituals to be transported wholesale to the Imperial Archives in Dadu, thereby preserving the imperial collections—books, paintings, scrolls, ancient calligraphies, and the like—nearly in their entirety.

Formal surrender took place a week or two later, but Bayan chose not to make his own formal entry into the Song capital until mid-March 1276. After the handover was secured, Bayan escorted the boy-emperor Gongdi, Junior Dowager Empress Quan Jiu 全玖 (1241 – 1309, Gongdi's birth mother), and a host of palace residents north to Dadu, never to see Lin'an again. Empress Dowager Xie had fallen ill and was permitted to join them later. All three were treated respectfully in their captivity: the two women subsequently became Buddhist nuns and the former boy emperor a prominent Buddhist monk in Tibet.

Khubilai and Bayan may initially have believed that the Song Dynasty had ended with the physical handover of Emperor Gongdi in early 1276, but they soon discovered otherwise. The Song court had secretly violated the terms of their surrender agreement on February 4 by spiriting the Emperor's two half-brothers, seven-year-old Zhao Shi 赵昰 (Emperor Duanzong 宋端宗, r. 1276 – 1278) and four-year old Zhao Bing 赵昺 (Emperor Bingdi 宋帝昺, r. 1279 – 1279) out of Lin'an, heading southeast to coastal Fuzhou. The Mongols would spend another three years pursuing by land and sea the last two child-claimants to the Song throne and their sizable retinue of loyalists and guards.[13]

Lin'an remained Lin'an by formal name throughout the Yuan Dynasty, but politically speaking, the city reverted to being just Hangzhou once again. The imperial capital, always officially "temporary" at West Lake, had finally returned north. War casualties and government relocation reduced the city's population by nearly half, from an estimated 1,100,000 inhabitants in 1205 to just 575,000 in 1290.[14] Yet for what until recently had been the 12th-Century world's richest and most populous city, that which remained in 1290 was still more than sufficient foundation upon which to rebuild.

Becoming Yuan

The Mongol conquest reunified China after 150 years as a divided empire, but loyalty to the Song Dynasty remained strong. As Yuan Emperor Shizu 元世祖 (r. 1279 – 1294), Khubilai attempted to implement benevolent rule with extensive use of northern Han Chinese in official positions. The Mongols were not a culture of sedentary clerks, and he fully recognized that their numbers—and skills—were simply too few to administer the empire on their own.

For the defeated Chinese, the memory of massacres in Fancheng and Changzhou rankled, as did the very fact that the occupiers were non-Han barbarians. These submerged resentments were still further inflamed in the early dynastic transition years by new desecrations in Shaoxing and Hangzhou. Some of the most egregious acts began in 1278 with a Tibetan Buddhist monk.

After Khubilai gained control of China below the Yangzi River, he remained supportive of Han Chinese religious practice, particularly Confucian and Buddhist temples. He designated Tibetan Buddhism as the dynasty's state religion, but this school of Buddhist practice was virtually non-existent in Southern Song China. In 1127, the new Emperor's general distrust of southern Buddhists led him to install Yang Lianzhenjia 楊璉真珈 (d. after 1311), a Tibetan Buddhist practitioner, as the Imperial Supervisor of Buddhist Religion in the former Southern Song territories. Yang's origins are uncertain, but he was likely either Tibetan or a Tangut from Xi Xia. Either way, his assignment to Lin'an as the senior Buddhism administrator put a "foreigner" and a proponent of an outside school of Buddhist practice in total control of religious funds and properties in the region.

In the period from 1278 to 1285, Yang interpreted in the broadest possible terms his charge to resurrect Buddhism in the south and install Tibetan Buddhism. He restored, converted, or rebuilt more than thirty Buddhist temples in the Hangzhou and Shaoxing areas.[15] He not only renovated temple buildings but recovered former temple lands and reconstructed lost Buddhist temples upon them, regardless what had been built in the interim.

In the Shaoxing area, near Kuaiji, a former Buddhist temple had been replaced by the mausoleum of Song Emperor Ningzong. Allowing greed dressed as religious zealotry to overrule common sense, Yang ordered Ningzong's remains exhumed and the temple rebuilt in its original place. Such an act constituted an unthinkable desecration of an imperial tomb site.

Excavating Ningzong's tomb and exhuming his remains apparently established a precedent with regard to the mausoleums of the five other Southern Song emperors buried in the same vicinity.[16] The gold, silver, and precious gems Yang's men removed from the imperial tombs provided funds for temple building and renovation. By one account, the raiders even drained the embalming mercury from the corpse of Emperor Lizong and detached the skull in order to retrieve a large pearl. The insult was allegedly then compounded by drinking from the skull before tossing it into a nearby lake.[17]

Although the precious tomb objects were confiscated for official government purposes, the mere act of desecrating the emperors' and other court officials' burial vaults enraged Song loyalists. Historical reports suggest that Yang also benefitted personally from what was little more than government-sponsored grave robbing. As offensive and ill-timed as those actions were so soon after the Southern Song defeat, Yang's worst was still to come.

In 1277, a fire of uncertain origin destroyed a number of buildings in the former Song palace at the foot of Phoenix Hill. Seven years later, at Yang's recommendation, Khubilai issued an edict authorizing the construction of five temples and a pagoda on the site of the former palace. Each of the five temples honored a different Buddhist sect, including Zen, Tiantai, and Tibetan.[18] Well enough, perhaps, but Yang was also said to have ordered the exhumed bones from the Song imperial tombs commingled and buried beneath a new, sixty-meter-high White Pagoda (白塔, Baita) on Phoenix Hill. By some accounts, Yang had the bones of cows and horses mixed together with the imperial remains.

Built with stones from the former palaces and standing atop the bones of defeated emperors, the White Pagoda represented a form of "esoteric sorcery intended to suppress the fortunate ambiance or potential spiritual power in an auspicious place...a permanent lock that sealed the divine merit accumulated from the former Southern Song emperors, neutralized any Song state's supporting spirits wandering around Phoenix Hill, and avoid[ed] any possible revival of the Song empire."[19] Soaring white and unavoidably visible over West Lake's southern shore, the structure's name, Pagoda for Suppressing the South (镇南塔, Zhennan ta) only added fresh daily insult to the injurious treatment of the imperial remains, a flagrant and sacrilegious reminder of the Song Dynasty's fall to barbarians.

The White Pagoda disappeared at or shortly after the end of the Yuan Dynasty. Historical accounts are unclear, one asserting that the despised structure burned to the ground after being struck by lightning and another stating that it was intentionally demolished by the anti-Yuan warlord Zhang Shicheng 张士诚 (1321 – 1367).[20] Either way, the more superstitious observer might surmise that the combined spiritual power of the emperors whose remains were ostensibly buried beneath the pagoda ultimately prevailed over the evil deeds of Yang Lianzhenjia and the Mongol invaders for whom he labored.

Two Southern Song Loyalists

By Confucian tradition, officials and educated elites who had served, were serving, or were aspiring to serve for one dynasty were morally forbidden by the dictates of filial piety from serving another. In times of dynastic transition, such men had limited options. The "true" loyalists (义士 yishi or 忠义 zhongyi) sacrificed themselves as martyrs by resisting, fighting to the death, or committing suicide. In the Southern Song era, many of these individuals had either committed suicide at Lin'an's fall or died later as part of the large force defeated by the Mongols as it fled south with the last royal heirs.

Others less committed to the ultimate sacrifice or burdened with family responsibilities refused to serve the new rulers, withdrawing into reclusion, resorting to artistic or literary endeavors, or turning to lay Buddhism. Literati in this second group regarded themselves as "leftover subjects" (逸民, yimin), loyalists without portfolio, as much embittered by the loss of their actual or prospective careers as they were by the end of the dynasty under which they had served. Two such men from the Hangzhou area, well-remembered for their actions as well as their various writings and works, illustrate the loyalist predicament.

Zhou Mi 周密 (1232 – 1298) was all but born into a position in the Song government. The six generations that preceded him had all served as Song officials, first from their native home near Jinan in Shandong Province and then from Wuxing (Huzhou) after

Zhou Mi's grandfather followed Emperor Gaozong's flight from the Jurchen Jin and re-settled the family.

Zhou enjoyed the comforts of family wealth in his early years, living on an estate, trav-eling with the family to his father's new posting in Fujian Province, and studying for the civil service examinations. In 1260, he capped his studies by achieving his *jinshi* degree. He doubtless looked forward to a life of official positions and the associated pleasures of traveling, exchanging poetry, meeting other educated officials of like mind, and dis-covering opportunities to enhance his family's already substantial collection of books, paintings, and antiquities.

Between 1261 and 1274, Zhou's official career rise was far from meteoric, but he freely admitted to more interest in literary matters than civil or administrative ones. In ad-dition, he approached officialdom as a lifestyle, describing the "pleasures of the brush, inkstone, lute, and cup—not a day passed without them."[21] His was the privileged life of the educated elite, a life of casual effort, of building a network of personal connec-tions, of favors given and favors received, and of side interests actively pursued. To his credit and his later good fortune, he developed a reputation for poetic talent as well as a connoisseur's eye for paintings.

When Lin'an fell to the Mongols, Zhou was the junior Prefect of Yiwu in the moun-tainous area well south of the capital. By the time he was able to safely reach his family estate in Huzhou, he found it in ruins, generations-worth of books, art, and antiquities burned or missing. Homeless, destitute, and jobless, he and his family took up residence in Lin'an at the home of one of his wife's relatives. Unwilling to take a position in the new dynasty, he associated at first only with Song loyalists like himself.

Over time, Zhou fell back on his aesthetic skills. Years of conflict, looting, and death had unlocked the paintings of wealthy collectors and flooded the market. At the same time, migrants from northern China now working for the Yuan court sought the finer trappings of their positions, and Zhou Mi the art connoisseur was well-qualified to assist them. Such work likely earned him a modest income and gifts or favors in exchange for his authentication and advisory services.

His wide-ranging connections gave Zhou entrée to dozens of private painting collec-tions, knowledge he transformed in 1296 into a book describing the contents of more than forty such collections. He titled the book *Record of Clouds and Mist Passing Before One's Eyes* (雲烟過眼録, *Yunyan guoyan lu*), a bitterly ironic allusion to Su Shi's description of recovering from overindulgence in artistic possessions: "It is like the mist and clouds that pass before one's eyes."[22]

As Zhou's circle of acquaintances expanded, some of them relented in their withdrawal stances and accepted positions in the new dynasty out of financial necessity. Zhu was typically uncritical of their decisions, but throughout the final two decades of his life, he steadfastly refused to surrender his loyalty to the Song Dynasty. On the contrary, he was so concerned that knowledge of events in the Song era would be lost to the fog of time, he began assembling a written collection of personal memories and anecdotes he heard from others. Referring to Lin'an as Wulin, one of its common colloquial names, Zhou's *Former Events in Wulin* (武林舊事, *Wulin jiushi*) remains an important historical source regarding life in Southern Song Lin'an, whether in the palace or in the daily affairs of the city's residents.[23]

Zhao Mengfu's 趙孟頫 (1254 – 1322) *yimin* experience took a different course, one that has been often remarked through the ages. Zhao's father Zhao Yuyin 趙与訔 (1213 - 1265) was a friend of Zhou Mi's, both families being among the elite of Huzhou. But where Zhou Mi was already 44 years old with an established career and a personal network behind him when Lin'an fell in 1276, Zhao Yuyin's son was only 22, serving in his first minor posting received through the hereditary "protection privilege" (蔭, *yin*, literally "shade") and an examination in the capital.

As not only a surviving subject of the Song Dynasty but also a lineal descendent of the Song royal family,[24] Zhao Mengfu was doubly compelled to withdraw from public service. He returned home, honed his musical skills on the zither (古琴, *guqin*), and devoted himself to intensive study of history and the arts. His social contacts narrowed during the years after 1276 to other educated and talented young men of his area who, along with himself, came to be known as the Eight Talents of Huzhou. Left without a dynasty to serve, they socialized together, held literary gatherings, and visited famous sites and temples. Zhou Mi was not among the eight, but he knew them all.

Ten years later in 1286, Khubilai (as Yuan Emperor Shizu) sent his representative Cheng Jufu 程鉅夫 (1249 – 1318) on a seemingly quixotic mission to recruit Zhao Mengfu and other of his hometown colleagues into government service. Prospects for success appeared grim, particularly since Cheng himself was a Song subject who had traitorously chosen to enter Yuan service shortly after Lin'an's fall. Shockingly, it was Zhao Mengfu who agreed to accept a position in the Yuan administration.[25] His fellow literati were stunned and criticized him sharply. Even members of his own family declared his decision unforgivable.

Zhao impressed during an audience in Dadu with Khubilai Khan, who later referred glowingly to Zhao as "a man at home among immortals."[26] One account from his biography in the official *Yuan History* (元史, *Yuan shi*) even claimed that after Zhao fell from his horse on a narrow path along the city wall, Khubilai ordered the wall moved and the path widened. His seemingly outsized favor with Khubilai may well have been as much the product of the former's Song-royalty lineage in service of the Yuan as of his intellect or administrative competence. Not surprisingly, Mengfu advanced rapidly within the Yuan court from his initial position in the Hanlin Academy and received positions of influence: in the War Ministry, on investigatory missions in Zhejiang, and as Vice-Governor of Jinan in Shandong Province in 1292.

In 1294, Zhao participated in preparing the annals for the reign of the recently deceased Khubilai. After a long hiatus away from the capital (1295 – 1309), during most of which he directed schools of Confucian learning throughout Jiangnan, he answered the summons to serve once again in Dadu. Under the patronage of Yuan Emperor Renzong 元仁宗 (r. 1311 – 1320), Zhao rose to the position of Director of the Hanlin Academy before retiring to Huzhou in 1319. He passed away there in retirement in 1322.

Unlike Zhou Mi, Zhao Mengfu beneficially influenced Mongol governance and policy as "an articulate proponent of humane government, advocating reforms in monetary policy, in the postal relay stations, and in the penal code, including the abolition of corporal punishment for officials."[27] Given Zhao's considerable reputation in 1286 and his Song imperial lineage, his acceptance of service under the Yuan opened the doors for other literati to do likewise, whether out of felt need to their nation or simply to relieve the financial burdens of unemployment. Thus, for example, six more of the Eight Talents of Huzhou[28] subsequently followed Zhao into Yuan service, as if Zhao's decision justified their own.

Yet Zhao, too, was ambivalent about his actions. In his poem "Guilt at Leaving the Hermit's Life," composed in 1288, he wrote:

> To stay in the mountains is called great ambition;
> Leaving the mountains, you become a small weed.
> It was already stated in ancient times.
> Why didn't I foresee all this happening?
> All my life I longed to go my own way
> And to give my ambition to hills and valleys.
> I paint and write for my own entertainment,
> Hoping to keep my nature wild.
> Unfortunately, I am trapped in a net of dust,
> I turn and get tangled up.
> I was a gull over the waters,
> Now a bird in a cage.
> Who cares about my sad singing?[29]

What Zhao himself could never have known when he first left Huzhou for Dadu was that his chief contributions in life would come not in civil administration but in the arts. His travels in the north would set him on a path that radically transformed Chinese painting.

The Crossroads of Eurasia

As nomadic peoples of the steppe, the new Mongol rulers had little use for city walls and gates, which in their experience were less about defending those within and more about keeping Mongol warriors out. In Hangzhou and in many other Chinese cities, walls were either dismantled entirely or simply left in whatever stage of disrepair they had reached at the end of the Song. The city's residents took to absconding with bricks and other wall materials for their own personal use. Yet even though Hangzhou lost its imperial luster under the Yuan, it was still a highly commercial and heavily populated city.

The government's lackadaisical attitude toward urban defense ironically coincided with a new kind of foreign invasion into Hangzhou. In the past, city residents might have seen an occasional Korean or Japanese visitor to their city, usually Buddhist monks or sea-borne traders. Ever since the days of Qian Liu and Qian Chu in the 10th Century, Hangzhou had maintained intermittent trade with those East Asian neighbors. Now, however, the Mongols' conquests into the Middle East and even Eastern Europe brought a new wave of non-Asian foreign traders into the city: Moslems, Nestorian Christians, and Jews.

Moslem traders had been commonplace in China since at least the Tang Dynasty, with their strongest presence in the port cities of Canton, Quanzhou (Fujian Province), and the Yangzi River city of Yangzhou. They had never been particularly numerous in Hangzhou/Lin'an,[30] but their numbers increased so substantially after 1276 that a grand new temple, the Phoenix Mosque (凤凰寺, Fenghuangsi), was constructed in 1281 on the former Imperial Way.[31]

Historical records indicate that the building site was an abandoned plot that had long been home to a lesser mosque. "The [Phoenix] mosque has its origin under the Tang... and was destroyed by fire towards the end of the Song. During the year [1281], there was the Grand Master ['Ala' al-Din who...stopped at Hangzhou. He saw what remained of the foundations and contributed generously for the re-establishment and the renovation to be undertaken."[32] Unfortunately, little is known about the mosque's great benefactor, 'Ala' al-Din. In another reflection of the increased Moslem presence in Jiangnan during the Yuan era, ancient records also suggest the construction of Suzhou's earliest known mosque "in the central part of the old city....connected with the well-known Sayyid family" in the second half of the 13th Century.[33]

In addition to erecting the Phoenix Mosque, Hangzhou's Moslem community also purchased prime land on the southeastern shore of West Lake for a cemetery, formerly an imperial park known as Jujing Yuan 聚景园. In 1921, during a road-building project alongside the lake, almost one hundred Moslem headstones were excavated. Many were lost in the decades that followed, but of the twenty-one that remain, seven have identifiable dates ranging from 1307 to 1351.[34] In the present day, a pavilion in the southeastern section of West Lake (in the Orioles Singing in the Willows park area) marks the tomb site of the Yuan-era Moslem poet Ding Henian 丁鹤年 (1335 – 1424), a quiet historical reminder of the Moslem heritage in Hangzhou.

Less well-known was the existence in Hangzhou of a Nestorian (景教, *Jingjiao*) church constructed in 1281 by Mar Sargis. The Church of the East, as the Nestorian community was called, was Turkic in origin, following the teachings of Nestorius (c. 386 – c. 450), the 5th-Century Archbishop of Constantinople. Nestorians arrived in Chang'an and Luoyang as early as the Tang Dynasty era[35] and reached the peak of their influence under the Mongol empire. The Nestorian building in Hangzhou was likely the first Christian house of worship ever constructed in that city, but hardly the last. Hangzhou would cultivate a complex relationship with Christianity in the centuries to come.

Unlike the Phoenix Mosque, the original Nestorian church no longer stands in Hangzhou. During the Japanese wartime occupation in 1942, missionary doctor Stephen Sturton (1896 – 1970) set out on an intensive private investigation to locate the church's original site and any remnants of its presence.[36] He ultimately determined its location to have been about three hundred yards west of one of the city's ancient eastern gates, replaced in his time by a modest fish and vegetable market.

In the year 1332, the Moroccan scholar and world-traveler Ibn Battuta (1304 – 1369) set out on an exploratory trip that would last fifteen years and take him through the Middle East, Afghanistan, Pakistan, India, Malaysia, the Philippines, and finally to China. He landed at the trading port city of Quanzhou in 1345 and traveled by river from there to Hangzhou. Ibn Battuta called the city El Khansa, indicating that more than a hundred years after the Song Chinese began referring to Lin'an as 行在 *xingzai*, their dynasty's "temporary residence," the term was still commonplace. In fact, anglicized variations of *xingzai* would continue in use by Western visitors for centuries afterward, morphing variously into Quinsay, Quinsai, Kinsay, Kinsai, and Kampsay, among others.

Although Ibn Battuta had already traveled widely,[37] he still expressed amazement in 1345 at Hangzhou's size and the diversity of its populace:

> This is the largest city I had ever seen on the face of the earth: its length is a journey of three days, in which a traveler may proceed on and find lodgings....When we approached this city we were met by its judge, presbyters of Islamism, and the great merchants. The Mohammedans are exceedingly numerous here. This whole city is surrounded by a wall: each of the six cities is also surrounded by a wall. In the first resides the guards, with their commander. I was told that, in the muster-rolls, these amount to twelve thousand. I lodged one night in the house of the commander. In the second division are the Jews, the Christians, and the Turks who worship the sun; these are numerous, but their number is not known: and theirs is the most beautiful city. Their streets are well disposed, and their great men are exceedingly wealthy. There are in the city a great number of Mohammedans, with some of whom I resided for fifteen days; and was treated most honorably.[38]

The Western Europeans Arrive

Fifty years before Ibn Battuta's brief stay in Hangzhou, the city's most famous medieval-Western traveler dictated his recollections of Yuan-era China. When the Venetian Marco Polo (马可波罗, Ma ke Boluo, 1254 – 1324) arrived in Dadu in 1275 at the tender age of 21, the Southern Song still controlled most of China south of the Yangzi River. By the time he arrived in Hangzhou in 1279, the Mongols had seized the former capital of Lin'an and effectively eliminated the Song royal family and the remaining loyalist opposition. Polo would remain in China for seventeen years, finally departing in 1291.

Doubts and issues abound with Polo and his famous travel report, dictated in around 1298 to Rustichello da Pisa (fl. 13th Century) while both were held as war prisoners in

Genoa. Was he ever in China? Did he visit all the places about which he wrote or simply repeat what he had heard from others? Why are so many facts exaggerated or incorrect, and why did he fail to mention so many obvious things like the Great Wall or the foot-binding of Chinese women?

Polo's descriptions of early Yuan Hangzhou, and his entire book in general, have been subjected to decades of intense scholarly analysis, parsing, debate, and even modern documentary attempts to retrace his precise travels. It is enough here to report some of what he claimed to have seen and, in Hangzhou's case, capture the awe in which he held the city. After all, what he dictated and Rustichello transcribed, accurate or not, astonished his medieval European readers and created long-lasting impressions of Hangzhou specifically and China generally.

To begin with, there is the matter of attention granted. By one analysis, out of the 232 chapters in Polo's *Travels*, the chapter on "Kinsay"[39] was the longest in the entire book. Polo wrote of "Yan-gui" (Yangzhou) in Chapter 60 that, "By special order of the grand khan, [he] acted as governor of this city during the space of three years." Yet he wrote barely a paragraph about Yangzhou and voluminously about Hangzhou, 150 miles away to the south. The same analysis states that what Polo termed "the City of Heaven"[40] occupies a seemingly disproportionate one twenty-fifth share of a travel book covering twenty-four years across Western Europe, the Middle East, Tibet, the Gobi Desert, China, Malaysia, India, and back again to Venice.[41]

Polo's account of a city "beyond dispute the finest and the noblest in the world" is suffused with exaggerations about the city's size ("an hundred miles of compass"), number of bridges ("twelve thousand"),[42] the location and size of West Lake ("inside the city" and with "a compass of some thirty miles"), market produce ("pears of enormous size, weighing as much as ten pounds apiece"), and population ("1,600,000 houses," which implies a population of seven or eight million people).[43] Yet his book contains the most detailed extant depiction of early Yuan Hangzhou by any non-Chinese visitor or resident.

Once Polo's account passes through its rather exaggerated beginning, presumably for effect, he quickly switches to describing the mansions and temples surrounding West Lake and the two islands in its middle. He then directs a notable amount of attention to the manner in which the city manages fire hazards and how it maintains civic cleanliness from paved roads and personal cleanliness from the three thousand hot baths in which the people "take great delight, frequenting them several times a month."[44]

Polo's account goes beyond merely describing the visible city. He addresses the people's use of geomancy and astrology, their funerary customs, and their requirement to post and maintain current above their doors the names in writing of all who live within each residence. He then returns his attention to the physical city, describing in detail the numerous markets and shops, the decaying city walls, the semi-deteriorated former palace of the Song emperors, and the various ways in which Hangzhou residents enjoyed pleasure-boating on West Lake:

And the Lake is never without a number of other such boats, laden with pleasure parties; for it is the great delight of the citizens here, after they have dis-
posed of the day's business, to pass the afternoon in enjoyment with the ladies
of their families, or perhaps with others less reputable, either in these barges
or in driving about the city in carriages.[45]

European readers could not but have been in awe of the canal-lined Kinsay described by Marco Polo, as if it were Venice as it perhaps aspired to someday be.
His description of such a magnificently rich and populous place, combined with
the not-too-subtle allure he infused in his description of the city's women of the
evening, made Kinsay an instant legend and a place most could only visit in their
dreams. Hangzhou may well have rewarded Polo in return. Alice Hobart Tisdale
reported in her 1909 visit to Lingyin Temple that a pavilion honoring five hundred
holy men (*arhats*) included among its honorees a statue of Marco Polo.[46]

Polo's *Travels* enlightened Westerners about China's wonders and attracted the attention of early Christian missionaries. Franciscan monks were among the first to
arrive in south China in the 1300s. The most famous was the Italian friar Odoric of
Pordenone (c. 1286 – 1331), who entered China in around 1325, about fifty years
after Polo's departure. He must have presented a striking foreign appearance to the
Chinese: small but severe, pale-faced, with a long, forked beard tinged with red. His
account of Cansay, as he termed Hangzhou, was brief in its specifics about the city
but nevertheless showed some striking similarities to Polo's "City of Heaven," with
its 12,000 bridges and its hundred-mile circumference.

While in Hangzhou, Odoric visited Lingyin Temple and later wrote of a remarkable experience there. When one of the Lingyin monks was asked to show the Franciscan monk
something interesting that he could transmit to the people of Italy, he retrieved a bucket of
table scraps and carried it into a garden-like area at the base of a hill near the temple.

> As we stood there he took a gong, and began to beat upon it, and at the
> sound a multitude of animals of diverse kinds began to come down from the
> hill, such as apes, monkeys, and many other animals having faces like men,
> to the number of some three thousand, and took up their places round about
> him in regular ranks. And when they were thus ranged round about him, he
> put down the vessels before them and fed them as fast as he was able. And
> when they had been fed he began again to beat the gong, and all returned to
> their retreats.[47]

An obviously bemused Odoric went on to say that those monkeys were believed by the
temple monk to be the souls of gentlemen whose good behavior had reincarnated them
as more noble animals, while the souls of boorish men returned in baser animals. No
matter how Odoric argued the point, he could not dissuade the Buddhist monk from
his views. Such is often the way of religious conviction.

The Franciscan friar ended his description of Cansay on an upbeat note sure to reinforce the grand imaginings Marco Polo had initiated:

> But if anyone should desire to tell all the vastness and great marvels of this city, a good quire of stationery would not hold the matter, I believe. For 'tis the greatest and noblest city, and the finest for merchandise, that the whole world containeth.[48]

When Hangzhou's old city walls were demolished in 1957, workers discovered two ancient gravestones of clearly Christian origin that had been used as building material for the walls. Dated 1342 and 1344, they identified the remains of, respectively, Caterina and Antonio, daughter and son of the (also deceased) Signor Domenico de Viglione.[49] Signor Viglione was likely one of the Franciscan monks from Italy whom Odoric reported visiting during his time in Hangzhou.

In the 1340s, the Florentine John Marignolli (before 1290 – after 1357) visited Campsay (his name for Hangzhou) during his travels through Yuan China. His too-effusive account reinforces those of Polo and Odoric but adds little of interest or insight:

> Campsay, the finest, the biggest, the richest, the most populous, and altogether the most marvelous city, the city of the greatest wealth and luxury, of the most splendid buildings (especially idol-temples, in some of which there are 1000 and 2000 monks dwelling together), that exists now upon the face of the earth, or mayhap that ever did exist.[50]

The Painting Revolution

While Marco Polo entertained Khubilai Khan in 1276 Dadu and began his travels within the new Yuan empire, Zhao Mengfu first quietly withdrew from the public sphere. Sequestration in his Huzhou hometown was far from a hardship, however. Located on the south shore of Lake Tai and nestled at the foot of the Tianmu mountain range, Huzhou was renowned in Song times for its cultural heritage, natural scenery, and agricultural productivity. As a popular adage of the Song era asserted: "When the harvest in Suzhou and Huzhou is good, the whole world will enjoy plenty." Only forty miles northwest of Lin'an, the city had become a residential favorite for members of the imperial clan, successful entrepreneurs, and wealthy migrants escaping from the north. Mongol general Bayan had also reputedly appreciated Huzhou's ambience as he patiently settled there while negotiating the Song surrender.

For Zhao Mengfu, the decade after 1276 had been a period of intense study and introspection for a brilliant young man. Only 22 years old, he would otherwise have been actively working to ascend the ladder of officialdom. Instead, as noted previously, he studied classical poetry and ancient paintings, wrote poems, practiced calligraphy and painting, and socialized with the Eight Talents of Huzhou and other local scholars. In those post-war recovery years, they abandoned politics to discuss the prevailing theories and practice of the arts and share ancient works with one another from their personal collections. Another Jiangnan literatus later succinctly described this pastime in his list

144

of "Fond Interests": "Freely displaying objects, but slowly putting them away."[51]

As much criticized as Zhao was for accepting service in the Yuan government, his ten years in the north (1286 – 1295) were revelatory. From each new imperial assignment, he expanded his personal network of officials and literati, many of whom shared with him the ancient paintings, calligraphy, and rubbings in their collections. In the capital, he also had opportunities to view works in the imperial palace collection, including those removed from Lin'an by the Mongols. By the time he returned to Huzhou in 1295 after pleading illness, he was prepared to explore a new form of artistic expression.

Shandong Province, where Zhao Mengfu had served as Vice-Governor, was also the native home of his Huzhou colleague Zhou Mi. Zhou had never seen his ancestral homeland. Having refused service to the Yuan Dynasty, he likely never would. For that reason, Zhao chose to paint a famous Shandong scene from memory as a gift to his friend. He completed *Autumn Colors on the Que and Hua Mountains* (鵲華秋色) in January 1296, "[his] first attempt to formulate a new pictorial language."[52]

The painting is oddly austere, clumps of trees like island oases on a featureless plain, a few stick-like fishermen in boats in the left foreground and right middle ground, and three or four "awkward houses" nestled among the trees. Colors are everywhere beige, pale blue, or a dark, muted green, except for the two oddly geometric Que and Hua mountains[53] (one like a flattened, loaf-shaped mound, the other distinctly conical), looming dark blue in the distance, isolated and alone behind everything else.

The primitivism in Zhao's painting projected a sense of antiquity and rejected Southern Song efforts at faithful depiction of the actual scenery. In doing so, he "transform[ed] the tradition of Tang and Northern Song from a revelation of the all-encompassing spirit that pervades the universe to an expression of personal feeling toward nature in the Jiangnan landscape." For Zhao Mengfu and those who came after him, representation gave way to personal expression of each artist's inner self. Literati painters who despaired of China under barbarian rule now had "a vehicle which permitted them to recall the glories of the Chinese tradition on the one hand and to express their personal tastes, dreams, and ideas on the other."[54]

Zhao Mengfu's innovations in *Autumn Colors* went still further. Once representation no longer asserted primacy, the painter's feelings could be measured in the expressiveness of his or her brushstrokes, just as calligraphy had been viewed across the ages as an outward display of one's inner spirit. To paraphrase Marshall McLuhan's aphorism of the 20th Century, the medium was now the message. Zhao then broke another tradition by inscribing his own calligraphy on the painting to explain his feelings and purpose. "Until this time,…a comment on the picture surface would have been strikingly out of place. When the function of painting changed to an intimate form of self-expression, not only was the artist freed to add his own remarks…but viewers were in effect invited to add theirs as well."[55]

In 1302, Zhao's ink painting *Water Village* (水村圖, *Shui cun tu*) reinforced and reaffirmed his break with artistic tradition. Ostensibly depicting a friend's hermitage, the handscroll represents the literati ideal of a reclusive scholarly retreat. The work is starkly simplistic, minimizing the variety of brushstroke types until the image appears little different from calligraphy, merging the burdens of representation with the freedom of inner expression. For Zhao, painting was calligraphy as much in form as in spirit, as he inscribed in a colophon on another of his paintings:

> Rocks are like flying white [cursive script], trees like seal script.
> To 'write' bamboo go back to the pa[-fen, i.e., clerical script] method.
> Only when a person is capable of understanding this
> Will he know that painting and calligraphy are basically the same.[56]

Zhao Mengfu was revolutionizing Chinese painting, nowhere more so than among the younger generation of Jiangnan literati. One of the earliest to emerge from Zhao's shadow was Jiaxing native Wu Zhen 吴镇 (1280 – 1354). Wu specialized in landscapes and bamboo, often adding poems about bamboo as colophons on his paintings. He lived a life so reclusive, scholars have asserted that he may never have traveled more than a few miles from his family home. A 14th-Century writer described Wu Zhen as "solitary" and "unsociable," but he added of Wu's painting: "His joy was forever in lofty mountains, beneath dense woods; his brushwork is therefore imbued with a feeling of profound distance and of detached, lofty ease. It is utterly lacking in the [worldly] air of the roaming scions of the wealthy and mighty."[57]

Another next-generation painter of renown was Wang Meng 王蒙 (1308 - 1385), a Huzhou native who happened also to be Zhao Mengfu's grandson. Wang almost certainly received early painting and calligraphic instruction from his grandfather. He pursued Confucian scholarship and, like his famous grandfather, accepted official positions in the dynasty (the Ming) that later succeeded the one into which he was born (the Yuan). He was an accomplished poet whose landscape paintings celebrated reclusion. He was also among the first to employ landscapes to personify specific individuals.[58]

Wu Zhen and Wang Meng, along with Jiangsu Province natives Huang Gongwang 黄公望 (1269 – 1354, from Changshu) and Ni Zan 倪瓚 (1301–1374, from Wuxi), comprised the celebrated "Four Great Masters of the Yuan Dynasty." As accomplished as they each were, they were all beholden to Zhao Mengfu, the Southern Song master whose revolutionary artistic vision charted a fertile new course for their work.

Molding Clay Figures

Before his initial departure from Huzhou in 1287 to serve the Yuan government in Dadu, Zhao Mengfu married Guan Daosheng 管道昇 (1262 – 1319), daughter of a local scholar-gentry family from Nanxun (Huzhou Prefecture). By the standards of the day, it was an unusually late first marriage; he was already 32 years old, and she was 24. Their marriage must have been one of mutual respect and maturity, since Guan traveled to Dadu when Zhao resumed work in the capital and even accompanied him on his assignments in Jilin and Lin'an.

As the daughter of a gentry family that had not been favored with sons, Guan Daosheng received a solid education and demonstrated sufficient talent in poetry, painting, and calligraphy to merit presentation as a suitable bridal match to Zhao Mengfu. No record exists that she received formal training in the arts before her marriage, but her life in the capital provided access to people of talent, training, and intellect as well as to the great art in private holdings and the incomparable palace collections. In addition, of course, she had the guidance of her husband, one of the greatest painters in the history of Chinese art.

It was not until after Zhao's furlough from the capital and return to Huzhou in 1295 that the first flowering of Guan's talent appeared. Her artistic skills developed into a widely acknowledged mastery of bamboo painting, a bold decision to "transgress propriety" by producing works featuring traditionally male-only subject matter. Her husband apparently supported her stance, since together they produced a handscroll titled *Orchids and Bamboo*.[59]

Such was Guan's reputation, in fact, that Emperors Wuzong and Renzong commissioned her to produce seventy or eighty bamboo paintings for themselves and the ladies of the imperial palace. Later, perhaps even defiantly, she wrote the *Manual on Painting Bamboo in Black Ink* to explain her techniques. Guan would later be celebrated "as a talented woman [and] also as a prominent figure in bamboo painting…one of the few women who is mentioned in early Western surveys of Chinese painting and whose work has been studied by modern Chinese scholars."[60]

Guan's innate calligraphic skills also evolved with time and practice until she was regarded as an outstanding talent in her brushwork, the equal of the best female calligraphers of the past. When Emperor Renzong learned of her talents and those of her son Zhao Yong 赵雍 (1289 – c. 1360), he commissioned an extraordinary family work. He requested that mother and son copy out the *Thousand Character Classic* (千字文, *Qianzi wen*)[61] in their respective calligraphy and that Zhao Mengfu produce six more copies, each in a different calligraphic script. The finished handscrolls were then lavishly framed with jade rods and added to the palace collection. It was an almost unimaginable family honor, magnified further when Renzong added, with implied but undeserved self-importance: "Later generations can know that in my reign not only was there an expert female calligrapher, but a whole family capable in calligraphy, which is extraordinary."[62]

The marital relationship between Guan and Zhao was strongly reminiscent of that between Li Qingzhao and Zhao Mingcheng in both love and mutual intellectual respect. Guan is believed to have given Zhao as many as three sons and six daughters, remarkable for her relatively late marriage at age 24, their wide travels as a couple, and her clearly active intellectual and artistic pursuits. But perhaps their love for one another is best demonstrated through the legendary story of Zhao's cautious poetic request to take two concubines into their household. Guan's graciously negative reply became a classic Chinese love poem, equally heartfelt when used in modern times as a wedding poem:

You and I have so much love	你儂我儂　忒煞情多
That it burns like a fire,	情多處　熱似火
In which we bake clay molded into a you and a me.	把一塊泥　捻一個你　塑一個我
We break both figures and mix them with water,	將咱兩個　一齊打破　用水調和
And mold again a you and a me.	再捻一個你　再塑一個我
I am in your clay; you are in my clay.	我泥中有你　你泥中有我
In life we share a single quilt.	我與你　生同一個衾
In death we will share one coffin.	死同一個槨

Zhao never asked about concubines again.

From 1299 – 1309, Zhao served the Yuan government as commissioner of education in the Jiangnan region, followed by a nine-year period back in the capital as a scholar and master calligrapher at the Hanlin Academy. Guan Daosheng fell ill in 1318 and took a serious turn for the worse in early 1319. Given permission to retire and take Guan home to Huzhou, the couple boarded an official boat for the journey. Before they had traveled any further than Shandong Province, Guan passed away. Zhao was devastated, and his health began to weaken not long after. He lived three more years, continuing his study and practice of calligraphy while painting mostly bamboo, Guan's favorite subject.

Consistent with the spirit of the final line of Guan Daosheng's poem about clay molds, the couple were buried together in 1322 among the mulberry trees at their country residence in Dongheng Village, Deqing, about twenty-five miles south of Huzhou. Their tomb site was restored in the 1980s.

Under Mongol Rule

Despite the humiliation and despair felt by so many of its citizens, Hangzhou benefitted in some ways from Yuan rule. Spared from major looting and destruction, the increased presence of Muslims, Jews, and Christians further internationalized the city. Trade flourished, and new cultures and cuisines entered the urban mix and broadened intellectual horizons.

Perhaps most significant, Khubilai (Emperor Shizu) embarked on a massive restoration and redirection of the Grand Canal between 1289 and 1292. Employing the forced labor of over two million people, the government oversaw construction of an entirely new and straightened canal section, known as the Huitong, that connected the Yellow River to the existing Wei Canal. The Huitong Canal cut across the open mouth of the network's formerly "sideways-Y" shape, reducing the length of the Hangzhou-to-Beijing trip by as much as 700 kilometers (420 miles).

Hangzhou now sat at the southern terminus of a domestic supply line linked directly to the capital. The *caoyun* grain transport system became the major lifeline between the agriculturally rich south, the capital, and the military defense forces in the north. Silks, teas, timber, porcelains, fine crafts, and of course, rice—all these and more poured into Hangzhou from points south and west, bound for delivery to the north. Imperial communications flowed through Hangzhou as well, since Khubilai had taken advantage of the Grand Canal's restoration to create a paved postal network running alongside the waterway, supported by 1,400 postal stations and as many as 50,000 horses.[64]

Yet these benefits also came with painful downsides. First on that list for many Hangzhou natives would have been the Yuan's caste-like social ranking system that placed Mongols first, Middle Eastern foreigners (known as 色目 *semu* or 色目人 *semuren*, "people of varied categories") second, northern Chinese (汉人, *hanren*) third, and the deeply distrusted southern Chinese (南人, *nanren*) last. Few southern Chinese could hope for an official position even if they were willing to serve the Yuan government. In fact, among the non-Mongols in higher official positions, fully one-third were *semuren*, a situation unheard of in Chinese history to that time.[65]

Nevertheless, there were opportunities, sometimes politically hazardous, for Han Chinese subjects of the Mongol Yuan such as Shaoxing's Yang Weizhen 杨维桢 (1296 – 1370). After famously withdrawing the ladder to his second-floor room for five years in order to study for the civil service examinations (and receive meals delivered by a pulley system), Yang achieved his *jinshi* degree in 1327. His up-and-down official career ended with agricultural administration and judicial positions in and around Hangzhou in the 1350s. Throughout, he rose to become one of the leading scholars, poets, and poetry society leaders of his time among Jiangnan literati despite a penchant for rather dissolute behavior. Although born into the Yuan, Yang accommodated himself freely to two rivals for the succeeding dynasty and accepted a position late in life with the victorious founder of the Ming Dynasty.[66]

In the first half of the 14th Century, Yuan governance deteriorated significantly. The Mongols cared so little for city walls that they forbade them for a time, leaving the residents feeling defenseless. They waged pointless military campaigns in places like Vietnam and Indonesia, depleted the imperial treasury, imposed regressive taxes, and created levels of inflation that reduced their paper currency to worthlessness. By refusing to place educated and talented southern Chinese in administrative leadership positions and insisting that all Chinese officials had to be employed under the supervision of a Mongol official, they lost a badly needed source of administrative skills and hamstrung the ones they did have. Corruption and inefficiency abounded, complicated by communication issues caused by the simultaneous use of Chinese, Uighur, and Persian scripts.

Khubilai's successor, his grandson Temür Öljeitü (Emperor Chengzong 元成宗, r. 1294 – 1307) ruled passably, but his death at age 41 without a male heir ushered in a twenty-six-year, conflict-riddled period that produced seven different emperors. When one emperor would favor sinicization of the dynasty, the reactionary next would favor traditional Mongol rule and practices. Governmental control deteriorated. As one example, the Yangzi River in the 1320s and 1330s became so infested with pirates preying on merchant ships that "commercial traffic...was virtually stalled by the brigands' vessels."[67]

When thirteen-year-old Toghan Temür ascended the Yuan throne as Emperor Shundi (元顺帝, r. 1333 – 1368), he could not have known he would be the last of his dynasty. His reign began badly, with a Regency so virulently anti-sinicization, it banned its Chinese subjects from keeping weapons, riding horses, and hunting. Shundi outlawed Chinese opera performance and astonishingly even proposed exterminating unmarried Chinese children and all others with the five most common family names (Li, Liu, Wang, Zhang, or Zhao).[68]

By the time some of those policies were reversed, disease and disaster followed: the Black Plague in the 1340s, famines from alternating droughts and flooding, and a virtual closure of the Grand Canal link to Beijing when the Yellow River overran its banks in 1344 and shifted its course.[69] Rebellions broke out in the north, only to grow and spread further in 1351 when the eight-month effort to regain control over the Yellow River provided fertile anti-Mongol recruiting ground among the tens of thousands of peasant conscripts.

By the 1350s, local anti-government armies were forming, and rebellious sects and warlords were emerging. The Mandate of Heaven was rapidly slipping away from the once-mighty Mongols less than a century after they had claimed it.

Chapter 8

THE PROSPEROUS MING

(1368 – 1644)

First Trip to West Lake[1]

The hills were like a lady's dark eyebrows, and the flowers were like her cheeks. The gentle breeze was as intoxicating as wine, and the ripples were as soft as damask silk. I had barely lifted my head before I felt drunk and overwhelmed. At that moment I tried to describe it but found myself speechless.

— Yüan Hongdao (1568 – 1610)

The Battle for Succession

As Yuan control over the Chinese empire weakened in the first half of the 1300s, the government struggled desperately to retain its hold over the sea salt monopoly. For centuries, as much as forty percent of the nation's salt had been extracted from the coastal marshes of northern Jiangsu Province and delivered to Yangzhou or nearby Taizhou 泰州, where taxes on its sale to wholesalers generated up to one-third of the empire's tax revenue.

In the 1340s and 1350s, salt thievery by gangs of smugglers grew rampant, compounded by corruption among officials, merchants, and even the soldiers posted to protect the government's trade. Into this illicit stew came four salt-smuggling brothers from the Taizhou area, led by their eldest, Zhang Shicheng 张士诚 (1321 – 1367). Gifted with the physical size and rough temperament that made him a feared but natural leader, Zhang's strength and fighting skills were betrayed in 1353 by his hair-trigger temper. Hearing one day what he perceived to be an insult from one of the government soldiers, he killed the man and then set a damaging fire to cover his escape.

After hiding with his brothers for a time in their home district, Zhang viewed organized

151

banditry as his only option. What began as a small group of ne'er-do-well recruits soon mushroomed into a ragtag army with thousands of equally disgruntled followers. Before long, they were preying on nearby villages and on the city of Taizhou, thieving homes and businesses instead of salt. Rather flaccid Yuan efforts to rein in Zhang's predations gave way to offers of appeasement and amnesty; Zhang's response was to murder the government envoys and continue marauding.

By year's end, his bandit army had seized control of Gaoyu, a market town sitting astride the Grand Canal about twenty-five miles north of Yangzhou. In less than a year, an underequipped peasant army had formed, gained a chokehold over the national lifeline, and posed a direct threat to the Yuan Dynasty. Military forces dispatched from Yangzhou failed to retake Gaoyu, and further efforts at appeasement only ended in more murdered envoys. With no other recourse, the capital sent a massive force under General Toghto (1312 – 1356) to recover Gaoyu and eliminate Zhang Shicheng. Despite stiff resistance from the rebels, Toghto appeared on the verge of victory when he was inexplicably relieved of his command in January 1355 and exiled to faraway Yunnan Province.

A miraculously rejuvenated Zhang Shicheng rejected further Yuan peace offers (and, of course, murdered still more envoys) and restored his army's strength. While still busily retaking territory he had lost to Toghto in northern Jiangsu, he sent his brother Zhang Shide 张士德 (d. 1357) on an exploratory foray across the Yangzi at year-end 1355. Within mere weeks, Shide captured Changshu, just thirty miles north of Suzhou. In March 1356, his force seized Suzhou as well; Shicheng took up permanent residence there the following month. Shide gained additional Jiangsu Province territories east and south of Suzhou and in much of northern Zhejiang Province from Huzhou to Shaoxing and, at least briefly in the summer of 1356, Hangzhou.

Meanwhile, the Yuan Dynasty was fatally fracturing into warlord states. To Zhang Shicheng's southeast, the pirate leader Fang Guozhen 方国珍 (1319 – 1374) controlled coastal Zhejiang, while Chen Youding 陈友定 (1330-1368) established himself in coastal Fujian Province. To Zhang Shicheng's west and southwest, the ex-monk Zhu Yuanzhang 朱元璋 (1328 – 1398) reigned over a large area in central and south-central China, with his capital at Nanjing. Still further west was another large state centered on Sichuan Province, under the rule of Chen Youliang 陈友谅 (1320 – 1363). While northern China had also fragmented among several Mongol leaders, the warlords of central and southern China were all Han Chinese. The deteriorated state of affairs under Mongol rule all but ensured that the next dynasty would be founded by one of these Chinese warlords.

Like Qian Liu before him, Zhang Shicheng played his political cards craftily, particularly after his brother was captured in battle by Zhu Yuanzhang's forces in 1357 and held for ransom. As he slowly starved himself to death, the imprisoned Shide managed to send Shicheng a two-fold message: do not surrender or join forces with Zhu Yuanzhang, and do ally with the Yuan in Dadu and Hangzhou. Zhang Shicheng followed this playbook, successfully negotiating an alliance which left him in near-total control of the territories he already held. While the Yuan government retained nominal control over Hangzhou, Zhang effectively controlled that strong-hold and Shaoxing as well. In 1357, the city restored and reinforced its deteriorated city walls to a height of thirty feet and a base width of nearly fifty feet[2] in prepara-tion for the coming conflict.

In 1359, Zhu Yuanzhang's forces under General Hu Dahai 胡大海 (d. 1362) laid siege to Shaoxing, whose defense was led by General Lu Chen.[3] The city was well-protected by high, crenellated walls and a surrounding moat, but the watery countryside and shallow waterways impeded the advance of any truly large-scale force. As events turned out, Hu's force was able to lay siege but proved inadequate to fully and effectively encircle the city. Lu Chen, in turn, personally led sorties out from behind the walls to engage and weaken the attackers, although he suffered wounds from at least one of these battles. Within the walls, strict measures were established to regulate equitable rice distribution, and open ground was put into cultivated use for the same purpose. Hu Dahai's attempts at persuasion with propaganda leaflets failed to generate dissent, and Lu Chen's humane treatment of battle prisoners even convinced some of them to declare allegiance to Zhang Shicheng.

As the siege dragged on, both sides offered prayers and sacrifices to their respective choice of gods. The attacking rebels chose to perform ceremonial rituals at the Temple of Yu the Great, but after they did not receive the divine assistance they sought, the angered soldiers simply toppled the god's statue. With the onset of the summer heat, an epidemic erupted in the latter half of May 1359 that sapped more strength from the already inadequate attacking force. Zhu Yuanzhang finally broke off the siege, cement-ing Lu Chen's reputation as a military leader. Lu continued as a commander in Zhang Shicheng's army until he surrendered to the Ming in 1366.

By the close of the 1350s, Zhang Shicheng had perfectly positioned himself as the Yuan Dynasty's logical Chinese successor. In this, he was further aided by the literati of Suzhou and Hangzhou, who saw in his alignment with the Yuan a signal that they could support him and even enter into his administrative service. He cleverly cultivated relationships with the local gentry and literati, seeking their advice and sharing their cultural interests. They in turn eagerly welcomed an end to Mongol rule and saw in Zhang a prospective dynasty-founder sympathetic to their interests. To that end, the former salt smuggler declared his Jiangnan domain Da Zhou 大周, the State (or Kingdom) of Greater Zhou.

To strengthen his defensive hold on Hangzhou, Zhang Shicheng altered the city's size and shape. He eliminated the southwestward extension of the walls created by Qian Liu, moving Phoenix Hill outside of the city by shrinking the wall's reach to no further than the southern foot of the multiple hills of Wushan. In the process, Zhang abolished four land gates and built one new southern gate, calling it Phoenix Hill Gate (凤山门, Fengshanmen), thereby reducing the number of land gates from thirteen to ten. This ar-rangement of ten gates would last for more than five centuries, into the early 20th Cen-tury. Zhang also added a new water gate on the south wall, called Phoenix Hill Water Gate (凤山水城门, Fengshan shuichengmen) to connect Hangzhou's canals with the Qiantang River.

153

By 1363, the end game of this dynastic chess match began to play out. Unfortunately, without the tactical brilliance of his brother Shide, Zhang Shicheng failed to deal a fatal blow against Zhu Yuanzhang when the latter turned his attention westward (from 1358 – 1363) to eliminate Chen Youliang. Attempts to seize some of Zhu's territory were made in 1363 and 1364 by another of Shicheng's brothers, Zhang Shixin (张士信, d. circa 1367), but he lacked Shide's military savvy and leadership skills. Shixin's forces had grown lazy and lacked their former fighting edge, perhaps softened by the pleasures and comforts of Jiangnan life. Consequently, they were repeatedly repulsed by Zhu's armies with stinging losses.

With his rivals to the west vanquished, Zhu Yuanzhang began preparing in 1364 for an offensive against Zhang Shicheng. Rather than attack Suzhou directly, however, Zhu's first move was north of the Yangzi. He quickly seized Shicheng's most distant Jiangsu Province territory, sealing him off from Yuan support out of Dadu. Zhu's lead general, Xu Da 徐达 (1332 – 1385), then began retaking the cities of Jiangnan that surrounded Suzhou, from Changzhou, Wuxi, and Changshu northward to Huzhou, Jiaxing, and Hangzhou southward. Huzhou fell on December 8, 1366; Hangzhou surrendered just one week later.

Xu Da gradually reduced Zhang Shicheng's territorial control to just the walled city of Suzhou, which stubbornly refused to surrender. It finally fell in October 1367 after Xu Da's ten-month siege ended with reports of cannibalism, thousands of deaths by disease and starvation, and mass suicides inside the city walls. Zhang's wife and concubines gathered in a palace tower and set it afire, while the self-declared ruler of the Da Zhou dynasty prepared to hang himself. However, Zhang was captured before doing so and transported to Nanjing, where he later died by execution or starvation.

The rest, as they say, is history. Zhu Yuanzhang solidified his hold over southern China before marching on the Yuan capital. On January 20, 1368 in Nanjing, Zhu Yuanzhang declared himself founding Emperor Taizu (太祖) of the Great Ming Dynasty (大明朝, Da Ming Chao), where "Ming" 明 signified "radiance" or "brightness." His reign name, Hongwu 洪武 ("abundantly martial" or "vast military power"), projected Zhu's intentions toward any further threats to his rule.

Zhu captured Dadu in September 1368, less than a year after defeating Zhang Shicheng in Suzhou. With the Mongols driven north, the new emperor had the Yuan capital torn down and replaced with a new city he called Beiping ("Northern Capital"). Meanwhile, he kept his primary capital city at Nanjing, his military base since April 1356. The new dynasty would not achieve full unified control of the empire until 1381, fully thirteen years after its birth.

Difficult Beginnings

However much Hangzhou's gentry and literati welcomed the departure of the Mongol Yuan, they soon discovered that the founding Ming Emperor was not going to shower them with favors. To the contrary, Hongwu responded to Zhang Shicheng's supporters in Jiangnan with vengeance. Some literati and their families were called to Nanjing and imprisoned or executed, while others were banished to distant corners of the empire. Thousands more families from around Hangzhou and Suzhou were ordered to relocate wholesale to Fengyang (Anhui Province), the city of Zhu's birth, which he envisioned transforming into a "Central Capital."

For the gentry families still left residing in Zhang Shicheng's former kingdom, Hongwu reclassified their prime holdings as government land and imposed backbreaking taxes, ranging as high as seventy percent of the value of the crops those lands produced. The new emperor may have been intentionally impoverishing his former foes, but he was also unintentionally causing widespread abandonment of highly fertile land as well as rampant tax evasion and related forms of tax-avoiding corruption.

In the realm of civil administration, Hongwu reinstituted the civil service examinations in 1370, the traditional path to officialdom long dominated by the scholars of Zhejiang and Jiangsu Provinces. However, the Emperor became so dissatisfied by the hugely disproportionate share of degrees awarded to southern candidates that he disbanded the examinations for fourteen years. Student scholars and aspiring officials of the greater Hangzhou area were largely cut off from access to the career paths they still aggressively pursued, even despite the Emperor's penchant for irrational suspicions and his capricious execution of officials who displeased him.

Hongwu allowed the examinations to resume after 1384, but he remained permanently wary of the examination system. As late as the final year of his reign (1397), he was outraged to discover that all fifty-one candidates judged to have passed the highest-level *jinshi* exam were southerners. He ordered the examiners to review their assessments carefully, only to be informed that the same fifty-one southerners were still the winning participants. After having two of the examiners executed and ordering a final review, the results changed: sixty-one Northerners, zero Southerners.[4]

For the people of northern Zhejiang, and particularly the educated elites, Zhu Yuanzhang's thirty-year reign may have been among the most difficult of any peacetime imperial era. Suspicion (and secret police) reigned in the Nanjing Court. In Hongwu's eyes, everyone around him was a hidden traitor or a potential rival. Those accused were severely punished or executed; those even marginally associated with the guilty suffered similarly. For example, Zhao Mengfu's celebrated grandson, the Yuan painter Wang Meng, died in 1385 during a six-year imprisonment after being linked, erroneously as it turned out, to an alleged conspirator. Suzhou native Gao Qi (高启, 1336 - 1374), arguably his era's greatest poet, was cut in half at the waist simply for writing a congratulatory poem to one of Hongwu's own hand-picked governors.

Backward or Forward?

Zhu Yuanzhang brought a complex personal background to the imperial throne. Born into abject poverty, doubly orphaned by disease at age 16, forced into beggarhood as a wandering monk just to survive, barely literate, and physically odd-looking if not simply ugly, he conceived of his new realm in strict Confucianist terms. In his view, the family unit and clan were paramount, as were loyalty, filial piety, and commitment to one's native place from one generation to the next.

Zhu Yuanzhang's traditionalist inclinations and desire to control the Jiangnan elites led him at times to overreach on policy. He actively sought to turn the sociocultural clock backwards, to revert China to a static, Confucian-agrarian society by borrowing from "the classicist's paradigm of a two-level society—self-sufficient agriculturists, ruled and civilized by humane generalists."[5] In that world, farmers would farm, as would their sons and the sons of their sons. Likewise for the descendants of merchants and artisans. Zhu sought to limit travel as well, requiring that special permits be secured for all unofficial travel greater than thirty miles from one's home.[6] On the cusp of one of China's great commercial and cultural awakenings, the Ming founding emperor was purposefully seeking to induce a national coma.

The Zheng 郑 family of Pujiang County, Zhejiang Province, serves as an archetype of the Hongwu Emperor's vision of Chinese society, especially in family life and lineage. At least as far back as the 1120s, the clan progenitor, Zheng Yi (fl. 1127 – 1130), settled into this mountainous area about sixty miles south of Hangzhou and prospered. On his deathbed, he insisted that his sons share the same stove; that is, not divide up the family property.

This and other of Zheng Yi's prescriptions were eventually collected into a set of family guidelines by the founder's great-great grandson, Zheng Dezhang (1245 – 1305) and read aloud to the clan members at mandatory monthly meetings. Dezhang's son formalized this arrangement further by committing fifty-eight such regulations into a text, the *Zheng Family Instructions* (郑氏规范, *Zhengshi guifan*). Reportedly first published in 1338, the list of regulations expanded through the Southern Song and Yuan Dynasty eras into 168 separate guidelines or stipulations.[7]

The *Zheng Family Instructions* was handed down from generation to generation, each clan family having its own copy. In line with Zheng Yi's deathbed command, the clan strictly enforced the principles of common property and prohibitions against private property ownership laid out in their guidebook.[8] Inside their ancestral hall, the Zhengs inscribed ten characters that defined their basic ethical and life precepts: loyalty, faith, family, fraternity, propriety, justice, honesty, shame, farming, and reading.[9]

When the Hongwu Emperor learned of this family's filiality and adherence to Confucian precepts—the ideal family lineage, so unlike his own tragic experience—he delivered to their village an inscribed tablet that read, "Number One Family of Jiangnan" (江南第一家, *Jiangnan diyi jia*). Hongwu's praiseworthy celebration of Confucian principles and their personification in clans like the Zhengs helped re-establish the primacy of traditional Chinese values and eradicate memories of life under Mongol rule. To the present day, Pujiang celebrates the Zheng clan's unique heritage as "The First Family of Southern China." In 2003, for example, then-Zhejiang Party Secretary Xi Jinping 习近平 (1953 –) convened a group of provincial leaders and department heads at Pujiang to study the Zheng family's remarkable history.[10]

Moving Forward

It was Hongwu's son, the Yongle Emperor 永樂帝 (1360 – 1424, r. 1403 – 1424), who snapped the Chinese empire awake once again during his two-decade rule. Three of his major programs brought direct commercial and economic benefit to Hangzhou and most of northern Zhejiang Province:

- By restoring and improving the Grand Canal, the Yongle Emperor returned the great waterway to active use and Hangzhou to its role as the southern terminus and transshipment point;

- By moving the imperial capital to Beijing and constructing a spectacular new palace complex, the Forbidden City, he increased the importance of Jiangnan agriculture as well as the *caoyun* grain transport lifeline to the north; and

- By building and outfitting in the Jiangnan region one of the greatest naval fleets in pre-modern history—over three hundred treasure ships and 27,000 men, commanded by the eunuch Zheng He 郑和 (1371–1433)—Yongle stimulated recovery of a vital regional economy sorely pressed by his father's economic oppressions.

As noted previously, Zhang Shicheng shrank the city's physical size and reduced the number of land gates from thirteen to ten.[11] There were now two gates each on the north and south walls and three gates each on the eastern and western sides of the city. A popular folk song[12] of early Ming times demonstrated Hangzhou's commercial recovery by linking each gate to the type of flourishing market in its vicinity (listed clockwise from the northwest corner of the city wall):

- Wulin Gate 武林门 – fish
- Genshan Gate 艮山门 – cocoons
- Qingchun Gate 庆春门 – night soil (fertilizer)
- Qingtai Gate 清泰门 – salt
- Wangjiang Gate 望江门 – vegetables
- Houchao Gate 侯潮门 – alcohol and spirits
- Fengshan Gate 凤山门 – horses
- Qingbo Gate 清波门 – firewood
- Yongjin Gate 涌金门 – paddle boats (for West Lake)
- Qiantang Gate 钱塘门 – incense

Beyond his economically stimulating projects, the Yongle Emperor undertook an extraordinary scholarly project that benefited Hangzhou's scholars and publishing houses. In 1403, he initiated the most ambitious publication enterprise ever undertaken in China to that time: compilation of a vast encyclopedia that encompassed all of the Chinese world's knowledge. Employing well over two thousand examination graduates and scholars with access to countless manuscripts and printed works f rom all fields of study, the editors published the *Great Canon of the Yongle Reign* (永樂大典, *Yongle dadian*) in 1407, with a preface written by the Emperor himself.

Unlike anything of its kind before, the encyclopedia consisted of 11,095 volumes (22,938 *juan*, or scrolls), totaling more than fifty million characters drawn, mostly verbatim, from over 8,000 sources. The entire work was maintained at the Wenyuan Hall in the Forbidden City for the use of imperial scholars, senior court officials, and occasionally the Emperors themselves.[13]

A second, similar project undertaken under Yongle's reign specified the written works with which examination candidates (and hence, future officials) were expected to be familiar as the basis of principled Confucian government. This effort produced two massive works for intending scholars and scholar-officials, the *Complete Commentaries of the Four Books and Five Classics*[14] (五经四书大全, *Wujing sishu daquan*) and the *Great Collection on Nature and Principle* (性礼大全, *Xingli daquan*) addressing orthodox Confucian philosophy. The two books were printed and widely distributed across the realm, effectively transforming them into national examination study guides.

Yongle's successor[15] and grandson, Emperor Xuande 宣德帝 (r. 1426 – 1435), was also a much-welcomed patron of scholarship and the arts. In the first year of his reign, he instituted crucial changes in the civil service examination system that would benefit Jiangnan scholars and seal the region's recovery for the next four or five centuries.

Examinations for the highest-level metropolitan (*jinshi*) degree would be held every three years and reopened to all qualified candidates. Degree awards would be granted subject to a quota arrangement that allocated fifty-five percent of the degrees to "southerners," thirty-five percent to "northerners," and the final ten percent to "in-betweeners." Since these quotas placed no limits on ranking levels, Jiangnan scholars in the qualifying fifty-five percent could, and did, dominate the rankings in each triennial class of graduates, yielding to them a disproportionate share of the best position assignments and career tracks.

For the families of Shaoxing and Xiaoshan, Hangzhou and Jinhua, Jiaxing and Huzhou, the Yuan-to-Ming transition years had been long and often painfully difficult. Yet in 1425, they were poised for four centuries of cultural, scholarly, and governmental leadership. Their fellow citizens would likewise enjoy a previously unimagined productivity and prosperity befitting "heaven on earth."

Zhejiang Painters Advance the Arts

While Zhao Mengfu and the Four Great Masters of the Yuan opened the gateway to more individualistic and personally expressive painting styles, many artists in the first century of the Ming era still chose to look back instead at the classical landscape painting traditions of the Tang and Song dynasties. Out of a renewed sense of loyalism, some focused their attention on the court painters of the Southern Song Painting Academy in Hangzhou.

Modern art critics have noted that Southern Song Academy landscapes exhibited an idealized atmosphere of romance and nostalgia. Wen C. Fong, for example, attributed this softening view of a "Camelot-like realm" in part to escapism from the cold reality of the loss of the north as well as a change of artistic mood induced by "the more luxuriant south." Fong further concedes that while neither explanation, separately or in combination, is fully explanatory of these stylistic changes, both were at least contributory.[16]

In 12th- and 13th- Century Hangzhou, the works of Ma Yuan 马远 (c. 1160 – 1225) and Xia Gui 夏珪 (fl. 1195 – 1224)[17] dominated the Southern Song court's landscape painting. So strong was their artistic influence that the Academy's collective oeuvre became known as the Ma-Xia style. Two hundred years later, when Hangzhou native Dai Jin 戴进, (1388-1462) looked for a post-Yuan, anti-Mongol model upon which to build a Ming landscape painting style, he settled on a revival drawn from the Ma-Xia style.[18]

Even as a relative youth, Dai Jin established himself as a profoundly talented landscape and figure-painting artist. His soaring reputation soon brought him an invitation to join the cohort of imperial court painters in Beijing in service of the Xuande Emperor 宣德帝 (r. 1426 – 1435). Jealous of Dai's talents and the admiration he received from court officials, his artistic colleagues conspired against him. They scoured his past works to find harmless depictions which they transformed by envy-warped interpretation into anti-government sentiment. These attacks persisted until the Emperor himself was convinced of their legitimacy. Dai Jin fled the capital and returned to Hangzhou, resuming his painting there and attracting numerous students and followers. The eunuch who first recommended Dai to the court was not so fortunate; he was executed, political collateral damage.

Although he based his work on that of Ma Yuan and Xia Gui, Dai brought new life to the Southern Song Painting Academy style. In his paintings, the presentation of unified space was less important than the surface itself and the brushwork therein, prefiguring the subsequent literati obsession with spontaneity in brushwork. Dai Jin has been described as "a very versatile painter who drew inspiration from diverse sources [and who] sometimes painted precariously close to the edge of control, creating a distinctively kinesthetic, movement-filled style that was fresh and new."[19]

Dai exerted immense influence over the Hangzhou area painters who followed or succeeded him in the same Southern Song-inspired style. Collectively, their work became known as the Zhe School (浙派, Zhe pai) style for their common residence in and around Zhejiang Province. Dai Jin is regarded as the school's founder, although some art historians regard it less a school of painting and more a collective linked together by geography. In any event, their style gradually gave way to the literati-driven work centered on Shen Zhou 沈周 (1427 – 1509), Wen Zhengming 文征明 (1470 – 1559), Tang Yin 唐 (1470 – 1524), and others in Suzhou who formed the influential and more critically celebrated Wu School of Painting (吴派, Wu pai).

Early in his reign, the Hongwu Emperor sought aggressively to eradicate all traces of Mongol rule. In its place, he wished to restore Han and Tang Dynasty traditions and his own particular view of proper moral order. One vehicle for achieving his national regeneration drive involved designating a set of secular sacrificial rituals which he would perform on behalf of the people, as well as rituals to be regularly performed by local officials.

Such rituals, inscribed officially in the *Sacrificial Statutes* (祀典, *Sidian*), were conducted at shrines, altars, and temples dedicated to model individuals, nationally or more locally, from Chinese history.[20] These individuals ranged from the obvious—past emperors and great sages like Confucius and Mencius—to "loyal officials, brave soldiers, persons able to withstand natural disasters or ward off calamities, who toiled in the founding of the state or died in its service." Early in his reign, Hongwu designated as worthies a number of individuals who helped establish his dynasty, enshrining them in a Temple of Meritorious Individuals at Jiming Monastery in Nanjing.[21]

At West Lake, an obvious candidate for sacrificial enshrinement was **Yue Fei**. In the nearly three hundred years since Yue's death in 1141, the State had done precious little to memorialize the illustrious Song Dynasty hero. Several efforts by his 12th- and 13th-Century descendants to establish a Hangzhou-area temple or shrine in his honor had regrettably ended in abandonment or ruin. In the 1370s, Yue Fei's refurbished tomb site was formally incorporated into the *Sidian* in honor of his loyalty to the nation, but it once again felt into a derelict state by the 1450s.

Finally, during the reign of Emperor Tianshun 天順帝 (r. 1457 – 1464), Hangzhou Vice-Prefect Ma Wei successfully pressed the throne for more imperial recognition of Yue Fei's loyalty and more formal support for Yue's tomb as a site of *sidian* ritual sacrifices. As part of that effort, Ma oversaw renovation of the temple building still extant on the site and even paid for repairs from his own salary. He was also the first official to represent visually and physically the story of Yue Fei's death due to Qin Hui's intrigues, albeit symbolically, by planting a cypress tree split down the middle. The character for cypress is the same *hui* 桧 as Qin's given name, so the severed tree standing before the temple represented a metaphorical drawing and quartering of the evil minister.

Yue's tomb site was embellished over the next half-century with inscribed steles and an arch, but its most notorious addition arrived in 1513, 372 years after Yue Fei's death. Three bronze statues depicted Qin Hui, his wife Lady Wang 秦王氏 (? – ?), and a co-conspirator in Yue's death, Moqi Xie 万俟卨 (1083 – 1157), each sculpted in submissive, kneeling positions. From the start, the three metal figures were so persistently and vigorously beaten and spit or urinated upon by angry visitors that they had to be replaced by cast iron replicas during the reign of the Wanli Emperor 萬曆帝 (r. 1572 – 1620). Around that same time, a fourth statue representing the complicit minister Zhang Jun 張俊 (1086 – 1154) rounded out the tableau of guilty parties.

Various honors and further embellishments accumulated at Yue Fei's tomb site throughout

160

the Ming era. In the 1530s, officials installed a stele alongside the split cypress. Inscribed in the stone were the four characters that by legend Yue Fei's mother had tattooed onto her young son's back: 精忠报国 (*Jin zhong bao guo*, "Serve the dynasty with unswerving loyalty"). In the 17th Century, more shrines and statues were added: first for Yue Fei's son, Yue Yun, then for his parents and daughter and continuing in an ever-widening circle of family and others associated with the hero's legend. Access to the temple was eased by land purchases as well, creating the foundations for what today is one of West Lake's most celebrated tourist sites.

The death and posthumous memorialization of another West Lake hero of the Ming era, Hangzhou native Yu Qian 于谦 (1398 – 1457, *jinshi* 1421), eerily parallels that of Yue Fei. During the reign of the Xuande Emperor 宣德帝 (r. 1425 – 1435), Yu's successful suppression of rebellions in the west gained him a high-level position in Shanxi Province. However, the Emperor's sudden death in 1435 led to the enthronement of his eight-year-old son as Emperor Yingzong 英宗帝 (r. 1435 – 1449) and the pernicious rise in influence of the eunuch Wang Zhen 王振 (d. 1449).

The boy-emperor Yingzong grew up fascinated by military exploits and aspired to make his mark in history through legendary conquests. When a new Mongol rise in the west developed in the late 1440s, Wang Zhen persuaded Yingzong, now 21 years old, to lead a pre-emptive strike against a 20,000-man force advancing on Datong (Shanxi Province) under the command of the tribal ruler Esen Taishi (1407 – 1455). Suppressing an emerging Mongol threat (reminiscent of the Yuan Dynasty) would earn the young ruler military glory and the people's gratitude.

Yingzong amassed a force said to have been 500,000 strong and personally led them north toward Datong in early August, 1449, accompanied by Wang Zhen as field marshal. The expedition was ill-conceived from the beginning, and the Ming forces were poorly organized. At an encampment at Tumu, Esen routed Yingzong's rear guard and surrounded the Ming army on September 1. Despite their overwhelming numerical superiority, nearly the entire 500,000-man army was obliterated. All the Ming generals lost their lives, Wang Zhen was killed (possibly by his own forces), and Emperor Yingzong was captured as a prisoner of war.

Panic-stricken courtiers in Beijing argued for immediate relocation of the capital to Nanjing, but Yu Qian staunchly opposed adding embarrassing flight to the already humiliating defeat at Tumu. Instead, he organized a strengthened defense at the capital and successfully fended off further Mongol advances. He also supported the ascension of Emperor Yingzong's younger brother to the throne as the Jingtai Emperor 景泰帝 (r. 1449 – 1457). Consequently, the value of the human asset Esen had planned to ransom back to the Ming court suddenly plummeted. After a year of negotiations in which Beijing demonstrated no serious interest in purchasing Yingzong's freedom, the Mongol leader simply released his captive in 1450 and returned north to his homeland.

Remaining the discarded ex-Emperor did not fit into Yingzong's plans, however. With the assistance of his former courtiers and followers, he organized a coup and retook the throne on February 11, 1457, adopting his second reign name as the Tianshun Emperor 天順帝 (r. 1457 – 1464). His younger brother and temporary predecessor was dead within a month, but he outlasted the man who had saved Beijing. Yu Qian was executed as a traitor only five days after Yingzong reclaimed the throne. He was quietly entombed at the family cemetery on Three Platform Hill (三台山, Santai shan) at the southwest corner of West Lake.

Fittingly, after the Yingzong/Tianshun Emperor died at age 37, his son and successor, the Chenghua Emperor 成化帝 (r. 1464 – 1487), rehabilitated Yu Qian posthumously. The Emperor also agreed to a proposal from Yu Qian's son to treat his father in a manner similar to Yue Fei, including a shrine and twice-yearly ritual sacrifices in accordance with the *Sidian*. In 1466, he even wrote in an imperial edict that he "cherished (Yu's) loyalty in his heart." A memorial temple and an inscribed stele were erected at Yu's tomb site in 1489. Periodic restorations such as those in 1537, 1560, 1590, and 1869 helped preserve the site into the modern era, with more recent renovations of the tomb, walkway, stone animals, archway and memorial temple in 1998, on the 600th anniversary of Yu Qian's birth.[22]

For literati throughout the Ming empire, West Lake was increasingly becoming more than just a place of scenic beauty or Buddhist contemplation. The lake and its surroundings were developing into an inspiring source of secular observance and patriotic remembrance, one that could conjure up thoughts (and poems) about heroic men and heroic deeds, about a glorious past, a troubled present, or an uncertain future.

...and Four Worthies...

The more Hangzhou grew and prospered under Ming rule, the more the city depended on West Lake for fresh water, and the more challenging grew the lake's maintenance. Surprisingly, land management around the lake became equally as important as water management due to private agricultural encroachment on the muddy but highly fertile shoreline. These unauthorized "land grabs," many of them performed by rich and powerful families, persistently threatened the lake's physical size and carrying capacity.

Failure of proper civil administration during the Yuan era, a hallmark of Mongol rule in the 13th Century, had only compounded the problem. West Lake was clogged with unrestrained water chestnut growth, and farming of fish, shrimp, and crabs occupied some sections of the lake. Illicit reclamation and cultivation of shallow shoreline areas had become so institutionalized that taxes were actually levied on those illegally transformed plots. Officials estimated that over 3,800 *mu* (more than 625 acres) of West Lake land had been expropriated and should be returned to the lake to restore its Song-era carrying capacity.

By the early 1500s, West Lake's deteriorating condition had reached a critical point. During periods of summertime heat or drought, lake waters regularly proved insufficient for badly needed irrigation in the fields east of Hangzhou. Equally problematic, waters normally drawn from West Lake were not reliably available to keep the city's canals adequately filled, seriously inhibiting routine urban transport and commerce.

In 1502, Sichuanese native Yang Mengying 楊孟瑛 (1459 – 1518) arrived in Hangzhou as Prefect, a position he retained for the unusually long term of seven years. Quickly recognizing the severity of the situation and West Lake's importance to the city's health and vitality, Yang studied the circumstances surrounding its use. The problem was more than a technical one, and the solution was more complex than mere silt dredging. Deeply entrenched interests would fight to preserve the status quo, a situation Yang summarized by writing that "benefits have accumulated for several dozen families but harm has been bequeathed to thousands and myriads of households."[23]

In his memorial to the throne requesting the necessary funds for his West Lake restoration project, Yang carefully laid out the history of earlier dredging and renovation projects and identified the existing problems created by the lake's deteriorated condition. He then outlined the process by which misappropriated land would be reclaimed (and for which amnesty would be granted and relocation costs compensated), presented cost and labor estimates for the work, and described how the project would be managed and the funds accounted for. He also quietly collected the support of other important officials and influential gentry and scholars to offset the objections that would surely arise from the powerful families with financial interests in the illegally confiscated land.

The Hongzhi Emperor 弘治帝 (r. 1487 – 1505) approved Yang's memorial, and work began in the early spring of 1506. The project took seven months to complete, employing 7,000 laborers.[24] The results were both restorative and transformative as West Lake was returned to its earlier size: "Dwellings, fields and orchards that had covered large stretches of the area…were replaced by the glimmering waters of the lake."[25] The project dredged enough mud and silt not only to restore and widen the deteriorated Su Causeway but also to build yet another six-bridge, north-south embankment parallel to and west of Su Shi's to discourage future encroachments. This last crosswalk over West Lake came to be known as Yang Causeway (杨公堤, Yanggongdi) in honor of its builder.

During his term of office, Yang Mengying also received approval to rebuild the badly dilapidated Three Worthies Shrine, which honored the contributions of Bai Juyi, Su Shi, and Lin Bu (he of the plum trees and cranes) to the character and beauty of West Lake. As part of the project, Yang further proposed adding to the shrine Li Bi, Tang-era builder of the original Six Wells, and renaming the structure the Shrine of Four Worthies. Zhou Xin, Hangzhou's city god, and Yang Mengying himself were subsequently added to the group, to be honored at what would be suitably renamed the Shrine of Six Worthies.

Yang Mengying's genius lay not only in hydrology but in his ability simultaneously to navigate the halls of influence and power. He restored West Lake's besmirched scenery to a beauty that reminded Ming literati once again of the fabled Xi Shi, made up or plain. He succeeded, and increasingly, they came—and invited their fellow elites to do likewise.

...and a City God

Legends and early Ming writings in Hangzhou tell a remarkable tale of supernatural spirit possession at the site of the City God's Temple on Wushan. According to those stories, a Daoist priest was suddenly possessed by a spirit who announced during the ritual celebration of the "old city god's" birthday that the heavenly lords had ordered him to be Hangzhou's new city god. The spirit gave his name as Zhou Xin 周新, a recently deceased surveillance commissioner[26] in the reign of the Yongle Emperor 永乐帝 (r. 1403 – 1424).[27]

The Chinese concept of a city god was an eminently practical one, dating back at least to the Tang Dynasty. Known as "gods of walls and moats" (城隍神, *chenghuang shen*), city gods were not gods or immortals in the traditional sense of the word. Rather, they were historical figures of the past, men who demonstrated extraordinary character and achievement in their time by demonstrating such traits as wisdom, integrity, loyalty, self-sacrifice, or service to the people. In most cases, they were local people, if not by birth then at least by residency or official position. Having been humans, they ranked at a relatively lower level of the heavenly hierarchy.

As the otherworld counterpart to this-world city magistrates and administrators, city gods were responsible for "all the spirits of the local dead, detection of good and evil among the living...and in the discovery of injustices in the lives of those already dead." Just as the local administrator "was the emperor's delegate to the people, the City God...was Heaven's delegate to the people and to their dead."[28] While they did not necessarily possess god-like powers, their earthly accomplishments were believed to give them influence with the more powerful heavenly gods. City gods were therefore called upon periodically to help protect their cities: to bring rain during droughts and end rain during flooding, relieve epidemics and insect infestations, facilitate good harvests, and generally promote the city's welfare when called upon in times of special need.

As far back as the Song Dynasty era, Hangzhou's city god was Sun Ben; little appears to be known about this individual. His temple, the Chenghuang Miao (城隍庙, City God's Temple) was originally located on Phoenix Hill. Around the time the Southern Song palace complex was constructed on that hill, however, the City God's Temple was relocated to nearby Wushan Hill. Sun Ben remained the city's resident protector and heavenly intermediary for at least the next 250 years until Zhou Xin's rather abrupt paranormal usurpation.

While not particularly famous, Zhou Xin's life was hardly without merit. His reputation as an honest and forthright official preceded his arrival in Hangzhou, as did admiration for his keen insight in divining judicial truths and resolving cases cleverly and justly. To some, he was the reincarnation of the legendary Judge Bao Zheng 包拯 (999 – 1062), a Song-era Sherlock Holmes, an investigator and case-solver. Lang Ying (b. 1487), a native of Hangzhou, described Zhou Xin in glowing terms:

> He was incorruptible and enlightened, resolute and honest. He removed local strongmen and heard cases of the aggrieved, often attending to the affairs

164

of unjustly wronged souls that had nobody to take care of them. Within he gained a reputation for being "cold-faced and cool as iron"....Outside people called him divinely enlightened.[29]

Zhou Xin's unjust end came at the hands of a corrupt military officer. When Zhou had a subordinate officer arrested for taking bribes, the accused's commander leveled a series of false accusations against Zhou, resulting in the latter's imprisonment and beating. When Zhou fiercely protested his innocence before the throne, Emperor Yongle injudiciously ordered his execution. Judging by Yongle's later support for Zhou's elevation as a city god, the accused's final words must have pierced the Emperor's conscience: "In life I am a straight official, in death I will be a straight ghost!"[30]

In 1503, the City God's Temple underwent major renovation in conjunction with special pleas to Zhou Xin to intercede with the Lord of Heaven for drought relief. The official in charge of that renovation was none other than future West Lake Worthy Yang Mengying.

Pirates Come Ashore

Even before Zhu Yuanzhang prevailed as imperial successor to the Yuan Dynasty, coastal Zhejiang suffered the predations of Fang Guozhen, the pirate-warlord of the southeastern coast. Fang and his followers had been raiding coastal towns and shipping lanes since 1348, seizing control over large cities like Ningbo and Wenzhou in 1355 and Shaoxing in 1358. In 1367, he surrendered to the new Ming Emperor, turning over a force of nine thousand soldiers, fourteen thousand seamen, and more than four hundred ships[31] that assisted in Zhu Yuanzhang's conquest of Fujian Province.

Despite the addition of Fang's naval force, the Ming Dynasty's lack of naval defense left towns and villages up and down the eastern coast exposed to sea-borne raiders. Smuggling flourished as well, depriving the state of tax revenues. In one decidedly non-military approach to reducing both scourges, Emperor Hongwu ordered the residents of Zhejiang Province to abandon the coast entirely and move as much as twenty miles inland. His son and successor, the Jianwen Emperor 建文帝 (r. 1398 – 1402) took an even more radical approach by banning foreign trade altogether.

Illicit trade, smuggling, and occasional Japanese raids continued into the 1400s, with Chinese merchant families becoming an active and integral part of these affairs. With little or no help from the central government, local officials carried the burden of dealing with smuggling and raiding, or making their own arrangements to benefit from it. When the celebrated Korean official and travel diarist Ch'oe Pu landed unexpectedly near Ningbo in 1488 after three storm-swept days at sea and a week of sail-less drifting, he described his biggest survival challenge as repeatedly having to convince local officials in Ningbo and Shaoxing that he was not a Japanese raider.

Ch'oe Pu's diary made no mention of inland pirate raids as he passed through Yuyao, Shaoxing, and Hangzhou on his escorted trip north to Beijing. In 1488, such activity was mostly in shipping lanes or along near-coastal villages. The larger market or port towns along the northern shores of Hangzhou Bay, such as Haining 海宁, Ganpu 澉浦, Haiyan 海盐, and Zhapu 乍浦, remained relatively free of bandit incursions as well. They had been well provided with rammed-earth and brick-faced walls more than a century earlier as part of the coastal defense system established by the Hongwu Emperor.

Into the 1520s and 1530s, coastal piracy and smuggling grew more widespread and threatening despite (and because of) repeated imperial bans against foreign trade. Local civil and military officials did little to control the problem, since they and others among the local gentry and merchant class either participated in the illicit activity or at least benefited from it, as did any number of common people who worked on the merchant ships. One pirate leader captured by imperial troops in 1534 had amassed a veritable flotilla of over fifty large ships, preying on the Zhejiang coastline for years. Yet local officials who tried his case were so lenient in their sentencing that the Emperor was forced to intervene.[32] Self-interest at nearly every local level simply overwhelmed efforts to enforce laws or imperial edicts.

Three major changes in southeast coastal piracy occurred in the 1540s that for Beijing transformed a troublesome local problem into a serious national threat. First, raiders who had formerly operated in small, independent bands recognized the benefits of cooperating, of acting in larger, more concentrated forces. Second, these larger groups found more readily defensible bases in the Zhoushan Islands, not far off the coast of Ningbo. Third, and perhaps most notoriously in the historical records, Japanese warriors began joining their Chinese counterparts. Before long, the pirate gangs would become known as *wokou* 倭寇, a derogatory term for the Japanese participants that loosely translated as "dwarf pirates" but served as well to deflect awareness of the generally majority participation of native Chinese in the looting and killing.[33]

By 1547, Emperor Jiajing 嘉靖 (r. 1521 – 1567) responded to memorials describing out-of-control piracy in Zhejiang and Fujian Provinces by appointing Zhu Wan 朱紈 (1494 – 1550) as military governor. Zhu's charge from the court to eradicate the pirates was doomed before it began, however. He was instructed to resolve the problem of banditry not by a military policing action but by putting a halt to all foreign trade. In effect, Zhu was not ordered to punish the perpetrators of smuggling and raiding but to suppress the trading activity from which the richest and most powerful local officials, merchants, and gentry profited. Intentionally or otherwise, he had been set up to fail. And yet, he nearly succeeded.

Zhu's first investigative stop was Zhangzhou, near Xiamen in Fujian Province, in November 1547. There he discovered a government military force in utter disarray: undermanned, undisciplined, and poorly equipped. Of the ten ships reported to the court for this outpost, only two were even serviceable. He also discovered just how deeply entrenched illicit foreign trade had become among the richest merchants and wealthiest families. Their flagrant disregard of court edicts had gone so far, they had fraudulently represented the construction of ferry boats for the public good as cover to build ocean-going merchant ships.

166

Zhu Wan's immediate response was brazenly undiplomatic and likely sealed his ultimate fate. He announced that, effective immediately, any individuals departing by sea would be summarily executed upon capture. By publicly naming some of the wealthy persons involved in the illegal trade, he turned a host of powerful families into adversaries who would pounce on the first opportunity to petition the court for his removal. His approach also drove the overseas trade back underground into smuggling, activity against which he did not have sufficient coastal resources to police.

Despite the odds, his strict enforcement policy, backed by a strengthened military and naval force, made surprising progress in suppressing banned foreign trade and piracy. In June 1548, his naval fleet conducted a successful surprise attack at Shuangyu 雙嶼, a pirate port in the Zhongshan Islands, destroying two dozen ships and rendering the port as unusable as they could manage. He memorialized the throne on his progress, rather undiplomatically writing "that it was easy to get rid of foreign pirates but difficult to get rid of Chinese pirates, that it was still easy to get rid of China's coastal pirates, but particularly difficult to get rid of China's pirates attired in caps and gowns."[34] Influential officials in the Jiajing Court were not amused and began actively arguing for Zhu's powers to be substantially curtailed if not removed altogether.

In March 1549, Zhu Wan scored a smashing victory at a major pirate base on the southern coast of Fujian Province, capturing more than two hundred pirates, 112 of whom were Chinese.[35] Exercising what he believed to be his rightful authority, he ordered ninety-six of the Chinese captives immediately beheaded.

Zhu's opponents in Beijing found their opening in this mass beheading. They argued that Zhu had seriously overstepped the bounds of his authority by executing without imperial permission nearly one hundred Chinese people who were just trying to make a living from trade. They successfully petitioned the Jiajing Emperor for Zhu's dismissal pending further investigation. As uncompromising as ever, Zhu committed suicide before the investigation could be completed. He was posthumously sentenced to death but formally rehabilitated in 1587.

Little was done to address the smuggling and piracy issues for the next six years after Zhu Wan's death. Trading transformed into raiding, however, when land-based merchants began abusing their positional leverage over the sea-borne traders by refusing to make payments or depriving them of access to food supplies. In 1552 and 1553, the area around Shanghai was repeatedly attacked by raiders, including the nearby market towns of Baoshan and Jiading.

Shanghai's first city walls were erected in 1553 after suffering its first *wokou* attack that year, and cities in Zhejiang began taking similar measures when they fell under assault. Already-walled coastal cities on Hangzhou Bay like Haiyan, Zhapu, Ganpu, and Haining reinforced their walls and added towers and other defensive measures between 1553 and 1555.[36] Pinghu, five miles from Hangzhou Bay and less than fifteen miles from Jiaxing, became in 1553 the first inland town to suffer damage from pirate attack. The city quickly marshalled its resources and had walls and a moat constructed by the following year.

Pirate attacks at Jiaxing in 1554 did not reach inside the city walls, but they caused substantial damage to suburbs that had developed as the city's population outgrew its walled area. In 1554 – 1555, city officials elected to improve Jiaxing's suburban defenses by constructing six new forts to guard approaches to the city and control access to the Grand Canal. Additional projects to raise the height of the city walls from fifteen feet to twenty-six feet and rebuild twenty-seven towers were completed in 1560 as long-term defense against *wokou* raids.[37] Several other inland cities built their first walls in 1554 and 1555, and the Grand Canal city of Tongxiang (Jiaxing Prefecture) finished its new walls in 1556 just days before first being attacked.[38]

While the larger walled cities were fending off attacks between 1552 and 1555—including even the great city of Hangzhou—market towns and smaller villages in the region suffered. Between 1553 and 1555, Xiaoshan incurred repeated pirate assaults, from east at the Qiantang River mouth westward to Xixing and the Xiaoshan district. Walls were erected at the county seat between December 1553 and April 1554, but the pirates returned again along the Xiaoshan plain in the fall of 1554, focusing particularly on wealthy country residences.[39]

In 1555, each of Zhejiang's six coastal prefectures—Jiaxing, Hangzhou, Shaoxing, Ningbo, Taizhou, and Wenzhou—suffered pirate raids, as did Huzhou. Hangzhou city withstood assault that year, but imperial troops remained inside the city walls while surrounding towns and villages were pillaged and thousands of people were massacred. When pirate groups realized that their approach could be seen from Leifeng Pagoda, they attacked and set its outer wooden structure afire. The exterior was never restored, leaving the brick shell a fire-scorched red that appeared to glow at sunset.

Unfortunately, Zhu Wan's successors proved serially ineffectual. Finally in 1556, the court appointed Hu Zongxian 胡宗憲 (1512 – 1565, *jinshi* 1538)[40] to the post of Supreme Military Commander, responsible for the entire eastern coastal defense, from Shandong Province to Canton. Hu's previous appointment had involved suppression of a Miao rebellion in Guizhou, useful military experience as well as valuable first-hand knowledge of the Miao peoples' fighting skills.

Hu Zongxian arrived in Zhejiang the year before his promotion and achieved noteworthy successes against the *wokou*, in part by subterfuge and in part by importing Miao fighters into his army. Hu initially targeted Xu Hai 徐海 (d. 1556), a former Buddhist monk in a Hangzhou temple and now one of the two major leaders of pirate armies.

The early months of 1556 were nearly disastrous. Xu Hai initiated several landings to draw Ming forces away from Zhapu (on Hangzhou Bay), where he intended to land more than ten thousand raiders. Unable to breach Zhapu's reinforced walls, Xu marched inland to Wuzhen, where he could then move on either Jiaxing to his east or Huzhou to his west. After several costly victories in the Wuzhen area, an injured Xu Hai headed with a depleted force for Tongxiang. The raiders camped outside the city walls and settled in for a prolonged siege to starve out the city while raiding the countryside.[41]

By enticing Xu with promises of gifts, imperial pardon, and peaceful surrender, Hu Zongxian was able to end the siege of Tongxiang. His negotiations with Xu Hai also sowed discord and distrust among other pirate leaders until they themselves overthrew and assassinated Xu Hai at Pinghu. Hu's Miao forces advanced on the squabbling pirates at that point, killing up to 1,600 *wokou* and executing their remaining leaders. Not long after this victory, the Emperor promoted Hu to supreme commander.

During the pirate Xu Hui's siege of Tongxiang in the fall of 1556, Hu Zongxian had been joined by a capable new commander named Qi Jiguang 戚继光 (1528 – 1588). Hu was impressed with Qi's abilities and petitioned for his promotion as an assistant regional commander.[42]

They complemented one another perfectly. Hu developed and executed a creative but aggressive repression strategy while Qi formed well-disciplined new regiments from Shaoxing-area recruits and refined his field tactics to better suit the pirates' hand-to-hand combat style. Still not satisfied with the battlefield results he was getting from his troops, Qi abandoned his recruitment from the Shaoxing area in favor of men from Yiwu, whom he viewed as more amenable to military discipline.

To eliminate Wang Zhi 王直 (d. 1560), a merchant turned pirate with a massive fleet of ships, Hu accepted the terms of Wang's offer to surrender only to incarcerate him in Hangzhou until the Emperor ordered Wang's beheading. Hu and Qi then organized a mass assault on the *wokou* stronghold on Zhoushan Island in 1558. While not entirely successful, the attack inflicted enough damage to force the pirates to abandon Zhoushan and scatter southward to Fujian Province, where Qi Jiguang took up the fight.

Qi's forces drove the pirates out of their stronghold near Taizhou in 1559, then advanced into Fujian in 1562 to eliminate several more bandit groups. His successes in the southeast led to more senior assignments battling Mongols in the north and repairing the Great Wall, enhancing its defenses by constructing over one thousand new watchtowers. After 1572, he drew upon his troop training experiences to write one of ancient China's most important military training manuals, the *Records of Military Training* (練兵實紀, *Lianbing shiji*).

Smuggling and piracy would continue plaguing eastern coastal China long after Hu Zongxian and Qi Jiguang suppressed the worst raiding of the 1550s and 1560s. As recently as September 1935, a bizarre newspaper report from Hangzhou told of a coastal raid in which forty bandits disguised as beggars kidnapped all thirty-one children from a village school, resulting in a sea chase in which only ten of the children were recovered and one perished.[43]

From the banning of foreign trade by the Hongwu and Jianwen Emperors and the rise of illicit foreign trade to the transformation of smuggling into outright piracy and violent pillaging of towns and cities, the future of the Chinese empire was playing itself out in coastal Jiangsu, Zhejiang, and Fujian Provinces. The Hongwu Emperor's earlier vision of a static, agrarian society could not withstand the irresistible economic pull of trade and commerce and the more vibrant and mobile society that would accompany it.

Commerce and Commercialization

When the Korean official Ch'oe Pu passed through Hangzhou for a several days' stay on his escorted way to Beijing, he remarked in his diary about the vibrant economy he witnessed in 1488:

> Houses stand in solid rows, and the gowns of the crowds seem like screens. The markets pile up gold and silver; the people amass beautiful clothes and ornaments. Foreign ships stand as thick as the teeth of a comb, and in the streets wine shops and music halls front directly each on another. There are flowers that do not fade through the four seasons and the scenery of everlasting spring all the year round. It truly seems a different world, as people say.[44]

By the early 1500s, agrarian society was giving way to an ever more urbanized one. The emergent commercial economy was based less on the sale of surplus goods beyond the needs for subsistence, and increasingly on production intended for sale at a profit. For urban residents, traveling merchants, and rural farmers producing agricultural goods or handicrafts, "The food they ate was what they bought, not what they grew."[45] Peasants who specialized in agricultural production or sericulture could also add to their farming income with secondary occupations such as embroidering, raising silkworms or mulberry trees, or operating a household loom to weave silk or cotton. Throughout Jiangnan, increased commercialization took advantage of a well-developed regional water transport network that facilitated the movement of goods and supported the development of market towns.

This societal transformation required a logistical lubricant, a vibrant merchant network to move handicrafts and surpluses to where they were needed or wanted. However, the development of a thriving merchant class required overcoming the stigma inherent in the centuries-old Confucian social model of *simin* 四民, the four categories of the people, which placed merchants (商, *shang*) at the bottom, beneath gentry-officials (士, *shi*), peasants (农, *nong*), and artisans (工, *gong*). An early-Ming handbook for magistrates expanded this list to add new occupations, but the new ordering—"officials, soldiers, doctors, diviners, gentry, peasants, artisans, and merchants"—still "managed to place the merchants in the lowest position."[46]

As commerce developed, this semi-official caste system shifted, elevating merchants to a position closer to scholars. The stigma of buying and selling relaxed as merchants grew wealthy, owned property, and increasingly vied with the well-educated for status, influence, and respectability. They lived comfortably, even luxuriously. By purchasing and collecting paintings, calligraphy, or antiquities of value, they could also aspire to the heightened cultural status of literati-officials.

Growing wealth in Jiangsu and Zhejiang Provinces enabled both scholarly and gentry families to more easily sacrifice one or more sons' time for, and absorb the associated expenses of, examination system preparation. As a consequence, candidates from both provinces came increasingly during the Ming and subsequent Qing eras to dominate the national competition for the coveted metropolitan (*jinshi*) degrees that paved the way to high official careers. By one analysis, of the 26,747 *jinshi* degrees granted in the Qing Dynasty era (1644 – 1911), Zhejiang candidates garnered 2,808 (10.5%) and Jiangsu's scholars captured 2,929 (11.0%). Combined, they totaled well over one-fifth of the national total for the entire Qing era.[47]

Needless to say, Zhejiang's *jinshi* winners did not come exclusively from Hangzhou. The late-Ming literatus Yuan Hongdao 袁宏道 (1568 – 1610) from Hubei Province commented poetically about the extraordinary number of provincial (*juren*) degree holders he observed in Shaoxing, all of them eligible to compete for *jinshi* degrees if they chose.

> I've long heard of Shanyin County,
> Today I'm here to see for myself.
> Their boat is square, their women's shoes tiny and pointy.
> More numerous than carp, the place is swarming with literati.[48]

In northern Zhejiang, silk continued as the area's primary industry. Raw silk was produced in the countryside, particularly in the rural areas surrounding Huzhou and Jiaxing and northward toward Suzhou. Farming families practiced sericulture in the manner of animal husbandry: purchasing sheets of silkworm eggs, raising silkworms from larvae, carefully tending their nutritional and environmental needs until they formed cocoons, and finally harvesting the cocoons before they hatched. Landowners planted thousands of mulberry trees, the leaves of which fed the growing larvae and encourage their maturation. Still other households undertook the laborious process of drawing the cocoon fibers into precious silk threads, from which others produced raw silk.

Weaving of the finest silk cloth and production of silk goods for high-end trade or imperial use took place in the largest cities. The early Ming government managed more than two dozen Imperial Silk Weaving Factories, of which thirteen were located in Zhejiang and Jiangsu Provinces. The most important factories initially operated in Beijing and Nanjing, but by the second half of the 15th Century, the three Imperial Silk Weaving Factories in Hangzhou, Suzhou, and Nanjing became the empire's most important sites.

Individual cities also developed concentrations of local handicraft production of high quality and national reputation. For example, Hangzhou became famous for its scissors[49] and oil-paper umbrellas, while the ink brushes (湖笔, *hubi*) manufactured in Huzhou and nearby Shanlian Town achieved an unsurpassed reputation throughout the empire.[50] The Longjing (Dragon Well) tea grown in Hangzhou's western hills was deemed one of China's finest, while Shaoxing's yellow-shaded rice wine known as 绍兴酒 (*Shaoxing jiu*) or just "*huang jiu*" (黄菊, "yellow wine") was widely regarded as among the top-level spirits in the nation. So enduring were these reputations and the associated production skills passed down over generations that in every case above, their elevated reputations persist in China to the present day.[51]

With the Ming-era expansion of trade and commerce came rising incomes and opportunities for leisure-time activity and conspicuous consumption. In Hangzhou, West Lake increasingly served less for crop production or fish farming and more for quiet Nature appreciation in the hills or on the water, visiting historical sites, or singing and drinking on pleasure boats. The lake area was already long recognized as a place of notable scenic views; the renowned Ten Views defined West Lake's "must-see" vistas as early as 1240.[52]

As more non-locals arrived on sightseeing excursions or religious pilgrimages to the temples surrounding the lake, inns, teahouses, restaurants, and hostels rose to meet their needs. One measure of Hangzhou's growing reputation as a tourism venue was the publication of West Lake travel texts organized by different touring routes. In the late 11th Century (1089 – 1090), Hangzhou native Yang Pan 杨蟠(1027 - ?) paired with Anhui-born Guo Xiangzhen 郭祥正 (1035 – 1113) to create *Matching Yang Pan's One Hundred Poems on West Lake*, (和杨蟠西湖百咏, *He Yang Pan Xihu baiyong*), a collection of paired poems to celebrate one hundred different locales and scenes of West Lake.[53]

Two centuries later, Hangzhou native Dong Sigao 董嗣杲 (active 1260 – 1278) borrowed Yang's and Guo's literary framework to create a "poetic walking guide" or "geo-poetic collection"[54] for one hundred sites and scenes at 13th-Century West Lake. A minor Song Dynasty official who chose Daoist monkhood on West Lake's Solitary Island over service to the Mongol Yuan, Dong prefaced each of his poems with a brief, gazetteer-like note "to inform his readers about the practices of site naming…or to provide practical spatial information useful for navigating from place to place along the lake."[55]

Titled simply *One Hundred Poems on West Lake* (西湖百咏, *Xihu Baiyong*), Dong's work led his readers on a counterclockwise sightseeing circuit of West Lake's famous locales and scenes in poetic form, "using the format of a pedestrian tour around the lake as the organizational scheme for his collection."[56] His one hundred poems did not constitute a touring guide *per se*, but their contents reflected the way sightseers of different social classes might "consume" the West Lake scenery and certainly prefigured the advent of books designed explicitly as tourism guides for the lake.

One of the earliest such guidebooks was the *Record of Touring and Sightseeing at West Lake* (西湖遊覽志, *Xihu youlan zhi*) by Hangzhou native Tian Rucheng 田汝成 (1503 – 1557), published in 1547. Another came from Shaoxing native Zhang Dai 張岱 (1597 – c. 1684), who provided his own tour routes and commentaries to guide visitors. Yet Zhang also complained about the very same tourists who were his guidebook's intended audience. He welcomed those among the literati and official classes who could properly appreciate the lake's natural beauty and its historical and cultural essence, but he disparaged those who treated the lake no differently from a teahouse or a brothel in the entertainment quarters. As for commoners, Zhang's views were captured on his pilgrimage to the island of Putuoshan, where he complained of the "unwashed, halitotic, defecating, urinating" crowd.[57]

Yu the Great's Successor Tames the Yellow River

Whether historians regard Yu the Great as man or myth,[58] there is no doubting the historicity of his celebrated Ming Dynasty successor, Pan Jixun 潘季馴 (1521 – 1595), the Huzhou native who tamed the Yellow River. For dozens of centuries, the mighty river celebrated as the cradle of Chinese civilization had also, and all too often, been the bane of its people. The source of the river's name comes from the yellowish silt carried from the Loess Plain in Shaanxi Province, measuring sixty percent or more of the river's downstream flow volume. From this constant deposition of silt onto a continuously rising river bed have come the events that caused the Yellow River to be known as "China's Sorrow" (中国的痛, *Zhongguo de tong*).

By one estimate, the past two thousand years have seen more than fifty major floods, myriad lesser floods, 1,500 or more embankment breaches that caused local flooding, and twenty or more shifts in the river's course.[59] Until the mid-16th Century, water management on the middle and lower Yellow River consisted largely of embankments to contain the water flow and periodic dredging to lower the river bed. Canals or channels were sometimes constructed in an effort to "drain off" some of the water-flow, but the number of floods and river course changes alone are sufficient measure of these efforts' overall inefficacy. The river remained its own master.

For centuries, the Yellow River had followed various courses to empty into the Bohai Sea, above the Shandong Peninsula. However, when some of the river dikes were intentionally ruptured in a failed effort to block the Jurchen Jin advance on the Song empire in 1128, the river branched southward to join the Huai River and flow into the South China Sea. The Yellow River's northern and southern branches co-existed until 1494, when the Ming court authorized a project to direct the river's flow entirely into the southern branch. Like the many past attempts at taming those waters, this one did little more than create a complicated new set of problems that endangered operation of the Grand Canal.

When Pan Jixun received his appointment as Imperial Commissioner of the Yellow River in 1565, he faced an almost impossibly complex problem. The Yellow River was flowing into the Huai River along sixteen different channels.[60] The largest channel met the Huai River near the city of Huai'an, creating a three-way intersection of the two rivers with the Grand Canal. In a geologic instant, silt from the Yellow River accumulated sufficiently to create a backflow on the Huai River that transformed a nearby land depression into a massive new reservoir, Hongze Lake 洪泽湖. Silt build-up in the lake caused even more flooding during periods of heavy water discharge, damaging agricultural land and even threatening some of the Ming tombs. Worse still, Yellow River silt raised the riverbed of the Huai River and caused blockages at the Huai'an section of the Grand Canal, threatening the supply of rice to the capital and to north China more generally.

Pan came to this assignment with the standard Confucian education and a *jinshi* degree (in 1550). With several years' experience as a prefectural judge and inspecting censor, he hardly seemed like the right person for such a complicated and vital hydrology project.

Yet what he brought to the problem was a keen intellect and an open mind, without attachment to the accepted (and marginally successful) solutions of the past. Those approaches to Yellow River silting had relied almost exclusively on diverting water away from the river into multiple channels, effectively spreading the silt across different outlets and dredging as necessary.

After study, measurement, and discussion about the behavior of water flows and silt deposition, Pan came to a radically opposite conclusion. He proposed instead to concentrate the flow of the Yellow River into one main channel running west of Hongze Lake and use river-edge or "thread dikes" (缕堤, lüdi) to narrow the waters even further, "binding water to wash away sand."[61] In Pan's judgment, spreading the river's flow had only slowed the current and allowed more silt to fall to the riverbed. In contrast, accelerating the river's flow rate would not only reduce silt deposition, it would also tend to scour and deepen the river channel. As Pan aptly phrased the process in his writings, "taming the Yellow River by means of the Yellow River."[62]

To supplement the dikes more closely bordering the river, Pan further proposed secondary "outer dikes" (遥堤, yaodi) up to a mile away that would prevent flooding if the inner dikes broke or overflowed. He also proposed construction of reservoirs to store clear water from the Huai River and other sources. Such clean-water reserves would enable river managers to release additional, silt-free water during seasonal periods of heaviest deposition or to increase natural scouring of the river bottom.[63]

Water commissioners and public works officials vehemently disputed Pan's theories and actively worked to impeach his actions and tarnish his reputation. Between 1565 and 1592, he served four separate terms in water management and put much of his theory into practice despite active opposition. Although he was unable to complete his entire program of Yellow River control, he charted the course for future work and expanded his successors' thinking about river management.

Pan's hydrologic approach helped manage the Yellow River for the next 250 years, but his ideas were not implemented without consequences.[64] Joseph Needham, the great historian of Chinese science, noted that pre-modern water management practices were designed to maintain the Grand Canal as "primarily a one-way channel, serving essentially the collection and concentration of grain-tax," since "governments in all dynasties invariably considered the interests of tax transport above those of irrigation or flood control. Fiscal appropriation always came first in their minds."[65] Other modern assessments of Pan's hydrology have concurred, arguing as one put it, that the court "immiserated and peripheralized western Shandong in order to maintain the imperial geography that linked the militarized north with the commercialized south."[66]

Pan's monograph, Overview of River Management (河防一览, Hefang yilan), completed in 1590, became an important reference source on river hydrology for centuries after his death. Later commentary on his monograph noted that "although changes in methods were afterwards necessary to fit changing circumstances, yet experts in river control always take this book as a standard guide."[67]

Pan Jixun may not have been the first scholar to see Yellow River management as a flow rate problem more than a water redistribution problem, but his genius lay in creating a pragmatic, observation-based engineering program and moving it successfully from concept to practice. Unlike Yu the Great, Pan Jixun was not a king or a demi-god, but like the first tamer of waters, he was a man of action whose revolutionary work charted the course for taming China's mightiest river.

High Ming

The closing decades of the 16th Century and the first decades of the 17th Century were particularly troubled times in Beijing. In 1573, ten-year-old Zhu Yijun 朱翊钧 (1563 - 1620) ascended the Ming throne as Emperor Wanli (万历帝, r. 1572 - 1620). His Regency period brought effective government and administrative improvements under Grand Secretary Zhang Zhuzheng 张居正 (1525 – 1582) and the boy-emperor's mother, Empress Dowager Xiaoding 孝定皇太后 (1544 – 1614), but after Zhang's death in 1582, nineteen-year-old Wanli seized full control of the throne to do with as he wished. Incredibly, his wish was to doing nothing, and to do so luxuriously. For the next thirty-eight years, China was governed by a spectacularly self-indulgent man who simply refused to govern, and who could react with dangerous unpredictability and fits of violence in the occasional times he was prodded into policy participation.

From 1589 nearly until Wanli's death, the Chinese government consisted of ministers who tried to guess what the Emperor wanted and self-serving eunuchs who did not much care. The administrative bureaucracy ground to a halt as thousands of prefectural and local government positions went unfilled. The military deteriorated similarly, even as military threats loomed yet again on the borders. In particular, a new wave of northern raiders called the Manchus began harassing the border territories under the leadership of Nurhaci (1559 – 1626).

Meanwhile, the leaderless nation was roaring. "New crops from America such as maize, sweet potatoes, and peanuts increased food production and the population reached over 100 million….[T]ax reforms and the spread of silver currency produced an economic boom….Technical advances improved the standard of manufactured goods, and…the demand for Chinese exports of luxury products rocketed, leading to the rise of a new class of extremely wealthy merchants, bankers, and businessmen…."[68] In Hangzhou and throughout Jiangnan, a new public-sphere dynamic was forming in which power and influence were increasingly shared among scholar-officials, literati who may or may not have held official positions, and a rising gentry class who helped fund local public projects and charitable endeavors.

Wanli's indifferently-spent reign years, 1572 – 1620, ironically coincided almost perfectly with an explosion in Chinese literary achievement. Two of China's greatest traditional novels, *Journey to the West* (西遊記, *Xi you ji*) and *The Plum in the Golden Vase* (金瓶梅, *Jin ping mei*), appeared between 1590 and 1610. Meanwhile, the increased number of publishers and market demand for published works led to two more classics resolving from multiple versions into their final forms during this period: *Water Margin* (水滸傳,

Shuihu zhuan, also called *Outlaws of the Marsh*) and *Romance of the Three Kingdoms* (三国演义, *Sanguo yanyi*). In 1598, the greatest of Chinese dramatic operas first appeared in performance under the title *The Peony Pavilion* (牡丹亭, *Mudan ting*).

The Song-Yuan-Ming transition and the attendant expansion of both population and wealth had created significant changes in family and career aspirations. Government growth was far outpaced by the massive increase in the number of candidates for new positions, all of whom had pored over the Confucian classics since adolescence in preparation for the civil service examinations. For the many who did not succeed at a level sufficient to sustain a remunerative career, one scholarly recourse beyond tutoring lay in the cultural sphere as creators, critics, and connoisseurs, where they reigned supreme.

Creators painted, produced poetry, plays, and short stories, sold their calligraphy, or wrote calligraphic inscriptions as a service. Critics criticized and squabbled, mostly with one another, while trying to steer public taste. But it was the connoisseurs who evolved into judge and jury, defining in every cultural sphere from painting and tea drinking to clothing fashion and garden design what was elegant (雅, *ya*) and what was vulgar (俗, *su*). Even the most mundane public activities were elevated to connoisseurship considerations: how to observe the moon on West Lake, which spring water to use for making tea, or how properly to place flowers in a vase and onto a table.

Less informed gentry merchants who elected to participate in the "taste race" deferred to the literati's judgment on these matters. As well, however, in a cultural market swarming with counterfeits, they depended on these scholarly elites for professional guidance and authentication on acquisitions of ancient books, paintings, calligraphies, rubbings, and inscribed bronzes and antiquities. The government might decide who became an official or not, but the literati decided for themselves who deserved membership in their community of properly refined souls.

Gao Lian 高濂 (1527 – c. 1603) offers a prime example of the growing literati class in Hangzhou. Son of a wealthy merchant family, he studied for the provincial examinations in order to bring to his family the status and honor of officialdom. After failing twice in the examinations, his family's wealth enabled him to reside comfortably along the shores of West Lake while pursuing alternate paths as a "commoner literatus" (布衣文人, *buyi wenren*, literally "scholar in plain cotton clothing").

Gao's educational background provided the foundation for his authorship of two plays, one of which was called *The Jade Hairpin* (玉簪记, *Yuzanji*). The play is a happy-ending love story representative of its time. Pan Bizheng 潘必正 is a young scholar so shamed by his failure in the official exams that he takes up residence with his aunt at a temple rather than return home. There at the temple he sees Chen Miaochang 陈妙常, a war refugee from a good family who sought a place as a Daoist nun after her family lost everything. They fall in love, but Pan's aunt sends the young man away to another exam to avoid a scandal for her convent. Love-inspired Pan passes the exam with honors this time and returns to wed Chen Miaochang. Despite being rather poorly received by the

176

critics of its time, *The Jade Hairpin* persists to the present day as one of Chinese opera's favorites, regarded by some as second only to *The Peony Pavilion*.

Beyond his work as a playwright, Gao is also remembered as the author of a "literati guide-book" titled *Eight Discourses on the Art of Life* (遵生八笺, *Zunsheng Bajian*), published in 1591. The rarified lifestyle suggested by the titles of these eight discourses are indicative of what a literatus of the late 1500s deemed should be worthy of his compatriots' attention:

- Discourse on sublime theories of pure self-cultivation;
- Discourse on being in harmony with the four seasons;
- Discourse on comfort on rising and resting;
- Discourse on extending life and avoiding disease;
- Discourse on food and drink;
- Discourse on pure enjoyment of cultured idleness;
- Discourse on numinous and arcane elixirs and medicines; and
- Discourse on remote wanderings beyond the mundane.[69]

It was a life most would envy but few could experience.

The career of Zhang Lian 张涟 (1587 – 1671) offers another example of the changing lifestyles of the middle- and late-Ming upper classes. According to the writings of his friend Wu Weiye 吴伟業 (1609 – 1671), Zhang was born in Huating (a district in modern-day Shanghai) but was commonly regarded as a native of Jiaxing. After studying painting in his youth, he put his knowledge and skills to work in the design of garden rockeries in the style of Yuan-era landscape paintings.[70]

From the imperial hunting parks of Qinshi Huangdi to the Impregnable Mountain park of Song Emperor Huizhou to the early private gardens of officials like Wu Wei, Bai Juyi, and Su Shi, oneness with Nature had held a special fascination among those whose financial circumstances permitted such preoccupations. Reclusion into Nature had already been an extreme option for Song and Yuan literati escaping dynastic uprooting or political turmoil, but by the mid-Ming, wealthy former officials turned their attentions to a more convenient solution.

Rather than suffer the time-consuming burdens of traveling to find a hospitable mountain retreat, they began constructing simulacrums of Nature in their own household settings or at nearby properties. Throughout Jiangnan, retired scholar-officials and wealthy merchants alike began creating magnificent and expensive private gardens that mimicked natural settings: lakes, waterfalls, mountains, ravines, caves, forests, and artificial rock formations of increasing complexity and surreality.

Like nearly every other element of cultured Ming life, garden design was subject to the strictures of connoisseurship. Guides like the *Craft of Gardens* (园冶, *Yuan ye*) by Ji Cheng 计成 (1582 – 1642), published in 1631, defined the contents and general design criteria for an elegant garden. Garden owners in turn viewed these settings as reflections of their elevated aesthetic taste and erudition.

177

Social and status pressures demanded the best professional guidance and construction, and Zhang Lian proved to be one of the best in late-Ming Jiangnan. He is believed by some modern scholars to have been influential in redirecting private garden design from "a rather ponderous and monumental style, with substantial buildings, fairly open spaces, massed plantings of a single type of shrub, tree or bamboo" to "a simpler, lighter style, with more delicate buildings, more mixed planting, and less imposing 'artificial mountains'."[71]

Strolling quietly through one's private garden, sitting in one place to admire the changing interplay of light and shade or the passing reflections of clouds on a pond, practicing calligraphy, taking tea and discussing poetry, or slowly unrolling a scroll painting to admire with colleagues: life could hardly have been much better for those privileged enough to live it. From Yangzhou to Suzhou, from Songjiang (Shanghai) to Hangzhou and Shaoxing, it nearly was heaven on earth.

For the next three hundred years, private gardens would burst into existence across Jiangnan and throughout China like the plants that flourished within them. Some gardens would blossom for many years, while others would eventually lie fallow for a while before disappearing or being rescued. Many would tragically be trampled to death by wars and occupations. Thankfully, some survived long enough to be restored in the present day to illustrate the literati ideals of an earlier time.

For some literati, though, the garden was as much a concept as a fixed physical space. Wang Ruqian 汪汝謙 (1577 – 1655), for example, owned two gardens at West Lake. A wealthy salt merchant from Huizhou with a reputation for poetry, patronage, and partying,[72] Wang named his properties the Unmoored Garden (不繫園, Buxi yuan) and the As You Like Pavilion (隨喜庵, Suixian). Unlike other gardens in Jiangnan, however, his "gardens" were pleasure boats that served the same purposes as the normal, land-based version. However, in his two gardens, he could enjoy all the scenery of West Lake any time he wished, alone or with friends of either sex.

Wang saw his boats as places for social congregation and entertainment, literary discussion, and poetry or art appreciation in the same way that a property owner viewed his stationary garden. In a sense, Wang's was a wealthy merchant's nose-thumbing response to literati posturing and their pretentious claims as sole arbiters of garden aesthetics. He defended his claim of boat-as-garden: "My garden is everywhere and has no stopping place; the sounds of songs cover the water to the east and the west," adding "What need is there to pile up rocks and dredge ponds, claiming them as one's own?"[73]

Around the same time, a literatus named Liu Shilong (*juren*, c. 1603) wrote an essay about his own garden. Like Wang Ruqian, Liu depicted his garden as the ideal entertainment center for fellow literati. His garden was lush with plantings: "peach and willow trees were for spring, paulownia and locust for summer, tangerines and oranges for fall, and pine and cypress for winter." Five mountain peaks, moon-viewing terrace, lotus pond, "bamboo-lined path," convoluted Lake Tai stones, mountain-topping pavilions peering over a roaring waterfall, fishing platform…everything a garden owner could dream of having.[74]

And a dream it was. Liu wrote in his "Record of the Garden that Is Not Around" that the name of his garden was Wuyou Yuan 乌有园, literally the Nonexistent Garden. In his view, his imaginary garden was superior to physical ones, limitless in size and composition, unending in variety, costing nothing to build or maintain, and passing down to posterity without suffering the ravages of time. Why go to the expense and trouble of building a thing so ephemeral as a garden, Liu Shilong wrote, when he could have such a perfect garden so easily and for all time? His essay finished with a not-so-disguised criticism of the garden mania he observed among the literati around him:

> Inside the garden, my body is always free from illness, my heart is always free from worries....My garden employs not shapes but ideas, and thus wind and rain cannot dilapidate it, water and fire cannot harm it....Those who visit my garden employ not their feet, but their eyes....And what their pure bosoms cherish, they can appreciate at their desks and mats and feel satisfied. I have my garden always and share my garden with others always. Those who read this "Record of the Garden that Is Not Around" should regard it thus.[75]

The Mystery of Miss Emotion

In and around Hangzhou, new wealth and expanding education spurred literary creativity and opened new opportunities for self-expression and cultural consumption. Women, who by Confucian mores were strictly confined to the "inner chambers" where they could practice only a limited set of household arts—and then only privately—were increasingly better educated and gradually transforming into creators as well as consumers of public culture. A prime example in Hangzhou of this cultural shift was a young woman whose tragically short life captivated Ming society but who, like Zhu Shuzhen before her, may never have existed.

Sometime around 1612, a striking poem began circulating among the literati of Jiangnan. The author was eventually determined to have been a young woman, age perhaps seventeen, who had written the following lines shortly before her premature death from illness:

> The sound of cold rain is unbearable through the lonely window,
> I light a lamp to leaf through *The Peony Pavilion*.
> Some in this world are even more stubborn in love than I,
> Xiaoqing is not the only heartbroken one.[76]

The anonymous young woman's poem suggested that her illness had arisen as a heartsick reaction to reading the story of Du Liniang 杜丽娘, the tragic heroine of *The Peony Pavilion* (牡丹亭, *Mudan ting*). She self-identified in her poem as Xiaoqing, so that name was adopted for her despite the possibility that she may merely have been punning with two characters, 小青 (*xiao qing*), that could be translated as both "young lady" and "Miss Emotion."[77] Some literati interpreted Xiaoqing's verse as proof that women were too emotionally fragile to read novels and hence should not be educated. Others, and especially the women of elite families, saw in Xiaoqing the living embodiment of Du Liniang, who dies for love in *The Peony Pavilion* only to be brought back to life by her great love, the young scholar Liu Mengmei 柳梦梅.

In the three years immediately following Xiaoqing's death, at least three authors pieced together modestly complete biographies of uncertain veracity. By those accounts, she was reputedly born in Yangzhou and sold as a "skinny mare"[78] (瘦馬, *shou ma*) into concubinage at the age of fifteen to Feng Yunjiang冯云将 (1572 – c. 1661). Upon his return home to Hangzhou, Feng's wife objected violently to the young girl's presence in her household and forced her to live in isolation at a small villa on Gushan (Solitary Hill), the former West Lake island home to Lin Bu and his cranes.

Xiaoqing passed the time mostly alone and nearly friendless, growing steadily more despondent as she wrote poems and painted. When she felt her health failing, she found an artist to paint her portrait. With proper ritual ceremony, she committed her spirit to the painted image, just as the fictional heroine Du Liniang does before her death in *The Peony Pavilion*. Mr. Feng was no doubt devastated when he discovered that Xiaoqing had passed away, but his jealous wife burned every trace of the young concubine she could find. All that was left were one painting and a handful of poems that Xiaoqing had secretly passed along to a servant for preservation, later collected and circulated under the title *Manuscripts Saved from Burning*.

Xiaoqing's story captivated almost immediately. "Within a decade of Xiaoqing's supposed death in 1612, she had become enshrined in popular imagination as the quintessential suffering heroine."[79] Her surviving poems were copied and circulated, biographies purporting to reveal her life story proliferated, and more than a dozen plays incorporated her story into their plot lines. Popular culture was metaphorically resurrecting her from death much as Du Liniang had been brought back to life by Liu Mengmei.

Xiaoqing's story transcended reality; her symbolism as a suffering heroine rendered factual truth irrelevant. A tombstone erected at West Lake reinforced her debatable historicity, providing a physical representation for those compelled by her story to validate her reality. Her status as a West Lake legend was reinvigorated again two hundred years later when a Hangzhou scholar-official, Chen Wenshu 陳文述 (1775 – 1845), ostensibly rediscovered and renovated her tomb site. Scholars have debated the facts and even the reality of her life to the present day, but for the romantic at heart, she remains Du Liniang's real-life counterpart, regardless.

Changing Attitudes

Jiaxing native Li Rihua 李日华 (1565 – 1635) provides another example of new wealth in the Ming era. Li's father, himself orphaned as a boy, had managed to attain sufficient prosperity to provide his son with a solid education in the Confucian classics. The young scholar honored his father's sacrifices by achieving his provincial (*juren*) degree in 1591 and his imperial (*jinshi*) degree the following year. His official career began propitiously with a six-year judgeship in Jiangxi Province, a three-year term as a magistrate outside of Kaifeng, and flood control management responsibilities on the Yellow River.

When Li returned to Jiaxing in 1604 to mourn his mother's passing, he turned the usual three-year leave allowance into a twenty-year withdrawal from official service. During those years, he practiced painting and calligraphy, cultivated his connoisseurship skills, and refined his taste for fine teas and the best spring waters for brewing. He also maintained a diary through many of those years, from which the entries between 1609 and 1616 have survived to depict "a gentleman of wealth engaging day by day in all the pursuits of his class."[80] The title of the published work, *Diary from the Water-Tasting Studio* (味水軒日記, *Weishui xuan riji*), advertised Li's passion for tea and his self-claimed powers of discrimination.

Li served in several more official positions between 1623 and 1628, but he is best remembered as a connoisseur, art critic, and diarist. He was also, at least for a time, married to one of his era's most radically famous courtesans, Jiaxing native[81] Xue Susu 薛素素 (c. 1575 – c. 1652). Aside from her natural beauty—for which she was duly praised—Xue Susu was lauded by the leading male painters of her time for her painting talents. She also demonstrated both knowledge and proficiency in music and poetry, essential elements of a courtesan's repertoire. What truly fascinated those who knew her, however, were her unladylike martial skills and her pride in showing them off.

From early adolescence, Xue Susu reveled in horseback riding and archery in the open fields outside the city walls. In the 1580s, she practiced her trade to modest notoriety in the famed Qinhuai courtesan quarters of Nanjing, but it was in 1590s Beijing where she ascended into the realms of celebrity. In modern terms, she became the city's leading socialite and hostess, entertaining her guests with a unique mix of poetry, music, and martial skills.

Ming literati were captivated by the combination of Xue Susu's beauty and androgyny. Even women remarked on her allure; Suzhou poetess Xu Yuan 徐媛 (1560 – 1620) described her in verse:

> Lotus blossoms as she moves her pair of arches,
> Her tiny waist, just a hand's breadth, is light enough to dance on a palm.
> Leaning coyly against the east wind,
> Her pure color and misty daintiness fill the moon.
>
> You tender and bewitching girl, skin smoother than jade,
> Fragrance wafts from every step the lotus makes.
> Slender waist can hardly withstand the morning breeze,
> Why not build a jade terrace and hide her in mansions of gold?[82]

Such a woman found no shortage of marriage and concubinage offers, and Xue readily availed herself of them. She married at least four times. Two of her partners were scholar officials from Jiaxing (Li Rihua and Shen Defu 沈德符, 1578 – 1642) and another was a wealthy merchant from Suzhou.

Ancient Chinese history includes several memorable tales of women warriors pressed into military action by family honor or circumstance: Xun Guan 荀灌 (303 – ?), Princess

Pingyang 平阳公主 (590s – 623), Liang Hongyu 梁红玉 (1102 – 1135), and, of course, the legendary Hua Mulan 花木蘭 (4th – 6th Century). Xue Susu was different from those predecessors: beautiful, cultured, artistically talented, and unabashedly martial…an androgynous unicorn among the genteel community of "skinny mare" courtesans. She would not be the last female knight-errant (女侠, *nüxia*) of pre-revolutionary China.

More important, Xue Susu's life prefigured societal changes that were gradually loosening the restrictive patriarchal regulations that bound women to the inner chambers. Courtesans might be freer to break new ground, but well-bred women (闺秀, *guixiu*) of elite and wealthy families were also finding new ways for their voices to be heard and appreciated without fear of shame or stigmatization. The next 250 years would see more Xue Susu's and Guan Daosheng's…and many more Li Qingzhao's who would see their poetry and prose published and praised rather than reducing it themselves to ashes for the sake of family propriety.

Prose Advances

> In the autumn of 1627, after [failing the civil service examination], I was tarrying in Nanjing when I idly picked out one or two remarkable situations I had heard of from past and present—items worth recording—and elaborated them into stories as a way of relieving the frustrations that oppressed me…. But whenever my [examination] colleagues visited me, they would ask me for one of my stories to read, and on finishing it, would invariably slap the table and exclaim, "What an amazing thing!" The news was spied out by a book merchant who begged me to let him publish the stories. And so I copied them out, put them together, and obtained forty stories.[83]

Thus in the preface to his second collection of short stories did Huzhou native Ling Mengchu 凌濛初 (1580 – 1644) explain not only how his two books came to be but also the genesis of their titles: *Slapping the Table in Amazement* (I and II) (拍案惊奇, *Pai an jing qi*). Storytelling in the common or vernacular language, long the domain of itinerant street performers and unimaginably distant from the dignified attention of the scholar-official class, emerged in the 1620s as an acceptable new form of literary endeavor thanks to Ling Mengchu and his Suzhou contemporary, Feng Menglong (冯梦龙, 1574 – 1646).

The fourth of five sons born into a distinguished Huzhou family of scholar-officials,[84] Ling Mengchu appeared destined from childhood to have a very promising career in officialdom. He was admitted to a local government school at the unusually early age of eleven and became a scholarship student at age seventeen. Inexplicably, however, he experienced nothing but repeated failure in the next-level provincial (*juren*) exams, at least four attempts without success.

As the product of a wealthy family, Ling could well afford a period of sowing-his-oats pleasure-seeking. He traveled from Hangzhou to Suzhou and Nanjing to establish his own personal network and start a family. He seriously contemplated withdrawing into semi-reclusion in Huzhou, but following the deaths and mourning periods for both of his parents, he traveled to Beijing in the hope of securing an official position through personal recommendation, his last remaining option. When that course proved fruitless as well, he left Beijing and headed south.

By the time Ling Mengchu arrived in Nanjing in 1627, Feng Menglong had already upended the Jiangnan publishing world. Like Ling, Feng had been born into comfort and a promising future. His gentry family provided him with a sound Confucian education, but (again, like Ling) multiple attempts in the civil service examinations garnered nothing but disappointment and frustration. Fond as he was of wine, women, and song, Feng took up residence in Nanjing and availed himself enthusiastically of the pleasures in the city's Qinhuai courtesan district. During those years of unemployment, he wrote a series of popular books and examination study aids as a source of income.

An inveterate collector of vernacular songs and stories, Feng Menglong published forty short tales in 1620 under the title *Stories to Instruct the World* (喻世明言, *Yushi mingyan*).[85] The book was such an overnight success, Feng quickly followed with two more story collections, *Stories to Caution the World* (警世通言, *Jingshi tongyan*) in 1624 and *Stories to Awaken the World* (醒世恆言, *Xingshi hengyan*) in 1627. Because each book title contained the same character *yan* 言, Feng's three books together became commonly known as *Sanyan*, or *The Three Yans*.

Ling Mengchu's first story collection, also consisting of forty tales, achieved equally unheard-of sales upon publication in 1628; it too led to a second edition of forty more stories in 1632. His two story books together became known simply as *Er pai* 二拍, *The Two Slaps*. Neither man originated most of their stories, preferring instead to reshape existing ones, and Ling readily acknowledged following in Meng's footsteps. Their genius lay in selecting the material, adapting it to vernacular speech, editing and reshaping the stories to the time in which they lived, grouping and sequencing the results, and adding introductions.

Where Feng Menglong's commentaries and story choices reflected his belief in a rigid moral code, Ling's tended toward a more situational and pragmatic morality, even ones based on common sense or tinged with tongue-in-cheek satire. For example, Ling Mengchu introduced one of his stories with the following:

> But the argument of greedy people fond of slaughter…runs as follows: "Heaven created animal life for our sustenance; hence it is no sin to eat meat." Now we don't know if the Lord of Heaven told them this personally, or whether they are simply announcing it on their own authority. But if our ability to eat animals is to be ascribed to Heaven's interest in our welfare, does that mean that, because tigers and leopards are able to eat human beings, Heaven created us for *their* benefit? We get stung by mosquitoes and flies. Does that mean Heaven created us for *their* consumption?[86]

Ironically, both writers ultimately got the official careers to which they had long aspired, through channels outside the examination system. Feng Menglong served admirably for four years (1634 – 1638) as a magistrate in Shouning County (Fujian Province) before retiring at the age of 64. Ling Mengchu gained an assistant magistrate's position in the still-minor market town of Shanghai, where he demonstrated remarkable valor in the struggle against piracy and wrote a treatise on coastal defense.

Ling's actions at Shanghai earned him a promotion in 1643, at age 63, to magistrate of Xuzhou Prefecture, a key defensive location in northern Jiangsu Province. In fighting the very next year that ended the Ming Dynasty, he died defending his jurisdiction from hostile Manchu assault. Ling's formal epitaph stated in closing, "His last words were: 'Spare my people!' which he shouted three times before he died."[87]

Ling Mengchu and his senior colleague Feng Menglong were raconteurs *par excellence*, who together introduced the vernacular short story into the Chinese literary milieu. Almost exactly three hundred years after they published their story collections, a writer from Shaoxing would follow in their footsteps, but with radically original stories that would reshape the modern literature of China.

The Jesuits Also Advance

In 1583, a 40-year-old Italian Jesuit sporting an aquiline nose beneath deep-set eyes entered the city of Zhaoqing in southeast China, dressed in the style of a Buddhist monk. Michele Ruggieri (1543 – 1607) had prepared tirelessly for this opportunity, spending most of the past four years on the nearby island of Macao learning Chinese language, grammar, and culture. He had occasionally joined Portuguese merchants in their trading visits to Canton and had even managed to establish himself temporarily in Zhaoqing the previous year before being forced to leave.

This time, however, Ruggieri had the benefit of a well-positioned sponsor, district magistrate Wang Pan 王泮 (c. 1539 – c. 1600, *jinshi* 1565), a native of Shaoxing. Recently installed in his official position at the administrative seat of Liangguang (today's Guangdong and Guangxi Provinces combined), Wang had offered Ruggieri modest residential accommodation in Zhaoqing in the hope of gaining the priest's intercession on a personal matter. According to Ruggieri's account, the magistrate had a wife and two concubines but no male heir after thirty years of marriage. Happily for both men's interests, a son arrived within a year of Ruggieri's arrival, followed auspiciously by a second son.[88] These results were reason enough for Wang to introduce other local officials and literati to Ruggieri, but a second reason proved even more compelling.

Ruggieri had arrived in Zhaoqing accompanied by a young acolyte named Matteo Ricci (1552 – 1610), recently arrived in Macao after a missionary assignment in India. Once the two were settled into their Zhaoqing residence, Ricci unraveled a world map drawn by the Belgian Abraham Ortelius (1527 – 1598) and hung it on their wall. He and Ruggieri soon discovered that this map with its continents and detailed longitude and latitude lines became an object of extraordinary fascination among the local elites who visited them. At Wang Pan's suggestion, Ricci began gradually translating names from the map into their Chinese equivalents.

Near the end of 1584, Ricci had a revised, translated version of his world map and Ruggieri had finished the first-ever Christian catechism in the Chinese language, the forty-three-page *Tianzhu shilu* 天主实录, or *A Veritable Record of the Lord of Heaven*. Wang Pan arranged for copies of Ricci's map and three thousand copies of Ruggieri's catechism to be printed and distributed among his friends and associates, marking the beginning of Jesuit proselytizing in China.

The following year, Wang Pan offered Ruggieri an even greater opportunity. He arranged for the senior Jesuit to travel to Canton, where he met Wang's brother, a silk merchant. The pair were joined by another Jesuit entrant into China, Antonio de Almeida (1557 – 1591), and the threesome traveled for two months from Canton to the Wang family home in Shaoxing. Ruggieri now found himself unexpectedly residing for six months in one of Ming China's greatest centers of elite scholarship and officialdom outside of the capital.

Although he only gained one convert to Catholicism—ironically, Wang Pan's aged father—Ruggieri and Almeida had represented their faith and Western scholarship well and attracted some notoriety. Perhaps a bit too much notoriety, because in early 1586, Wang Pan wrote Ruggieri asking him to return with Almeida to Zhaoqing. The two Jesuits did as they were asked, traveling back south in the company of Zheng Yilin, Wang Pan's successor in Zhaoqing and another native of Shaoxing. They were back in Guangdong where they started, but Ruggieri, Ricci and Almeida had crossed their first hurdle toward a more substantial presence in China. Word would spread about these Westerners with their religion and their maps and their knowledge of the planets and stars.

Ruggieri returned to Rome in 1588, but Ricci and Almeida remained in Zhaoqing for another year until local officials ordered them to return to Macao. The two Jesuits departed Zhaoqing as asked but headed instead for the more remote district of Shaozhou in northern Guangdong Province, where they enjoyed a relatively peaceable residence. Almeida passed away from illness in 1591, but Ricci was joined at Shaozhou three years later by Lazzaro Cattaneo (1560 – 1640). That year, 1594, was marked by Ricci's critical decision to abandon Buddhist monks' dress for that of the secular scholar class. Ricci also began his collaboration with Cattaneo that year to develop the first system of *pinyin*[89] and tone markings as an aid to Westerners for learning Chinese language.

Ricci had long since set his sights well beyond Shaozhou to Beijing and the imperial palace. After two failed attempts to establish a foothold in Nanjing, he finally managed a precarious presence there in 1598, thanks in part to his reputation as a man of science and as the "author" of the celebrated world map. An unsuccessful attempt to enter Beijing with Cattaneo in late 1598 nearly killed Ricci from illness, but he recovered and set out again from Nanjing in 1600. He failed this time to achieve an audience with the Wanli Emperor, but his reputation gained him access to the capital and a number of literati officials resident there. One connection proved especially valuable, a recent and highly-placed[90] *jinshi* graduate (1598) from Hangzhou named Li Zhizao 李之藻 (1565 – 1630).

Li's intellectual connection with Ricci upon their first meeting in 1601 was nearly immediate. Having joined several friends to visit Ricci at his Beijing residence, Li was struck by the world map hanging on the wall. Several years earlier, he had produced his own geographical description of China, accompanied by his own maps of the fifteen provinces, but this European map was something else altogether. Li Zhizao pressed Ricci for details on the longitude and latitude lines and, after doing his own calculations, conceded that the world was indeed spherical as Ricci's map contended.[91]

No sooner had Li seen Ricci's map than he wanted to create a fully Chinese-inscribed version. He prevailed upon the Jesuit priest to collaborate in expanding the European map's size and content, placing China at the center and adding more descriptive information about foreign countries as well as the sun and stars. Their new map, some five feet high and fifteen feed wide, was ready for woodblock printing in 1602 and titled *The Map of the Universe and the Thousand Countries* (坤輿万国全图, *Kunyu wanguo quantu*). It was the first Chinese map ever to display the existence and shape of the American continents.

Ricci's network of officials grew substantially while he remained in Beijing. In 1602, he met and became friends with Yang Tingyun 楊廷筠 (c. 1557 – 1627, *jinshi* 1592), another native of Hangzhou. Two years later, in 1604, Xu Guangqi 徐光启 (1562 – 1633) passed his *jinshi* examination in the capital and finally met Ricci. Xu was by now already a Catholic convert, having been baptized the previous year in Nanjing by the Jesuit João da Rocha (1565 – 1623). These three Confucian-educated Chinese scholars—Li Zhizao and Yang Tingyun from Hangzhou and Xu Guangqi from Shanghai—would become known in the history of Chinese Catholicism as "the Three Great Pillars"[92] of the Catholic Church in China.

For the next several years, each of these three men pursued their separate official careers, although Xu Guangqi and Li Zhizao continued collaborating with Ricci whenever possible on scientific and mathematical matters. Xu delved enthusiastically into Euclid's *Geometry* and worked several hours daily with Ricci for six months to translate the first six of Euclid's *Elements* as 几何原本 (*Jihe yuanben*), published in 1607. Ricci later described their joint effort on Euclid as 口譯筆受 (*kouyi bishou*), literally "mouth giving, brush receiving."[93] As a baptized Catholic, Xu also built a chapel in Shanghai and founded a mission there, first manned by Lazarro Catteneo, Ricci's old friend from Shaozhou.

Li Zhizao, on the other hand, studied astronomy with Ricci, developing what the latter deemed a high level of skill in producing astrolabes. Between 1606 and 1610, Li published illustrated works on spheres and astrolabes and a mathematical treatise in which he introduced the notion of circles as infinite-sides polygons, a conceptual precursor to the calculus of Newton and Leibniz.

In contrast, Yang Tingyun actively pursued his career assignments without much concern over Ricci or Catholicism until he retired in 1609 after seventeen years of official service. A devout Buddhist, he returned to Hangzhou to pursue his own religious studies and even began a series of lectures on Buddhism from a location on the shores of West Lake. His intellect was of a much less scientific and mathematical bent than Xu's or Li's; he persisted to the end claiming that he never understood all of Ricci's talk about "circles and hypotenuses."[94]

In 1610, Li Zhizao fell so seriously ill, he believed he was on his deathbed. Ricci attended to his friend day and night, agreeing to Li's request that he act as executor of the dying man's last will. During those last days, Li also accepted conversion to the Catholic faith. In an unexpected twist, Li recovered but Ricci fell ill and died only a few months later in May.

The next year, when Li's father passed away in Hangzhou, Li returned home for the usual mourning period. When Yang Tingyun came to offer condolences, he was surprised to see that Li had removed all traces of Buddhist images and statuary. Furthermore, Li had not called upon a Buddhist monk for his father's funeral rites but instead had invited Lazzaro Cattaneo and Nicolas Trigault (1577 – 1628) to attend to those duties. At Li's insistence, Yang engaged the two Jesuits about their religion and then invited them to his residence for more extended discussions.

Ultimately convinced by Cattaneo's and Trigault's arguments, Yang Tingyun asked for conversion, only to be rejected. He could not be baptized as a Catholic, the Jesuit priests informed him, unless and until he foreswore his concubine, the woman who had given him his only two sons. After much internal debate and struggle, Yang relented and arranged for his former concubine's care. He converted to Catholicism in 1611, although he chose not to divorce himself as completely from Buddhism as had his friend Li Zhizao. Yet as one of his first acts as a new Christian, Yang joined Li in inviting Cattaneo to take up residence in the new mission they were founding in Hangzhou. After a temporary stay alongside West Lake,[95] Cattaneo moved into the new mission residence constructed for him inside the city walls, not far from the Qiantang Gate.

For the next few years, Yang succeeded in gaining as many as one hundred new converts to Catholicism, mostly from among his extended family, friends, and associates. Meanwhile, Li Zhizao enthusiastically pursued his post-retirement work of translating Western mathematical and scientific works. He also memorialized the Wanli Emperor in 1613 with a recommendation that the court establish a school for the translation of foreign books, noting that many things he had learned from Ricci were nowhere to be found in Chinese books. In this proposition, Li was more than two centuries ahead of his time, since the first such translation school would only come into existence in 1865 at the Jiangnan Arsenal.

The first high-level resistance to the Jesuits' missions arrived in 1616, spearheaded by another native of Hangzhou, Shen Que 沈漼 (d. 1624, jinshi 1592). As the newly installed Vice-Minister of Rites in Nanjing, Shen initiated a series of three memorials that year arguing for the expulsion of the foreign missionaries. Shen presented a full litany of accusations against the foreign Jesuits: residing in China illegally, undermining Confucian orthodoxy, subverting Chinese astronomy, disguising themselves as Chinese to act as spies, holding secret meetings, practicing alchemy, acting as a seditious and heterodox sect, and representing a malign influence on the Ming tombs and imperial palace in Nanjing by the proximity of their residences. According to Shen Que, the Jesuits had even stolen for their religion's use the Chinese words for "heaven" (天, tian) and "great" (大, da), traditionally applied to the emperor.[96]

Shen's third memorial personalized his attacks, naming Alfonso Vagnone (1566 – 1640) and Alvaro Semedo (1585 – 1658) in Nanjing and Sabatino de Ursis (1575 – 1620) and Diego de Pantoja (1571 – 1618) in Beijing. Li Zhizao, Yang Tingyun, and Xu Guangqi wrote memorials and published written defenses of the Catholic faith and its followers, but their efforts proved futile. The Wanli Emperor's edict of February 3, 1617 ordered the four Jesuits named by Shen Que to be chained, caged, and carted to Canton for return to Macau and their residences in Nanjing and Beijing closed or destroyed.

In advance of this decree, however, Xu Guangqi in Shanghai and Yang Tingyun in Hangzhou were quietly welcoming eight foreign Jesuits and six of their Chinese coadjutors into their homes, where they took refuge for the next five years until the crisis passed. The consequences could have been much worse, but famines, earthquakes, and the appearance of two comets in November 1618 occupied the court's attention and may have been interpreted as heavenly suggestions that they reconsider their anti-Catholic actions.[97] The Jesuit refugees in Hangzhou and Shanghai maintained low profiles and passed those few turmoiled years quietly and safely. Shen Que's reward for his anti-foreign crusade was promotion to Grand Secretary in 1620, placing him at the apex of Chinese officialdom until his retirement in 1623 and death in 1624.

Despite Shen Que's civil assault, the 1620s proved a productive time for the Jesuit missions. Nicolas Trigault returned from a European trip with seven thousand Western books, materials for a massive translation project Yang Tingyun had hoped but ultimately failed to organize. A year after his retirement from official life in 1625, Yang established a Christian school in Hangzhou and also built the city's first Catholic church complex, located inside Wulin Gate, and a second one near the Qiantang Gate; neither are extant today. He passed away in 1628.

The irrepressible Li Zhizao actively continued his translation and publishing work right up to the time of his death in 1630. He produced books and translations on Aristotelian logic, wrote about and interpreted the contents of the Nestorian stele, and edited *Tianxue chuhan*, the *First Collection of Learning from Heaven*, a 1628 compilation of works by Ricci, Pantoja, Giulio Aleni (1582 – 1649), and others, as well as works on water technology by Xu Guangqi and on mathematics and astronomy by Ricci, de Ursis, Xu Guangqi, and Li himself. These last pieces included recent reports on Galileo's telescopic discoveries of Jupiter's moons and Saturn's rings.

With Xu Guangqi's passing in 1633, the last of the Three Pillars were gone, as were Ruggieri (1607), Ricci (1610), Pantoja (1618), de Ursis (1620) and Trigault (1628); the aging Catteneo would stay on in Hangzhou until his death in 1640 at the age of 80. Others like Vagnone, Semedo, and Aleni had dispersed across the Chinese empire or to the capital. Brilliant new arrivals replenished the Jesuits' numbers, and some of them would achieve unprecedented influence for a time in the Qing court. Regardless, Hangzhou had become their safe haven and a home base of sorts, and that city, too, would see new Jesuit arrivals to build upon and carry forward their predecessors' religious and secular work.

End of the Ming?

The final years of the Ming Dynasty were troubled ones, indeed. The Wanli Emperor's refusal to govern his realm for thirty-five years had done great but not irremediable harm to the military, bureaucracy, and treasury. His immediate successors, however, were spectacularly ill-equipped to right the Ship of State: Taichang 泰昌帝 (r. 1620 – 1620) barely lasted a month on the throne before dying, likely by poisoning, and Tianqi 天啓帝 (r. 1621 – 1628) was an illiterate 15-year-old utterly dominated by another self-serving eunuch, Wei Zhongxian 魏忠賢 (1568 – 1627).

By the time the well-meaning but perpetually indecisive Chongzhen Emperor 崇禎帝 (r. 1627 – 1644) took the throne in 1628, the empire had reached a state of chaos. A terrible famine struck the land, causing bandit groups and local warlord armies to spring up in much the same way they had before Zhu Yuanzhang founded the Ming Dynasty. Nature, or the heavens, only compounded Chongzhen's problems. The 1630s and 1640s are recognized by modern climate scientists as one of the coolest periods of the "Little Ice Age" that impacted China for much of the final two hundred years of the Ming.[98] The Yellow River flooded multiple times, and droughts and famines devastated the populace.

Meanwhile, on the northern borders, a powerful new Jurchen tribe rose in the 1590s under Aisin-Gioro Nurhaci 愛新覺羅 · 努爾哈赤 (1559 – 1626), who consolidated his might by subsuming the Mongols into his forces. In 1616, he declared himself the founding emperor of a reconstituted Jin Dynasty and soon began attacking Ming bases in the northeast, above the Great Wall. The Ming court responded in 1618 with an expeditionary force intended to push the invaders back northward, but that effort failed disastrously and left Nurhaci's forces in control of virtually all northern and eastern territories beyond the Great Wall. Nurhaci celebrated his victories by constructing a new capital for himself at Mukden (modern Shenyang 沈阳) in 1625. By the mid-1630s, his people had adopted a tribal identity for themselves: the Manchus.

During this same period, a bandit leader from Shaanxi Province emerged from deeply impoverished rural circumstances. Li Zicheng 李自成 (1606 – 1645) accumulated a militarized following numbering in the tens of thousands as he rampaged his way through Henan and Anhui Provinces. He then turned northwest into Gansu Province before setting his sights on Chengdu (Sichuan Province) in 1637. Fortunately, Li's assault was turned back in a devastating defeat at the hands of the Ming army.[99]

Li Zicheng spent the next few years regrouping in Henan Province, aided in his recruitment by a devastating famine in 1640 that left the people with nowhere else to turn. His army grew steadily as he ravaged the region, taking small towns, executing any officials he could capture, pillaging anything of value, and welcoming still more followers from the ranks of the desperate common people. From 1641 to 1644, Li's "bandit army" of 400,000 or more soldiers seized control of major city after major city in north central China: Luoyang, Kaifeng,[100] Xiangyang, Xi'an, Taiyuan, and Datong. As he advanced toward Beijing in February 1644, Li Zicheng formally declared himself the Great King of his new dynasty, the Da Shun 大順朝. On April 22, 1644, his army encamped at the site of the Ming emperors' tombs, just twenty-five miles north of Beijing.[101]

The next day, they stood outside the walls of the Ming capital, and after only a day's pause, they launched their assault on April 24. One of the city's southern gates was opened for the attackers, reputedly by eunuchs seeking to collaborate, and Li's soldiers poured into the city. Before the day was out, the Empress committed suicide and the half-drunk Chongzhen Emperor executed most of his daughters and concubines. Early on the morning of April 25, the Emperor climbed the hill in the imperial park and hanged himself in the pavilion at the crest, ironically named the Pavilion of Imperial Longevity. He was just 33 years old. The next day, Li Zicheng entered the Forbidden City and seated himself alongside the throne. He chose not to declare himself emperor of a new dynasty until he could be reasonably certain Chongzhen and his three imperial princes were all dead.

The Ming Dynasty had ended. Or perhaps not. The Song Dynasty had not disappeared five centuries earlier when the northern capital was lost to the Jin; it had simply reformed in Hangzhou. Ming loyalism was still strong below the Yangzi River, and Li Zicheng had achieved no hold or loyalty anywhere in the south. In addition, a sizable Ming army still operated at full strength only 100 miles northeast of Beijing. And then there were the Manchus in the northeast, held in check by Ming forces but likely salivating over the chaos and military weakness they were witnessing from just outside the northern border.

Far away to the south of the Yangzi River, the people of Hangzhou, and throughout Jiangnan, watched and waited, fearing the worst.

Distribution of known Liangzhu Culture excavation sites between the Qiantang River (lower middle) and Yangzi River (upper section of display image), with Lake Tai (Taihu) in the center. Compare sites to modern city locations in Map 2.

Artistic rendition of Liangzhu "capital city", regarded by some as the original site of Hangzhou when the present-day area was still submerged by ocean waters. Note the water-filled nature of the terrain.

Bell tower (left) and memorial tomb entrance (right) for tomb of Yu the Great at Kuaiji Mountain, Shaoxing. Massive statue of Da Yu hovers over the nearby hilltop.

Walkway to Yu the Great's tomb.

The Da Yu statue atop Kuaiji Mountain can be seen from miles away.

Statue of Wu Zixu, God of the Tidal Bore, in the Wu Zixu Temple on Wushan, Hangzhou City.

Exhibition Hall of Wang Xizhi's Calligraphy, Shaoxing City.

Replica of Lanting xu, Wang Xizhi's "Preface to the Poems Collected at Lanting Pavilion" in 353 CE, displayed at the Exhibition Hall of Wang Xizhi's Calligraphy.

Entrance arch to Wansong Academy, Wushan Hill, Hangzhou. Note that upper portion of the arch is shaped like the character 品 (pin), signifying moral character (品德 , pinde) or moral conduct (品行 , pinxing).

Life-size diorama portraying Liang Shanbo and Zhu Yingtai as Wansong Academy students.

Pavilion and tomb of Su Xiaoxiao at Xiling Bridge, West Lake, Hangzhou.

*View of Bai (Juyi) Causeway across the northern portion of
West Lake with the cityscape behind.*

Looking toward the northern hills of West Lake with Baochu Pagoda on the hilltop.

Summer lotus flowers and Baochu Pagoda.

View of the western hills bordering West Lake.

West Lake in haze or mist. The large center island is Three Pools Mirroring the Moon; the stone pagodas are in the water near the island's left end. Running diagonally from left to center of photo is Su (Dongpo) Causeway.

View south and west of West Lake with Leifeng Pagoda. Photo taken from City God's Temple on Wushan.

Panoramic view of West Lake from City God's Temple.

Memorial Hall for Su Shi (Dongpo) on Su Causeway.

View of Bai Causeway with Leifeng Temple rising behind on the lake's south shore.

Stairway to the restored Leifeng Pagoda.

Preserved brick ruins from the base of the Leifeng Pagoda after it fell in 1924.

From inside Leifeng Pagoda, a carved diorama depicting the moment when the handsome young pharmacist's assistant Xu Xian offers his umbrella to the minor gods Bai Suzhen (White Snake) and Xiaoqing (Green Snake).

Entrance to City God's Temple, Wushan, Hangzhou City.

Statue of Zhou Xin 周新 *, worshipped as the City God of
Hangzhou since the early 15th Century.*

Chapter 9

TRANSITION – THE SOUTHERN MING

(1644 – 1660)

Glow of Sunset upon Thunder Peak[1]

The ruined pagoda at home on the banks of the lake,
Shambolic as a drunken old man.
Extraordinary feelings are to be found here amid the shards,
What need does it have for the arts of man?

– Zhang Dai (1597 – c. 1684)

From Bright (明) to Clear (清) [2]

In his final days, Emperor Chenzhong transmitted urgent messages to General Wu Sangui 吴三桂 (1612 – 1678), ordering his army to come to the defense of the capital. Wu's force had been stationed at Shanhaiguan, the famed pass at the far eastern end of the Great Wall, roughly 175 miles from Beijing. His charge at Shanhaiguan was simple: protect the Chinese empire from new threatening invaders from the north, the Manchus.

Chenzhong's order placed Wu in an impossible predicament. If he abandoned his position and marched to the capital's rescue, he would leave an open door for a massed army of Manchu troops to rampage uncontested through Hebei Province and southward along the Bohai seacoast into Shandong Province. Yet he could hardly allow Beijing and the imperial family to fall victim to the bandit Li Zicheng. Complicating matters further, Wu Sangui's father (himself a retired general), his family, and his beloved concubine, Chen Yuanyuan 陈圆圆 (1624 – 1681), all resided in Beijing. To make matters still worse, both Li Zicheng and the Manchu general Dorgon[3] (1612 – 1650) had each already made generous offers for Wu to join their sides against the other one, and against the Ming.

Family, love, and dynastic loyalty ultimately won out, particularly once Wu learned that Beijing had fallen and that Li Zicheng was holding his father captive. Wu's army was the largest remaining Ming military force, but he remained concerned that it might still be insufficient to defeat Li's massed bandits and save the capital from its rapacious usurper. Consequently, he turned to General Dorgon with an offer: aid the Ming army in retaking Beijing, and the next Ming emperor would reward the Manchus liberally with territory and treasure.

For Dorgon, the opportunity was beyond anything he could have imagined. Wu Sanguai was offering him a free pass south of the Great Wall and practically opening the gates of Beijing for his troops. Why accept a bit of land and some gold and silver when he could easily seize the throne and have the whole empire? Not surprisingly, he consented to Wu's offer.

Enraged by Wu Sangui's rejection, Li Zicheng led a force of 100,000 out of Beijing, intent on eradicating Wu's army. By the time the two armies met not far from Shanhai Pass, Wu's force had been supplemented by Dorgon's troops as well as 20,000 – 30,000 local militia volunteers. Li's army was shattered on May 27, 1644 and driven back toward Beijing. Wu and Dorgon followed in hot pursuit. When Li re-entered the capital on May 31, he initiated a murderously vindictive rampage, pillaging all the palace valuables he could melt down and carry. On June 3, he ascended the throne and proclaimed himself Emperor of the Great Shun Dynasty even as he set fire to his own palaces. The next day, he led his forces out of Beijing, fleeing west toward Shaanxi, his native province.

Wu Sangui and General Dorgon arrived at Beijing's gates on June 6, two days after Li's sudden departure. When he discovered that Li had executed his father and family and that Chen Yuanyuan had secretly and safely escaped, the emotionally outraged Wu abandoned all sense of political perspective regarding the situation he himself had created. With Dorgon's encouragement, Wu headed westward in pursuit of the imperial imposter, possibly not even entering the capital city onto whose doorstep he had just delivered a Manchu general and troops.

That same day, Dorgon completed one of the most remarkable conquests in world history. Carried ceremoniously into the Forbidden City on an imperial palanquin, he dismounted before the assembled courtiers and simply announced the Manchu conquest. The Ming Dynasty was over, he declared, ended by the death of Emperor Chongzhen several weeks earlier. The Manchus claimed to have delivered the Chinese empire from the murderous and rapine clutches of a bandit usurper, and they were now accepting the Mandate of Heaven to rule. Nurhaci's six-year-old grandson Aisin Gioro Fulin, for whom his uncle Dorgon was a Regent, would soon arrive to ascend the throne of the new Qing Dynasty as the Shunzhi Emperor 順治帝 (r. 1644 – 1661). Northern China had fallen for the third time in five centuries to northern peoples whom the Han Chinese people still viewed as barbarians.

For anyone wondering how the Manchus would rule, they needed only look at Beijing.

Barely a week after taking control of the city, Dorgon issued an edict declaring that all males must immediately shave their heads in the Manchu style, leaving only the hair at the back part of the head to be grown and braided into a queue. The Chinese reaction to such a blatant violation of filial piety was immediate, emotional, and vocal. Centuries of tradition asserted that one's human body was a gift from one's parents; no part of that gift should be voluntarily damaged by cutting or tattooing. The opening paragraph of the *Classic of Filial Piety* (孝经, *Xiao jing*) states unambiguously: "Our bodies, down to every strand of hair and bit of skin, are received from our parents, and we do not dare to injure or wound them. This is the beginning of filial piety."[4]

The edict amounted to an unforced error on Dorgon's part, seriously threatening his efforts to establish a new civil administration. Two weeks later, the order for head-shaving was rescinded, but not the accompanying regulations requiring men and women to dress in the Manchu style. These early signals clearly suggested the Manchus' intention not to supplant Han culture but to graft elements of theirs onto the Chinese one. Despite these immediate outward changes, the Manchu Qing dynastic style from the earliest days of the conquest of Beijing reflected "a public stance of being more Chinese than the Chinese"[5] themselves.

A common paraphrase of Karl Marx asserts that history repeats itself twice, first as tragedy, and then as farce. From the Northern Song alignment with the Jurchen Jin to the Southern Song alliance with the Mongols to Wu Sangui's emergency mutual aid pact with the Manchus, Chinese imperial history had indeed played out Marx's sequence from tragedy to farce. By desperate trial and persistent error, China's rulers discovered at first hand that the enemy of one's enemy can indeed be a perilous friend. It would take time, and more pain would be endured, but that lesson would not be forgotten.

From North to South

After capturing Beijing, the Manchus debated their next strategic move. Should they secure both sides of the Great Wall but remain primarily in the north, or should they solidify their hold on the half of the Ming empire north of the Yangzi River? Unifying the entirety of China seemed well beyond their means, perhaps as much militarily as administratively.

Meanwhile, the northern invaders pursued mop-up operations in the territories they already held. Wu Sangui, now aided by armies under the command of two of Dorgon's brothers, Ajige (1605 – 1651) and Dodo (1614 – 1649), continued his western pursuit of Li Zicheng's army until that force effectively dissolved and its leader was dead, either by suicide or execution, in mid-summer 1644. With Li Zicheng defeated, Dodo was recalled to Beijing, leaving Wu Sangui in charge of pacification as Prince of the Western Territories.

When Dodo arrived in Beijing in late 1644, he discovered that the most critical strategic decision had already been made. He was placed in command of an army a quarter-million strong with orders to cross the Yangzi River and conquer the rest of the former Ming empire. As had already been the case in the north, the advancing army would be commanded by Manchus (with key Han Chinese advisors), employing Mongol cavalry as strike forces and Han Chinese as foot soldiers. "[I]t was the combined force of arms—Manchu, Mongol, and Chinese—under resourceful, determined Manchu leadership, that built the [Qing] empire."[6]

Just ten days after capturing the northern Jiangsu city of Xuzhou in May 1645, the Manchu army on May 12 reached the outskirts of Yangzhou, on the north bank of the Yangzi River. Dodo sent his representative under flag to the city wall to request a surrender, but that envoy was killed by an arrow. Dorgon also sent letters to Yangzhou's commander, Shi Kefa 史可法 (1601 – 1645), in an attempt to achieve a peaceful surrender, but those messengers were also executed and the letters burned. One of Ming China's richest and most highly cultured cities, populated by about one million citizens and some of the empire's finest gardens, settled in for a siege with a defensive force of approximately forty thousand soldiers.

Shi Kefa's treatment of the Manchu envoys and surrender offers had only enraged Dodo. The attacks began on May 13 with cannon fire and human wave assaults, indicating that Dodo was unconcerned about casualties among his troops. On May 20th, the city wall was breached and a north gate opened. Ming soldiers abandoned their posts, discarded their weapons, and searched out places to hide. The Manchus had already covered the south gate and had even engaged hundreds of boats on the Yangzi to ensure that few could escape to safety. After unsuccessfully trying to cut his own throat, Shi Kefa was captured and taken to General Dodo's quarters. When he still refused to join the Manchu side, he was beheaded in front of his own captured troops.

What began as the military conquest of a fabulous fortress city soon transformed into one of the most hideous massacres in Chinese history. Looting began on the first evening of the city's occupation, but passive theft gave way to coercion and violence as the looters increasingly doubted peoples' claims that they had no more valuables to surrender. Fires broke out, but the damage was limited by heavy rainfall that night. The next day, pillaging gave way to wanton rape and murder. Residents who emerged from hiding after declarations they would be spared if they gave themselves up were chained in groups of forty or fifty and paraded through the city. A diary of the sacking by Wang Xiuchu 王秀楚 (fl. 1645) described the horrific scene:

> The women wore long chains around their necks, clumsy as a string of beads. They stumbled at every step. They were covered with mud. Here and there on the ground lay small babies who were either trodden under the hooves of horses or the feet of men. The ground was stained with blood and covered with mutilated members of bodies. The sound of sobbing was heard everywhere on the open fields. Every gutter and pond was filled with corpses, lying one upon another. The blood turned the water to a deep greenish-red color, and the ponds were filled to the brim.[7]

After six days, the troops were ordered to cease their rampages and sheathe their swords. Corpses were collected and buried, and the remaining injured and starving were attended to. By some estimates, 800,000 people died in Yangzhou in just those six days. No one on the opposite side of the Yangzi River could have failed to see in Yangzhou the scale of devastation witnessed at Fancheng and Changzhou 370 years before at the hands of northern invaders. The effects from Yangzhou proved just as chilling and, in the long run, would be just as hatefully remembered.

On June 8, Dodo's armies were arrayed outside the walls and gates of Nanjing. This time, there would be no fighting. The city gate opened and a contingent of more than one hundred Ming officials, led by Qian Qianyi 钱谦益 (1582 – 1664), came forth to offer their peaceful surrender. After negotiation, Manchu troops and their lead commander marched quietly into Nanjing on June 16, 1645.

Even as the Manchus were establishing themselves in Nanjing, Dodo's armies pressed southeastward under the command of his nephew, Prince Bolo (1611 – 1652). The massacre at Yangzhou and the uncontested surrender of Nanjing must have weighed heavily on the Ming officials and soldiers in Jiangnan's major cities, since they fell with ease before the oncoming invaders. The Jiangsu cities of Changzhou, Wuxi, Changshu, Suzhou, Jiading, and Songjiang fell successively in June, Hangzhou in the early days of July, and Shaoxing on July 13.

On its face, Jiangnan was now Qing. Among the scholar-official and gentry class, however, Ming loyalism generated continued resistance. Organized attempts to create and sustain a competing Southern Ming Dynasty persisted, first under the Prince of Fu (Zhu Yousong 朱由崧, 1607 – 1646) and then the Prince of Lu (Zhu Yihai 朱以海, 1618 – 1662), but they ultimately collapsed under the pressure of overwhelming Manchu force. Dodo's edict in June 1645 calling for universal adoption[8] of the Manchu-style male hairdress (shaved head and queue) only amplified anti-Manchu sentiment. Each male now had to make a painfully visible, anti-Confucian declaration of disloyalty to their former dynasty.

The hair-style edict spawned innumerable personal crises, arguments and violence between adopters and refusers, and several organized but scattered rebellions.[9] In the Jiaxing district of Xiushui, for example, the Manchus installed as magistrate a medicine salesman named Hu Zhichen. In order to encourage compliance with the new hairstyle edict, Hu shaved his head in the Manchu style. He was immediately scorned by the elites as a low-class collaborator and ridiculed by the people residing in the nearby villages. Resistance coalesced behind two local men, one a military commander and the other a member of the gentry, resulting in Hu's assassination.

After a groundswell of support for their loyalist cause, the two leaders declared Xiushui as the new loyalist capital of the prefecture, in place of Jiaxing. Not yet satisfied, the assembled militia of Xiushui marched on Jiaxing, where such loyalist sentiments were not as strong. The city's residents not only defended the walls against the assault from Xiushui, they began killing Ming loyalists still resident inside the city. The attempted loyalist takeover of Jiaxing failed, but Xiushui remained loyalist for a time and the entire region fell into a "collaborators versus loyalists" chaos:

> All of the formerly arrogant elements who had viciously threatened the villages did everything in their power to wreak revenge on enemy households. People were killed, fires set—all through the countryside it was like this. For a full ten days this mutual slaughter continued, until the corpses were stretched all across the deserted fields.[10]

As one writer from Taicang[11] summarized the confusion and conflict caused throughout Jiangnan by Dodo's edict:

> After those of us in the city cut our hair, it was only the country folk who continued as before. Those who had hair did not visit the city. Those who had shaved their hair did not go into the countryside. If they were seen, they were in either case killed. The countryside and the city were blocked off from each other.[12]

Across the Qiantang River in Xioashan, despair over the new northern invaders turned into countless suicides among women and children even before their actual occupation. Many were recorded in a Xiaoshan County gazetteer in a chillingly bloodless form of enumeration:

> Mrs. Zhao, née Zhang, fearful of rape and death at the hands of the invading Manchus, drowned herself and her young son in Xiang Lake.

> Mrs. Wang, née Dai, drowned herself in Xiang Lake.

> Mrs. Lai, née Cheng, drowned herself in White Horse Lake.

> Mrs. Lai, née He,
> Mrs. Lai, née Huang,
> Mrs. Lai, née Ren,
> Mrs. Shen, née Lai,
> in a suicide pact all threw themselves down a well west of Xiang Lake and drowned.

> Yang Shoucheng, his wife, née Tang, and their son threw themselves in Tiger Village Pond and drowned.

> Weng Sun and eighty-nine members of the Shen lineage drowned themselves in the Qiantang River.[13]

For the common people of Jiangnan, life mostly went on as it always had. They would bend to the will of whomever reigned over them, just another of life's vicissitudes to be dealt with as it came. For the more youthful students, Confucian studies continued in the hopeful assumption that the examination system and career ladder of officialdom would persist. Merchants could reasonably anticipate the resumption of normal trade activity once armed conflict ended and the new dynasty had established its administrative bureaucracies. It was the Confucian-educated elites, the scholar-official class—whether aspiring, already serving, semi-retired, or retired—who faced some of the most painful personal decisions about how to respond to the new dynasty. Their stories are myriad...a few selected accounts illustrate the different ways they responded.

A Garden's Unplanned Use

Nothing in Qi Biaojia's 祁彪佳 (1602 – 1645) charmed life pleased him more than the spectacular garden he had constructed in his native Shaoxing. Son of a *jinshi* (Qi Chenghan, *jinshi* 1604), Biaojia was nothing short of a Confucian prodigy: *juren* winner at age 16, *jinshi* degree holder at 20, and "majestically handsome" as well.[14] A successful if not quite stellar official career followed for a decade, after which he returned on sick leave to Shaoxing in 1635 to enjoy a comfortable life as a bibliophile and connoisseur of collectibles. Inspired during a visit to nearby Yü Mountain (虞山, Yüshan) where he had played as a boy, Qi purchased a huge plot of land that spread broadly over three faces of the hill.

For more than two years, Qi Biaojia lavished his time, attention, and family fortune on the creation of his manufactured wonderland, which he named Allegory Garden (喻园, Yu yuan). Unlike the Chinese gardens typically associated today with a family's living quarters, Allegory Mountain by Qi's own account was at least a mile (three *li*) from his residence, requiring frequent travel between his home and the hillside construction site. He had already visited every garden he could manage, discussed garden design with his scholarly colleagues, and invited their suggestions.

The result was spectacular, a garden that "occupied three sides of the mountain and overlooked ten *mu*[15] 亩 (1.65 acres, or about 72,600 square feet) of level land. Half the area was covered by water and rocks; half by the house, flowers, and trees. The lot included two halls, three pavilions, four covered walkways, belvederes, embankments, galleries, and chapels. It also boasted a multistoried building for his fine library of over 31,500 [volumes]."[16]

Allegory Garden was clearly the prideful joy of a wealthy man already known for his civic involvement, charitable contributions of medicines, and support for famine relief. Nonetheless, his garden marked him as the most elite of the elites in his area. It was a place that drew the finest of Shaoxing's citizens to visit, socialize, and attend performances, facts that Qi carefully recorded in his diary—no doubt with a smile of achievement. One comprehensive study[17] published in 2006 identified nearly two hundred writers who authored among them almost one thousand pieces, mostly poems, celebrating the scenic and aesthetic marvels of Qi's garden estate. Their encomiums preserved Allegory Garden in literary memory long after its physical existence had ended.

After his mother's death in 1644 and following the fall of Beijing, Qi accepted a position as Governor of Suzhou in the Southern Ming government of the Prince of Lu.

In early 1645, Nanjing surrendered to the Manchu invaders, and then Hangzhou fell and the Prince of Lu's reign ended in flight. Qi Biaojia returned to Shaoxing convinced that martyrdom by suicide was his only viable option. He secretly prepared a will, informed his family that he was retiring to bed, and then drowned himself in the pond he had constructed in Allegory Garden. His son buried him on the garden grounds in a coffin that Qi had already supplied for himself. He was just 44 years old. His will instructed his family to turn over the entire garden to the monks at a nearby temple to help fund their operations.

A single note follows Qi's final entry in his diary: "My grandfather's diary ends on this day. During the 5th watch of the 6th day, he died a martyr."[18]

A Small Matter

For some in the Jiangnan area, the Manchu mandate for head-shaving provoked even greater resistance than the rise of the new "foreign" dynasty. Yang Tingshu was a highly esteemed teacher from the Suzhou area who was imprisoned in 1647 on suspicion of connections to an anti-Manchu uprising in Songjiang, south of Shanghai. At his hearing, the magistrate informed Yang that his treatment would be lenient if he simply cut his hair and shaved his head.

"To cut off my head is a small matter," he is said to have replied to the judge. "To shave my head is a great matter."

The magistrate ordered that the small matter be carried out; Yang Tingshu was beheaded in Wujiang as a resister and Ming loyalist. His legend was further enhanced when a report circulated that his last words were: "I was born a man of the Great Ming, and I shall die as a spirit of the Great Ming." Key to that report, and Yang's elevated standing as a martyred refuser, were specious claims that the final half of that pronouncement came from the mouth of his already-severed head.[19]

"Never Surrender!"

Although Wang Siren 王思任 (1575 – 1646, *jinshi* 1595) was born in Beijing during his father's official posting there as a physician, Shaoxing was the family's native place. Like Qi Biaojia, Wang was a precocious scholar who attained his *juren* degree at age 19 and his *jinshi* degree at age 20. His official positions included assignments as a magistrate in Shanxi Province and later in Nanjing. His service won the acclaim of the common people but aroused sufficient resentment and jealousy from other officials that they conspired to impeach him on spurious charges. In 1606, he retired back to Shaoxing for three years before taking a new position again in faraway Shanxi Province.

A pattern of excellent service followed by contrived allegations of illegality or inappropriate actions dogged Wang's career for the next thirty years. He would leave a position, regain a new (and sometimes lesser) one, succeed again, and be impeached by jealous colleagues or powerful local figures whose wrongdoings Wang had uncovered. His penchant for writing with biting sarcasm about those officials' ineptitude or mediocrity demonstrated writing talent but only amplified his opponents' dislike.

At around age 60, he retired to write his autobiography and enjoy his large family in Shaoxing: five concubines, seven surviving sons, and at least five grandsons.[20] In 1645, the 70-year-old Wang accepted a position as Minister of Rites at the Prince of Lu's temporary court in Shaoxing. Aggressively anti-Manchu, he swore never to shave his head and posted a sign on his door declaring "Never surrender!"[21] As Prince Bolo's Manchu army neared Shaoxing in pursuit of the Southern Ming "pretender," Wang fled into the surrounding hills. He took up quiet residence at a hut located close by his family's burial ground, where he starved himself to death out of loyalty to his lost dynasty. He was posthumously honored in a shrine of local worthies.

Unable to Resist, and Repenting Belatedly

The most committed loyalists either fought to the death or surrendered to fate by committing suicide. They numbered in the tens of thousands. For many others, however, various forms of withdrawal from officialdom, and sometimes altogether from society, provided both self-preservation and passive resistance to the new Qing Dynasty. Older Ming loyalists could withdraw into seclusion more easily, many having already served the Ming in their earlier years, established themselves financially, and seen properly to their parents' burials and mourning periods. Younger men who had been anticipating official careers in the Ming were the most awkwardly positioned, trapped in a moral vise between the filial demand for loyalty to one's dynasty and loyalty to—and care for—one's aging parents and family members.

Participation in the elite lifestyle of Shaoxing was practically Chen Hongshou's 陳洪綬 (1599 – 1652) birthright. Born in Zhuji, the great-grandson of a high-level official and grandson of a jinshi (Chen Xingxue, jinshi 1577), he received the Confucian training befitting his expected future: study of the Confucian classics, command of multiple calligraphic styles, knowledge of the great poets and painters, aesthetic discernment, and at least a modest degree of skill in versifying and painting. As early as age four, young Chen revealed his greatest talent from among those disciplines by painting "a seven-foot picture of Guan Hou 关侯 (God of War) on the wall of the house of his future father-in-law."[22]

Nevertheless, his and his family's goals were for officialdom, and that meant passing the provincial (juren) examinations, followed by the metropolitan and imperial examinations for the coveted jinshi degree. Chen's father died when the boy was just nine years old; by age fourteen, he was already producing artworks for sale in Shaoxing markets. The lowest-level prefectural degree (shenyuan) came in 1618, at age nineteen, but attempts in 1624, 1627, and 1630 failed to capture the next-level juren degree.

Meanwhile, his older brother had inherited the family estate, leaving Chen and his wife ignominiously occupying a small corner of the property. Throughout the 1630s, his primary source of income came from paintings he produced explicitly for sale in the marketplace, including figures and scenes found in novels and plays and playing cards used at drinking parties. His lifestyle ranged from "bohemian" and "unorthodox" to periods of "prolonged aesthetic dissipation."[23]

In the early 1640s, Chen purchased a position at the Imperial Academy in Beijing in hopes of gaining entrée into Ming officialdom. He turned down the only offer he received there, as a court painter, and returned home to Shaoxing in 1643. Three years later, as Prince Bolo's troops approached Shaoxing, Chen Hongshou fled for safety to a remote Buddhist temple. "In the summer of [1646], I regret to have fled for my life to the mountains and valleys," he later wrote in a poem. "Then I shaved my head and threw on the black garb of a monk."[24]

As the chaos and sackings receded, he abandoned temple life and resumed residence in Hangzhou as a professional painter. Having achieved no social status through examination success and making a living from selling his paintings (a practice regarded by elite literati as undignified), he was regarded as little more than a craftsman. Embittered by his fate—unable to serve, but unentitled to withdraw or resist by virtue of never having served, or even qualified to serve—he drank heavily and acted the *kuangshi* (狂士), the unruly or "mad" scholar. He sometimes produced paintings that presented scholar-elites, so praised for their resistance by reclusion, in harshly sarcastic forms. Born to a life among the elite, he could only live in their shadows. In one poem, he wrote:

> In my hometown, people treat winners and losers so differently
> That I dare not return to my thatched hut.
> Don't I understand the causes?
> In my heart I feel so ashamed.[25]

During a period of temple residence in the Yunmen Mountains, Chen produced a still-extant scroll painting, *Yaji* (雅集, *Elegant Gathering*) that he signed as "The Monk Who Regrets" (僧悔, Seng hui), along with a seal impression "Hui chi" (悔迟, "Regretting Belatedly"). His portrait works were intricately tied to theatrical figures, and his paintings increasingly adopted an "all the world's a stage attitude" toward life, including his own. He repeatedly questioned his own motivations, understanding full well that his brief commitment as a Buddhist monk was less about faith than it was about self-preservation. Although he might not easily face his ancestors in the next life over matters of dynastic loyalty (for not having simply committed suicide), he could point proudly to his continuing recognition as a great painter of his era whose works survive and are esteemed to the present day.

Resisting with Brush and Ink

As a well-educated man who lived through one of imperial Chinese history's most contentious transitions, Zhang Dai 張岱 (1597 – c. 1684, courtesy name Tao'an) is unusually famous for someone who had few noteworthy accomplishments to his name. Born into wealth and scholarship in late-Ming Shaoxing, Zhang experienced no meaningful successes in the examination system. He held no government offices, never won any battles or even served in the military, made no scientific discoveries, nor introduced any new theories

216

of philosophy, political science, religion, or governance. He admitted as much in the mock obituary he wrote for himself in 1665, about twenty years before his death:

> Zhang Dai....In his youth he was a fop. He had a great love of ostentation, being fond of luxurious quarters, pretty maids, beautiful boys, fresh clothes, fine foods, fast horses, painted lanterns, fireworks, opera, music, antiques, and flowers and birds. At the same time, he was excessive about tea and abusively fond of oranges, and was a bookworm and a poetry demon. He toiled at these pursuits for half a lifetime, when all turned into a dream-illusion.[26]

His self-criticism rings with regret for wasted time, the pleasures of wealthy excess, and a life of underachievement, yet he was among the most personable and insightful chroniclers of his time. His form of dynastic loyalty came not from bold action but from his writing, where he strove mightily for almost forty years to record for posterity all that he believed had been lost with the fall of the Ming. And it is through Zhang Dai's extant works that modern scholars have better understood elite life in late Ming China and the travails of the Ming–Qing transition.

Zhang Dai began writing his first book, a collection of biographies titled *Profiles of Righteous and Honorable People*, in 1618, at age 21. Even as he was working to see that book published in 1627, he conceived his life's project: to produce a history of the Ming Dynasty from its inception under Zhu Yuanzhang in 1368 and progressing through the reigns of fifteen Ming emperors to that of the then-current emperor, Chongzhen. By long tradition, the official history of each dynasty was written by the dynasty that succeeded it, but Zhang had no special reason to think that Chongzhen would be the Ming's last emperor. More likely, he perhaps believed that information collected during the Ming reign by a serious historian like himself would prove a valuable aid to the next dynasty's eventual writers of the Ming history.

After Nanjing fell to the Manchus in 1645, the Prince of Lu established a short-lived Southern Ming court at Shaoxing. Zhang Dai accepted an invitation to serve, but after just two or three months in a minor official position, he left in frustration. He then gathered up a few books from his family home on Dragon Mountain and abandoned Shaoxing in the summer of 1646 for a remote mountainous area about forty miles to the south. He also took the draft manuscript and materials for his Ming history, leaving behind in Shaoxing a family library containing thirty thousand volumes. After his hurried departure, the troops of Ming General Fang Guo'an ransacked his family's abandoned home, ripping up the books to light fires or wad up inside their armor to blunt arrow strikes. "Thus," Zhang wrote, "the collection I had accumulated for the span of forty years was all lost in a matter of days."[27]

When he finally returned home in 1649, Zhang Dai found nothing but ruins. He was 52 years old, formerly well-off but now nearly penniless. He rented a small plot of land on Dragon Mountain in a place whose name, Happiness Garden, reminded him of visits as a young boy with his grandfather but now simply mocked his fate. He described himself as a changed man, shaken to recall his formerly carefree and profligate ways and viewing the entirety of his new circumstances as just punishment:

> How extravagant things were! Today's suffering is retribution for that. This bamboo hat is retribution upon my skull, and sandals are retribution upon my heels—dues for hatpins and fine-soled shoes. My monkish robe is retribution for furs, coarse hemp for fine linen—dues for light and warm clothes. Coarse greens are retribution for meat, and coarse grain for rice—dues for tasty delicacies. A grass mat is retribution for a bed, and a rock for a pillow—dues for gentle comforts. Rope is retribution for hinges, a round jar for windows—dues for living comfortably on the high and dry. And smoke is retribution upon my eyes, manure upon my nose—dues for captivating smells and sights. The road is retribution upon my feet, my sack upon my shoulder—dues for sedan chairs and attendants. Each and every category of sin can be seen from each and every sort of retribution.[28]

Chastened and suffering, perhaps, yet still alive, unlike so many among the Ming loyalist elites who died fighting or chose honorable suicide. Zhang Dai would take up writing once again, rationalizing his continued existence as essential to completing his "true" version of Ming history, uncorrupted by Manchu perspectives and propaganda as he believed the official histories would undoubtedly be. In this, Zhang was fashioning himself after Sima Qian 司马迁 (c. 145 – c. 86 BCE), China's greatest ancient historian, who opted for castration over execution in order to finish his celebrated *Records of the Grand Historian* (史记, *Shiji*).

Zhang went still further to justify himself, naming his Ming history *The Stone Casket* (石匮书, *Shigui shu*). This odd-sounding title alluded to the storage vessels used by historians in Sima Qian's time to preserve and protect the source materials upon which they relied. It is tempting to imagine that Zhang viewed his "unadulterated" Ming history as a source that future historians would rely upon and store in their stone caskets.

From 1649 to about 1655, Zhang Dai produced his first draft of *The Stone Casket*, a monumental work of 2,500,000 characters. Because Emperor Chongzhen's death marked the end of the dynasty in 1644, he knew there would be a sequel describing the Ming fall and the failed efforts to create a Southern Ming. He completed his Ming history in the 1670s, adding another half-million characters for the sequel.

Meanwhile, family affairs interrupted in a way that propelled Zhang's authorial life in an entirely new and highly personal direction. Two of his sons demonstrated sufficient scholarly promise in their studies that their father accompanied them to Hangzhou as they sat for the provincial (*juren*) examinations in 1654. As subsequently disappointed as Zhang undoubtedly was when his sons both failed that year's exams, he was thrown into despair by a visit to West Lake:

> [I] have been kept far from West Lake for twenty-eight years. Nevertheless there has not been a day that West Lake has not been a part of my dreams, and the West Lake in my dreams has, in fact, never been gone for a single

day….[I]n 1654 and 1657, I went back to West Lake, and…of that whole stretch of lakeside villas nothing was left but shards of broken tile. So all those things that were present in my dreams were, in reality, not there beside West Lake at all. As for the view from Broken Bridge,[29] all those delicate willows and tender peach trees of olden days, all those pavilions for singers and dancers, were as if washed away by a vast flood, and not one in a hundred was spared. I therefore fled from the place as quickly as I could, saying to myself that it was because of West Lake that I had come there, but now I could see things were in such a state that I should strive to protect the West Lake of my dreams….[30]

The wreckage Zhang Dai saw at West Lake inspired another way for him to capture for posterity the glory that had so recently been the Ming Dynasty. In 1646, Zhang Dai produced his greatest literary work, *Dream Reminiscences of Tao'an* (陶庵梦忆, *Tao'an mengyi*). In 123 short, topical essays, he recalled multiple aspects of his life prior to 1645, setting them implicitly against the years since the Manchu conquest of the Chinese empire. Drawn largely from memory, *Dream Reminiscences* wanders among such topics as watching the Qiantang River tidal bore, tasting spring waters for tea brewing, visiting the incense market at West Lake, observing the grave-sweeping rituals of Shaoxing's residents, hanging and viewing decorative lanterns, and building and losing his family's library collection.

Zhangs's commentaries in *Dream Reminiscences* could evoke sadness and regret, but they could equally demonstrate a fierce, on-point sarcasm. In his "Ghost Festival at West Lake" (西湖七月半, Xihu qiyueban) vignette, he skewered the preening social behavior of the people who in his Ming years boarded rented boats at West Lake for moon-viewing on the seventh night of the seventh lunar month. He divided the participants into five types:

- The first type: "…ostensibly looking at the moon but actually not seeing the moon at all."
- The second type: "…to left and right they stare and gaze, present beneath the moon but really not looking at the moon at all."
- The third type: "…they, beneath the moon, both look at the moon and hope that other people are looking at them looking at the moon."
- The fourth type: "…they look at the moon, they look at those looking at the moon, and at those not looking at the moon, but they aren't really looking at anything."
- The fifth type: "they look at the moon, but their air of looking at the moon remains unseen by others, nor do they make a point of looking at the moon."[31]

Zhang Dai's was presumably the fifth, properly moon-viewing type. Of course, his type did indeed look at the moon while making a point of not looking at the moon, so that the uncultured masses would notice them looking as though not looking, all the while telling themselves that none of this really mattered.

Recalling how subjects of the Ming partook of the natural beauties of West Lake, Zhang Dai produced another remembrance work on that subject. Titled *Dream Pursuit of West Lake* (西湖梦寻, *Xihu mengxun*), the book functioned as a literary travel guide, organized into geographical sections around Xihu while offering a collection of poetry and prose pieces relevant to the sites in each section.

Dream Pursuit of West Lake was a special form of travel aid, one that enabled its readers to experience West Lake with the "proper" Ming literatus mindset. The book constituted yet another element of Zhang's quiet resistance program, preserving the Ming world view and aesthetic against the "northern foreigners" who might someday obliterate all memory of Han Chinese civilization as he knew it. History would ultimately demonstrate that he was not entirely wrong in his estimation of the Manchus.

Zhang Dai's closing act of cultural preservation and rebellion by literary means came with his collection, *Portraits of the Eminent Worthies of Zhejiang during the Ming Dynasty Whose Lives Embodied the Three Eternals*[32] (明於越三不朽明贤圖赞, *Ming yuyue sanbuxiu mingxian tuzan*). In this work, Zhang combined individual portrait images with posthumous textual commemorations in prose and verse in an effort to immortalize more than one hundred Zhejiang Province natives, including friends and members of his extended family. Only six of his profiles were women, all of them confined to the "Virtue" category. Embittered to the end, Zhang's preface of 1680 pointedly excluded the standard reference to the corresponding Qing imperial reign year (Kangxi's nineteenth). The completed work was not published before Zhang's death and remained unknown and unpublished until its first appearance in print two centuries later, in 1888.[33]

Frederick Mote wrote in a memorable 1973 essay[34] that few physical remnants of China's past remain in their original form; most are rebuilt or reconstructed replicas. He argued instead that, in China, "The past was a past of words, not of stones....It constantly scrutinized that past as recorded in words, and caused it to function in the life of its present." He added, "Chinese civilization did not lodge its history in buildings.... In short, we can say that the real past...is a past of the mind; its imperishable elements are moments of human experience. The only truly enduring embodiments of the eternal human moments are the literary ones." The numerous written records of Qi Biaojia's Allegory Mountain and Zhang Dai's literary efforts to capture the essence of his lived experience through the late Ming offer two prime examples of preserving in words a lost garden, lost worthies, and a lost lifestyle.[35]

The Great Collaborator…and a Wife Who Disagreed

When Qian Qianyi led a sizable cohort of Nanjing officials through the city gates in peaceful surrender to Prince Dodo on June 8, 1645, he fully understood the personal ramifications of his actions. At age 63, he was widely regarded as one of the great figures of his time. A *jinshi* in 1610, examination supervisor in Zhejiang, Hanlin academician, court supervisor of instruction, and an esteemed poet and literary critic, he was one of the leading intellectual lights of the fallen dynasty.

After the horrific massacre at Yangzhou less than two weeks prior, Qian and his colleagues concluded that Nanjing could not withstand a Manchu assault and that the Ming fall was a foregone conclusion. Better to suffer personal shame and public criticism, they believed, than accede to hundreds of thousands or even millions of senseless deaths and untold destruction. True Ming loyalists throughout the south might have found a way to forgive Qian his decision to surrender; some might even have been secretly relieved. However, few could excuse their citizen-leader for what he did next.

Once Prince Dodo and his senior commanders entered Nanjing, Qian began collaborating with them regarding a peaceful takeover of the entire Jiangnan region. He crafted a slogan urging the people to accept the new Manchu rule: "Heaven favors [the Manchu rule] and the people embrace [the new Qing Dynasty]." When Prince Dodo described his plan to select and install local officials in each city and town as "pacification commissioners," Qian provided the names of dozens of suitable candidates and actively helped recruit them into service. In an effort to gain acquiescence by the populace, he also crafted a painfully obsequious statement of support for the new dynasty that welcomed the Manchus as the nation's saviors from radical rebels and welcomed restorers of civil order:

> Is there anyone else who could have mounted such a campaign against banditry and saved the world with their sense of obligation, who could have routed the rebels who defied Heaven and avenged the unthinkable death of our emperor, who could have cleared away the shame and expelled the evil, surpassing in eminence all that has gone before, as the Great Qing has done? Is there anyone else who could care for the graves of our emperors and restore their ancestral temples, who could provide relief for the provinces and diminish the suffering of the people, who could summon the orphaned imperial servants and restore administrative authority, anyone whose benevolence is as deep, whose intentions as lofty, whose humanism as exhaustive or whose sense of obligation as thorough as the Great Qing?[36]

The new pacification commissioners were armed with Qian Qianyi's statement of support as they took up their positions throughout the lower Jiangsu and northern Zhejiang Province areas.

Throughout this time, and even before the surrender at Nanjing, Qian had taken these actions despite the vocal opposition of his brilliant and beloved consort, Liu Rushi 柳如是 (1618 – 1664). It is said that as the Manchus crossed the Yangzi River to besiege Nanjing, Liu had argued vehemently that Qian should simply withdraw and refuse to serve a Manchu dynasty. Some accounts asserted that Liu even encouraged him to commit honorable suicide,[37] in which martyrdom she presumably would have joined. The Qing-era poet Yuan Mei (1716 – 1798) later versified on their predicament and wrote disparagingly of Qian Qianyi's decision to collaborate:

> All thought [Qian Qianyi] a peerless scholar among the officials of his age,
> But this new husband of hers was only a second-rate man.
> ....

Qian gave himself the title "Disciple of Poetry,"
And the two lovers burnt incense to that ancient sage, Buddha.
Liu, the courtesan, proved greater than a court full of scholars,
But Qian preferred romance to his place in history.
....
Then one day the dust of war swirled over the land,
And holding knife and noose, Liu urged Qian to die.
She said, "Life is brief, why not rest in peace?"
(And his failure at that moment decided history's verdict).
A pity that although Qian lived to such a great age,
In paintings, at least, he had to make way for his wife![38]

Although Qian chose a path other than suicide or withdrawal into reclusion, their story as a couple before, during and after these events was one that lived on through the ages. Ironically, Qian Qianyi's willingness to serve two dynasties would arise some one hundred years hence and help instigate one of the most devastating literary inquisitions in China's imperial history.

Liu Rushi's talents and life story were altogether the equal of Qian's if not surpassing his. Born in Jiaxing[39] to a family named Yang, she was sold into concubinage at a young age and then to a brothel in southern Jiangsu Province. By the age of just 15, her beauty and intellect marked her as a special talent and led to the first of several extended relationships among the elites of Jiangnan society. This first arrangement occurred in 1633 (at age 15) with Chen Zilong 陈子龙 (1608 – 1647, jinshi 1637),[40] a scholar-official and esteemed poet from Songjiang who was ten years Liu's senior. History suggests that they were intellectually and emotionally quite compatible, but Chen's first wife forced the young concubine to leave.

By the latter 1630s, Liu Rushi cemented another consort-mentor relationship, this time with the much older Wang Ruqian, the playboy salt merchant and proud owner of the floating "Unmoored Garden" on West Lake. Wang was more than forty years older than Liu, but he traveled actively around Jiangnan and introduced Liu to the cream of Ming society. Wang gradually withdrew from the relationship after about three years together, which greatly angered the young courtesan. He compensated for the separation by introducing her to yet another scholar-official, Qian Qianyi, in around 1639 or 1640.

By now, Liu Rushi was widely known throughout the region for her beauty, her painting skills, and especially her poetic talents, having already published several collections of her work. "As a consort, she was the archetypal woman of excellence: beautiful, romantic, committed to affairs, pursued by many, and very proud...[S]he was a brilliant beauty as well, a regular guest at literati parties."[41] In her first meeting with Qian Qianyi in late 1640, she dressed as a man and submitted a selection of her poetry to his critique. Popular belief contends that Qian believed she was a man and was favorably impressed by the poems put before him.

By year's end, Liu Rushi had taken up residence at Qian's estate. Thirty-seven years older than the young courtesan, Qian was so utterly taken by her beauty and talents that he took her as his second wife in July 1641. In the social world of the literati class, she stood as her husband's near-equal, boldly dressing in male clothing with enough regularity that others began punning on her chosen name by calling her 儒士 *rushi*, that is, "Confucian gentleman." Liu had her own boat in which she frequently traveled to West Lake and other venues in the region, and she also traveled to several of China's sacred mountains.[42]

In the second half of the 1640s, the couple collaborated on their greatest work. Qian built a five-bay tower for Liu Rushi at his home in Changshu[43] as a combination study, library, and workspace. Qian named the building the Tower of Crimson Clouds (绛雲樓, *Jiangyun lou*), equating Liu with an immortal fairy descended from the heavenly skies. It was in this magnificent library that Qian and Liu jointly authored their *Collection of Poetry from Successive Reigns* (列朝诗集小传, *Liechao shiji xiaozhuan*), a massive anthology accompanied by two thousand biographies of the represented poets.

A late 17th-Century biography of Liu Rushi described her peer-like working relationship with Qian Qianyi in mildly idealized but informative terms:

> Once [Qian] had retired from the world of embroidered curtains and jasper chambers he would spend day and night closeted here in close conversation with Liu [Ru]shi....In old age, Qian's obsession with reading and with books became even more pronounced and as he went about his editing and his checking of textual variants...it was only Liu [Ru]shi that he would ever consult. Whenever the slightest furrow crossed his brow or his brush paused as it plied its way down the page, Liu [Ru]shi would immediately leap to her feet and proceed upstairs to consult some book and would open it up to point with her slender finger to precisely the right passage, never once making a mistake. On other occasions, when Qian's use of an allusion proved wrong or infelicitous, she would correct whatever he had written.[44]

Liu Rushi is regarded by modern scholars as not only the editor and commentator on the selections from female poets in *Collections of Poetry from Successive Reigns* but also the author of their respective biographies. In her radical position as a courtesan-editor, and presumably with Qian Qianyi's awareness if not consent, Liu "place[d] the emphasis firmly on the courtesans' [poetry] work, giving them pride of place at the expense of gentry ladies."[45] Hers was a bold elevation of courtesan poetry over that of the genteel women of the inner chambers.

The couple had a daughter together in 1649, upon whom Liu fervently doted. In fact, she insisted upon her daughter's betrothal at age ten that the young boy "marry in" and reside at the Qian family's residence for the next four years. Qian Qianyi and Liu Rushi remained happily together for twenty-four years in a clearly companionate relationship until his death at age 83 in the summer of 1664.

Following his death, Qian's family members and clansmen descended upon his widow, demanding money from the estate and claiming that she had no survivor's rights as a former courtesan and second wife. Soon they began demanding that the entire estate be auctioned, with the proceeds distributed across the clan membership. With nowhere else to turn, Liu invited the entire clan group to a banquet, at which she promised to address their demands. After everyone was seated, the besieged widow withdrew to her chambers and hung herself, barely a month after her husband's death.[46] The family refused to bury her remains alongside Qian's at Yushan Mountain in Changshu, but her tomb is located nearby to his.

Liu Rushi's intelligence and fierce independence, her bold demands to be treated equally with the literati males of her time, and her aggressive promotion of the poetry of Ming females made her an early hero of women's rights in China. The life and spirit of this daughter of Jiaxing would offer an important source of inspiration to the women of late 18th-Century and early 19th-Century Zhejiang.

West Lake at the End of the Ming Dynasty[47]

From its early transformation from salt-laden lagoon to fresh water source to scenic pleasure spot and tourist vista, West Lake sustained a complicated relationship with the city to its east and, by extension, to the national culture. Where once Bai Juyi and Su Shi had acted to sustain the lake as a water source, the latter's three hundred poems about Hangzhou had immortalized West Lake as something much more, a natural work of art imbued with deep human meaning. "If Su Shi the prefect physically saved West Lake, it was Su Shi the poet who elevated its landscape from the ranks of ordinary reservoirs and made it a unique site on the cultural map of imperial China."[48]

Yet West Lake became so attractive as a place of pleasurable distraction and conspicuous display that the fall of the Southern Song Dynasty was attributed in part to the lake's deleterious effects on the strength and moral fiber of the dynasty. Those who sought aggressive military action to retake the north from the Jurchen Jin claimed that West Lake's pleasures had softened and distracted the emperors and their courts. In their view, the lake that Su Shi had compared poetically to Xi Shi had exerted its destructive wiles over the Southern Song just as that legendary beauty had done in bringing King Fuchai and the Wu State to ruin.

The Yuan Dynasty years saw substantial deterioration in West Lake's condition, particularly since the Mongol rulers viewed the Song literati lifestyle with undisguised disdain. However, their lack of attention to West Lake's maintenance reduced it nearly to extinction. Hangzhou scholar Tian Rucheng described the lake's former condition in his 1547 *Record of Touring and Sightseeing at West Lake* as having become ninety percent cultivated land:

> West of the Su Embankment the higher elevations became farmland while those lower down were turned into ponds. Patches of land were crisscrossed by roads like fish scales, and there was no room left. East of the embankment all that remained was a narrow waterway that flowed like a belt.[49]

Such was the situation when Yang Mengying set out at the beginning of the 1500s to reclaim the West Lake as a body of water. Yang's work was eminently successful in reclaiming the lake, but scenery in the surrounding areas fell into a deteriorated condition once again by the 1580s. This time, a local official prevailed upon the eunuch Sun Long 孫隆 (1525 – 1594), director of the Suzhou and Hangzhou Imperial Silk Factories, to finance renovation work on the embankments, roadways, temple buildings, and horticulture around the lake. Himself immensely wealthy, Sun drew upon the silk factory's massive financial resources as well to fund a full-scale makeover. Even as he labeled Sun Long a profligate, Zhang Dai praised this work in his *Dream Reminiscences of Tao'an*:

> As part of his lavish refurbishment of the lakeshore, Sun Long had an outdoor terrace built and upon this one can take in the cool breeze or stroll beneath the bright moon. One can also have a banquet laid out here for one's guests, and not a day goes by that is without the sound of flutes and singing or without an opera performed....Sun Long expended several hundreds of thousands of *taels* on prettifying the lake, and in this regard his efforts were not inferior to those of the Academician Su Shi.[50]

Just five decades after Sun Long's massive renovation project, the final years of the Ming era left the West Lake under-maintained and damaged once again, evidenced by Zhang Dai's despairing observations when he visited the lake with his sons in 1654. Even worse, the Manchu choice of Hangzhou as a major garrison site in 1647 and their decision to locate that armory in the city's northwestern section had effectively made them West Lake's caretakers.

Like the Mongol Yuan, the Manchus viewed Jiangnan as the source of a morally destructive and socially disordered lifestyle to be discouraged under their rule. In Hangzhou's case, that meant, in part, restricting the people's formerly free-wheeling and licentious use of West Lake. Instead, the garrison soldiers converted the lake area into drilling and horse-grazing grounds. The hillside villas went unrepaired, and the celebrated willow and peach trees lining the three famous dikes were chopped down and used as firewood. Without the tree roots to hold the embankment soil together, the causeways began deteriorating as well.

As had happened centuries before, West Lake began to shrink again, leading once more to illegal encroachments that converted the exposed lakebed into cultivated land. Such circumstances were not unusual in northern Zhejiang, where countless smaller lakes disappeared in favor of (legal and illegal) encroachment for revenue-generating agricultural purposes. By at least one count, the number of lakes in the Ningbo-Shaoxing plain (south of the Qiantang River from Ningbo to Xianshan) had decreased by land reclamation from 217 in the Song Dynasty to 199 at the start of the Ming Dynasty and to just 44 by the 20th Century, "and those that remained had reduced surface areas and water storage capacity."[51]

Larger lakes suffered as well. Thousand-year-old Mirror Lake (鉴湖, Jian hu) near Shaoxing had been encroached out of existence by the end of the Song Dynasty, and Xiang Lake in Xiaoshan suffered repeated bouts of encroachment and industrialization (for brick-making) until it, too, disappeared for a time. After 1984, when the lakebed clay was nearly exhausted, Xiaoshan's local government restored Xiang Lake to its present-day size.[52]

When Suzhou native You Tong 尤侗 (1618-1704) visited West Lake in 1649, just two years after the Manchu occupation began, he described the water as silt- and weed-filled, adding:

> None of the countless branches and catkins [from the willow and peach trees] were left. There were only broken roots jutting from the weeds. From afar I could see the dilapidated Lake Heart Pavilion[53] (*Huxing Ting* 湖心亭)— it was all but collapsing into the water. The pavilions and towers around the lake were all in a state of ruination. In the past there were silk cables and ivory oars, fragrant carriages and precious horses, gentlemen with purple flutes, and beauties with red rouge. What have become of them now! All that confronted me were some lone crows flying past the setting sun, and a few lines of migrating wild swans crying sadly on the desolated marsh.[54]

In the cycle of decay and restoration that characterized West Lake's existence, the lake reached yet another low point in the first decades of the Qing Dynasty.

Chapter 10

QING DYNASTY – THE FIRST CENTURY

(1644 – 1735)

A stone-paved pathway hidden deep in myriad bamboos
Tempts me to climb with an old friend to Meditation's home.
Suddenly, as we unbar the gate, our eyes delighted see
Beyond the Lake the city's smoking hearths; beyond the River, hills.[1]

— *Wei Fang-t'ai (1650 - 1728)*

City within a City

As if the Manchu head-shaving edict in the summer of 1645 had not already caused enough upset and disruption, a new edict soon led to the greatest upheaval in Hangzhou since the construction of the Southern Song palace complex more than five hundred years earlier.

In late 1646, the Manchu conquerors had forcibly evicted all Han Chinese citizens from the entire northeastern quarter of Xi'an, and similarly in the southeastern quarter of Nanjing. In their place, the new rulers established military garrisons, surrounded by their own high walls and accessible through a limited number of gates. These "Tartar cities," as they came to be called by Westerners, served as Manchu-only residential districts for garrison soldiers and their families, creating what historian Frederick Wakeman termed a "Manchu apartheid."[2]

By the end of the dynasty, over one hundred of these garrisons would be established across the empire.[3] Perhaps surprisingly, many of their occupants were neither Manchus nor Mongols. They were northern Han Chinese who had lived under Manchu rule and made up the vast majority of the Qing infantry. While the Manchus maintained their own homogeneous army corps known as the Eight Banners,[4] the massed troops of Chinese foot soldiers were known as the Green Standard army, whose commanders were nearly always Manchus.

In 1647, it was Hangzhou's turn to accommodate the forced construction of a garrison inside its city walls. The Manchus chose the northwestern section of the city as their new military outpost, requiring that all Han Chinese residing in those 420 acres (more than 13% of the walled city's total area)[5] be removed—forcibly, if necessary. In their place came five or six thousand soldiers, along with their wives, children, and parents. At one point, a commander of the new Hangzhou garrison memorialized the throne that nearly 1,500 buildings had been seized for residential use, repurposing, or just demolition.[6] The civic disruption was enormous, creating a near-instantaneous mass of displaced persons seeking shelter in a city already long known for overcrowding.

Meanwhile, garrison walls seven feet thick and rising thirty-five feet high[7] were completed in 1648, with six gates for entrance or exit. This restricted area contained the seven-acre headquarters and residence of the garrison commander, along with offices for other senior officials and their staffs, a parade ground, a military academy, and residential accommodations for as many as 20,000 military and their family members. Despite the high walls and conversion of the lake shore to military uses, Hangzhou's new influx of Manchu "immigrants" nevertheless enjoyed the city's most convenient access to West Lake. The garrison's land seizure had swallowed Qiantang Gate within its confines, providing the Manchu population with the quickest and easiest access to the most preferred points along the lake's northern shore.

As perhaps a final insult directed at the Ming loyalists still remaining in Hangzhou, the Manchus appointed a Ming turncoat named Tian Xiong 田雄 (d. 1663) as the commanding general of the new garrison. Tian would lead the Manchus in the recapture and pacification of eastern Zhejiang Province and the Zhoushan Islands over the next several years.

A Survivor Takes the Throne

From the time of his ascendency to the Qing throne in 1638 as a compromise choice at the age of just five,[8] the Shunzhi Emperor's 順治帝(r. 1644 – 1661) reign was largely guided by a Regency under his uncle, Prince Dorgon. Dorgon oversaw the military conquest of Ming China and suppressed the Southern Ming restoration effort and other anti-Manchu movements across the empire. He also ordered creation of the physically and socially segregated Manchu city in the northern half of Beijing which established the pattern of "Manchu apartheid" across the empire's garrison network. Yet it was he as well who reinstituted the triennial civil service examination system in 1646.

Upon Dorgon's death in the last days of 1650, the twelve-year-old Shunzhi took over a Chinese empire still churning with conflict, rebellion, and the tribulations of a dynastic transition. The young Emperor also faced heated bouts of factionalism at court, unresolved remnants of the power struggles that had originally placed him on the throne as a compromise ruler. He strove to be a good leader by learning Chinese, welcoming discussions with capable advisors, restoring the Hanlin Academy, and fighting factionalism and corruption. What he could not counteract was a fearsome, unseen enemy that changed the arc of Chinese imperial history: smallpox.

While the Manchu people were not immune to smallpox, cases in the nomadic north were not common and epidemic outbreaks were rare. Increased contact with the more sedentary and urbanized Chinese below the Great Wall heightened the risk of contagion, a circumstance about which the Qing court was well aware and greatly feared. In fact, during the Shunzhi Emperor's seventeen-year reign, nine separate outbreaks of smallpox in Beijing[9] caused him to withdraw each time to specially prepared and isolated quarantine shelters known as *bidousou* (避痘所; literally, "place to avoid pox"). In Shunzhi's case, his two *bidousuo* were islands surrounded by water.

Despite these extraordinary precautions, Shunzhi nevertheless contracted the disease. Shortly before his death, he decreed that no one should succeed him on the throne who had not already contracted smallpox and survived. Thus, upon Shunzhi's passing, the court obeyed his order and chose as the next emperor the only one of his four living sons who satisfied that criterion, the eight-year-old Xuanye 玄燁 (1654 – 1722). That fortunate young man would occupy the Qing throne for sixty-one years, longer than any emperor in history. As the Kangxi Emperor 康熙帝 (r. 1661 – 1722), he would also be celebrated as one of imperial China's greatest rulers.

Crossing the Boundaries – Women Poets

As calamitous as were the changes resulting from the Manchu conquest of the Ming, those events hardly paused one of the great cultural shifts of 17th-Century China— the public rise and acceptance of the literary gentlewoman (闺秀, *guixiu*). Where Li Qingzhao suffered the exceptional circumstances of widowhood and the privations of dynastic conflict and Liu Rushi benefited from loosened social strictures applied to concubines, the wives and daughters of elite families had long been captives of their household's inner quarters, seldom seen and rarely heard. Women's traditional education since the Han Dynasty, to the extent anything formal was provided, had generally focused on moral instruction and cultivation of the four womanly values (四德, *si de*): virtue, speech, demeanor (i.e., ritual conduct and physical charm), and household work. "From her first birthday to her last breath, a woman was taught *fu-tao* [妇道, *fudao*, female virtues]: how to be a wife."[10]

From the last decades of the Ming through the first decades of the Qing, the *guixiu* of the Hangzhou area figured significantly in the new levels of respect and broadened distribution given to women's poetry and prose. The educated wives of Jiangnan's elite families were increasingly seen in public or traveling with their husbands, staking out positions concerning public and civic affairs, expressing dynastic loyalty, and networking and congregating socially with one another and in small groups. Such women were appreciated as additions to their families' social capital, contravening the traditional attitude that "a woman without talent is virtuous" (女子无才便是德, *nüzi wucai bianshi de*).[11] While no one individual can be said to have initiated this opening-up trend, several contemporaneous early exemplars and influencers were Huang Yuanjie 黄媛介 (c. 1620 – c. 1670) from Jiaxing, Shang Jinglan 商景兰 (1605 – c. 1676) in Shaoxing, Gu Ruopu 顾若璞 (1592 – c. 1681) in Hangzhou, and Wang Duanshu (1621 – after 1701) in both Shaoxing and Hangzhou.

Reminiscent of the dynastic conflict travails of Li Qingzhao, **Huang Yuanjie**'s life was a study in breaking women's traditional domestic boundaries. Life began well enough for a young woman born into a well-established but financially stressed Jiaxing family. Huang Yuanjie received an early education, as did her brother and elder sister. Yuanjie subsequently entered into an arranged marriage[12] to an aspiring but ultimately failed Ming scholar named Yang Shigong 杨世功, forcing the young woman to take on students and sell her poetry and paintings to support their family. Her artistic and poetic reputation grew, but the Manchu conquest in the 1640s upended the modest life[13] she had fashioned as the primary breadwinner for her husband and two children.

During the 1640s, Yang and his family moved from place to place in Jiangsu Province in an effort to escape the Manchu conflict. Some accounts suggest that Yuanjie may have been kidnapped during this period and possibly raped, sold into a brothel, or both.[14] Following the change in dynasties, the family settled near West Lake in Hangzhou, where Huang resumed her production and quite successful sale of artworks, poems, and even her calligraphy. As she traveled about Jiangnan selling her works, which were much in demand at high prices, she brandished an openly public persona and befriended other educated and talented women of her time.

Her growing reputation eventually garnered the attention of the official world in the capital, in particular a high-level minister named Shi Shen. Aware of Huang's financial difficulties, Shi Shen invited her to travel to Beijing to tutor his daughter in the Classics and the arts, even sending along the money to pay for her boat travel with her children. Along the way, her son Yang Delin drowned as the boat reached Tianjin. Less than a year later, her daughter Yang Benshan passed away as well. Devastated by the loss of her children, Huang Yuanjie fell ill and left the capital. Her failing health forced her to interrupt her return trip with an extended stay near Nanjing where she, too, died about six months later.[15]

Huang's literary and artistic accomplishments, her frequent (and unaccompanied) travel, and her well-developed social-professional network of like-minded woman of talent "opened a way for other women to combine domesticity with a career, literary achievements with feminine virtue, and respectability with sociability and mobility."[16]

As the daughter of a distinguished scholar-official family,[17] **Shang Jinglan** was the beneficiary of both an education and a choice marriage match with the equally wealthy and respected Qi Biaojia. About half of her husband's official career involved positions in Fujian Province and in Beijing; Shang accompanied and resided with him (and away from Shaoxing) for most of that time, broadening her experiences, cultural exposures, and contact network.

Her husband's obsessive interest in Shaoxing's garden culture after his retirement from official life in 1635 included social visits to numerous private gardens, often in the company of his wife. These excursions provided Shang Jinglan with further networking opportunities among the wives and daughters of elite families. During these visits, the women enjoyed the same socializing as their husbands and fathers: drinking tea or wine, composing or exchanging poetry, listening to instrumental performances, admiring paintings and antiquities, or watching the performances of theatrical troupes. Over time, Shang began forming loose communities of her peers.

During the two years Qi spent constructing Allegory Mountain, Shang was often at his side, helping plan the garden's design.[18] Her husband's diary contains references to groups of women meeting at the garden after its completion and receiving distinguished female visitors like Liu Rushi and Huang Yuanjie (who stayed with the Qi family at Shang's invitation for an entire year). For the final thirty years of her widowhood following her husband's suicide in 1645, Shang focused on her family's welfare while cultivating a distinguished literary circle drawn from the women of Shaoxing, Hangzhou, and Jiaxing. She worked diligently to educate her daughters as well as her sons in literary tradition, and she was widely esteemed for the impromptu poetry composition outings she convened for her four daughters, one sister, and two daughters-in-law:

> On days when she had free time, [Shang] would ascend a hill overlooking water, and ordering her daughters-in-law and daughters to take pens and pack ink stones, would proceed to have them set rhymes and choose topics. Everyone talked of these marvelous occasions.[19]

As her life crossed over from Ming to Qing, Shang Jinglan stood near the forefront in expanding her own freedom of movement, associating with other women both socially and culturally, and promoting a scholar-official style of education for the young women in her family.

Although she was thirteen years older, **Gu Ruopu**'s life in Hangzhou paralleled Shang Jinglan's in several ways: born into a gentry family, product of a literary education, married in 1606 into another gentry family (that of Huang Maowu 黄茂梧, 1590 - 1619), and widowed with two sons and two daughters in 1619 after just thirteen years of marriage. Gu's father-in-law stepped in at this juncture, arranging to further her education so she could oversee the Huang boys' preparation for the civil service exams. Gu committed herself to her sons' education, even having a boat converted into a floating study in a quiet corner of West Lake to isolate her oldest son from noise and distractions.[20] She not only fulfilled her maternal responsibilities to the Huang family sons but also set out on a program of education for the women in both her natal and marital families, some of them relatively distant kinship relations.

Gu was an accomplished poet and writer in her own right, but she is remembered most for her strong advocacy of women's literary education and her influence in that regard in the Hangzhou community. She was also a fierce proponent of women's writing, asserting in the preface to her own works that it was a woman's calling to do so. In her view, female beauty and virtue arose from and was enhanced by literary education. As more women

231

and their daughters followed the leads of Shang Jinglan, Gu Ruopu, and others, "attitudes among the literati changed as talent, beauty and virtue combined to form a new ideal of femininity and elite men valorized...gentlewomen as intellectual companions."[21]

The youngest of the women discussed here, **Wang Duanshu** was the second daughter of Wang Siren, the Ming loyalist from Shaoxing who starved himself to death. As a young girl, Duanshu's reading abilities so confounded her father that he sent her for tutoring along with her eight brothers, whom their father famously deemed less capable than their sister. Her family knew her as an exuberant spirit who liked dressing up as a soldier and "commanding" the family's maidservants in military formations.

Wang entered an arranged marriage with an official named Ding Shengzhao 丁聖肇 (1621 – c. 1700), betrothed virtually from the time of their same-year births. The couple lived in Beijing, but they returned to Shaoxing after 1644 due to the Manchu invasion of the north. Impoverished by her father's suicide, Duanshu resolved to support her family by "plowing with her tongue,"[22] that is, tutoring and writing. The family eventually settled in Hangzhou and circulated among the leading lights of the region, especially with Zhang Dai and Li Yu 李漁 (1610 – 1680), both of whom aggressively supported women's education in literature and aesthetics. Wang's network of equally stellar female acquaintances included the cultural leaders Liu Rushi, Shang Jinglan, and Huang Yuanjie. Although she lived as an elite gentlewoman in a literatus family, she largely ignored the restrictive traditions imposed on women of the inner chambers. Instead, she was outspoken and outgoing, freely exchanging poetry with anyone with whom she engaged.

Throughout her post-Ming years, Wang Duanshu was celebrated for her poetry and equally for the quality of her paintings and calligraphy. Like Liu Rushi and Qian Qianyi, she and Ding Shengzhao lived as intellectual partners and co-equals. Wang had little or no interest in the household matters typically expected of women and even arranged (and paid for) a concubine for her husband.[23]

In the first half of the 1650s, Zhang Dai and a supportive cohort of forty-six other Zhejiang literati[24] financed publication of Wang Duanshu's prose and poetry, titled *Red Chantings* (吟紅集, *Yinhong ji*). The work was surprisingly positively received, perhaps a result of its focus on dynastic loyalty rather than romance.[25] Regardless, the collection helped burnish her authorial reputation among Jiangnan's literati to such an extent that some began referring to Wang as an "honorary man."[26] Such recognition from the male-dominated literary world led to the publication of five more collections of Wang's poetry and prose. Regrettably, only *Red Chantings* remains extant today.

Wang Duanshu's well-earned esteem also paved the way for her most renowned work as editor of a monumental anthology of women's poetry, predominantly from the Ming era. *Classic Poetry by Famous Women* (名媛詩緯, *Mingyuan shiwei*, published 1667) contained biographies and critical commentary on two thousand poems from over one thousand women writers in forty-two volumes (卷, *juan*), including the work of courtesans as well as gentlewomen (in separate sections, of course).[27] *Mingyuan shiwei* was the product of a quarter-century research and compilation project on Wang's part, exhaustive in her effort to ensure that the rising female voices of her dynasty would not be lost—in much the same spirit that Zhang Dai memorialized his remembered glories of the Ming reign. Her husband, Ding Shengzhao, authored one of the book's four prefaces, a nod to Confucian marital propriety, while another was provided by Qian Qianyi, still the most esteemed literary critic of his time despite his acquiescence to the Manchu dynasty.

From among the many poems Wang Duanshu wrote throughout the course of her life, perhaps the most compelling is one where she looks back wistfully at the life she lived and the times in which it occurred:

Telling My Story[28]

> So unexpectedly the prime of my life has passed,
> As white hairs appear on the sides of my temples.
> The flowing water goes its way, never to return:
> And blue hills stand blocking my way forward.
> I look out over the heaven and earth's expanse,
> Within which I cannot call a single speck my own.
> This world lacks people with a discerning eye,
> Who can tell the foolish from the wise?
> They delight in the crooked, don't love the straight:
> Comparable to the curved bow and the taut string.
> The lotus flower springs from the tip of my tongue,
> But purse and chest are ashamed of the single coin.
> I myself know that one must mind one's time,
> Once the party is over, one's ashamed over its vanity!
> At dawn one plans to travel to Qin and Jin;
> At dusk one thinks of going to Qi and Yen.[29]
> I sigh that I lack the ambition that soars;
> Tired and weary, I can only struggle on.
> I always feel as stupid as the cuckoo bird,
> Ashamed of trying to fill the sea with pebbles.[30]
> The azure heaven cannot be questioned;
> Who says that the wise will come first?

The Brush Is Deadlier than the Sword – A "Ming History" Story

While Zhang Dai's attempt to preserve his Ming Dynasty memories in *Dream Reminiscences of Tao'an* was perhaps political by inference, such was decidedly not the case for Zhuang Tinglong's (莊廷鑨; d. 1655) audacious *History of the Ming* (明史記略, *Mingshi jilüe*). Born into a well-off merchant family in Nanxun Town, Huzhou Prefecture, Zhuang was a promising, Confucian-educated student at the Imperial College. Tragically, he fell blind at a young age, ending his hopes for an official career.

After returning home, the young man learned of the financial difficulties of Zhu

Guozhen's 朱国祯, (1557 – 1632, *jinshi* 1589) family. Zhu was a highly respected scholar and official in the Ministry of Rites at the capital, but his family in Nanxun had fallen on hard times since his death. He had already compiled information toward a history of the Ming Dynasty before dying with the work not completed, and now his family was offering his unfinished work for sale. For the visually impaired Zhuang Tinglong, the opportunity for guiding the work to completion with his name on it appealed to his desire to accomplish something memorable. With his father's consent and financial backing, he purchased Zhu's unfinished history as the starting point and organized a cohort of a dozen or more paid scholars to build upon it.

The end result, completed and published by Zhuang Tinglong's father in 1660 (five years after Zhuang Tinglong's death), could never become the Ming history of record. A dynasty's official history could only be produced and approved by its successor dynasty. However, the dynastic loyalism that inspired Zhuang Tinglong's history heavily colored its contents. The book's "disparaging references to the Manchus and its stubborn use of Southern Ming reign titles for the years after 1644 constituted an intolerable challenge to the authority of the new regime."[31] According to Hummel, "certain passages…alluded to the conquerors as still under Ming rule, referred to Manchu emperors by their personal names, and reckoned time in terms of reign titles of the Southern Ming princes—all acts designated by the new rulers as treason."[32]

Wu Zhirong 吴之荣 (d. 1665), Huzhou's local magistrate at the time and now a subject of the Qing Dynasty, informed Huzhou Prefect Chen Yongming 陳永命 (d. 1662) about the book's slanderous content. In doing so, he mistakenly (and apparently intentionally) implicated another local merchant named Zhu Youming 朱佑明 in place of the book's original author, the historian Zhu Guozhen. When the Prefect chose to take a bribe from the Zhuangs rather than take action against the book, Wu Zhirong elevated his report to a higher official. Word finally reached the palace in Beijing, where the eight-year-old Kangxi Emperor ruled under a Regency headed by the courtier and military commander Oboi 鳌拜 (1610 – 1669).

Investigative officials sent by the court to Huzhou arrested everyone involved, however marginally.[33] Writers, contributors, editors, proofreaders, booksellers, individuals who owned a copy of the book, officials who failed to report its existence—all were swept up in the literary dragnet. Zhuang Tinglong's father was imprisoned in Beijing and died before his trial, while others among the publishers and booksellers were executed. Most of the remainder of the Zhuang family were executed as well, while the wrongfully accused Zhu Youming and his three sons were beheaded as part of an indiscriminate massacre that also claimed Zhu's wife by suicide.

Several of the collaborating writers and their families' sons also suffered execution; a fortunate few managed to bribe their way out of trouble. In all, more than one thousand persons were arrested. Seventy persons were executed, and others were punished by exile to remote areas of the empire. Perhaps the most bizarre punishment was left for the already deceased Zhuang Tinglong. His corpse, and that of one of the contributing writers, were exhumed from their graves and ritually dismembered.

Several officials were removed from office, and others were executed. Huzhou Prefect Chen Yongming was relieved of his post and hung himself before arriving at his new position-in-exile. Such was Regent Oboi's retaliatory fury that he had Chen's corpse returned to Hangzhou for dismemberment. The only beneficiary from the entire case was its originator, the whistleblower Wu Zhirong, to whom the court granted the entirety of the Zhuang family estates.

The message from Beijing to those in Jiangnan with residual loyalist leanings was more than crystal clear. The Manchu Qing response was so obviously intended to intimidate that no one could fail to see its similarities to the Manchu-inflicted massacre at Yangzhou in 1645. Try as they might, the Manchus would never be Chinese. They were barbarian outsiders, ruthless and intolerant. This "Ming History" case of 1663, not yet even twenty years into the dynastic reign, also signaled ominously that fearsome literary acquisitions would be part of the Qing Dynasty's governance portfolio. Huzhou in 1663 would prove not to be an anomaly, only a forerunner of worse to come.

Winning Back the Empire

Although the Qing Dynasty dates officially from the year 1644, China's Manchu rulers discovered that gaining control over such an immense and varied empire required far more than capturing Beijing and Nanjing. Loyalist outbreaks in Jiangnan,[34] driven in fair part by Dorgon's head-shaving edict, were put down in the late summer months of 1646. Naval-based attacks emanating from Fujian Province under Zhu Yihai (Prince of Lu) and Zheng Chonggong (more popularly known as Koxinga) lasted until the Qing armies fended off the latter's grand plan to retake Nanjing in August 1659.

Zhu Yihai remained alive and a symbolic resistance figure in Fujian Province and off the coast of Xiamen until 1662, and the Southern Ming base there was not captured by the Qing forces until 1663. Even then, the Qing ascendance across the southern empire—from the Pacific Coast to far west Yunnan Province—was more nominal than actual, with real control ceded to the rulers of what could only be called fiefdoms. Almost twenty years after the fall of Ming Beijing, the Manchu government truly controlled less than half of the land they ostensibly ruled.

In 1669, the fifteen-year-old Kangxi Emperor emerged from his eight-year Regency to take control of the palace court and the government. Like all imperial reign names, his was filled with sorely needed promise: "Healthy (康, *kang*) and Prosperous (熙, *xi*)." After imprisoning the overbearing Regent Oboi, the young Emperor set out first to gain military and administrative control of his empire. What had begun as military governorships given to Chinese warlord-defectors when the Manchus lacked the manpower to administer the entire empire had evolved into claims of hereditary rights to rule. By 1670, Kangxi identified three "fiefdoms" he needed to eliminate in order to assert his rule:

- In the southeast, the coastal region occupied by today's Fujian Province, under the rule of Geng Jingzhong 耿精忠 (d. 1682), inherited in 1649

235

from his father, Geng Zhongming 耿仲明 (1604 – 1649);

- In the deeper south, the territory now comprised of Guangdong Province, under the rule of Shang Zhixin 尚之信 (1636 – 1680), following his father, Shang Kexi 尚可喜 (1604 – 1676); and

- In the southwest, the modern-day lands of Guangxi Zhuang and Guizhou, Hunan, Yunnan, and Sichuan Provinces, portions of Gansu and northern Shaanxi Provinces, and Chongqing, all still under the rule of an increasingly independent and assertive Wu Sangui.

The precipitating event of the so-called Rebellion of the Three Feudatories[35] was a request in 1673 from Shang Kexi in Guangdong Province to be permitted to surrender his governorship and return north to his native home in present-day Liaoning Province. The Kangxi Emperor was receptive and asked Geng Jingzhong and Wu Sangui to follow Shang's example in return for other rewards. The two military governors tentatively agreed but procrastinated over self-claimed difficulties and complications. In reply, the Emperor elevated tensions by transforming his request into an order. Wu's response was dramatic: he declared himself the head of a new Zhou Dynasty, effective with the start of the lunar New Year, 1674. The rebellion thus began with Wu Sangui claiming that he would be the true Han Chinese successor to the late Ming, suggesting that Ming loyalist resistance was still alive.

As Wu gathered allies in the west and consolidated his control south of the Yangzi River, Geng Jingzhong moved north, first attacking and then seizing control over Wenzhou in coastal Zhejiang. Unbelievably for the people of Zhejiang, the dynastic succession conflict had returned to their province, twenty years after most believed the matter settled, however unsatisfactorily. Geng's three-pronged advance took Zhuji and Shaoxing as well as Yiwu, Jinhua, and Quzhou by October 1674. It was a mark of the Qing military's ineffectuality that Geng's relatively modest army gained control of nearly the entire province other than Hangzhou.

The Kangxi Emperor's gamble paid off when the Qing army managed to hold the line against further territorial losses until both Geng Jingzhong and Shang Zhixin surrendered their governorships in 1677 and Wu Sangui died in 1678. Wu Shifan 吴世璠 (1663 – 1681), Sangui's grandson, continued the western rebellion for several years before finally admitting defeat and committing suicide in 1681.

Kangxi had ignored the warnings of his court advisors and boldly gone all-in, putting his reign and potentially his dynasty's continuing existence in play. His territorial reclamation work was not yet quite complete,[36] but he was now clearly the emperor of "all under Heaven."

Inspecting the South

In addition to eliminating the warlords and their fiefdoms, the newly ascendant Emperor identified two other priorities for the opening years of his reign: controlling the Yellow River floods and restoring the Grand Canal after the damage and neglect it suffered during the dynastic conflict years. Both of these objectives were critical to the national well-being and economy, and both involved complex issues of hydrology and engineering. They also provided impetus (and imperial justification) for one of Kangxi's greatest legacies: the grand inspection tour (巡狩, *xunshou*).

Chinese history offered multiple precedents for traveling emperors intent on seeing their lands and subjects at first-hand. Emperor Shun 帝舜 (c. 2294 – 2184 BCE) reputedly traveled to the nation's sacred mountains to offer ritual sacrifices, and the great unifier of the Chinese nation, Qin Shihuang (r. 221 – 210 BCE), roamed his conquest lands, including a legendary visit to the tomb of Yu the Great at Kuaiji Mountain. Emperors Han Wudi (r. 140 – 87 BCE), Sui Yangdi (r. 605 – 618), and Tang Gaozong (r. 626 – 649) had all made use of inspection tours to reinforce their rule first-hand and receive the people's adulation in the process.

Kangxi, however, would take imperial touring to an entirely new level. During his reign years from the end of the Three Feudatories Rebellion in 1681 until his death in 1722, Kangxi undertook 128 such tours out of the capital, nearly half of them hunting tours in his native northern homeland. His inspection tours included six trips southward into Jiangnan, three westward into Shanxi and Shaanxi Provinces, and three eastward to the secondary Manchu capital at Shenyang (Liaoning Province). "During this forty-two-year period, there were eleven years in which Kangxi spent more than two hundred days on the road and twenty-four years in which he spent more than one hundred days traveling."[37]

In 1684, Kangxi unexpectedly transformed his ceremonial "Eastern Tour" to sacred Mount Tai into an impromptu "Southern Inspection Tour" that took him as far south as Suzhou and Nanjing before returning to Beijing after sixty days outside the imperial capital (November 5, 1684 to January 4, 1685). Five years later, in 1689, he commissioned his "Second Southern Inspection Tour" traveling via the Grand Canal all the way to Hangzhou and across the Qiantang River to Shaoxing and Mount Kuaiji. This time, Kangxi stretched the duration of his tour to seventy-one days, departing Beijing on January 28 and arriving back at the capital on April 8, the day after his thirty-fifth birthday. It was during this second tour, with his inaugural visit to Hangzhou, that a temporary imperial palace was first built on Solitary Island, near the north shore of West Lake.

Over the thirty-three-year balance of his reign, the Kangxi Emperor would conduct four more Southern Inspection Tours (in 1699, 1703, 1705, and 1707), each one terminating at Hangzhou before returning northward via Nanjing, Yangzhou, and the Grand Canal. These "inspection tours" were traveling extravaganzas, no matter how hard Kangxi tried to discourage their being treated as such. A massed fleet of ships coursed down the Grand Canal and back, comprised of dozens of boats containing hundreds of passengers and crew. Each city along the way competed in providing the grandest possible reception, as described by one writer as the Emperor reached Suzhou on his Third Southern Inspection Tour:

> On 13 April 1699 the [Kangxi Emperor's] imperial flotilla entered Suzhou

prefecture. Those gathered along the route to greet the procession were stretched on continuously for hundreds of *li*; however, they were most numerous in Suzhou. The various local officials were in front. Government students and licentiates were behind them. Local elders were next, finally followed by ordinary residents. People came by water and by land. Above each boat flew a yellow banner saying, 'XXX from YY district welcomes the imperial procession.' The same [banners showing people's names and places of origin] could also be seen on land. Virtually all of the large thoroughfares were finely festooned, some with yellow damask. Lavishly adorned stages, one hundred paces wide, were set up in front of Suzhou's old postal relay station and at the foot of Tiger Hill, and lantern-bedecked arches and pavilions stretched across bridges and alleyways.[38]

There is no reason to believe that Hangzhou's reception would have been any less well-attended, festive, and extravagant.

Kangxi's first visit to the Hangzhou/Shaoxing area consumed nine days of his 1689 Southern Tour: four days in Hangzhou city (February 28 – March 3, 1690), one day each in Shaoxing and Xiaoshan (March 4 and 5), two more days in Hangzhou (March 6 – 7), and a final day in Shimenzhen, Jiaxing Prefecture (March 8).[39] Despite time spent reviewing Yellow River and Grand Canal water management projects and issues, the Emperor's southern tours were more political affairs than hydrologic inspections. Having spent his youthful years gaining command of Chinese language, studying the Confucian classics, and refining his calligraphy and poetry composition skills, he hoped to lower the barriers between his court and the local literati class. By his own behavior, he sought to demonstrate that his rule would be as much Chinese as Manchu and would preserve Han culture and traditions.

Although he also stayed in the military garrison on his first visit to Hangzhou, his primary aims were introductory. He held audiences with local officials and civic leaders as well as members of the local elites and the common populace. He also granted gifts, rewards, and tax remissions to deserving individuals, schools, and temples, and he observed ceremonial rituals and protocols.

Significantly, Kangxi committed a portion of his first Hangzhou visit to crossing the Qiantang River with a full retinue and traveling by horseback to Shaoxing and the nearby tomb of Yu the Great. His initial proposal for this excursion and sacrificial offering to Da Yu was the source of fierce debate among his ministers, who had no forewarning of Kangxi's plans. The Emperor's attending ministers argued that no such imperial ritual existed for Yu the Great and suggested instead that Kangxi send an appropriate representative to offer a sacrifice. Not surprisingly, the Emperor had his way.

At dawn on March 4, 1689, Kangxi approached Yu's tomb on foot and led his imperial retinue "in the formal ceremony of three kneelings and nine prostrations, after which the sacrificial text was read and the sacrifice performed." The Emperor's ritual observance at Kuaiji Mountain "emphasiz[ed] his concern for unifying the empire, attending to river conservation work, and recruiting able men for his government."[40] In addition, his personal imperial veneration of Yu the Great's tomb laid claim to a symbolic Qing connection with the lineage of China's past emperors. As one modern commentator aptly summarized Kangxi's six tours,[41] they constituted a "ritualized appropriation of a 'Chinese' empire."

In his last two days in Hangzhou, the Emperor busied himself with meetings and awards granted to military officers and observed a garrison display of military formations and battle skills such as horse-riding and archery. Not only was Kangxi making a point about maintaining Manchu military traditions and battle readiness, he was also ensuring that his time spent in Hangzhou would not be perceived as merely luxuriating in the famously majestic scenery and other of the city's pleasurable offerings.

Wang Hui's 汪翚 (1632 - 1717) twelve-scroll, chronologically arranged depiction of the Kangxi Emperor's Second Southern Inspection Tour, the 1689 *Illustration of the Kangxi Emperor's Southern Tour* (康熙帝南巡图, *Kangxi di nanxun tu*), immortalized the entire journey. Wang and a supporting cohort of painters began their work in 1691 and finished the twelve scrolls about four years later. The completed work was nothing short of monumental: each scroll over two feet wide, the longest (Scroll XII) exceeding 85 feet in length. Their combined length has been estimated to exceed 650 feet, with depiction of more than 37,000 human figures.[42] As Maxwell Hearn noted, "Created under the supervision of Jiangnan artists and officials, the painting…confirms the emperor's success in recruiting Southern scholars and enhances his image as a patron of the arts and devotee of Southern culture."[43]

Scroll VIII illustrated the Emperor's crossing from Jiangsu Province into Zhejiang Province, departing from Suzhou and passing Jiaxing and Shimen before stopping for the evening at the canal-side town of Tangqi 塘栖镇, about fifteen miles north of Hangzhou in what is now the city's Yuhang District.[44] In the final section of this scroll, the walls of the former Southern Song capital loom vaguely in the distance.

If viewers of the Southern Tour scrolls expected the next scroll to present Kangxi's glorious entry into Hangzhou and a visual appreciation of West Lake, they would have been sorely disappointed. Despite other scrolls offering views of important Jiangnan cities like Yangzhou, Nanjing, Zhenjiang, Changzhou, Wuxi, Suzhou, Jiaxing, and Shaoxing, Scroll IX utterly bypasses Hangzhou and West Lake. Instead, the ninth scroll begins with the Emperor's entourage crossing the Qiantang River beyond the city walls for their ceremonial visit to the tomb of Yu the Great.[45] Some have speculated that the pictorial omission of Hangzhou and West Lake reflected the Emperor's deep concern that his Inspection Tour not be immortalized as a holiday junket.[46]

Scroll IX opens with a crowd of people, horses, ox carts, and goods unloading from a flotilla of river boats onto the southern shore of the Qiantang River. Their path passes through Xiaoshan and turns eastward along teeming canals and through tilled lands. Prosperous market towns are filled with busy, canal-side shops and tea houses, arched bridges, and hundreds of robed and hatted (and exclusively male) pedestrians. Women are only seen through residential windows and standing in doorways, or occasionally socializing among themselves in a quiet courtyard.

The final sections of Scroll IX portray Shaoxing and the mountainous area beyond containing Yu the Great's temple complex. In addition to the city walls and western gate, Wang Hui's depiction of Shaoxing features Fushan 府山 (Prefectural Mountain), the *yamen* offices at the hill's southern foot, the Prefectural School, and a distant, hill-topping pagoda. Unrolling the scroll further, the Emperor and a sizable entourage of court and local officials approach Yu the Great's temple complex, surrounded by imposing mountains. Kangxi finally makes his first and only appearance in Scroll IX, humbly approaching the tomb on foot to lead the ritual ceremony.

The Emperor's first stay in Hangzhou clearly whetted his appetite for return visits. He repeatedly went to great lengths to distinguish his stated seriousness of purpose from the reputation of the city for leisurely and extravagant entertainment and immoral behavior.[47] He was so worried about appearances on his first visit to West Lake in 1684 that he wrote, almost apologetically: "We stopped by the [West] Lake merely because it was located on the way to Yu's mausoleum [in Shaoxing]. Some may think that we are enjoying sightseeing here; we are concerned about this."[48] In a poem written five years later during his next visit, Kangxi still wrote defensively:

> West Lake was a place of painted boats and music in the past, my trip is to visit local places and inspect the mountains and waters. Never have I stopped my horse to enjoy food; I merely drank a cup of spring water at Hupao [monastery].[49]

During his southern tours, particularly in Jiangnan, the Kangxi Emperor also sought to promote discipline, strict moral order, and military preparedness to the Han Chinese and reinforce those same Manchu values among the soldiers and their families stationed in the region. Qing emperors and their advisors greatly feared that their garrison troops in places like Suzhou and Hangzhou would lose their military edge to the strength-sapping casual delights and soft, undisciplined lifestyle of the region.

On his week-long stay at Hangzhou during his Third Southern Inspection Tour in 1699, Kangxi offered up a personal demonstration of his martial expectations from the men of the Hangzhou garrison. After he, a few princes from among his family retinue, and some of his imperial guards had demonstrated their archery skills, he led a second exhibition of shooting from horseback. The Emperor showed outstanding deftness in hitting his mark even when his mount unexpectedly veered from his head-on gallop.[50] His message to local officials and military commanders alike was the primacy of traditional Manchu military values and the critical need to maintain them before all else. No imperial edict from Beijing could have conveyed as well the signals that his presence and demonstrated abilities sent.

"Ten Views" Save West Lake

The Kangxi Emperor would return to Hangzhou three more times after his 1699 tour, arriving during his Fourth, Fifth, and Sixth Southern Inspection Tours in 1703, 1705, and 1707. His multiple visits to Hangzhou no doubt contributed substantially to West Lake's recovery from its deteriorated condition at the beginning of his reign, but his West Lake activities in 1699 also re-legitimized it as a sightseeing venue.

As early as the Tang Dynasty, poets had begun glorifying specific sites in the West Lake vicinity for their scenic beauty. They might single out the everyday view from a particular locale, and perhaps add qualifiers for time of day (e.g., dawn or sunset), season of the year, weather conditions (e.g., foggy or misty, snowy or snow-covered), phase of the moon, or even the presence of certain sounds or smells. The process of signifying sightseeing spots accelerated in the Song Dynasty era, prompted by painters as well as poets. Among the earliest to enumerate and codify in writing the ten scenes most highly esteemed by West Lake connoisseurs was Zhu Mu 祝穆 (d. 1255) in his guide to touring sites.

A portfolio of ten sites that demonstrated the most refined appreciation of West Lake's natural beauty gradually coalesced into a semi-formal list of "must-sees" for visitors.[51] Their names alone indicated how various environmental and temporal qualifiers were incorporated and how, when, and under what conditions these "Ten Views" were best seen according to the cognoscenti:

- Spring Dawn at the Su Causeway (苏堤春晓, *Sudi chunxiao*)
- Summer Breeze Stirring Lotuses at Qu Winery Garden (曲院风荷, *Quyuan fenghe*)
- Autumn Moon over the Peaceful Lake (平湖秋月, *Pinghu qiuyue*)
- Lingering Snow on Broken Bridge (断桥残雪, *Duanqiao canxue*)
- Leifeng Pagoda in the Sunset (雷峰夕照, *Leifeng xizhao*)
- Twin Peaks Piercing the Clouds (双峰插云, *Liangfeng chayun*)
- Orioles Singing in the Willows (柳浪闻莺, *Liulang wen ying*)
- Fish Viewing at Flower Cove (花港观鱼, *Huagang guanyu*)
- Three Ponds Mirroring the Moon (三潭印月, *Santan yinyue*)
- Evening Bell from Nanping Hill (南屏晚钟, *Nanping wanzhong*)

Widespread awareness of the Ten Views created a virtual travel guide for those who wished to achieve the cultured "West Lake experience." (See Appendix A for a brief description of each view above.) As one more means to demonstrate his knowledge and appreciation of traditional Chinese culture during his 1699 stay in Hangzhou, Kangxi set out to visit each of the ten sites. Much more than merely visit, however, he put his imperial imprint on every site in a masterful act of cultural appropriation. At each viewing spot, the Emperor wrote its name in four large characters (see list above) which were then inscribed onto stone steles and mounted under new pavilions. The Manchu Qing Dynasty had effectively seized ownership of the "Ten Views" tradition, forever fixing their titles in stone.

In 1722, the Kangxi Emperor's eleventh son, Aisin Gioro Yinzhen 胤禛, succeeded his father to the throne as the Yongzheng Emperor 雍正帝 (r. 1722 – 1735) and reigned for just thirteen years before his death at age 56. He never traveled to Hangzhou, but he accomplished an unexpected physical renewal of West Lake to complement the Kangxi Emperor's symbolic elevation of the Ten Views. In his first year as Emperor, he issued an edict ordering Li Wei 李衛 (1687 – 1738), the Governor of Zhejiang Province, to dredge and restore the lake to its previous size and depth. It would be the largest such reclamation and renovation effort since Sun Long's projects 130 years earlier. During the years of his governorship (1727 – 1732), Li Wei also oversaw compilation of a literary companion to the rehabilitation work, the *Gazetteer of West Lake* (西湖志, *Xihu zhi*), published in 1734.[52]

In 1727, the Yongzheng Emperor issued another edict ordering Hangzhou officials to take extra care in maintaining the Ten Views pavilions and steles installed by his father in 1699. By virtue of those inscribed stones and their protective pavilions, Kangxi's co-optation of West Lake's scenery had indeed turned into Manchu responsibility for the lake's (and their own imperial heritage's) well-being.

For the people of Jiangnan, the work associated with Yongzheng's edicts announced Qing acceptance of West Lake as a scenic tourist site, despite the Manchus' early disinclination to glorify it as the Ming literati had done. Yet however much support the Yongzheng Emperor gave to West Lake's maintenance and appearance, it paled by comparison to the Ming-like love affair one his sons would soon form with Xizi Hu 西子湖, the great beauty Xi Shi's Lake.

From the Earthy...Li Yu 李漁 (1610 – 1680)

Li Yu was born to be a scholar, just not a Confucian one. From an early age, Li was a precocious reader and learner, a blessing and a hope for a merchant family from which no scholar had emerged for the past nine or more generations. The young man excelled in his studies and passed his first-level licentiate (秀才, *xiucai*) exams with such skill that his examination papers were copied and circulated among Ming officials in Zhejiang. Unfortunately, he fared poorly in his first and only attempt at the provincial (*juren*) examinations in 1639 Hangzhou. His second opportunity in 1642 was pre-empted by the advance of Manchu armies into the Ming empire, a misfortune only exceeded by his mother's death that same year. His father had already passed away in 1630.

As the Manchu armies advanced into Zhejiang in 1644 – 1645, Li Yu abandoned his family's ancestral home in Lanxi (less than fifteen miles from Jinhua) to hide away in the mountainous wilds of Zhejiang. As the conflict eased, he found a minor clerical position in Jinhua, and a temporary safe haven for his wife and child in the home of Jinhua's Assistant Prefect, Xu Xicai 許檄彩. By the time he was safely able to return to his home village at Lanxi, he discovered little but burnt ruins.

An intelligent young man with readily apparent talents, Li took stock of his circumstances: parentless, his family's wealth lost, stolen, or put to the torch, low scholarly status as a mere first-level graduate, and no prospect of an official career as a Ming subject in a new and foreign dynasty. Seeing few options, he turned his sights toward Hangzhou, his best hope for a career and the means to support his family more comfortably. He would write; it was his only monetizable skill.

And write he did. He refashioned himself as the Old Bamboo-Hatted Man (i.e., Fisherman) of the Lake (湖上笠翁, *hushang liweng*) and published his first play in 1651. Between 1651 and 1658, Li Yu wrote five more well-received plays and completed three successful collections of vernacular short stories: *Silent Operas* (无声戏, *Wusheng xi*), *Priceless Jade* (连城璧, *Liancheng bi*), and *The Twelve Towers* (十二楼, *Shi'er lou*). "Li Yu's plays and short stories are distinctive not only for their originality, parody, and lively dialogue, but also for the way that the author-narrator-commentator—who was identified with Li Yu by name—incessantly interrupts the reader, baits her, and delights in outsmarting her."[53]

Arriving in Hangzhou unknown and penniless, he needed just ten years to become a celebrity who entertained celebrities. No longer constrained by the pressures and obligations of examinations and an official career, he simply shaved his head and passed through the dynastic transition as if it had never happened. He earned enough income to support a growing family, but he also demonstrated a lifelong propensity for spending beyond his means that kept him under constant financial pressure. Nevertheless, he established a solid literary reputation as a writer and playwright upon which he built a long-lasting career. He also accumulated a substantial store of social capital that proved even more valuable.

In 1658, Li Yu relocated his family to Nanjing, ostensibly to address claims of rampant pirating of his published works in Jiangsu Province. He completed and published his *Twelve Towers* short story collection in Nanjing and wrote four more plays, but much of his attention drifted away from writing. At his residence, he opened a combination publishing house and bookstore where he could produce and sell his books along with items like stationery of his own design. He began trading on his name and reputation, traveling across the Chinese empire to entertain wealthy officials and merchants (who eagerly welcomed him) and seek their patronage.

During his travels in the 1660s, Li Yu received two talented young concubines as gifts,[54] Qiao Fusheng 乔复生 (d. 1672) and Wang Zailai 王再来 (d. 1673 or 1674). Both were mere adolescents, and both demonstrated special talents in singing and performing. Li set about training them to perform scenes from his plays, using grounds at his Nanjing residence that he was already transforming into a magnificent garden and theatrical space he called the Mustard Seed Garden (芥子园, *Jiezi Yuan*). The garden's name derived from a philosophical passage in a Buddhist sutra stating that a mountain can be inserted inside a mustard seed. Li adopted the name as well for both his bookstore and his publishing house.

Meanwhile, Li's two young performers attracted widespread attention, as did Li's inventive theatrical presentations in which he himself sometimes participated. His small troupe brought important visitors from near and far into his residence, expanding his personal network still further. Soon he began taking his troupe on the road, offering performances to high officials and wealthy merchants that became one of his most successful sources of income.

Li had reached the peak of his personal fame. He was renowned for his literary and theatrical creativity and also widely acknowledged as an expert in garden design. He capitalized on his fame with the publication in 1671 of an eclectic and witty treatise on "the art of life." *Temporary Lodge for My Leisure Thoughts*, or simply *Leisure Notes* (闲情偶寄, *Xianqing ouji*), is "a curious collection of several hundred essays on topics that range from theater direction to heating, choosing a concubine to balustrade design, the art of walking to pomegranate trees."[55]

Among many other topics, *Leisure Notes* includes Li Yu's theories about garden architecture and design and is also noteworthy for his advocacy of universal women's education. Li presented a detailed curriculum of basic readings and desired skills in music, the arts, and calligraphy in a program for young women that one biographer termed "the first of its kind in Chinese history."[56] In his customarily dry, tongue-in-cheek manner, he introduced his thoughts on teaching women to read: "Females find reading and writing difficult only at the point of entry. Once they have got their foot in the door, they are quicker than males, because males lack concentration, while females pay undivided attention."[57]

Tragically, both of Li's talented young performers died from illnesses at around age nineteen, Qiao in 1672 and Wang just over a year later. Li was financially impacted and emotionally devastated by both deaths, especially Qiao's, who had given him a daughter. He wrote dozens of mournful poems in both of their memories.

In the spring following Wang's death, Li Yu began exploring a return to Hangzhou for a peaceful retirement. Seeing Zhejiang and West Lake again must have softened his heart and inspired nostalgia for his earlier times in the former Song capital. In 1675, he accompanied his two sons to Hangzhou as first-time candidates in the provincial examinations. Li purchased land on a hillside overlooking West Lake the following year, and in 1677 he sold his bookstore and Mustard Seed Garden residence and moved back to Hangzhou. He called his new residence The Winding Garden (紗园, Zheng yuan), but his happy return to his native area was marred that same year by the death of his wife of fifty years.

Ironically, the book that in 1679 would forever preserve Li Yu's Mustard Seed Garden for posterity came not from his brush but from a work commissioned in Nanjing by his son-in-law, Shen Xinyu 沈心友. More than three years prior, Shen had commissioned a painter and family friend from Jiaxing named Wang Gai 王改 (1645 – 1710) to create a painting manual. The result was magnificent: five chapters (with multiple, detailed subsections) covering basic theories on the use of color and the painting of trees, landscapes (mountains, water, rocks), persons, and buildings, with samples of landscapes produced by famous masters. In early 1680, the book was finally published as the *Mustard Seed Garden Manual of Painting* (芥子園畫傳, *Jiezi yuan huazhuan*), with a preface by Li Yu dated December 24, 1679.[58]

Response to the painting manual ran well beyond expectations, so much so that Li asked his son-in-law to commission a second, supplementary manual to include "plants, grass, flowers, insects, and feathered and furry creatures."[59] This second volume was published in 1701, too late for Li Yu to enjoy its contents.[60] He passed away more than twenty years earlier, in 1680. His public legacy was still not yet complete, however.

In 1693, a ribald and remarkably explicit, twenty-chapter sexual comedy achieved its first formal publication under the name 肉蒲团 *Rou Putuan*; in English, *The Carnal Prayer Mat* or *Prayer Mat of the Flesh*. The novel presented the carnal escapades of a young man named Weiyangsheng ("Before Midnight Scholar")[61] who sets out on a quest for sexual satisfaction with the empire's most beautiful women. In the book's early chapters, a monk warns Weiyangsheng about the retributions that accompany serial sexual seduction. The profligate young scholar replies that while the monk spends his days sitting on a prayer mat, he only wishes to spend his time on a prayer mat of the flesh.

The novel charts Weiyangsheng's increasingly convoluted escapades, including a variety of erotic sexual experiences rendered in unusual detail. In the end, however, moral retribution prevails. A young woman whom Weiyangsheng marries and abandons is sold into prostitution and eventually commits suicide when Weiyangsheng unknowingly arrives sometime later to sample her services. Shocked into awareness of what he has done, the regretful young man returns to join the monk on a prayer mat of his own. He ultimately castrates himself to eliminate any further temptations of the flesh. The book was officially banned but nevertheless circulated widely throughout the Qing era and entered Japan in around 1705.

Although no irrefutable proof of *The Carnal Prayer Mat*'s authorship has yet been discovered, there is widespread agreement that Li Yu is the probable source. As Patrick Hanan summarized the situation: "So distinctive is his brand of fiction that, although the novel has never actually been proved to be by Li Yu, one has only to read it alongside his stories to feel the truth of the attribution."[62] Scholars believe Li produced the manuscript in around the year 1657, during his years in Hangzhou when his literary productivity was at its highest. If so, the novel was published posthumously, more than a dozen years after his death and nearly forty years after it was written. *The Carnal Prayer Mat* remains alongside *The Plum in the Golden Vase* (金瓶梅, *Jin Ping Mei*, 1610) as the two great erotic novels of classical Chinese literature.

To the Divine...the Jesuits (1640 – 1720)

The Jesuit presence in Hangzhou continued through the final years of the Ming Dynasty and well into the Qing era despite the passing of Yang Tingyun, Xu Guangxi, Li Zhizao, Lazzaro Catteneo, Nicolas Trigault, and others. Each in his own way had contributed to a religious foundation upon which a new generation of scholarly Jesuits would build after the fall of the Ming. A number of them visited or lived in Hangzhou, but Martino Martini (1614 – 1661) and Prospero Intorcetta (1625 – 1696) left marks on the city that can still be seen today. These two were also among the first Westerners whose written works brought informed understanding and appreciation of Chinese history, geography, and culture to the educated classes in Europe.

Once the Manchu armies had taken Hangzhou and Shaoxing in 1645, they continued a southeastern march into Fujian Province in hopes of capturing the fleeing Prince of

Lu (Zhu Yihai), one of the last remaining members of the Ming royal family. As they reached the coastal Zhejiang city of Wenzhou, they encountered an Italian Jesuit priest who had posted a large-character sign on his door declaring: "A doctor of the Law of God, from the Great West, dwells here."[63]

Inside that door waited Martino Martini (Chinese name: 卫匡国, Wei Kuangguo) and a group of his local converts who had fled to his compound for protection. The priest quite possibly feared for all their lives at the hands of the "northern barbarians" who were overrunning the Chinese empire and massacring the people so indiscriminately. As a relative newcomer to China, having only arrived in Hangzhou a year earlier, he had decided for safety's sake to travel among the Prince of Lu's Ming loyalist followers.

Martini greeted the Manchus at his door with a display of Western books, various scientific and astronomical instruments, and Western religious statuary.[64] The Manchu commander's response was simplicity itself. Would the priest profess loyalty to the Manchu rule by complying with the head-shaving and dress decrees? The Jesuit accepted those terms without hesitation. He soon had his head shaved in the Qing style, after which he was respectfully escorted safely back to Hangzhou.

In addition to his religious studies, Martino Martini had arrived in China with a deep grounding in mathematics and especially its application to geography and cartography. He was also an intellectually curious and enthusiastic traveler who took every available opportunity to see and document this new country that was still such a mystery to Europeans. Those who knew him described him in glowing terms: tall and strong, full-bearded, amiable, quick to laugh, and intelligent but able to explain difficult concepts in understandable ways. One of his literatus acquaintances in Lanxi wrote of Martini: "He is great in personality, of illuminated mind and splendidly charitable. To look at him he seems an angel. He is what is called a perfect man."[65]

From the Jesuit missionary base in Hangzhou, Martini traveled and proselytized throughout northern Zhejiang, from Jinhua and Lanxi in the southwest to Shaoxing and Ningbo to the southeast. During this time, he collaborated with local literati[66] on translations into Chinese of European religious and philosophical works. He also had opportunity to travel to Beijing, visit the Great Wall, and continue on to Shanxi and Shaanxi Provinces before returning to Hangzhou in 1650. All the while, he was absorbing and recording geographical and historical information.

In 1651, Martini received orders to return to Rome and report on the work of the Jesuit missions in China. While in Europe, he published his three principle works (all in Latin):

- *Sinicae Historiae Decas Prima*, a history of ancient China from its earliest times through the Han Dynasty era (202 BCE – 220 CE).[67] From the most ancient myth stories through the Xia, Zhou, Qin, and Han Dynasties, this work stood as the most comprehensive and detailed ancient Chinese history of its time for European historians and scholars. Martini's history also precipitated panicked reconsideration in Europe of the historicity of the Christian Bible and its use in determining the dates of such Biblical events as the Great Deluge and Creation.

- *De Bello Tartarico Historia*, a detailed account of the late Ming Dynasty and its fall, drawn from various first-hand reports and information obtained from former government officials, soldiers, literati, and other missionaries. Martini's account describes "the suffering of the peasants and their heroic defense of their traditions and nationality," "provides detailed descriptions of the Chinese landscape and cities," and "conducts an acute analysis of the reasons for the...fall of the Ming."[68] *De Bello Tartarico Historia*'s detailed and partially first-hand treatment of such recent historical events in China took Europe by storm; the book was soon republished in nine different European language translations.[69]

- *Novus Atlas Sinensis* (*New Atlas of China*), a comprehensive, province-by-province geography of the Chinese empire, complete with seventeen maps (a national map, one map for each of fifteen provinces, and a map of Japan) and extensive commentary on each province's climate, geographical features, major cities, and famous sites. The *New Atlas* was first published in 1655 Amsterdam and traveled in translation across Europe in nine additional languages. Martini's *Atlas* remained the standard geographic and cartographic China sourcebook in Europe and stood uncorrected for more than a century. His work in this field gained him remembrance in the West as the "father of Chinese geography."

While Martini's three books left a major intellectual mark in European understanding of the Chinese empire and its history, he left a mark of a different kind upon his return to Hangzhou in 1658, accompanied this time by Prospero Intorcetta. The first Christian church in Hangzhou, dating to the 1620s and early 1630s, had been built at Guan Bridge, quite close to Qiantang Gate. However, most of that area had since been subsumed into the Manchu garrison in 1647. The original church was now crowded into a small space, and its location so close to the garrison and the soldiers who lingered about the area discouraged followers from visiting.

Zhejiang Governor Tong Guoqi 佟国器 (d. 1684) was sympathetic to the Christian church, especially after his wife converted to that faith. He urged the returned Martini to build a finer church at a better location and helped with financial support both personally and from wealthy followers in the community. Martini was thus able to purchase a suitable plot of land at Heavenly Water Bridge (天水橋, Tianshui qiao), near Yang Tingyun's family residence.[70]

Construction began in 1659 on a Romanesque-style church with the name Our Lady of Immaculate Conception. By 1661, the church interior was put to use even as construction continued. Sadly, Martini died from cholera in June of that year and never saw the fully completed church or heard the praises for its architectural and decorative beauty.[71] Humbert Augery (1618 – 1673) succeeded Martini in Hangzhou and oversaw

247

completion of the Hangzhou cathedral in 1663. The Europeans named the new building "Church of the Savior," but its Chinese name *Chaoxing tang* 超性堂, translated as something closer to "Church of the Supernatural." The name by which the church was later known, the "Cathedral of the Immaculate Conception," was not adopted until the mid-nineteenth century.[72]

Even after his death, Martino Martini continued to make waves. In 1679, Yang Tingyun's Christian son donated a sizable plot of land for a Catholic cemetery at the northern foot (the "back side") of the hills containing the Lingyin and Tianzhu temples.[73] Eighteen years after his death, Martini's corpse was exhumed from its gravesite near his church to be honorably relocated to the new site. The Jesuit priest Phillippe Couplet (1623 – 1693), himself dubbed "the Confucius of Europe" for his knowledge of Chinese spiritual philosophy,[74] described the rather macabre scene that ensued:

> The body of the Jesuit Martino Martini is still intact: no hair has fallen from his head nor whisker from his face. There is no sign of putrefaction. There were people who cut his hair and nails, who washed his face and applied cosmetics to it. His body was placed in a wooden chair in a corner of the upper nave. There are numerous visitors, including friends of the deceased, and all of them declare: the Jesuit is protected by the people and by the divinities because of his sublime virtues.[75]

In 1676, the Sicilian Prospero Intorcetta, recruited by Martini during his European tour in the 1650s, took up the post at Hangzhou following Augery's death. Intorcetta was an intellectual leader in a Jesuit society widely known for its powerful scientific and religious scholarship, but he was also an aggressive missionary. He oversaw the construction of new churches in Jiaxing, Huzhou, Ningbo, Wenzhou, and Taizhou and renovated and expanded the Hangzhou church's existing seminary and library.

Undoubtedly Intorcetta's most celebrated enhancement of the Cathedral complex came with the commissioning of seventy-two painted images depicting key Biblical scenes to explain the formation of the Catholic Church and its most important precepts. Beneath each image, he arranged for written inscriptions relating its story and explaining its meaning. In this way, Intorcetta knew he could engage the illiterate masses through the illustrations while providing deeper context for the literati classes. The use of pictorial or cartoon images would become one of the routine ways to communicate with the peasant and worker masses through much of the 20th Century.

It was also under Prospero Intorcetta's watch that the Jesuit Cemetery, Dafangjing, 大方井, was built on the Yang family's donated land. Intorcetta purchased additional land to expand the cemetery's size and allow for the burial of nuns from the Sacred Heart and Sisters of Charity convents and priests of other religious orders. At the cemetery site, he built an arch-like gateway (牌楼, *pailou*) at one end of a traditional "spirit walk" (神道 , *shendao*), with an underground crypt at the other end of the walkway. Inside the crypt were placed the cremated remains of Jesuit priests, including those of Martini and eventually Intorcetta himself.[76]

In addition to his church-building and other missionary work, Intorcetta's Hangzhou years contained their share of political intrigue. During Kangxi's first visit to Hangzhou on his 1689 Southern Inspection Tour, the senior Jesuit priest boarded a small rented boat in which to approach the Emperor's floating palace ship and pay his respects. Kangxi, already well familiar with the Jesuits from their substantial presence at the court in Beijing, invited Intorcetta aboard for a brief audience and the grant of a few small gifts. Much to his guest's surprise, Kangxi asked to be guided to the Cathedral building, located only a short distance from the docking place of his imperial ship.

Intorcetta rushed to reach the Cathedral first so he could position himself kneeling before the church building as Kangxi's ship floated past. He repeated this obeisance with a deep bow of greeting when Kangxi's boat passed by the Cathedral again on that day's return route. The Emperor was sufficiently pleased with the Jesuit's homage that he sent his own representatives to the Cathedral two days later to show their respects to the Lord of Heaven and donate a gift of twenty silver pieces to the church.[77]

In the autumn of 1691, Prospero Intorcetta put his political capital from 1689 to good use. Zhang Penghe 张鹏翮 (1622 – 1666), the newly installed Governor of Zhejiang Province, decided to enforce an earlier but largely ignored edict from 1669 (the final year of Kangxi's Regency) that prohibited the building of Christian churches and banned Chinese people from converting to that religion.[78] Zhang ordered Martini's Cathedral to be transformed into a temple and the statuary and crucifixes destroyed, declaring illegal in Zhejiang Province any further observance of the subversive Western religion. Intorcetta quickly fashioned a letter explaining these events to the Jesuits in Beijing and asked that they appeal his case to the Emperor. A memorial outlining Zhang's actions and the Jesuits' defense quickly made its way to Kangxi.

Zhang Penghe's actions backfired spectacularly when the Emperor issued two responding edicts in March 1692, subsequently known as the Edicts of Toleration. The first edict permitted the Jesuits to practice their religion in their churches as they wished. The second document granted the same privileges to Chinese Christians. For the Jesuits, these two rulings were interpreted as receiving carte blanche to practice and proselytize their faith throughout the empire. Three months later, Intorcetta traveled to Beijing to express his gratitude to the Emperor, who received him graciously on two separate occasions, the second of which was an imperial dinner feast. Kangxi delivered to Intorcetta yet another imperial order during this visit, requiring Zhang Penghe to repair any damage done to the Cathedral.[79]

Just ten days after Intorcetta's return to Hangzhou, a fire raged through the city and damaged much of the Cathedral's interior. The religious images painted on the walls were ruined, but the library and its print woodblocks survived unharmed. Uncontrolled fire had partially but only temporarily achieved what Zhang Penghe could not.

In his late sixties and burdened by restoration of the fire-damaged church, Prospero Intorcetta passed away quietly from illness in October 1696, age 71. He died believing that the Jesuits would prevail in China; he would never know that in 1724 they were evicted en masse from the Chinese empire (except in Beijing) by Kangxi's son and successor, the Yongzheng Emperor. In 1730, the Hangzhou Cathedral was converted into an ancestral temple. Kangxi's inscription on the gate, "Built by Order of the Emperor" (provided on his 1699 Southern Inspection Tour), was then replaced for the next 134 years by characters announcing "Temple of the Celestial Empress."[80]

Tilling and Weaving

In the year 1145, a Song Dynasty magistrate serving in the district of Yuqian, about 25 miles west of Hangzhou, traveled to the capital (Lin'an) with an unusual gift for Emperor Gaozong. Lou Shou 楼璹 (1090-1162), a native of Ningbo, carried with him two silk-scroll paintings in which he had depicted scenes from the working life of the rural citizens whom he served as a government official in the Jinhua area.

One of the scrolls contained twenty-four chronologically-sequenced scenes related to the production of silk, starting with women collecting mulberry leaves for feeding each year's batch of silkworms and ending with women weaving silk cloth on a home loom. The second scroll followed the same step-by-step presentation, but its twenty-one images illustrated the toilsome process of men planting and harvesting rice. Each panel in both scrolls also contained an eight-line, five-character poetic inscription from Lou Shou's brush. Together, the *Pictures of Tilling and Weaving* (耕织图, *Gengzhi tu*) depicted the ancient Jiangnan adage about the distribution of household work: "Men plow, women weave."

As quaintly charming a gift as these two scrolls might have seemed, they were not intended to idealize rural life in the manner of *American Gothic*.[81] To the contrary, Lou's two scrolls were a bold political statement—part plea, part warning—reminding the Emperor and his new reign of the importance of farming[82] and that even he, in his elevated position, served the people. This message was implicit in the images but was "made explicit in the accompanying poems, many of which comment almost exclusively on social relationships among farmers, bureaucrats, and the emperor."[83] A hardworking populace able to see peacefully to their own needs was, by implication, the surest sign of a successful reign.

Lou Shou's message may also have been intended to convey an important additional message to all the northern Chinese now resettling from their dry-farming wheat-lands into the fertile, water-rich south. The south, and Jiangnan in particular, may have been mythologized as "the land of rice and fish," but these imported northern officials should not mistake that adage to mean that rice grew magically or that fish simply jumped miraculously into nets and cooking pots. The common people were the indispensable handmaids of those miracles.

Gaozang received the scrolls graciously and instructed that they be hung in the imperial residential quarters, perhaps as a symbolic reminder of the social contract between ruler and ruled. He also ordered that copies be made and delivered to local officials as educational devices about the processes for sericulture and riziculture as well as reminders of their duties toward the welfare of the common people.

Before delivering his scrolls to the Emperor, Lou Shou had actually produced a second copy of his work. Those scrolls he left in the hands of his two sons, who wisely decided to preserve their father's paintings by having them faithfully inscribed in stone from which additional copies were produced as rubbings. The originals were eventually lost, but versions believed to have been faithfully drawn from a copy of the two originals were painted in around 1350 by a little-known painter named Cheng Qi 程棨. These, too, were inscribed in stone and occasionally copied. Although the two *Pictures of Tilling and Weaving* scrolls were included in the Yongle Emperor's great *Yongle dadian* encyclopedia in the early Ming era, their existence was largely forgotten[84] until the Kangxi Emperor became aware of them on his first visit to Hangzhou in 1689.

For a foreign ruler anxious to establish his royal bona fides and demonstrate his unflagging concern for his Chinese subjects' welfare, *Pictures of Tilling and Weaving* were an unexpected gift. To help navigate the politically churning waters of literati Jiangnan, with its lingering waves of Ming loyalist sentiment, he could use these 600-year-old images from Hangzhou's rural environs to demonstrate his imperial commitment to traditional Chinese society. They also illustrated his firm support of the region's—and the empire's—two great sources of surplus economic production and taxes, silk and rice.

Kangxi commissioned the court's premier painter, Jiao Bingzhen 焦秉貞 (fl. 1689-1726), to paint a fresh version of Lou Shou's original scrolls. Jiao chose to balance the two scrolls with twenty-three color images each, reducing sericulture by one panel and increasing riziculture by two panels.[85] As a student of the Jesuit Johann Adam Schall von Bell (1591 – 1666), he also incorporated Western painting techniques into his revised version.

The Emperor was clearly pleased with Jiao Bingzhen's artistic reinterpretation of Lou Shou's scrolls. He ordered printing woodblocks to be prepared that included with each image Lou Shou's original poem and a new poem composed by the Emperor himself. Kangxi also added a new, forty-one-column preface for the scrolls.[86] His introductory remarks feel simultaneously empathetic but effusive to excess about his consideration of the common people's welfare, as in the following translated excerpt:

> During each of my inspection tours to the provinces I listened to folk songs, and I was also happy to observe agricultural activities, the characteristics of lands in the north and south, the correct way of sowing seeds for millet and glutinous rice, the differences between the early and late seasonal breaks, and the method of catching and exterminating unfledged locusts. I often love to inquire about these things and to get to know about them all very clearly. When administering to affairs of state, I constantly speak about these things to all my statesmen and officers.... [W]oodblocks have been engraved for the purpose of preservation [of Lou Shuo's illustrations], in order that they be shown to our descendants and subjects, so that they may all know that every single grain which they eat is the result of difficult work and every piece of cloth that they wear is not easily manufactured.[87]

251

In the closing sentence above, Kangxi echoed sentiments often voiced by and to past emperors about the primacy of agriculture and sericulture in the political and moral order of the imperial realm. In the Southern Song, Emperor Gaozong himself declared, probably just rhetorically, that "rearing silkworms should be done in the imperial palace, so that all will know the hardships of farm work."[88] Mao Zedong's late 1960s exhortations that the educated elite go down to the countryside and learn from the farmers and workers seemingly drew from a similar philosophical wellspring.

By imprinting his poetic voice on each panel, Kangxi effectively repurposed the Song Dynasty version to reinforce the propaganda elements of his southern touring initiatives. Kangxi's new and retitled *Imperial Pictures of Tilling and Weaving* (御制耕织图, *Yuzhi gengzhi tu*)[89] were completed in 1696 for distribution to government officials throughout the Qing empire.

During the 1700s, these didactic-political icons took on a life of their own. The Yongzheng and Qianlong Emperors, Kangxi's son and grandson, published new editions during their reigns, each adding their own set of new, four-line poems. Scenes painted in a similar genre soon appeared in both Japan and Korea, and Giuseppe Castiglione (1688 – 1766), the famous Italian Jesuit painter at the imperial palace, painted another set in European style. Images inspired by or copied from Jiao's scrolls migrated onto textiles, fans, ceramics, embroidery, porcelain tea sets, lacquerware, ink cakes, and tea packages. Wallpaper at the Halbturn Castle in Austria even included similar scenes of tea cultivation.[90]

No other region of China remotely rivaled Jiangnan for raw silk production, and few areas north of the Yangzi River had the climatic conditions and water abundance to cultivate significant amounts of rice (wheat, soybeans, and potatoes were more commonly grown in the north). Yet thanks to Lou Shou and his close observation of peasant farming outside of Hangzhou, the particular agricultural and sericultural methods and technologies of Jiangnan came by the eighteenth century to represent, indeed idealize[91] and valorize, the rural agricultural life of the entire empire.

The Kangxi Emperor transformed these images into generic representations of peasant life in China, largely severing their connection to Hangzhou and the surrounding area. As those images and others like them migrated into the West, foreigners in the 19th and 20th Centuries came to imagine (mistakenly) an entire nation of Chinese peasants wading through rice paddies and weaving silk.

In the Banana Garden

The literary inspiration of late-Ming poetesses like Shang Jinglan and Wang Duanshu blossomed in a banana garden in the 1660s and gave new status and credibility to women's writing in the Qing era. Up to that time, small groups of women from elite families had occasionally gathered quietly to enjoy the recreational pastime of shared poetry composition. Unlike the public poetry clubs of the male literati, however, the women's versions were privately held within their household quarters. Furthermore, participation was almost exclusively limited to female family members: mothers, daughters, daughters-in-law, nieces, and cousins.

In the early 1660s, Gu Zhiqiong 顧之瓊 (fl. second half 17th Century), a niece of women's education advocate Gu Ruopu, decided to organize a poetry club in Hangzhou for her daughter, Qian Fenglun 钱凤纶 (1644 – 1703). Herself the daughter of a scholarly family, Qian received a scholar's education and showed early promise as a painter of bamboo. By the age of sixteen, she was married to a young student who happened also to be Gu Ruopu's great-grandson.

Seeking to cultivate her daughter's literary talents and provide her with engaging female companionship, Gu Zhiqiong recruited four suitable women of poetic talent: Lin Yining 林以宁 (1655 – after 1730), Chai Jingyi 柴静仪 (d. 1680), Chai's daughter-in-law Zhu Rouze 朱柔则 (1662 – 1722), and Xu Can 徐灿 (1610 – 1678), the wife of Grand Secretary Chen Zhilin 陈之遴 (1605 – 1666). All hailed from Hangzhou except Suzhou native Xu Can, and all were the daughters of *jinshi* degree holders except Chai Jingyi, whose father held the *juren* (provincial level) degree. Chai's family status was hardly a concern, however, as the other women readily acknowledged her superior talent.

This new poetry group adopted the name Banana Garden Poetry Club (蕉园诗社, Jiaoyuan shishe), and the members became known as the Banana Garden Five (蕉园五子, Jiaoyuan wuzi). Historians have never been able to locate a specific Banana Garden site if there was one, but banana trees were often planted beside scholars' studios for the gentle sound of raindrops falling onto their magnificent, large leaves. For as long as the members remained in the Hangzhou area, they met once or twice a month at one another's residences, or in public spaces, to compose poetry together.

To their credit, the members of the Banana Garden Five saw their meetings as the gendered equal of male poetry gatherings, as evidenced in the following excerpt from one of Qian Fenglun's extant poems:

A Feast at Chai Jingyi's Home One Day in Winter

Sitting together in a beautiful mansion of iris and orchid.
Our talk and laughter bring us great pleasure just like the spring breeze,
In harmony we engage in literary pursuits.
Books lie scattered in the ornate chamber,
Zithers and lutes are placed on yew tables.
As the birds leave, silence descends on the courtyard,
As the clouds disperse dark shadows fall on the curtains.
Reclusion keeps the hurly-burly of the world far away,
Being aloof our thoughts transcend mundanity.
Time flies like a shuttle speeding on the loom,
I worry that our happy get-togethers will be over too soon.
Now that we are tipsy we break into loud songs,
Having enjoyed to the full such "admirable virtue!"⁹²

Qian Fenglun clearly signals the women's enjoyment of the prerogatives of the elite male world: scattered books, fine musical instruments, untrammeled minds withdrawn from worldly concerns, day-long recreation, and plentiful drink. Descriptive though it is, her poem also unapologetically "transposes the male scholars' world and their tradition of gathering in literary circles into a female context."[93]

Marriage and/or travel with their husbands to new official positions eventually separated the Banana Garden Five, and their activities ended. After several years' hiatus, however, Lin Yining resurrected the group as the Banana Garden Seven (蕉园七子, Jiaoyuan qizi), consisting of herself, Chai Jingyi, Qian Fenglun, and four new members: Gu Si 顾姒, who had kinship ties with the Gu, Qian and Lin families in Hangzhou; her niece, Feng Xian 冯娴; Mao Ti 毛媞, daughter of the famous poet Mao Xianshu 毛先舒 (1620 – 88); and Zhang Hao 張昊 (d. age 25).

The Banana Garden poets were active in Hangzhou's literary circles from the 1660s through the 1680s and remained persistent in the public nature of their activity. One Hangzhou scholar recorded his memories of the Banana Garden Seven's appearances at West Lake:

> When the weather was warm and bright in spring, pleasure boats with brocade screens would crowd the lake; both tourists on the water and on land would vie with each other in showing off their finery. Everyone would wear glittery earrings, jade jewelry in the shape of feathers, and silk robes trailing with pearls. Only Chai Jingyi would go out in a small boat with Feng Xian, Qian Fenglun, Lin Yining, and Gu Si, all of them gentlewomen. Wearing simple outfits made of raw silk and their hair tied in a bun, they would busy themselves with ink brush and paper. When the women on pleasure trips in other boats around them saw them, they lowered their heads with shame, realizing that they could not live up to them.[94]

There is no denying that these were privileged gentlewomen (*guixiu*): educated, financially secure, and at ease to pursue poetry writing as a recreational activity. Nevertheless, they dared break the bonds of tradition that constrained women of their class to hide behind the doors of their inner chambers, compose poetry solely for their own private amusement, and refrain from public display or self-promotion. The Banana Garden Poetry Club in both its iterations is widely regarded by scholars as the first public organization of its kind in China to have been created by women, for women.[95]

Born out of the female literary community in Hangzhou, the Banana Garden poets' open visibility paved the way for, and likely inspired, later groups elsewhere, such as the ten female members of the Clear Brook Poetry Club (清溪吟社, Qingxi yinshe) in Suzhou, the Plum Blossom Poetry Club (梅花詩社, Meihua shishe) in Jiangyin, and the Washing Flower Poetry Club (浣花詩社, Huanhua shishe) in Sichuan Province. Literary gatherings like the Banana Garden Poetry Club broke new ground that supported women's writing (and literary consumption) through the rest of the Qing Dynasty and even helped make possible the emergence of female novelists in the 18th and 19th Centuries.

Wife, Mother, Painter

Although more and more women from elite or gentry families were gaining recognition and support for their poetry, relatively few were celebrated or remembered for their painting. In the Yuan Dynasty era, Guan Daosheng was praised for her art and remembered as one of China's greatest female painters; her daughter Guan Daogao 管道杲 (1262 – c. 1319) was also recognized for her artistry. In the closing years of the Ming era, the courtesans Xue Susu and Liu Rushi were well known for their painting skills, and no less an authority than Wu School of Painting founder Shen Zhou reportedly proclaimed Qi Shenning (d. 1477, mother of the great Wu School painter Wen Zhengming) to be "the Guan Daosheng of the present age." Modern scholars have found little supporting evidence for Shen Zhou's claim, however.[96]

Through the Ming and Qing eras, gentry women increasingly joined courtesans in being inculcated in the worlds of poetry and painting. More and more daughters were educated and trained so as to present desirable marriage prospects. Elite and wealthy families in turn sought brides who could educate the next generation—and especially begin the early education of any male children. More young women were literate and could write poetry, and some found further self-expression in painting. In one Chinese biographical dictionary[97] of more than 31,000 Chinese artists, 1,046 are women. Among those, the social positions of 527 are identifiable as gentry and 45 as courtesans; many of the remainder may well also have been from gentry or scholarly families. Yet among those in the Qing Dynasty era, one woman painter garnered particular eminence: Jiaxing native Chen Shu 陈书 (1660 – 1735).

Chen Shu was born into an old-line Jiaxing family who traced their local ancestry back more than five hundred years to the Song Dynasty. She was precociously intelligent, known for harassing her brothers so she could memorize their lessons and recite the Classics. Even as a child, Chen Shu enjoyed producing faithful copies of paintings and calligraphy when she saw them among her family's holdings. When her father passed away early and her mother chose not to remarry, she earned income for the family by sewing and also tutored her younger brother.

Chen married into the Haiyan (Jiaxing) family of a widower named Qian Lunguang 钱 纶光 (1655 – 1718) and bore four sons (the first of whom died from smallpox at age five) and a daughter. Her husband was moderately accomplished as a calligrapher and poet, and the couple shared common interests in the arts that included his poetic inscriptions on some of her paintings. Due to her husband's work helping his aging father at his position in the district schools of Quzhou and his subsequent death in 1718, Chen took primary responsibility for her children's early education, "pawn[ing] her clothing and [selling] her jewelry and paintings" to provide adequately for their schooling.[98]

Her eldest son, Qian Chenqun 钱陈群 (1686 – 1774), was the most successful of Chen's children. After attaining his *juren* degree in 1714 and the *jinshi* degree in 1721 (the penultimate year of Kangxi's reign), Chenqun progressed from the Hanlin Academy to director of education in the capital from 1835 – 1842 and then vice president of the Board of Punishments for the following ten years. He also officiated examinations in Jiangxi Province and metropolitan examinations at the capital, and in 1751 he traveled with Qianlong on that Emperor's First Southern Inspection Tour.

Chen Shu twice visited her son in Beijing and was apparently made known to Emperor Yongzheng. She was highly regarded for her landscapes and flower paintings but was also adept at portraying human figures and writing poems. Chen's son periodically gave gifts of his mother's paintings to Yongzheng. In turn, Yongzheng sent gifts of silk and ginseng to Chen Shu in gratitude for her son's dedication and service to the empire.[99]

As Chen Shu's health declined in her mid-70s, Qian Chenqun petitioned Emperor Yongzheng for leave to visit his mother in Jiaxing. Upon hearing this news, Chen Shu objected, arguing that her son's service to the nation was more important than preserving an old woman's comfort. She insisted instead on traveling to Beijing, which she did in October of 1734, only to die there the following spring. Qian Chenqun was not present at her death; despite her declining health, she had instructed her son to attend to his assigned duties away from the capital.

After his mother's (and Emperor Yongzheng's) death, Qian Chenqun demonstrated his filial piety by giving some of his mother's paintings as gifts to Emperor Qianlong. Qianlong apparently received them with pleasure, retaining them for the palace and sometimes inscribing his own poems on them. Perhaps most famously, Qianlong wrote a second colophon onto one of Chen Shu's works, *Spinning and Teaching the Classics at Night* (夜访授经图, *Yefang shoujing tu*). In that painting, Chen Shu depicted her son as a young boy studying at night by lantern light while she sat nearby weaving in order to make ends meet,[100] a classic illustration of motherhood and filiality. The first colophon had been inscribed by her adult son Chenqun, the studious boy in the painting:

> Hard at work by the latticed flame,
> The night lamp glows bright.
> From the child by her knee,
> The sound of reading echoes the sound of her wheel.
> While her hands are busy with the needle,
> Her ears hear his recitations.
> You know my kindly mother
> Is my teacher too.[101]

In his mother's biography, Qian Chenqun wrote that Chen Shu "filled three volumes with poems, but was too modest to permit them to be published, and was so skilled in the depiction of landscapes, figures, and flowers that people vied for her works."[102] Arthur Hummel's biographical dictionary asserts that twenty-three of Chen Shu's paintings appear in the imperial catalog of the palace collection,[103] possibly establishing her as the best represented woman painter in the imperial collection of anyone in Chinese history.[104]

Chen Shu was not born into an artistic lineage, nor was she married to a famous painter. She developed her own oeuvre from the rich cultural world around her in Jiaxing and from her time in Beijing, and she passed on her knowledge to her sons, grandchildren, and students. Yet her lasting fame comes as much from her life and personal character. "The praise that Chen Shu's paintings elicited from connoisseurs on the highest levels of society down through the years was…a response to her complete persona: filial daughter, dutiful wife, devoted mother, strict teacher, and talented painter….an exceptional woman [who] achieved success in the most conventional ways."[105]

Quelling a Paper Rebellion from Jiaxing

The Kangxi Emperor reigned for sixty-one largely effective years until his death in 1722. His rule was marked by a calming of the populace. Outright loyalism ended, but a smoldering hatred lingered. Kangxi retained the civil service examination system, reduced taxes, secured the northern and western borders, struggled to reduce bureaucratic corruption, welcomed advances in science and technology from the West, and fully embraced Han Chinese history and culture. He also instituted a private and secretive communication system[106] with select, highly trusted officials from whom he demanded frank and unvarnished reports about persons, conditions, and events throughout the empire.

One of Kangxi's gravest failures, however, concerned the imperial succession. He had long favored his second son Yinreng 胤礽 (1674 – 1725) as heir-apparent, but that young man fell into such a depraved and disturbed lifestyle that his father had him arrested. On his deathbed in 1722, Kangxi had still not publicly proclaimed a successor. Thus, when his fourth son, Yinzhen 胤禛 (1678 – 1735), emerged after the Emperor's passing claiming to have been so named, his prospective ascension to the throne was tarnished by doubt and insecurity. As the self-proclaimed Yongzheng Emperor, Yinzhen responded with a small-scale reign of terror directed against his uncles and nineteen brothers. As one historian delicately described the results, "Most of them did not die natural deaths."[107] The succession chaos also left Yongzheng defensive about his right to rule.

By the time of Yongzheng's reign, the angry loyalist writings of the mid-1600s had largely been forgotten, including those of a literatus from Tongxiang (Jiaxing Prefecture) named Lü Liuliang 呂留良 (1629 – 1683). Lü had been a brilliant student when the Ming Dynasty fell,[108] and he continued with his studies and even participated in the provincial examination system under the new dynasty. By 1666, however, he ceased his examination efforts, declared that he would never serve under the Qing, and practiced as a physician for eight years.

After 1674, Lü focused on classical studies, teaching, and writing. His essays, which he sold through a bookstore he opened in Nanjing, were read as study aids by many examination candidates, but he sprinkled them with disparaging, anti-Manchu comments. Widely respected for his scholarship, he resolutely rejected multiple offers for official positions or participation in special examinations and ultimately withdrew into reclusion as a Buddhist monk. At his death in 1683, his last will declared "that he should not be buried in any clothes of Manchu design."[109]

More than four decades after Lü's death, a few of his essays reached a 50-year-old licen-

257

tiate named Zeng Jing 曾靜 (1679 – 1735), a minor official in Hunan Province. Those essays ignited an anti-Manchu spark in Zeng, who like many officials was well aware of the hideous succession rumors swirling around the Yongzheng Emperor. Zeng sent one of his students, Zhang Xi, to visit Lü's descendants in Jiaxing in hopes of obtaining more of his writings.

Inspired by further anti-Manchu rumors and backstopped by Lü's writings, Zeng conceived a quixotic plan to overthrow the Qing Dynasty. To instigate the rebellion, he engaged Zhang Xi to deliver a lengthy letter on his behalf to Yue Zhongqi 岳鍾琪, (1686 – 1754), the Governor-General of two northern provinces and, not coincidentally, a lineal descendant of Song military hero Yue Fei. Lü's message to Yue Zhongqi was filled with vitriolic charges against Yongzheng's reign: fratricide and perhaps regicide, capricious persecution and arbitrary execution of officials, drunkenness, insatiable greed, uncontrolled sexual behavior, and tolerance for sycophancy.

Yue Zhongqi received Zeng Jing's letter in October 1728; both its author and the bearer refused to divulge their names. The Governor-General sent off a secret letter to Beijing notifying Emperor Yongzheng of these unusual events. Fearing the Emperor's possible reaction, he held back Zhang Xi's letter as too offensive to be shared. In the meantime, he feigned agreement with the plot until Zhang Xi revealed his own name as well as Zeng Jing's. Thus began a series of investigations, arrests, and document seizures at the Lü home in Jiaxing. The overthrow plot was quickly traced all the way back to Lü's two surviving sons and several grandsons, all of whom were arrested.

By early December, all the individuals who possessed Lü Liuliang's writings or who aided and abetted Zeng Jing's search for those materials were packed off to Beijing by Zhejiang Governor Li Wei, who oversaw the local investigation. Lü's writings collected by the investigators were sent as well. Court investigators also arrested and interrogated Zeng Jing and Zhang Xi and members of their families. After determining that the rebels were, as Yongzheng described them, "completely laughable people," Zeng and his mother and two sons and Zhang Xi with his father, older brother, and one cousin, were also transported to Beijing.[110]

Faced with wild claims from an obviously unthreatening "rebel" with a few enablers but no apparent following, the Emperor might have simply had the ineffectual group executed and been done with the matter. Instead, however, Yongzheng opted for an imperial "teachable moment." He crafted an eighty-three-page, point-by-point rebuttal of the accusations made against him and had it read aloud to his gathered court officials.

As additional seized materials were delivered into his imperial hands, Yongzheng professed disgust over the shocking nature of some of Zeng's allegations, knowing that such a low-level official was not their sole originator or perpetrator. In April 1729, he ordered hundreds of copies of his rebuttal distributed, nine copies each to every garrison commander, provincial governor, and provincial commissioner of finance, education, and justice. He regarded Zeng Jing merely a fool taken in by rumors, but he characterized the deceased Lü Liuliang's treason as "guilt of the vilest kind," indicative of "the collapse of the

Through the summer of 1729, Yongzheng engaged in a remarkable series of written exchanges with the still-imprisoned Zeng Jing. The Emperor had apparently decided to persuade the lowly official of the falsehoods and errors in his prior beliefs rather than simply execute him. Provided with substantial documentary evidence, Zeng finally relented in a lengthy essay of his own that he called *My Return to the Good*. As a show of imperial mercy, Yongzheng not only ordered Zeng's release in February 1730 but also arranged a minor official position for him in his home province of Hunan.

Having won Zeng's concession, the Emperor had the entire case record printed as a two-volume book of over five hundred pages, titled *A Record of How True Virtue Led to an Awakening from Delusion*. Hundreds of copies were printed for court officials, and hundreds more were sent to governors and senior officials in each province. Each provincial governor also received a second copy to be recopied as often as necessary to ensure that local officials, licentiate students, and every local school had one.

With Zeng Jing and Zhang Xi both set free (contradicting his advisors' recommendations that they be executed as traitors), Yongzheng's attention turned back to the "vile" family of Lü Liuliang in Jiaxing. In January 1733, the Emperor issued his ruling. Lü's last surviving son, age 70, was beheaded, as were the disinterred corpses of Lü himself and his deceased firstborn son. All of Lü's grandsons over the age of sixteen were exiled as slaves to Manchu military garrisons in the far north, and the family's properties were confiscated and sold to fund public works in Zhejiang Province. Lü's writings were confiscated and banned under Qing rule.

Lü Liuliang, the Ming loyalist and refuser from Jiaxing, suffered his second death (by posthumous beheading) fifty years after his first, never knowing that he had inadvertently fomented an attempted rebellion. Nor would he ever know the damage he caused to his family's estate and his descendants' well-being. As for Zeng Jing and Zhang Xi, their escape from punishment would be short-lived. Yongzheng's son and successor, the Qianlong Emperor, would view their roles far more harshly; both would be ordered executed by slicing ("death by a thousand cuts") in the early months of 1736.

Perhaps this entire drama would not have played out as it did, and would have ended much more simply, quickly, and with far fewer fatal consequences, had the Kangxi Emperor just made his choice of successor clear and widely known.

"High Qing" Hangzhou[112]

The extraordinary agricultural, sericultural, and mercantile productivity achieved in Jiangnan during the Ming Dynasty barely paused for the dynastic transition. Hangzhou, the beating heart of northern Zhejiang, was spared from serious conflict damage and soon recovered from the urban displacements caused by the Manchu garrison constructed inside its walls. As the intransigence of Ming loyalism diminished and economic life moved on, Hangzhou resumed its commercial vitality and thus helped the satellite cities around it to regain theirs. As a consequence of the Kangxi Emperor's repeated visits to the city, and especially to West Lake, religious and recreational tourism revived and expanded despite the earlier Manchu aversion to what they saw as its character-weakening effects.

Through the years of the Kangxi Emperor's reign (1661 – 1722), Hangzhou stood as one of the most populous and wealthiest cities in the world, ranked seventh among the world's cities in population in 1720 (estimated 316,000) by one data-based analysis.[113] In the Chinese empire of that time, only Beijing's population exceeded Hangzhou's. The city operated as the southern terminus of the Grand Canal's national supply line, conveying goods of all sorts to the national capital and to markets in Jiangnan and points north. Conversely, wheat and other grains from the north flowed down the Grand Canal and through Hangzhou terminal to reach markets in the deeper south and southwest.

About seventy miles to the east, Hangzhou's deep-water port at Zhapu handled exclusively (by imperial edict) the abundant maritime trade with Japan and Korea and "substantial quantities of Chinese silk export[ed] to Southeast Asia, Japan, and Spanish America."[114] Goods and materials landing at Zhapu reached Hangzhou in one day via a series of inland canals and guard stations that followed the upstream westbound path of the Qiantang River. Such was Zhapu's importance to the provincial capital's mercantile economy and international trade that the Qing government installed a separate naval garrison in that small but high-walled town in 1728.

Within Hangzhou's city walls, manufacturing, trade, and culture flourished in a synergistic relationship. As one of the empire's three locations of Imperial Silk Weaving Factories (along with Suzhou and Nanjing), silk production constituted the city's primary business. These factories produced the highest quality tribute silks for the imperial family and the Qing Court, whose demands necessitated a substantial increase in the production capacity (number of looms) in those locations.[115] Hundreds of factory looms processed raw silk by dyeing, weaving, and embroidering high-quality textiles for domestic use as well as export.

These operations depended in turn on farmers in outlying rural areas—especially around Jiaxing and Huzhou—to raise silkworms, harvest their cocoons, spin silk yarn, and plant and tend the mulberry trees whose leaves fed the worms in their larval stage. Where weaving had once been primarily an urban-centered operation, developments in loom technology allowed weaving to spread as private family businesses into Jiangnan market towns around Jiaxing and Huzhou.[116] Thousands of independent, family-operated looms now wove raw silk for the open market, where the imperial factories increasingly sourced their raw silk. As cotton farming spread rapidly over the drier eastern coastal areas of Jiangnan in the Ming and Qing eras, cotton weaving only added further to Hangzhou's manufacturing base.

Silks and cottons and their associated markets provided a strong financial base for the local economy. Fine handicrafts evolved, particularly with jade carving, silk fans, umbrellas, and scissors. With a highly educated populace, arts and antiquities markets proliferated, as did book shops and book publishing. In its time as the capital of the Southern Song, Hangzhou (Lin'an) had been the center of Chinese publishing, albeit much of what it published was in the service of the government. However, the city managed through succeeding centuries to sustain itself as a leading center of book publishing.

In the Qing era, Hangzhou's publishing industry ranked third in size in the empire, behind Nanjing and Suzhou, and was especially esteemed for the quality of its works involving color. Local book shops and book markets prospered as well, with some publishers even hanging new editions at the city gates[117] to attract a reading audience. Huzhou book merchants were especially well-known for the heavily laden book boats[118] (书船, *shuchuan*) in which they trolled Jiangnan's canals, both urban and rural, making new publications and old editions available to the reading public, rich or poor.

In a city of such wealth and cultivation, retail trade flourished as well. In addition to the shops along the Southern Song Imperial Road, an active market developed at the northern foot of Wushan (Wu Hill) along Hefang Street. Here, shop after shop offered famous local products like silks and silk fans, but also herbal medicines, teas, dried fruits and fish, Shaoxing wine, and more. With all of these, of course, came an abundance of restaurants and tea houses.

For early Westerners who visited Qing Hangzhou in the 18th and early 19th Century, Marco Polo's city by the lake seemed always to be a revelation, a measure of just how special the city was.

> This is one of the richest and largest Cities of the Empire. It is chiefly considerable on account of...the Trade it carries on of the finest Silk in the World.... The Streets are very narrow, but the Shops are convenient, and the Merchants are reckoned very rich....Tho' there are large Gardens in the City, and the Houses have but one Story, it is surprising how populous it is. The great Streets are crowded like those of Paris, with the Difference, that you see no Women there.[119] (*Jean-Baptiste Du Halde, 1687*)

> The streets of this city are very narrow, but well paved; and the houses, which are two and three stories high, being uniformly built of brick, have a very neat appearance. The warehouses of the merchants exceed any I ever saw, both for splendor and magnitude; while the shops are fitted up, both within and without, in a style of the greatest elegance. Their goods, whether enclosed in packages, or displayed to view, were disposed in the most pleasing and attractive mode of arrangement.[120] (*Aeneas Anderson, 1793*)

> In the city of [Hangzhou], being particularly famed for its silk-trade, we were not surprised to meet the extensive shops and warehouses; in point of size and the stock contained within them they might be said to vie with the best in London. In some of these there were not fewer than ten or twelve persons serving behind the counter; but in passing through the whole city not a single woman was visible, either within doors or without....In every shop were exposed to view silks of different manufactures, dyed cottons and nankeen....

The rest of the houses, in the public streets through which we passed, consisted of butchers' and bakers' shops, fish-mongers, dealers in rice and other grain, ivory-cutters, dealers in lacquered ware, tea-houses, cook-shops, and coffin-makers; the last of which is a trade of no small note in China.[121] (*John Barrow, 1793*)

The shops in the main streets have their fronts entirely removed by day, so that the passenger may have an opportunity of seeing and of forming a good idea of the wares which are for sale. I observed many shops where gold and silver ornaments and valuable Jade stone were exposed for sale. Old curiosity shops were numerous, and contained articles of great value amongst the Chinese, such as ancient porcelain jars, bronzes, carved bamboo, jars cut out of the beautiful Jade stone, and a variety of other things of like description. I observed some large silk-shops as I passed along, and, judging from the number of people in the town wearing silk dresses, they must have a thriving trade. Everything, indeed, which met the eye, stamped [Hangzhou] as a place of wealth and luxury.[122] (*Robert Fortune, 1852*)

Two additional commentaries specific to West Lake and its surroundings during the Qing Dynasty are also of interest.

We had a splendid yacht and another made fast to it to serve as a kitchen; the dinner began the instant we went on board and ceased only when we stepped a-shore. It consisted of at least a hundred dishes in succession, among which were excellent eels, fresh caught in the lake and dressed in a variety of ways; yet the water was clear as crystal. Vast numbers of barges were sailing to and fro, all gaily decorated with paint and gilding and streaming colors; the parties within them apparently all in pursuit of pleasure. The margins of the lake were studded with light aereal buildings, among which one of more solidity and of greater extent than the rest was said to belong to the Emperor.[123] (*John Barrow, 1793*)

The western lake is about three or four miles at its greatest length, and a little less in breadth. The great line of the western city-wall comes down to within a few yards of the waters, for a mile or more in extent. Beautiful temples, dilapidated pagodas, the country-houses of the wealthy, a few pack-houses and stores of the more opulent merchants, ancestral temples, ancient tombs and monumental arches, long rows of temporary resting-places for depositing the coffins containing the bodies of individuals who had died at a distance from their own native district, villages and gardens scattered over the undulating hill-sides, and coppices of luxuriant vegetation now shedding their sere leaves in the autumnal breeze, formed a fine panorama of picturesque scenery.[124] (*George Smith, Bishop of Victoria, 1858*)

As the Scottish botanist Robert Fortune summed things up in the early 1850s, "When comparing [Hangzhou to] the towns of Shanghai and Ningbo, the former is a trading place and the latter is a place of great wealth. Hangzhou has both of these advantages combined."[125]

"High Qing" Shaoxing

In the Qing era, the city of Shaoxing could take immense pride in its 4,000-year-old historical connection to Yu the Great and its rich, 2,500-year civic, cultural, and economic history. Like much of Jiangnan to its immediate north, the Shaoxing plain was water-rich and agriculturally fertile, leading British Consul E.H. Parker to write in 1884 that "this is without exception the fattest stretch of land I have ever seen in China or elsewhere."[126] The former capital of the Yue State in the 5th Century BCE may have been cast into Hangzhou's shadow during the Southern Song Dynasty, but Shaoxing found its own flourishing path to prosperity that went well beyond its shared regional specialization in fine silk and cotton textiles.

As much or more than Hangzhou was renowned for Longjing tea, Shaoxing brewers were recognized as the empire's premier producers and purveyors of "yellow wine" (黄酒, *huangjiu*). In fact, the city was so inextricably associated with *huangjiu* that the drink was commonly referred to as "Shaoxing yellow wine," or just "Shaoxing wine." According to one account, the Shaoxing urban/rural complex hosted more than two thousand wine-producing operations in the late Qing era. It is even said that Cao Xueqin 曹雪芹 (1715 – 1764), author of the "great Chinese novel" *Dream of the Red Chamber* (红楼梦, *Hong lou meng*), once jibed about seeing his novel to completion, "If anyone is in a hurry to read my novel, all he's got to do is keep me daily supplied with roast duck and good Shaoxing wine and I'll be happy to oblige him."[127]

Dating back to at least 500 BCE, Shaoxing wine is produced from glutinous rice using the waters of nearby Mirror Lake (鉴湖, Jianhu), adding yeast for fermentation along with other ingredients. The early fermentation matures for three years or more in large, mud-sealed, earthenware jars and emerges with a sweet fragrance and the amber hue that gives it the "yellow wine" description. In traditional brewing, the clay storage pots were inscribed with flower designs so that Shaoxing wine came also to be called "carved flower wine" (花雕酒, *huadiao jiu*). The preferred method of consumption is for the wine to be gently warmed, but Shaoxing wine is also a key flavoring ingredient in such popular Chinese cooking dishes as Drunken Chicken, braised fish, and braised pork belly (one of Mao Zedong's favorite dishes).

Multiple gradations of Shaoxing yellow wine developed over time by adding more rice during fermentation to increase the percentage of alcohol. These modestly higher-proof varieties are called "added rice wine" (加饭酒, *jiafan jiu*). One of the great traditional uses of Shaoxing wine came to be known as "daughter red" wine (*nü'er hong jiu* 女儿红酒). Families with a newborn daughter would purchase the finest grade of Shaoxing *huadiao* wine and further embellish the jar with landscapes, dragons and phoenixes, Eight Immortals crossing the sea, and other good luck symbols. The family then buried the wine jar for eighteen years. At the time of their daughter's wedding, when the lucky color red appeared everywhere from lanterns and table decorations to the bride's dress and red gift envelopes (红包, *hongbao*), the bride's parents would retrieve the long-maturing wine and serve it to their wedding guests.

Yellow wine was far from Shaoxing's only famous domestic export. The city evolved over time into a national center for the production of tinfoil spirit money. Dozens of tinfoil workshops in Shaoxing transformed ore from Yunnan Province into tin ingots about one centimeter in thickness, then set about pounding them repeatedly for up to two weeks until they were paper-thin. These paper-like tin sheets were then distributed to peasant households throughout the Shaoxing area where they were pasted onto a yellow bamboo-paper backing and folded to mimic the ancient, boat-shaped gold or silver nuggets known as *yuanbao* 元宝, symbolizing great wealth.

By one estimate from 1932 -1933, Shaoxing hosted more than one hundred tinfoil workshops staffed by more than two thousand workers.[128] Traveling through the Shaoxing area in the 1920s, Harry Franck wrote that "On the narrow sloping space between [the moat and city wall] thousands of sheets of brown paper were spread out to dry, before being made into 'spirit money'…Between 70 and 80 percent of the people of Shaoxing are supported through the making of this false wealth." He also remarked that Shaoxing usually "resounds" from the beating of tin ingots into the paper-thin sheets which then join "the constant processions of squeegeed sheets, eighty pounds in each small package, trotting through the streets."[129]

Yet of all the agriculture products, potent potables, textiles, and handicrafts that flowed from the Shaoxing region, none were more notorious in the Ming and Qing eras than the educated men themselves. According to one adage, there were three things one could find anywhere one traveled in Qing China: sparrows, bean curd, and Shaoxing natives.[130] The reason for their ubiquity across the empire was unusual if not unique: they were members of a homegrown network of legal clerks, known as "Shaoxing masters" (绍兴师爷, *Shaoxing shiye*), who populated government offices (*yamen*) across the empire.

The educational background of most government officials centered on the civil service examination system, which focused far more on the Confucian Classics than on the practical matters of bureaucratic administration. By the Qing era, the highest-level degree holders (*jinshi*) were a truly rarified lot, so steeped in their "ivory tower" studies that one could only wonder at their practical knowledge or ability to apply their learning to actual governmental administration.

Consider that in 1850, about two million candidates sat for the first-level exams every year; about 30,000 (1.5 percent) were awarded licentiate degrees. From among that group, perhaps 1,500 (5 percent) would succeed in the triennial provincial (*juren* degree) exams. Only 300 from among those 1,500 *juren* holders would achieve the highest (*jinshi*) degree in the triennial metropolitan exams. In other words, just one out of every 6,600 candidates (one one-hundredth of one percent)[131] would be eligible for the most responsible official positions.

Yet this multi-level sieve of human talent, operating on a scale unmatched in global history, sorted and ranked by a somewhat impractical skill set: capacity for memorization, calligraphic style and clarity, and intimate familiarity with the ancient Confucian classics and commentaries. Successfully passing through this tortuous sifting process could rarely be achieved without absolute immersion and unwavering devotion to the Confucian Classics and the rigid stylistic demands of the exams themselves rather than the practicalities of civil administration.

Lack of relevant, pragmatic training and frequent reassignment from one location to another meant that officials often arrived at their posts with limited knowledge of administrative rules, regulations, and practices and even less knowledge of the district for which they were responsible. Consequently, they were forced to rely on the already-present secretaries or legal specialists (collectively called *muyou* 幕友, literally "friends behind the curtains") to conduct ordinary, day-to-day operations or navigate the legalistic vagaries of the office. And surprisingly often, those clerks were part of the "Shaoxing network."

From the late Ming onward in the imperial era, Shaoxing men followed a path to government service through the purchase of clerical positions or acceptance of a clerk's assistant position after earning a lower-level degree. Shaoxing native Gong E, himself a Qing-era legal advisor for nearly four decades, "claimed in the 1790s...that 'no fewer than ten thousand Shaoxing families were engaging in the *muyou* profession.'" A 1773 official report from Shandong counted 199 legal advisors across the entire province, with 112 (56 percent) identified as natives of Shaoxing prefecture.[132] Zhejiang legal secretaries dominated the profession nationally, and Shaoxing men predominated in that group.

Not to say that Shaoxing was unable to produce successful exam candidates, however. In the Ming era, an impressive 977 Shaoxing Prefecture scholars achieved a *jinshi* degree, second only to Ji'an Prefecture in Jiangxi Province.[133] Over the course of the Qing Dynasty, Shaoxing produced the sixth most *jinshi* degree holders, 505, out of 185 prefectures; Hangzhou ranked first on that score (1,004 *jinshi*), with Suzhou second (785 *jinshi*)[134] By comparison, analysis from the 1892 *Complete Register of Qing Officials* revealed that 499 Shaoxing men (out of 6,987 total) served as clerks or sub-officials, while Hangzhou had 163 and Suzhou 116 in those positions.[135]

For those unsuccessful in the civil service examinations, or those who simply chose not to participate, legal advisor offered an easier path to a semi-official position with hidden influence and opportunities for "extra" income. What James Cole referred to as Shaoxing's "vertical administrative clique"[136] was self-perpetuating, since the city's new clerical candidates found easy entrée among their fellow townsmen who already held such positions. From the lowest county-level *yamen* to the prefectural capitals, Shaoxing natives knew and communicated with one another in a common dialect that facilitated the business of bureaucratic governance. While the legal and administrative intricacies of their field and the relative lack of knowledge of their superiors made for job security, they could also be turned to more self-serving and remunerative (if not always strictly legal) ends.

Not surprisingly, the sheer number of Shaoxing clerks and their ability to navigate or even manipulate the Qing legal system made them objects of widespread distrust if not outright disparagement. A mid-Qing scholar from Yuyao wrote that "the Shaoxing locale has many evil people habitually proficient as corrupt clerks...who make a talent of their inclination for litigation." He added with obvious disdain for the quality of their work that the local prefect had even ordered some of them beaten after reviewing their legal briefs.[137] Martino Martini commented on the reputation of Shaoxing clerks at the beginning of the Qing Dynasty, writing that "There are no legal counsels...more cunning or sly in all of China," an ambiguous if not cautiously admiring sentiment. Martini's views were echoed by another Jesuit, Jean-Baptiste Grosier (1743 – 1823), who also wrote that Shaoxing natives "are said to be the greatest adepts at chicanery of any in China," so that astute governors and prefects were sure to include them among their secretarial staffs.[138]

Because local (county-level) officials and their secretaries were often paid only nominal salaries that rarely even covered expenses, Qing-era administrative personnel faced constant pressure to find revenue sources in tax collection and judicial administration. To generate funds, *yamen* officials "charged a variety of fees for public service and practiced extortion on a widespread scale....[that] could well be characterized as in business to sell administration at the highest marketable rates."[139] This behavior was naturally less than endearing to the common citizen and led to another, perhaps envy-tinged adage that summed up the overall sentiment: "Shaoxing has hills but no wood, water but no fish, and men but no righteousness."[140]

Chapter 11

QING DYNASTY – THE SECOND CENTURY

(1735 – 1842)

I left West Lake thirty years ago, but I cannot help feeling homesick for it, and each time I revise my garden, I play at creating an imitation of the lake, constructing a dike, digging wells, making an Inner and Outer Lake, a Flower Harbor, Six Bridges, and Southern and Northern Peaks. While I am building these, I am always thinking, "Isn't it difficult to succeed at imitating the creations of nature when using the abilities of a human?"

— *Yuan Mei (1716 – 1798),*
on building his Harmony Garden to mimic West Lake[1]

Another Imperial Visitor

When the 57-year-old Yongzheng Emperor died in 1735 after a twelve-year reign, he left no doubt about his successor. He had long since decided on Hongli弘历 (1711 – 1799),[2] his fourth son (and Kangxi's favorite grandson) as the heir apparent, keeping his choice secret in a sealed box to be opened only upon his death. However, Yongzheng also kept a transitional thumb on his son's rule by establishing a four-person Regency to guide him. Hongli ascended the Dragon Throne at age 25 as the Qianlong Emperor (r. 1736 – 1795), respectful of the Regency but determined to follow in his grandfather Kangxi's footsteps, figuratively as well as physically.

Early in his reign, Qianlong manifested a wanderlust not unlike that of his grandfather. In 1741, he undertook a modest first step by traveling north to the Imperial Summer Resort and hunting grounds at Chengde (known then as Rehe 热河 or Jehol). Two years later, he visited the ancient Manchu capital at Mukden (present-day Shenyang), followed by tours to Shanxi Province in 1746, Shandong Province in 1748, and Shanxi and Henan Provinces in 1750. Not only were these tours relatively short in distance, they carefully avoided southern tours that might be deemed recreational excursions that his Regents might oppose.

Finally, in 1749, circumstances for a southern tour began to converge. The last of Qianlong's four Regents resigned, and in the autumn of that year, the court received a memorial signed jointly by seven high-ranking Jiangnan officials requesting that the Emperor visit their region. "Day and night we plead," they wrote, "awaiting a visit from the imperial procession, stretching our necks and standing on tiptoe....The populace is of one mind: they eagerly wish to welcome [the imperial procession]. This truly emanates from the utmost sincerity of the entire provinces' gentry, elders, scholars, and commoners."[3]

The Emperor was well aware of Jiangnan's importance economically, governmentally, and culturally. That southern region contained sixteen percent of China's arable land but generated nearly thirty percent of the empire's cash tax revenue, thirty-eight percent of the tax revenue submitted as grain, and well over sixty percent of the tribute grain that fed the capital.

Jiangnan degree holders filled the court and national bureaucracies out of all proportion to their share of the population, a result of their disproportionate receipt of *jinshi* degrees in the triennial examinations. Jiangnan men also occupied large numbers of the better first assignments for new graduates as a result of their extraordinary proficiency in the examinations. Between 1645 and 1795, the metropolitan (national) examinations were held sixty-one times; the highest-scoring candidate, known as the *zhuangyuan* 状元, hailed from Jiangnan on fifty-one of those occasions.[4]

Zhejiang and Jiangsu had wealth, prestige, agricultural riches, and unmatched influence in administrative and cultural affairs. Given its past of anti-Manchu sentiment and Ming loyalism, Qianlong could not afford to ignore Jiangnan for long. Lacking his grandfather's pressing concerns over water management to shield himself from accusations of placing pleasure over duty, Qianlong found a new rationale for a southern tour: the Dowager Empress's upcoming 60th birthday in 1651.[5]

> Wherever We travel on an imperial tour of inspection, We always accompany the Empress Dowager in enjoying the sights. The famous sights of Jiangnan are pre-eminent in the realm, and if We were personally to accompany the Empress Dowager's procession there to see the beauty of the hills and streams as well as the abundance of the people and their products, it would well suffice to bring pleasure to Her venerable bosom.[6]

In so many words, the Qianlong Emperor justified a southern expedition on the grounds of a filial son granting his 60-year-old mother a precious birthday gift. Any incidental sightseeing in the midst of the Emperor's efforts to conduct the business of government would then be attributable to the feminine interest in such ephemeral entertainments. Like his grandfather Kangxi, Qianlong would ultimately commission six Southern Inspection Tours, in 1751, 1757, 1762, 1765, 1780, and 1784. The Dowager Empress (Imperial Consort Xiaoshengxian 孝圣宪皇后, 1692 – 1777) would accompany the first four of these recurring gifts from her ever-filial son before her death in 1777.

The Qianlong Emperor's Hangzhou itinerary in the First Southern Inspection Tour mirrored his grandfather's, especially in its side excursion to Shaoxing to pay sacrificial homage at the tomb of Yu the Great. His nine-day stay in the city by West Lake demonstrated as well Qianlong's enthusiasm for the scenery, culture, cuisine, and pleasures of his kingdom's southern climes. Then again, where Kangxi's primary objective as an early-Qing emperor was to project the unifying power of a new ruling authority, Qianlong's concerns were more about moral and political suasion of Jiangnan's citizenry.

In addition to meeting with local officials, recruiting scholars, administering special examinations, inspecting water works, sacrificing to local deities, and granting various honors, gifts, and tax remissions, Qianlong strove to present a military presence. The Emperor manifested this reminder of authority in several ways. First, at Hangzhou and all major cities along the route, the Emperor and his court invariably arrived on horseback. They traveled locally the same way as a reminder of the Manchu military heritage. Second, at garrison sites like Hangzhou, Qianlong conducted military reviews and observed drills and exercises, usually carried out by a mixture of Manchu banner and Green Standard (Han Chinese) soldiers. Naval exercises were conducted at Zhapu as well, although most often in the presence of Qianlong's designated representatives.

Third, Qianlong reiterated the importance of military preparedness and chastised those who fell short in his judgment. He fretted constantly over the Hangzhou and Nanjing garrisons for their soft military discipline and their adoption of Han Chinese ways. Like his grandfather, Qianlong feared that the daily pleasures and easy life of Jiangnan would induce laxity among the Manchu troops and even lead to their loss of ethnic identity.[7]

During each visit to Hangzhou, Qianlong enjoyed the use of the Wenlan Palace on Gushan (Solitary Hill), the island near the north shore of West Lake on which Lin Bu had tended his crane and plum trees in the early 11th Century and where many common people had once lived as well. After the Southern Song signed a peace agreement with the Jurchen Jin in the early 1140s, Emperor Gaozong's mother (Empress Dowager Wei) was allowed to return south along with the coffins of the deceased Emperors Huizong and Qinzong. In celebration, Gaozong ordered the island cleared (except for Lin Bu's grave) and a new Daoist temple[8] and accompanying gardens were built there to commemorate his mother's release.[9]

In the 15th Century, the West Lake Academy of Classical Learning and its associated library had occupied the former temple grounds. Prior to the Kangxi Emperor's fourth Hangzhou visit in 1705, a temporary palace was constructed on the island hillside. Although the height of Solitary Hill measured only thirty-eight meters (about 124 feet), its foremost position near the northern shore offered magnificent views over West Lake and the southern hills beyond. In 1727, Kangxi's vacant temporary palace had been transformed once again into the Shengyin Temple, so Qianlong's resurrection of southern inspections necessitated construction of a suitable new residence for his first visit in 1751. A dock built along the island's south shore and crowned with an imperial gateway welcomed the Emperor as West Lake delivered him to his temporary Hangzhou palace.[10]

Qianlong was among the most literarily expressive of Chinese emperors, conveying his thoughts and sentiments across well over forty thousand poems during his reign. Not surprisingly, West Lake inspired its own share of imperial verse, although often couched in terms that downplayed his viewings as mere leisure, as in this poem from his second Hangzhou visit in 1757:

> According to the people's wishes,
> We once again visit a renewed Su [Shi's Embankment].
> In the wake of disaster, We remain seriously concerned.
> This is the primary reason for our spring tour of inspection.
> How is touring [Su] Embankment frolicking at West Lake?[11]

Despite his declared avoidance of sightseeing, Qianlong managed in his visits to experience the Ten Views of West Lake just as his grandfather had done. He composed his own new poems for all ten views and ordered steles erected to commemorate his arrival at each site.

In 1764, Suzhou-born court painter Xu Yang 徐扬 (1712 – after 1777) received a commission to produce a twelve-scroll depiction of the Emperor's inaugural (1751) Southern Inspection Tour. Once again, Qianlong was following the inspection tour precedents established by his grandfather. However, where Wang Hui had emphasized the distances traveled by Kangxi and conveyed a sense of movement across various terrains in order to survey the southern realm, Xu Yang's scrolls were more focused on specific destinations in "a series of monoscenic historical tableaux."[12] Unlike Wang Hui's work, Xu's also employed Western painting techniques like foreshortening and fixed-point perspective.

After two years, Xu's drafts were approved and he set to work on silk. He submitted the finished set of scrolls for mounting in November 1769 and presented them triumphantly to Qianlong in mid-1770 for the Emperor's 60th birthday celebration. As had been the case with the Kangxi Emperor's record of his Second Southern Inspection Tour, scenes and events exclusive to Jiangnan occupied fully five of the twelve resulting scrolls (Scrolls VI to X in both cases), or almost forty-two percent of their number.

Scroll VII depicted the imperial entourage's approach from the Jiangsu-Zhejiang border to Jiaxing; Scroll VIII displayed the glories of Hangzhou and West Lake; and Scroll IX covered Qianlong's travel from Shaoxing to the tomb of Yu the Great. Scrolls VII and VIII are lost; Scroll IX resides in Beijing's National Palace Museum. Fortunately, Xu Yang produced paper copies of all twelve scrolls soon after the silk versions were completed. Paper copies of Scrolls VII and VIII are held at the Beijing Historical Museum.[13]

During each of his last four Southern Inspection Tours (1762, 1765, 1780, and 1784), Qianlong altered the route from Jiaxing to Hangzhou with a detour through Haining. The Qiantang River tidal bore had persisted through the centuries as a periodic threat to human life along the Hangzhou Bay coastline as well as a threat to highly productive local agriculture and sea salt manufacture. Both of these harvests were significant tax sources for the empire, yet every attempt to strengthen the seawalls had ended up an eventual failure against the erosive power of the tidal surges.

On its surface, this addition to the Emperor's itinerary appeared to be an imperial review of a seawall reinforcement project begun by Kangxi and even more heavily financed by Yongzheng. In 1727, Yongzheng also underwrote construction of a tidal bore viewing platform from which to offer annual sacrifices to the god of the tides. Qianlong assumed personal responsibility for these rituals on each of his four visits. Unfortunately, neither his sacrifices nor those performed in the intervening years by Ministers of Rites measurably affected the strength of the tidal bores or the damage they caused.

Qianlong's four Haining visits ultimately convinced him that a fish-scale (overlapping stone) barrier was the only feasible solution.[14] He therefore financed, along with substantial local and sea salt merchant contributions, a twenty-mile stretch of seawall built with overlapping stones, completed in 1783. The stone seawalls did not always prevent tidal surges from inundating the Haining area, and the new barriers also proved rather costly to maintain. Not until the 20th Century would construction technologies advance sufficiently to put truly effective barriers in place.

Qianlong used the seawall project as an important justification for his last two Southern Inspection Tours (1780 and 1784), much as his grandfather had done with the Yellow River flood control effort. While his physical presence was hardly necessary to the project's completion, the Emperor in his *Record of the Southern Tours* claimed an active managerial role:

> On Our southern tour in 1780, We personally visited and inspected [the seawalls]. Although We ordered the governor-general and governor to build seawalls made of fish-scale bonded stone masonry…, We also instructed them to leave the old wooden walls in place as a second line of defense….Now in 1784, We have issued another order to extend Zhejiang's stone seawalls. During this southern tour of 1784, We personally visited and directed the construction, sparing no cost and ordering the wholesale conversion of the seawalls into stone.[15]

Qianlong's insistence on personal involvement in the seawall project and his four site visits transformed Haining into a literati tourist site for viewing the tidal bore. No longer content to watch the partially spent but still impressive tidal bore on the Hangzhou shores of the Qiantang River, late 18th-Century literati began traveling eastward to Haining to celebrate poetically the incoming tidal flow (and their own self-congratulatory viewing of it) from the Emperor's observation points.[16] From this time forward, the tidal bore was more to be consumed as a leisure experience and less to be feared as a source of natural disaster.

The Emperor's repeated visits to Haining also unwittingly spawned a curious and long-lasting folk rumor about the Emperor's birth origins. According to the gossipy (and historically unsubstantiated) tale that arose in the 1780s, Qianlong was actually the son of a Haining family named Chen 陈 whom the Yongzheng Emperor had "acquired" in exchange for an unwanted imperial daughter. In some tellings, both children were even born on the same day.

The Haining Chens were an extraordinary scholarly family, even by Jiangnan's elevated standards. Between the 16th and 19th Centuries, thirty-one Chen family members obtained *jinshi* degrees, and an astonishing 103 were *juren*. Three of these super-achievers served their respective emperors as Grand Secretaries, while hundreds more earned official ranks. Chen Zhilin 陈 (1605 – 1666, *jinshi* 1637, husband of Banana Garden poetess Xu Can) served as the Shunzhi Emperor's Grand Secretary in the 1650s, while Chen Shiguan 陈世倌 (1680 – 1758, *jinshi* 1703) served similarly for the Qianlong Emperor through much of the 1740s and 1750s.[17]

Depending on the source,[18] either Chen Shiguan or his father, Chen Xian 陳詵 (1642 – 1722, *juren* 1672) ostensibly fathered the child whom the lurid story claimed to be the eventual emperor. These rumors arose because Qianlong visited the Chen family in each of his four Haining stopovers and stayed at their Garden of Tranquil Waves (安澜园, Anlan Yuan).[19] Popular novels appeared and built upon idle speculation that the Emperor's visits to Haining were subconscious "returns home," further cementing a tawdry tale as speculative fodder for a movie adaptation in 1929.[20]

An Imperial Tea

When Lu Yu surveyed and ranked the varieties of tea cultivated during the Tang Dynasty, he noted the tea grown by the monks of Lingyin and Tianzhu Temples in the western hills beyond West Lake. However, the great tea connoisseur apparently held their tea in relatively low regard, perhaps due to his era's preference for caked teas over loose-leafed ones. Nor in the Tang era was the spring water of Longjing (龙井, Dragon Well) particularly celebrated. In the Zhejiang region, Lu had favored the teas of the Huzhou area and spring waters found in Wuxi and Suzhou, among others.

By the Northern Song, Su Shi mentioned several local teas in his writings about Hangzhou, but Longjing's received no special recognition in his commentaries. As literati tea connoisseurship began pairing spring water quality with tea leaves as essential for the finest drinking experience, the combination of Longquan (龙泉, Dragon Spring) waters with the tea leaves grown nearby rose in the taste-testers' rankings. The Longjing tea-drinking experience benefited from natural circumstances, but carefully controlled seasonal timing of tea-leaf picking added to the drink's delicacy. The relatively new technique of dry-pan frying rather than steaming the leaves enhanced the taste experience even further. By the close of the 16th Century, tea aficionados were proclaiming the fine qualities of the Longjing-area teas.

A Qiantang County gazetteer from the early 1600s was among the first documents to formally acknowledge tea grown in the Dragon Well vicinity as a "local product," describing it as "green in color," having "a fragrance like that of soybean flower" with a distinctive taste that was "sweet and delicious."[21] However, it was only in the late Ming, as tea preferences fully evolved from tea cakes and soupy tea broths to leaf teas steeped in hot water, that connoisseurs began to include Dragon Well tea among their favorites. Finally, the Zhejiang gazetteer of 1736 saw the first official recognition of a local product called "Longjing tea," citing it as superior to any other local teas.[22]

Teas from the western regions of China had been essential products of Chinese trade with northern and western tribal peoples since at least the Song Dynasty, particularly the tea-for-war-horse exchanges with the Tibetans and Mongols.[23] Varietal tea comparisons and the "refined" drinking experience remained a literati fascination, while less differentiated consumption gradually became popular with commoners. Nevertheless, the persistent writing of Jiangnan literati in praise of Dragon Well tea as the preferred beverage of the educated elite elevated it to a national status symbol; the only higher status could come from an imperial blessing. That imprimatur was achieved with the Qianlong Emperor's Southern Inspection Tour visits to Hangzhou.

Qianlong is said to have visited the Longjing vicinity during four of his six visits to Hangzhou, and several stories purport to explain Qianlong's connection to Longjing tea. During a visit to Hugong Temple at the base of Lion's Peak Mountain (狮峰山, Shifeng shan), he was treated by one account to a drink of tea that he found so instantly appealing that he claimed for himself the eighteen tea bushes on the hill from which his leaves had been picked. A ringed set of eighteen tea bushes stands there today, claimed to be the same bushes from more than two centuries ago. The bushes were marked as the Emperor's Tribute Tea Trees, and Longjing tea was given the title Gong Cha 貢茶, Emperor's Tribute Tea, or simply Imperial Tea. Ever the aspiring poet, the Qianlong Emperor also produced eight poems about Longjing in each of his four visits to that area.

Poem Written while Making Tea at Longjing[24]	坐龙井上烹茶偶成
Fresh tea made with Longjing's spring water,	龙井新茶龙井泉，
The way the tea is cooked gives it a unique taste.	一家风味称烹煎。
The small tea plant sprouts from fertile soil,	寸芽生自烂石上，
Tea leaves are picked and roasted before Spring rain comes.	时节焙成谷雨前。
Why do we praise only the Palace tea?	何必团凤夸御茗，
When I drink this delicious tea that purifies my heart.	聊因雀舌润心莲。
I wish to call upon an eminent monk to discuss Buddhism,	呼之欲出辨才在，
Unfortunately, I can only use writing to express my thoughts.	笑我依然文字禅。

Another story linking Qianlong to the fame of Longjing tea asserts that during one visit, the Emperor picked some tea leaves for himself and held them in the sleeves of his robe. Upon his return to Beijing, he visited his mother who had fallen ill. She detected the fragrant scent of the leaves and asked for tea to be brewed from the now-flattened leaves.

She felt much better after drinking the tea, so her filial son ordered that his mother be presented the finest Longjing tea leaves every year thereafter.

Teas harvested from the Lion's Peak are still regarded today as the finest among those grown in the vicinity, and Longjing Tea remains one of China's most celebrated teas.[25]

Books...Books...Books

Although much of China's publishing centered on Lin'an during the Southern Song era, Zhejiang had already established itself as a book-producing area as much as four centuries earlier, in the Tang Dynasty. By that time, carved woodblocks were already being employed to print multiple copies of poetry collections by the likes of Bai Juyi. Even during the interim Five Dynasties era (907 – 960) of Wuyue, Hangzhou was a major center of woodblock printing, including the famous 84,000 sutra copies stowed away in pagoda bricks and tiles by Qian Shu. In the Northern Song, while Kaifeng was still the capital, "almost half the books for the Imperial College [in Kaifeng] were printed in Hangzhou."[26]

Paper production and papermaking technology advances arose from Zhejiang as well. In the Song Dynasty era, raw materials like "rice straw, wheat straw, the mulberry bark, hemp, rattan and bamboo" were plentiful, and "paper-making factories were spread everywhere in Zhejiang Province."[27] Bookbinding techniques advanced in and around Hangzhou, and China's premier writing-brush makers operated nearby in Huzhou. In such an environment, bookstores proliferated, as did book collectors. By Emperor Qianlong's time, Jiangnan (especially Nanjing, Suzhou, Huzhou, and Hangzhou, along with Jianyang County in north-central Fujian Province) stood as the empire's centers of book production and collecting.

Beyond the literary purges and human punishments exacted by Kangxi on Zhuang Tinglong in 1663 Huzhou and Lü Liuliang in 1729 Jiaxing, Qianlong found further sources of concern during his reign. In 1768, the Emperor rediscovered the writings of Qian Qianyi, the man who helped deliver Jiangnan to the Manchu conquerors. Qianlong complained openly of Qian's persistent denigration of the Manchus and their culture, infuriated that such criticisms came from an unfilial man who professed loyalty to two dynasties. In one poetic expression of his views, the Emperor wrote:

> Although throughout his life Qian continually talked about loyalty,
> he served two dynasties;
> Having no principles as to when to take office and when to retire,
> How can his literary productions then be worthy of attention?
> It really makes one spill out the wine in disgust.[28]

The Emperor's disgust soon manifested itself in literary excision. In the summer of 1769, he ordered empire-wide confiscation and destruction of Qian Qianyi's writings and printing woodblocks from all sources—publishers, private collections, libraries, bookshops, and street vendors. In a bizarre but emphatic final twist, Qianlong commissioned biographies of thirty-three Ming loyalists in the *Record of All Officials Who Died Out of Loyalty to the Fallen Dynasty* (胜朝殉节诸臣录, *Shengchao xunjie zhuchen lu*) and awarded various honors to over 3,750 more loyalists who in Qian Qianyi's day had remained properly steadfast in their opposition to the Manchus.[29]

What happened next has been the subject of historical conjecture and debate, but the events themselves constituted both the literary apex and the literary nadir of Qianlong's reign. In 1772, the Emperor issued a new directive demanding that officials at all levels throughout the empire submit information and copies of all "valuable" library holdings in their jurisdictions, defined in the edict as "any preserved book which clarifies the essential methods of government or which concerns human nature."[30] The many hundreds (if not thousands) of private book collectors were urged by the edict to do likewise.

On its face, Qianlong's goal in this collection effort was audacious, ambitious, and self-glorifying: to produce a complete, state-sponsored compendium of the greatest written works of Chinese history, from the classics and treatises on governance to works of history and philosophy. He expected this new compilation to succeed Ming Emperor Yongle's encyclopedia of 1407, the *Yongle dadian* (永樂大典), as the greatest literary compendium in Chinese history and thus showcase the glories achieved under Manchu reign.

The initial submissions merely trickled in as responders remained uncertain of the purpose or feared punishment for some items they might have owned. Qianlong persisted, cajoling, remonstrating, and even shaming some officials by name until books began pouring into the capital. It was a measure of Jiangnan's wealth and strong academic traditions that more than half of the books submitted by provincial governors came from Zhejiang (34%) and Jiangsu (18%); another 15% came from the Governor-General of Liangjiang 两江 (Jiangnan plus Jiangxi Province).[31]

In 1773, as the review for books worthy of inclusion in the proposed encyclopedia was well underway, the Emperor issued another edict granting the project its formal name, *The Complete Book of the Four Treasuries* (四庫全書, *Siku quanshu*). A staff of over seven hundred, including nearly four hundred scholars and scholar-officials, ultimately culled through well over ten thousand different submissions. With Qianlong's approval, the editors chose 3,593 titles[32] for inclusion in the compendium, grouped into four "treasuries": Classics (经, *Jing*), History (史, *Shi*), Philosophy (子, *Zi*), and Fine Literature (集, *Ji*). Hand-copied in their entireties, these chosen books produced a work of almost 80,000 scrolls, comprising over 36,000 volumes and an estimated 800 million words (characters).

The first *Siku quanshu* was completed in 1782 and placed in the Wenyuan Hall 文源阁 at the Summer Palace (圆明园, Yuanmingyuan) in Beijing. It was a literary triumph of nearly unimaginable magnitude, unsurpassed in size by any other compendium of knowledge in world history until Wikipedia approached a billion words in 2007. The second full copy of the *Four Treasuries* was delivered to the Wenshuo Hall 文渊阁 in the ancient Manchu capital of Mukden (present-day Shenyang). The third and fourth copies were placed, respectively, in the Wenyuan Hall 文渊阁 of the Forbidden City in 1784 and the Wenjin Hall 文津阁 in Chengde's Summer Palace in 1785.

To ensure that the Emperor and his court would be able to access the *Four Treasuries* wherever he might have temporary residence, Qianlong had three more copies produced and dispatched to Jiangnan, with one each stored in Zhenjiang (the Wenzong Hall 文宗阁), Yangzhou (the Wenhui Hall 文汇阁), and Hangzhou (the Wenlan Hall 文澜阁, Wenlan ge) at Solitary Hill on West Lake. Wenlan ge, the Hangzhou library for the *Four Treasuries*, was built in 1783 specifically for that purpose and was situated on the south shore of the island, at the foot of the hill on which the emperors' temporary residence, the Xinggong Palace 行宫, had been constructed.

During the course of the *Siku quanshu* project, the manuscript compilers reviewed a number of books that were deemed worthy but not of sufficient merit or originality for inclusion in the *Four Treasuries*. Though omitted, nearly 6,800 such works were duly recognized by their inclusion in an associated, 200-scroll "attachment" to the main work, published in 1793 as the *Annotated Catalog of the Complete Imperial Library*, (四庫全書總目提要, *Siku quanshu zongmu tiyao*). This supplementary work cataloged, with bibliographic details, the entire list of 10,000-plus titles considered as serious candidates for the *Four Treasuries*, whether included or not.

What did not appear in the *Annotated Catalog* were another 3,000-plus books screened by the court's scholars and determined to contain seditious, anti-Manchu material. As early as 1774, Qianlong had voiced skepticism about the too-pure nature of the books already received at the capital. In a September 1774 edict, he wrote:

> Now of the over ten thousand volumes submitted by the several provinces none has been singled out as offensive. How is it possible that among such a quantity of books bequeathed by former generations not one should contain a trace of sedition?

In the same edict, Qianlong promised no harm to the remitters but also made clear his intentions regarding seditious materials infecting his realm:

> [O]ne need not fear evil consequences in producing them. I want the books, not to do harm to their owners, but to seek out the defects in the works themselves....I decreed to the governors-general and governors of Kiangsu and Chekiang that if they suspected the books to contain words either subversive or involving lèse majesté, they should not let them be preserved to mislead posterity. When these works reach here, I shall only have them burned, and you may inform the owners that the books had better not be preserved, but this will in no way incriminate them. Much less will the officials by dispatching them be held blameworthy.[33]

Works believed potentially seditious began arriving in Beijing by the thousands after the 1774 edict, beginning a literary inquisition that lasted nine years in its most aggressive form, until 1783. Works with few instances of minor anti-Manchu content were officially "corrected," while those deemed too seditious to be preserved were added to an index of banned books. Governors were informed of these illicit books and ordered to collect and destroy any additional copies in their jurisdictions. Wherever possible, the print woodblocks were to be seized and submitted or burned as well. In 1778, over 52,000 woodblocks already received at the capital were summarily destroyed.[34] In 1783, an imperial index of banned books, the *Siku jinshu*, was issued to high-level officials across the empire.[35]

Was the *Siku Quanshu* merely the incidental result of a vanity project conceived in 1771 to celebrate Qianlong's sixtieth birthday and his mother's eightieth that year? Was it intended simply as a political statement of Qing (Manchu) superiority to the Ming, or was it perhaps a demonstration of literary openness and benevolence gone wrong? Did the Emperor conceive the *Four Treasuries* from the start as cover for a literary inquisition? Or did the inquisition arise opportunistically when he realized that the massive collection effort could be used to array the "pure" and the "tainted" plainly before him and "cleanse" (or "erase") the latter?

Regardless of his true motivations, the Qianlong Emperor had simultaneously glorified and devastated Chinese literary history. His actions also marked West Lake's Solitary Hill as the holding site of a sacred national treasure, one that the citizens of Hangzhou would go to remarkably heroic lengths to preserve and protect over the next 150 years.

A New Island in West Lake

Zhejiang Governor Li Wei had overseen major dredging of West Lake in the mid-1720s, but by 1800, the lake desperately needed renewal once again. This time, the task fell to Zhejiang Governor Ruan Yuan 阮元 (1764 – 1849). A native of Yangzhou, Ruan grew up in an official family with traditions on both the military side (his grandfather) and the scholarly side (his father). As a result, he became at age twenty-five (in 1789) an uncommon scholar-official: a civil *jinshi* with skills in horsemanship and shooting.

After early assignments in Shandong Province, Ruan arrived in Hangzhou in 1795 as the newly appointed Director of Education. His well-educated wife, Kong Luhua 孔璐华 (1777 – 1833),[36] joined him in the provincial capital. As a 73rd-generation descendant of Confucius, her presence added no small amount of social capital to Ruan's official administration.

Ruan Yuan's position provided him with opportunities to promote works for publication and explore the bountiful library treasures of the region. Over the course of his two-year stay, he discovered and collected 160 rare and worthy books that had escaped the collection net of Qianlong's *Four Treasuries* project.[37] His memorials to the Jiaqing Emperor 嘉庆帝 (r. 1796 – 1820) on these books eventually became part of a new imperial work, *Summary of Books Not in the Four Treasuries* (司库未收书目提要, *Siku Weishou Shumu Tiyao*), that included titles Ruan had uncovered.[38]

In 1799 - 1800, Ruan Yuan returned to Hangzhou, this time as the newly installed Provincial Governor. While much of his time was consumed with matters of coastal defense and initiating repairs to famous tombs such as those of Yu the Great and Su Shi, he also undertook a badly needed restoration of West Lake. Under Ruan's oversight, the silt recovered from the lake bottom was piled up at a single location in the lake, forming a mound of mushy land that projected above water level. The small new island, the third such in West Lake's open waters, sat sandwiched between the shore-hugging Solitary Island to its north and the Three Pools Mirroring the Moon to its south.

Since the land was too soft for habitation or building upon, it served as a wildlife sanctuary and became known as Ruan Gong Dun, (阮公墩, "Lord Ruan's Pier").[39] Ruan thus became the fifth and last government official in Zhejiang—along with causeway namesakes Bai Juyi, Su Shi, Zhao Yuchou, and Yang Mengying—whose name is enshrined in the manmade infrastructure of West Lake. Ironically, not one of them was a native of Hangzhou or even from Zhejiang Province, yet their names have remained an honored presence into the modern era.

In addition to founding or reinvigorating schools and their libraries in Haining (Anlan 安澜Academy), Qiantang (Chongwen 崇文 Academy), and Hangzhou's Shangcheng District (Ziyang 紫阳 Academy), Ruan Yuan established a school on the shore of West Lake for advanced study of the classics. He called the new institution Gujing Jingshe 诂经精舍, "literally 'a place to concentrate on the essence of the classics.'"[40] Ruan adopted an active management role, carefully selecting the scholars who would deliver the school's lectures as well as the students privileged to receive them.

Gujing Jingshe was an ivory tower research center of the first order, but it was also open-ended and outward-looking. Students were not tested on the Classics, and they faced no restrictions on the length of their studies. The school was well supplied with classical texts, but it also maintained books on practical scientific, governmental, and judicial fields as well as mathematics and Western scholarship.

Gujing Jingshe Academy began active operation in the 1820s, was destroyed during the Taiping Rebellion, and continued after rebuilding until the new educational system was introduced in 1904. Under the leadership from 1868 – 1898 of the renowned philologist and classicist, Huzhou native Yu Yue俞越 (1821-1906), the Academy distributed esoteric research through its own publications, produced brilliant alumni, and paved the way for modern educational reform.

New Literary Vistas

Women's poetry clubs of the late 1600s (like the Banana Garden poetry club in Hangzhou) were largely of, by, and for close-knit circles of local women, requiring little or no male involvement. Breaking the boundaries between literati males and talented (and aspiring) women would require a radical individual, a literatus willing to "lower" himself by publicly dignifying women's literary abilities. He would also have to endure the inevitable allegations of immoral behavior, of philandering disguised as guidance.

That individual finally arrived in the late 1700s, a century after the Banana Garden outings, in the form of arguably the greatest Chinese poet of the 18th Century. Yuan Mei 袁枚 (1716

– 1798) was born and raised in Hangzhou, the only son in a family of modest means. Yuan's youth was dominated by his mother, grandmother, and an aunt, so much so that he was said to have shared a bed with his grandmother until at least the age of twenty.[41]

Yuan garnered his *juren* and *jinshi* degrees, respectively, in 1738 and 1739, the latter at the impressive young age of 23. His assignment to the prestigious Hanlin Academy was cut short, however, when he proved unable to pass several Manchu language examinations. Instead, he was routed into the national bureaucracy with several modest positions in Jiangsu Province between 1742 and 1748. After a brief assignment in Nanjing in 1748, he resigned from official life, determined to make a living by writing.

In Nanjing, Yuan Mei purchased a run-down garden residence where the Cao family had lived just two decades before.[42] Yuan called his residential preserve Harmony Garden (随园, Sui Yuan) and rebuilt it with plentiful reminders of his hometown's West Lake: pavilions, a causeway-like separator over the water, and a humped bridge similar to West Lake's Broken Bridge. "Here [in Nanjing] I can live at home and yet live beside the [West] Lake," he wrote. "Live away from my native place, and yet all the time live there."[43]

Over the next forty years, Yuan Mei wrote and published poetry collections, essays, and "strange stories" of the supernatural, produced a book on the art of cooking and consuming fine food, traveled widely, painted, and hosted literary gatherings at Harmony Garden. His renown as a premier poet, essayist, and critic won him fame, fortune, and a wide range of influential contacts. He also acquired multiple young women as concubines over the years and became widely known for his liberality and sexual profligacy.[44] Consequently, Yuan's late-in-life decision to begin taking on female disciples, none of them daughters of his family clan, prompted no small amount of social outrage.

For much of his life, Yuan Mei had taken a keen interest in the poetic development of his two younger sisters and other women in his family. Through written exchanges with his numerous social contacts, he had also encouraged the wives and daughters of other families to pursue literary educations and develop their poetry skills. In around 1783, at age 67, Yuan accepted his first female student-disciple, Chen Shulan 陳淑兰 (1766 – 1820). His arrangement with Miss Chen soon prompted requests for mentorship from other women poets. He accepted several more, including the Hangzhou sisters Sun Yunfeng 孙云凤 (1764 – 1814) and Sun Yunhe 孙云鹤.

In 1790, during a visit to Hangzhou, Yuan convened the first formal gathering of some of his female disciples[45] at the West Lake residence of Qing official Sun Jiale 孙嘉乐 (1733 – 1800), father of Sun Yunfeng and Sun Yunhe. The two young women invited eleven other women to this poetry convocation, each of whom brought samples of their work. During a lakeside banquet, Yuan discussed poetry composition, answered questions, encouraged them to publish their work, and generally kept his female audience enthralled by his patient attentiveness. As Sun Yunfeng described the scene (poetically, of course): "Asking about words, they left wine glasses idle. / Talking about techniques, they did not notice dishes getting cold."[46]

Two years later, Yuan conducted another gathering at the Sun family's residence on West Lake, followed by a similar meeting in Suzhou. In both gatherings, he read and commented on works either brought by the attendees or produced extemporaneously at the meeting. While estimates of Yuan's female following range as high as fifty disciples (many of them from Hangzhou), his second of two published collections of his followers' works, titled *Selected Poems by the Female Disciples from the Sui Garden* (隨園女弟子詩選, *Suiyuan nüdizi shixuan*), contained pieces by twenty-eight women.

In 1796, the 80-year-old Yuan further infuriated his scandalized critics by commissioning an illustrated version of the first meeting in Hangzhou, *Painting of Thirteen Female Disciples Asking Yuan Mei for Advice at Lake Tower* (十三女弟子湖楼请业图, *Shisan nü dizi hulou qingye tu*). The scroll painting opens with the two Sun sisters chatting as they pass under a willow tree on a private, fenced property. They are walking toward several small groups of Yuan's disciples, each group engaged in a different activity: playing a *qin* (zither), picking an orchid, brush writing on a banana leaf, ink-painting a picture of plum blossoms, reading a book, contemplating a small stand of bamboo (perhaps for a poem), and fishing in the garden pond. Last to appear is Master Yuan Mei, seated in a pavilion with brushes and blank paper, preparing to write perhaps the very colophon that followed the portrait.[47] Another painting of three more female disciples was added later, along with another colophon by Yuan.

Yuan Mei was not alone among male literati of his time in advocating for women's literacy and recognizing their poetic and painting talents. Chen Wenshu 陳文述 (1771 – 1843), more than fifty years Yuan Mei's junior, had thirty or more female disciples from the Hangzhou area, while Ren Zhaolin's 任兆麟 (fl. 1776 – 1823) Clear Brook Poetry Club cultivated another following of ten female poets in and around Suzhou.

Yet no cultural voice of the times could rival Yuan Mei's. As perhaps the nation's leading cultural light of the 18th Century, Yuan's strong advocacy for women's education and artistic talent, including publication of his disciples' collected work, provided substantial impetus to women's changing roles in 19th-Century and early 20th-Century China. He was vigorously attacked for these views (and personally for his nontraditional behavior with his female followers) in 1798 in a famous literary broadside from the brush of historian and classical revivalist Zhang Xuecheng 章学诚 (1738 – 1801). Zhang's lengthy diatribe, titled "Women's Learning" (妇学, "Fuxue"), "did little to change the outpouring of writing from learned women," however.[48]

More and more women were finding the courage to employ their talents in ways that were shattering traditional boundaries. And once again, many of those groundbreakers were coming from the Hangzhou area. In 1767, sixteen-year-old Hangzhou native Chen Duansheng (1751 – 1796) began writing a remarkable tale of women's frustrated aspiration. Her story employed a popular Jiangnan-area form of mixed storytelling and ballad singing known as *tanci* (弹词, literally "plucking rhymes").[49]

Titled *Love Reincarnate* (再生缘, *Zaisheng yuan*, also translated as *The Destiny of Rebirth*), Chen's story followed the fictional Yuan Dynasty life of a beautiful and talented young woman from Yunnan Province named Meng Lijun 孟丽君.[50] Meng refuses a marriage arranged by the evil manipulations of a rejected suitor's powerful family and, dressed as a young man, escapes with her maid. Taking the male name Li Mingtang, Meng Lijun passes the imperial examinations with the highest honors, rises to the position of prime minister, and demonstrates her impeccable skills as a court official and advisor until the emperor begins to suspect his prime minister's gender.

Chen finished sixteen chapters of this tale, the story much more convoluted than suggested above, by her mid-twenties. At that point in her writing, the author was faced with a major decision about plot direction, whether to have Meng Lijun carry on with her gender deception or face the emperor's anger and punishment by divulging the truth. Meanwhile, the press of Chen's own life issues—marriage, the death of her mother, and relocation to the northwest due to her husband's exile after an examination scandal—caused her to abandon the story for about a decade. Finally, she added one more chapter not long before her premature death in 1796 at age 44. However, that last chapter still left her *tanci* story unfinished and Meng Lijun's fictional fate hanging in the balance.

Several decades later, the *tanci* writer Liang Desheng 梁德绳 (1771 – 1847) wrote a three-chapter conclusion to Chen's story. Meng Lijun reveals her identity, receives the emperor's praise for her abilities, abandons her cross-dressing, and marries her original beloved, himself now a high official. Liang hailed from a literary family in Hangzhou, the daughter and granddaughter of important officials. A talented writer of poetry, she married a scholar-official whom she outlived by nearly thirty years. Liang also cultivated a close patron-student relationship with Zhejiang Governor Ruan Yuan; one of her daughters married one of his sons, and Ruan also wrote a preface to Liang's collection of her poetry.

Several other writers produced endings to Chen Duansheng's *Love Reincarnate*, but it was Liang Desheng's version that gained popular acceptance. The completed work circulated in manuscript form until it finally reached print publication in 1821 under the title *A Woman Hero* (*Jingui jie*). The story was transformed into an immensely popular opera in 1921 Shanghai and remains today a favorite tale in the Suzhou storytelling art form of *pingtan*.

Liang Desheng's other important contribution to evolving women's literature concerns her niece, Wang Duan (1793 – 1839). When her married sister died at an early age, Liang took charge of Duan's well-being, especially her education. The young girl demonstrated remarkable literary talent, producing mature verse as early as six years of age. Already the daughter of a scholar and later the daughter-in-law and mentee of Chen Wenshu, Wang Duan was the beneficiary of an unusually privileged education and literary guidance. In addition, her arranged marriage with Chen Peizhi 陈裴之 (1794 – 1826), while tragically abbreviated by Chen's early death at age 32, was an intellectually companionate and mutually supportive one.

An accomplished poet and editor in her own right, Wang's most interesting literary venture was her *Selected Poems of Thirty Ming Poets* (明三十家詩選, *Ming sanshi jia shixuan*), a collection of works and commentaries on thirty male writers from the Ming Dynasty. Such was her knowledge and literary judgment that she successfully broke a cultural boundary that proscribed women from editing or venturing critical analysis on the works of male writers. She dared even to declare her controversial choice of Gao Qi (高启, 1336 – 1374)[51] as the greatest male poet of the Ming era.

Wang Duan is also commonly believed to have drawn on her excellent knowledge of history to write what may have been the first novel by a Chinese woman, titled *An Unofficial History of the Yuan and the Ming Dynasties* (元明逸史, *Yuanming yishi*). Perhaps deeming it a step still too far, she burned the manuscript before her death in 1839.

Among the many literary women friends from Hangzhou who supported Wang Duan's groundbreaking work, perhaps none were closer than Wu Zao 吳藻 (1799 – 1862). Wu was born into a merchant family and married into another one. Unfortunately, neither her parents nor her husband appreciated her literary talents, a source of great personal frustration that allegedly plagued her unhappy marriage. Subsequent biographers sometimes compared her to Zhu Shuzhen, even suggesting she was the Qing-era reincarnation of the great Song poetess.

Wu Zao was a master of *ci* (song lyric) poetry, but she is most celebrated for a brilliantly conceived, gender-bending drama extraordinary for her times. Titled variously *Drinking Wine and Reading "Encountering Sorrow"* (饮酒读骚, *Yinjiu du Sao*) or simply *The False Image* (乔影, *Qiaoying*), the play features a woman poet named Xie Xucai 谢絮才, a direct reference to a brilliant poetess of the 4th Century named Xie Daoyun 谢道韫.[52]

In Wu Zao's drama, Xie Xucai is a woman dressed as a man, sitting before a portrait of a woman (herself) dressed as a male scholar. In the monologue, she laments her literary fate: unappreciated and unknown, lacking a mentor, a talent destined to be lost to time. When the play was performed to immediate acclaim by a male actor in 1825 Shanghai, the presentation became a man performing as a woman dressed as a man, wishing she were a man as she looked at the painting of a woman dressed as a man. When Xie Xucai introduces herself, she asserts her fine literary skills but decries her anonymity because of her gender:

> Were I to let loose what is in my heart, I would resemble an egret flying on top of the clouds. But unfortunately, I was born in the wrong age, and so I resemble an ailing crane shut in a cage. Alas, I'm shackled in this body, and I can only lament and sigh about it.[53]

She later adds, "I have a man's ambition and a woman's sorrow and frustration."[54]

As if that much gender identity layering was not enough, the protagonist drinks wine while reading the famous poem "Encountering Sorrow" by the Chu State poet Qu Yuan 屈原 (c. 340 – 278 BCE). In that poem, Qu has been banished from the capital and "figuratively casts himself as an abandoned woman in order to describe the frustration of an exiled courtier whose desire to serve goes unfulfilled."[55] The historical fact that Xie Daoyun (Xie Xucai's alter-ego) was also the daughter-in-law of the illustrious Shaoxing calligrapher Wang Xizhi adds still more literary context to Xucai's theatrical laments.

Wu Zao declared herself in the final words she gave to Xie Xucai: "I cannot tell the reflection in the portrait from my own form, for they have already become one."[56] Wu so openly lamented during her lifetime not being born male that scholars have occasionally speculated on her sexual identity. Regardless, her *Drinking Wine and Reading "Encountering Sorrow"* illustrated once again the sociocultural constraints faced by educated Chinese woman of the Ming and Qing Dynasties. More important, the play demonstrated how those traditions were increasingly being challenged in the middle and later years of the Qing by the *guixiu* 闺秀 (gentlewomen) and *cainü* 才女 (talented women) of Hangzhou.

In her fictional character Meng Lijun, **Chen Duansheng** accessed a female cross-dressing tradition and blatantly asserted women's capacity to achieve the highest levels of competent officialdom (an opportunity that Meng Lijun could only gain through deception). **Wang Duan**'s deep study and understanding of Ming poetry provided her with the intellectual foundation and artistic judgment to break new ground for women in literary criticism. Unfortunately, her self-assurance was perhaps insufficient to release what might have been the first novel published by a female Chinese author. **Wu Zao** would employ the ancient *tanci* storytelling form in a radical new and artistically complex way to plead the same case as Chen Duansheng for women's rights and opportunities outside the household inner chambers.

These Zhejiang women were certainly not alone in late-Qing China, but they clearly stood among the frontrunners of an unfolding movement that could no longer be turned back.

British Boots on the Ground

Much as the Kangxi, Yongzheng, and Qianlong Emperors had feared, the military discipline and readiness of Manchu garrison forces in Jiangnan gradually declined over the decades. The causes were many—poor leadership, inadequate pay, infrequent military exercises, outdated equipment—but falling into the Jiangnan lifestyle proved to be at least as much of a factor. The senior command position at Hangzhou's garrison grew so undemanding in the 1700s and 1800s that it often became a relaxing and comfortable last assignment for near-retirees or imperial clan family members. Between 1796 and 1850, Hangzhou garrison commanders died on average within 18 months after leaving their posts, and more than sixty percent of them died either in office or shortly thereafter.[57]

As the 18th Century merged into the 19th, inspection reports on the Hangzhou garrison expressed dismay over the troops' lack of military preparedness. Manchu banner soldiers at Hangzhou and Zhapu "had come to cherish expert knowledge of local history, ancient ruins and relics, literature inspired by the beauty of West Lake, and had themselves begun to generate no small amount of poetry and painting celebrating the local landscape." The military ethic in both garrisons looked even worse, reflecting "a fascination with the aesthetics of Chinese culture, and the taste for trivia that can best be fostered by those who neither reap nor sow...[such as] kites, praying mantises, birds and bird cages, tops, folk songs, classical poetry, opera, and tea house entertainments."[58]

Looking back through time, the renowned novelist Lao She 老舍 (1899 – 1966), himself of Manchu origin, was even more scathingly critical of his ethnic ancestors:

> In the last days of the Qing Dynasty, the life of the bannermen, apart from consuming the grain and spending the silver supplied by the Chinese, was completely immersed, day to day, in the life of the arts....[E]verybody knew how to sing arias from the classical opera, play the one-stringed accompaniment, perform recitations with the drum, and chant the popular tunes of the day. They raised fish, birds, dogs, plants and flowers, and held cricket fights. Among them were many with outstanding calligraphy, or some talent at landscape painting, or writing poetry....They didn't have the strength to defend the borderlands..., but they developed a very intimate relationship with their pets and their culture.[59]

Perhaps none of this unreadiness would have mattered had the British not developed an unquenchable thirst for Chinese tea, as well as silks and porcelain. After the Qianlong Emperor's rather haughty dismissal in 1793 of George Lord Macartney's equally haughty, multi-part demands for a mutual trade relationship,[60] the silver imbalance arising from such a one-sided exchange relationship led the British to introduce opium as their prime export and monetary counterbalance.

Opium addiction ravaged the Qing world of the early 1800s and generated a variety of responses from the capital. In 1821, the year the Daoguang Emperor 道光帝 (r. 1821 – 1850) ascended the throne, Ruan Yuan conducted mass arrests of opium merchants in Canton, but to little avail. New legislation proved ineffectual, withdrawal treatment was insufficient for an estimated 12.5 million opium users, and ferreting the illicit trade out of a bureaucracy infested by drugs and money made local enforcement impossible.

Finally, Governor Lin Zexu 林则徐 (1785 – 1850) traveled to Canton in 1839, gained control over and destroyed the foreigners' existing opium supplies, and demanded that they immediately cease importing the drug. Drug traders' anger, compounded by an unrelated Chinese death in Hong Kong at the hands of drunken British sailors, led in late 1839 to a brief naval skirmish at Canton in which the British boats easily prevailed (but was misleadingly reported to the Daoguang Emperor as a great Chinese victory).

When the British realized that Lin Zexu would not yield to their naval pressure at Canton, they opted for a strategy that applied greater pressure closer to Beijing. Thus began the First Opium War. The British naval Captain Charles Elliot (1801 – 1875) cruised China's southeastern coast, firing at will as he sailed northward toward Zhoushan, the largest in a cluster of islands off the coast of Ningbo and Hangzhou Bay. The British had long coveted Zhoushan as a trade port, dating back to its specific inclusion as one of Lord Macartney's trade relations "requests" submitted to the Qianlong Emperor in 1793. In addition to its potential as a trade port, Zhoushan also offered strategic value as a staging point for possible military invasion of China along the coast, at or above Hangzhou Bay.[61]

After blockading the ports at Xiamen (Fujian Province) and Ningbo, a British force of twenty-two warships and twenty-seven transports anchored off Zhoushan Island on July 4, 1840. The next day, they occupied the walled city of Dinghai, the island's main port. The fleet moved on northward to blockade the mainland port at Tianjin, which protected a direct path to Beijing. In response, the Daoguang Emperor proposed a tentative agreement with the British but demanded that the details be worked out back in Canton. Believing their pressure strategy had worked, the British left Tianjin waters on September 25 and returned all the way south, abandoning Zhoushan Island as well. Of the 3,600 troops who had been temporarily stationed on the island until the fleet's southward return, about 1,300 had fallen ill and 150 had died.[62]

Negotiations in Canton resulted in the Chuanpi Agreement (穿鼻草约) in January 1841, calling for British possession of Hong Kong and payment of six million dollars in reparations for the opium destroyed by Lin Zexu. Daoguang subsequently rejected this treaty. Several small skirmishes occurred around Canton during the following few months, each time falsely hailed in Chinese reports to the Emperor as great victories.[63] Meanwhile, British patience wore thin and pressures mounted from London for the return of Chinese trade, including opium. In the summer of 1841, British naval forces sailed northward once again with a force of 9,000 troops, this time planning to blockade the Yangzi River, cut off the Grand Canal supply line of rice and salt to Beijing, and sail to the doorstep of Nanjing.

The British naval force seized the port at Xiamen in late August. On September 26, they arrived for the second time at Dinghai on Zhoushan Island. The city was now better fortified but still mounted no cannons, so the British heavily shelled the city's defenses from their water positions before sending ground troops against the walls and gates. Dinghai was captured on October 5, after which British forces occupied Zhenhai (on the coast, opposite Dinghai) on October 10 and the port city of Ningbo on October 12.

While the British quartered at Ningbo for the winter, Chinese officials organized a counterattack by local Green Standard troops and reinforcements, including aboriginal peoples dressed in tiger skins, brought in from more distant provinces. Their attack was launched on the pre-chosen, geomantically auspicious,[64] but horribly rainy day of March 10, 1842. Despite a strategically well-conceived, multi-front assault plan, the recapture effort failed badly on all fronts from confused, inept, and underequipped execution.

As detailed in the diary records of Bei Qingqiao 贝青乔 (1810 – 1863),[65] a scholarly poet-patriot from the Suzhou region, ground troops from northwest China could not understand orders issued in Mandarin and then got so badly lost they did not participate in the attack. Many of the Chinese combatants were armed only with spears and knives; others misunderstood their orders and failed even to use their matchlocks. Most fell easily before the well-armed British soldiers; others were lured into ambushes or into areas planted with land mines. One senior commander at Zhenhai was even said to have collapsed in an opium reverie, perhaps a fit state considering the underlying causes of the conflict.

The accompanying Chinese naval forces fared no better. A fire raft assault on the British fleet failed when the rafts were set alight too far distant from the enemy ships, and the Qing naval flotilla designed to attack the British fleet at Dinghai simply sailed up and down the coast and never engaged. A plan to use northern Chinese as naval assault troops was foregone due to their repeated bouts of seasickness, while a 276-boat fleet of Yangzi River fishermen were unfamiliar with the reefs around Zhoushan and then could not advance when the tide was running against them at the designated time for their "water-braves" assault.

An astonishing plan to outfit nineteen monkeys with firecrackers and then throw them onto the British ships in the hopes of starting fires or exploding their powder-magazines was abandoned when no one dared approach the foreign fleet closely enough to toss the monkeys (who, it was said, were left to starve to death). Another proposed plan before the attack involved leaving smallpox-inoculated sheep and cattle for British foragers to find and carry back to their encampments, but this dreadful form of warfare was thankfully never implemented.[66]

With little to fear from the Chinese forces they had seen so far, the British decided on a land assault at the Manchu garrison city of Zhapu, seventy miles east of Hangzhou but only ten miles from Jiaxing. The garrison was manned by 7,000 – 8,000 troops, about one quarter of whom were Manchu banner soldiers. Zhapu thus became the site of the first-ever, full-scale ground assault against a city located on the Chinese mainland by a European military force. It would also be the Europeans' first serious encounter with native Manchu troops—and vice versa.

The opening salvo took place on May 18, 1842. Captain W.H. Hall (c. 1797 - 1878), aboard the British ship *Nemesis*, described the landward scene as they approached Zhapu:

> The view of [Zhapu] and the adjacent hills from the sea, as you approach the coast, is very remarkable. The town and its extensive suburbs are situated near the western extremity of a small promontory, stretching east and west for the distance of between four and five miles. The suburbs, which appear to be the principal resort for merchants and traders, and contain the most wealthy shops, run along the edge of the beach, partly at the foot of the hills which rise on either side, and partly occupying a low flat between them. The actual walled town stands about half a mile in the rear.[67]

The British fleet, headed by seven warships and several transports, discharged ashore 2,200 mixed British and Indian troops along with 110 officers. Most of the town's Manchu defenders had positioned themselves in the hills outside the walls, but they quickly retreated back toward the city when they were unable to slow the foreigners' steady advance. Hall noted as well that many of them "were even seen deliberately cutting their own throats as our men were advancing upon them."[68]

Fighting renewed the next day until the only contested location outside the city walls was the Tianzun Temple, where a force of about three hundred Manchu soldiers had prepared to make their defensive stand. The British suffered several casualties trying to enter the temple grounds and several more as they attempted to take the temple's central hall. When cannon fire failed to breach the temple walls, they used gunpowder explosives to create enough wooden debris to set the building on fire. From the sound of gunfire inside the burning building, Hall believed a number committed suicide, so that only fifty soldiers were taken prisoner.

Meanwhile, the British established cannon on the hills they had taken the previous day and began uncontested shelling of the town. Zhapu was enclosed in a wall about three miles in circumference, bordered outside by a modest moat. British grenadiers met little opposition as they scaled the city walls near the east gate. They followed along the ramparts and simply opened additional gates for the troops waiting beyond the walls.[69]

Once inside the city, the British were shocked to see the results of "self-destruction of whole Tartar families; the women destroying their children, drowning them in wells, and throwing themselves in afterwards; the husbands hanging and poisoning their wives, and deliberately cutting their own throats." The first Chinese-European battle on mainland China had ended in two days. Hundreds and likely thousands of Chinese soldiers, their families, and townspeople had died. The British suffered thirteen dead and forty-five wounded, modest losses but still more than they had expected. The inner walled garrison now stood empty of Manchu troops, occupied only by "the Chinese rabble who plundered it and frightened the few [Manchus] who remained."[70]

Both sides behaved honorably with regard to prisoners. The British set up a field hospital in Zhapu to care for the Manchu wounded before turning them over to the Chinese negotiators. In return, eleven prisoners were returned to the British, although Captain Hall indicated in his memoir that only two of the eleven—one British and one Indian—belonged to the *Nemesis* fleet. Those men had previously been kidnapped in Zhoushan and carried off to Hangzhou, but when they were transported back to Zhapu, the British fleet had already left. The captives were therefore returned to Hangzhou for five days before finally being safely transported by sedan chair to Ningbo via Shaoxing.[71]

For all the horror of conflict and "self-destruction" witnessed by Captain Hall, he concluded his account of the Zhapu campaign with admiration for the town's pastoral setting:

> The country about [Zhapu] is perhaps one of the finest and most beautifully cultivated spots in the world. It resembles in some respect, the prettiest parts

of Devonshire. The low hills immediately adjoining the town—the rich, luxuriant, well-watered plain beyond, interspersed with numerous hamlets and villages, with their curiously-shaped blue-tiled roofs, and intersected by canals and causeways, formed a very attractive panorama.[72]

Zhapu was the first stop in a British advance that subsequently took Wusong (June 16), Shanghai (June 19), and Zhenjiang (where they suffered over 1,600 casualties, July 21) before threatening the walls of Nanjing on the Yangzi River.[73] At that point, the Qing government signed the Treaty of Nanjing on August 29, 1842, ceding Hong Kong to the British, exacting reparations, and opening the first five Chinese cities as treaty (i.e., trading) ports.[74] While largely forgotten in the larger diplomatic scheme of the First Opium War, Zhapu was the first occasion in which Manchus and Europeans took real-world stock of one another's full military capabilities and began adjusting their thinking accordingly.

A final note. Well before launching their assault on Zhapu, the British had seriously contemplated sailing upriver to seize Hangzhou. Two of their ships had begun reconnoitering the upstream route before returning, discouraged, to Ningbo. Hall's account explained why:

> The tides were found to be so strong at the mouth of the river, that it was impossible to attempt to push even a steamer up with any degree of safety. [One of the British ships] made the attempt to enter the river's mouth, but became wholly unmanageable, and was very nearly carried upon a sand-bank where she would probably have been lost....But no power of steam and sails combined was sufficient to stem the current.[75]

Ironically, it was the ravaging river and tidal flows driven by water god Wu Zixu, swallower of Cao'e and her father, target of Wuyue King Qian Liu's three thousand arrows, and destroyer of seawalls, that dissuaded the British fleet from advancing on the capital of Zhejiang Province in the early 1840s.

Chapter 12

THE TAIPING REBELLION

(1853 – 1865)

Autumn Moon on the Smooth Lake[1]

A jade-disc moon lights up, the lake is pure and still.
A glass of one colour
Drenches the inverted shadow of the river in the hills.
Beyond the flowers the Jasper Palace glints brighter,
Earth has no scene so clear and cool.

With a smile picking the lotus I ride the little boat,
Drunken scoop up handfuls of ripples,
Quivering a thousand acres of gold.
Want to call Su Shi the immortal to versify with me,
Damped by the dew on the cassia flowers, the collar of our gowns chilled.

— Mo Fan (16th Century)

The Taiping Heavenly Capital

In the early days of March 1853, Qing Emperor Xianfeng 咸丰帝 (r. 1850 – 1861) faced what every past dynasty had faced at least once: an existential crisis. Outside the walls of mighty Nanjing—guardian of the Yangzi River, founding capital of the Ming Dynasty, protector of wealthy Jiangnan eastward and gateway to interior China westward—stood the terrifying sight of a peasant army 700,000 – 800,000 strong, perhaps even more than one million. Untrained and unfunded peasants, wild men (and women) whose refusal to shave their heads and braid their hair in the required Manchu style had earned them the condescending nickname "long-haired devils" (长毛鬼, *changmao gui*), supplied and armed only with what they had been able to loot or seize along their conquest path.

The notion was incomprehensible, preposterous. Yet there they were, camped before the impregnable walled city. Nanjing was nothing if not monstrous, surrounded by massive walls more than forty feet wide at the base and sixty-five feet or more in height. Thirteen gates penetrated its twenty-mile, crenellated circumference, guarded from above by over thirteen thousand battle stations. Outside the walls, just to the north and northwest, ran the Yangzi River, while the Qinhuai River 秦淮河 wrapped itself around the city's western and southern walls.

Inside those walls, however, the Qing government had precariously little in the way of defense beyond the walls themselves. The city's military force, only thirty thousand or so to begin with, had been stretched thin from sending troops westward in earlier failed attempts to halt the rebels' steady advance from the south. They now numbered less than two thousand regulars and several thousand from the city's Manchu garrison, plus whatever they could muster by way of mercenaries and ad hoc militia organizing. This ragtag agglomeration would be hard-pressed to hold Nanjing under the best of circumstances, and the current situation hardly qualified for that assessment.

The first Taiping forces had arrived on March 6, but over the next few days, these were followed by wave upon wave of rebel battalions. They quickly seized control of Yuhuatai Hill 雨花台山 to the south, from which they began shelling the city wall using cannons and ordnance left behind by retreating Qing soldiers. On March 12, the Taiping river armada sailed into view. They anchored along the city's north side and quickly seized control of the Pukou 浦口 port on the opposite bank of the Yangzi River.

While Qing Governor-General Lu Jianying 陸建瀛 (1776 – 1853) frantically dispatched messengers seeking reinforcements that never came, the Taipings prepared for battle. They constructed military barracks and began planting thousands of sharpened bamboo stakes in the grounds outside the city gates. More important, the coal miners who had joined their crusade were busy tunneling on the city's northern border, preparing the way for huge explosive charges intended to breach the city walls.

On the night of March 18, hundreds of mounted Taipings rode from south to north along the western wall, holding torches aloft. Qing soldiers rushed to that side and opened fire, believing the assault had begun. Indeed, it was about to, but not where they stood shooting at mounted figures designed to look like Taiping fighters. The real assault soon began at the north wall, where three massive tunnel explosions created the desired breach in the defensive wall. Taipings rushed in, but Qing soldiers and local residents joined forces and managed to regain control of the breach.

Their heroic efforts came to naught, though. A handful of rebels who had managed to enter the city came upon a sedan chair containing a Qing official. As the bodyguards of this important personage fled, the rebels killed anyone left behind, including the sedan chair's passenger. They little realized at the moment that they had just dispatched the Governor-General. Their luck held even further when those same fleeing bodyguards quickly spread word that Governor Lu was dead and the city had fallen. As more soldiers abandoned their posts and withdrew into Nanjing's inner-walled military garrison,

Taiping rebels began scaling the undefended south walls and opening the gates. They were assisted by hundreds of other rebels who had already been resident in the city for weeks, dressed as Buddhist monks and staying in the city's temples.

The next morning, Taipings massed outside the garrison and attacked, overwhelming those inside—bannermen, regulars, and their families. No one who was caught was spared as the vengeful violence raged. Only a few lucky dozens managed to sneak their way out of the garrison and disappear into the main city area. At least one subsequent investigation concluded that the massacre had resulted in more than thirty thousand deaths.[2]

Despite the horrors of the garrison massacre, the Taipings maintained close order and discipline: no raping, no opium smoking, no killing of common people. They did, however, burn, damage, or deface Buddhist, Daoist, and Confucian statues and artifacts wherever they found them, in monasteries and temples, in public venues or in private shops and homes. Many of the places of worship were themselves burned or destroyed, including the Porcelain Pagoda,[3] one of Nanjing's most famous nearby sites. They also obliterated every trace—seals, documents, books, clothing—of the Manchu occupation.

Ten days later, Hong Xiuquan 洪秀全 (1814 – 1864) descended from his dragon ship in full imperial regalia and entered Nanjing, renaming the "Southern Capital" as Tianjing 天京, the "Heavenly Capital." He then declared it the home of the Taiping Heavenly Kingdom (太平天国, Taiping tianguo) and himself as the Heavenly King (天王, Tian wang).

For defensive reasons, Taiping armies were quickly sent further east to take a nearly evacuated Zhenjiang 镇江, about forty miles away. Before those forces could advance further toward their planned assault on Suzhou and Shanghai, however, they were re-called to Nanjing to help defend a Qing threat approaching from the west. Meanwhile, separate rebel expeditions in May 1853 headed west, targeting Sichuan Province, and north, intent on capturing Beijing and driving the Manchus entirely out of China.

The western expedition achieved some successes, but it never reached Sichuan and was recalled to Nanjing's defense in 1856. From May 1853 to May 1855, the northern expedition advanced toward Beijing and could quite possibly have taken the city. Even the Qing court had regarded the city as lost, instructing all tax revenues to be sent to Manchuria. Unaccountably, however, the Taipings chose to move east and attack Tianjin, a decision that ultimately led to that army's defeat and near total decimation.

After advancing almost non-stop over 1,200 miles, from the mountainous southern areas of Guangdong and Guangxi Provinces to Nanjing, the Taiping movement ground to a halt. For the next six years, while Hong Xiuquan eschewed active field leadership and basked in the glories of his heavenly title, the Taiping capital suffered internal conflicts and power struggles. To the credit of the Manchu Banner and Green Standard troops, they moved to encircle and threaten Nanjing in 1853 and again in 1856. Meanwhile, the Qing government regrouped, building new armies and retaking at least some of their lost cities and territory to the west and south.

291

By the summer of 1859, instead of sitting on a throne in Beijing's Forbidden City, the Heavenly King found his capital besieged by Qing troops. In fact, the Imperialist forces had now been positioned outside Nanjing for so long, they had constructed a new canal that "stretched for about 45 miles through the outskirts and bristled with over 40,000 guards stationed in over 130 camps."[4] By this time, however, two important Taiping leaders—Hong Rengan 洪仁玕 (1822 – 1864) and Li Xiucheng 李秀成 (1823 – 1864)— had emerged. Together, they would conceive and execute a brilliant strategy to extricate the seat of the Heavenly Kingdom from its encirclement, using Hangzhou as bait.

The Taipings

The origin story of the Taiping Rebellion has often been told.[5] Hong Xiuquan, a village teacher and thrice-failed examination candidate from the mountainous area north of Canton, fell ill in his home village in 1837 and experienced hallucinatory dreams caused by a high fever. When he awakened, he recalled from his dreams an elderly, golden-bearded man who instructed Hong and his "Elder Brother" to drive the demons out of their kingdom. When he later read a pamphlet handed out by Christian missionary preachers in Canton, he concluded that his fever-dreams were a message: he was the son of the one God and the younger brother of Jesus, commanded by his Father to drive the Manchu devils and non-Christian idolaters out of the land.

He began preaching his beliefs for a new Christian kingdom, delivered from the rule of the Manchus and the idolatry of Daoism and Buddhism. A new society of God worshippers built upon Hong's ideas gradually formed in neighboring Guangxi Province in the 1840s. When this new, anti-Manchu cult drew the attention of local Qing officials for its heterodox beliefs, their militant persecution of the believers transformed the group from religious adherents into guerrilla fighters and finally into an armed force. The rebels won surprising early victories in their encounters with Qing troops and began their march northward, gaining arms and thousands of adherents after each victory.

Converts to the Taiping cause were generally not converts in the religious sense. They were poor and downtrodden peasant farmers, miners, the unemployed and unemployable, malcontents, criminals, grifters, and the like. Joining the Taipings was far less a matter of faith than a matter of hopelessness, a case of "nothing left to lose" coupled perhaps with vague hopes for a societal revolution. Their desperation was only compounded by the ravages of opium, the economic and subsistence pressures of a demographic explosion that expanded the population from 150 million to 430 million in the past hundred years, and a wave of natural disasters through the 1840s.[6]

The Great Feint

In late April 1859, Heavenly King Hong Xiuquan welcomed the arrival at Nanjing of his trusted cousin, Hong Rengan, whom he quickly crowned the Shield King 干王 (Gan Wang). When Xiuquan had fallen delirious with fever back in 1837, Rengan had sat at his bedside. When Xiuquan began preaching the doctrine of his God-worshiping society, Rengan had been one of his earliest converts.[7] Even after Xiuquan left his Guanlubu

Village home on his first proselytizing crusade in April 1844, his young cousin remained at home as a teacher and generated as many local converts as he could.

For most of the period from 1851 until his arrival in Nanjing, Hong Rengan had been living in Hong Kong, associating with and learning from Christian missionaries and avoiding the Qing police who sought him. It had taken him a harrowing year of solitary overland travel through war-devastated countryside to reach Nanjing, and now he sat quietly as a council of Taiping leaders argued how to survive the Heavenly Capital's encirclement.

Finally, Hong Rengan spoke. The Qing army had concentrated massive resources around the city, he argued. To draw a meaningful portion of them away, he proposed a diversionary tactic. A force of Taiping rebels would march west along the northern bank of the Yangzi River, then turn southeast at rapid pace to capture the unsuspecting and thinly guarded city of Hangzhou. Such a drastic and deeply symbolic loss would necessitate a substantial Qing response drawn from the forces gathered at Nanjing. When the Qing forces approached Hangzhou, the Taipings would then abandon the city and march double-time back to Nanjing, where they could attack the Qing encirclement from the rear while forces inside the city rushed out to do battle.

Hong Rengan's plan was enthusiastically endorsed and adopted, not only by the leadership council but by the man who would have to execute it, Li Xiucheng, the Zhong Wang (忠王, Loyal King). A native of the Wuzhou 梧州 area in easternmost Guangxi Province, Xiucheng later described himself in a deposition written just before his execution:

> My family was destitute and had not enough to eat. We lived by tilling the land, cultivating mountain [slopes] and hiring out as laborers, keeping to our station and accepting our poverty. At the age of eight, nine, and ten I studied with my uncle, but my family was poor and I could not study longer.[8]

Despite his lack of education or training, this part-time charcoal-maker from an impoverished mountain village had an innate ability for organizing and motivating and an equal aptitude for military tactics. He joined the Taiping movement in its early days of 1851 for its promise not of heaven but of meals, after which he rose steadily to high command as the rebels repeatedly succeeded in their battles with the Qing armies.

Li quickly demonstrated his insightfulness, questioning the value of liberating Nanjing if the Taipings were only going to continue concentrating their forces and followers there. Rengan's reply revealed the rest of his grand plan:[9] forget about the north and west and look eastward, targeting the most fertile lands of the empire and its richest cities: Hangzhou, Shaoxing, Suzhou, Songjiang, and Shanghai.

With all the wealth they could seize from those cities, Hong continued, the rebels could then purchase a fleet of steamships and take the eastern coastal provinces of Fujian and Guangdong, perhaps even Hong Kong. After that, they would take control of everything south of the Yangzi River, not only cutting China in half but robbing Beijing of its essential rice supplies. At the last, he believed, the Christian foreigners in Shanghai would certainly cooperate with the God-worshiping, Bible-reading Taipings to overthrow the anti-Christian Qing government and rid China of the idolatrous Manchus.

Desperation forced planning and coordination to begin immediately. By early 1860, everything was in place for the daring strike. Li Xiucheng left Nanjing with a force of about 6,000 men, escaping the surrounded city in the only way possible: disguised in Qing army uniforms confiscated after earlier battles. They arrived outside Hangzhou unmolested on March 11, 1860, having covered a hostile, indirect, and mountainous route of at least 175 miles in four weeks.

In order not to reveal their limited strength, the rebels encamped in the hills surrounding Hangzhou and erected a multitude of banners to suggest a massive "long hairs" attack. To inflate the perception of their invading force even further, they "took wooden images from temples, dressed them up in Taiping uniforms, and positioned them on hills round the city, in stockades, with banners flying."[10] As they had at Nanjing in 1853, the rebel forces began their attack against the main city gates while tunneling under the wall to set explosive charges. On March 19, 1860, their explosives breached Hangzhou's wall, and the rebels entered the former capital city of the Southern Song Dynasty. Their actual attacking force numbered only around 1,250 men.

The next six days demonstrated almost everything that was wrong with Qing Dynasty China. Faced with a small force not even intent on permanent occupation, civilized Hangzhou fell into utter chaos. The local militias broke and ran immediately, stopping only long enough to loot whatever they could grab and carry. Government officials abandoned their offices nearly as quickly, joining the retreating militia in ransacking the residences of the city's richest families. While residents fought their own militias to protect life and property, the Manchu banner forces retreated into the safety of their walled garrison.

Amid all the chaos, thousands of Hangzhou's women followed the long-standing dictates of Confucianism: commit honorable suicide rather than be ravaged and dishonored. One estimate put the number of Hangzhou citizen deaths at 60,000, another at 60,000 – 100,000.[11] A *yamen* official present at the attack later wrote of wild cries for the deaths of Qing "demons," wanton rape, and killings of those who had no money to surrender. "At every intersection," he wrote, "the dead bodies piled up as high as mountains. Everywhere you looked, with every third step you had to jump over a corpse in order to pass."[12]

After six unsuccessful days attacking the inner walled garrison, the Taiping occupiers simply awaited the Qing military response. Back in Nanjing, the Qing commanders learned of Hangzhou's fall and doubtless imagined that the rebel force must have been enormous to have taken a city of that size. Consequently, the Qing force surrounding Nanjing sent about a quarter of its troops marching to Hangzhou under the command of Zhang Yuliang 張玉良 (d. 1861) even as Li Xiucheng began preparing to march his men back to Nanjing.

When the Qing troops arrived at Hangzhou, they found the city occupied by a force of unknown size. Li Xiucheng later explained the climax of his great ruse:

> After entering the city we fought for several days without taking the Manchu garrison. Then, as expected, General Ho and General Chang [Zhang Guo-liang 张国梁, 1810 - 1860] sent troops from Chiang-nan [Jiangnan] for the relief of Hang-chou, under the command of Chang Yü-liang. At the Wu-lin Gate of Hang-chou, the two sides made contact, and we knew that [General] Ho's and Chang's forces were divided and that they had fallen into our trap. The following day at noon, we used flags and pennons newly made in Hang-chou, in order to deceive the enemy. This is a device for withdrawing with insufficient troops. Unexpectedly Chang Yü-liang fell into the trap, and we had been gone for a day and a night before he dared to enter the city. Thus we were able to withdraw without hindrance.[13]

Having nothing better to do after re-occupying the abandoned city, the Qing troops looted whatever was still left worth taking. Remarkably, Qing officials celebrated the entire Hangzhou incident as a victory over the rebels, despite the death of perhaps ten percent of the civilian population and as much as twenty percent of the garrison population. Ruichang, commanding general of Hangzhou's garrison, was promoted with a hereditary rank; another general from the nearby garrison of Zhapu 乍浦镇 received the appellation "protecting hero." The ancient sage of war, Sun Wu, would certainly have admired Li Xiucheng for executing a plan so effectively that the losers actually convinced themselves that they were the winners.

Li Xiucheng's force made its way through the Tianmu Mountains 天目山 and arrived outside of Nanjing on April 23. Other rebel forces converged on Nanjing from the north and west, bringing the total Taiping troop strength to as many as 150,000 soldiers and cavalrymen, substantially outnumbering the Qing siege force and effectively surrounding the surrounders.

On May 1, 1860, a battle signal announced the Taiping assault on the Qing camps outside Nanjing's walls. Rebel soldiers streamed out of the walled city at the same time the outside forces attacked. Fighting was fierce for two days, followed by two days of rain when the action grew even more fevered. A full-scale assault on May 6 broke the Qing resistance and imperial soldiers fled, many eastward toward Zhenjiang. The imperial army's siege of Nanjing may not have ended the rebellion, but it slowed the Taiping advance for several years. More important, the siege bought the Qing empire time for new and better-trained private armies to form under commanders like Zeng Guofan 曾国藩 (1811 – 1872) and his young assistant, Li Hongzhang 李鸿章 (1823 – 1901).

In the near term, however, pressure on the Taiping capital had been relieved. The rebels were free to make their next moves. Additionally, Qing government officials and military forces had been soundly defeated and roundly embarrassed at Hangzhou, revealing fundamental weaknesses and foreshadowing worse to come. For Hong Rengan, the events at Hangzhou must surely have confirmed for him the feasibility of his plans to overrun Jiangnan. He would not wait long to make his next move.

Hardly had the Taipings' victory celebration ended at Nanjing when Li Xiucheng set forth on the next phase of Hong Rengan's grand plan. By May 20, Li's army arrayed itself outside the walls of Changzhou; the city fell six days later. They captured Wuxi, just twenty-five miles west of Suzhou, three days after taking Changzhou. On June 2 (1860), the rebel army arrived at Suzhou and simply walked through the already-opened gates.

Hong Rengan and Li Xiucheng next transmitted letters to the British and French officials in Shanghai announcing their plan to approach the city peacefully in order to discuss mutual interests, including trade relations. Shanghai, whose foreign delegations had long professed diplomatic neutrality, proved to be far less welcoming than Suzhou.

On August 17, 1860, a force of about three thousand Taipings marched into Shanghai's outer settlements. They encountered but overcame modest opposition from Qing imperial soldiers who then fled back to the foreign settlement with tales of a massive rebel invasion. Consequently, when the Taipings reached the walled city, Li's envoys were showered with heavy fire from French and British guns and Sikh sharpshooters. The rebels retreated to safety, puzzled by the deadly greeting they had just received.

Two days later, French troops poured forth from the settlement, intent on clearing the wealthy mercantile suburbs nearby where Taipings could gather for an assault. Their methods were as horrifying as anything ever ascribed to the rebels or imperial troops—looting shops, raping women, setting every structure ablaze, and shooting or bayonetting men, women, and children indiscriminately. Even reports later published in the English-language *North China Herald*[14] were aghast at the Westerners' atrocities.

A deeply disillusioned Li Xiucheng now realized that the foreigners' lack of interest in any sort of collaborative relationship had punctured Hong Rengan's grand plan for a Manchu-free Heavenly Empire. Taking matters into his own hands—and widening the rift between himself and Hong Rengan—he ignored orders from the Heavenly King to march north to Beijing. Instead, Li left troops to hold the rich Jiangnan cities he had already taken and moved the rest of his forces southwestward, up the Yangzi River valley.

Li Xiucheng's objective was to reinforce the Taipings' strategic but threatened hold on the city of Anqing 安庆,[15] located on the north bank of the Yangzi, about 150 miles up-river from Nanjing. The Taipings had first captured Anqing in February 1852, but it had been under heavy siege since early summer of 1860 by a new army formed and led by Zeng Guofan. Li Xiucheng now planned to coordinate with Chen Yucheng 陈玉成 (1837 – 1862), the Brave King (英王, Ying Wang). Their two armies would sweep westward along either side of the Yangzi River, free Anqing from Zeng's assault, and continue on to take the lightly guarded but even more pivotal tri-cities of Wuchang 武昌, Hanyang 汉阳, and Hankou 汉口 (together comprising modern-day Wuhan 武汉). They planned to execute a pincer attack on opposite sides of the Yangzi: Chen at Hankou on the north bank, Li at Wuchang on the south bank.

With control of the Jiangnan territory east of Nanjing (other than Shanghai) already assured, Li reasoned that the Taiping capital needed Anqing as the defensive linchpin of its western flank. Capturing the Wuhan tri-cities would be even better, since they further backstopped Anqing, controlled the strategic meeting point of the Yangzi and Han rivers, and provided a gateway to Sichuan Province. Of course, Nanjing's welfare served Li's personal interests as well, since the Heavenly Capital defended the western flank of his new Jiangnan fiefdom. He could deal with stubborn Shanghai later.

Unfortunately for the Taipings, even the best laid plans were just waking dreams; reality intervened. Chen Yucheng's army chose to bypass Anqing and head toward Hankou. Meanwhile, Li's troops were forced into a circuitous but not necessarily unwelcomed route that slowed their advance but enabled them to absorb a large number of new recruits in Jiangxi and Hubei Provinces. By the time he reached Wuchang in June 1861, Li's army had grown by at least another three hundred thousand.[16]

Li was also two months late arriving at Wuchang. By then, Chen had long since withdrawn most of his force from Hankou and returned to assist Anqing.[17] Thanks to Li's delay, the Qings had been able to substantially reinforce Hankou and its two sister cities. The Qing naval hold on the Yangzi also prevented Li from contacting Chen's residual forces still stationed fifty miles away at Huangzhou 黄州. Convinced he was unable to take Wuchang without Chen's force simultaneously attacking Hankou across the river, particularly with three hundred thousand raw, untrained, and underequipped new recruits, Li decided to retrace his path back to Jiangnan. His first major targets would be Hangzhou and Ningbo, but his ultimate target was Shanghai.

Hangzhou Falls a Second Time

Even as Li Xiucheng was marching around Anhui, Jiangxi, and Hubei Provinces to the west, Taiping forces led by Li's cousin, the 6'6" (198 cm.) giant Li Shixian 李世贤 (1834 – 1865) had already been active in far southwestern Zhejiang. Dubbed the Attendant King (侍王, Shi Wang), Li Shixian had provided rear cover for Li Xiucheng's advance toward Anqing by capturing several second-tier cities and tying down the Qing troops in Quzhou 衢州 in southwestern Zhejiang Province.

Li Xiucheng's massive force, now as many as 750,000 men, re-entered Zhejiang Province near Quzhou in late September 1861. After an unsuccessful assault on that city, Li moved northeastward to join forces with Li Shixian and his 100,000-man army at Yenchow 严州 (present-day Jiande 建德). The two cousins then mapped out their battle plans. Li Shixian would move eastward on a southerly route below the Qiantang River, and Li Xiucheng would head northeast toward Hangzhou on the river's north bank.

After finally completing the conquest of Quzhou and Yenchow, Li Shixian began a successful campaign across lower Zhejiang Province that put him on a path toward Lishui 丽水 and ultimately Taizhou 台州, one of the province's most important coastal cities. At the same time, Li Xiucheng's northeastern movement brought him to Hangzhou's doorstep on October 26, 1861 with the capture of the nearby towns of Lin'an 临安 and

Yuhang 余杭. Before moving directly on the former Southern Song capital, however, Li dispatched part of his force across the Qiantang to take Xiaoshan 萧山 and Zhuji 诸暨 (near Shaoxing) to protect his southern flank.

Prior to launching his assault on Hangzhou, Li ordered thousands of message-bearing arrows to be fired over the city walls announcing that no civilians or Qing soldiers would be killed or molested if the city surrendered peacefully. Neither the city officials nor the Manchu garrison commanders accepted the offer. Li completed his tight encirclement of the city and began the siege, fending off several Qing reinforcement attempts with relative ease. Hangzhou's gates were closed and barricaded; the city was now cut off from supplies and outside communication.

In mid-November, Qing troops under Zhang Yuliang arrived with badly needed reinforcements for the besieged city. Characteristic of the imperial military's persistent comedy of errors, a marksman within the garrison managed fatally to shoot Zhang outside the door of his own field headquarters; the Qing rescue effort of Hangzhou evaporated. Hope for rescue among the city's residents diminished still further on November 1, when a separate wing of Li's army gained control of Shaoxing with only minimal conflict, thereby blocking any line of rescue from Ningbo.

As Li Xuecheng's siege continued into December, food supplies in Hangzhou began running dangerously low for the garrison, the remaining urban residents, and the hundreds of thousands of refugees who had fled inside the city walls.[18] Supplies for the attacking Taipings were nearly exhausted as well. Li had even contemplated abandoning the siege until he learned from Hangzhou refugees that "soldiers and residents fought each other for food scraps or wandered around looking for tree leaves and pieces of leather to eat. Some even resorted to cannibalism."[19] In his *Record of 1861* (辛酉记, *Xinyouji*), first published in 1880, Hangzhou native Zhang Guanglie 张光烈 (b. 1854) wrote of eating tree bark, horse feed, and grass roots, adding: "There were those whose suffering was even worse, and they starved to death in the roads. Before they had breathed their last, the meat on their thighs was hacked away by other people."[20]

The first break in the siege stalemate came on December 28, 1861, when a few Qing soldiers and militiamen desperately scaled the walls to escape starvation. More soldiers followed, and the rout quickly began. Taiping soldiers ascended the undefended outer walls and, once inside, simply opened four of the city gates, often escorted by local people who were relieved to be rid of the Qing forces.

In the first days of occupation, utter chaos reigned. Suicide by hanging or drowning ran rampant, particularly among women. Zhang Guanglie, who was then only seven years old, subsequently recorded in *Record of 1861* the hangings among his female relatives and the deaths of eighteen members of his extended family. Far more traumatic, he personally witnessed his mother's death from stabbing and decapitation by a Taiping rebel,[21] an event that propelled him to adopt the name Guanglie, or "Shine Brightly on the Martyr" and later to build a garden he named Lie Yuan 烈园, the Martyr's Garden.[22]

298

The Taipings soon had control over the main city area, known as the Outer City, while the Manchu troops remained withdrawn inside their walled garrison, the Inner City. Provincial Governor Wang Yuling 王有龄 (1810 – 1861) retreated to his *yamen* office, where he hung himself in the rear garden before Li Xuecheng could meet him. Li offered a generous surrender amnesty to the Manchu Banner force inside the garrison— freedom to leave unharmed, by boat, with all their valuables—but his entreaties were summarily rejected. With no other alternative, the Taipings attacked the Inner City walls several days later; the garrison fell on December 31, 1861. Manchu General Ruichang committed suicide, as did ten thousand Manchu soldiers and civilians.

Under Li's orders, the remaining soldiers were imprisoned; Manchu civilians were left free and unmolested. He also arranged for coffins and burials for the dead Qing soldiers. For Governor Wang Yuling, whose actions as Hangzhou's leader had clearly won Li's respect, Li had his corpse attired in full military dress and transported back to his hometown by a flotilla of fifteen boats attended by five hundred men.[23]

During Li Xiucheng's siege of Hangzhou, Li Shixian's southern route troops captured Taizhou and then moved up the Zhejiang coast to encircle Ningbo by the end of November. With rebel forces camped outside the city gates, the Taipings faced their "Shanghai problem" of 1861 once again. As one of the first five treaty ports in China in 1842, Ningbo was actively occupied and used for trade—and missionary work—by foreigners, particularly the British and French. As they had outside of Shanghai in August 1860, the Taipings assured foreign officials in Ningbo that their settlements would not be disturbed and that all foreigners' lives and property would be protected from harm.

This time, the British and French both elected to maintain neutrality in what they still regarded as a Chinese civil war. They increased their naval presence around Ningbo and threatened and intimidated Taiping representatives in the hopes of discouraging a rebel assault, but in the end, they stood down. The risk of conflict between rebels and foreigners decreased significantly, however, when Ningbo's Chinese officials and military leaders simply abandoned the city to its fate. On December 9, the Taipings marched into the city without a fight. Although they were generally welcomed by the civilian residents, uncertainty and fear led more than seventy thousand people to flee into Ningbo's foreign settlement the next day.[24]

For the first time, the Taipings now had direct access to a seaport and all that came with it by way of trade. Perhaps most important, they could more easily procure military supplies from foreign sources, whether legitimate, stolen, or smuggled. Over the longer term, the rebels could even contemplate the purchase or construction of ships and creation of a Taiping Navy.

Li Xiucheng now controlled virtually all of Jiangnan east of Nanjing, south of the Yangzi River and north of Fujian Province, with only Huzhou and Shanghai still in Qing hands. With Jiangnan came immense mercantile and agricultural wealth, access to sea trade and international relations, and control over the entire lower section of the Grand Canal. Had Li been content with the territory he already commanded,

Chinese imperial history might have taken a very different course. But his mind had long since been made up: he wanted Shanghai's river ports and control over the mouth of the Yangzi. For the Westerners in Shanghai's foreign settlement, and for their home governments, that would be one step too far.

The Game Changes

Early in 1860, an American mercenary sailor and general roustabout named Frederick Townsend Ward (1831 – 1862) presented an audacious proposal to two of Shanghai's civil and business leaders, *daotai* Wu Xu 道台吴煦 (1828 – 1860) and wealthy banker Yang Fang扬枋 (1810 – 1865). With their financial backing, Ward said, he would organize a defense force for the city, employing Western, Filipino, and Indian mercenaries whom he would train and equip. Shanghai would no longer have to depend solely on the undependable, underequipped, and too often ineffectual Qing army troops. Wu and Yang accepted his offer.

Ward managed by mid-year to assemble a small band of Western and Southeast Asian mercenaries. After gaining battlefield experience in several Qing counterattacks outside of Shanghai, Ward's new foreign force shocked everyone by retaking the major walled city of Songjiang on July 16, 1860, just two weeks after the Taipings had captured it. They were less successful at Qingpu, where the rebels turned them back twice in brutal, high-casualty losses. Worse, Ward's troops were only barely managing to retain control of Songjiang against repeated Taiping counterassaults.

Li Xiucheng's first advance on Shanghai in August 1860, although intending no harm to the Western residents, had nevertheless unnerved the foreigners and Chinese residents alike. British Royal Navy Admiral James Hope (1808 – 1881) responded with negotiation backed by force: he captained a well-armed fleet of ships up the Yangzi River to Nanjing in early 1861 and secured a truce. The Taipings agreed to refrain from approaching Shanghai any closer than two days' march from the city, or about thirty miles. In return, the British promised to remain neutral in the Taiping–Qing conflict. The Heavenly King accepted those terms, but promised to abide by the agreement only for the balance of that year (1861).

The quiet period gained by Admiral Hope's gunboat diplomacy was just what Frederick Ward needed to reassess his tactical strategies and needs. He reconstructed his army as a mixed foreign and Chinese force, increased its size to six thousand soldiers, and equipped it with his first battlefield steamship, the *Cricket*. Despite the defensive potential of this new army, French and British officials still objected to Ward's involvement, mostly on the grounds that he threatened their neutrality arrangements by recruiting Westerners into his force. Like any experienced adventurer, Ward proved to be far nimbler than the bureaucrats and stodgy military officials who stood in his way. When they had him arrested in April 1861 for violating the foreign directives regarding neutrality, he simply forfeited his American citizenship and accepted Chinese citizenship.

300

As the truce period neared its end in late 1861, Liu Xiucheng's forces began massing outside of Shanghai for a second attempted assault. A large force came down from the north and positioned itself at Wusong 吴淞, threatening Shanghai's waterway to the Yangzi River. More troops approached from the west, out of Suzhou, while Li led his force out of Hangzhou and threatened from the south. Ward's force, now known as the Ward Corps of Disciplined Chinese, surprised the Taipings in January 1862 by re-taking Wusong while managing to keep a precarious hold on Songjiang. Shanghai still remained under serious threat, however, as the Taipings torched their way through the city's outskirts and filled the skies with smoke.

When word reached the foreign settlements of yet another massive rebel force approaching out of Suzhou, British and French military leaders decided they had seen enough. On February 13, they formally abandoned their neutrality and adopted a joint defense plan for Shanghai, incorporating their respective land and naval forces along with Frederick Ward's troops. Throughout the spring of 1862, they successfully conducted joint operations to reclaim a number of nearby small towns in an effort to clear a thirty-mile safe zone around Shanghai. Ward's force was so integral to these efforts that the Qing governor of Suzhou rewarded them with the official name "Ever-Victorious Army" (常勝軍, *Changsheng jun*).[25]

Qing army commander Li Hongzhang arrived in Shanghai in early summer 1862 and quickly became the most important new player in the eastern China theater. Zeng Guofan in Anqing had ordered his young protégé to recruit a new army of his own and deliver it to the eastern front, putting the two men and their forces along the Yangzi River but on opposite sides of Nanjing. By April, Li Hongzhang's entire force of nine thousand troops and support personnel, known as the Huai Army, were delivered from Anqing to Shanghai by the suddenly less neutral British, who authorized the Mackenzie, Richardson shipping company to assist.[26] By June, the Ever-Victorious Army—newly equipped with three more steamships[27]—and Li's Huai Army were busily clearing rebels from the remaining unrecovered cities within the thirty-mile radius. In August, they held off Li Xiucheng's last-ditch assault on Shanghai, bending but not breaking as they finally stopped the Taiping advance around the Hongqiao 虹桥 suburbs.

Frederick Ward would be killed in action near Ningbo in September that year and replaced by British Major General Charles Gordon (1833 – 1885). Over the next two years, Li Hongzhang and Gordon would collaborate effectively to drive the Taipings out of eastern Jiangsu Province and all the way back to Nanjing.[28]

The Battle for Zhejiang – Eastern Front

The French and British in Ningbo could hardly help noticing the surprising successes achieved by Ward's Ever-Victorious Army, both alone and later in combination with Li Hongzhang's Huai Army. Abandoning their studied neutrality in Zhejiang Province, the British began forming an "Ever-Secure Army" under Captain Roderick Dew (1823 – 1869), and the French organized an "Ever-Triumphant Army." The French handed command of their new Franco-Chinese force to naval officer Albert Edouard le Brethon de

Coligny (1833 – 1863), but Zhejiang's true counterpart to Frederick Ward turned out to be an unlikely customs inspector in Ningbo named Prosper Giquel (1835 – 1886).

Born in Brittany, in the seaport town of Lorient, Giquel was destined for a life far from his native France. He joined the French navy in 1852, became a Knight of the Legion of Honor in 1855 for his service in the Crimean War, and made his way to Canton as an ordnance officer during the Second Opium War (the so-called Arrow War) of 1856 – 1860. To the Chinese, he must have cut an intriguing figure: a full head of unusually curly hair that receded over a strikingly high and wide forehead, deep-set eyes, the type of sharp, aquiline nose that led Chinese people to refer to Westerners as "big noses" (大鼻子, *da bizi*), and a broad mustache running from cheek to cheek over a full but neatly-trimmed beard.

Giquel's mastery of French, English, and newly-acquired Chinese led him into the employ of Robert Hart (1835 – 1911), Inspector-General of the Imperial Maritime Customs Service. Among the many Westerners in China of his day, Hart was arguably one of the most sympathetic and forward-thinking supporters of China's cause. In an open letter published in the *New York Sun* (September 24, 1912), Sun Yat-sen cited "men of the calibre of the late Sir Robert Hart" whom China had "most trusted" for "hav[ing] shown in the past that unselfishly they have the interests of China at heart."[29] Hart's attitudes and perceptions would be reflected in Giquel's life's work in China.

After two years as a mid-level official in occupied Canton's military government, Prosper Giquel arrived at his Customs Office post in Ningbo in the fall of 1861. He hardly had time to assume his new responsibilities as the office's director, however, when the Taipings arrived outside the city walls in December. With little other choice, he closed the office and headed for the safety of Shanghai, itself threatened by Li Xiucheng's early-1862 advance. For the next six months, Giquel commanded a Franco-Chinese artillery unit formed for Shanghai's protection by army captain Jacques Marie Paul Tardif de Moidrey (1826 – 1872). He also observed Frederick Ward's mixed corps in action during this period.

By the time Giquel returned to a liberated Ningbo in May 1862, he was well-prepared to make the case for a Ward-like contingent in that city. Within weeks, he received authorization and financial backing from the city's leading officials and gentry to begin organizing. Since his responsibilities to reopen and administer the Ningbo Customs House prohibited Giquel's assumption of command over the new force, French naval officials assigned le Brethon to that position.

Giquel, whom the Chinese by now called Ri Yige (日意格), acted as liaison and fund-raiser with Ningbo's civic leaders. Le Brethon handled the military recruiting, training, equipping, and liaising with French military command in Ningbo and Shanghai. For financial reasons, le Brethon's force began with even fewer men than Ward had in 1860, less than 500 in total.[30] Aside from money, their biggest obstruction early on came from the British, especially in the person of Vice Admiral James Hope. Having decided to support Ward's contingent, the British had already begun forming another such mixed corps for Ningbo – under their command.

Adopting Shanghai's defensive plan of a cleared thirty-mile radius around Ningbo, Giquel and le Brethon headed northwest in July to reclaim the cities of Yuyao 余姚 and Shangyu 上虞. For a new and lightly trained force, Yuyao was a daunting first objective: walled three miles around and moated where not bordered by a river, and held by as many as ten thousand rebels. However, the new Franco-Chinese force was augmented by mixed, British-led troops under a Major Morton, imperial troops from Canton, and a supporting British Royal Navy presence under Captain Roderick Dew.

Le Brethon opened the assault on Yuyao on July 31, 1862, but heavy rains and a lack of coordination among the various attacking forces caused the first day's effort to falter, with casualties and recriminations. Working more effectively together the next day, the combined force breached the walls and swarmed into the city. Most of the Taipings fled westward, toward Shaoxing. After le Brethon left Yuyao on August 8, command of the mixed Franco-Chinese force holding that city was handed to Tardif de Moidrey, who successfully withstood a concerted counterattack from the rebels during the August – September period.

Giquel had since returned to Ningbo and successfully secured promises of continued financial backing until the Taipings had been entirely driven from Zhejiang Province. While Giquel was no doubt persuasive in his own right, he was coincidentally aided when Frederick Ward was mortally wounded at Qiqi while fighting to protect Ningbo from a renewed assault. For the citizens of Ningbo, the French certainly looked like their next best option.

In short order, Giquel and Tardif de Moidrey expanded the mixed Franco-Chinese force to over a thousand men. In mid-November, they left for Shangyu, less than twenty miles due west of Yuyao. The gruesome march route felt longer than it really was. Giquel described in his diary that along the way, "Decapitated and dismembered bodies of men, women, and children lined their path," arrayed so as "to intimidate them."[31] Although Giquel's elbow was permanently injured in the fighting, they took Shangyu from the rebels in just two days, with artillery support from two of Captain Dew's cannons. Incapacitated for further combat, Giquel retired to Ningbo to oversee his unit's resupply. In Shangyu, le Brethon planned his next and most challenging advance yet on the Taipings: taking back the city of Shaoxing.

By late December 1862, a notably enlarged Ever-Triumphant Army set forth for Shaoxing, a city as well-defended by the rebels as any in Jiangnan. King Goujian's capital city 2,400 years earlier was now surrounded by walls thirty-five feet high and fifteen miles in circumference and a moat over one hundred fifty feet wide.[32] Le Brethon's plan was straightforward, mixed with an element of psychology. He would begin with a full-scale but likely unsuccessful assault in the hope that the results from Yuyao and Shangyu would cause the Taipings' resolve to crumble into flight and abandonment. Failing that outcome, he would encircle the city, block their canal-based supply lines, and starve them out.

Confident in their fortifications, the rebels deflected the first assault in mid-January 1863 and held their positions. The Franco-Chinese force had arrived at Shaoxing with just three cannons, one of which had been seized from the Taipings when they took Shangyu. Le Brethon personally directed the positioning and targeting of that cannon when it suddenly exploded "at the first discharge…carrying away the whole upper part of his body and causing instantaneous death."[33] With Prosper Giquel unable to return to the battlefield, the French placed Tardif de Moidrey in charge.

Le Brethon had been well-respected by Roderick Dew and well-liked by the men he led. Tardif de Moidrey shared neither of those leadership accomplishments. In fact, the latter failing may have cost him his life. He organized a second direct assault on Shaoxing on February 19, but hardly had the fighting begun when de Moidrey was felled by a bullet to the back of his head. The leaderless assault collapsed almost immediately when most of the troops simply refused orders to advance against the rebel defenses.

Command of the Ever-Triumphant Army now fell to another naval officer, Paul d'Aiguebelle (1831 – 1875). During the continued encirclement of Shaoxing, d'Aiguebelle's force actually grew in size to over two thousand men, and the frustrated French military command quietly supplied two more heavy guns to support another assault. Concern among the rebels inside the city walls only grew as their attackers' strength increased and their own supplies dwindled. When a last-resort attempt to turn d'Aiguebelle with a colossal bribe failed, the Taipings simply abandoned the city on March 14 and retreated to Xiaoshan. Le Brethon's original strategy had succeeded, at the price of three field commanders, two dead and one (Giquel) decommissioned.

The Battle for Zhejiang – Western Front

While the French, British, and Chinese were gradually clearing the rebels from cities and towns to the east of Hangzhou, an important Chinese military leader was emerging far to the city's west. Even as Zeng Guofan finally retook Anqing on September 3, 1861, General Zuo Zongtang 左宗棠 (1812 – 1885) was proving increasingly successful against the Taipings in Anhui and Jiangxi Provinces. Zuo's troops now occupied the three-way juncture of Anhui, Jiangxi, and Zhejiang provinces, guarding Zeng Guofan's eastern flank from Li Shixian's rebels in Zhejiang. Like Li Hongzhang's Huai Army, Zuo's force—called the Xiang Army—consisted of five thousand men he himself had recruited.

After Anqing, events moved suddenly and, for Zuo, propitiously. At Zeng Guofan's recommendation, the Imperial Court on December 27, 1861, named Zuo commander-in-chief of Zhejiang's military forces, such as they were. Two days later, Hangzhou fell to the rebels and provincial governor Wang Youling 王有齡 (1810 – 1861) committed suicide. Within weeks, a court edict, with Zeng's support, named Zuo to replace Wang as Governor of Zhejiang Province. His first orders were to take back Zhejiang and Fujian provinces from the rebels.

At this point in early 1862, the fate of the Qing Dynasty rested almost entirely in the hands of just three military leaders operating in the south: Zeng Guofan to the west of Nanjing along the Yangzi River, Li Hongzhang to the east, also along the Yangzi River in Shanghai and Jiangsu Province, and Zuo Zongtang to the south. It was Zuo from among them who would figure most prominently in Hangzhou's and Zhejiang's future.

By most accounts, Zuo Zongtang rose from a large family of poor-to-modest means in Hunan Province. He achieved his provincial (*juren*) degree in 1832, but when he failed three times to gain the vaunted metropolitan (*jinshi*) degree, he settled into a quiet life of teaching, farming, and raising his four sons. Everything changed in 1852. Zuo began working with Hunan Governor Zeng Guofan to form local militia and create defenses against bandit groups who ravaged the land in the wake of the Taiping rebels. Two years later, he was placed in charge of a provincial effort to train military recruits, manufacture guns, and build ships.[34] These last experiences would bring him into the sphere of military practice and were instrumental in his later assignments.

Zuo was repeatedly remarked by his contemporaries for his striking appearance and demeanor. Boulger described him in 1885 as "short and corpulent," with "small, crafty eyes [that] brightly light up a countenance remarkable for its rough-cut but wasted features" and a thin moustache "which in idle moments he has a habit of twirling." He had a stern and commanding demeanor, "never suffering contradiction from any of his subordinates."[35] Although Zuo was widely honored for incorruptibility and frugality, Boulger also conjectured with seeming certainty that Zuo was a "woman-hater" with a disturbing coldness even toward his own mother. Rigid to a fault in his application of military discipline, he was nevertheless "much beloved by his soldiers."[36]

Given his new titles and orders from Beijing, Zuo pushed forward into Zhejiang Province almost immediately, establishing his first beachhead to the west of Quzhou on February 18, 1862, five months before le Brethon began his initial assault on Yuyao. Moving southeast, Zuo's Xiang Army captured Suian on March 6 after a particularly bloody battle, Changshan 常山 on March 20, Jiangshan 江山 on April 13, and Shimen 石门 on April 23. These first actions cut a southeasterly swath through Taiping-held western Zhejiang, clearing the way for their first major-city target, Quzhou. Opposing them, headquartered further east along the Fuyang River in Jinhua 金华, was Li Xiucheng's "giant" cousin, Li Shixian.

After his rapid advance on Quzhou, Zuo Zongtang paused to regroup and assimilate new recruits and scattered remnants of the Zhejiang army into his trained force. He wanted to be fully prepared to attack a position that the rebels had been occupying for months and fortifying with dozens of stockades outside Quzhou's walls. On July 1, 1862, Zuo's army managed to capture about thirty of these stockades on a single day. Almost unbelievably, the Taipings simply evacuated the city, having hardly put up a serious fight.

As unlikely as the recapture of Quzhou had been, Li Shixian's ill-advised recall to the Heavenly Capital turned the Taiping loss of Jinhua, Zuo's next target, into a veritable comedy of errors. After Zuo's advance stalled for several months at Longyou 龙游, just a few miles east of Quzhou, he split his force and invested Tangxi 汤溪 on the outskirts of Jinhua. A surprise rush on the gates of Tangxi on February 27, 1863, killed six thousand rebels and seized the town; the next day, Longyou fell to Zuo's assault. As both Xiang Army forces advanced on Jinhua, the rebels defending that city learned about Tangxi's fall and fled for Longyou even as the remnants of Longyou headed for Tangxi. Amid all the confusion and chaos, the rebels at Lanxi 兰溪 and Yiwu 义乌 abandoned their towns as well. Zuo ended up occupying all five towns, two without firing a shot, and killing more than ten thousand aimlessly fleeing Taipings.

The way forward was now clear. Zuo continued on toward Hangzhou, taking Tonglu 桐庐 and Zhuji and sending part of his force toward Ningbo to clear rebels from the southern side of the Qiantang River. A great pincer movement had been formed by the eastern and western front advances, and they were now ready to close on Hangzhou.

Hangzhou Recovered

Hangzhou promised to be the first time Zuo Zongtang would conduct joint battle operations with the foreign-led Franco-Chinese army. The situation did not bode well, since Zuo had been consistent in his opposition to the presence of foreign armies on Chinese soil or allowing them command over Chinese soldiers. Even after the Ever-Triumphant Army became an irrevocable fact, he vehemently opposed increasing their strength beyond 2,500 men. He may have wished to see the Franco-Chinese unit dissolved, but he also realistically feared turning loose a band of trained mercenaries who might join the rebels if the money was right.

When Zuo and d'Aiguebelle met for the first time in late March 1863, the Frenchman came dressed in full military regalia as though he was fighting in the service of the King of France. At their next meeting, Zuo was apparently won over by his counterpart's respect for Chinese etiquette: d'Aiguebelle had shaved his beard and exchanged his French military dress for proper Chinese military attire. [37] They would gradually discover professional respect for one another and collaborate quite effectively.

The Xiang and Ever-Triumphant armies continued to consolidate their positions through the spring of 1863, clearing the Taipings from cities and towns in Zhejiang until the Hangzhou and Huzhou vicinities were the last remaining major objectives. More good news for Zuo arrived in early June 1863 when he received imperial appointment as Viceroy of Zhejiang and Fujian provinces while retaining his Governor's position in Zhejiang.

Bad news followed soon after. The previous summer, his troops had been so badly stricken with a cholera outbreak that half his troops had been incapacitated. [38] This time it was malaria, and once again the epidemic was fearsome. D'Aiguebelle was barely able to achieve anything more through the summer than maintain his defenses. Zuo was infected as well, sickened so badly that as late as December he still could not safely ride a horse.

When operations resumed in the fall, Zuo and d'Aiguebelle combined to attack Fuyang 富阳 on September 18 and gained control just two days later. The defeated rebels headed downriver to Hangzhou. Next came Yuhang, held by a strong rebel force only twenty miles from Hangzhou. The assault began on January 3, 1864 and was repulsed; Zuo suffered heavy losses. Another attempt on February 4 failed as well. Zuo wisely pulled back and refocused on Hangzhou, leaving enough troops at Yuhang to keep the rebels penned up inside.

When Jiaxing was retaken on March 24 by Li Hongzhang's Huai Army force out of Jiangsu Province, Zuo welcomed the return of some of his forces he had earlier dispatched to assist. Having spent the last two months investing Hangzhou, he ordered the attack to begin on March 31. Rain and wind swept the city and West Lake that day, and the rebels defended furiously into evening. At around midnight, Zuo's men managed to scale the walls at several points and throw open a gate on the city's north side.

Hangzhou returned to the imperial fold the next day, April 1, 1864. Not long after, the Taipings abandoned Yuhang as well. Rebels who fought their way out of either city fled north, heading for Huzhou.

Last, but Not Least

Eight years earlier in July 1856, with Taiping rebels threatening just thirty miles to the west of Huzhou, American shipping and railroad magnate Robert Minturn (1836 – 1889) approached the walls of that ancient city by boat. He was cordially refused entry, but he nevertheless remarked on the battle preparations he had seen:

> Hoo-chow was…strongly fortified…The walls were in thorough repair, the outworks on the canal had been put in order, all the cannon were mounted, and we saw a great many of the forty thousand soldiers who had been collected and quartered in and about the city. The gate of the city was more rigidly guarded than even the barrier…It is surrounded on three sides by hills, the highest of which are about 1000 feet high, and are covered with monasteries.[39]

Minturn's cursory military assessment proved quite accurate. Huzhou endured a two-year siege by the Taipings before finally falling in May 1862, around the same time Ningbo was retaken from the rebels and Zeng Guofan began his long siege to recover Nanjing. With Hangzhou now back in Qing hands and mop-up operations actively clearing the areas east, west, and south of the provincial capital, Zuo Zongtang turned northward toward Huzhou, the Taipings' last major stronghold in Zhejiang. He attempted a full-out assault in April but was repelled by the Taipings' well-fortified positions under the command of General Huang Wenjin黄文金, (1832 – 1864), known as Du Wang堵王 (Wall King).

Through the summer, Zuo cleared outlying towns near Huzhou, including Deqing and Anji. Li Hongzhang applied additional pressure from the north, investing Changxing just northwest of Huzhou along the Lake Tai shoreline. Because many of the dislodged and displaced from the various Taiping losses had retired to Huzhou, the rebel force defending the city had swollen to around 100,000.[40] Their desperation could only have magnified as Charles Gordon led the Ever-Victorious Army's recapture of Yixing and Jintan along the western boundary of Lake Tai in March, imperial troops under rebel-turned-Qing-commander Cheng Xueqi (程学启, 1828 - 1864) retook Jiaxing, also in March, and Li Hongzhang and Charles Gordon combined to regain Changzhou in May.

News of the Heavenly King's suicide (June 30, 1864) and the fall of Nanjing to Li's and Zeng's armies on July 19 marked the beginning of the end. For the Taipings who had not already fled south into Jiangxi Province and chosen instead to fight, Huzhou was now their last stand. For Zuo Zongtang, Huzhou represented his last chance to add to his Hangzhou success and share in the imperial rewards that Zeng and Li would doubtless receive for Nanjing's restoration to Qing control.

Zuo's anticipation only grew when news arrived that the Heavenly King's heir-apparent, Hong Tianguifu 洪天贵福 (1849 – 1864), had somehow escaped Zeng Guofan's clutches at Nanjing and secretly slipped into Huzhou. Equally enticing, the notorious Shield King, Hong Rengan, had been in Huzhou since springtime. Zuo and Li Hongzhang had needed the first half of the summer just to clear the numerous forward posts with which Huang Wenjin had surrounded Huzhou before his opponents' arrival. By the end of July, they finally had Huzhou surrounded.

For the first and only time in the fourteen-year-long rebellion, the Qing Green Standard Army, Zuo's Xiang Army, Li Hongzhang's Huai Army, the British (800 men under command of a Colonel Reynolds), and the Ever-Triumphant Army would join forces in a combined assault. Even Gordon's since-disbanded Ever-Victorious Army was represented in the person of Colonel Bailey, who stayed on to command a heavy artillery unit for Cheng Xueqi's Green Standard force. Prosper Giquel completed the reunion, having recently rejoined Paul d'Aiguebelle and the Franco-Chinese force. Like d'Aiguebelle, Giquel quickly formed a friendly working relationship with Zuo Zongtang that would continue into the post-war years.

Pressured by Beijing to secure Zhejiang after the fall of Nanjing, Zuo began his assault on Huzhou on August 8. The weather throughout the Lake Tai area was so insufferably hot and humid, uniformed soldiers collapsed from the heat. Firearms and cannons dangerously overheated as well, and they sometimes exploded when in use. The Taipings repelled the first wave of full-scale attacks on August 8, August 9, and August 14, inflicting heavy casualties on the allied forces. Zuo regrouped for several days after the third failure, then launched a combined artillery and ground assault on August 17 that continued virtually non-stop for ten days. Huzhou suffered multiple fires on August 27 and fell the next day.

Amid the chaotic fighting that began inside the city walls, thousands of rebels poured out of the gates, heading west into the surrounding hills for Guangde in nearby Anhui Province[41] or southwest toward Jiangxi Province. By one estimate at the time, as many as half of the rebels successfully escaped Huzhou.[42] Worse, Shield King Hong Rengan and Hong Tianguifu, the fifteen-year-old Heavenly King, were among them. Still worse, at least for Zeng Guofan, he had previously reported by memorial to the Emperor that the successor Heavenly King had been killed at Nanjing.

A disappointed Giquel wrote angrily in his journal on August 26 that the allied generals had exhibited more interest in clearing Zhejiang Province of rebels than in completely eradicating the rebellion for the Empire's benefit:

> Everything is useless. The mandarins only wish for one thing: to see the rebels gone. They have a real chance to finish off the rebellion. To allow it to move to the [other] provinces is to perpetuate it indefinitely. But what do they care; let the others suffer.[43]

Among the Taiping defenders in Huzhou had been as many as a dozen Westerners—English, Austrians, Greeks, Germans, and French—mostly sailors, and about evenly divided between mercenaries and individuals who claimed they had been kidnapped and forced either to fight or be decapitated. One of their number, an English soldier named Patrick Nellis, achieved a modicum of temporary notoriety when he recounted his story in *The London and China Telegraph* newspaper in January 1865.

Nellis claimed he had been kidnapped outside of Shanghai and transported in chains to Huzhou where he was given a fight-or-die option.[44] He and other Westerners fought for the Taipings, but most of their promised compensation never materialized. In the last days of fighting, one of the Westerners was fatally injured. The rest managed to escape during the chaos of the city's abandonment on August 27 – 28 and make their way by boat out of the area. Nellis wrote that the Heavenly King's son "was not in the city, and I never heard of him." He did, however, have an interesting encounter with Hong Rengan, who asked Nellis in halting English "...what I was. I said an Englishman. He said he had never met a good foreigner....I did not see him again.[45]

With Huzhou finally in hand, the rich and fabled Jiangnan area fell once again under Qing rule. The rebellion was far from over across the empire, but for Hangzhou and its satellite cities like Huzhou, Shaoxing, and Jiaxing, the time had finally come for recovery and return to a semblance of normalcy.

Loose Ends

As defeated rebels congregated in Anhui Province or headed further southwest into Jiangxi Province, Qing officials worried about the survivors rekindling the rebellion under the leadership of the young Heavenly King and Hong Rengan or other escaped generals. Concerted efforts began to capture the missing generals and kings (*wang*), along of course with the son of Hong Xiuquan, now the second Tian Wang.

By the same token, a greatly relieved Beijing court, on behalf of the child-Emperor Tongzhi, rushed to reward the triumvirate of generals now openly referred to as "Zeng, Zuo, Li." Despite their loyal service to the empire, they together also constituted a possible threat: the most powerful and effective military leaders in China, heading personal armies and not overly beholden to the throne.

On the Taiping side:

- **Li Xiucheng**, the Loyal King, escaped Nanjing before its fall on July 19, 1864, but he was captured three days later at Fangshan 方山 (Square Mountain), just south of the former Heavenly City. After writing his confession, he was executed by order of Zeng Guofan on August 7, three weeks before the fall of Huzhou.

- **Hong Rengan**, the Shield King, fled in the company of Hong Tianguifu as they made their way to Guangde in Anhui Province. When that city fell under attack, they fled together again. They were camped near Shicheng 石城县 in Jiangxi Province on October 9 when Qing soldiers discovered them. Hong Rengan was captured, but Tianguifu and a small entourage managed to escape yet again. Rengan was executed in Nanchang on November 23, 1864.

- **Hong Tianguifu** continued on southward in Jiangxi Province. Nearly captured again, he escaped but lost the rest of his entourage. He cut his long hair, traveled incognito until he found harvesting work with a farmer, and was finally captured on October 25. The second and last Taiping Heavenly King died from "death by a thousand cuts" on November 18, one week shy of his fifteenth birthday.

- **Huang Wenjin**, the Wall King and Taiping commander at Huzhou, died from battlefield wounds at Changhua town, about fifty miles west of Hangzhou.

- Perhaps most remarkable, a notorious Taiping general named **Yang Fuqing** 杨辅清 (d. 1874), nicknamed the Yellow Tiger, escaped all the way to Shanghai. There he boarded a ship to America and settled into a new life as a gang boss in Los Angeles for several years. He is believed to have been killed in 1874 when he returned to Fuzhou to organize an anti-Qing espionage ring.

On the Qing and Western side:

- **Zeng Guofan** received the title of First Class Marquis Yiyong (一等毅勇侯) and was awarded the high honor of a two-eyed peacock feather to be worn on his mandarin hat, one of the highest marks of imperial recognition.

- **Li Hongzhang** received an imperial yellow jacket after retaking Suzhou, but by 1865 he had garnered the official first-class rank of earl and the right to wear the two-eyed peacock feather. The yellow jacket symbolically represented the Emperor's ceremonial bodyguard.

- **Zuo Zongtang** received the beloved yellow jacket from the Emperor after the conquest of Hangzhou, followed by the same earldom title as Li Hongzhang at the close of the Zhejiang campaign. He returned to Hangzhou after the fall of Huzhou, but another promotion as Viceroy and Governor-General of Fujian and Zhejiang sent him off to Fuzhou Province.

- **Charles Gordon** was awarded the imperial yellow jacket after his role in recapturing Suzhou, coupled with the Chinese rank of viscount. He had previously refused politely to accept rewards of money and gifts of the Emperor's calligraphy on yellow silk. He received several promotions from the British Army as well. Gordon left China in November 1864 and later died in battle in the Sudan in 1885. He has been forever remembered in the West as "Chinese" Gordon.

- **Prosper Giquel** assumed command of the Ever-Triumphant Army at Huzhou in August 1864 when d'Aiguebelle left the front and returned to Hangzhou. Just six weeks later, after the fall of Huzhou, Giquel's army was decommissioned. He was nevertheless raised to the rank of lieutenant-general and would soon be given entirely new responsibilities at the behest of Zuo Zongtang. Giquel would later receive the imperial peacock feather award and, like Gordon, the imperial yellow jacket.

A Sidebar on Chicken

One of the best known and most popular dishes in American Chinese restaurants, General Tso's Chicken, is named after General Zuo Zongtang. On Chinese menus in the West, it will probably appear like this: 左宗雞, (Zuo zong ji), using the traditional character for chicken (*ji*), or it could look like this: 左宗鸡 (Zuo zong ji), using the more modern and simplified form for the character *ji*. Either way, the English usually comes out in the old-fashioned, Wade-Giles transcription. Not General Zuo's Chicken, but General Tso's Chicken, or even General Tsao's Chicken.

There is no doubt that the savior of Hangzhou did not invent the dish named after him, and the likelihood he ever tasted chicken served this same way is also nil. Some restaurateurs and food-lovers in modern Hunan promote Zuo's connection as part of the legend, but there is no evidence to support their claim. In fact, the strongest evidence points toward Taipei, New York City, and Henry Kissinger!

Although Jennifer 8. Lee popularized the topic of General Tso's Chicken via her book and TED Talk on Chinese food, a more exhaustive treatment of the issue comes from Fuchsia Dunlop.[46] By Dunlop's account, the dish originated with a Hunanese emigrant named Peng Changgui 彭長貴 (1919 – 2016). His culinary training had come in Changsha (Hunan), where he apprenticed with a master Hunanese chef named Cao Jingshen. During the war years of the 1930s and 1940s, Peng relocated to Chongqing, temporary seat of the Nationalist government, and established his own reputation as a master chef. After the fall of Chiang Kai-shek's Nationalist government in 1949, he moved to Taipei and opened his first restaurant, Peng Yuan (Peng Garden).

Peng says he first prepared an early version of the dish in 1952[47] after he began catering government receptions and meetings. He named the dish General Tso's Chicken in honor of Zuo Zongtang, still known in the 1950s by the Western spelling Tso Tsung-t'ang. Chef Peng's choice of General Zuo expressed the reverence Hunanese people still felt toward their great military hero and native son. Peng's christening decision also gave his dish a sense of authenticity as well as an air of (admittedly false) historicity.

In 1974, Peng Changgui opened his first American Chinese restaurant in New York City, serving Hunan-style cuisine and hoping to catch the wave of newfound popularity of things Chinese after President Nixon's 1972 visit. He was unfortunately ahead of his time with regard to American acceptance of genuine Chinese food, but he persisted despite an initial failure of his business. He tried again on East 44th Street near United Nations Plaza, where he found his biggest promoter in Henry Kissinger. Peng related his story: "Kissinger visited us every time he was in New York...and we became old friends. It was he who brought Hunanese food to public notice."[48]

Peng's original version of General Tso's Chicken was straightforward but unsweetened: "Deep-fry seven or eight small pieces of starch-coated chicken until crispy, let them drain of oil, and then stir-fry them with red pepper and soy sauce."[49] However, the chicken dish he had prepared in China did not quite suit American tastes, so Peng added a bit of sugar to his hot, sour and salty dish.

As enthusiasm for Chinese cuisine blossomed in the 1970s and interest in Chinese regional dishes expanded, General Tso's chicken became a staple on American-Chinese menus. It also grew sweeter and sweeter, so much so that a retired Peng Changgui later shrank back in disgust when Jennifer 8. Lee presented him with a photo of the Americanized version into which his dish had evolved. "莫名其妙!" ("*Moming qi miao!*"), he exclaimed. "This is all nonsense!"[50] Perhaps more consistent with the bafflement expressed by this idiomatic Chinese would be: "What is *that* supposed to be?"

Ironically, while many Westerners recognize the association of the name General Tso (or Tsao) with their Chinese restaurant chicken order, few if any would know the name Zuo Zongtang, who he was, or what he did. At least they have never forgotten him in Hunan. Hopefully not in Hangzhou, either.

Chapter 13

RECOVERY AND OPENING

(1865 – 1895)

Coming Back Late from a Trip to the Lake	On the Lake, Singing about the Moon[1]
I'm in love with the scenery of	*Deep in the night the sky*
the West Lake.	*is clear, cool breezes rise;*
Mountain peaks carry	*On the lake, someone sings*
the evening sun,	*"Strolling in the moonlight."*
Returning birds flutter in	*Water trickles and flows,*
bamboo dew,	*shallow and clear.*
Falling fruit echoes by	*Moon white, endless void,*
the celery pond,	*threads of mist evaporate;*
Leaves rest in the quiet	*Water, light moonlight,*
of the breeze,	*two circles linked together.*
Fish swim in the cool of	*The moon, the moon's reflection,*
water's depths.	*two sights unsurpassed.*
A pavilion half-lit, a moonlit scene,	
Lotus mist inflames us with its perfume.	

– *Two poems by Zhu Shuzhen (1135 – 1180)*

China in 1865 was itself a battlefield casualty. Magnificent cities emptied and in ruins. Invaluable art, historical documents, and cultural treasures damaged or lost. Centuries-old architecture, especially Buddhist and Daoist temples and pagodas defaced, desecrated, or destroyed; ancient statuary mutilated or burned. More than twenty million[2] dead from disease, exposure, starvation, warfare, indiscriminate slaughter, or suicide, their corpses filling lakes, canals, and wells, littering the streets, or left in cheap coffins lining the banks of rivers and waterways. Agricultural land, carefully husbanded over centuries, abandoned. The Grand Canal, China's centuries-old lifeline between north and south, neglected, silted over into uselessness.

The rebellion was a true peasant movement, built on centuries of economic and feudal oppression, facilitated by a corrupt and governmentally inept dynasty, triggered by a poor man who dreamed he was a god—or at least the son of one. For China, the earth had moved…but at a horrible cost. And still the war was not ended. By mid-December 1864, Zuo Zongtang had marched southeast to coastal Fujian Province, where Li Shixian still commanded as many as two hundred thousand rebel soldiers. Zuo led a difficult and drawn out campaign that only secured Fujian in February 1866 when a massive assault on the Taiping stronghold of Jiaying (modern Meizhou in Guangdong Province) ended with more than ten thousand rebels dead and sixty thousand surrendered. The Taipings were finally neutralized, reduced to little more than bandit groups across the southernmost provinces.

The Qing Court looked down at its bleeding wounds and peered up at the foreign vultures circling overhead. British…French…Americans…Germans…Russians…and, increasingly, Japanese. Each eyed China's vast territory, resources, and markets as opportunities. Some innocently, for trade; others more aggressively, for economic exploitation; and some voraciously, as ripe for occupation. Recovery—perhaps survival—was going to require some changes.

The Aftermath

For the war's survivors, recovery meant dealing with life's dearest necessities while coping with the psychologically scarring memories of deprivation, death, even massacres. Shaoxing native Zhang Daye 張大野 (1854 – ?) later recalled events at Bao Village, where a local militia under Bao Lishen 包立身 (1838 – 1862) had successfully held off the Taiping rebels for eight months before succumbing in July 1862:

> When Bao Village fell, since they could not easily kill off the thousands of men and women in the village, the bandits drove them into various houses; then they wrapped up cotton with bamboo mats, poured oil inside, erected the mats all around the houses, and set fire to them. The fire raged for eleven days and nights. Most of the people who died were from Hangzhou; next were the natives of Bao Village; people from Shaoxing took up about one-tenth. Afterward, corpses were scattered all over the place, maggots spread into the woods, and the horrible stench could be smelled from a dozen leagues away.[3]

Another account describes events at White Sands Village (白沙村, Baisha cun), where many Hangzhou residents had first fled the approaching rebels and hidden in a large cave. The refugees put up a spirited resistance when the Taipings arrived in the area, so the attackers simply blocked the cave entrance with wood and flammable materials, set it ablaze, and stood by as more than three thousand men, women, and children perished inside.[4]

Frederick D. Cloud, an American Vice-Consul, described Hangzhou's horrendous aftermath:

> The Great Street, with its splendid rows of magnificent shops, was one long stretch of charred debris, among which were the mangled remains of thousands of men, women and children. The canals were so full of the bodies of those who had committed suicide during the first few days of the reign of terror that those later wishing to end their existence could not find sufficient water in which to drown themselves. Terror-stricken, the people rushed out of the western gates and threw themselves into West Lake in such great numbers that "one could walk out into the lake for a distance of half a *li* on dead bodies." It is estimated that fully 600,000 people were either murdered or committed suicide during the occupation of the T'ai P'ing rebels.[5]

Despite their likely post-traumatic distress, new and returning officials and gentry began tackling the most pressing matters in Zhejiang's cities and towns: burying the dead, ensuring adequate food supplies, and restoring population and agriculture. Work to lay the dead to rest began almost immediately in Hangzhou. As Provincial Governor, General Zuo Zongtang led the recovery effort in Zhejiang even as Beijing pressed him to move his troops against the Taiping forces still infesting Fujian and Guangdong Provinces.

Only a few months after retaking Hangzhou, Zuo approved formation of a broad-based Benevolence Association comprised of gentry, literati elites, and local officials. The Association was tasked with addressing multiple near-term needs, from burials to medical services and schools. The collaborative, quasi-governmental nature of this charitable organization marked the increasingly active role of the non-official citizenry, particularly at its most elite and moneyed levels. Beijing receded into the background as the province mounted its own resources for recovery, a trend that would only strengthen over the decades leading to 1911.

A long history of charitable burying organizations, often appearing instantaneously in times of disaster, provided the framework for the Association's response. Hangzhou's burial sub-bureau set for itself a time frame of three months for having all of the dead interred. To achieve this objective, unclaimed corpses were collected, placed in government-provided coffins, and given proper (if unmarked) burial sites. Countless new cemeteries also sprang into existence around the Hangzhou region for more than a decade after 1864.

Bones, sadly plentiful, were gathered by workers who may literally have been paid by the pound. As many as fifty-seven mass gravesites on the hills or near temple grounds around West Lake sheltered those tragic remains.[6] In Zhang Guanglie's tragic case, he wrote in *Record of 1861* that his mother's long-lost corpse, still wrapped in a reed mat, was only found and buried with her husband on Dragon Well Hill in 1878, looking down upon West Lake seventeen years after her murder.[7]

Concurrent with these burials were efforts to honor the dead collectively with a Manifest Loyalty Shrine. Retired officials and gentry pooled their resources to purchase and transform two adjacent but grievously damaged literati gardens—Governor Jin's Estate and Gao Garden—into ritualized memorial grounds. Although local people visited the grounds, the new formal goal for these gardens was less about the traditional notions of escape and forgetting and more about contemplation and remembering. No longer privately held, these restored and repurposed "gardens" also served as leisure spots and tourist sites.[8]

On the food supply issue, the prefect of Yenchow (today's Jiande) described the problem and hypothesized at least a partial solution, but also one that illustrated his regionally restricted perspective:

> After the Taiping wars vast areas of agricultural land were laid waste and various cities and towns reduced to a shambles. Villages far and near are very sparsely populated and ridges and furrows are all covered with thorns and weeds.... To rehabilitate this area it is vital that immigrants be attracted.... The only [locally] available immigrants are the shack people, who for generations have cultivated mountains and have not mingled with the common people....Previously they were compelled to depend on mountains for a livelihood because of the shortage of irrigated paddies, but today irrigated paddies are waiting for them to till. They will be willing to come down from the mountains to till the paddies which will offer them far greater incomes.[9]

Some recently dismissed soldiers from Zeng Guofan's and Li Hongzhang's armies may have chosen to settle in Zhejiang rather than return to their native places, but their numbers were wholly inadequate to restore the province's harvest. Such vast wartime population losses dictated the only feasible solution for restoring the regional agriculture base: massive peasant immigration from outside the immediately affected area. Throughout Zhejiang, Jiangsu, and Anhui Provinces, newly established immigration bureaus actively sought and warmly welcomed waves of settlers from elsewhere—not that the newcomers were always received so happily by native survivors, however. Peasants from Shaoxing and Ningbo sought land in northern Zhejiang and southern Jiangsu, while those from coastal Wenzhou and Taizhou headed for the area around Jiaxing.

Meanwhile, peasants from less affected regions outside Zhejiang, like northern Jiangsu and Hunan Province, flooded into the area. Many headed for the outlying reaches of Huzhou and down the Qiantang and Fuyang River valleys toward the battered cities of Fuyang, Jinhua, and Quzhou. By one estimate, one county in Hunan Province alone sent over a million emigrants into the war-blighted area in just two generations.[10]

The very riches and land productivity that had attracted the destruction of war were now operating in the service of its restoration. As a Zhejiang Province history phrased it poetically, "Once the valley became hollow, the wind was bound to blow in."[11] But the process would be slow, and fraught with native resentment. When German geographer Baron Ferdinand von Richtofen (1833 – 1905), inventor of the term "Silk Road" and an uncle of the famed "Red Baron" flying ace of World War I, surveyed the region southwest of Hangzhou in the early 1870s (well more than five years after war's end in Zhejiang), he praised the area's natural fecundity but wrote:

The valleys, notwithstanding the fertility of their soil, are a complete wilderness. In approaching the groups of stately white-washed houses that lurk at some distance from underneath a grove of trees, you get aware that they are ruins. Eloquent witnesses of the wealth of which this valley was formerly the seat, they are now desolation itself. Here and there a house is barely fitted up, and serves as a lodging to some wretched people, the poverty of whom is in striking contrast with the rich land on which they live. The cities I have mentioned…are extensive heaps of ruins, about a dozen houses being inhabited in each of them…The roads connecting the district cities are now narrow footpaths, completely overgrown in many places with grasses fifteen feet high, or with shrubs through which it is difficult to penetrate.[12]

Von Richtofen claimed during his travels through the region to have casually inquired in different locales as to the survival rate from the rebellion. In his estimation, the typical response was "three in every hundred." Yet he also witnessed positive signs of immigration, mainly from Ningbo and Shaoxing.[13]

The larger cities of northern Zhejiang—Hangzhou, Jiaxing, Shaoxing, Huzhou—faced enormous recovery challenges of their own, from infrastructure repair and rebuilding of damaged or destroyed housing stock to economic restoration and repopulation. Hangzhou Prefecture had reported a population of about 3.2 million in an 1820 census, and had likely grown to well over 3.5 million by the late 1850s. A subsequent report published in the Republican era identified a native population of only 720,000, a population loss of nearly eighty percent even fifty years after the war's end.[14] Similarly, Ho Ping-ti estimated the population losses in the cities of Hangzhou and Jiaxing at seventy percent and sixty-eight percent, respectively.[15]

The major cities, and Zhejiang Province as a whole, would gradually recover and prosper, but they (along with Nanjing, Yangzhou, and Suzhou in Jiangsu Province) would no longer be the shining stars of the Yangzi Delta region. The ground beneath them had shifted eastward; Shanghai's formidable rise would soon overshadow them all.[16]

Rebuilding the City, Restocking the Library

The first decade following the Taiping occupation of urban Hangzhou was one of restoration and recovery. By several estimates, as much as eighty percent of the city's building stock had been leveled. Contemporary observers wrote in horrific terms of "the scourge of the rebellion"[17] and "a withering plague"[18], leaving the diminished city "a waste and howling wilderness"[19] and "a wilderness of ruins"[20].

Rebuilding was slow, heavily dependent on local resources. Nevertheless, walls and gates were repaired, canals cleared, housing gradually rebuilt, and market commerce re-established. The tilled fields stretching eastward from the city returned to cultivation, and small shops and skilled trades resumed operation along the suburban waterways.[21]

In 1879, one observer estimated the city's population at 800,000. Suburbs soon reappeared even as the city walls were reinforced, with gates that closed strictly at sundown and reopened just as strictly at sunrise. Late returnees desperate to re-enter the city could nevertheless do so at one of the gates by risking, "for about a penny," a ride in a basket elevator: "a windlass with a basket suspended," a ratchet-less mechanism operated by a man who might be half asleep or "under the influence of liquor," leaving the occupant "hung between heaven and earth,…wondering whether he should proceed upward or fall suddenly downward."[22]

Two years later, a walk through the city found "business streets…almost impossible of traverse, because of their crowded state…vendors of all kinds of wares cried them to the limit of their lung power; men carrying on yokes fitted to their shoulders…, beggars…, children crying…, coolies shouting…, learned gentry in long robes…, artisans carrying tools, errand men or boys with their parcels, children going or returning from school…, a veritable pandemonium."[23] From her wide photographic travels across China, the irrepressible Isabella Bird (1831 – 1904) marveled by 1895 at the city's merchant wealth and described at least some streets as "broad, light, and well flagged." She added, "Hangzhou impresses one with a general sense of well-being. I did not see one beggar."[24]

One of the leaders in Hangzhou's reconstruction was Ding Bing 丁丙 (1832 – 1899), son of wealthy scholar and bibliophile Ding Ying 丁英 (d. 1855). Well before the devastations wreaked upon Hangzhou by the Taipings, Ding had already suffered a devastating personal tragedy of his own. Having married a young poetess named Ling Zhiyuan 凌祉媛 (1831 – 1852), he lost his bride to illness when both of them were barely twenty years of age. In 1854, two years after Ling's death, her widowed husband published in her memory eighty-two of her poems, written between 1845 and 1852, under the title *Drafts of Poems and Song Lyrics from the Green Snail Shell Loft* (翠羅閣诗词稿, *Cuiluoge shici gao*).[25] Ling's poetry collection would be just the first of many books Ding Ling published over his lifetime.

Before the rebellion reached Hangzhou in the early 1860s, Ding Bing had already been, like his father, active in philanthropic affairs for feeding the hungry and repairing temples. Once Hangzhou had finally been recovered from the Taipings, Ding returned to his hometown and devoted himself to the recovery effort. The list of his involvements was impressive: "rebuilding the academies and other public buildings; repairing bridges, temples, and shrines; dredging waterways and repairing dikes; heading the Zhejiang Printing Office; establishing a foundling home; supervising the charitable ferry and life-saving association; setting up gruel stations and homes for the destitute; and collecting money for relief as needed."[26]

As Hangzhou returned to life, surviving soldiers and families who formerly occupied the Manchu Garrison trickled back into their old neighborhood. Perhaps two thousand of the more than ten thousand Manchus who occupied the garrison before 1860 now sought to restore their lives and livelihoods. Instead, they found their homes and neighborhoods in ruins, victimized by the war.

With the imperial treasury badly depleted, the garrison community had nowhere to turn except charity. A few Manchus of mercantile means were able to assist, and limited restoration took place. The Qiantang Gate exiting onto West Lake was restored to its former condition, as were the garrison's (inner city) walls and five gates.[27] The commanding officer's residence and grounds, including a temple and an academy, were also repaired. The scars of war ran long and deep, however, and not just to the physical city. As late as 1872, *Shenbao* reported Manchu soldiers dying of fright at the sight of ghosts roaming the area, presumably suicide victims or perhaps direct casualties from the first assault on Hangzhou in 1861.[28]

As early as 1852, the Qing court had begun permitting the sale of Manchu banner land, providing a temporary boost to banner soldiers' income at the expense of the land's continued use for growing vegetables. Additional financial pressures on the imperial treasury led to cuts and elimination of various special grants to field officers and (in 1862) reduction in the payment allowance to each man and wife, regardless the number of their young children. Poverty grew to epidemic levels inside the garrison, so that "the population first pawned everything they owned to buy food....Hunger drove adults and children out of the garrisons into the countryside in search of food, and...many died in the cold night temperatures....[W]ithin a few years, bannermen and former bannermen would be found in carpentry, weaving, pottery, mechanics, and other skilled trades."[29]

Never popular with the city's Han Chinese to begin with, the diminished Manchu community was now publicly scorned and largely left to fend for itself. The garrison soldiers could never be forgiven for their sheer cowardice and ineffectuality in 1861, and even less so for turning on the very people they had been paid for decades to protect as they fled Hangzhou. Lack of a Confucian education and absence of marketable skills left many of them capable of little more than menial physical labor. In his *Hangchow Journal of 1870*, David Lyon put it succinctly: "The Tartars are but a feeble folk compared with what they were before the Taiping rebels razed their city to the ground."[30]

Unbeknown to that struggling remnant, their time had passed; a cruel new era had begun for the once-proud descendants of invincible horse warriors. Almost fifty years later, the 1918 annual report of Hangzhou's YMCA addressed the Manchus' collective circumstances as a distressing charitable matter:

> In a segregated part of the city live the remnant of the once lordly rulers, parasites, and oppressors of the Chinese people, the Manchus. They are now a pathetic people. Their income is now cut off, they are socially ostracized, and since they have never learned to work, they are reduced to a state of poverty. Their children have been deprived of all opportunity to study or education, and they are growing up as street urchins and professional beggars. A year ago, the Association started a free summer school for these unfortunate children.[31]

Less mundane early recovery projects also drew the attention of city officials and some of the scholarly elite as well. New schools needed to be established or old ones salvaged from their ruins. The provincial examination halls that accommodated up to thirteen thousand *juren*-seeking aspirants once every three years had to be restored. Temple halls and defaced or destroyed statuary required renovation or replacement. Even the sacrosanct temple and tomb site of Yue Fei suffered intentional harm. Among the damaged items before Yue Fei's tomb were the stone attendants' statues lining the approach, all of which were decapitated, and the kneeling statues of Qin Hui and his wife and two colleagues, all of which were damaged.[32]

Perhaps the most esoteric and revealing of the many restorative efforts concerned the Wenlan ge imperial library. Ding Bing and his brother, Ding Shen 丁申 (d. 1887), were among the many citizens who fled Hangzhou in the early 1860s and headed north into Jiangsu Province. The two men were steeped in scholarly and book-collecting traditions; their ancestors had even contributed books to the Qianlong Emperor's grand literary collection project, the *Four Treasuries* (the *Siku quanshu*). The Ding family's collection had been destroyed in 1861 when the rebels executed their "false capture" of Hangzhou, but their successful printing business sustained the brothers' connection to the world of books.

While traveling in northern Zhejiang in 1862, Ding Bing happened to notice a curious sheaf of papers being used as package wrappers. His experience and trained eye told him that he was looking at materials from the Wenlan Library on West Lake's Solitary Hill, home of one of the great *Four Treasuries* sets. Knowing the Taipings had already invested the city, he concluded that rebels or thieves must have entered the building and were desecrating if not scattering or destroying its invaluable contents.

Unable or unwilling to risk re-entering Hangzhou themselves, the brothers traveled to Shanghai. There they met with a book dealer named Zhou Huixi 周匯西 and financed a secret mission to retrieve as much of the *Four Treasuries* material as possible. Zhou gained entry to the rebel-held city by convincing the Taipings that he sought only to collect and protect written-upon papers. Such respect for the written word was an accepted Chinese tradition. No writing was to be debased by common use or put to an improper purpose.

The Ding brothers' success, though not total, was measured by sheer volume: approximately 6,600 recovered volumes of the full, 36,000-volume set were transported for safekeeping to Shanghai, only returned to Hangzhou in 1864 after the rebels had been driven from the city.[33] That same year, even as mass burials, care arrangements for the newly orphaned, and treatment for disease, exposure, or starvation took place, recovery of Hangzhou's share of the empire's literary intellectual property began.

The Ding brothers and their fellow literati continued their search for missing *Four Treasuries* volumes. Some, it turned out, had been salvaged by other scholars and hidden away during the conflict; these were now freely returned to their former archive. With literati on the alert in Shanghai and throughout Jiangnan, stolen volumes were ferreted out from street markets and recovered amid illicit efforts to sell or trade them.

Meanwhile, local fund-raising efforts supplied enough capital in 1880 to restore the gutted and partially roofless Wenlan Palace library to a semblance of its former glory. When the restoration was completed the following year, the recovered volumes were returned to their former home. For the next eight years, Ding Bing bought, borrowed, or had transcribed every still-missing volume he could identify, adding over 2,500 more recovered works to the collection by 1881.[34] He simultaneously rebuilt an extraordinary personal and family library, including hundreds of rare and ancient books that in 1909 became a cornerstone of the Jiangsu Provincial Library collection in Nanjing. Isabella Bird wrote of Ding Bing's collection in 1895 as "the finest private library in China," stored, organized, and classified "admirably," and (perhaps a bit over-enthusiastically) "open freely to anyone who introduces himself by a card from an official."[35]

Returning the re-compiled *Four Treasuries*, perhaps the finest literary product of the Qing era, to its hallowed place on the shores of West Lake reaffirmed Hangzhou's intellectual position in the realm. The efforts of the Ding brothers and others among the Hangzhou literati and gentry communities signaled their deep commitment to literary and cultural preservation under even the most trying circumstances.

Silk Recovers

As the greater Hangzhou area recovered from the Taiping conflict, attention naturally turned to its major industries, especially sericulture and silk production and weaving. Throughout the Ming and Qing dynasties, Chinese sericulture had centered in northern Zhejiang and southern Jiangsu provinces, especially around Jiaxing and Huzhou. Weaving concentrated in the same broad area, along with the Imperial Silk Weaving Factories in Hangzhou and Suzhou.

From the 14th through 18th centuries, Chinese silks supplied the imperial court and the domestic market virtually unopposed by imports, but growing international competition presented entirely new challenges in the 1800s. Silk production was well-established in Japan by 600 CE,[36] in Byzantium around the same time, in southern Italy by 1050, throughout Italy by the 1400s, and in the 1500s in Lyon, France, where sericulture and weaving grew by the 1700s to dominate local industry. Although China continued to export high-end silk to Europe, French silks from Lyon developed new, non-Asian styles and designs and supplanted Florence and other Italian cities as Europe's silk production center into the mid-1800s. Invention of the punch card-driven Jacquard loom in 1804 further industrialized French silk weaving and posed a distant but nonetheless existential threat to China's silk export trade if not to its Chinese manufacture.

By a quirk of nature and fate, French sericulture came to a sudden and unplanned halt, beginning in 1845, five years after the First Opium War and five years before the start of the Taiping Rebellion. The causes were threefold: a microsporidium, a virus, and a fungus,[37] the last of which left dead silkworms encrusted in white spores, looking like sugar candies. All three "invaders" created epidemics that spread uncontrollably through France's silkworm population. Incredibly, other infestations attacked Europe's mulberry trees at nearly the same time, causing a near collapse in French silk production by the 1860s.

With the dramatic fall in French raw silk production, demand for Chinese raw silk rose accordingly through the 1850s, growing to at least 50% of the total international trade volume. Exports out of Shanghai in 1858 were 1,300% greater than in 1842, when the city was first opened as an international treaty port. Initially, even the Taiping conflict benefitted Shanghai's silk merchants, since the rebel army's seizure of Nanjing in 1853 left their city as the primary export center. Silk production was seriously disrupted from 1860 – 1864, however, while the rebels controlled most of Jiangnan's prime silk-producing territory.

If luck is nothing more than the intersection of coincidence with preparation, coincidence had occurred in Europe and post-Taiping Jiangnan was prepared to rebuild its silk industry. The Jiaxing and Huzhou areas recovered gradually, their silk output greatly diminished for the better part of the first decade of recovery. New mulberry trees were planted and new settlers in the area established small, family-based operations. Learning curves had to be traversed, however, since repopulation of the vacated land brought in willing but inexperienced outsiders who lacked sericulture knowledge. In Hangzhou, where imperial silk factories had operated since the early years of the Song Dynasty, weaving capacity had suffered enormous damage from the rebel occupation. Hangzhou's Imperial Silk Weaving Factory had counted as many as 750 looms in operation in the 1700s, but that number reached only 115 in post-war 1870.[38]

By the mid or late 1870s, much of the silk producing area in Zhejiang had fully recovered. Customs commissioners reported that "a great number" of mulberry trees had been felled by the Taipings, but in the prime silk producing city of Nanxun (near Huzhou), "the inhabitants are so active and the trade so prosperous that all traces of the rebel occupation have entirely disappeared." In the late Qing years, the town was home to so many nouveau riche merchants that high society in Shanghai began describing them condescendingly as "four elephants, eight cows, and seventy-two dogs." The "four elephants" of Nanxun were the fabulously wealthy and influential Liu, Zhang, Pang, and Gu family clans.[39]

In the nearby town of Anji, "the people are raising silkworms, and the mulberry trees are flourishing. Recently mulberry trees have been planted even in the hills." Around Jiaxing, old mulberry groves were restored and entire new areas planted: "In the past, only the southwest *hsiang* had mulberry trees, but now to the east of the city, for 20 – 30 *li* by water, there is absolutely no unclaimed land left, and the peasants do [sericulture] as their regular occupation." At coastal Haiyan, "Mulberry...trees grow everywhere, in the fields and along the walls...There is not one person who does not practice sericulture. The techniques have all been learned from [Huzhou]."[40]

For the silk producers of Jiangnan, recovery was motivated as much by opportunity as by tradition. The total collapse of France's sericulture industry, which in 1853 had produced an incredible fifty-seven million pounds of cocoons,[41] now installed China once again as the dominant export market for raw silk. The dramatic reduction in shipping time and costs resulting from the Suez Canal's opening in 1869 further magnified European demand, another felicitous coincidence for China's silk producers. America's sudden, post-Civil War demand for raw silk, which came to rival that of France, provided yet another driver of the recovering Chinese silk trade.

International demand for one of the lowest of low-technology, downward-scalable, low-barriers-of-entry industries—raising silkworms and harvesting their cocoons—was peaking just when the people of Jiangnan needed it the most. While certainly much welcomed at the time, such windfalls often come at a price of their own.

Novel Ideas

In 1877, a twenty-four-chapter sequel to Cao Xueqin's 曹雪芹 (1715 - 1764) classic novel *Honglou meng* 红楼梦 (*Dream of the Red Chamber*) appeared in Beijing's literary marketplace. Titled simply *Honglou meng ying* 紅樓夢影 (*Shadows of "Dream of the Red Chamber"*), the book's author was identified by the pseudonym Unofficial Historian of the Cloud Raft (云槎外史, Yuncha waishi). The book's preface offered no better insight into authorship, and it, too, was signed anonymously by the Idler at West Lake (西湖散人, Xihu sanren).

Honglou meng ying was hardly the first or only sequel to *Honglou meng*. In fact, one scholar noted that there are at least eleven other extant sequels, adding that all of them were at least begun if not completed before *Honglou meng ying* first appeared.[42] Furthermore, the novel itself is not considered a great literary work, nor does it match the quality of over 1,100 extant poems written by its author. What made this particular sequel special was the novel's unique approach and content, as well as the identity of its author, the latter fact not known with certainty until 1989.

In that year, the unexpected discovery in Japan of a lost section of the sequel author's published poetry collection confirmed the pseudonymous Cloud Raft Historian as Gu Taiqing 顧太清 (1799 – 1877), an ethnic Manchu from Beijing.[43] In that moment, Gu became the author of the earliest extant novel written by a Chinese woman. The same recovered manuscript section also revealed the preface-writing Idler at West Lake as Shen Shanbao (沈善宝, 1808–1862), substantiating the linkage between Gu Taiqing and the writing women of Hangzhou.

Gu Taiqing was born in or near Beijing to a distinguished Manchu banner family that had suffered a recent official disgrace. Although Gu was well-educated and showed early promise as both a poet and painter, she was relegated at age 24 to concubinage in the family of a Manchu prince named Yihui 奕会 (1799 – 1838), a great-grandson of Emperor Qianlong. Their relationship was matrimonially fruitful, evidenced by three sons and two daughters, and they shared interests in poetry and painting. When Yihui's first wife died, he took no new wife and no additional concubines, content in his companionable relationship with Gu.

In 1835, Gu Taiqing's literary interests connected her with two of Liang Desheng's daughters in Hangzhou, Xu Yunlin 许云林 and Xu Yunjiang 许云姜, both of whom were well-versed in poetry, painting, and even seal carving. They in turn introduced Gu to a network of "at least a dozen or more women from Hangzhou and its environs"[44] that included Wang Duan, Wu Zao, and most especially, Shen Shanbao,[45] who wrote that at their first introduction, the two women almost "fell in love" with one another.[46]

Shen became Gu's closest friend and most fervent supporter.

Gu's happy life ended abruptly in 1838 with Yihui's unexpected death and Gu's expulsion from the household by her stepson. She was forced to sell her jewelry and move with her children to the suburbs, but her sympathetic Hangzhou friends consoled and assisted her through the emotional and domestic hardships. The following year, this network of literary women established their own poetry group in Beijing, called the Autumn Red Poetry Club, that included Gu Taiqing in its membership. Her stepson's death in 1857 without a male heir eventually changed Gu's fortunes once again when her late husband's family accepted one of Gu's grandchildren as their heir and welcomed her back into their fold.

Despite these challenges and the household burdens of raising five children, the thirty-year period from 1839 to 1869 proved to be Taiqing's most prolific. In addition to her poetic output during this span, she launched her effort to create a new sequel to the immortal classic, *Dream of the Red Chamber*. Unlike Chen Duansheng, who wrote her first sixteen chapters of *Love Reincarnate* (*Zaisheng yuan*) in just two years, Gu appears to have written much more intermittently. She and Shen Shanbao exchanged dozens of poems with one another during these times, and according to Gu, it was Shen whose persistent "nagging" motivated her finally to complete her sequel in around 1861.[47]

Shadows of "Dream of the Red Chamber" was not published until 1877, around the time of Gu Taiqing's death and fifteen or more years after its completion. Although it did not generate much critical response at the time, Gu's sequel is recognized today for her literary approach. She preserved the original *Red Chamber* story's ending, eschewing the supernatural or reincarnation devices of previous sequels that brought original characters back to life. She "evolved" some characters to meet her storytelling needs, but overall, she retained and extended the original story's narrative threads. Unlike nearly all the earlier sequels, Gu also retained the tragic atmosphere of the original novel's conclusion, eschewing a happily-ever-after ending.

Although she built upon an existing story and set of characters rather than an entirely new narrative, Gu Taiqing produced a sequel novel unlike any that preceded hers. The first-known novel written by a Chinese woman was thus a novel of domestic manners. *Honglou meng ying* illustrated and valorized the lives of Qing-era women and addressed their domestic realities, including child rearing, music-playing, matchmaking, weddings, banquets, and even childbirths. "Her work is distinctive in the many autobiographical elements that she infuse[d] into it, such as her appreciation of music, the insertion of her own poetry, and interest in such matters as childbirth and child rearing."[48]

In the years following Gu Taiqing's death in 1877, yet another groundbreaking work of female fiction was also forming in the Jiaxing district towns of Tongxiang and Haining under the authorship of a woman of Hangzhou origin. Her name was Zhou Yingfang 周颖芳 (1829 – 1895), her chosen literary genre was *tanci* (mixed storytelling and ballad singing), and her subject was the great Song Dynasty military hero Yue Fei, entombed and enshrined on the north shore of her hometown's West Lake for many centuries.

Like so many of the best-educated women of the Ming and Qing eras, Zhou Ying-fang was born into a prominent family of scholars and officials. Her grandfather had been Governor of Yunnan Province, and her father and brother were officials. Zhou's well-educated mother also came from an official family, although her father (Yingfang's maternal grandfather) had died in disgrace for having set free Hong Xiuquan, the soon-to-be Taiping Heavenly King, after his arrest in 1851 in Guangxi Province during the early stages of Hong's rebel organizing. Zhou's mother Zheng Zhenhua 鄭貞華 (1811 – 1860) had actually published a well-received *tanci* narrative of her own.

Zhou Yingfang received a solid education in history as well as the arts and was married into another prominent family, the Yan's of Tongxiang. Her husband, Yan Jin (严瑾, 1827 – 1865), obtained a position in the southern province of Guizhou in the 1850s, where he proved particularly well-suited for local military leadership. Zhou and the Yan family relocated to Guizhou,[49] but Yan Jin died in battle while fighting off a Miao rebel attack in 1865. The family returned to Tongxian only to find their former home in ruins as a result of the Taiping occupation of the Hangzhou region.

Now widowed and motherless (Zhou's mother had committed suicide in 1860 when the Taiping rebels first captured Hangzhou), herself the mother of a son and three daughters, Yingfang rejected the notion of widow-martyrdom and relocated with her children to Haining. She remained widowed and lived a life of reduced but not impoverished means, successfully raising her children (the son into officialdom, the daughters all educated and married to officials) and pursuing her personal literary interests. She wrote and published poetry from her Studio of Ink Fragrance (硯香閣, Yanxiang ge) and found time to read histories, including a 1744 fictionalized account of Yue Fei's life titled *The Complete Biography of Yue Fei* (說岳全傳, *Shuoyue quanzhuan*), the book which formed the literary counterpoint to her *tanci* narrative of the Yue Fei story.

Although Zhou Yingfang's *Biography of Dedication and Loyalty* (精忠传, *Jing zhong zhuan*) only reached publication in 1932 Shanghai, she completed her *tanci* manuscript in 1895, the same year in which she passed away. According to her book's preface, she "wrote the fiction on and off and on for twenty-eight years in her cottage, as a recreation in difficult times."[50] Before the book was published by Shanghai Commercial Press, it was Zhou Yingfang's adult children and their spouses who proofread the preprint copy.[51]

Zhou's manuscript was far from another standard tale of military battles and heroic stands by a man loyal to his nation and his ruler, however. Instead, Zhou radically altered the storytelling focus, giving equal if not more weight to the forgotten household women Yue Fei left behind during his military affairs. Hers was a story by a woman about women, about their support of family, endurance of hardships, and abilities to manage household affairs. Yue Fei's politicized military career and famous battles are more than paralleled by the continuing life of his household, with dinners, wedding ceremonies, childbirths, and household affairs interspersed and juxtaposed with reminders of the ongoing warfare. Beyond the traditional virtues of obedience and chastity, Zhou's characters demonstrate that "strength, endurance, generosity, forbearance, competence, flexibility, and mobility also make up womanhood."[52]

Prior to the Taiping onslaught, the gentlewomen of Ming and Qing Jiangnan had been fomenting an educational and literary rebellion of their own. From the days of Liu Rushi, the Banana Garden Poetry Club, Shang Shilin, and Gu Ruopu to those of Chen Duansheng, Liang Desheng, Wang Duan, and Wu Zao, women were increasingly asserting their rightful place in the realms of literary creation, criticism, and consumption.

In the second half of the 19th Century, Hangzhou area women continued pushing against their traditional literary boundaries. They actively prodded and promoted the creation of Gu Taiqing's first-ever, female-authored Chinese novel. In Zhou Yingfang's *tanci* narrative, they reminded their fellow male citizens that even in times of war and male heroism, it was women's abilities and strength that held the homeland together for their return. Collectively, they set the stage for a woman writer and revolutionary from Shaoxing who would soon shatter every restrictive barrier and open the cultural doorway into the 20th Century.

Hangzhou's Great Millionaire

While millions suffered and died during the civil war years, the conflict and its aftermath provided singularly rich opportunities for a few. One of the rebellion's greatest beneficiaries was born a peasant, worked as a child cowherd in Anhui Province, became arguably the richest man in Hangzhou, fell into bankruptcy, and died two years later, allegedly from depression. Yet he left behind a famous medicine hall and an extraordinary residence in the heart of Hangzhou that remains today one of the city's most remarkable tourist sites.

At just fourteen years of age, Hu Xueyan 胡雪岩 (born Hu Guangyong 胡光墉, 1823 - 1885) resettled in Hangzhou as an apprentice in a private bank.[53] Born with a seemingly inexhaustible entrepreneurial spirit, the young banker made the acquaintance of salt merchant Wang Youling and befriended him financially at an early stage in both their careers. As Wang rose through the provincial bureaucratic ranks and ultimately to Governor of Zhejiang Province, he assisted Hu in turn, helping the latter build his nascent banking empire. In addition, Hu served (profitably, no doubt) as Wang's intermediary in procuring military supplies for the province.

When Governor Wang committed honorable suicide after the Taiping rebels took Hangzhou in the final days of December 1861, Hu Xueyan lost perhaps the most influential contact in his growing network. Unperturbed, however, he quickly turned to Wang's successor, Zuo Zongtang, the new Governor-General of Zhejiang and Fujian Provinces. Zuo had not yet begun the reconquest of Zhejiang, but he understood that his military skill set would prove inadequate to the bureaucratic, administrative, and monetary challenges of provincial governance. Thus began a mutually beneficial, twenty-year working relationship between the two men.

For the next several years, under imperial orders, Zuo moved through Zhejiang and on into Fujian, driving the Taiping rebels before him. Throughout this period, he relied heavily on Hu Xueyan, "deputizing him to obtain supplies and foreign arms and ammunition, to help in the work of reconstruction at Hangzhou, and to handle the job of transporting military supplies."[54] During this period, Hu even took a lead position in assembling a large fund, the interest from which financed operation of a fleet of two dozen ferry boats to transport people back and forth across the Qiantang River.[55]

On June 25, 1866, less than five months after his climactic defeat of the rebels at Jiaying (modern Meizhou, Guangdong Province), Zuo submitted his memorial to the imperial throne recommending the creation of a military arsenal and ship-building center at Fuzhou, where Hu had already relocated at Zuo's request. His plan received imperial authorization just three weeks later.

Zuo's military star had ascended to such heights that he received further imperial instructions in September. The court ordered him to take command of military forces in distant Shaanxi and Gansu Provinces and douse the flames of the four-year-old Dungan Revolt among the Hui Muslims. Before his departure for the northwest, Zuo put Hu Xueyan in charge of purchasing materials and hiring workers for the new Fuzhou Arsenal.

Furthermore, Zuo secured for Hu the responsibility for procuring weapons and ordnance for his campaigns in Shaanxi and Gansu, including loan financing and provision of non-military industrial materials. Hu Xueyan processed millions in transactions and bulk silver shipments to those remote provinces over a period of a dozen years. Well before the Dungan Revolt ended in 1877, Hu was already a rich man, having amassed assets by 1872 in excess of twenty million taels by one contemporary estimate.[56] His Fukang Bank had become one of the city's most powerful financial institutions, and his business interests had expanded into real estate, pawnshops, salt, and shipping.

Riding the wave of his immense wealth less than a decade after the Taiping Rebellion, Hu set out to build a monument to himself and a home for his family and his numerous concubines (said to have been a dozen or more). On almost eleven *mu* 亩 (over 78,000 square feet, or about 1.75 acres) of prime Hangzhou city land, he began construction of a magnificent, thirteen-building residence and garden. Built in classical Chinese style from the finest materials, the complex also incorporated the latest in Western touches, including the use of chandeliers, large mirrors, colored glass windows, and excavation of a below-level basement. When work completed in 1875, Hu's palatial residence boasted more than sixty thousand square feet of living space, Hangzhou's highest building of its time (the Yu Fengtang), China's largest man-made cave in the Zhi Yuan 芝园 garden rockery, and an artificial waterway running through the residence.

Even as Hu's personal palace was under construction, he set out on the business venture for which he is still best remembered: a pharmacy for traditional Chinese medicine (TCM). In 1874, he founded Hu Qingyu Tang (胡庆余堂), a medicine hall at the busy foot of Wushan Hill. Hu Qingyu Tang operated on three simple principles: high quality medicines, ethical treatment of customers, and fair pricing. The pharmacy achieved near-immediate success and was soon regarded as China's premier medicine hall south of the Yangzi River. Its operation continues to the present day, expanded in 1991 to include a Museum of TCM on the site of the original store at the corner of Hefang Street and Daijing Alley.

Hu's life and career reached its peak in the latter half of the 1870s. He was awarded a red cap by Beijing, an honor usually restricted to officials with the title of governor. In addition, he was permitted the honor of riding a horse into the Forbidden City while wearing yellow, symbolic actions of singular rarity. But with great wealth sometimes comes an insatiable desire for still more, and into this temptation fell "Red-capped Merchant" (红顶商人, *Hong ding shangren*) Hu Xueyan in 1883.

European silk production had recovered somewhat in the later 1870s, thanks in part to the scientific researches of Louis Pasteur in France; Japanese production of raw silk expanded as well. The rapidly globalizing silk trade now subjected the Chinese silk industry to unfamiliar price and profitability swings dictated by world market conditions, a circumstance that invited speculation and profiteering. Enter Hu Xueyan, who in 1881 and 1882 perceived an opportunity to corner the silk market and add to his already immense fortune.

Believing that Europe would suffer poor raw silk production in 1883 as had happened in 1876,[57] Chinese speculators began buying and hoarding silk bales, bidding up prices even further in the process. When that forecast proved spectacularly untrue the following year, demand for Chinese raw silk fell, prices plunged, and rotting silk inventories overflowed warehouses. Hu Xueyan had placed some of the market's biggest bets on a strong silk market for 1883; a report by Customs Commissioner Edward Bangs Drew (1865 – 1908) in October 1882 suggested that Hu was already holding 14,000 bales of raw silk.[58] By comparison, total silk exports from Shanghai had been estimated at 57,000 bales in the 1873 - 1874 production year.[59]

Hu suffered massive investment losses when raw silk prices collapsed. Meanwhile, Chinese banks that had extended credit to silk merchants and speculators experienced runs and declared bankruptcy, including Hu's own Fukang Bank in 1884. In what seemed an instant, Hu's fortune was gone, and he found little empathy and no support from Beijing. He died the following year, still deep in debt. In January 1886, a court edict ordered officials in Hangzhou to seize whatever assets and properties remained. Not long after, Hu Xueyan's eighty-two-year-old mother committed suicide and joined her son in the hereafter.[60]

Hu's spectacular Hangzhou residence changed private hands several times in the ensuing years, and for brief periods of time reportedly even housed schools and factories.[61] Years later, the mansion became home to multiple families, with well over one hundred people in residence. Government-sponsored renovation began in 1999, and Hu Xueyan's former home was opened to the public as a historic site in January 2001.[62]

The Pot Begins to Boil

China in the 1890s was already a far different place than it had been in 1850. The regions most impacted by the Taiping civil war had recovered with substantially diminished populations. By one recent study, the estimated population of 17.05 million in 1893 Zhejiang Province, three decades after the war's end, still remained almost forty-four percent below its 1851 population of 30.28 million. The story was much the same in the adjacent provinces of Jiangsu (-30.7%), Anhui (-38.6%), Jiangxi (-42.4%), and Fujian (-26.6%).[63]

Despite these massive population loss, home-grown companies, some government-supervised, had formed in such key industries as finance, textiles, shipping, mining, and ironworks. Merchants no longer occupied the bottom of the Confucian social hierarchy below scholar-officials, peasants, and artisans; they were joining the elites, if not becoming them. "Commercialization encouraged the fusion of merchants and gentry into a vigorous, numerically expanding elite whose power rested on varying combinations of land ownership, trade, usury, and degree holding."[64]

In Zhejiang and Jiangsu Provinces, officials and gentry had increased their independence from Beijing and were moving aggressively to manage local affairs locally. "Post-rebellion reconstruction fostered a rapid and permanent expansion of elite-managed, quasi-governmental local activities....Lines between local and national concerns began to blur, and assertive elites began to engage in new kinds of competition with official representatives of the state."[65]

Aside from these societal shifts within the Jiangnan population, foreign influences and involvements created additional changes and amplified social pressures for change. Missionary hospitals introduced Western medical practice and pharmaceuticals. Western medical schools trained doctors and nurses. Missionaries and educated elites opened schools for both boys and girls, adding science, mathematics, geography, and even foreign languages to the curriculum. Chinese scholars began translating Western books in numerous technical subject areas, and occasionally even works of pure literature.

Like the proverbial frog in the pot set above the flame, the Qing government was in danger of not recognizing its gradually changing circumstances from these trends until the boiling point was reached. By then, it would be too late.

Chapter 14

GOOD INTENTIONS, UNSOUGHT

(1865 – 1895)

Suddenly, they turned their heads and looked back at the city. There were houses on the hilly slopes, stacked layer upon layer. Temples, towers, and terraces of varying heights looked like immortal palaces amidst falling flowers…All enthusiastically praised the vista by saying that inside the city and along the lake were the scenes of a thousand fan paintings.[1]

– Xihu Laoren (Old Man of West Lake, 13th Century)

In the end, recovery in Zhejiang Province from the Taiping uprising was largely funded and engineered by the officials and people of Zhejiang. Beijing offered little assistance: the Qing treasury was badly depleted, rebellion continued but had moved northwest into Shaanxi, Gansu, and Xinjiang provinces, and the military stood in tattered disarray. Neither was any international rescue plan or humanitarian aid program in the offing, nor would it likely have been accepted or its motives trusted.

Yet by the same token, the events of the previous quarter-century – opium wars, forced opening of treaty ports by invasion of Beijing (and the Forbidden City) by the Eight Powers' forces in 1860, Western participation in the defeat of the Taipings, and growing enthusiasm for Chinese teas, silks, and porcelains – had heightened Western awareness of the Middle Kingdom's very existence (and vice versa).

Christian missionaries began arriving in earnest with the opening of the first five treaty ports in 1842. Their public preaching and dissemination of printed materials in cities, towns, and rural villages contrasted with the more secular Westerners who traveled the rural outskirts of those coastal cities in hunting parties, enjoying plentiful opportunities to bag deer, pheasants, ducks, and other small game. For many Chinese, their first en-

330

counters with these Westerners bemused or befuddled. "The inhabitants of these parts… have already divided European visitors into two classes, the 'bird shooting' foreigner, and the 'book-distributing' foreigner," wrote the Bishop of Victoria in 1858. [2]

From the start, the long-range objective of the "book-distributing foreigners" for mass religious conversion was clear. Many, if not most, viewed their proselytizing as a pseudo-military conquest, casually adapting military language to their pursuits. Arthur Evans Moule quoted a Church Missionary Society conference resolution in 1858 stating that: "We consider the immediate *occupation* of Hang-chow" from which, joined with the missionaries in Ningbo, could be made "a common and united *advance on* the interior of the empire (*emphasis* added)."[3] Missionaries' rest and recovery periods back in their home countries were *furloughs*, and newly arrived missionary personnel were *reinforcements*.

For the most deeply religious foreigners, China beckoned as a grand opportunity, a land of idolaters ripe for Christian conversion and (in their minds, at least) for civilizing. Perhaps no one could have made this condescending, crusader-like conquest attitude more brutally clear than Joseph Edkins (1823 – 1905) in a published letter of 1869 to the British Minister in Beijing:

> Are we wrong then in having come to China? Must we apologize to the Chinese for all the defeats we have inflicted upon them, and the changes we have made amongst them socially and politically, and forthwith take our departure?…Shall we not rather be told that it is too late now even to moot the question whether western nations ought or ought not to force their intercourse on an unwilling heathen people? The thing has been done, is being done, and will continue to be done. The nations of the west seem to be brought hither by a necessity over which they have no control. They bring their commerce, their civilization and their religion with them; and it is beating the air to argue against the introduction of them, simply because they will produce revolutions.
>
> China, it is admitted on all hands, needs a revolution. Its ignorance, its superstition, its pride, its exclusiveness—all require to be changed. Until this is done, foreign intercourse of any kind will be a perpetual source of danger to individuals, and of complications between the governments. The Christian religion is the only means by which such a change can be brought about, and in time it will effect this change in China, as it has done in the nations of the west.[4]

Uninvited though they were, and whatever their racial attitudes and ultimate motivations, Western missionaries would have a significant impact in Hangzhou and the surrounding area for the next hundred years. The days of China's practiced insularity and "We have no need of your manufactures"[5] would soon be gone, whether by choice or by force.

Foreigners on a Mission

As the year 1858 drew to a close and the Taiping conflict raged well to the west, American Presbyterian minister John L. Nevius (1829 – 1893) decided it was time to sally forth from his Ningbo mission station on the exploratory first steps of his own conquest. His objective was Hangzhou, well-known as a hospitable outpost for Jesuit missionaries two centuries before. By Chinese law, Nevius's excursion was prohibited, since the 1842 Treaty of Nanjing limited foreigners' travels to five port cities (Shanghai, Ningbo, Fuzhou, Xiamen, and Canton) and only such areas around them as could be visited and returned from in a single day.

Nevius and two Ningbo colleagues, Rev. William A. Russell (1821 – 1879) and American Consul C.W. Bradley (1806 – 1863), succeeded not only in reaching Hangzhou's walls but in entering the city itself, much to the surprise of its inhabitants and the dismay of its officials. As they walked the city streets and admired West Lake, they were closely observed until finally escorted to the government *yamen*. City officials politely but firmly escorted the three men canal-side for an immediate return trip by canal boat to Ningbo. A group of chained criminals served for their fellow passengers—a barely veiled signal of their future welcome.

Undeterred, Nevius struck out for Hangzhou again in February 1859, assisted by several of his Chinese converts. This time, however, he was prepared for an unarmed, one-foreigner foray into the city, planning to stay until he was evicted. Outside the city walls, he unexpectedly met another foreigner with similar intentions, Rev. J. S. Burdon (1826 – 1907). Together, and with their Chinese Christian assistants, they mounted a successful two-foreigner invasion of the city. Nevius somehow secured temporary lodgings in one of the many temples perched on Wushan (City God's Hill) in the southern part of Hangzhou and stayed for nearly a month. He then traveled back to Ningbo to retrieve Mrs. Nevius; they returned to Hangzhou together in April. Their new accommodations outside the city walls at the Liuhe (Six Harmonies) Pagoda proved to be short-term when Nevius managed to arrange new quarters at another temple in the Wushan hills.

Husband and wife moved quietly back inside the city, with Mrs. Nevius transported in a closed sedan chair.[6] The Reverend then called at the *yamen* and presented himself to city officials, who received him more cordially than he probably had any right to expect. With their furniture transported from Ningbo, the couple had barely settled in as the only foreigners in Hangzhou when faraway events rudely intruded. What began in Canton in 1856 as a conflict over Chinese seizure of the British ship *Arrow* expanded into armed warfare that spread north along the Chinese coast to Tianjin in 1858 and ultimately into the Eight Powers occupation of Beijing in 1860.

Conflict in the north amplified the ever-present resentment and hatred of foreigners across the empire, forcing Hangzhou's officials to deal with the Nevius's lone presence in their city. To pressure their foreign residents into leaving, *yamen* officials twice arrested the Daoist monk who had rented them rooms. Officials then informed the couple that their landlord would suffer severe harm unless they left forthwith. Their departure would undoubtedly have happened anyway, since the Taiping rebels ransacked the city for the first time not long afterward. Thus, for the duration of the Taiping Rebellion in Zhejiang, Hangzhou was free of missionary foreigners but ruinously victimized by the civil war.

Meanwhile, events in Beijing proved that the Nevius's bold actions had only been a year or two ahead of their time. The Second Opium War (1856 – 1860) ended with the Convention of Beijing, a one-sided agreement whose terms legalized foreign travel anywhere in China. Furthermore, the treaty permitted foreign missionaries and their converts to proselytize openly, practice their religion freely, and purchase residences as well as land upon which to establish churches and chapels. The doors to the Chinese empire had been flung open to Christianity, and the missionaries at the Zhejiang gates rushed in as soon as the Taipings had been cleared from the province.

John Nevius was no longer in Ningbo, having taken up residence in coastal Chefoo (modern Yantai), Shandong Province. Others quickly took his place in Hangzhou, however. The year 1864 saw the arrival of Protestant missionary Rev. George E. Moule, and the next two years brought three more ministers to the city. But it was in 1867 that the first trickles became a tidal wave. In that year alone, at least nineteen foreigners arrived to convert Hangzhou to Christianity, fifteen of them as a single party led by J. Hudson Taylor, founder of the new China Inland Mission. In the period from 1864 to 1874, at least forty-four identifiable foreign missionaries, including equally committed wives, arrived in Hangzhou, plus another six in Shaoxing.

Every foreign missionary who entered Zhejiang Province likely had experiences or made observations about which they could (and often did) write or lecture. Some wrote to educate the people of their home countries about China and its people and culture. Many others wrote less but contributed to the advancement of education and medical care or such social causes as eradication of opium use, promotion of women's rights, or elimination of foot-binding. Their names have mostly passed quietly into missionary record books, their letters and diaries boxed up and gathering dust in university library archives. Yet at least a few of those individuals' life stories and accomplishments are worthy of special note.

The Ghost-Talker of Ningbo – Mary Ann Aldersey

Londoner Mary Ann Aldersey (1797 – 1868), known in Chinese as Aidisui 艾迪綏, received her introduction to Chinese language from London Missionary Society founder Robert Morrison (1782 – 1834) while still in her twenties. However, her life's work as a missionary educator only began at age 40 with a Bible school for girls of Chinese descent in Jakarta, Indonesia. When Ningbo opened as a treaty port five years later in 1842, she relocated there, becoming in the process the first-known unmarried Western woman ever to stand upon the lands of the Middle Kingdom. She was accompanied from Jakarta by three young girls: two of her former Chinese-Indonesian students, Ruth Ati and Christiana A-Kit, and Mary Ann Liesk, a twelve-year-old Scottish lass whom she had adopted at the request of the girl's parents.

Strong-willed, fiercely independent, and fearless, Miss Aldersey opened a girls' school in Ningbo, quite possibly the first ever established in China. Ten years after her arrival, and thanks to the acquired-dialect abilities of Ati and A-Kit, the school's enrollment had expanded to forty students, a surprising achievement given Aldersey's bizarre reputation among many Ningbo natives.

Ningbo's five miles of encircling walls, normally occupied mostly by soldiers and beggars, provided both elevated views over the city and countryside as well as a place for uncrowded walks. Miss Aldersey strolled along those walls at dawn every day, year-around, carrying with her a ladylike bottle of smelling salts to obscure the city's less desirable fragrances. Local people were certain her wall-walking served for communicating with spirits, evil or otherwise, aided of course by her mystical smelling salts. "Rumors abounded that Mary Ann had murdered all her own children and now wanted theirs. They said she took out her pupils' eyes before killing them."[7]

From a missionary standpoint, Mary Ann Aldersey was an early and active promoter of the budding cultural movement for Chinese women's education. To her male missionary colleagues, she demonstrated that educating girls was equally or more effective than establishing boys' schools in accessing Chinese families in their homes. Aldersey not only inspired Western missionary organizations to actively recruit female spouses and young single women for China, she served as a role model for those intrepid women.

Doctor Apricot – David Duncan Main

Of all the many Christian missionary workers resident in Hangzhou from the 1860s through the 1930s, Dr. David Duncan Main (1856 – 1934) left the inarguably greatest mark on the city and its people. Perhaps no events better measure Dr. Main's enormous impact than those on the weekend of September 8 – 9, 1934, seven years after his final departure from China. A memorial service in honor of Main's sudden passing a week earlier in Buxton, England took place on the grounds of the multi-building hospital complex he created. The Hangzhou funeral observance was attended by "a remarkable gathering of pastors, doctors, students, and patients, while the Chinese were present in large numbers."[8] The next day, a second memorial service at the nearby Leper Chapel brought such emotions to the sufferers whom Dr. Main had tended that those who rose to speak could only choke back sobs and retire, "the[ir] unspoken testimonies...more eloquent than any words."[9]

Born in 1856 Scotland, David Duncan Main became a horse-riding enthusiast while working summers at his brother-in-law's farm. It was a skill he would unexpectedly employ to advantage in adult life. He also developed a teen-aged interest in medical missionary work, undertook several years of medical training at Glasgow University and the Edinburgh Medical Missionary Society, and in 1881 married the aptly named Florence Nightingale Smith (1856 – 1942).

Although Main had hoped for a position in India, the just-married couple accepted their Church Missionary Society (CMS) assignment to Hangzhou. They arrived in Shanghai, unmet, in November 1881 and found their way to Ningbo. Another missionary on honeymoon there escorted them as far as Shaoxing. The final leg of their journey to Hangzhou was capped by sedan chair rides across the Qiantang River in December.

Doctor and Mrs. Main fell to work immediately, taking over supervision of a sixteen-bed opium treatment center and medical dispensary first opened by Dr. James J. Meadows (1835 – 1914) in 1869. They were soon inundated with patients of all sorts, finding large crowds of people waiting anxiously outside their gates every morning. Not having yet mastered the local dialect but insisting on meeting personally with each patient, they relied on assistants to act as their interpreters. They also began traveling to suburban villages and two CMS out-stations as much as thirty miles distant, tending to medical needs outside the city.

Word spread quickly in Hangzhou about Dr. Main's diagnostic and surgical skills and his wife's nursing abilities, enough so that his clientele began to include scholars and government officials. Although he had managed to expand the original opium refuge modestly, he foresaw the need for a larger hospital. Bishop George E. Moule (1828 – 1912) apparently agreed, since the necessary financing soon arrived from CMS. In what little spare time he had, Dr. Main designed the new hospital building and oversaw its construction. The grand opening of The Hospital of Universal Benevolence occurred in May 1884. "The British Consul attended, and there were Mandarins, Chinese officials, city merchants, missionaries and native Christians, and an even larger crowd of old patients. The male guests were received…in the waiting room of the new hospital…[while the women]…were received and entertained by Mrs. Main at her own house."[10]

Dr. Main's review of operations for the year 1885 reported over ten thousand patient visits, including seventy-nine attempted suicides by opium, of which sixty were saved.[11] Over the next several years, the Mains added to their hospital with a dedicated opium refuge, a Leprosy Hospital, a Home for Lepers' Children overseen by Mrs. Main, and a Medical Training College. To facilitate medical training, Dr. Main and his assistants began translating several English-language texts on medical treatment, surgery, and midwifery into Chinese.[12]

Dr. Main's medical treatments by now drew Manchu patients from the garrison and *yamen* as well, including an instance where he saved the Provincial Governor's life from a case of smallpox that had been misdiagnosed. However, it was his horseback riding skills and Western saddlery that really won over Hangzhou's Manchu population. Years later during the Boxer Rebellion in 1900, the Dowager Empress Cixi ordered all foreign missionaries and Christian converts killed. The Manchu generals in Hangzhou who allegedly ignored her edict were friends and patients of Dr. Main's.

After a furlough back in Scotland in 1890, the Mains returned and set to work on a hundred-bed Women's Hospital, opened in 1894. They later added a Convalescent Home for Tuberculosis, a Leper Home for Women, a Children's Home for Orphans, and a Nurses' Home for the hospital's expanding staff. When Isabella Bird visited Main's hospital complex in 1896, she described the men's and women's buildings as "of the latest and most approved European type…abreast of our best hospitals in lighting, ventilation, general sanitation, arrangement and organization." Bird noted the size and professional quality of the twenty-six-person staff and further praised the Women's Hospital (under Mrs. Main's charge) for its "highly varnished floor, flowers, pictures, tables, chairs, and harmonium [like a] pleasant double drawing room in a large English mansion."[13]

After another furlough in 1900, the returning couple enjoyed a riotous, celebratory reception from crowds "who escorted him to his home with flags and banners waving, rockets firing, and other demonstrations of an affectionate welcome."[14] As if they had not already accomplished enough, the Mains engineered further additions to their medical complex, including a Maternity Home, a Training Home for Midwifery, a Fresh Air Home, and an Isolation Hospital for patients suffering with contagious diseases. In 1911, the hospital added electric lights, running water, and its first X-ray machine.[15]

On his final furlough in 1921, Dr. and Mrs. Main secured funding for his crowning achievement: the Christian Medical College of Hangzhou. Opening day celebration for one of the finest medical schools in China took place on October 8, 1924. By the time of his retirement three years later, the hospital with all its annexes accommodated five hundred beds.[16] Dr. Main's hospital complex continues operation today under the name The Second Affiliated Hospital, Zhejiang University School of Medicine, on Jiefang Road.

Few foreigners asked for so little and gave so much to the Chinese people through the years of self-strengthening and revolution as Duncan and Florence Nightingale Main did for forty-five years. The people of Hangzhou so sincerely appreciated his medical and humanitarian care that they called him Dr. Apricot (杏子医生, *xingzi yisheng*). This nickname alluded to the legendary 3rd-Century physician Dong Feng 董奉 from Fujian Province, who is said to have declined payment from his patients after he successfully treated them. He asked only that they plant from one to five apricot seeds at his residence, the number depending on the seriousness of their illness. He was ultimately surrounded by an apricot forest, whose fruits he then traded for rice.[17] In later times, physicians in China came to be referred to as "from the apricot forest" and hospitals as "apricot forests."

The Teachers - Mary Vaughan and Louise H. Barnes

On December 18, 1887, Miss Mary Vaughan (1849 – 1909) arrived in Hangzhou, the city to which she had been assigned by the Church Missionary Society. As the home-schooled daughter of a CMS minister in Brighton, Vaughan had spent the first thirty-eight years of her life in social service work for her father's parish, caring for her father, and sharpening her formidable foreign language skills. After just eight months in Hangzhou, she passed her first Chinese language exam and eagerly set out on her missionary path as an educator.

In 1889, Vaughan began visiting CMS out-stations dressed in Chinese attire. She taught young children and grew increasingly interested in the more remote town and village work. In 1895, she joined forces with Miss Louise Barnes (1855 – 1927), who became a lifelong friend. They made numerous visits together over the following years to the towns and villages of the "river district" southwest of Hangzhou, opening girls' day schools in the more receptive districts. But all the while, Vaughan dreamed of someday creating a girls' school in Hangzhou itself.

Around 1906, with the invaluable assistance of Dr. Duncan Main, Mary Vaughan's dreams began to take physical shape. Funds were raised, plans were drawn, land was purchased, and construction began on a boarding school to provide young women with education beyond the middle school level. Most of the construction took place under Dr. Main's watchful eye while Vaughan was on a health furlough back in England. She recovered slowly and not fully, but nevertheless set out again for China, traveling with her close friend Louisa Barnes in mid-August 1907.

Arriving in Hangzhou, the two women found a shining new, three-story Girls' High School, but no Duncan Main. Vaughan politely refused to enter the school for her first look without the man who had made the school possible. While she awaited Dr. Main's return from a much-needed summer rest in Japan, she left Hangzhou to visit old friends in the river district. Her frail constitution was not up to the task, however, and she fell seriously ill. Vaughan was hurriedly returned to her residence in Hangzhou, where she passed away on January 8, 1908. She never once set foot in the school that she had conceived and toward whose construction she had personally donated.

One year later, on February 13, 1909, "a beautiful spring day, flags flying, Chinese guests [and numerous missionaries] crowding in,...[for] the opening day of the Mary Vaughan Girls' High School...Dr. Main took the chair and formally opened the school."[18] Principal for the new school was none other than Louise Barnes, who in earlier years had opened and overseen two of her own charitable day schools for girls.

The "advanced curriculum, with English language...textbooks, as well as plush new facilities" at Mary Vaughan High School for Girls attracted the daughters of wealthy and educated families. While many Hangzhou-area elites sensed the changing times and evolving push for female emancipation, being forward-thinking did not mean sacrificing their daughters entirely to a new cultural order. Missionary school reputations for strict discipline and adherence to traditional codes of female morality, obedience, and filiality made the decision for more advanced education rather more palatable.[19]

In August 1909, Barnes wrote to the CMS Board that among her twenty-five students, eleven were from Christian convert families and most of the remainder came from elite scholarly or official families. In fact, she proudly announced, three of those students were the great-granddaughters of the late Marquis Zeng Guofan. Their attendance was already proving to be an extraordinary inducement for other high officials to follow suit with their daughters.[20]

Zeng Baosun 曾寶蓀 (1893 – 1978), one of Zeng Guofan's great-granddaughters, would later travel to England under the explicit charge of Louise Barnes and enter the all-female Westfield College, University of London. Zeng Baosun's firsts would include first female Chinese student at the University of London (1913) and first Chinese woman to earn a Bachelor of Science degree (1916) abroad. After further study in teacher training and education at both Oxford and Cambridge, she and Barnes returned to Zeng's native Hunan Province to form the Yifang 藝芳 School for Girls[21] in 1918, modeled on the curricular concepts of the Mary Vaughan School. In a fascinating bit of role reversal, Zeng Baosun served as Yifang's first principal and Louise Barnes as an English teacher. Louise Barnes passed away from heart failure in Shanghai in 1927, aged 72.

Rumors and Resentments

While Christian missionaries opened numerous schools, medical dispensaries, opium refuges, and hospitals in the Hangzhou area, their presence was often unwelcomed and treated with all manner of enmity and suspicion, some of which manifested as conspiracy theories arising from xenophobic superstitions.

Rev. Arthur Evans Moule of the Church Missionary Society wrote of rumors circulating through Hangzhou in 1867 that Christian priests were luring children into their premises in order to slay and pickle them. Another fear passing among the people at that time asserted that members of the Presbyterian Mission were kidnapping and drowning women in a newly-built water storage tank.[22] The following year, when Hudson Taylor attempted to expand his China Inland Mission (CIM) from Hangzhou into Yangzhou, he and his foreign colleagues were variously accused of stealing the eyes of the dying, eating children, and cutting the fetuses out of pregnant women to make secret potions or medicines.[23]

Similarly, Rev. D. N. Lyon described an outbreak around Hangzhou of a "paper man craze" in 1876. Its proponents claimed that foreigners were creating human-shaped paper figures, imbuing them with a spirit force, and sending them out at night to cut men's queues. According to this rumor, the victims would then invariably die within a few months. Alternatively, those same paper figures were said to slip into homes, settle onto the chests of their chosen victims, and steal away their breath until they expired. Countermeasures included Daoist charms braided into a man's queue, painting crosses on streets and doors (since Christians were believed to be immune thanks to the crucifixes they wore), and banging on gongs at night to ward off those papery spirits.[24]

While rumors and placards stirred up emotions and occasionally incited violence, they inevitably failed to achieve the desired result of driving away such determined foreigners. Nevertheless, they fueled lingering resentments that could be, and sometimes were, easily rekindled. The missionaries' own actions occasionally created problems as well by sudden, unexpected arrivals in new cities and towns, or by inadvertently violating Chinese traditions and beliefs.

By way of example, Rev. E.B. Inslee's 1867 arrival in Hangzhou marked the opening of missionary work in China for the American Presbyterian Church (South). Within just a few years, three other ministers (M.H. Houston, John L. Stuart, and Ben Helm) had joined him. They then jointly secured land for a residence on Wushan, home to the City God's Temple and numerous lesser temples and shrines. Their chosen neighborhood was also occupied by the homes of city officials and provided delightful views of West Lake from above the hot, teeming streets. On their purchased land, the missionaries constructed a residence, a chapel, and a day school for boys.

The missionaries' presence on the hill was certainly noticed but went largely unremarked until 1873, when the family of the provincial treasurer suffered the loss from illness of his wife and one son. After engaging a *fengshui* expert to seek the cause of the family's misfortune, the grieving official received the geomancer's professional conclusion: one or more of the foreigners' buildings (apparently the boys' school)[25] had disturbed the *fengshui* of the hill dedicated to the worship of the city gods.

The Presbyterians declined when they were asked to give up their land on Wushan, even after being assured they would be compensated with land at a more geomantically acceptable location. Local officials increased their pressure by arresting the former land-owner along with everyone else involved in selling the land to Inslee and his colleagues. Even the stone mason who brokered the sale was beaten and imprisoned.[26]

When those guilt-inducing pressure tactics failed to achieve the desired departures, city officials personally delivered a letter to the American Consul in Ningbo, thereby elevating the dispute into a diplomatic matter. Negotiations and written communications between consular officials and missionaries ensued,[27] finally resulting in the requested relocation and compensation of eleven thousand Mexican silver dollars from the provincial treasury for construction of new buildings to replace those foregone on City God's Hill. At the new site, the Presbyterian missionaries quickly erected two residences, a boys' boarding school and a girls' boarding school, and two chapels.[28]

Those events recalled similar but more violent incidents several years earlier. By far the worst occurred in 1868 when the expansion-driven Hudson Taylor[29] led a group of CIM missionaries out of Hangzhou into Zhenjiang, intending to establish a station across the Yangzi River in Yangzhou. On July 20, Taylor, his wife and four children, and six more foreigners (including two unmarried young women)[30] took up residence in Yangzhou and staked their residential claim.

Grumbling crowds soon gathered at their gate, placards appeared on nearby walls, and rumors of stealing the eyes of the dying and cannibalizing young children spread. Uneasy peace prevailed until August 22, when two more foreigners arrived at the missionary residence, followed almost immediately by wild rumors of twenty-four newly-missing Yangzhou children. That same afternoon, the unrest could no longer be contained.

As their residence came under violent assault, Taylor and one colleague rushed to the office of the city prefect for assistance after being badly stoned during their escape. Inside the missionary residence, the attackers destroyed furniture and set fires in the lower level, forcing the foreigners hiding upstairs to jump from the second-floor windows. One of their party was struck by a thrown brick and lost permanent sight in one eye, and two of the ladies were badly injured in their fall.

Action by city officials eventually calmed the situation, but the incident became a minor diplomatic crisis when the Prefect of Yangzhou balked at Taylor's demand for reparations. In the end, the situation was only settled, at least to the foreigners' satisfaction, after the British Consul sailed upriver from Shanghai accompanied by an intentionally threatening gunboat. The British press expressed outrage that uncontrolled missionaries in China had nearly started a war, and there were calls in Parliament to require all British missionaries to withdraw. Foreign Secretary the Earl of Clarendon put it politely but succinctly: "Her Majesty's Government cannot delegate to Her Majesty's Servants in foreign countries the power of involving their own country in war."[31]

An incident of similar but less diplomatically inflamed nature occurred with Northern Baptist Horace Jenkins (1832 – 1908) in Jinhua in 1869. In one of the more amusing dispute resolutions, literati in Jinhua who were frustrated by their inability to achieve their eviction ends by legal means simply relocated the entire house leased by Horace Jenkins to "a temple, where it was 'deposited for safe-keeping'."[32] Other incidents occurred with James J. Meadows (1835 – 1914) and Dr. Arthur W. Douthwaite (1848 – 1899) in Huzhou (1874), and with Samuel Dodd (1832 – 1894) in Jiaxing (1877). In the last instance, Christian missionaries were forcibly expelled from the city without redress or restitution.[33]

These incidents often followed a common pattern. One or more foreigners appeared in the town unannounced and left quietly. They then returned, rented a residence, and moved in. The local people (sometimes spurred on by literati and/or officials) disputed the foreigners' presence, and conflict or violence ensued. The local authorities intervened, and the people were ordered to accept the foreign presence in accord with the latest "unequal treaty" signing.

On some occasions, the missionaries' ill-timed appearance unknowingly violated local customs or practice. For example, G.W. Painter and John Stuart were chased out of a small village in 1891, threatened with bamboo pole beatings and showered by a hail of stones, mud, and hurled clamshells. Their mistake was arriving during the peak of the silkworm raising season. The negative *fengshui* arising from their mere "foreign" presence might endanger the productive growth and transformation of the silkworm larvae into plump, plush cocoons.[34]

Through the ensuing decades of recovery, revolution, and post-imperial Republicanism, Christian religious, educational, and medical presence would persist despite occasional flare-ups of national resistance like the Boxer Rebellion. Christian missions would found and enhance hospitals, fund and develop universities, organize chambers of commerce and YMCAs, promote women's education, and campaign against opium use and foot-binding. Regardless, their presence was more often resented than welcomed, viewed as another price of power imbalance and national weakness.

Christian missionaries were tolerated to the extent their secular services (schools, hospitals, sanitoriums, orphanages) were personally or socially beneficial, but neither the missionaries nor their religion fully assimilated into Chinese culture. They were outsiders—accepted and even appreciated at most for honest intentions—and they would remain outsiders until they were later disinvited and their institutions co-opted and partially if not fully secularized. The seeds they had sown were not just religious ones, however. Inadvertently mixed in among them were seeds of self-strengthening and anti-imperialism that ultimately sprouted as national self-determination.

Chapter 15

THE IMPERIAL AGE ENDS

(1895 – 1911)

Walking in Spring by West Lake[1]

North of Lone Hill Temple, west of the Jia Pavilion,
The water's surface has just smoothed, the foot of the cloud low.
Wherever you go new-risen orioles jostle for the warmest tree:
What are they after, the newborn swallows that peck at the spring mud?

A riot of blossoms not long from now will be dazzling to the eye,
The shallow grass can hardly yet submerge the horse's hoof.
Best loved of all, to the east of the lake, where I can never walk enough,
In the shade of the green willows, the causeway of white sand.

– Bai Juyi (772 – 846)

Eyes Awakened

One of the lessons Qing military leaders learned during the Taiping Rebellion was the importance of modern naval technology. Western artillery had proven instrumental in driving rebel armies from walled cities and towns by shelling them from the floating platforms offered by steamships. One of the earliest known Chinese attempts to explore this new steam-driven technology came in 1864 when Zhejiang Governor-General Zuo Zongtang commissioned a group of Chinese engineers to build a Western-style steamship at Hangzhou's West Lake.[2] The results, although less than stellar, informed Zuo's understanding of the necessary course of action.

Rejecting British recommendations that the Qing court purchase steamships from England, Zuo submitted a memorial to the throne dated June 25, 1866. In it, he proposed the creation of a ship-building dockyard, arsenal, and school of marine engineering and navigation at coastal Fuzhou 福州, in Fujian Province. Zuo also outlined a radical start-up plan: purchase the necessary machinery from foreign sources and employ foreign engineers, technicians, and advisors (chiefly Prosper Giquel and Paul d'Aiguebelle) for five years to create a Chinese cadre of trained shipbuilders and navigators. By July 14, Zuo held the imperial edict of approval in his hands. Unable to remain in Fuzhou himself, he also chose as his successor in administering the Fuzhou Arsenal Shen Baozhen 沈葆桢 (1820 – 1879), son-in-law of Lin Zexu.

During the five-year term of Giquel's management, from 1869 – 1874 (d'Aiguebelle resigned in 1869), the navy yard at Fuzhou Arsenal employed up to seventy French engineers and launched fifteen ships. Nineteen more ships were completed from 1875 - 1897 under Chinese administration of the yard, making shipbuilding one of the Chinese empire's first modern industries. Along with the Fuzhou Arsenal ships, China's naval self-strengthening efforts included purchase of battleships from foreign nations, particularly Germany and Britain. Efforts were also made to modernize the empire's ground forces, including Li Hongzhang's Huai Army. The Japanese regarded the Chinese military strength as formidable; knowledgeable Westerners believed China could now prevail in a conflict with Japan. Such proved not to be the case, however.

By 1894, tensions between Japan and China over control of Korea flared into armed conflict on the Korean peninsula in late July. War was declared by both sides on August 1. Chinese ground losses in Korea, a Japanese incursion into Manchuria, and two crushing naval defeats (at Yalu River on September 17, 1894 and Weihaiwei 威海卫 in Shandong Province in January/February 1895) shocked Chinese officials and the educated elite. Self-strengthening had failed, leaving their nation with a humiliating defeat in just eight months, coming at the hands of a much smaller and condescendingly regarded nation. For stunned Chinese nationalists like the activist-journalist Liang Qichao 梁启超 (1873 – 1929), the sudden and deflating end to the conflict woke the Chinese nation from its "dream of 4,000 years."[3]

Hangzhou's Forced Opening

On April 17, 1895, Li Hongzhang signed the Treaty of Shimonoseki, marking the ignominious end of the Sino-Japanese conflict. In addition to recognizing Korean independence and yielding Taiwan and the Liaoning Peninsula to Japan, China was forced to pay Japan huge reparations in silver. Furthermore, Article 6 of the Treaty ordered that, effective in six months from the signing date, the cities of Shashi, Chongqing, Suzhou, and Hangzhou "shall be opened to the trade, residence, industries, and manufactures of Japanese subjects" and that "steam navigation for vessels under the Japanese flag, for the conveyance of passengers and cargo, shall be extended to the Wusong River and the Canal, from Shanghai to Suzhou and Hangzhou." The Treaty also permitted Japanese subjects "to [transport] imported merchandise into the interior of China" and "be free to engage in all kinds of manufacturing industries" in all of the existing and new treaty ports.[4]

Under the terms of existing "most favored nation" agreements, such rights automatically applied as well to Britain, Germany, France, and the United States. The terms of Shimonoseki devastated the sovereignty China had so jealously guarded for centuries. The doors had been opened not just to the four named cities, including Hangzhou, but effectively to the whole empire. And not just for Japan, but for the major industrialized nations of the West.

Hangzhou officials were now forced to negotiate with Japanese representatives for the site of a new foreign settlement. Fearing that their recent enemy would demand a location within the city walls, Hangzhou's negotiators were relieved to learn instead that the Japanese site of interest was four miles north at Gongchenqiao 珙晨桥 (in present-day Gongshu District 拱墅区), a three-arched bridge and the wharf where the Grand Canal ended and goods were unloaded.

The surrounding area was already well-populated, host to everything from restaurants and teahouses to temples and brothels, but by at least one Westerner's account, the Japanese concession zone was nearly uninhabitable. After relegating all the foreigners to concession land four miles north of the city walls, the evicted former inhabitants "rooted up all their mulberries, and left behind a large bald square swamp,…crawling with snakes, humming with mosquitoes, and reeking of malaria." For the Japanese "victors" of the recent war, the city prepared the evacuated land "by cutting the nice large square swamp into equally attractive little square swamps and intersecting them by a network of projected roads…[that] went nowhere in general."[5]

In the end, the 120-acre Japanese section of the foreign concession zone was never significantly developed. By 1925, their concession contained a consulate, a post office, and a few warehouse buildings operated by the Japan-China Steam Navigation Company.[6] The Westerners' concession areas were even less developed, home to little more than an Imperial Customs House.[7]

The Japanese ultimately confined their commercial interests to North China and the Shanghai area, largely foregoing development in their new concessions at Suzhou and Hangzhou. In 1935, over 29,000 Japanese nationals resided in Shanghai, with 14,500 more in Qingdao; the corresponding count in Hangzhou was twenty-nine.[8] The Western powers likewise chose to focus elsewhere, seeing Shanghai as their best option in the Yangzi Delta and looking further inland for opportunities in more resource-rich areas.

Aside from a cotton mill and a silk-reeling factory, Hangzhou's foreign concession area by the late 1890s was more gambling warren and red-light district than commercial-industrial zone. The hoped-for influx of foreign industry and capital into Gongchenqiao had failed to materialize. Lacking central government investment, Hangzhou's industrialization outside of silk and cotton textiles tended toward modest commercial and consumer enterprises: "electric companies and flour mills…match, soap, candle, camphor, paper, and a few machine factories; or brick kilns, food-processing plants, and printing presses."[9] Wang Liping summarized the city's overall situation: "As it entered the twentieth century, Hangzhou was a stagnant, marginalized city, struggling to reposition itself in a drastically changed world."[10]

Educational Reform Takes Root

Liang Qichao was not alone in assessing the results of the Sino-Japanese War as an awakening from a "dream of 4,000 years." Intellectuals and educators throughout China began searching for paths to educational reform. In Shaoxing, a potent voice for New Learning came from one of the city's civic and charitable leaders, Xu Shulan徐樹蘭 (1837 – 1902).

Xu's father had provided financial support to government troops during the Taiping conflict, and Shulan's post-rebellion philanthropy followed suit. In addition to focusing on water supply and control issues, he founded charitable homes for orphans and widows and assisted in famine relief.[11] In 1897, in response to the nation's defeat in the Sino-Japanese War, he established one of the early schools for foreign learning, the Shaoxing School of Chinese and Western Studies (绍兴中西学堂, Shaoxing Zhongxi Xuetang).

One of his school's most brilliant students and a future president of Beijing University, Jiang Menglin 蒋梦麟 (1886 – 1964), wrote frankly (and rather astonishingly) in his autobiography about how the expanded academic environment at Zhongxi Xuetang profoundly impacted his understanding of the natural world:

> The first and most surprising thing I learned in this school was that the earth is round like a ball....I was dumbfounded on being further told that lightning is created by electricity and is not the reflection from the mirror of a goddess; that thunder is a by-product of the same electricity and not the beating of a drum by the god of thunder. In elementary physics I learned how rain is formed. It made me give up the idea that a gigantic dragon showers it from his mouth like a fountain high above in the clouds.[12]

Seven years after founding Zhongxi Xuetang, Xu Shulan also created arguably the earliest version of a public library in China, the Guyue Cangshulou 古越藏書樓. Xu donated the land, the building, and a private collection of more than 70,000 volumes, created rules for organization, management, and use of the collection, and opened it to the public at no charge.[13]

In the closing years of the 19th Century, Hangzhou Mayor Lin Qi 林啓 (1839 – 1900) also surveyed Hangzhou's academic landscape with equal concern. The city housed six traditional schools of higher learning, but Lin viewed them all as inadequate to the vital challenges of new learning to foster national strengthening.[14] His solution, actively supported by Zhejiang Governor Liao Shoufeng 廖寿丰 (1836 – 1901) and the local gentry, came in the form of a new school whose name, Qiushi Academy (求是書院, Qiushi shuyuan), drew from the ancient phrase 实事求是 (shishi qiushi), "seeking truth from facts."

Qiushi Academy opened in 1897 with thirty students. Most of them had already begun climbing the traditional academic ladder of the civil service examination system but were now seeking "pragmatic" knowledge. Working out of a temple building, students received instruction in subjects that prefigured a modern engineering school: agriculture, mining, manufacturing, and the like. The student body expanded quickly as enthusiasm grew for reform and self-strengthening. In 1903, Qiushi Academy became Zhejiang Higher Education Institute. By 1907, enrollment exceeded three hundred students.[15] Change was in the air, especially among the young.

The same year (1897) that Qiushi Academy opened, Western Christian educators in Hangzhou founded the Hangchow Presbyterian College, building upon already well-established roots. As early as 1845, Presbyterian missionaries had formed the Ningbo Boys Academy in that newly-opened port city. Their academic objective at the time was strictly religious, seeking to train native Chinese converts as ministers.

The school moved to Hangzhou in 1867, where it maintained a modest and somewhat precarious presence as the Hangzhou Presbyterian Boys' School. The school's fortunes improved considerably in 1880 when Junius H. Judson (1852 – 1930) arrived to take over its administration. Judson revised the curriculum, elevated the academic standards, enhanced the physical plant with new laboratories, and extended the high school program to six years, effectively transforming it into a junior college. In 1897, the school became the Hangchow Presbyterian College. Although the college closed for an entire term in late 1900 due to safety concerns during the Boxer uprising, it resumed operation soon after with new equipment and a growing enrollment.

The Qing government's abolition of the civil service examination system in 1905 further spurred the school's growth and expansion. In 1906, the Board of Directors approved exploration of sites for a larger campus outside Hangzhou's city walls. Their search led to acquisition of an idyllic setting about five miles southwest of the city:

> At present about eighty-five acres of land have been purchased on the Hangchow [Qiantang] River....There is a plateau one hundred feet above the level of the river's mean tide, which will form the campus, and from this the hills rise upwards to a height of four hundred feet. On the east is a stream of spring water sufficient to supply all our needs, and the river front has a beach of sand and pebbles suited to swimming and bathing, while in front, to the southeast, is the Hangchow Bay, and to the southwest are chains upon chains of beautiful hills.[16]

The new campus would not open for another five years. For the moment, however, Zhejiang Higher Education Institute and Hangchow Presbyterian College would continue to operate on parallel tracks. Their paths were not yet set to intersect, although that day would eventually arrive.

In addition to its role as an early progenitor of modern Zhejiang University, a historically curious but little-known sidebar emerged from the original Ningbo Boys' Academy. The school's first graduate to be ordained as a minister, Jin Linyou 金麟友 (d. 1866), was assigned as a pastor to the church in Yuyao. Tragically, Jin and his wife fell victims to cholera in 1866, leaving behind their two-year-old daughter, Jin Yunmei 金韻梅 (1864 - 1934) and seven-year-old son. The two orphaned children were then raised by missionaries Dr. Divie B. McCartee (1820 – 1900) and his wife Juana.

More than twenty years later, the young girl, known in the West as Dr. Yamei Kin, would achieve distinction in 1888 as the first Chinese woman to receive a medical degree in the United States. She graduated at the head of her class from the Women's Medical College of the New York Infirmary in 1885.[17] Dr. Kin is generally credited as the first person to introduce tofu to American food scientists, having been asked by the U.S. Department of Agriculture in 1917 "as part of a wider effort to develop new sources of protein for American soldiers during World War I."[18]

A Dramatic Appeal for Women's Education

At the outset of the Qing Dynasty in 1648, Han Chinese residents and businesses occupying a sizable area in the northwestern district of Hangzhou's walled city had been forcibly evicted in order to construct the Manchu Garrison. The new occupants—Manchu officials, soldiers, and their families—were segregated from Hangzhou's Han Chinese residents by a gated inner wall for both physical security and ostensibly to preserve their culture, language, values, and social practices from Han influence.[19]

Over the succeeding two and one-half centuries, evolving social and cultural movements among the much larger native Chinese population inevitably penetrated Hangzhou's garrison walls. One such area of influence was the incipient struggle for women's education, specifically schools and school attendance for young girls. Christian missionaries and Chinese activists alike pursued this objective, often by creating and operating the primary and middle schools they sought. However, no one in Hangzhou was prepared for the news story they read on December 30, 1905.

Eighteen months earlier in June 1904, a Manchu woman named Guaerjia Huixing 惠興 (1870 – 1905) decided to open a new private school for Manchu girls. She set out on a fund-raising campaign among the Manchu population in Hangzhou, but the donations she secured were not nearly sufficient to begin her work. Widowed at age nineteen with a son (Jin Xian) still to raise, she had few resources of her own. Huixing pushed bravely forward regardless, naming her school Zhenwen Women's School 贞文女子學校 (Zhenwen nüzi xuexiao), loosely translated as the Women's School of Purity (zhen as in zhenjie 贞洁, chastity or virtue) and Progress (wen as in wenming 文明, civilization).[20]

On June 26, 1904, Huixing "...assembled many famous local people to discuss establishing a women's school." In the midst of her impassioned speech about the importance of education for national development, she "... suddenly exposed one of her arms in front of all the people and cut a piece of flesh from it. She swore: '... If the school has to be closed one day, I will die with it.'"[21] The school struggled during its first year of operation, running out of money several times and barely staying afloat. Frustrated by her inability to garner financial support or even collect on private donations she had been promised, Huixing fulfilled her threat by committing suicide (by opium poisoning) in the final days of 1905, leaving behind a solemn but hopeful letter to her pupils.[22] She was just 35 years old.

Within weeks, Huixing's actions became a national *cause celebre*. Some lauded her passion and support for women's education as chivalrous. Others saw her cutting of flesh as a transparent allusion to ancient Confucian prescriptions about female filial piety: caring for one's parents' or in-laws' nourishment by serving one's own flesh as a last resort. Calls for public honors for Huixing's martyrdom on behalf of women's education, still a too-radical notion among conservative officials, were ultimately recognized but redirected toward her chaste widowhood, a more politically palatable virtue.

A memorial ceremony on February 2, 1906 at a girls' school in Beijing drew five hundred attendees, with speakers praising Huixing's sacrifice on behalf of the nation. One speaker gushed hyperbolically that Huixing was "the greatest woman in women's circle in China's six thousand years of history."[23] Huixing in death was no longer a "hated Manchu woman"; she was now appropriated as a national heroine and martyr of the Chinese people.

Before the end of 1906, plays celebrating her life were already being written and performed in Beijing and Tianjin to raise money for Zhenwen Academy. Even Empress Dowager Cixi attended performances of two different Huixing plays at the Summer Palace. Not coincidentally, the court issued new "Regulations for Womens' Schools" in March 1907 in support of women's education.[24] Meanwhile charitable contributions for the school poured in from across the nation. Zhenwen Academy reopened in April 1907 to a new life under a new name: Huixing Women's School. Enrollment rose immediately to sixty students, and construction began on multiple new campus buildings.[25] Remarkably, the Hangzhou Huixing Middle School continues in operation today— on Huixing Road, naturally—still located within the boundaries of what was once the Manchu Garrison.

The movement for women's education began with individuals like Gu Ruopu, Shang Jinglan, Yuan Mei, and Chen Wenshu and was seconded by Western missionaries after 1842. However, its rapid expansion in the 1890s prefigured the social and political revolutions soon to come. In 1877, Western missionary societies had reported a national total of just thirty-eight girls' schools and 524 students; by 1896, less than two decades later, those figures had grown eightfold to 308 schools and nearly thirteenfold to 6,798 pupils.[26] In 1907, two years after Huixing's suicide, the Qing government reported the existence of four hundred Chinese girls' schools, nearly all of them primary school level.

A handful of post-primary schools had been established for young women who wished to continue their education, but they were strictly vocational in nature. In Hangzhou, for example, young women could attend schools for sericulture, handicrafts, nursing, or midwifery.[27] After 1907, post-secondary options for female students still remained limited by imperial law to normal schools, that is, training schools for kindergarten or public girls' school teachers. Those who once taught or were taught in the privacy of household "inner chambers" could now at least be teachers or students in the public domain.[28]

It would be another twenty years before an education leader from Shaoxing would begin removing the last barriers to women's full educational opportunity. But at the dawn of the 20th Century, women's learning was fast evolving from household-focused, centered on female virtue, and demonstrated only in the privacy of the inner chambers to supporting personal desires for public self-actualization and greater socioeconomic productivity. The objectives of women's education were rapidly expanding from "for the self" and "for the family" to include "for the nation."[29]

China's First Female Travel Writer

Writing about long journeys and visits to famous sites within China evolved over the centuries into a culturally respectable form of self-expression among the scholar-official class. Such prose writing was an exclusively male domain, since women seldom traveled and were strongly socially discouraged, if not forbidden, from such public forms of self-expression. These barriers were shattered in 1904 with the publication of *Travels of 1903* (癸卯旅行记, *Guimao lüxing ji*) by Shan Shili 单士厘 (1858 – 1945).

Born in Haining, Jiaxing Prefecture, into a family of scholars and high officials, Shan Shili was the unfortunate victim of her mother's early death. However, she was also the fortunate recipient of a thorough education in classical poetry, painting, and history from her maternal uncle, Xu Renmu 許仁沐, a scholar and author of numerous books. Xu also inculcated in his niece the traditional values of all gentlewomen (闺秀, *guixiu*): to be sexually virtuous, demure, unpretentious, submissive, and filled with filial piety.

At the relatively late age of 29, Shan married into another open-minded and scholarly family, that of Qian Xun 錢恂 (1853 – 1927) of Huzhou. In 1890, just five years into their marriage, Qian Xun traveled to Western Europe as an attaché to a diplomatic mission through England and France, and then on to Italy. Shan Shili remained in China at that time with her young children. When Qian Xun returned home and related the story of Marco Polo's travels,[30] Shan Shili's imagined life lay spread out before her.

Wish fulfillment first arrived in 1899 when Qian Xun was assigned to oversee Chinese students in Japan. Over the next four years, Shan Shili made several journeys back and forth between China and her husband's residence in Japan, meeting educated Japanese women and learning the language with sufficient fluency to do translations. Her two sons and several grandchildren resided in Japan with her, as did a daughter-in-law (Qian Fengbao) who in 1901 may have been the first Chinese woman to study in Japan.[31]

After Shan Shili joined her husband in 1903 on his diplomatic travels in Korea and Russia, she incorporated travel observations and her thoughts on political events, women's issues, women's traveling, and modern Chinese life in *Travels of 1903*. In particular, she declared her conviction that "the barriers to female mobility [were] social and psychological rather than physical."[32] Published in 1904 with a preface by her husband,[33] Shan's book was groundbreaking, as much essay as travelog.

In his preface, Qian Xun declared his wife's written record of her 1903 travels as "an accomplishment that no Chinese women [sic] had ever managed before."[34] In her own preface, Shan wrote that her book "might benefit [women] readers by widening their scope of knowledge," adding, "If women of my country were to chance to read this diary and aspire to travel themselves, then my wish would be satisfied."[35] Was ever there written a quieter call to arms?

After Russia, Qian Xun and Shan Shili continued their diplomatic journeys, which took them to Holland and Italy for Qian's ambassadorial postings between 1907 and 1909. Writing of her European travels in her second travel book, *Notes on the Quiet Return Home* (*Guiqian ji* 归潜记), Shan shifted her focus to the new artistic world that suddenly opened before her: gothic architectural treasures, Roman antiquities and statuary, classical and contemporary paintings, even traditional Western depictions of female nudity.[36]

Her uncle's long-ago lessons in art served her admirably as she strove to provide her readers with a visual sense of these works. Her rapidly developing aesthetic and intellectual appreciation of Western art and architecture were evidenced by her claim to having visited St. Peter's Basilica in Vatican City as many as thirty times.[37] Her essays also reflected an impressive degree of scholarly research as she tackled topics ranging from Greek mythology to Marco Polo to the history of Western religions.

Because Qian Xun predeceased his wife by sixteen years, Shan Shili's sons supported her in Beijing through her later years, during which time she continued ceaselessly to write. Through it all, she encouraged women to broaden their intellectual horizons, calling avidly for universal education for Chinese women and vigorously opposing foot-binding. Yet she also advised women to preserve the *guixiu* values by which women had abided for countless centuries. One could argue that although Shan Shili lived an admirably revolutionary life, she was never herself a true revolutionary. *That* woman, more than fifteen years Shan Shili's junior, arrived in Japan from Shaoxing in 1904, the same year Shan published her *Travels of 1903*.

Hangzhou Inspires

For at least a dozen centuries, poets, painters, and scholars had found creative inspiration in Hangzhou and in its waters and surrounding hills. In the late spring of 1908, a wealthy American couple found one of their most important charitable causes in Hangzhou, and their eighteen-year-old son discovered his life's mission.

David B. Gamble (1847 – 1923) had the great good fortune to be born the son of James Gamble (1803 – 1891), one of the co-founders with William Procter of the famed Procter & Gamble Company. After his own career was cut short by illness, David and his wife, Mary Huggins Gamble (1855 – 1929), invested much of their time on the religious training and worldly education of the three Gamble boys: Cecil (1884 – 1956), Sidney (1890 – 1968),[38] and Clarence (1894 – 1966). The boys' religious education centered around the Presbyterian Church, where their father held a seat on the Presbyterian Board of Foreign Missions. The young men's wide-ranging secular education included a four-month-long family tour through Europe in 1902.

In 1906, after the American Presbyterian Mission approved construction of a college in Hangzhou, they enlisted Robert F. Fitch (1880 – 1953) to barnstorm

America as a fundraiser for the new school. Fitch, the son of a well-known China missionary,[39] had grown up in China and had been stationed in Ningbo as principal of a boys' school. Along his fundraising way through the U.S. in 1907, he met the Gambles, who expressed such great interest in the prospective Hangchow Christian College that Fitch invited them to visit the city and inspect the planned campus site. Thinking bigger, the senior Gambles mapped out a 1908 East Asia itinerary for themselves and their two younger boys, Clarence (age 14 in 1908) and Sidney (age 18). They would spend four weeks in Japan, two weeks in China, three weeks in Korea, and finish with six more weeks in Japan. The younger Clarence served as family journal-keeper, and although both boys took photographs, Sidney proved to have the finer eye.

The Gambles arrived in Shanghai to the warm greetings of Robert Fitch on May 9, 1908. Two days later, they stepped aboard the boat that would transport them through the Yangzi delta plain and Grand Canal into northern Zhejiang. On their first full day in Hangzhou (May 13), Fitch and the Gambles traveled by sedan chair to the planned campus site, stopping along the way to photograph the Leifeng Pagoda and the neighboring Jingci Temple as well as the Liuhe Pagoda alongside the Qiantang River.

Over the succeeding six days, the Gambles wandered the city market, visited a Christian girls' school, rowed on West Lake, met Duncan Main and toured his hospital complex, explored Lingyin Temple, took in the view from atop the Qiantang Gate, and browsed the wares at a Chinese pharmacy. Five more days back in Shanghai, including a visit to Yu Garden (豫园, Yuyuan), and the family was on its way to Korea and Japan. Before departing China, the Gambles pledged a donation of $7,500 toward a dormitory (later named Gamble Hall) at the new Hangchow Christian College. The Gambles subsequently made additional donations for a sports field and a swimming pool, both named after them.

Upon his return to America in fall 1908, Sidney Gamble enrolled in Princeton to study labor welfare and labor economics. After graduating with a Master's Degree in Social Economics from UC Berkeley, he returned again to Hangzhou in 1917 to join Robert Fitch on a harrowing exploration up the Yangzi River into remote areas of Sichuan Province and the Tibetan borderlands. Later that year, Sidney settled in Beijing to conduct a social survey for the YMCA that led to his first academic publication, *Peking: A Social Survey* (1921).

The path for his life's work was set: additional field research visits to China from 1924 – 1927 and again in 1931 – 1932, resulting in five more published books on Chinese family and village life.[40] Sidney Gamble's works are still regarded as classics in the field of Chinese sociology and anthropology, but his lifelong enthusiasm for Chinese culture and life, his love of photography, and his innate human empathy and artistic sensibility combined to make his archives[41] of over 5,000 photos equally valuable to posterity. And it all began in 1908 with a visit to Hangzhou, where young Sidney Gamble fell in love with China.

Reform and revolution filled the air in *fin de siècle* China. From Shanghai to Hangzhou and around the Yangzi Delta area, the scent was palpable. Internal reform, anti-imperialism, anti-Qing and anti-Confucian sentiments, anti-opium and anti-foot-binding crusades, universal education, and women's rights and education…all were catching fire and spreading. One early sign of the times was promoting the wider use of the vernacular language instead of the elite classical language. A Western missionary journal noted the appearance in September 1901 of "a paper or magazine" in the "colloquial" or common language, published by "a few young men in Hangzhou."[42]

In 1903, a new periodical, produced by Zhejiangese students in Tokyo (most of them former students at the Qiushi Academy), captured the revolutionary zeitgeist. Its very name, *Tide of Zhejiang* (浙江潮, *Zhejiang chao*), suggested the well-known image of the surging Qiantang River tidal bore sweeping away outmoded tradition, archaic ways, Manchus, and foreigners in its onrushing waters. The coming tide was, they hoped, the tide of revolution.

Among the intellectual leaders of the early revolutionary movement was Zhang Binglin 章炳麟 (1869 – 1936), proud son of a scholarly family in Yuhang 余杭 (now a district of Hangzhou City). After years of classical studies, Zhang reacted to the Qing Dynasty's failures in the Sino-Japanese War (1894 – 1895) by promoting national reform. When the Hundred Days Reform movement of 1898 collapsed, he wrote scathingly of the conservative opposition and sharply criticized Empress Dowager Cixi 慈禧太后 (1835 – 1908). Forced soon after to flee the country for safety, he headed to Japan (soon to become the favored destination of anti-Manchu student activists and revolutionaries). Along with his writings, Zhang demonstrated his revolutionary commitment with the most visible anti-Manchu act possible: he severed his queue.

In 1900, he published the first version of *Book of Persecutions*, (訄書, *Qiushu*), his stridently anti-Manchu essay collection. The following year, Zhang publicly reinforced his break with the Qing court. His August article, published with the openly inflammatory title "On the Correct Hatred of the Manchus" (正仇满论, "Zheng chou Man lun"), argued that only revolution, and not reform, could put the nation on the proper path to national strength.

Zhang fled to Japan again in early 1902 to avoid arrest. While there, he helped organize a revolutionary assembly with another provocative name: "Meeting to Commemorate the 242nd Anniversary of the National Destruction of China," an undisguised reference to the end of the Ming resistance in 1660 and the death of the last legitimate Ming heir to the throne.[43] Although the planned meeting was blocked by Japanese authorities, no one could question Zhang's revolutionary bona fides, or his daring.

Having returned to Shanghai in 1903, Zhang's overt radicalism peaked. In an "open letter," he aggressively attacked the positions espoused by Kang Youwei 康有为 (1858 – 1927), leader of the Qing reformist movement. In doing so, he made dismissive references to past Qing emperors by using their personal names and referring to the current Guangxu Emperor 光绪帝 (r. 1875 – 1908) as ignorant: literally, as a person unable to distinguish beans from noodles.[44] The Shanghai newspaper *Subao* 苏报 quoted Zhang's open letter and other of his writings on June 29. He was arrested by the Shanghai International Settlement police the very next day.

Two weeks later, Zhang Binglin and five other defendants appeared in court, charged with sedition in what came to be known as the *Subao* Case. When hearings began in early December after resolving some jurisdictional disputes, Zhang freely admitted that he wrote the articles in question but had no involvement in their publication in *Subao*. On May 21, 1904, the Settlement court handed down its guilty verdict and a sentence of three years' hard labor and permanent exile from the International Settlement. Zhang devoted much of his prison time to intense study of Buddhism and became a devout follower and philosophizer for the balance of his life.

Meanwhile, the notoriety surrounding the *Subao* Case elevated rather than suppressed revolutionary fever, creating more opposition press and helping sell out multiple printings of books like Zou Rong's 邹容 (1885 – 1905) government-banned *The Revolutionary Army* (革命军, *Geming jun*).[45] Growing enthusiasm for radical reform and pragmatic, non-Confucian, "Western learning" (西学, *xixue*) in subject areas like science, medicine, philosophy, economics, and literature drove increasing numbers of Chinese students to Japan—from just nine in 1896 to one thousand in 1903 and fifteen thousand in 1906—where they fed on one another's revolutionary fervor.[46]

Upon his release in 1906, Zhang Binglin was personally escorted by representatives of Sun Yat-sen's 孙中山 (Sun Zhongshan, 1866 – 1925) new Revolutionary Alliance (同盟会, Tongmenghui) to a ship headed for Japan. At the other end of the voyage, he was greeted and feted by two thousand overseas Chinese students. A Han Chinese subject of the Manchu Qing Dynasty who had openly criticized the Beijing government, insulted the honor of the Kangxi and Qianlong emperors, belittled the current emperor, and in so many words called for the overthrow of the dynasty, was now a revolutionary hero.

In Tokyo, Zhang took over editorial management of the official organ of the Revolutionary Alliance, the *People's Journal* (民把, *Minbao*) until the Japanese government banned it in 1908. The contagion of revolutionary fever for self-determination was spreading, and among the younger generation of educated elites, a full-scale outbreak was brewing. The "tides of Zhejiang" were swelling.

Foreign Railroad Rights Derailed

Beyond opening the Fuzhou Arsenal in the late 1860s for shipbuilding, Chinese intellectuals and the Qing court recognized the inevitability of new technologies such as steam-powered industrial machinery, macadamized roads, telegraphy, and telephony. Each of these technologies brought complex challenges, not only in ownership and implementation but in their uprooting of traditional ways of life and forms of employment. In the early 1900s, no form of industrialization was more essential to China's future, and more provocative in its implementation, than railroads.[47] Zhejiang Province, with Hangzhou as its center, proved to be a flashpoint.

As early as 1863, a mostly British consortium petitioned the Qing government for the right to build a Shanghai – Suzhou railway. Five years later, Sir Rowland Macdonald Stephenson (1808 – 1895) proposed a line from Shanghai to Nanjing, and from there to far southwestern Yunnan Province, ultimately to link up with a British-Indian network. With persistence and no small amount of duplicity, the British managed in 1876 to build a ten-mile demonstration line northward from Shanghai to Wusong 吴淞 on the Yangzi River.[48] After a year of controversial operation, however, the Chinese government bought the foreign-operated line solely in order to dismantle it.

As with the Germans to the north, the British in Shanghai viewed railroads as a potential gold mine. Virgin soil on which to create a national railway network promised profitable opportunities for financing, construction, operation, and shared or even full ownership of a large part of the new rail system, as well as access to China's interior lands. European nations and consortiums engaged in what amounted to a territorial race for influence and profits.

In 1898, the newly-formed British & Chinese Corporation[49] obtain several railway development concessions from Beijing, including a Shanghai – Nanjing line through Jiangsu Province and a Suzhou – Hangzhou – Ningbo line prospectively linking Suzhou with the major cities of northern Zhejiang. In spite of strenuous opposition from gentry and officials in Jiangsu Province, negotiations for the Shanghai – Nanjing line continued until an agreement signed in 1903 authorized project financing of 3,250,000 English pounds through the British & Chinese Corporation. Work on the Yangzi Delta's first major rail line began in 1904; the Shanghai – Suzhou section went into operation in 1906, with the whole line operational in 1908.

Meanwhile, opposition to British financing and control over the prospective Suzhou – Hangzhou – Ningbo line swelled in northern Zhejiang. The gentry class rightly viewed railroads as a Chinese national asset and British involvement as both blatant imperialism and a threat to the nation's future strength. Appeals to Beijing to revoke the Suzhou – Hangzhou - Ningbo concession went nowhere; the Qing government feared alienating a foreign power. Even though the cancellation effort fell short, an anti-imperialist, rights recovery movement had been born.

In 1903, Zhejiang's provincial representatives contended that the original concession agreement required the British to "take prompt steps" to survey and lay out the planned route for the line. A hurried survey might have taken place shortly after signing back in 1898, but no report had ever been produced and no construction work initiated.[50] The British had simply pocketed the concession. Provincial gentry now argued that the concession agreement should be nullified by this breach. They firmly believed the province could self-finance by selling shares in the new railway line, enabling Chinese citizens to fund a Chinese railway designed, built, operated, and owned by the people and government of Zhejiang.

While officials in Beijing sparred with the British & Chinese Corporation over the status of the original concession, hundreds of Zhejiang merchants and gentry met in the second half of 1905 to form an independent Zhejiang Railway Company with its own board of directors. Their actions were precipitated by yet another reported request for a railroad concession from an American group seeking to link Hangzhou with Jiangxi Province to the southwest. In September, with imperial authorization, the new Zhejiang company began soliciting subscriptions, gathering enough financial support (two million yuan pledged in the first ten days) to begin construction on modest segments of the new railway line under the watchful eye of a Chinese engineer trained in the United States.

Those first efforts, named the Jiangshu Line and planned to be linked to the proposed Shanghai line, began in 1907 at Gongchenqiao, the terminal wharf of the Grand Canal, about five miles north of the city wall. This inaugural effort at rail development somewhat mirrored an earlier Japanese request to build a 3.5-mile line from their foreign concession at Gongchenqiao Bridge southward through Jianggan District, a proposal quickly rejected out of concern that it would draw business toward the foreign concession area and away from the city.[51]

In 1907, the new, Chinese-constructed rail line began at the Grand Canal's endpoint, skirted the wall on Hangzhou's east side, and then curled south and west another five miles to the small town of Zhakou 闸口, a busy market town with a wharf on the Qiantang River. Connecting the Grand Canal with the Qiantang River would enhance commercial transport into interior Zhejiang as well as Anhui and Jiangxi Provinces. Because the resulting railway line curved gently around Hangzhou's eastern boundary, all five of its stations were inconveniently located outside the city wall. The Jiangshu Line proved to be a useful learning experience, but poor construction limited engine speeds to no more than ten miles an hour over a railway line less than twenty miles in length.[52]

Spurred on by aggressive protestations from local Zhejiang and Jiangsu officials and gentry, negotiations continued in Beijing with the British. However, under the proposed agreement issued on October 20, 1907, the Suzhou–Hangzhou–Ningbo line would still be financed and controlled by the British. Two days later, mass protests against that agreement broke out in Hangzhou. Zhejiang's provincial leaders sought nothing less than the removal of all British involvement or influence. Further discussion in which Zhejiang representatives were called upon to participate finally achieved a somewhat convoluted but grudgingly acceptable arrangement on November 29.

Under terms of the new agreement, not signed until March 1908, British & Chinese Corporation would provide financing of 1,500,000 pounds sterling, secured by a combination of subscriptions already collected, future earnings of the Zhejiang Railway Company, and surpluses from British-controlled railways in northern China. By the common consent of all parties, the British loan would be taken on not by Zhejiang Railway Company but by the national Board of Posts and Communications which would, in turn, provide financing of up to 10,000,000 *yuan* to Zhejiang Railway and a similar company for Jiangsu Province. In addition, chief engineering responsibility would shift to a Zhejiang-chosen British subject, and the line itself would adopt a new route and name: the Shanghai–Hangzhou–Ningbo line, no longer to connect to Suzhou.[53]

The 112-mile, Shanghai-to-Hangzhou leg of the new line was completed and put into operation in August 1909. The next year, a new gate for the railway line was cut through the city wall, enabling passenger trains to terminate inside Hangzhou's walls at the new City Station (城站, Chengzhan, built in 1910) rather than outside the walls at Qingtai Gate Station.[54] What had until now been a three-day boat trip via a complicated canal network became a three-hour train ride, bringing the two cities into connections both obvious (day tourism and shopping) and unforeseen (revolutionary networking).

The rail link to Ningbo received less attention, perhaps because there would be no bridge of any kind crossing the Qiantang River until 1937. Small sections of the Hangzhou–Ningbo leg were completed in 1912 and 1914, but full connection on the southern side of the Qiantang between Xiaoshan 萧山 and Ningbo would still not occur until 1936. The Shanghai–Hangzhou railway line would also be extended in 1937 to reach Changsha in Jiangxi Province and Zhuzhou in Hunan Province. The railway segment into the interior provinces became known as the Zhegan Line.

The rights recovery movement in Zhejiang showed the growing provincial willingness to assert home interests before those of the imperial throne. The battle to develop and control national assets also demonstrated the increasing voice and activism of merchants, gentry, students, and teachers in fashioning local policy and the growing public sentiment against foreign intervention and imperialism. Even for less activist citizens, purchasing railroad stock became a form of patriotic resistance to foreign intrusion. Unrecognized at the time, Zhejiang's railway movement was also grooming leaders for bigger things soon to come.

"Competes with Men" [55]

Shan Shili lived her broadened life by following in her husband's footsteps and adhering to female norms like the Three Obediences (三从, *sancong*), which prescribed that a woman follow her father and elder brother in youth, follow her husband in marriage, and as a widow, follow her son. Qiu Jin 秋瑾 (1875? – 1907)[56] charted a completely independent path and obliterated numerous such traditions on her way to becoming a national, if not world-historical, figure.

Qiu Guijin 秋闺瑾 was born in Xiamen 厦门, a coastal city of Fujian Province in southeast China, while her father, Qiu Shounan 秋寿南 (1850 – 1901, *juren* 1873), served as a legal secretary. The Qiu family were modestly well-off and respected citizens of Shanyin (Shaoxing), the native place of the legendary filial daughter Cao'er. The paternal lineage traced back to several successive generations of scholar-officials; her mother's family sported a similar scholar-official heritage.

Qiu Guijin's well-traveled formative years included time spent in Xiamen, in her family home in Shaoxing, and such other places as her father's employment dictated, including Hunan Province. Her upbringing reflected all the contradictions expressed later in her adult life. She was well-educated in reading and writing of poetry and literature, endured having her feet bound, and was trained in *guixiu* traditions like embroidery. Yet she also demonstrated an unconventional female enthusiasm for archery (and later, fencing), horseback riding, swords, martial arts stories, and wine drinking, traits patently reminiscent of Liu Rushi and earlier female knights-errant.

The first defining event of Qiu's adult life came in 1896 when the family consummated her arranged marriage to Wang Tingjun 王廷鈞 (1879 – 1909), the youngest scion of a wealthy Hunan merchant family. Wang was not only Qiu's junior by four years, he was her decidedly intellectual inferior. Nevertheless, she submitted to the marriage and soon became the mother of two children, son Wang Yuande 王沅德 (1897 – 1955) and daughter Wang Guifen 王桂芬 (1901 – 1967). Her life retreated into the mundane world of the traditional Chinese wife: running a household, dealing with in-laws, raising and educating children, and writing occasional poetry.

In 1902 or 1903, the family relocated to Beijing where Wang Tingjun took up an official post, acquired not through examination or merit but by purchase. Life in the more cosmopolitan imperial capital opened Qiu's social sphere to other well-educated and well-informed women who shared their wide-ranging reading and discussion interests. At home, however, Qiu increasingly despised her husband's intellectual shallowness, his arrogance and condescension toward others, his gambling and carousing, and particularly his disinterest in the welfare and future of the nation. She wrote ominously to her brother that her husband's "behavior is worse than an animal's...he treats me as less than nothing."[57]

One reputed marital clash in Beijing had Wang Tingjun abandoning Qiu to visit a brothel with his friends. In retaliation, she dressed as a man (a forbidden behavior) to take her maid and children to a Beijing opera performance. An embarrassed Wang Tingjun slapped his wife in the face when she returned home. Afterwards, she moved into a hotel and wore men's clothes more regularly, drinking in public and reading revolutionary literature.[58] Frustrated with both the material comforts and restrictions in her life, she grew increasingly radicalized. In February 1904, Qiu freed her feet (and, metaphorically, her soul) from the bindings of her childhood, effectively declaring independence from her *guixiu* life.

Finally, in June 1904, Qiu undertook the second defining action of her life. Inspired by the support and encouragement of Hattori Shigeko (1872 – 1952), whose husband was a visiting Japanese professor in Beijing, Qiu pawned her dowry jewelry for cash, abandoned her husband and children, and boarded a ship in Shanghai, bound for Tokyo. In Japan, a nation where by 1904 ninety percent of the female population already attended school,[59] she joined the first wave of Chinese women seeking on their own to advance their education through "foreign learning."

Just before she left for Tokyo, Qiu Guijin renamed herself Qiu Jin ("Autumn Jade"), dropping the 闺*gui* character (meaning boudoir or women's chambers). She would no longer stand for being the brilliant jade jewel of someone else's inner chambers. From Qiu's perspective, the only way for a woman to take on men's roles was to become a man—even if it meant dressing as one.

No doubt bearing the heavy emotional load of leaving her young children behind in China, Qiu Jin lamented poetically while on the seas, heading for Japan.

Regrets: Lines Written en Route to Japan

> Sun and moon have no light left, earth is dark;
> Our women's world is sunk so deep, who can help us?
> Jewelry sold to pay this trip across the seas,
> Cut off from my family I leave my native land.
> Unbinding my feet I clean out a thousand years of poison,
> With heated heart arouse all women's spirits.
> Alas, this delicate kerchief here
> Is half stained with blood, and half with tears."[60]

While still aboard the same ship, she wrote another poem that announced her patriotic and revolutionary focus. She titled her poem for context and motive, while her eight written lines describe her intent:

Written in the Boat Amid the Yellow Sea upon Seeing the Japanese Military Map for the Russo-Japanese War and upon a Japanese Co-traveler's Request for a Poem as a Gift

> Coming and going with the wind over endless miles,
> A lone body sailing on the East Sea carries the thunders of Spring.
> How could one bear to stand by and see that the map of Chinese land
> shifts in its colors of belonging?
> Or to let the rivers and mountains be torn into wreckages and scorched
> into ashes!
> Muddy liquor cannot melt the anguished tears shed for the pain of the
> country,
> Saving it from dangerous times depends on the talents of millions.
> With the blood of multitudes offered in devotion,
> Heaven and earth must be re-mapped into healing energies.[61]

She was preparing to re-map *tianxia* 天下, the Qing Dynasty's "all under heaven," using "the blood of multitudes offered in devotion."

Qiu Jin's two years in Japan were a whirlwind of activity. She studied Japanese language and joined Sun Yat-sen's new Revolutionary Alliance (Tongmenghui, 同盟会), lectured on revolution, promoted women's rights and equality, and wrote articles against foot-binding and in favor of women's education. She sought not only her own emancipation but the same freedoms as men for all women. As one modern commentator wrote, Qiu

...blamed women themselves, as well as male-dominated society, for their traditionally subservient position. Women had failed to study and leave inner compartments. Thus they had abdicated their naturally equal rights and abilities by acquiescing in training that destroyed any thought of independence.[62]

In the personal realm, she took on another new name, "Female Knight-Errant (or Swordswoman) of Mirror Lake" (鉴湖女侠, Jianhu nüxia), alluding to a famous lake in her hometown of Shaoxing.[63] At other times, she called herself by equally provocative and assertive nicknames: Jing Xiong 竞雄 ("Competes with Men") and Dushu Jijian 讀書擊劍 ("Read Books, Practice [Strike with] Sword").

Qiu regularly dressed like a man[64] or wore a Japanese kimono, and she practiced martial arts, military drilling, and marksmanship. She also carried a Japanese sword, experimented with explosives and bomb-making, and began developing contacts in other groups like the Revolutionary Restoration Society (光復會, Guangfuhui). Woman warrior Qiu Jin wished to lead the revolutionary fight against the hated Manchus, and her troops would surely include the millions of China's long-oppressed women.

To a Western reader, Qiu Jin's self-presentation as a swordswoman or knight-errant might make her seem the poseur. In fact, she was assuming for herself the near-mythic mantle of legendary Chinese women warriors. As far back as 500 BCE in Qiu's own home area of Shaoxing, King Goujian of Yue was said to have engaged the mysterious Maiden of Yue 越女 (Yuenü), self-proclaimed inventor of "the way of the sword," to train his troops before conquering the Wu State.[65] The *Ballad of Mulan* originated in the 4th or 5th Century CE, the fearsome female warrior Liang Hongyu 梁红玉 (1102 – 1135) died battling the Mongols at the end of the Southern Song Dynasty, and the Ming female general Shen Yunying 沈云英 (1624 – 1660) fought to defend Beijing from the Manchus in the 1640s.

Closer to Qiu Jin's time, in 1878, came *The Tale of Heroic Sons and Daughters* (儿女英雄传, *Ernü Yingxiong Zhuan*) by the Manchu Red Bannerman Wen Kang (文康, c.. 1798 – c. 1870).[66] The story's martially accomplished heroine, He Yufeng 何玉凤, who hides her identity by calling herself Shisanmei (十三妹, "Thirteenth Sister"), sets out to avenge her father's death at the hands of a court official. During her travels, she rescues a young scholar named An Ji 安骥 from a band of thieving monks and then frees from the monks' den the maiden Zhang Jinfeng 張金鳳 and Zhang's captive parents. He Yufeng ultimately sees justice served for her father, after which Yufeng ("Jade Phoenix") and Jinfeng ("Golden Phoenix") become companionate wives to the successful official An Ji. Unlike Thirteenth Sister, however, Qiu Jin would never return to the world of husband, household, and domestic affairs.

When the Japanese government issued a ban on political activity by Chinese students in late 1905, Qiu Jin and many others returned to China. She traveled first to Huzhou to accept a position at the Xunxi Girls School (女学浔溪, Xunxi nüxue) in present-day Nanxun, teaching Japanese language, science, and personal hygiene. After just three months, worried administrators asked her to leave out of concern that she was also actively espousing revolution to the students.

Qiu headed next for Shanghai, a growing hotbed of revolutionary fever. There she met up with her cousin, Xu Xilin 徐锡麟 (1873 – 1907), also a native of Shaoxing and now a leader of the Zhejiang branch of the Restoration Society. While in Shanghai, Qiu Jin wrote against foot-binding, arranged marriages, and lack of women's education for her new *Chinese Women's Journal* (中国女报, *Zhongguo nübao*). Unfortunately, the magazine failed to secure enough funding to publish more than two issues. Never content to slacken her pace, she also experimented in Shanghai with explosives, at one point injuring herself when one attempt went awry.

Throughout the 1905 – 1906 period, Qiu also sought to channel her revolutionary message to Chinese women through a radical poetic performance piece she titled *Stones of the Jingwei Bird* (精衛石, *Jingwei Shi*).[67] The Jingwei Bird in Chinese mythology is the reincarnation of the Sun God's daughter, who drowned in the sea. In her second life as a small bird, she is determined to prevent further drownings by filling the sea with small pebbles and sticks. Tragically, the Jingwei Bird dies, exhausted by the effort. In Qiu Jin's telling, the Jingwei Bird's mighty efforts against insurmountable odds called to mind Chinese women's struggle in the existing cultural milieu, "urging what seems impossible as what is not yet but *can* be."[68]

Qiu Jin finished only the first six of *Jingwei Bird's* twenty planned acts, but her completed preface spells out her criticisms of the sisterhood in no uncertain terms:

> I live in an era of transition. Taking advantage of the light of the dawning civilization and the paltry knowledge I possess, I have thrown off the yokes of the past. Yet I am often pained that my sister compatriots remain in a World of Darkness, as though drunk or dreaming, oblivious to the changes around them. Even though there are now schools for women, few enroll in them. Let me ask you, of our twenty million women, how many still grovel at the feet of tyrannical men?....Toadying for favor, they ingratiate themselves to men—obeying their commands like horses or cows. They are no more than the servile and shameless playthings of men. But though they are subjected to immeasurable oppression, they are unaware of their pain; though suffer abuse and humiliation, they have no shame. They are completely blind and ignorant, saying with idiotic serenity: this is our fate.[69]

In September 1905, Xu Xilin's revolutionary fervor led him to establish the Datong School (大同学堂, *Datong xuetang*) for girls in Shaoxing, at least partly as cover for the fifty guns and twenty thousand rounds of ammunition he had purchased to effectuate a bank-robbing scheme.[70] Remarkably, the plan to raise funds for the Restoration Society by robbing local banks was apparently abandoned not for its impracticality but for lack of anyone who could drive a getaway vehicle. Xu also had to be dissuaded from another self-destructive plot to celebrate the opening of Datong School by massacring all the officials invited to attend.[71]

By 1907, Xu's Restoration Society had conceived a new plan for the revolutionary overthrow of the Manchus and their dynasty. That same year, he arranged a faculty position at Datong for Qiu Jin, marking the third and final defining event of her life. While ostensibly directing a girls' school program, Qiu made contacts with revolutionaries in Hangzhou and elsewhere in the province, including Jinhua and Quzhou. She busied herself raising funds to support the movement, building and training a revolutionary militia, and instructing the school's female pupils in military drill. Most important to their cause, Qiu Jin, Xu Xilin, and others mapped out the details of a coordinated plan for the uprising they believed would kick-start a national revolution against the Qing Dynasty.

With Xu now embedded in neighboring Anhui Province as head of the Police Academy in Anqing 安庆, their plan called for Xu to instigate the rebellion on July 19, 1907, by assassinating Anhui Governor Enming 恩銘 (1846 – 1907). At the same time, revolutionaries in Jinhua and Quzhou would rise, helping draw Manchu garrison soldiers from Hangzhou to assist in quelling the outbreak. Qiu and the Shaoxing area revolutionaries would then enter Hangzhou and, aided by sympathetic military compatriots recruited into their cause, take control of the garrison and thus the Zhejiang provincial capital. In Qiu's view, their spark would certainly ignite the national fire of a revolutionary uprising.

Even the best-laid plans can fail, but Xu Xilin's assassination plot proved to be comically amateurish. When word of his revolutionary plot leaked out, Xu panicked and put the plan into motion almost two weeks early, at the Police Academy's graduation ceremony on July 6. As the program began, Xu (acting without his customary eyeglasses) and one co-conspirator opened fire on Governor Enmin with four pistols as they announced the revolution, spraying bullets everywhere. Despite hitting Enmin with multiple shots, they failed to kill him on the spot and exhausted their ammunition.

While Xu tried to recruit the school's 280 students who sat stunned before the stage, the rest of the government officials escaped and took the injured Governor with them. A small group of students, perhaps as many as forty, joined Xu as they headed for the Academy's armory. Xu was unable to open some of the storerooms, and those he opened contained ammunition mismatched to his pistols. They found other, large-caliber guns, but the students had not yet received training in their use.[72]

Although Xu managed to hold out for several hours of gunfighting against government troops, he and nineteen students were ultimately captured. Xu was questioned under torture before being executed the next day. The *North China Herald* reported the grisly news that Xu's heart had been removed from his body and his decapitated head mounted for public display.[73] Governor Enmin died from his wounds, but the Anhui uprising had sputtered badly. Far worse, Xu Xilin's broader revolutionary plan and his connection to Shaoxing and Qiu Jin had been revealed.

By July 12, Qiu Jin knew that garrison troops from Hangzhou were on their way to arrest her at the Datong School. Fellow revolutionaries pleaded with her to go into hiding, but she refused, declaring that she was prepared to spill her own blood for the cause. Instead of fleeing, she arranged for dispersion of the group's guns and ammunition and counseled her students to go into hiding.

That same day, Qiu Jin wrote her final poem, recognizing her imminent fate and despairing of her fellow revolutionaries' inability to overthrow the Qing and restore a Han dynastic reign (as referenced by the allusion to Luoyang and weeping bronze camels):

> In the blink of an eye, the most opportune moment is over.
> My bold ambition is not fulfilled, to my bitterest regret.
> We dropped our whips into the sea
>   to check its ruthless inundation.
> We raised our swords to the sky
>   to sharpen them on the moon.
> No clay to seal up Hangu—
>   imperiling armored horses.
> Copious tears in Luoyang—
>   shed by bronze camels.
> Having my flesh reduced to dust,
>   my bones ground to powder,
>   such fate is now a banality.
> I only hope my sacrifice will help to
>   preserve our country.[74]

On the morning of July 13, several hundred government soldiers surrounded the Datong School. Brief fighting broke out, two students were killed, and Qiu Jin and a handful of her students were arrested. Despite being tortured, she remained silent before her interrogators. Refusing to write a confession, she was said in newspaper reports to have written only the phrase, "Autumn rain and autumn wind, they make one unbearably sad (秋风秋雨愁杀人, *Qiufeng qiuyu chou sharen*)." The Chinese character for autumn, 秋 (*qiu*), is the same as that of her family name. While historians have yet to locate any concrete evidence for Qiu Jin's authorship of this poetic farewell,[75] that seven-character phrase has nevertheless remained a persistent element in her biography.

Following a brief mock trial, Qiu was beheaded in Shaoxing on July 15; she was just 32 years old. Ironically, Xu Xilin was nearly forgotten to history while Qiu Jin rose almost instantly to heroic stature. Her peaceful surrender, her stoicism under torture, and her seemingly too-hasty execution generated sympathy with both the public and the regional press.

By a paradoxical quirk of history and gender, the woman whose own revolutionary plan was never activated would, by her sacrificial death, damage the Qing government's cause far more than her male cousin who actually assassinated a governor.

Revolutionary Days

The Taiping Rebellion and its aftermath had badly shaken the empire, but the Qing Dynasty had survived and the nation slowly recovered. Regardless, the sudden, crushing loss to the Japanese in 1895 and the failure of the Hundred Days' Reform in 1898 signaled unmistakably that Manchu rule was incapable of adapting to the changing worlds of geopolitics and technology. Powerful Western nations were forcing open the gates and spreading the scourge of opium, and closer to home, the Japanese and Russians threatened. Military technology, steam-driven industrialization, railroads, telegraphy, electrification, modern finance—all were upending thousand-year-old lifestyles. The old Chinese world was turning upside-down.

Good-faith efforts at revolutionary change by the Qing government, such as abandonment of the civil service examination system in 1905, either stalled or left aspiring candidates and families of the gentry and scholarly elite unmoored, uncertain where to turn.[76] What were thousands of Confucian-trained scholars to do with their *shengyuan*, *juren*, or *jinshi* degrees? What of the next generation—their sons, and even their daughters? In 1907, Hangzhou's examination halls were demolished, replaced by a provincial normal school for prospective teachers. What were they supposed to teach, and where?

In 1911, the inevitable revolution finally arrived. Anti-Manchu uprisings had been a regular feature of the domestic Chinese political scene since at least 1895, when an attempted rebellion in Canton failed before it could even begin. In the fifteen years from 1895 to 1910, more than a dozen such uprisings erupted.[77] Some started but failed, others were disrupted before they could be carried out.

Like most of the previous attempts, the planned October 1911 uprising in Wuchang (one of Wuhan's tri-cities) targeted forced seizure and control of a city. Launched in the early evening of October 10, the revolutionaries gained command of the entire city by the next day. They immediately declared themselves the Military Government of Hubei of the Republic of China and chose a new governor (Li Yuanhong 黎元洪, 1864 - 1928) from among their number.

This time, success in Wuchang prompted similar uprisings elsewhere. Within two weeks of the Qing government's expulsion from Wuchang, local government overthrows had taken place in Changsha (Hunan Province), Xi'an (Shaanxi Province), and in Jiujiang (Jiangxi Province). Three more provinces—Jiangxi, Shanxi, and Yunnan—fell by month's end.

In Hangzhou, fear and chaos bred of revolutionary change were at least as prevalent as hope. The weeks before the revolution were fraught with fear that the Manchus would not surrender their garrison. Dr. Duncan Main wrote of the civil unrest:

> Last week, when people were panic stricken and coolies had to carry away everything and everybody...the situation became most serious. Fear spread like wild fire, and shopkeepers began to shut up their shops, and work and business practically ceased. Then there was a raid on the rice shops and rioters made a disturbance for two days. At night we could hear them wildly running through the streets shouting and calling out when their burdens became too heavy to carry, and then there was general looting among themselves. Even

the women and children shared in the spoils and in the early hours of the morning could be seen with baskets and bags taking what they could.[78]

An eyewitness account by Frank W. Bible, from the faculty at Hangchow Presbyterian College, paints a similar but rather deadlier picture:

> The three weeks preceding the actual Revolution in Hangchow [on November 4] witnessed an almost indescribable panic among the people of that city; fugitives by tens of thousands left, fearing that the Manchu garrison would shell the city as soon as attacked....Then with the outbreak at Wuchang the people have endured the most terrible suffering known since the Taiping rebellion. For many months tens of thousands of people have had no work; the death rate has been very high....The horrors of the situation were intensified by an epidemic of both typhus and famine fevers....and it is no exaggeration to say that for some time people died by the hundreds daily. The local supply of coffins was exhausted and the surrounding towns and cities had to be drawn upon.[79]

In Hangzhou, near-chaos already reigned, with schools and some factories shut down in late October. The evacuation of the Governor's family to Shanghai offered just one measure of the local Qing officials' precarious hold over the city by the beginning of November.

On November 3, the night before Hangzhou's uprising, members of the Zhejiang Provincial Assembly presented Manchu Governor Zengyun 增韞 (1869 – 1946), with an ultimatum demanding three immediate actions: declare Zhejiang's independence from the Qing government, begin demolishing the inner walls separating the Manchu garrison from the rest of the city, and recognize the bannermen as Han Chinese. When Zengyun rejected demands that were impossible for him as a loyal Manchu to satisfy, the uprising began the next evening.

When a second appeal for a bloodless, non-destructive surrender was rejected by the garrison's military leaders, the revolutionaries began a midnight shelling of the military compound from positions on nearby Wushan.[80] Duncan Main summarized the brief conflict:

> At midnight the revolutionaries fired mounted guns from the city hill, hitting the Tartar General's Yamen and at last, knowing they could not hold out against their enemies, they quietly threw out their arms and ammunition on the street and surrendered! This is the way the revolution took place in Hangchow, and practically throughout Chekiang there has been no fighting or resistance to the rebel forces. Everywhere the white flag is flying.[81]

The senior Manchu commander surrendered in order to minimize the damage and loss of life among the garrison's residents. Another commander named Guilin was quickly executed, however, when the Republicans discovered that he had secretly hidden a sizable arms cache for a possible counter-revolutionary action. Six years earlier, Guilin's had been one of the strongest public voices in support of the Huixing Girls' School and the broader cause of women's education.

Two militant groups led the way in seizing key installations in Hangzhou: the New Army and the Dare-to-Die Corps. Ironically, the New Army evolved out of a Qing government military reform and modernization program instituted in 1905. Just as Qiu Jin had successfully recruited some of their men to her cause, the Revolutionary Alliance and a locally reborn Restoration Society now sought converts within these troops, and especially among the military academy graduates who had studied in Japan. The individual who cemented the link between the New Army activists and the Revolutionary Alliance was the reformer Zhu Fucheng 諸輔成 (1873-1948). In Zhu's hometown of Jiaxing, the Qing prefect simply abandoned his position and fled to Shanghai, after which Jiaxing announced its independence without conflict.[82]

Overthrow by force of one government did not automatically guarantee smooth formation of a new one, either in Hangzhou or for Zhejiang Province more generally. Accusations of pro-Manchu leanings and repeated outbreaks of factionalism among Revolutionary Alliance, Restoration Society, and New Army members soon devolved into assassinations. Circumstances in Zhejiang were further complicated by a summer season of heavy rains and flooding in coastal areas that decimated rice and cotton crops. News of the revolution spurred desperate villagers to resolve their subsistence needs by forming bandit groups and preying on wealthy landowners.[83] Order and governance would be restored, but the process was fraught with recriminations and bloody conflicts that foreshadowed national governance difficulties for more than a decade.

The Republic of China, with Sun Yat-sen as its provisional president, was declared on December 29, 1911, effective January 1, 1912. It was also on that same effective date that the official date in the new Republic of China was accepted as January 1, 1912 in accordance with the Gregorian (Western) calendar. Governmental abandonment of the traditional lunar calendar marked the start of a new era, although warlordism in the subsequent years kept the lunar calendar in use in some parts of China.[84]

On February 12, 1912, Empress Dowager Longyu 隆裕皇太后 (1868 – 1913) signed the abdication agreement on the child-Emperor Puyi's 溥仪 (1906 – 1967, r. 1909 – 1911)[85] behalf. Regardless how the Revolution was still playing out in each province, creation of a new national government promised a fresh start and the hope for unity, order, reform, and modernization.

Drum Tower, Hangzhou City.

Cliffside Buddha carvings on the approach to Lingyin Temple.

Main hall, Lingyin Temple.

Statue of Mad Monk Ji Gong, worshipped in a separate, dedicated hall at Lingyin Temple.

Jingci Temple complex, viewed from Leifeng Pagoda.

Statue of King Qian Liu, first king of the Wuyue State during the Five Dynasties period (907 – 960), on the King Qian Temple grounds, West Lake.

Liuhe (Six Harmonies) Pagoda, along the Qiantang River.

Three of the five Qian-family kings, all of whom are honored in the King Qian Temple. Qian Liu takes the seat of honor as the founder of this reign period in Hangzhou.

Entrance hall for the Yue Fei tomb and temple.

Honor (spirit) walk, statues, and steles approaching the tomb of Yue Fei (left) and his son Yue Yun (right).

Cast iron statues of the "evil" Qin Hui and his equally wicked wife, Lady Wang, who together engineered Yue Fei's unjust execution and have been reviled ever since.

Night view of entrance to the Phoenix Mosque complex on
Zhongshan Middle Road, Hangzhou.

Memorial arch and burial vault at the ancient Jesuit cemetery, which once held
the cremated remains of Martino Martini and Prospero Intorcetta.

Cathedral of the Immaculate Conception church, Hangzhou.

Statue of Ming poet and women's education advocate Yuan Mei, located at Wansong Academy where Yuan had once been a student.

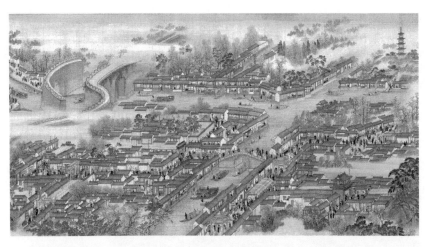

View of Shaoxing City as depicted by Wang Hui in Scroll 9 of the Qianlong Emperor's Southern Inspection Tour. Image extracted from Wikimedia Commons, accessed at https:// commons.wikimedia.org/wiki/File:Wang_Hui_and_others._Emperor_Kangxi_Touring_ the_South._9th_handscroll_of_a_set._1691-98_Palace_mus._Beijing.jpg

View of the Qianlong Emperor's visit to the tomb of Yu the Great, as depicted by Wang Hui in Scroll 9 of the Qianlong Emperor's Southern Inspection Tour. Image extracted from Wikimedia Commons, accessed at https://commons.wikimedia.org/wiki/File:Wang_ Hui_and_others._Emperor_Kangxi_Touring_the_South._9th_handscroll_of_a_ set._1691-98_Palace_mus._Beijing.jpg

Tea plantation field in the hills west of West Lake.

Fish pond and halls at the former residence of Hu Xueyan.

Tomb site and statue of revolutionary Qiu Jin near Xiling Bridge, Solitary Hill (Gushan), West Lake.

Entrance plaza to Lu Xun Village, Shaoxing City.

Wine shop, Shaoxing.

Night market on Hefang Street, near the foot of Wushan in Hangzhou.

Memorial sculpture of Lin Huiyin, near the Yang Causeway at West Lake.

View of the first Qiantang River bridge crossing, looking southeast toward Xiaoshan's Binjiang District from atop the Liuhe Pagoda.

Chapter 16

TROUBLED TRANSITION YEARS

(1911 – 1919)

Ten Miles of Lotus Flowers[1]

Twin lakes and piled up hills make a scene of transparent beauty.
Among them are three autumns of cherry blossoms,
Ten miles of lotus flowers.
Melodies from a Tibetan flute play with the clear sky,
Songs of the water chestnut float through the night.
Laughing and flirting are the fishermen and lotus girls.
Thousands of horse-riders hold straight the Governor's banners.
Intoxicated, he listens to the bamboo flute and drum,
Writes poems in praise of the rosy clouds.
On another day I shall paint this scene into a picture.

– Liu Yong (987 – 1053)

While the Chinese nation struggled in 1912 to establish a new form of central government, one of the first orders of business in Hangzhou required little debate: dismantling the Manchu garrison and evicting the Manchu soldiers quartered there. For more than two centuries, that walled-off compound had occupied a sizable portion of the northwestern corner of the ancient walled-city area, bordering West Lake's eastern shore. The real question was one of urban planning: whether and how to redesign, reconfigure, and repopulate the vacated space. The answer would define Hangzhou's future to the present day.

West Lake – A (Very) Brief Social History

West Lake had primarily functioned in the Tang (618 – 907), Wuyue Kingdom (907 – 960), and Northern Song (960 – 1127) eras in the most pragmatic of ways, as Hangzhou's main source of fresh water and for crop irrigation, harvesting water plants, and supplying adequate water to the urban canal network. This is not to say that the lake went unvisited or overlooked. To the contrary, West Lake was the common people's venue for traditional and religious celebrations. Similarly, the literati class increasingly held out the lake and surrounding hills as a site for excursion and as a beatific landscape worth celebrating in paintings and verse. Yet as often as provincial governors Bai Juyi and Su Dongpo praised the lake's natural beauty in their poetry, they are remembered more for the pragmatic results of their dredging, plant removal, and water management oversight.

During the Southern Song period (1127 – 1279), "West Lake, the city water supply source" first truly became "West Lake, the tourist site." Population migration and urban crowding, the influx into Lin'an of educated and well-heeled northern elites, and increased wealth and leisure time among the populace fostered growing social acceptance of short (half-day to two- or three-day) pleasure excursions (遊 you, "roaming for pleasure"). Yet the sheer visual and psychic separation between the lake and Hangzhou's residents caused by the city walls conflicted with the lake's scenic beauty and near proximity. Inevitably, officials, literati, and gentry merchants began employing brief West Lake excursions for socializing, release from the stresses of crowded urban life, or immersion at one level or another in Nature.[2]

Through the years of the Southern Song, scholar-officials and artists celebrated West Lake's scenic grandeur as befitting the urban seat of the dynasty. No well-educated literatus from elsewhere in China could fail to be aware of Xihu's historical and cultural aura or its connections with the lake's immortal Three Worthies: Lin Bu, Bai Juyi, and Su Shi (Dongpo).[3] Nor would such a scholar refrain from an excursion on the lake if the opportunity presented. The dynasty, the capital, the lake, and the literati were engaged in a perpetual embrace of mutual reputational enhancement.

Literati celebration of West Lake as a scenic site expanded still further during the prosperous Ming and Qing dynasties. Effusive appreciation and multiple repeat visits from Qing Emperors Kangxi and Qianlong in the 17th and 18th centuries only magnified the lake's allure, creating new "must see" sites by their very presence and writings, especially their calligraphic canonizations of the Ten Views. The numerous temples in the lake area stood equally important as Buddhist and Daoist pilgrimage sites, drawing tens of thousands of visitors every year from Zhejiang and the surrounding provinces.

For the people of Hangzhou, however, West Lake remained more of a day trip or country excursion than an integral part of the city. The busiest markets operated well inside the walls, following north-south along the imperial Great Street, east-west near the foot of Wushan (City God Hill), and near the northern and eastern gates. Unless one climbed atop one of the city's western gates (like Qiantang) or scaled the Wushan hills in the southern precincts, West Lake was invisible, hidden behind that thirty-foot-high wall. Xihu's quietly rippling waves may have lapped the city's shoreline beneath its western walls, but they were not psychologically part of the city's everyday life for most commoners.

This sense of city–lake separation was further exacerbated in 1648 when the conquering Manchus walled off their military garrison, the *Qiying* 旗营, with its own twenty-foot-high inner wall. For the next 250 years, city residents wishing to visit Xihu had three choices of gates by which to exit through the western wall: Qingbo Gate 清波门 toward the south end of the wall and lake, Yongjing Gate 涌金门 more central to the lake itself, and Qiantang Gate 钱塘门 at the lake's northeastern section, closest to many of the most popular historical and scenic sites. However, passing through Qiantang Gate meant passing through the breadth of the garrison and being subjected to searches and other harassments that discouraged urban-lakeside interaction.

The Lake Enters the City

As the revolutionary dust settled in Hangzhou, movement leaders seized control of the garrison, asserting public ownership of the land and evicting all the Manchus residing therein. In a letter to her sister Alice Tisdale Hobart (1882 – 1967), Wayland Academy teacher Mary Nourse (1880 – 1971) described the eerie events that followed Hangzhou's night of revolution:

> During the night we heard shooting, but by morning everything was quiet; the white band of revolution was on every man's arm. In the afternoon I went with a group to see what had happened to the Manchu garrison....It was empty. What became of the Manchus no one knows. There were no signs of violence, just empty houses and courts. In a few days, men armed with shears stood at every street corner to cut off the queue of any man who refused to cut his own.[4]

The new government's plan for the garrison's vacated land was straightforward in concept but not so simple in execution: create a modern New Business District (新市场, Xin shichang). Proposals for transformation of vacant fields in the Qiying into a market area had been floated as early as October 1909 during the Zhejiang Provincial Assembly's first annual meeting, but those were never acted upon.[5] A brief extract from minutes of the 1909 Assembly meeting nevertheless states the case quite clearly:

> The Qiying area is located in the center of Hangzhou city, and is very close to West Lake, separated only by a wall. Therefore, market construction on the Qiying site would not only invigorate commerce, but also promote West Lake.[6]

Regaining control of the entire garrison area after the 1911 Xinhai Revolution presented grand new opportunities for a much more radical and impactful urban renewal on ten times as much[7] lakefront area. The job of refashioning Hangzhou and charting its physical course into the future fell to Zhu Fucheng, now director of Civil Administration for Zhejiang Province.

Product of an elite Jiaxing family, Zhu spent almost two years studying in Japan in 1905 – 1906. Like so many young Chinese men (and women) of that time, he connected with other revolution-minded individuals and joined the Revolutionary Alliance (Tongmenghui) before returning to Jiaxing as both a teacher and founder of separate primary schools for boys and girls. In addition, he took active roles in the Jiaxing anti-opium crusade, the business community, flood relief work, and agricultural programs to combat a devastating regional infestation of rice borers. In 1909, Zhu earned a seat in the newly formed Zhejiang Provincial Assembly; a year later, he rose to vice president of that body.[8]

While Zhu provided visionary guidance and acted as political liaison for the New Business District, Hangzhou native Ruan Xingyi 阮性宜 assumed responsibility for technical planning and implementation. Another product of overseas education in Japan, with engineering experience from the Hangzhou–Ningbo–Shanghai railway construction project, Ruan's earliest decisions were necessarily conceptual and strategic. How would the former garrison land be accessed and used, and how would the land interact with West Lake? In other words, how would the lakefront area be opened, and to what purpose?

Ruan Xingyi implemented a plan of radical revision: demolish the garrison's inner walls and the western section of ancient wall running alongside West Lake,[9] construct a broad lakeside avenue (Hubin Lu 湖滨路, or Lakeshore Road) where the wall once stood, and create an entirely new grid network of major and minor streets, irrespective of where and how the garrison streets were located previously. Four primary streets would each be sixty-three feet wide, while twenty-three secondary streets would each be exactly half that width.[10] Eight of the new roads were designed to run east-to-west to reinforce the connection between West Lake and downtown commerce and transport, with one of them reaching as far as the railway arrivals at City Station.[11]

Plans for land use demonstrated even more forward-thinking ideas and a clear intent to integrate West Lake into the New Business District. The area between Hubin Lu and the lakeshore, until recently used by the Manchus as military training grounds, would now be occupied by a string of public parks. Boat docks would be strategically placed to accommodate the desires of visitors to experience the lake as countless generations of literati and gentry had done before.

Away from the lakeshore area, land in the New Business District would be reserved for such civic institutions as a library, a theater, an exhibition hall, and a combination athletic field and public meeting venue. Education buildings and hospitals would be constructed on lands formerly occupied by Confucian academies and temples. The balance of the land not already reserved for such public institutions would be auctioned for private ownership, and "any individual with Chinese citizenship was entitled to bid for the land."[12] Various tax incentives were offered as well to encourage rapid redevelopment and discourage warehousing of vacant lots.

As clearly as the New Business District represented modern urban development, it served equally as an intentional act of historical and ethnic erasure.

Such large-scale urban renewal naturally caused displacements, particularly among the former garrison residents. Land sales began on December 1, 1914, and forcible removal of any remaining Manchu residents started soon after, running from December 19 – December 26. Although the resulting homelessness problem was addressed by construction of a block of new residences, Manchus in Hangzhou and elsewhere "quickly fell to the lowest stratum of Chinese society…identified in the public consciousness with poverty and unskilled labor."[13]

By 1920, most if not all of the former Qiying land had been sold. Steadily rising land prices in the New Business District and plans for extension of Lakeshore Road into a fully lake-encircling thoroughfare (completed in 1922) were a further measure of the plan's success. The residents of Hangzhou City coined their own form of recognition for the positive changes, adopting the popular new saying: "*Xihu rucheng* 西湖入城," "West Lake entered the city."

With all the renovation and renewal accomplished around West Lake's eastern shore, the New Business District gave birth to a concentration of commercial enterprises serving the tourism industry. Once the Shanghai–Hangzhou railway link was completed in 1909, Shanghai's residents began viewing Hangzhou as a resort, sometimes referring jokingly to the city as "Shanghai's back yard."[14] Restaurants, teahouses, hotels, performance halls, and other travel service businesses rushed into the new commercial area. By one account, the number of hotels in Hangzhou grew from fifteen before 1911 to ninety-one by 1927.[15] Retail trade followed, whether for souvenirs and snacks or for upscale goods attractive to well-heeled visitors. West Lake had not only entered the city, the city was increasingly becoming an adjunct to West Lake.

As commerce and excitement grew around the New Business District, activity in the centuries-old market district at Wushan and along the Great Street correspondingly diminished. Yet even as the New Business District was transforming the city's west side, completion of the Chengzhan 城站 (City Railway Station) in 1910 precipitated growth of a new, east-side market area. The new railroad station was quickly surrounded by more hotels, restaurants, and shops catering to the tourist trade.

Visitors from Shanghai flocked by train to Hangzhou, enjoying day trips, weekend excursions, and spring and fall holidays. This circumstance illustrated the absolute inversion of these two cities' fortunes in the years since 1840. In the past millennium, Shanghai had grown from a fishing village known as Hudu 沪渎 to a market town with a protective wall only five kilometers around to a bustling port trading town of as many as two hundred thousand residents. Even at its most populous, however, it was still a commonplace as recently as the first half of the 19th Century to refer to Shanghai as "little Hangzhou" or "little Suzhou."[16]

The impact in Jiangnan of the Opium Wars and especially the Taiping Rebellion was inestimable. Shanghai grew explosively and internationalized; Hangzhou shrank just as explosively and suffered massive devastation. Together, these conditions spurred a role reversal that converted Hangzhou and Suzhou into prime tourist venues heavily patronized by Shanghai's expanding urban population.

The new Shanghai – Hangzhou railway accommodated this increase in passenger traffic with special offers and even produced its own sightseeing guides for first-time visitors. The contrast between the two cities could not have been greater. As Wang Liping astutely observed, Shanghai was now the very model of Chinese modernity, while Hangzhou served as the paragon of preserved tradition.[17] As Wang also noted, "Places like modern Hangzhou presuppose the existence of places like Shanghai."[18]

As the crowds on and around Xihu grew, however, the West Lake experience changed. Quiet contemplation, poetic musing, and religious observation gave way to boat rides, scenic photography, and culinary sampling. The typical visitor no longer arrived steeped in the lore of the lake. More and more often, they lacked deep awareness of past poems and paintings and were incapable of deciphering the obscure cultural references and allusions that had thrilled Ming and Qing literati merely for their ability to acknowledge and exchange them. Visual and commercial experiences were gradually replacing the previously more historically and culturally-centered written ones. "The gaze of the literati was replaced by the gaze of tourists, who came only as consumers of culture," unwittingly experiencing the "phenomenon of cultural creation in the name of tradition."[19] West Lake became a site for visitors to consume the sophisticated lifestyles and aesthetic tastes of the literati. "Sight-seeing without any purpose was itself the purpose."[20]

Hangzhou and the West Lake were witnessing the birth of modern tourism in China, accessible to greater and greater segments of the population regardless of their wealth or education. Foreigners also began hearing more about the captivating scenery and historical charms of the city on the lake and its ancient reputation as "Heaven below." In October 1920, for example, the great mathematical philosopher Bertrand Russell (1872 – 1970) visited Hangzhou for two days and gave a lecture on education at the Zhejiang Teachers College. He also acted the tourist during his brief stay, seeing West Lake by boat on the first day and by sedan chair on the second day. "It was marvelously beautiful," he wrote in his autobiography, 'with the beauty of ancient civilization, surpassing even that of Italy."[21] Although deeply felt on the superficial, visual level, Russell's assessment contained no indication that he understood anything of Xihu's sociocultural content or context.

Qiu Jin's First Five Burials

Qiu Jin's hasty trial and her execution just two days after her capture at the Datong School in 1907 had inflamed anti-Qing passions and generated widespread sympathy for her fate. The Zhejiang officials most immediately involved in her case ultimately encountered substantial career difficulties, and the magistrate who passed her death sentence eventually committed suicide,[22] perhaps experiencing for himself the sorrows of autumn wind and rain. Even Zhejiang Governor Zhang Zengyang 張曾敭 (1852 – 1920) came under fire; one Hangzhou newspaper printed a prophetic cartoon of a ship under sail in a heavy storm with the caption: "The autumn wind and the autumn rain presage the coming storms. Zhang's sail will be sent to obscurity in the tides of Zhejiang."[23] Not long afterward, Governor Zhang was transferred to distant Shanxi Province.

Much of the press sided with the revolutionary martyr as well. Despite these outpourings of sympathy and even allegiance, her decapitated corpse was virtually untouchable. What to do about burying and memorializing such a controversial anti-government figure, especially a woman?

Stories of the treatment of Qiu's dead body vary in detail, but they all agree on the general sequence of events. Her execution took place at Xuantingkou 軒亭口 (Pavilion Intersection), a market crossroad in Shaoxing; a memorial stele would be erected at the site in 1930.[24] Because her family went into hiding and dared not claim Qiu's body, her corpse remained exposed for a time at the execution site. Later reports suggested that a cleaning woman from Datong School finally wrapped Qiu's body in a straw mat. Not long after, a local charitable association placed her in a cheap coffin and buried her in a pauper's cemetery on nearby Fushan Hill, where she remained interred for the time being.

In life, Qiu Jin had enjoyed the financial and emotional support of two sworn sisters, Xu Zihua 徐自华 (1873 – 1935) and Wu Zhiying 吴芝瑛 (1867 – 1934).[25] Almost immediately upon Qiu's death, Wu Zhiying began shaping the Qiu Jin legacy—not the renegade, sword-bearing, male-clothes-wearing revolutionary fighter, but the martyred anti-Manchu heroine, poetess, and supporter of women's rights and education. In short order, Wu penned three essays for publication in Shanghai: a biography, a memoir, and a "Sacrificial Prayer for Qiu Jin."[26] After 1911, it was also Wu Zhiying who wrote the preface for the first edition of Qiu Jin's collected works.

Several months after the execution, Xu Zihua and Wu Zhiying quietly arranged for Qiu's remains to be disinterred from Fushan Hill and transported to Hangzhou by Wu's husband and Qiu's brother, Qiu Yuzhang 秋譽章 (1873–1909). There, on the shores of West Lake, the two women arranged construction of a more fitting tomb for their martyred friend. The widowed but comfortably wealthy Xu Zihua selected and paid for the burial plot by the lake, thereby fulfilling a mutual commitment with Qiu Jin about burial near Xiling Bridge. Wu Zhiying financed the burial in "a modest tomb...constructed in the fairly typical Yangtze-delta style of a half-dome supported by cylindrical form" with an accompanying carved stele reading: "Swordswoman of Mirror Lake" (鉴湖女侠, Jianhu nüxia).[27] Wu also wrote the tomb inscription. Qiu's second burial took place on February 24, 1908.

The well-attended memorial service in February and the burial site itself attracted the curious as well as those fostering anti-Qing sentiments, much to the annoyance of government authorities. Before long, local officials ordered the tomb demolished and the body removed. Qiu Yuzhang retrieved his sister's remains once again and had them carried to her husband Wang Tingjun's hometown of Xiangtan, Hunan Province. When Wang died in 1909, husband and wife were buried together, a reunion Qiu Jin would likely not have welcomed.

In mid-1912, after the revolution Qiu had dreamed of initiating had finally been achieved, provincial officials in Hunan relocated her tomb once again—to an honored site in Changsha. This resting place proved to be transitory as well, since only a few months later, Qiu Jin was posthumously recalled to West Lake. There, on October 27, 1912, she was given a national hero's burial on Solitary Hill, not far from Xiling Bridge. A new, tomb-facing Pavilion of Wind and Rain (風波亭, Fengyu ting) celebrated her life's memory.

On December 8 – 9, 1912, Sun Yat-sen visited West Lake and honored Qiu Jin in a speech, adding a four-character memorial plaque inscription that read 巾幗英雄 (*Jinguo yingxiong*); in English, "Female Hero." Qiu's final resting place in death had become the political symbol she aspired to be in life. At least now her oddly peripatetic remains could rest in peace…for the time being.

Huzhou Helps the New Republic

As the founder and leader of the Revolutionary Alliance, Sun Yat-sen was the natural choice to head the new Republic of China. He accepted the role as a provisional leader on January 1, 1912, but it was hardly a unified government. The Tongmenghui operated as a loose alliance, and the various New Armies that effectuated the Qing overthrow in province after province did not constitute anything like a military force under unified command – except in North China, where the powerful Beiyan Army operated under the leadership of Yuan Shikai 袁世凱 (1859 – 1916).

In return for securing the Empress Dowager's (and the child-emperor Puyi's) abdication in February, Yuan Shikai assumed the presidency of the Republic of China when Sun Yat-sen resigned, as previously agreed upon. Thus began a five-year period marked by creation of a National Assembly, formation of the Guomindang 袁世凱 (GMD)[28] political party, and establishment of a capital in 1912 (first at Nanjing, then in Beijing). Unfortunately, those same years also saw the assassination in March 1913 of a GMD leader, Song Jiaoren 宋教仁 (1882 – 1913), followed by armed revolt against Yuan Shikai in July 1913, flight to Japan for safety by Sun Yat-sen in November 1913, and the declaration by Yuan Shikai of a new Empire of China with himself as Emperor (1915 – 1916).

Chaos reigned when Yuan Shikai died of natural causes in 1916. Military strongmen around the nation established their own fiefdoms and clashed with one another for additional territorial control. A decade-long warlord era had begun, and it would be the common people who suffered most from the confusing cycles of forced allegiances, military occupations, and re-occupations. Throughout this period of upheaval, two men from Huzhou played major roles in both the events of the moment and in charting the path for future events. Their names were Chen Qimei and Zhang Jingjiang.

Chen Qimei 陈其美 (1878 – 1916) was another of the many young Chinese men of his time who studied in Japan—in his case, at the Tokyo Police Academy in 1905 – 1906. There he joined the Revolutionary Alliance and made the close acquaintance of Sun Yat-sen (ten years his senior) and an even closer acquaintance, bordering on mentorship, with another student (ten years his junior) from the Ningbo area, Chiang Kai-shek (蔣介石 Jiang Jieshi, 1887 – 1975). Very likely, Chen provided encouragement for Chiang's enrollment in the Revolutionary Alliance.

When the Japanese government began expelling revolution-leaning Chinese students in 1906, Chen left for Shanghai. Chiang Kai-shek remained behind in Japan, spending most of the years from 1908 – 1911 in a military academy. Back in Shanghai, Chen Qimei expanded his circle of contacts among activists, gentry leaders, rich businessmen, and even Shanghai underworld organizations like the infamous Green Gang.

Despite his rather frail appearance, Chen proved himself a leader by "his strong personality, his intelligence, and his courage….he was a born organizer, a man of action, a conspirator ready for anything, even assassination."[29] When uprisings rolled across China in late 1911 like a fast-moving storm, Chen led the assault on the Jiangnan Arsenal in Shanghai on November 3 and seized control of the Manchu garrison, ascending afterward to military governorship of the city. Two days later, after Chen Qimei called him home from Japan, Chiang Kai-shek led the revolutionary force that took the garrison in Hangzhou.[30]

Like Sun Yat-sen, Chen Qimei fled for Tokyo in mid-1913 when uprisings against Yuan Shikai's rule failed. Chiang Kai-shek headed for Japan as well, further tightening the bond between Chen and himself during their exile. In 1916, Chen returned once again to China to lead resistance efforts against Yuan's attempts at instituting a new imperial reign. On May 18, he was killed by an assassin's bullets in Beijing, almost certainly on the orders of Yuan Shikai. Despite his early death at age 38, Chen Qimei brought his protégé, his fellow Zhejiangese Chiang Kai-shek, into the political-military arena.[31]

One of the most important but unlikely contacts Chen had cultivated in Shanghai prior to the Revolution was Zhang Jingjiang 張靜江(1877 – 1950), a wealthy antiques dealer from the Nanxun district of Huzhou. Born into one of the most elite and longest-lineage families in the region, Zhang suffered congenital maladies that affected his ability to walk as well as his eyesight. Nevertheless, as a young man he studied the Chinese classics, practiced calligraphy, and even rode a horse. Spurred on by his own youthful accomplishments, he found the audacity to change his given name to Renjia人傑, proclaiming himself to the world as an "outstanding personality."[32]

The Zhang family's multi-generational wealth came largely from the salt and silk trades, but Jingjiang's father harbored very internationalist views toward the academic and business education of his five sons. Two years after marrying the equally well-educated Suzhounese Yao Hui 姚蕙 (d. 1918) in around 1900, the 25-year-old Zhang Jingjiang departed for Paris, having managed through personal and family connections to be included in a sizable diplomatic delegation. With plentiful free time to explore the City of Light, he conceived a business plan to open a shop in Paris and import a wide range of Chinese goods, from silks, fine crafts, and jades to works of art, calligraphy, and antiquities.

When his personal fund-raising efforts back home bore insufficient fruit, Zhang Jingjiang turned to his father (Zhang Baoshan 张宝善, 1856 – 1926) for 300,000 silver dollars in financial backing. Over the next decade he established and ran a hugely profitable import business that eventually added offices in New York, London, and Shanghai.[33]

As the shops' offerings increasingly gravitated toward antiquities, Zhang was forced to make periodic journeys by sea back to China. While aboard the *S.S. Tonkin* in 1906, Zhang Jingjiang discovered to his delight that Sun Yat-sen was among the ship's passengers. Zhang wanted to do more than just meet the reformer with the growing reputation; he wished to discuss revolutionary philosophy, particularly his interest in anarchy as the solution to China's reform problems. Sun Yat-sen, on the other hand, sought to avoid Zhang, fearing from the latter's participation in a government delegation that he might be a spy.

Zhang persisted while aboard ship and, after several discussions, became completely enamored of Sun's vision for China and the revolutionary struggle necessary to achieve his goals. In fact, he committed so wholly to Sun's cause that he promised virtually unrestricted financial backing, on the spot. They agreed on the simplest of communication plans: if Sun telegrammed the letter "A," Zhang would immediately send him 10,000 yuan, if a "B," 20,000 yuan would be delivered, 30,000 yuan for a "C," and so on up to at least the letter "E."

Sun apparently regarded Zhang Jingjiang's pledge with a fair degree of skepticism. Perhaps it was a showy display of ostentation, or idealism parading as pragmatism, or just plain eccentricity. As desperate for funding as he always was, Sun nevertheless failed to call upon his too-enthusiastic supporter until March 1907 in Hanoi, when he happened to relate his *S.S. Tonkin* encounter with Zhang Jingjiang to a friend, Hu Hanmin 胡汉民 (1879 – 1936). Hu persuaded Sun that there was little risk in sending a meaningless telegram containing the letter "A," even if seen by Qing government agents. To their surprise, Zhang wired them 10,000 yuan. Not long after, Sun tried again, using "B" and then "C"; the requested funds followed in short order. Zhang Jingjiang quickly became Sun Yat-sen's largest and most reliable financial backer, replying to one of Sun's letters of gratitude by saying he required neither thanks nor explanation for how the funds were used.[34]

Zhang Jingjiang also provided the financial support for Sun Yat-sen's failed uprising attempt in Guangdong Province in April 1911, seven months before the successful Wuhan uprising. Years later, Sun formally recognized Zhang's support for the Revolution with an inscribed scroll in his calligraphy reading "A man of loyal heart and chivalrous mind" (丹心下跪, *Dan xin xia gui*).[35]

When Chen Qimei died in 1916, Chiang Kai-shek had turned to Sun Yat-sen as his mentor and advisor; when Sun passed away in 1925, Chiang placed much of his confidence in Zhang Jingjiang. The two had met as early as 1912, since both men along with Chen Qimei circled closely in the political, financial, and military orbits around Sun Yat-sen. In fact, they grew close enough and of sufficiently like mind in those early years to perform a ritual of sworn brotherhood.[36]

Their relationship only expanded and intertwined further in the succeeding years. When Yuan Shikai ordered Chiang's arrest in 1914, it was in Zhang's Shanghai residence where Chiang stayed until he could escape to Japan. It was Zhang Jingjiang who introduced Chiang to the Shanghai underworld groups like the Green Gang, thugs whom Chiang would later recruit as allies. It was through Zhang Jingjiang's household, particularly his second wife Zhu Yimin 朱逸民 (1901-1991),[37] that the still-married Chiang met and successfully courted 13-year-old Chen Jieru 陳潔如 (1906 – 1971), who became his second wife in 1921 at age 15. And it was Zhang Jingjiang whom Chiang asked in 1922 to see to his two sons' education should he not survive military conflict in support of Sun Yat-sen in Guangdong Province.

Following Sun Yat-sen's death from cancer in 1925, Zhang ascended to important roles in the new Nationalist government, becoming known as one of the "Four Elder Statesmen of the Guomindang." He maintained his alliance with Chiang and shared the leader's stance in opposition to the nascent Communist Party. Yet he remained so mysteriously a behind-the-scenes power figure that the venerable *New York Times* described him in 1928 as an invalid who controlled the GMD's inner circle:

> This man, so little known outside of China that his name is unfamiliar to most newspaper readers in America and Europe…is, unhappily, so crippled that he is always carried from room to room by devoted attendants….[38]

Despite a growing antipathy and separation between the two men over personal matters,[39] Zhang was named Chairman of the National Reconstruction Committee (for infrastructure development) in February 1928 and retained that office for ten years. In November of the same year, he became Governor of Zhejiang, his native province, a position he held until resigning in January 1930 at Chiang Kai-shek's instigation.

During these partially overlapping tenures, Zhang focused on an extraordinarily broad range of economic development projects. He authorized construction of highways and road networks, dredged waterways and built dams, initiated regional bus companies, developed electric power plants and power distribution networks, worked with RCA to create China's first radio network, and developed major new railway lines as well as shorter, single-purpose lines to support expanded coal mining operations. Under Zhang's watch, Hangzhou benefited with a new highway connecting the city to Shaoxing, a modern new power plant to generate and distribute electricity, and the Zhegan Railway line connecting Zhejiang to Jiangxi Province.

In his later years, Zhang Jingjiang turned increasingly to Buddhism for spiritual solace.

When war broke out with the Japanese in 1937, he left Nanxun with his family for Hong Kong. From there, the family sailed first to Europe and then, in 1939, to America, where they settled into residency in the Riverdale section of the Bronx, New York City. Zhang's health gradually deteriorated, as did his eyesight, until he passed away on September 3, 1950. The frail little man from Nanxun with poor eyesight and a pronounced limp had left a giant imprint on Republican-era history and a beleaguered but industrializing nation.[40]

Preserving a Classical Art Form

Throughout the pre-Revolution period 1895 – 1911, the reformers of the era increasingly disparaged Confucianism and cultural traditions in the name of modernization and self-strengthening. Along the northern shore of West Lake, a group of scholars formed a traditionalist barricade of their own to preserve seal engraving (篆刻 *zhuanke*), one of China's singular, 3,000-year-old art forms.

In a manner loosely parallel to the development and proliferation of private gardens in China, seals began as symbols of imperial power and gradually marked the relative authority and power of high officials on down to lower-ranked levels. By the Ming and Qing dynasties, seals were as much about antiquities and aesthetics as they were practical signifiers of status or power; the personal seals of the literati class demonstrated instead one's erudition and aesthetic sensibilities. Ancient seals or those of famous individuals became collectors' items, objects of study and academic discourse for their inscriptions, choice of calligraphic style, and execution of carving/presentation technique. Such classical seals impressed on the colophons of scroll paintings instantly identified the writer and, in some cases, added substantial value to a painting.

As much as they admired seals as *objets d'art*, connoisseurs also revered the act of seal engraving. As a fine art with inseparable links to centuries of classical painting and calligraphic exposition, seals "epitomized the high culture of the literati lifestyle" that (in the view of its knowledgeable practitioners) warranted "preservation and transmission of not just seal carving, but the very literati lifestyle that had produced the seal as a social technology."[41] Nevertheless, modern society increasingly rendered seals archaic, if not obsolete.

Sensing the potential death of a beloved art form and its associated life style, four seal carving scholars in Zhejiang Province—Ding Ren 丁仁 (1879 – 1922), Ye Ming 叶铭 (1867 – 1948), Wang Fu'an 王福厂 (or Wang Ti 王禔, 1880 – 1960), and Wu Yin 吴隐 (1867 – 1922) formed the Xiling Seal Engraving Society (西泠印社, Xiling yinshe) in 1904. Their stated mission included not only seal studies but also preservation of metal and stone inscriptions. Ding, Ye, and Wang all hailed from Hangzhou; Wu was from Shaoxing. Most of those who joined the Society in its formative years were from those same cities or nearby areas of Zhejiang Province.

In the Society's first few years, members contributed personally to create a capital base from which to develop their headquarters property on Solitary Hill. The name of their new society, Xiling, alluded directly to the nearby Xiling Bridge connecting Solitary Hill to the northern shore of the lake. The choice of that specific locale served a two-fold purpose. First, the site's garden-style setting, replete with traditional-style halls, pavilions, rockeries, and a small pond, hearkened back unmistakably to the era of the literati elite. For West Lake visitors today, no other venue on or near West Lake so effectively recalls and physically preserves elements of the traditional literati lifestyle.[42] Second, the Xiling Seal Engraving Society's location serves an honorific and historical purpose, related to one of seal carving's most esteemed scholars and practitioners, Ding Jing 丁敬 (1695 – 1765).

By most measures, Ding Jing would be considered a brilliant eccentric.[43] Born in Hangzhou to a family of means, Ding chose to study traditional Chinese culture widely and intensively, but not with the usual intentions toward the civil service examination system. He became recognized as an intellectual and connoisseur of the arts, ranging from poetry and calligraphy to book collecting, antiquarian studies, and seal carving. He rarely traveled, spending most of his life in Hang-zhou and rejecting all opportunities for an official position. Instead, he earned a modest income from making and selling wine, leaving time to pursue intellectual interests, explore ancient inscribed ruins and relics found in the Hangzhou area, and exchange art work with friends and associates. On occasion, he and his literati colleagues met on Solitary Hill, near Xiling Bridge, to discuss their studies and en-gage in spirited debates.

Drawing on his explorations around Hangzhou, Ding published a study, *A Record of Wulin [Hangzhou] Metal and Stone Inscriptions* (武林金石錄, *Wulin jinshi lu*), describ-ing more than three hundred ruins and relics around Hangzhou, as well as inscrip-tions on a variety of stone and metallic monuments. In the area of seal engraving, Ding's antiquarian studies led him to favor the simplified ancient characters com-mon to the Han Dynasty era, inscribed primarily in straight lines. The Zhejiang School he founded remains one of China's two dominant styles of cutting characters for seal engraving.[44] The most renowned of Ding's followers, all from Hangzhou, became known as the Eight Great Seal Artists of Hangzhou.[45]

In 1913, the Xiling Seal Engraving Society hosted its first-ever formal event, a celebra-tion of the 1,560-year anniversary[46] of the Orchard Pavilion gathering that inspired Wang Xizhi's calligraphic masterpiece. A new building and pond were constructed in 1915, and another building was added in 1922 to house some of the Society's most valued artifacts.[47] However, as West Lake became more and more a tourist site, the Xiling Society buildings gravitated toward the market demand for casual enjoyment: a teahouse, seating areas, and a shop to sell low-cost seals and associated books, rubbings, and paraphernalia—traditional culture as commodity. In 1929, the grounds were even "borrowed" by the municipal government for the West Lake Expo's hygiene exhibition. Nevertheless, seal arts were surviving into the new era, indicated by their inclusion in Chinese fine arts exhibitions in Shanghai (1929) and Nanjing (1937).

The Xiling Society's property was largely abandoned during the Japanese War but recovered enough afterwards to celebrate (albeit, three years late) the Society's fortieth anniversary in 1947. In 1951, the Society turned the grounds and operation over to the new Communist Party government. Although the Xiling site suffered some damage during the 1960s, it was subsequently restored by the Hangzhou city government. In 1999, the name "Xiling Seal Society" was elevated to national trademark status; a new China Seal Studies Museum was also created that same year. In 2001, the Xiling Seal Society's preservation was guaranteed by its classification as a "Key Cultural Relic Protection Unit," and in 2009, UNESCO added Chinese seal engraving to its Intangible Cultural Heritage of Humanity list with the Xiling Seal Engraving Society's crucial assistance.

More than a century after four seal-carving connoisseurs transformed their passions into a formal association of like-minded scholars, their vision for cultural preservation of an ancient Chinese art form had survived, formally recognized and internationally celebrated.

The Flower Painter: Wu Changshuo

When the Xiling Seal Engraving Society made its formal public debut in 1913, the members chose as the association's leader an individual esteemed for his knowledge and mastery not only of seal carving but of the "three perfections" of the traditional literatus: painting, poetry, and calligraphy.

Wu Changshuo 吳昌碩 (1844 – 1927) was a man of the Qing Dynasty. He was born in Huzhou in the decade preceding the Taiping Rebellion, when the sons of scholarly families devoted themselves to study of the Confucian classics and aspired to excellence in the arts as well as the civil service examination system. Wu's father, Wu Xinjia (1821 – 1868, *juren* 1851) guided his youngest son into the world of classical studies at an early age. An accomplished poet and seal carver, Wu Xinjia also introduced his son to those traditional literary-artistic endeavors and engendered in Changshuo a lifelong interest in seal engraving as well as epigraphy, the study of ancient carved inscriptions.

The advance of the Taiping rebels into the Huzhou area in 1860 disrupted the young man's student life and tragically destroyed his home life. By the time he and his father were able to return to their hometown, they did so as the sole survivors of what had been a nine-person family. Despite post-war struggles and privations, Changshuo resumed his studies and, in 1865, assumed a private-school teaching position in the nearby town of Anji. Although he signaled his lifelong commitment to epigraphy by christening his residence the Seal Script Cloud Pavilion, his main artistic focus narrowed to another classically Chinese tradition: bird and flower painting, particularly plum blossoms.

During the 1860s, Wu Changshuo sat for and passed the lowest level civil service examination, achieving the title of *shengyuan* 生員 (licentiate). From the late 1860s into the 1890s, he traveled through Suzhou, Shanghai, and Hangzhou, meeting and studying with accomplished painters and seal carvers including, in Hangzhou, the great master of Chinese epigraphy, Yu Yue 俞樾 (1821 – 1907) and, in Shanghai, the painter Ren Yi (任頤, 1840–1896).

In 1894, at age fifty, Wu enlisted for front-line military service in the Sino-Japanese War; a few years later in 1899, he was appointed to his first (and only) position as a government official. He resigned after just one month, unable and unwilling to deal with the petty politics of official life. He returned to Shanghai and his established circle of literati colleagues, determined finally to devote himself to painting and calligraphy.

Wu spent the balance of his lifetime living in Suzhou and Shanghai, developing his artistry in "botanical subjects: plum blossoms, orchids, bamboos, pine trees, narcissus, peonies, gourds, wisteria, fruit, and vegetables. He also occasionally painted figures and landscapes."[48] He rose to become the leader of a new school of early modern painting labeled the Shanghai School (海派, *haipai*), whose artists combined traditional themes with new styles of presentation. Wu has been described as "a powerful artist who used the strong color and forms typical of the Shanghai School to structure compositions based on the calligraphic brushstrokes that wonderfully unite the painting with the poem that so often accompanies it (and sometimes dominates it). His earlier work is richly colorful...always fresh and vigorous, raising the Shanghai School to a new level of achievement."[49]

Throughout the first decades of the twentieth century, Wu's work was highly popular and much in demand, especially among Japanese art collectors. Books depicting his paintings began appearing in China and Japan through the early to mid-1920s, and the famous Japanese department store Takashimaya featured public exhibitions of his works in 1921 and again in 1925.[50] In addition to being the first president of the Xiling Seal Engraving Society, he was director of the Shanghai Calligraphy and Painting Association.

Wu's ability to bring together elements of classical painting, calligraphy, seal carving, and epigraphy marked him as a master of traditional styles and a bridge toward a new, modern era. In his later years, Wu suffered pain in his hands that prohibited seal engraving, but he continued his painting and remained honored for his life's work, the full fruits of which did not truly emerge until his fifties.

One amusing anecdote from the last year of Wu's life has him traveling to Hangzhou in 1927, where he decided to pay a call on his friends at the Xiling Seal Engraving Society headquarters on West Lake. When he arrived, he was surprised to see other visitors bowing and burning incense in front of a bronze bust. To his amazement, the figure so honored was his own, sculpted by the Japanese artist Asakuro Fumio (1883 – 1964).

Wu Changshuo's life experiences carried him through the horrors and dislocations of the Taiping civil war, the struggle for national self-strengthening, defeat at the hands of the Japanese in 1895, the failed government reform effort in 1898, the humiliations of the Boxer Rebellion and the onerous reparations exacted by the Western powers in its aftermath, and finally the 1911 Revolution and the ensuing warlord era. Yet through it all, he remained dedicated to the most refined and delicate of arts, seal carving and painting of flowers and birds.[51] Perhaps he really was China's last literatus.

Education Reform Advances

Once the civil service examination system ended by imperial decree in 1905, study of the Confucian classics no longer held its "make-or-break" position in Chinese education. In response to the changed circumstances and the needs of the Republic, the Qiushi Academy, now the Zhejiang Higher Education Institute, began adding elements of the "new learning": the Agricultural Institute in 1910 and the School of Engineering Technology in 1911.

By 1927, these new departments in the school had expanded to include programs for such subject areas as (in Agriculture) botany, farming, forestry, and sericulture, and (in Engineering) chemical, civil and electrical engineering. These more technical disciplines added to a liberal arts curriculum consisting of domestic and foreign languages, history, mathematics, philosophy, political science, and psychology, as well as a medical school program. Schools of Education and Economics followed in 1929.

In nearby Zhakou, southwest of the walled city and overlooking the Qiantang River, the campus of Hangchow Presbyterian College was also taking shape. On Erlongtou (二龙头, Second Dragon Head Hill), academic and administrative buildings, dormitories and faculty housing, a library, sports facilities and fields, water reservoirs, and even a hill-topping observatory sprouted like mushrooms and soon dotted the hillside. The adjacent Sanlongtou (三龙头, Third Dragon Head Hill) just to the west hosted additional residences as well as modest tea plantations and a bamboo grove. Sitting on the campus grounds, students and staff could look out over the Qiantang River and admire the natural wonder of the somewhat depleted tidal bore as it reached their stretch of the river. Perhaps not surprisingly, the school's college literary magazine was christened *The Tide*.

Enrollment the first year (1911) amounted to 117, with thirty-one students in the college and eighty-six in the middle school. Although English language dominated classroom instruction, the school's official language position dictated that the use of English should be carefully tempered so as not to impede students' learning. Tragedy struck the campus late in the first year when a malaria epidemic infected nearly every pupil and caused the death of two students.[52] The highlight of the school's early existence arrived on December 10, 1912 with a visit to the campus and a speech to the students from Dr. Sun Yat-sen. A second honor came when the grandson of Zeng Guofan donated several thousand valuable books to the school's library.[53]

In 1914, the school was renamed Hangchow Christian College (之江大学, Zhijiang daxue), but it retained its junior-college curriculum and status through the decade of the 1910s. Warren H. Stuart (1879 – 1961), one of the four China-born sons of Hangzhou missionary John Linton Stuart (1849 – 1913), was appointed Acting President in 1916 and retained the school's presidency until 1922. Not until November 26, 1920 did the trustees approve the school's charter under the laws of the District of Columbia as a degree-granting four-year college, following which the school celebrated commencement of its first two Bachelor's Degree graduates in 1922. Aside from strengthening the school's faculty, Stuart expanded the Board of Directors from six to nine members so that the first three Chinese members could be added.

Like many Western-founded schools of the era, administrators sought to foster physical education as well as sports competition. Teams both intramural and inter-collegiate were formed for football, basketball, tennis, and track. On May 11, 1918, the school even hosted an East China Intercollegiate Track and Field competition. Hangchow Christian College also initiated an intercollegiate debate team in 1919. Attempts to start varsity crew faltered, not for lack of participants but for lack of competition.

Hangzhou was far from alone in China's education revolution, which rapidly spread across the country. Much of the national movement was pioneered or guided by Shaoxing native Cai Yuanpei 蔡元培 (1868 – 1940), "the Father of Modern Chinese Education." Born into the Qing Dynasty not long after the Taiping Rebellion ended, Cai Yuanpei's life can be divided into three phases—traditionalist, revolutionary, and educational leader/reformer—that closely tracked the radical changes and revolution of his time.

Born into a mid-level mercantile family, Cai devoted his early studies to the Confucian classics, like all young scholars of the 1880s and 1890s. When his father's early death threatened to derail the eleven-year-old Yuanpei's education, his *juren* uncle stepped in both directly and through additional tutors to prepare his nephew for the civil service examinations. Devoted to his studies and eminently capable, Cai rewarded his family's sacrifices by passing his first-level exams at age 17 and gaining his *juren* degree in 1889. He achieved the highest-level, *jinshi* status only one year later at age 22, an extraordinary accomplishment at any time in imperial Chinese history.

After two years in junior positions in Shanghai and Zhejiang Province, Cai was recalled to Beijing in 1892 as a Hanlin scholar. In 1894, he was inducted as a compiler into the vaunted Hanlin Academy, a surefire pathway to a career in high officialdom. However, his nation's defeat in the Sino-Japanese War (1896) pierced Cai's faith in the Qing government and opened his feelings toward ideas of reform. Collapse of the Hundred Days' Reform movement in 1898 cemented his belief that essential national reform could never be achieved within the existing governmental structure. Only radical action would change China, and advancing the people's education would be vital in that new political world.

Cai began his life's second phase not long after resigning from the Hanlin Academy in 1898 and returning to Shaoxing, now a growing hotbed of revolutionary sentiment. He accepted supervisory and Japanese language teaching positions at two schools, the latter at the South Seas School in Shanghai. During this period, he began assimilating educational reform ideas and formulating more concrete views on curriculum and textbooks as well as female education.

In 1902, educators in and around Shanghai founded the reform-minded Chinese

Educational Association with Cai Yuanpei as its president. That same year, a student strike at South Seas School led to the resignation of numerous students and progressive teachers, many of whom joined Cai at the Patriotic Girls' School,[54] now renamed simply the Patriotic School. For the next four years, Cai was an active revolutionary, leading the Patriotic School, joining the new Restoration Society, and heading the Shanghai section of Sun Yat-sen's Revolutionary Alliance. By at least one account,[55] Cai was involved in building explosive devices and even training groups of female students at the Patriotic School as assassination teams.

Discouraged with the revolutionary movement, Cai Yuanpei traveled to Berlin in 1906 for three more years of study at the University of Leipzig. His German education culminated with an undergraduate degree in 1910. More important, it exposed him to a broad array of Western liberal arts studies. When the Revolution broke out in November 1911, Cai was still in Germany, now 43 years old and no longer the active revolutionary of 1902 – 1906. Instead, he began the third and greatest phase of his life when he received a surprise invitation from the new provisional government of China to assume the post of Minister of Education.

From January to July 1912, Cai Yuanpei initiated sweeping and radical reforms in China's primary education, instituting female learning below the university level and promoting textbooks that addressed Confucian principles rather than exhaustively studying directly from the Confucian Classics. Reducing the workload from Confucian studies also opened up the curriculum for other desirable subjects, such as the natural sciences.

Conflicts with President Yuan Shikai caused Cai to resign his position and return to Europe for further study, first to Leipzig, and then to Paris and Lyons when World War I erupted in Europe. Cai returned to China in 1916 following the death of Yuan Shikai to accept an invitation as chancellor of Peking University (北京大学, Beijing daxue, Beida 北大 for short).

Some of Cai's best friends, knowing Beida's reputation as "a den of gambling and debauchery for those awaiting civil service postings,"[56] tried to discourage him from accepting a "no-win" position. Instead, he entered the campus by horse-drawn carriage on January 4, 1917, returning the bows of the gate guards and servants who lined up to greet him. His message was clear: things were going to change. A few days later, in his inaugural address as Chancellor, he announced that Beida would now be a place of study, research, contemplation, and debate, not just a diploma-issuing pleasure palace for government office aspirants. To make sure his statement of university educational philosophy was clear, he informed students that those who disagreed should leave to find their "education" elsewhere.[57]

Cai wasted little time in stamping his reformist imprint on China's most famous university. Seeking to institute a more democratic institution, he created a ten-person faculty advisory council to make policy decisions on curriculum, faculty evaluations, and various student administrative matters. He streamlined the curriculum, enhancing the humanities and natural sciences while disbanding the business and engineering departments. Cai also brought into the faculty new instructors like Chen Duxiu 陳獨秀 (1879 – 1942) and Hu Shih 胡適 (1891 – 1962), based not on their political leanings but on their academic and research accomplishments. Regardless, Beida did not operate in a vacuum, and external events soon brought new complications and challenges.

May Fourth Propels A Cultural Movement

Although provincial governments and local gentry had achieved modest successes in railroad rights recovery, foreign powers from Japan to Europe still viewed the post-1911 Chinese nation as a fertile target for imperialist actions. Some of their interests were driven by desire for natural resources, others by control of and profit from infrastructure assets, creation of favorable if not one-sided trade arrangements, or access to untapped commercial markets. Chinese intellectuals continued to despair of their country's weakness and the repeated humiliations suffered at the hands of foreign countries.

On January 18, 1915 the Japanese government initiated a blatant diplomatic assault on Chinese sovereignty by presenting the government of Yuan Shikai with its infamous Twenty-One Demands. Organized into five different groups, these declarations addressed Japanese territorial claims over land and ports in Shandong Province, authority to finance and construct new railways in the northeast and Manchuria, and rights for Japanese residency, financing, foreign advisors, policing, and commercial development of natural resources in Manchuria and Eastern Inner Mongolia. One of the Twenty-One Demands even required the Chinese government to announce publicly that "No bay, harbor, or island along the coast of China may be ceded or leased to any Power."[58]

After three months of largely unsuccessful negotiation, Yuan Shikai acceded to most of the Japanese demands on May 7, 1915. The popular Chinese response was immediate outrage, including mass defection from Japan of up to four thousand Chinese university students. The very date of Yuan Shikai's signing, May 7, became instantly memorialized as National Humiliation Day. The following year, a flailing Yuan Shikai failed in his effort to declare himself emperor of a new Han Chinese dynasty and passed away in June.

By 1915, World War I was already consuming Europe. The Japanese government sided with the British after war broke out the year before, offering to police the Pacific waters against German ships in return for control over German possessions it could seize in Micronesia. In August 1914, Japan officially declared war on Germany and Austria-Hungary; China did likewise in August 1917 but did not enter the conflict in a military capacity.

When the French had earlier asked for wartime labor support in May 1916, however, the Chinese government responded by sending over forty thousand manual laborers to France, mostly from Shandong Province. When the British asked for similar manual labor support the following year in order to free up more Englishmen for front line combat, Beijing shipped off another one hundred thousand men, along with hundreds of students to act as translators. Another two hundred thousand men provided similar non-combat, manual labor support on the Russian front.[59]

It was for these unarmed men, common laborers who filled sandbags, repaired roads and rails, dug trenches, unloaded cargo at shipyards, and even removed dead bodies from battlefields that Cai Yuanpei helped re-establish the Diligent Work and Frugal Study program during his war years in Europe.[60] China's first experiment in mass education helped train those volunteers and acclimate them to the foreign military environment under which they worked.

When war ended in 1918, both Japan and China were represented among the victors at the Paris Peace Conference. The Chinese delegation expected at a minimum to see Liaoning Province returned from German control, but word reached Beijing in late April that the "Great Powers" were planning to cede control of that province (including the city of Qingdao) to the Japanese.[61] Several Beijing student organizations quickly convened and called for mass demonstrations against the treaty terms to take place on May 7, 1919, National Humiliation Day; virtually every student body in Beijing was prepared to join in. News from Paris grew steadily worse, with indications that China's peace conference representatives were capitulating to the proposed terms with hardly a complaint. As tensions mounted in Beijing, the local government acted to suppress the student outcry.

The consequences were almost inevitable. The students moved their mass protests forward to May 4. At 1:30 that afternoon, more than three thousand students from thirteen different colleges and universities brought their protests to Tian'anmen Gate— there was no Square as yet—before beginning their marching and chanting through the Beijing streets. Most of the protest was non-violent, although the residences of two Chinese government representatives to Japan were set afire and thirty-two students were arrested by police.

The next two months witnessed more student protests and demands for release of those arrested on May 4. The protesters created a citywide Student Union of Beijing that included middle school students and was—for the first time—coeducational. Cai Yuanpei actively supported the students' protest, resigning the presidency of Peking University (along with the chancellors at several other colleges) after the government declared its plans to prosecute the arrested students. At least one student committed suicide in protest.

Another student strike on May 19 spread to multiple cities including Shanghai (May 23), Suzhou (May 28), Hangzhou and Nanjing (May 30), and Ningbo (May 31), followed on June 5 by a protest march of over one thousand students from fifteen girls' schools in Beijing. More student strikes erupted in Shanghai (also on June 5) and again spread rapidly to Hangzhou and multiple other cities.

Overall, the response to May Fourth in Zhejiang Province was largely limited to Hangzhou, Ningbo, and Wenzhou. As early as May 12, students from middle schools and normal (teacher training) schools had organized demonstrations, but when the provincial government announced early and immediate closure of schools for summer vacation, the schools emptied. This muted response did not, however, reflect lack of awareness or interest among Zhejiang's students. Rather, new student journals sprouted that summer, including sixteen in Hangzhou, three in Shaoxing, and two in Huzhou. Ten more periodicals started up between the last quarter of 1919 and the first quarter of 1920.[62] While many were short-lived, they were aggressively anti-traditional and would soon be instrumental in cultural and educational debates.

The cumulative pressure of these successive events was determinative at Versailles. In direct contravention of orders received from Beijing to sign the treaty, the Chinese delegation announced their unanimous refusal and tendered their immediate resignations. China went down in history as the only represented country that refused to sign the fatally flawed Treaty of Versailles, the agreement that inadvertently paved the path to World War II.

Beijing's university students finally called an end to their strikes on July 22, having achieved apologies from the government and the release from prison of their thirty-two previously arrested classmates. Cai Yuanpei agreed to resume the presidency of Peking University effective September 20, 1919. Not long after his return, he took the radical step for which he is perhaps best remembered: he admitted female students to the university in early 1920.

Cai himself had helped propel the movement toward coeducation at Beida, speaking publicly about the importance of education for girls and women and citing the coeducational practices of foreign universities as models. His speeches gave rise to the first direct, written request for admission from Deng Chunlan (1898 – 1982), the sister of one of Beida's male students.[63] Pressure increased to admit female students to the University, becoming even greater during the student actions associated with the May Fourth Movement. By early 1920, Cai had admitted six women as students, with three more permitted to audit classes. The number of female students grew somewhat slowly, however. By 1926, only sixty-one of the over 1,800 students at Peking University were women.[64]

The effects of the May Fourth Movement in China on the national psyche and student activism were inestimable, but perhaps the greatest impact was felt on another, already-existing arts and literature revolution. The rapidly evolving "New Culture Movement" (新文化运动, Xin wenhua yundong) would be motivated by the spirit of May Fourth, spearheaded to a great degree by natives of Hangzhou and Shaoxing, and enthusiastically adopted by newly-activist university students across the country.

Chapter 17

A "New Culture" Rises

(1919 – 1927)

In spring flowers and willows compete in beauty, while lotus and pomegranates bloom in summer. In autumn the fragrance of cassia floats in the air, and in winter jade-like plums bloom amidst the whirling flakes of auspicious snow. The scenes of the four seasons are ever changing, and these things that gratify the heart and give pleasure proceed endlessly apace.[1]

– Wu Zimu (13th Century)

Denounce Filial Piety!

In October 1919, not long after Hangzhou's colleges had resumed operation following the summer's early forced closures, a student at the Zhejiang Provincial First Normal School received an urgent letter from his family in Jinhua. Shi Cuntong 施存统 (1899 – 1970) learned that his mother's health was failing; she did not have long to live. Raised in the highly conservative social climate of the Qiantang River valley southwest of Hangzhou, he was the dutiful son, steeped in the Confucian tradition of filial piety.

Dropping his studies, Shi rushed back to Jinhua, where he found that his mother was indeed gravely ill. He also discovered that she was being left mostly unattended, with little care or consolation. Shi Cuntong offered to pay for nursing assistance, but his father told him to save his money. Those funds could better contribute to a more elaborate funeral and burial for his mother, his father explained, and thus redound positively to the family's social status. The young man now found himself trapped in a Confucian conundrum. He could not be the filial son by respecting his father's decision and also be the filial son to his mother by easing her dying days.

Perhaps Shi Cuntong had in mind the burdens of filial piety on daughters as well.

402

He was likely familiar with the tale of the sacrificial daughter Cao'E who died retrieving her father's drowned corpse from the river. He probably also knew the locally honored legend of Miaoshan, the rebellious third daughter of a king, who donated her eyes and arms to her father so he could live.[2] Then there was the story of Ding Bing's young bride, Ling Zhiyuan, who wrote in a poem that she prayed for the gods to substitute her in death for her seriously ill mother; her mother recovered unexpectedly, and Ling died not long after, equally unexpectedly.[3]

After several days in Jinhua mulling over his filial dilemma, Shi Cuntong came to a revolutionary decision: he returned to Hangzhou. Not simply to resume his studies, but to write a virulent attack against the doctrine of filial piety. "It was too late to try saving my mother," he later wrote. "I thereupon resolved to save all other women who in the future might find themselves in similar circumstances."[4] His essay would take aim at the very foundations of Confucian culture.

The May Fourth Movement at First Normal School had already spawned a new activist group called the Zhejiang New Tide Society (浙江新潮社, Zhejiang xinchao she). Comprised of a strange-bedfellows mix of liberal students from Hangzhou First Middle School and disaffected conservatives from First Normal School, the New Tide students published the first issue of their weekly newspaper of the same name, *Zhejiang New Tide* (浙江新潮, *Zhejiang xinchao*) on November 1, 1919. The paper was an instant hit, selling out within a few days of publication. The eagerly awaited second issue contained Shi Cuntong's bombshell—an essay entitled simply "Decry Filial Piety!" (非废, "Fei xiao").

 Shi's piece was not so much a plea for women's rights and welfare as an attack on his paternal lineage and its dictatorial wielding of patrimony. In the young man's view, private ownership of property and the economic power held by male heads of households in dispensing that property via inheritance created an asymmetric power balance between fathers and sons. Sons, and their mothers, were thereby deprived of their independence as well as their rightful possessions. They were not free people; they were owned by the patriarchy, which exercised its power in part through the dictates of filial piety.

The provincial government reacted predictably and forcefully. The New Tide Society students were expelled from their schools, as were sympathetic faculty members. When the President of Zhejiang First Normal was forced to resign, the students seized control of the campus and held it until the end of January 1920, when government troops retook it by force. Provincial officials also forced the principal of First Middle School to resign.

Shi Cuntong withdrew from the school and traveled to Shanghai. Unable to return home to Jinhua, he found new roots after meeting Chen Duxiu in Shanghai. Those two, and several others, formed a local study group to discuss Marxist theories. Shi and Chen would be among the small group who founded the Chinese Communist Party (CCP) in July 1921. After some early connections to Chiang Kai-shek's Guomindang, Shi aligned himself with the more centrist wing of the CCP and worked with Zhou Enlai 周恩来 (1898 – 1976) in Chongqing during the Japanese war. He rose to Deputy Minister of Labor in 1949 and remains today an honored revolutionary hero in his hometown of Jinhua.

A New Culture

Four years before the events surrounding the May Fourth Movement of 1919, Chen Duxiu founded a magazine called *New Youth* (新青年,*Xin qingnian*), one of the many journals and newspapers springing from the ferment of the time. In the opening issue of September 15, 1915, Chen published his own essay, "A Call to Youth" (敬告青年, "Jinggao qingnian"). His editorial was a *cri de couer* to students across the nation, acknowledging issues like foreign imperialism but insisting that no problem posed a greater threat to China than traditional culture. He called for a "new culture," instructing his readers to:

- 自由非奴隶 (*Ziyou fei nuli*) – Be free and not a slave;
- 进步非保守 (*Jinbu fei baoshou*) – Be progressive and not conservative;
- 进取非退隐 (*Jinqu fei tuiyin*) – Be a leader, not a laggard or follower;
- 世界非锁国 (*Shijie fei suoguo*) – Be open to the world and not isolationist;
- 实利非虚文 (*Shili fei xuwen*) – Be pragmatic and not theoretical; and
- 科学非想象 (*Kexue fei xiangxiang*) – Be scientific and not superstitious.[5]

New Youth captivated student readers and quickly became the leading voice of the "New Culture" movement. Radical essays about cultural reform appeared one after another. In one such essay, Chen Duxiu famously wrote that China must replace "Mr. Confucius" with "Mr. Science" and "Mr. Democracy." In January 1917, Hu Shih 胡適 (1891 – 1962) submitted an essay calling for increased use of vernacular language or plain speech (白话, *baihua*) in all forms of writing, from poetry to newspapers.[6]

The next month, in an article titled "The Family System as the Basis of Despotism" (家族制度為專制主義之根據論, "Jiazu zhidu wei zhuanzhizhuyi zhi genju lun"), Wu Yu 吳虞 (1872 – 1949) penned a scathing attack on filial piety as the means by which "the family and state collaborated to keep the individual bound and gagged emotionally, intellectually, and spiritually."[7] Later that year, Chen Duxiu wrote about the objectives of "the Army of Revolution in Literature" a blatant, three-point assault on literary traditionalism:

1. To destroy the painted, powdered and obsequious literature of the aristocratic few, and to create the plain, simple and expressive literature of the people;

2. To destroy the stereotyped and monotonous literature of classicism, and to create the fresh and sincere literature of realism; and

3. To destroy the pedantic, unintelligible and obscurantist literature of the hermit and the recluse, and to create the plain-speaking and popular literature of a living society.[8]

By the time *Zhejiang New Tide* began publishing in November 1919, such periodicals were part of an expanding movement that began with *New Youth*. The height of the May Fourth protests may already have passed by then, but Shi Cuntong's denunciation of filial piety added still more fuel to the New Culture fire among Hangzhou's students. More significant, his notoriety helped link the student activist movements in Hangzhou and throughout Zhejiang with those in Shanghai, Beijing, and elsewhere.

Increasingly, the student readers of *New Youth* and dozens of similar periodicals were being immersed in a new cultural environment. Cai Yuanpei, as perhaps the nation's premier educational leader, sided with the students as well, and not only in words. No supportive action on his part could have been more potent than his hiring of both Chen Duxiu (as Dean of the College of Letters) and Hu Shih (as a lecturer) onto the Peking University faculty. Cai's support and the articles flowing from these radical publications were building upon the student rebellions of the May Fourth Movement and further spurring the students' awakening activism.

Yet of all the many influential articles that appeared in the pages of *New Youth*, none had more impact on Chinese culture than a fictional work authored by a self-described cynic.

A Madman's Diary

On May 15, 1918, a strange short story appeared in *New Youth*, written mostly in vernacular language[9] by a Shaoxing native under the pseudonym Lu Xun. Titled "Diary of a Madman" (狂人日记, "Kuangren riji"), the story presents the paranoid musings from the found diary of a man who "has gone elsewhere to take up an official post." The diary's thirteen entries record the missing man's realization that everyone around him is a cannibal. They may all feast on one another someday, but right now he believes that he is their intended prey. Even his elder brother is a cannibal who has already eaten his little sister. When he looks to his classical texts to chart the course of this behavior over time, he is suddenly able "to see words between the lines,[10] the whole book being filled with the two words—'Eat people'." Believing he is being driven to suicide so he can be eaten, the writer finishes with a despairing but hopeful entry: "Perhaps there are still children who have not eaten men? Save the children...."

"Diary of a Madman" stunned *New Youth*'s readership.[11] Here was a writer likening four thousand years of Confucian teachings and the struggles for examination success and official position to cannibalism, to so viciously consuming one another that none could "ever hope to face real men" (i.e., foreigners). To prove his point, the madman (as he refers to himself) recalls Xu Xilin, Qiu Jin's revolutionary partner, of whom it was commonly said that his heart and liver were eaten by his executioners in 1907. He also refers to an ancient prescription of filial piety that sons and daughters should cut and feed their flesh to parents who are starving or in need of meat for nourishment from illness.

The closing line, "Save the children...," not only called for revolutionary social change but quickly became the hallowed slogan of those efforts. The story itself marked the birth of a new era in Chinese realist fiction and propelled the New Culture movement to the forefront of Chinese arts and literature.

Lu Xun 鲁迅 (1881 – 1936)[12] was born Zhou Zhangshou 周樟壽 in Shaoxing. He grew up in a well-established local family, with a Hanlin scholar grandfather (Zhou Fuqing 周福清, 1838 - 1904) and a literatus father (Zhou Boyi 周伯宜, 1861 – 1896), and two younger brothers, Zhou Zuoren 周作人(1885 – 1967) and Zhou Jianren 周建人 (1884 – 1984). His mother, Lu Rui 鲁瑞 (1857 – 1943), was a village countrywoman who had taught herself how to read.

At age seven, his parents set their first-born son out on the standard educational path toward the civil service examinations: studying the *Four Books* and *Five Classics* (四書五經, *Sishu wujing*), reading traditional poetry and learning to write his own, and mastering the arcane complexities of the eight-legged essay (*bagu wen*, 八股文) used in the examinations. Lu Xun was a dutiful young scholar, but he also enjoyed the outdoors and showed keen interest in the natural world and in drawing and tracing. However, two family incidents in his youth left deep marks on him that would color his adolescent thinking and later appear in his writing.

In the first, repeated failures in the provincial (*juren*) examinations led his father to approach *his* father (Lu Xun's grandfather) about bribing an examination official. The illicit act was accidentally discovered,[13] resulting in the family's public disgrace. Lu Xun's father was stripped of his degree, and his grandfather imprisoned and nearly executed in Hangzhou.

The second incident resulted from the first. Lu Xun's father responded to his personal and family disgrace with bouts of drinking that drastically imperiled his health. Doctors prescribed traditional medicines comprised of obscure herbs, forcing young Lu Xun into humiliating pharmacy searches for the required ingredients. At times, the boy resorted to pawning out-of-season clothing for enough money to secure the ingredients, always with the hope of recovering the pawned items before they were needed again.

At age 17, Lu Xun aspired to attend the Qiushi Academy in Hangzhou, but financial straits forced him to choose the low-cost and ultra-conservative Jiangnan Naval Academy (江南水師學堂, Jiangnan Shuishe Xuetang) in Nanjing. At around this time, the clan family leader changed Lu Xun's formal name from his birth name, Zhou Zhangshou, to Zhou Shuren, alluding to the adage that it takes ten years to nurture a tree, but a hundred years to train a man.[14] He left the Naval Academy after just six months and enrolled in the nearby School of Mines and Railways, where he received his first exposure to foreign literature and languages (English and German). Three years later, in 1902, he sailed to Japan on a government scholarship, first to study Japanese language and then to enroll in a Japanese university. It was around this time that he cut off his queue.

After a brief visit home to Shaoxing for an unwanted arranged marriage, Lu Xun returned to Japan to begin medical school studies at Sendai in northern Japan. His objective was to return to China with the modern medical knowledge that had been so lacking during his father's illness years earlier. After a little more than a year, he abandoned his studies at Sendai and returned to Tokyo to study literature. He later described the classroom incident during a current-events presentation at Sendai that he claimed caused him to redirect his career. One slide showed a bound Chinese man about to be beheaded as a Russian spy by Japanese soldiers while surrounded by strong and healthy-looking fellow Chinese gathered to watch the spectacle. He wrote:

> [A]fter seeing this film, I felt that medical science was not such an important thing after all. People from an ignorant and weak country, no matter how physically healthy and strong they may be, could only serve to be made examples of, or onlookers of utterly meaningless spectacles, and such a condition was more deplorable than dying of sickness. Therefore our first important task was to change their spirit, and at that time I considered the best medium for securing this end was literature and thus was determined to promote a literary movement.[15]

In 1909, Lu Xun (still known as Zhou Shuren) returned to China and accepted a position in Hangzhou at Zhejiang First Normal College as a lecturer in the sciences. At odds with the school's Confucian-oriented presidents (one of whose resignations he facilitated), he returned home as dean of Shaoxing Middle School. After the 1911 Revolution, he briefly headed the new Shaoxing Normal College before Cai Yuanpei, as the new Minister of Education, reached out to his fellow Shaoxing comrade with a position in Nanjing, and then in Beijing when Yuan Shikai relocated the national capital. Despite Cai Yuanpei's departure over disagreements with Yuan, Lu Xun stayed on in the Ministry of Education and made significant contributions: upgrades at the Capital (Peking) Library, a new National History Museum, and a new Library of Popular Literature.

Remarkably, Lu Xun was a reluctant writer of fiction, having to be repeatedly cajoled by friends into submitting work for *New Youth*. In the 1922 preface to his first short story collection *Call to Arms*, Lu Xun described with an allegory his ambivalence toward submitting his first work of fiction ("Diary of a Madman") to *New Youth*. Suppose, he said, a group of people were locked asleep in a windowless, iron room with no way out. They will soon die of suffocation, but they will not suffer because they are asleep. If, somehow, one were able to wake at least a few of them by shouting, they would only die in insufferable agony instead of peacefully in their sleep. Would awakening them have been a kindness?

When Lu Xun finally shouted, countless numbers of his fellow citizens indeed awakened.[16] After he submitted "Diary of a Madman" under the pseudonym Lu Xun (adopting his mother's family name, Lu), he became nationally known by that name. In 1920, Cai Yuanpei invited him to join the Peking University faculty as a part-time instructor in literature; he also taught at Peking Woman's Normal College. Even with this workload, Lu Xun continued leading the New Culture literary wave. The period from 1918 – 1926 brought an outpouring of memorable short stories drawn from his own life experiences and observations in and around Shaoxing, including among others, "Kong

Yiji" (1918), "Medicine" (1919), "The Story of Hair" (1920), "My Old Home" (1921), "Happy Family" (1924), "Soap" (1924) and "New Year Sacrifice" (1924).

Between December 4, 1921 and February 12, 1922, Lu Xun also published a serialized short story in the *Beijing Morning News* entitled "The True Story of Ah Q" (阿Q正傳, "Ah Q zhengzhuan"). "Ah Q" would be his only novella, but it would be his masterpiece, arguably the first in modern Chinese literature. Where "Diary of a Madman" critiqued traditional learning in China, Lu Xun now leveled a savage attack on what he saw as the willful blindness of his fellow Chinese people, the cruelties of the social caste system, and the utter ineffectuality of the educated elite. His story was nothing less than an assault on the national character of his time.

The story's protagonist, Ah Q, is something of the town[17] laughingstock, an uneducated man who lives in a local temple and performs odd jobs around the village in the last weeks before the 1911 Revolution. Ah Q's defining characteristics are levels of self-regard and self-delusion so bloated that his every social interaction is either an opportunity for silent condescension or a silent proclamation of personal victory, no matter how much he is outwardly abused or humiliated. Lu Xun presents him psychologically, so the reader sees the world through Ah Q's eyes and "hears" his thoughts.

Ah Q is the perpetual victim. The action is comical, at times outright slapstick, and even the tragic ending contains as much humor as pathos. Lu Xun's intention, of course, was biting social criticism: the semi-anonymous and clan-unattached Ah Q represented the Chinese Everyman of his time. Even his abbreviated name, the English letter "Q," could be viewed as a shaved head with the Manchu braid (ironically, a "queue") hanging from it.

As Lu Xun presents the Chinese national character through Ah Q, his countrymen are plagued (both personally and nationally) by inflated self-regard and grudge-bearing, unrelenting condescension toward one's (perceived) "lessers" and obsequious obeisance toward one's (perceived) "betters," and a willful blindness to reality that, like Ah Q, transforms every humiliation and loss into an empty "spiritual victory." Yet within every incident illustrating Ah Q's failings lies the kernel of its solution, of the changes that Lu Xun believed were necessary in Chinese character and society to strengthen the nation. The fact that Lu Xun published the story under the pseudonym Ba Ren 巴人[18] only enhanced its impact, since readers everywhere were captivated by the identity of the mystery author.[19]

The nearly instantaneous acclaim for "Ah Q," propelled in great part by French novelist Romain Rolland (1866 – 1944), raised international awareness of Lu Xun's literary oeuvre. As a consequence, he was approached in 1927 about being nominated for a Nobel Prize in Literature at the request of a Nobel Academy member. Lu Xun politely but firmly demurred. He wrote in reply that "China still really had no person who should receive the Nobel Prize," arguing self-effacingly that a Nobel Prize simply given for "our yellow skin… would be sufficient to promote the Chinese sense of false glory to make us think we really could walk shoulder to shoulder with the great authors of other nations."[20]

In 1926, at the peak of Lu Xun's fame as a New Culture realist, he left Beijing and his university teaching positions. Increasing politicization and warlord protest activity, particularly at the Women's Normal College, led to violence and the death of two of Lu Xun's students. Toward the end of that year, he accepted a teaching position in Xiamen and left behind his life as a fiction writer. What he took with him to southeastern China were his reputation as one of the nation's leading intellectuals, a student named Xu Guangping 許廣平 (1898 – 1968) with whom the still-married Lu Xun was deeply enmeshed in a love affair, and the early signs of tuberculosis.

A "Sinking" Feeling

While Lu Xun continued making literary waves in 1921 Beijing with his *New Youth* stories about the nation's collective psyche, another young man from Zhejiang was plumbing the depths of the individual psyche. Yu Dafu 郁达夫 (1896 – 1945) hailed from Fuyang, just twenty miles southwest of Hangzhou. His father and grandfather were doctors, but Yu Dafu's relatively comfortable early life was upended by his father's death when the boy was only three years old. He nevertheless moved forward academically in Fuyang, first with traditional private school studies and then a new-style public primary school.

At age 15, he took up middle school studies in Hangzhou and was subsequently admitted to Hangzhou Presbyterian College[21] before being expelled for his involvement in a student strike. In 1913, he began a ten-year stint in Japan by enrolling at Tokyo Imperial University to study economics, becoming part of the continuing Chinese student diaspora there. Yu Dafu spent his four preparatory years in Japan utterly immersed in Western, Japanese, and Russian literature; Yu himself claimed to have consumed over a thousand titles.[22]

His life in Tokyo apparently mixed academics with deadening debauchery. The after-effects he suffered from the pleasures of drinking, womanizing, and gambling included guilt, loneliness, and self-recrimination. Out of these experiences also came, in 1921, a semi-autobiographical short story collection, aptly titled *Sinking* (*Chenlun*, 沉淪), that won Yu Dafu lifelong fame. The book consisted of three stories, "Sinking" (沉淪, "Chenlun")," "Silver-Gray Death" (銀灰色的死, "Yinhuise de si"), and "Moving South" (南迁, "Nanqian"). Yu's stories shocked readers with their interior monologues of despair and their sexual frankness. C.T. Hsia described the title story as "a mawkish tale of adolescent frustration and guilt" whose "daring and originality at once captivated the younger audience and enraged moralists, who found its decadence highly corruptive."[23]

The main character in "Sinking," an unnamed Chinese student in Japan, struggles with overwhelming loneliness and extreme sexual frustration. He lives alone in a small inn, staying well apart from other students, Chinese or Japanese. After a bout of voyeurism involving the innkeeper's daughter and a night of tortured guilt over his behavior, he temporarily escapes his temptations by moving into a Buddhist temple. His sexual desires are triggered again, however, when he overhears another couple in their love-making, so he decides to visit a brothel where he is mostly ignored by a waitress. Further convinced of his own uselessness, he drinks himself senseless.

The next morning, he strolls along a seaside beach contemplating whether to simply walk into the sea and disappear. His final words suggest his decision: "O China, my China, you are the cause of my death!...I wish you could become rich and strong soon!....Many, many of your children are still suffering."[24]

The narcissistic central figures in Yu Dafu's three *Sinking* stories were walking metaphors for China's turn-of-the-century weakness: "thin, pale, bespectacled, and dragging a sickly body…excruciatingly vulnerable and fearful of possible rejection," "emaciated-looking and slightly hunchbacked," and experiencing shame "at both the racial level (being a Chinese in a superior Japan) and the sexual level (inadequate masculinity and failure to live up to the ideal of a conscientious, abstinent scholar)."[25] *Sinking* thus joined "Diary of a Madman" and "The True Story of Ah Q" among the literary emblems in the New Culture movement that spurred Chinese students' calls for change.

The Cartoon Revolution

More than just opening new literary doors, the New Culture Movement opened artistic eyes and broadened aesthetic horizons, encouraging new ways of employing traditional arts and styles by integrating Japanese- and Western-inspired forms. Perhaps the finest example of integrating and blending old and new, Chinese and foreign, religious and secular, can be seen in the public emergence in the 1920s of Feng Zikai (丰子恺, 1898 – 1975) and his renowned *manhua* 漫画 (cartoon or sketch, from the Japanese *manga*).

In 1924, rumors reached the editor of the Shanghai-based *Literature Weekly*, Zheng Zhenduo 郑振铎 (1898 - 1958), about the unusual work of an artist-teacher at the local Lida Academy. Hoping to discover new forms of representation to enliven his publication with something original and even radical, Zheng wanted to see this work for himself.

Instantly captivated by Feng Zikai's austere and straightforward presentation of classical themes, Zheng Zhenduo returned home with a selection of Feng's works. He later wrote that he "felt an irrepressible sense of delight; it was as though I have captured some new territory." Indeed, he had. *Literature Weekly* received such enthusiastic feedback on Feng's sketches that Zheng began calling them "Zikai *manhua*."[26] Their style was fresh, simple, cogent, and instantly recognizable, not least from the Western letters Feng used to sign his work: "TK" (for Tsi-kai, as Feng's given name was anglicized at that time). Feng's work would revolutionize pictorial culture in 20th-Century China, transforming cartoons into both an art form and a vehicle for mass communication.

Feng Zikai's father, Feng Huang 丰鐄 (1865 – 1906) celebrated his son's birth in 1908 in Shimenwan 石门湾, a small town near Jiaxing, as the long-hoped-for continuation of the family lineage after the earlier birth of six daughters (two other brothers had died in childhood). The Fengs were an educated and well-off family, proprietors of a silk dyeing business whose income allowed Feng Huang to pursue the traditional civil service examination path to a government career. After several failed attempts to gain his provincial (*juren*) degree, he finally succeeded in 1902, only to see the examination system abolished in 1905. Rather than turn back to the family business, he lapsed into the consolations of alcohol, opium, and tutoring his only son.

As the family's "little emperor," Zikai showed little interest in the Classics but great enthusiasm for the illustrations and woodblock prints they contained. When his father died from tuberculosis, the eight-year-old family scion began copying and tracing figures from one of his father's many books, the *Mustard Seed Garden Painting Manual*, and even coloring them using dyes from the family business. Zikai's mother stepped in to direct her son's education toward the humanities and a career in teaching. That path lay in Hangzhou, where the young man enrolled in Zhejiang First Normal School. It was here that one of Feng's teachers suggested the new name of Zikai[27] for the young man who until now had been called by his birth name, Feng Ren (丰仁).

The choice and timing of his enrollment at First Normal proved fortuitous. In Feng Zikai's third year, he fell under the spell of a newly arrived art and music teacher named Li Shutong 李叔同 (1880 – 1942). Li had studied Western painting and music at the Tokyo School of Fine Arts and had been an early and controversial proponent for painting nudes in Chinese artistic training. At First Normal, he guided Feng Zikai away from tracing and toward drawing and sketching, and to drawing physical objects, not just copying old paintings.

Married (to Xu Limin, 1896 – 1983) and now responsible for his aging and ailing mother in Shimenwan, Feng graduated from First Normal and took on art teaching positions in Shanghai. Two years later, in 1921, he traveled to Japan in order to advance his art education. Although his funds ran out in just ten months, he gained valuable exposure to Japanese and Western art and Japanese, English, and Russian languages. He found time as well to dabble in violin playing, attend Kabuki theater performances, and browse museums and old bookstores. Feng also discovered the work of Takehisa Yumeji (1899 – 1934) at this time; he would later allow that Yumeji's paper-and-ink work greatly influenced his own. In particular, the book *Yumeji's Collected Paintings: Spring* (and later the similarly-named *Summer*, *Autumn*, and *Winter* volumes) illustrated new ways to merge poetry and painting in a modern style.

Back again in China, Feng accepted a teaching position at the newly formed Chunhui High School in Shangyu (Shaoxing), a hotbed of intellectual and political ferment in the 1920s. The school's location at White Horse Lake "was nothing less than idyllic, and memoirs and poems about the area…generally describe it in terms of Tao Yuanming's utopian 'Peach Blossom Valley'."[28] Amidst the Walden-like tranquility of that setting, Feng Zikai began experimenting with a new phase in his work: sketching scenes to illustrate selected lines from classical Chinese poetry. The source of his inspiration, however, sprung not from White Horse Lake, but from West Lake.

On an earlier excursion from Chunhui High School to visit a friend in Hangzhou, Feng had hoped to complete a few sketches of West Lake in moonlight, a favorite scenic setting (along with mist or rain) of the literati class. Try as he would, he could not find the inspiration for a satisfactory rendering of the lake and returned to his room for the evening. His friend, however, happened to recite some lines of Bai Juyi's while leafing through the sketches Feng had already made but rejected.

> The moonlight is like water,
> The water like the sky.
> Where is the person who watched the moon with me?
> The scene is cast in shadow as it was last year.

Forgetting the lake itself and focusing on Bai's poem, Feng was able to create the sketch that captured what he felt. Realizing the hidden power of scenic descriptions in poetry, he began an entire series of works, "new paintings from old poems."[29] Some of his drawings depicted literal translations, while others offered reinterpretations or even new perspectives on classical poetic lines. Feng continued this practice of turning poetic verse into paintings through the 1920s and intermittently throughout his life. In 1943, his "paintings from poems" *manhua* were published as a collection entitled *Poetry in Paintings*. However, as the decade of the 1920s drew to an end, his private life, public role, and the subjects of his art would turn in new directions.

The Opera Revolution

Traditional Chinese opera represents another artistic field where multiple cultural trends combined with external events in the 1920s and 1930s to form an entirely new, popular, and long-lived theatrical style. Born in the rural peasant villages outside of Shaoxing and nurtured in the Hangzhou – Huzhou – Jiaxing area, Yue Opera (越剧, Yueju), sometimes called Shaoxing Little Opera, rose to become one of modern China's best loved operatic forms. As one writer summarized it, "If Peking opera is the prime theatrical style in Chinese opera, Yue opera is the second."[30] With its all-female performance troupes, Yue Opera signaled a major shift in Chinese women's rights and their societal roles as public performers and culture consumers, "a concentrated expression of the historical rise of women in public culture in modern Chinese society"[31]

Chinese opera traces its roots at least as far back as the Southern Song (1127 – 1279) and Yuan (1271 – 1368) dynasties. Throughout the Ming and much of the Qing Dynasty, Suzhou-style Kunqu (崑曲) Opera dominated, rivaled and then surpassed by Peking Opera (京剧, Jingju) in the latter half of the Qing era. Across those centuries, myriad other local opera styles developed, characterized by the use of local dialect, local tunes, and sometimes even local storytelling traditions. By the 19th Century, official studies found over three hundred different styles of operatic storytelling in China,[32] many of them drawing upon the same historical stories and legends for their repertoire.

During the Qing Dynasty, Chinese opera performance was an entirely male domain, regardless whether the role was masculine or feminine, young or old. The Manchu conquerors viewed many operas as decadent and even as a contributing factor in the Ming collapse, so strict limits were placed on story lines and content. Women who dared to participate in such performances were regarded as little more than licentious sexual provocateurs. Consequently, Qing-era men and boys took on all the female parts, cross-dressing and sometimes winning particular fame as female impersonators. Such was the case in major regional operas as well as lesser, local opera styles.

Gender restrictions also applied to attending opera performances. Women in well-to-do families might occasionally be permitted to watch from a suitably screened vantage point within their family's private residential compound. In rural areas, women might have occasion on a religious or festival holiday to view opera scene performances staged in public marketplaces. However, public audiences in theaters or teahouses were generally all-male.

In the mid-1800s in the rural area south of Shaoxing, peasant farmers in the town of Shengxian 嵊县 (modern day Shengzhou 嵊州) developed a local storytelling style for light diversion while laboring in the fields. They often told bawdy tales, sprinkled with earthy vernacular language, that stressed the hardships of rural life. Over time, a few young men picked up enough of a story repertoire to supplement their income with occasional performances presented to rich landowners and merchants. As the number of performers out of Shengxian increased, they traveled to nearby large cities such as Ningbo and Hangzhou. Their success waxed at first, but it waned in the pre-revolutionary years of the early 1900s.

Fortune struck on the frosty evening of March 27, 1906 in Dongwang Village, just outside of Shengxian. Three separate pairs of traveling storytellers stopped for the night at the residence of Chen Wanyuan 陈万元, a well-known patron who regularly welcomed overnight stays by wandering troubadours. When his fellow townspeople asked for a performance, Chen suggested that all six storytellers act on their story together on stage. The four-hour performance that resulted was an instant sensation. As word spread, other storytellers began forming acting troupes and their numbers grew. Using only a drum and a wooden clapper and with few props or costumes, people around Shengxian began referring to this new storytelling style as "little opera" to differentiate it from the more elaborate "Shaoxing major opera" (绍兴大班, Shaoxing daban).

Shengxian little opera spread outward through Zhejiang during the 1910s, reaching Shanghai for the first time in 1917. When its popularity began to decline, the opera troupes remade themselves in 1919 on the heels of the May Fourth Movement and in light of the new emphasis on women's rights and freedom. They adopted a new repertoire, focusing on traditional romantic stories with heroic female characters. Shanghai theaters and teahouses once again welcomed them; by 1925, as many as fifteen different venues hosted little opera performances. But the truly radical change was quietly forming back in Shengxian, well beyond the range of Shanghai's awareness.

As mixed-gender performances slowly grew in popularity, a Shengxian merchant named Wang Jinshui, manager of the Shenping Theater in Shanghai, perceived the increasing need for a reliable supply of female little opera artists. The obvious solution: establish an opera training school for girls. Wang opened his new school in 1923, committing his own daughter to the program and offering an attractive package of enrollment incentives. The school succeeded in its recruiting but was rather less successful in its first efforts at all-female public performances. By the following year, however, the troupe had refined its presentation and began winning over an enthusiastic following in eastern Zhejiang, from Ningbo to Hangzhou. The opera revolution in Shaoxing and Shanghai was only just beginning.

Who's Buried in Wu Song's Tomb?

The New Culture Movement's experimentation with new forms of expression could not simply expunge two or three millennia of cultural achievement, nor did it seek to do so. Countless myths, legends, stories, poems, operas, paintings, and historical events were deeply embedded in Chinese culture and in the hearts, minds, and imaginations of the people. However, they could be adapted or repackaged in surprising and creative ways. One of the more peculiar of these manifestations appeared at Hangzhou's West Lake in 1924, thanks in part to an entirely unexpected sponsorship.

The sources are a bit murky, but they suggest that several workers in the West Lake vicinity happened upon a tombstone during an excavation. The marker's inscriptions improbably identified the deceased as Wu Song 武松, one of the numerous heroic figures in the novel *Shuihu Zhuan* 水浒传, variously known by the English names *Outlaws of the Marsh*, *Water Margin*, and *All Men Are Brothers*. The novel has most often been attributed to Shi Nai'an 施耐庵, (c. 1296 – c. 1372), possibly a native of Hangzhou,[33] and has long been considered one of the Four Great Novels of classical Chinese literature.

Outlaws of the Marsh tells the tale of a band of 108 outlaws who gathered together at Liangshan Marsh in Shandong Province under the leadership of the rebel Song Jiang 宋江.[34] This small but heroic force sets out to defend the country from foreign invasion by the Khitan Liao and to assist in putting down the anti-Song rebellion instigated by Fang La. Many of the novel's seventy chapters[35] trace the exploits of individual members of the troop, including several chapters devoted to Wu Song.

Wu Song's introduction to *Water Margin*'s readers begins with the escapade for which he is most famously recalled: killing a man-eating tiger with his bare hands. Having left an inn late one day rather than stay overnight, Wu Song ignores the innkeeper's warnings of a fierce tiger roaming the nearby mountain ridge he has to cross in his travels. Signs along the way convince Wu that the tiger warnings are more than just idle talk or an innkeeper's trickery, but he forges boldly ahead anyway. During a moment's rest, the dreaded tiger appears and a fearsome struggle ensues. Wu Song emerges exhausted but victorious after kicking the tiger in the face, punching it dozens of times, and finally beating the prone animal with his broken cudgel for good measure. He would forever after be renowned as the man who killed a tiger by sheer bravery and strength.

Wu Song's story continues with his enrollment in Song Jiang's "band of brothers," leading troops against the barbarian Liao and fending off Fang La's rebels in a battle at Muzhou 睦州.[36] Wu decides to retire in Hangzhou after this final conflict and lives out his life as a reclusive Buddhist monk in the Liuhe Temple.

414

Among the thousands of visitors to West Lake in 1924 was the notorious "Big Ears" Du Yuesheng 杜月笙 (1888 – 1951), leader of the Green Gang (青帮, Qing bang), a powerful Shanghai-based criminal organization. He and his cohorts happened to notice the grave marker for Wu Song. However unlikely it was that the grave actually held the corpse of Wu Song,[37] Du Yuesheng decided that such an amazing fellow deserved a more honorable burial. He therefore financed the construction of an elaborate burial site at Xiling Bridge, not far from a similar mound for Xue Susu.

Wu Song's tomb site included the traditional domed mound, a short passage leading to the tomb, and a memorial arch. A stone stele mounted in front of the tomb mound read, "Tomb of Song Patriot Wu Song" (宋义士武松之墓, Song yishi Wu Song mu). The entire configuration grandly celebrated a character who existed in fiction but probably never in flesh and blood. The tomb's contents were irrelevant; only the recognition of heroism against tigers and national enemies mattered.

Wu Song's tomb was damaged in the 1960s but fully restored in 2004. At West Lake today, the site is not readily visible and is easily overlooked by the excited crush of tourists around Xue Susu's tomb. However, a short walk westward from there will recall the memory of the tiger-killing hero.

Numerous stories and movies have since recalled the 108 outlaws and Wu Song's legend, including Pearl Buck's translation of *Shuihu Zhuan* as *All Men Are Brothers*. Noteworthy as well, Wu Song and his brother's marital problems occupy the opening pages of *The Plum in the Golden Vase* (金瓶梅, *Jin Ping Mei*), another of China's great classical novels of the Ming-Qing era. More recently, a satirical short story by Ha Jin titled, "A Tiger-Fighter Is Hard to Find"[38] employs the Wu Song tiger-slaying episode to offer a literary commentary on modern heroism and media.

Chapter 18

THE NATIONALIST ERA

(1927 – 1949)

Settled Snow on Solitary Hill Island[1]

On the white stone of the hilltop six-cornered blossoms spread.
On the blue-black of the water's surface, one solitary topknot.
A purple wind molds the cloud, the shell of morning cracks:
A white jade turtle lifts the sun out of the bowl of ice.
Plum blossoms there's no better time to pick than braving the cold:
Bamboo leaf wine why shouldn't we tread a frozen path to buy?
If Lin Bu left a mark to last a thousand years
It's all because the finest views are here on West Lake.

– Gao Deyang (1368 – 1398)

A Train to Hangzhou

Following the death of Yuan Shikai in 1916, the Chinese nation lapsed into a precarious period of regional factions and warlord-dominated cliques. The military strength of Yuan's Beiyan army enabled his successors to maintain a semblance of central government, but the decade from 1916 – 1926 witnessed constant military conflict as warlord factions fought with one another for increased power. This period was reminiscent of the Five Dynasties and Ten Kingdoms era (907 – 960), the decades immediately following the fall of the Tang Dynasty. This time, however, there had been no Qian family to steer Hangzhou's course safely through troubled political seas.

Even as student demonstrations and strikes flared over the terms of the Versailles Treaty in 1919 and Cai Yuanpei pursued revolutionary educational reform at Peking University, a new movement was quietly organizing in Shanghai. The Bolshevik Revolution in

1917 Russia and the social-economic writings of Karl Marx spurred essays about Marxism as a governing philosophy for 20th-Century China. Ideas about communism spread widely but thinly across the nation, so that by mid-1921, the Chinese Communist Party (CCP) consisted of only fifty-seven members. For the Western powers in Shanghai, however, the Russian Revolution provided more than sufficient cause to be wary of any Marxist-based organizing movements in the China whose future they still hoped to shape to their own interests.

Shanghai's International Settlement may have appeared a haven of stability in July 1921, but for the twelve CCP representatives who chose to meet there secretly on July 23, the risks were still substantial. With schools closed for summer vacation, the group met in an upper floor classroom of a girls' school in the French Concession.[2] He Shuheng 何叔衡 (1876–1935) and a young Mao Zedong 毛泽东 (1893 – 1976) represented Changsha at this meeting, the first plenary session of the CCP. Neither Chen Duxiu nor Li Dazhou 李大钊 (1889 – 1927), the two founders and leading voices of the Party, were able to attend.

Lively and sometimes contentious discussions ensued for a full week as the group sought to establish its organizing principles. According to Philip Short,[3] a decision to relocate the July 30 session to the residence of Shanghai CCP representative Li Hanjun 李汉俊 (1890 – 1927) proved nearly fatal. During that day's meeting, a stranger peered through the window and then hurriedly excused himself for being at the wrong address. The meeting broke up almost immediately, the participants dispersing quickly into the Shanghai streets. Not long after, Chinese and French Concession police detectives arrived but found nothing despite a four-hour search.

Because the French Settlement authorities remained on continuous high alert and surveillance, the First Congress members hatched an ad hoc plan to complete their meeting thanks to a Jiaxing connection. As related by Xiao Yu 萧瑜 (1894 – 1976),[4] a friend of Mao's from Changsha, the delegates would each purchase train tickets for Hangzhou, intending to visit West Lake as tourists. When the train stopped in Jiaxing on its way to Hangzhou, they would leave the train and casually mix with the platform crowd. Meanwhile, the wife of one of the delegates would rent a boat on South Lake (南湖, Nanhu), on the outskirts of Jiaxing, where the meeting could be completed.

The boat was furnished with a table upon which mahjong sets had been placed. A large wooden screen near the open end of the boat hid the table and those seated around it. The delegate's wife acted as lookout: when other boats passed nearby on the lake, she tapped on the screen with her folding fan. Inside, mahjong tiles would be shuffled loudly enough for their clacking to be heard by passersby.[5] At the end of that day on South Lake, the First National Congress closed with Chen Duxiu named the CCP's Secretary-General in absentia. Afterwards, Mao and Xiao Yu continued on to Hangzhou. Mao's first opportunity to view the famous West Lake scenery would be far from his last.

Peking University's Zhejiang Leadership Continues

Admitting women students was only the latest of Cai Yuanpei's educational reforms at Peking University after he returned to its presidency in September 1919. He fought aggressively to maintain the school's independence and bolster its academic and faculty credentials. He invited Lu Xun into the faculty as a lecturer and continued to strengthen the humanities departments, not just by faculty hires but with a stellar cast of guest lecturers and visiting professors: John Dewey (1859 – 1952), Bertrand Russell (1872 – 1970), Swedish art historian Osvald Siren (1879 – 1966), birth control activist Margaret Sanger (1879 – 1966), and Indian poet-playwright-philosopher Rabindranath Tagore (1861 – 1941).

Unfortunately, troubles could not be kept at bay. In March 1921, the university closed for six months over a wage strike, a result of the government not having paid the faculty for three months. Students demanded the school reopen and marched to the presidential palace on June 3, only to suffer brutal beatings by military police. The negative publicity from that event forced the government to negotiate, and classes finally resumed. Repeated instances of government interference compelled Cai Yuanpei to resign again in 1923.

Although Cai soon returned as Peking University's chancellor and remained in that position until 1927, he spent much of the mid-1920s in Europe. Freed to undertake broader intellectual pursuits, he forged another remarkable imprint on China's academic life in 1928 as the founder and first president (from 1928 – 1940, the year of his death) of the Academia Sinica,[6] the nation's most elite science and technology research and publishing organization of that era. *The New York Times*, in Cai's obituary notice, described him as a "Chinese elder statesman, educator and publicist" and labeled him "the Father of the Chinese Renaissance."[7] If any further evidence of this titular honor is necessary, it should be noted that another of Cai's remarkable accomplishments was co-founding the National Conservatory of Music. In 1956, that institution would become the Shanghai Conservatory of Music.

As Cai Yuanpei reduced his presence in Beijing and his active role in day-to-day administration, Jiang Menglin assumed effective leadership of the university. Like so many of the faculty's leading lights, Jiang Menglin was a son of Zhejiang Province,[8] born in Yuyao, between Shaoxing and coastal Ningbo. After beginning his traditional-style education in a private school, he studied at Xu Shulan's Sino-Occidental School in Shaoxing and then at a Catholic school in Shanghai before moving to the Zhejiang First Normal School in Hangzhou. In 1908, he enrolled at the University of California, where he majored in education. After graduation, he traveled to New York to study at Columbia University under John Dewey and earn his doctorate in education.

When five major educational reform groups formed the Society for the Promotion of New Education in January 1919, Jiang Menglin served as editor of their journal, *Xin jiaoyu* 新教育, *The New Education*. The Society's educational philosophy featured prominently in the magazine's masthead: "Individual Development and Social Progress."[9] Jiang and his fellow New Education and New Culture reformers distanced themselves and their spheres of operation from the government, creating an independence that Ming- and Qing-era literati had never enjoyed. *New Education* supported these efforts

418

under Jiang Menglin's leadership, in part by coordinating its editorial content with John Dewey's extended China visit and lecture series from 1919 – 1921.[10]

After Jiang's years at Peking University, he was appointed director of the Zhejiang Provincial Department of Education in 1927. The following year, he became President of Zhejiang University in Hangzhou as well as Minister of Education under the new Nationalist government. In 1930, he resigned from the Nanjing Ministry when he was appointed President of Peking University, a position he held until 1937. During the nomadic war years, Jiang Menglin remained instrumental in keeping China's university education alive, working jointly in Changsha and then Yunnan Province with senior administrators from Qinghua and Nankai Universities.

Where Cai Yuanpei had strenuously promoted humanities education as the major need of his time (during and through the New Culture Movement era), Jiang had foreseen the importance of whole-person education. He advocated not only for universal compulsory education but also for vocational and remedial education, increased physical and artistic/aesthetic education, and development of students' individuality, social consciousness, and sense of citizenship. Chinese education had been radically transformed in the three decades from 1905 to 1935, and among the greatest leaders of that change had been Cai Yuanpei and Jiang Menglin, two Zhejiangese men from the neighboring cities of Shaoxing and Yuyao.

The Pagoda Came Tumbling Down

During the warlord-dominated decade, Hangzhou submitted to the rule of military governor Lu Yongxiang 盧永祥 (1867 - 1933), a native of Shandong Province, from August 1919 to September 1924. A former commander of Yuan Shikai's Beiyang Army, Lu and his neighboring warlord in Jiangsu Province, Qi Xieyuan 齐燮元 (1885 - 1946), engaged in brief armed conflict over control of Shanghai that began on September 1, 1924. Qi prevailed, and Lu fled Zhejiang on September 18, thanks in major part to an attack from the south by another warlord, Sun Chuanfang 孙传芳 (1885 – 1935).

Sun Chuanfang had held the military governorship of Fujian Province for about eighteen months when he joined in the attack against Lu Yongxiang. With the warlords of Jiangsu and Zhejiang engaged in conflict, Sun saw opportunities that might even extend as far as Beijing. As he marched his Beiyang Fourth Army north into Zhejiang, Hangzhou residents experienced the chaos and uncertainty of impending conflict.

Elmer Mattox (1869 – 1963), who served as President of Hangchow Christian College and was associated with the school for forty years, wrote about the Hangzhou of September 1924:

> This section was thrown into great confusion; people became panic-stricken and tens of thousands flocked to the shelter of the foreign settlements in Shanghai....For the six weeks during which the fighting continued,...schools could not open, meetings were forbidden, and the only work that missionar-

ies could do was...caring for the wounded and the refugees.[11]

Hangzhou was fortunate this time. Lu Yongxiang abandoned Hangzhou peacefully and, on September 25, 1924, Sun Chuanfang marched toward the city on the road running along the Qiantang River below the Hangchow Christian College campus. That same day—some say at the exact time Sun triumphantly entered Hangzhou[12]—Leifeng Pagoda collapsed into rubble on the south shore of West Lake, leaving only the stub of the first floor standing. It was only after the pagoda's fall that Wuyue king Qian Chu's secret—the insertion of 84,000 copies of a Buddhist sutra in the hollowed-out cores of the floor tiles—was finally uncovered.

Leifeng Pagoda's fall after nearly 950 years seemed the most ill of omens and the most freakish of coincidences. To some, a pagoda is a pagoda is a pagoda, but Leifeng Pagoda was more than that. It was a fairy tale, simultaneously a legend and an imperial icon, a place of alleged miraculous power and a fortress against evil.

Leifeng's collapse was easily explainable yet nevertheless wholly unexpected. Qian Hongchu's pagoda had long suffered the usual ravages of age, war, and fire. The monument was set ablaze during a Northern Song rebellion and restored in the late 1100s. Burnt again in the mid-1500s by Japanese bandits, only the pagoda's inner brick core remained standing, a gently tapering, nearly conical structure topped with a platform. Left unreconstructed, various plants, trees, and ivies grew on the platform and down the pagoda's fire-reddened brick facing.

As a ruin, the pagoda gradually took on a unique fame of its own, celebrated by literati poets and even by the Kangxi and Qianlong Emperors during their Southern Inspection Tours.[13] Both Emperors had been instrumental in standardizing, immortalizing, and promoting the famous "Ten Views of West Lake," one of whose scenes was "Leifeng Pagoda in the Sunset" (雷峰夕照, Leifeng xizhao). Former Zhejiang Governor Li Wei once described the decaying pagoda in the Qing era with near-Keatsian reverence:

> The solitary tower remains proudly erect, with its red-brick walls covered in verdant creepers. When the evening sunlight falls on it, the beautiful-ly decorated platform at the top of the pagoda is set off perfectly by the mountains behind; it is as though one had opened up a gold mirror, from which peals of fire are about to fall. The most resplendent palace could not compare with it.[14]

Alongside this rich history, mystical lore concerning Leifeng Pagoda also arose from a fairy tale-like story commonly known as *The Legend of White Snake* (白蛇传, *Bai she zhuan*). The story was retold in multiple, generally consistent versions until it finally coalesced with the short-story version, "The White Maiden Locked for Eternity in the Leifeng Pagoda," written by Feng Menglong.

The plot involves two minor gods, White Snake and Green Snake,[15] who have attained enough magical powers to change their forms and exercise other feats of magic. Tired of life on Mount Emei,[16] they decide to go exploring and head for Hangzhou, having long heard descriptions of the area's beauty. On arrival, the two snakes assume the appearance of beautiful young women, calling themselves Bai Suzhen 白素貞 and Xiaoqing 小青. While they wander about West Lake admiring its scenery, a rain storm erupts and catches them unprepared. Luckily for the two beauties in disguise, a handsome, unmarried pharmacist's assistant named Xu Xian 許仙 gives them shelter under his umbrella.

Bai Suzhen falls in love with Xu, the two marry, and they move (with Xiaoqing in tow) to Zhenjiang, where Xu Xian opens a medicine shop of his own. The shop is extraordinarily successful because Bai Suzhen secretly imbues the medicines they sell with extra healing powers.

One day, a monk named Fa Hai 法海 enters the shop and informs Xu that his wife is actually a demon. The young man rejects this fabulous notion, but the monk later provides him with a strong wine. Have Bai Suzhen drink this wine until she loses consciousness, Fa Hai instructs, and you will see her true form. The ruse works, but Xu Xian is so shocked by his wife's true snake form, he collapses in shock and dies. White Snake and Green Snake fly back to Mount Emei to retrieve a magical fungus that restores Xu to life. His love for Bai Suzhen now exceeds his fear of her true form.

Fa Hai, who also has magical powers, persists with several unsuccessful efforts to rid the mortal world of the two demons until he finally defeats them. He captures the two snakes in his alms-bowl and chants as he buries it beneath Leifeng Pagoda:

> When the West Lake is drained of its water
> And rivers and ponds are dried up,
> When Thunder Peak [Leifeng Pagoda] crumbles,
> The White Snake shall again roam the earth. [17]

Yang Lianzhenjia's infamous White Pagoda in early-Yuan Hangzhou, built atop the buried remains of Southern Song emperors to suppress their anti-Mongol spiritual power, may have provided imaginative inspiration for the White Snake legend at Leifeng Pagoda.[18] Countless versions of the White Snake story have appeared over time, including multiple operatic versions, movies, television series, and children's books. When the story was not being retold or refashioned for new media, it provided a recognizable source of literary allusion on good versus evil and the power of unconditional love.

The mythical, demon-restraining power of Leifeng Pagoda and the story's connection with magic-infused medicines also spawned superstitious belief in the pagoda's healing power. Over the centuries, visitors to West Lake chipped away at the ancient bricks of the exposed inner shell or removing entire bricks, believing that in powdered form they possessed special healing powers against diseases and fetal miscarriages. With enough bricks removed from the reachable lower levels, coupled with the slow ravages of wind, weather, and time without reinforcement or repair, Leifeng's collapse—but not the timing—was inevitable.

The 20th-Century fall of Leifeng Pagoda generated an entirely new set of metaphorical interpretations. One of the earliest came from Lu Xun, who wrote in "The Collapse of Leifeng Pagoda" (dated October 28, 1924) that he had never been much impressed with the "Leifeng Pagoda at Sunset" view. He added with a dose of rather cranky cynicism that everyone in the country should be pleased about the pagoda's collapse because Fa Hai was nothing more than a meddlesome monk who should have minded his own business.

The following February 6, Lu Xun added another dose of biting sarcasm in "More Thoughts on the Collapse of the Leifeng Pagoda." He wrote that China suffered from "a sort of 'ten-site disease', or at least an 'eight-site disease'....Look through any county annals, and you will find the district has ten sites, if not eight, such as 'Moonlight on a Distant Village,' 'Quiet Monastery and Clear Bell,' 'Ancient Pool and Crystal Water.'"[19]

To cite just one example consistent with Lu Xun's thesis, the Haining vicinity was transformed from a rural backwater into a late 18th-Century sightseeing venue due in fair part to the Qianlong Emperor's repeated seawall and tidal bore visits. As a consequence, local or visiting literati rediscovered earlier sets of Haining area "views" and spawned multiple new series such as: "Eight Scenic Views of Haichang," "Twelve Scenic Views of Xiachuan," "Four Scenic Views of Zunjing Pavilion," and "Ten Scenic Views of Luoxi."[20]

Lu Xun's explicit calling out of the "ten views" tradition shattered hallowed conventions surrounding the seven-hundred-year-old, imperially certified "Ten Views of West Lake." Ten years later, the "Ten Views" could be openly satirized, as one writer did by suggesting alternative West Lake views with titles like "Dancing in the Jinguo Hotel" and "Purchasing Antiques at the Yue [Fei] Tomb."[21]

Turning his attention back to the pagoda's ruin, Lu Xun's second article excoriated his fellow countrymen for wrecking public property for "some trifling personal gain" only to patch over the traditions that caused the ruins. He closed with a call for new attitudes in a revitalized and changing nation: "We want wreckers who will bring about reforms, for their hearts are lit up by an ideal."[22]

In the 1960s, author Eileen Chang (Zhang Ailing 張愛玲, 1920 – 1995) alluded to the events of September 25, 1924 by entitling her semi-autobiographical novel *The Fall of the Pagoda*. The story line does not involve Hangzhou or West Lake, but as David Derwei Wang wrote in his introduction to the novel, "Chang finds in the fall of the Pagoda a series of associations—from the collapse of a phallic symbol to the tumbling of patriarchal authority; from Chinese feudalism to Chinese nationalism—and brings it to bear on her own concerns."[23]

Heading North

Warlord Sun Chuanfang established himself as military governor of Zhejiang Province in late September 1924. Over the next twelve months, he expanded his domain to include four other provinces: Fujian, Jiangsu, Anhui, and Jiangxi. With his headquarters in Nanjing and control over some of the richest and most productive lands in the country, Sun's position looked increasingly like that of Hong Xiuquan, the Taiping Heavenly King, less than a century earlier. However, Sun Chuanfang was no more of a welcomed presence in Hangzhou than his warlord predecessor Lu Yongxiang had been. Military control, regardless under whose command, ran directly counter to the desires of Zhejiang's intellectual and gentry leaders for provincial autonomy.

One of the keys to Sun's conquest of Zhejiang had been the support of Xia Chao 夏超 (1882 – 1926), a native of Qingtian in southeastern Zhejiang. A graduate of the Zhejiang Military Academy, Xia had cleverly navigated the political waters of post-1911 Zhejiang and risen to police chief for the entire province. In 1919, he had backed Lu Yongxiang as military governor in return for preserving his own power base, but after supporting Sun Chuanfang's overthrow of Lu in 1924, he was rewarded with the civil governorship of the province as well as retaining his post as provincial police chief. Still not satisfied with his position, Xia found opportunity to advance further while Sun's attention turned to installing himself in Nanjing as the head of a united "League of Five Provinces."

A poor harvest in 1925, compounded by both drought and floods, further weakened Sun's support among Zhejiang's gentry. Sensing opportunity, Xia Chao turned receptive to entreaties from Chiang Kai-shek. Chiang had already launched his Northern Expedition (北伐, Bei fa) against Sun Chuanfang's stronghold in Jiangxi Province in July 1926, so Chiang's representatives approached Xia Chao about carefully reducing Sun's border forces in southern Zhejiang areas adjacent to Jiangxi. Hoping to catch Sun by surprise and take Shanghai in the process, Xia declared Zhejiang's independence and adopted a new constitution on October 16. He was further backed by Hangzhou activists who declared their support for Chiang Kai-shek's Nationalist government in Guangdong Province. Xia was rewarded with command of the 18th Army unit of the GMD's National Revolutionary Army (NRA).

Xia set out for Shanghai in October 1926 with a force of 6,000 – 10,000[24] mostly untrained men, but Sun managed to get their route blocked before they could reach the city. After some minor skirmishes in the Shanghai suburbs, Xia fell back with his forces to Jiaxing. On October 20, Sun's emergency reinforcements engaged Xia's defenses at Jiaxing and routed them before day's end. Many of those who fled were captured and summarily executed that same evening. Xia failed to escape as well. Tracked down and hauled from his fleeing motor car, Sun ordered that he be shot there on the street and his decapitated head delivered to Nanjing.[25]

Despite the failure of his uprising, Xia had created a helpful distraction for Chiang Kai-shek's Northern Expedition efforts. Through October and November 1926, separate Nationalist forces progressed northward through Jiangxi and Fujian Province. After the Fujian provincial capital of Fuzhou surrendered to the NRA on December 9, Sun's position was seriously weakened. Chiang Kai-shek's armies were converging on Zhejiang from the southeast, south, and southwest.[26]

Sun Chuanfang attempted to shore up his Zhejiang regime in the final months of 1926 by installing new military and civil governors, the latter (Shaoxing native Chen Yi 陳儀, 1883 - 1950) to replace the traitorous Xia Chao. To strengthen his position in Jiangnan, Sun quickly forged an anti-Nationalist alliance with Zhang Zuolin (张作霖, 1875 – 1928) in Manchuria, but his frantic moves proved too little, too distant, and too late. Chiang Kai-shek and his representatives managed to turn key local military leaders to their side, including Chen Yi. On December 19, a group of Zhejiang's civil leaders meeting in Shanghai declared their province independent and autonomous and presented a written declaration to that effect to both Sun and Chiang.

Sun retaliated with an all-out, four-division thrust[27] down the Qiantang and Fuyang River valleys, pushing Chiang Kai-shek's Nationalist forces back to Quzhou, near the Jiangxi Province border, in early January 1927. Only fast action by the NRA's First Army unit in Fujian Province provided reinforcements sufficient to halt Sun's armies just ten miles from Quzhou and launch a counterattack on January 20. The two armies battled furiously for four days in the Lanxi and Jinhua areas from January 29 to February 1. Sun's forces attempted a counterattack at Tonglu which failed, as did a last-ditch attempt with reinforcements to hold the line at Fuyang. The line broke and Sun's defeated soldiers headed northeast toward Hangzhou and Shanghai, looting their way through the mostly emptied towns in their paths.

On February 17, Hangzhou's military and civil governors both left the provincial capital and headed for Shanghai. "The night of February 17 was a night of terror, with retreating Northern troops looting and burning the shops of the city on their way out. Finally, by noon of the 18th, Chiang Kai-shek's Southern troops had marched in and quiet was restored. The people welcomed the troops with open arms."[28]

An interesting sidebar to the Hangzhou evacuation by Sun's troops appeared in the American press on February 28, 1927. An unnamed Presbyterian missionary claimed to have witnessed a large group of Sun Chuanfang's soldiers demanding money from the city's Chamber of Commerce the day before they evacuated the city. Dissatisfied with delays in the Chamber's response, the defeated soldiers "marked out a section of the city a mile square, containing the best shops...and immediately looted everything in sight."[29] When they returned to the Chamber of Commerce office, they were given $40,000 in cash. The next morning, armed groups of Hangzhou residents hunted down as many of Sun's soldiers as they could find. "Hundreds were butchered in this man hunt," according to the missionary. He noted as well that Chiang's Northern Expedition troops were "smartly uniformed" and "well armed" and "generally refrained from looting when they reached Hangchow, except in the homes of foreigners."[30]

More troubles followed as Sun's retreating soldiers were being transported to Shanghai "in cold cattle cars."[31] Their train stopped in Jiaxing, where they were met by city officials who asked the commanding officer not to permit the defeated soldiers to leave the train. Their request was ignored as soldiers, many of them mercenaries, poured out of their crowded train cars and headed into Jiaxing to take whatever they wanted and do whatever they wished. Their behavior in the cities and towns in northern

Zhejiang would stand in sharp contrast to Chiang Kai-shek's victorious Northern Expedition troops, who would soon be welcomed into those same places.[32] Having secured Zhejiang Province by mid-February, NRA forces moved on Shanghai, which fell on March 22, and Nanjing, which fell the next day.

Chiang Kai-shek promptly relocated the Nationalist Government from Canton to Nanjing. Fighting north of the Yangzi River and in western China would continue for almost two more years until the closing days of December 1928. In the meantime, Chiang shattered the tenuous arrangement of cooperation between the GMD Nationalists and the increasingly potent Chinese Communist Party. On April 12, 1927, he authorized the Shanghai Massacre[33] (also known as the April 12 Incident or April 12 Massacre) of Communist Party members; the associated purge continued for the next two or three years. A quote commonly attributed to Chiang at the time asserted that he would rather mistakenly kill one thousand innocent people than allow one Communist to escape.

Chiang Kai-shek's Northern Expedition ended in 1928 with the nominal reunification of China under a Nationalist government centered in Nanjing, with Generalissimo Chiang at its head. The coming Nanjing decade would demonstrate that China had not yet achieved real unification—or real strength.

West Lake Shows Off

Removal of Sun Chuanfang and creation of a centralized national government in Nanjing provided Hangzhou with a welcome period of relative stability. Since the arrival of railroad passenger service, the city's post-1911 economic recovery and expansion had progressed noticeably. Population figures of the era demonstrate Hangzhou's progress, increasing from around 140,000 in 1911 to nearly 820,000 in 1928, an annualized growth rate of almost eleven percent. Yet the city had not noticeably industrialized to accommodate the employment needs of so many people, relying heavily instead on small merchant operations and tourism.

West Lake by the closing years of the 1920s had been fully transformed into a tourism and resort area. The decision by newlyweds Chiang Kai-shek and Soong Meiling 宋美齡 (1898 – 2003) to celebrate their honeymoon with a stay at the lakeside Cheng Villa in December 1927 only further publicized West Lake as eastern China's premier resort area. For Western visitors, the popular 1918 sightseeing guidebook of Robert F. Fitch[34] went through repeated new editions in 1922, 1928, and again in 1935 to keep pace with the city's rapidly changing tourism offerings.

In the opening pages of his 1922 edition, Fitch left no doubt about whom he saw as his intended readers. Titling the first chapter "How to Get to Hangchow and Where to Stay," he wrote exclusively about the improvements in transportation between Shanghai and Hangzhou from houseboats (a week's travel time) to steam tugboat (thirty-six hours) to railroad (four and a quarter hours), identifying three acceptable hotels and noting that "the best train is the afternoon express, leaving Shanghai at the North Station."[35] In 1925, a Western writer for *Travel* magazine described his arrival by train on the teeming Hangzhou station platform:

> The usual, or rather more than the usual amount of hubbub and confusion is there to greet one. Third and first-class passengers, silk clad and cotton clothed, coolie, mandarin and modern business man crowd and elbow one another, while heavily laden luggage coolies, perspiring under staggering loads, shrilly out-shout the general din with cries of what in other lands is commonly known as 'gangway'.[36]

Hangzhou was fast becoming the weekend playground of Shanghai's Westerners and well-heeled Chinese citizens. This perception was further reinforced by their discovery of the pleasures (and heat relief) afforded by summer-long stays in the Western-style resort villas at Moganshan 莫干山, located northwest of Hangzhou in the Tianmu Mountains.

In October 1928, the city on the lake took its boldest self-promotional step yet when the provincial government, under the leadership of Governor Zhang Jingjiang, approved plans for a West Lake Exposition. First proposed in 1922 in connection with the completion of the New Business District and the lake-encircling roadway, proponents of the 1929 Exposition conceived the event as a spur to economic development and growth as well as a celebration of the new Nationalist government.

Grand design responsibility for the Expo site was handed to Liu Jipiao 刘既漂, (1900–1992). Only 28 years old, Liu nevertheless brought to the table an impressive resumé: studies at L'Ecole Nationale des Beaux Arts in Paris, contributor to the Strasbourg Expo in 1924, and chief architect of China's pavilion at the 1925 Paris Expo, where he married Western Art Deco and Chinese cultural images into an award-winning design. Back again in China, Liu was already well known as a co-founder (with Cai Yuanpei) and Head of Design of the new Hangzhou National Academy of Art.

China had previously participated at the Panama Expo in 1915 and the Philadelphia Expo in 1926, but Hangzhou West Lake would be the nation's first opportunity to host an international exposition. It turned out to be a memorable performance. Across the northern side of the lake and on Solitary Island, Liu Jipiao arrayed two museums and eight exhibition halls, each of the latter having a specific focus such as industry, agriculture, silk, art, education, and hygiene/sanitation. Additional exhibition spaces were provided for specialized government administrations and technologies: roads, communications, and aviation. Liu made use of a number of already existing buildings along the lake shore and on the northside hills, but he created eye-catching entrance gates, ticket kiosks, arches, towers, and building decorations that fused Chinese architectural styles with the latest in Art Deco architecture.

Not to say that everyone appreciated Liu Jipiao's architectural vision or the use of "sacred" West Lake as a public exhibition venue. During a sightseeing visit to Hangzhou a dozen years later in 1941, Lin Yutang 林语堂 (1895 – 1976) stayed at a lakeside hotel and visited Tiger Spring in the western hills. On his way there, he took note of "a structure resembling a lighthouse...[from] a commemorative hall left over from some exhibition." In his short essay, "The Monks of Hangzhou," he wrote that if he had command of an artillery battalion, he would first target "this insult to the face of West Lake" for obliteration and would likely be celebrated by posterity with the following humorous lines:

> Green are the trees along West Lake's shore
> Only this blemish the senses abhor.
> General Lin, his anger unbounded,
> With his cannons this eyesore pounded.[37]

The First West Lake Exposition opened on June 6, 1929 and closed over one hundred days later on October 20, drawing an estimated twenty million visitors in four months. Attendees were treated to more than just exhibition halls: airshows by planes capable of landing and taking off on the lake, numerous lectures, and competitive events ranging from table tennis and cycling to Chinese chess and Go.[38] While most of the exhibitions and visitors were of Chinese origin, a number of foreign delegations and a selection of foreign products were also displayed.

Perhaps not as grand as the Paris Exposition four years earlier, the West Lake Expo nevertheless proudly introduced the new, post-1911 Hangzhou, and greater China, to China's own citizens and to the world at large.

University Education Evolves

Early on, the new Nationalist government set its sights on education and instituted major changes at the university level. The former Ministry of Education became the University Council (大学院, Daxueyuan) in 1927, with Cai Yuanpei at its head. The next year, the Zhejiang Higher Education Institute became the National Zhejiang University (国立浙江大学, Guoli Zhejiang daxue)[39] to reflect the school's heightened status and broadened offerings.

In 1927, the American Board of Directors at Hangzhou Christian College confronted a new directive from Nanjing, applicable to all foreign mission schools. In order to continue operation, the College was now required to install a Chinese national as its president, restructure its Board to be majority Chinese, admit both female and male students, and make religious education and religious service attendance elective or voluntary. George Fitch complied by resigning the college presidency, but in June 1928 the American Board formally rejected the limits being imposed on religious instruction and observation. Three days later, the Board ordered the school closed, in opposition to the wishes of the faculty in Hangzhou.[40]

Not until September 1929 did the Senior Middle School and Junior College achieve compliance with the new directive and receive authorization to re-open. Almost two years later, in July 1931, the Senior College successfully registered and re-opened as the (private) Hangchow College of Sciences and Humanities (私立之江文理学院,Sili Zhijiang wen lixue yuan). Hangzhou native Li Pei-en 李培恩 (Baen E. Lee, 1889 – 1958), a 1910 alumnus, was named as the school's President.

In 1932, Hangchow College opened a new library and a new science building, followed between 1933 and 1935 by additional faculty living quarters, a central administration building, and a materials science laboratory. In 1936, construction finished on the school's hallmark building, the red-brick Economics Building with its traditional clock tower. The building was funded as a memorial to a student who was waylaid and killed by bandits not far from the campus while on his way back to the school from Shanghai.[41]

Two Literary Influencers in 1930s America

The First West Lake Exposition in 1929 represented just one way for China to re-introduce its post-imperial self to the world via an event entirely of its own making. The Expo enabled Hangzhou, and the nation at large, to feature its culture and commerce, and to tell its story in its own way. At the same time, however, two American women living in China in the 1920s and 1930s, one world-famous and the other largely forgotten today, were also telling their versions of China's story. It would be their "sentimental and middlebrow"[42] stories as much as any newspaper reporting that would shape mid-to-late 20th-century Western popular perceptions and stereotypes about China.

As author of numerous works of literary fiction about life in turn-of-the-20th-Century China and the first woman ever to receive the Nobel Prize for Literature, Pearl Buck (1892 – 1973) hardly needs introduction. Born Pearl Sydenstricker, she was the daughter of American missionaries Absalom (1852 – 1931) and Caroline Stulting (1857 – 1921) Sydenstricker. When her parents arrived in China in 1880, they were sent to Hangzhou as their first posting. For the next three years, they divided time between Hangzhou and Suzhou, after which they settled into mission work in Zhenjiang, Jiangsu Province, only 40 miles from the provincial capital at Nanjing. Pearl grew up in Zhenjiang, but she certainly knew about Suzhou and Hangzhou from her parents' early experiences in those two cities.

After marrying the agricultural economist John Lossing Buck (1890 – 1975) in 1917, Pearl Buck lived for a time in Anhui Province before moving to Nanjing, where she taught English literature and began her writing career. Her first two works, *East Wind, West Wind* and *The Good Earth* were published in 1930 and 1931, respectively. Her moving tales of the lives of the common people in China were astonishingly successful in America and the West.[43] Movies based on her work only magnified their reach and influence. Buck was extraordinarily prolific, producing well over two dozen novels (nearly all set in China), three autobiographies, and countless short stories, along with children's books and numerous works of non-fiction. Five of her fictional works were produced as Hollywood movies.

Equally influential in 1930s popular culture were the China-based novels of Alice Tisdale Hobart (1882 – 1967). In 1908, the same year Sidney Gamble's family visited

428

Hangzhou, Alice Nourse took leave from her employment with the Chicago YWCA to visit her Baptist missionary sister Mary in Hangzhou. Mary Nourse had taken up teaching at Hangzhou's Wayland Academy after completing her graduate studies at the University of Chicago in 1905.

In her autobiography *Gusty's Child*, Hobart described her first sighting of Hangzhou's grand city wall, depicting a barrier rather different from what the modern reader might imagine:

> And there it was rearing itself out of the flat fields. It did not seem a man-made thing of brick and mortar. More like earth, in the process of the centuries petrified into the semblance of brick, but keeping the precious life-giving properties of earth to nourish the swinging vines and gnarled trees which...I could see growing on its perpendicular outer face. Only the parapet, clean-cut geometrically precise, retained a man-made look.[44]

In 1910, two years after her first visit, Alice returned again to Hangzhou (just as Sidney Gamble would do in 1917), joining her sister as a teacher at Wayland.[45]

Marriage among Western missionaries was a commonplace event in early 20th-Century China, where a small and insular expatriate community of single women (nearly all of them teachers, doctors, or nurses) intermingled with single or widowed missionary men. In Alice Nourse's case, however, her expatriate connection occurred with an executive from Standard Oil Company of New York named Earle Tisdale Hobart (1886 – 1968). They met in Hangzhou and married in Tianjin in 1914, after which Hobart's oil industry career took him to Manchuria, Changsha, Nanjing, and Shanghai before they returned to the United States in 1927. As Alice followed her husband and his work from place to place, she tried her hand at writing: an encounter with bandits in Manchuria (*Pioneering Where the World Is Old*, 1917), life as an expatriate wife in Changsha (*By the City of the Long Sand*, 1926), and experiences in Nanjing during the Northern Expedition (*Within the Walls of Nanking*, 1928).

Although she never returned to China, Alice Tisdale Hobart continued to write successful popular novels set in the country where she had lived and traveled for seventeen years. In 1933, she published *Oil for the Lamps of China*, the story of an oil company executive troubled by his consuming commitment to his work. Hobart's book proved to be such a bestseller in 1934, "second in influence and sales only to Buck's *The Good Earth*,"[46] that it was quickly produced as a movie of the same name in 1935. She continued for much of her life to write novels—set mostly in China, ten in all—achieving estimated lifetime sales in the range of four million copies.

In Hobart's 1967 obituary notice,[47] *The New York Times* referred to its own Book Review description of *Oil for the Lamps of China* as "a novel of amazing scope." The article summarized Hobart's life's work by stating that "each [of her novels] reflected her craftsmanship as a storyteller, her concern for humanity, her sympathy for the underdog, and her fundamental optimism." More darkly though, the obituary included a brief excerpt from Hobart's most famous book that inadvertently reflected the condescending views about China she had also helped perpetuate: "For a long time I've felt China's going down into some dark struggle," *The Times* quoted. "I used to think of the West coming to China as a light, illuminating darkness. It's not going to be like that. It's going to be a hard travail to get the West born in the East, if it ever is." It was an oddly politicized editorial choice for an obituary selection from a writer's life's work.

The two women writers whose work did more than anyone to shape early American popular culture perceptions of China and Chinese people, for better or worse, both had Chinese roots in Hangzhou.

Like Mother, Like Daughter

The abrupt departure of Qiu Jin from her husband's family home in 1903 left plentiful emotional scars on Wang Guifen, her abandoned daughter.[48] By the same token, her mother's heroic life, fight for gender equality, and ultimate sacrifice for her country must have installed an offsetting pride in her daughter's heart. Known by her courtesy name Canzhi 燦芝, Qiu Jin's daughter grew up in Xiangjiang (Hunan Province) with her grandmother and brother. As a youngster, she demonstrated the same preferences as her mother for physical activities and exercise.

After receiving her early education at Yifang Girls' School in Hunan and the Patriotic Women's School in Shanghai, Wang Canzhi matriculated from Daxia 大夏 (now East China Normal) University in 1927. After graduation, she took a position as principal of a school in Shanghai founded and named in her mother's honor, Jing Xiong ("Competing with Men") Women's School.[49]

During her time working at Jing Xiong, Wang Canzhi took two major steps to enhance and reinforce Qiu Jin's memory. After visiting her mother's West Lake tomb and pavilion on Solitary Hill in 1928, she lamented poetically the degree to which the site had deteriorated:

> The walls have fallen, the tiles broken, surely no longer able to shield autumn
> wind and autumn rain;
> The long weeds are tangled and the wild flowers drooping, sadly I sigh over
> my mother's efforts long forgotten.[50]

Wang submitted a petition seeking restoration of her mother's tomb and memorial site. In this request, she seconded an earlier petition by a well-connected local member of the gentry[51] (and uncle of the not-yet-famous Zhou Enlai) for installation of a pavilion, inscribed stele, and memorial hall for the late revolutionary heroine. Cai Yuanpei added his influential voice in support and, although the memorial hall was never built, a new pavilion was constructed atop Fushan Mountain in Shaoxing and named for Qiu Jin. Cai himself wrote the "Record of the Memorial Stele for Martyr Qiu" that was inscribed on the stele erected at the crossroad site of Qiu's execution.

Wang Canzhi's second major step in honoring her mother's memory involved editing her mother's writings. Published in 1929, the *Collected Writings of Qiu Jin, the Woman Martyr* (秋瑾女侠遗集, *Qiu Jin nüxia yiji*) contained over two hundred of Qiu Jin's poems and essays. Perhaps most significant to her mother's place and perception in history, *Collected Writings* opened with a sizable portfolio of photographs, including several depicting Qiu Jin in the iconic poses for which she is still famously remembered.

Despite Wang's emotional reconnection and commitment to her mother's memory, she was nevertheless her mother's daughter: restlessly independent, willing to study in a foreign land, and harboring deep disregard for traditional female roles. Late in 1928, she applied for and received government financial assistance to study aeronautical science and engineering at New York University.

Separation from her native country as well as from the mother she never had clearly weighed heavily on Canzhi while she was in New York. Two of her poems written at that time are titled "Missing My Mother While Studying Abroad in New York" and "Longing for Mother While in New York." The latter piece opens with the following lines: "A brilliant star falls, / One morning, a tragic parting. / Before I could know my loving mother, / You have given your life to the revolution. / And I have no way to beckon your spirit."[52] She returned to China in 1931, celebrated as the nation's first female aviation expert.[53] She then worked in the Nationalist government's Ministry of Aviation as an instructor on aviation and technology.

Much later, in 1953, Wang Canzhi produced a historical novel centered on her mother's biography, *The Story of Qiu Jin in Revolution* (秋瑾革命傳, *Qiu Jin geming zhuan*). As final testimony to her family heritage, she published her novelized biography under the name Qiu Canzhi.[54] In December 1967, having taken her mother's family name as her own, Qiu Canzhi died and was buried in Taipei.

In 1927, the ever-insightful Lu Xun offered his own particularly critical view on Qiu Jin's tragic demise. Looking back twenty years to her martyr-like death, he suggested in the publication *Yusi* that Qiu had been "clapped to death" (就是被這種劈劈拍拍的 拍手拍死的, *jiushi bei zhei zhong pipipaipai de paishou pai side*). Unique phrasing, to be sure, but deeply meaningful from a man who shared the same hometown and knew her personally. Because Qiu Jin had been so notoriously recognized and praised by her fellow student revolutionaries during her years in Japan, Lu Xun proposed, the unremitting adulation, the *pipi paipai* (劈劈拍拍) clapping as he termed it,[55] had gone to her head and made her reckless.

Lu Xun nevertheless participated in public remembrances to Qiu Jin and graced her with his highest honor: inclusion in one of his short stories, "Medicine." On its face a story about the superstitious healing power of an executed martyr's blood, Lu Xun's 1919 story recalls his own childhood experiences procuring ineffectual healing potions for his sickly father. Yet embedded in the short story is also a paean to Qiu Jin's martyrdom, as well as recognition that her death alone was not enough to miraculously "heal" pre-revolutionary China. The allusions are clear,[56] from the temporal setting in autumn

431

(*qiu*) to the martyr's name, Xia Yu 夏瑜 ("summer jade" to Qiu Jin's "autumn jade"), to Xia Yu's execution ground, barely disguised on a faded plaque whose visible characters 古_亭口 (*gu _ ting kou*) needed only the missing second character 轩 (*xuan*) to identify the *Xuanting kou* crossroads site of Qiu Jin's execution in Shaoxing.

An Architectural Couple

Qiu Jin presented herself to the *fin de siècle* world as a tradition-breaking radical: abandoning her family, aggressively seeking education, cross-dressing with impunity, and taking up arms in the cause of republicanism. Yet perhaps no one better and more gracefully foretold the dawn of the "New Woman" in 20th-Century China than Lin Huiyin 林徽因 (1904 – 1955), who powered her way to new heights of feminine influence and respect by virtue of her remarkable intellect, aesthetic sensibility, and indomitable spirit. Her story is at once inspirational and romantic, marked as well by monumental hardships and suffering.

Life began in Hangzhou with the utmost of ease for Lin Huiyin.[57] Born into a wealthy family whose native place was near Fuzhou in Fujian Province, she was the granddaughter of the late-Qing Hanlin scholar and Zhejiang government official Lin Xiaoxun 林孝恂 (d. 1914) and daughter of the even more accomplished Lin Changmin 林長民 (1876 – 1925). Her father was among the early cohort of young Chinese men who learned English and Japanese and then traveled to Japan for post-secondary education, gaining his degree in law and politics at Waseda University in 1909. Following the 1911 Revolution, Lin Changmin assumed a leadership position in drafting the new Republic of China constitution.

Back in Hangzhou in the meantime, daughter Huiyin had been receiving a modern education since the age of four, including several years at a British-operated secondary school where she gained fluency in the English language. Consequently, when her father was asked in 1920 to observe post-war reconstruction in Europe as part of China's League of Nations Institute, it was only natural as an advocate of women's education that he asked his sixteen-year-old daughter to accompany him. Huiyin enrolled at St. Mary's College in Cambridge, developed an interest in architecture (said to have been spurred by a schoolmate studying architecture),[58] and the following year met the first love of her life.

Xu Zhimo 徐志摩 (1897 – 1931) was not only seven years Lin Huiyin's senior but was already married and the father of two sons. Born in Haining and educated at Hangzhou High School, Xu had studied law at Tianjin and Peking Universities, achieved an undergraduate degree in history from Clark University in Massachusetts, and studied economics at Columbia University before entering King's College in the hope of studying with Bertrand Russell.[59] There at Cambridge, Xu devoted his academic attentions to the study and translation of English and French Romantic poetry and his personal attentions to a blossoming young beauty from Hangzhou.

Despite the presence in London of his wife Zhang Youyi 張幼儀 (1900 – 1988), Xu became hopelessly enamored of Lin, possibly even proposing marriage. They became close friends, inspiring Xu to write highly romanticized poems that are still remembered and even memorialized today, such as his renowned "Farewell to Cambridge" (1931) and this parting verse for Lin Huiyin, titled "Coincidence" (1926):

> I am a cloud in the sky
> Quite by chance reflected in the heart of your wave.
> > No need to be surprised,
> > And still less to rejoice;
> In the blink of an eye my image will disappear.
>
> We met by chance one dark night at sea,
> You were voyaging your way, I mine.
> > It is well enough to remember,
> > But still better to forget
> The light we shed, each on the other, crossing paths.[60]

Lin Changmin heartily disapproved of this budding romance and returned his daughter to China in 1921. Xu Zhimo, apparently fearing a lost opportunity for true love, divorced Zhang Youyi the following year and returned to China as well.[61] In the meantime, Huiyin's father quietly arranged his daughter's marriage to Liang Sicheng 梁思成 (1901 - 1972), the son of Liang Qichao; the two fathers had met and developed a strong friendship earlier in Japan. Their children's engagement knitted together two of Zhejiang's most scholarly, forward-thinking, and accomplished families and created a husband-wife partnership that would go down in modern Chinese academic history.

In June 1925, the young (but not yet married) couple attended summer school classes at Cornell University, where Huiyin registered herself under the English name Phyllis Lin. In the fall, they registered together at the University of Pennsylvania, Liang Sicheng in the School of Architecture (which did not yet accept females) and Huiyin in the School of Fine Arts. Despite the restrictions about formal enrollment, they both took many of the same architecture classes. After graduating, Liang Sicheng moved on to Harvard to study Chinese architecture and Lin Huiyin chose theater set design at Yale. In March 1928, the couple married in Canada[62], then honeymooned in Europe for several months to visit art museums and famous architectural sites.

The young newlyweds returned to China in 1929 to found the Architecture Department at Northeastern University in Shenyang, with Liang as its head. They modeled their department after the one at the University of Pennsylvania but added classes on Chinese architecture and art history. They soon added two fellow alumni from Pennsylvania and another from the Massachusetts Institute of Technology (MIT) to build the department's faculty and expand its curriculum.

In 1930, Lin Huiyin contracted the tuberculosis that would plague her throughout the rest of her life. The following year, after leaving Shenyang due to Japanese military action in Manchuria, Lin stayed for a time in Beijing, recuperating from a bout of the disease and writing memorable poetry and short stories. Xu Zhimo visited her there in a free moment away from lectures he was giving in the city, after which he wrote his last poem to her, titled "You Are Leaving":

> You are leaving
> And I, too, shall go,
> For here we must part company;
> You take that road,
> Rest assured as you go;
> Watch the streetlamps on the horizon,
> You need only follow
> The line of the lights.

Later that same year, Xu boarded an airmail plane headed to Beijing in order to attend a lecture Lin Huiyin was presenting on Chinese architectural art to a group of foreign diplomats. The airplane crashed in bad weather in Shandong Province and Xu Zhimo perished. Lin Huiyin wrote her own poem in Xu's memory:

> After you are long gone,
> I will move forward in great strides,
> For the night dew in this wilderness is fresh;
> Do not worry
> About that which is deep in the clouds,
> Just hope that the wind blows,
> And mercury from the stars
> Flows into the sea of clouds;
> You will forever
> Light up the bottom of my heart
> Like a luminous pearl.
> I love you![63]

Their story is still regarded as one of the great and tragic love stories of 20th-Century China.[64] Xu Zhimo's poem, "A Second Farewell to Cambridge," is commonly taught to Chinese school children and was commemorated in 2008 by placement of a stone at the foot of a bridge on the University of Cambridge campus, engraved in Chinese with the first and last lines of Xu's poem: "Quietly I am leaving, / Just as quietly I came /… I shake my sleeves, / Not to bring away a patch of cloud."[65]

Lin's and Liang's entry into the new Society for the Study of Chinese Architecture in 1931 marked the beginning of their joint pursuit and monumental documentation of China's architectural history. They were motivated in fair part by the discovery in Nanjing of a manuscript copy of a rare treatise on architectural craftsmanship for imperial palaces, the *Yingzao Fashi* 營造法式 (*State Building Standards*) written in 1103 by the Song architect Li Jie 李誡 (1065 – 1110).[66]

In March 1932, the couple put their first major stamp on Chinese architectural scholarship in the *Bulletin of the Society for Research in Chinese Architecture*. Lin Huiyin published "On the Principle Characteristics of Chinese Architecture," presenting Chinese wooden construction and timber framing as a unique structural system not radically different from that of modern steel and reinforced concrete. In so writing, Lin also offered a pointed counterargument against Western attitudes that Chinese architecture was simplistic and had little of practical or scholarly value to offer. In the same month's bulletin, Liang Sicheng wrote "Architecture of the Tang Dynasty," in which he fashioned an evolutionary and life-cycle history of Chinese architecture from the Tang era (618 – 907) to the present day.

Between 1931 and 1937, Lin Huiyin's non-architectural activities demonstrated the range of her fertile intellect and the sheer capacity of her life. In addition to her academic work, she wrote poetry and several short stories. In "Ninety-Nine-Degree Heat," for example, she juxtaposed daily life in the sweltering Beijing summer of both the leisured rich and the working poor, "achiev[ing] a panoramic observation of life...in terms of social class, politics, economics, gender, and psychology."[67] Lin also served as the "charismatic hostess and the guiding spirit" of a weekly cultural gathering that became known as "Madam's Salon."[68] As historian John Fairbank, a close friend and welcomed guest along with his wife Wilma at Madam's Salon, wrote admiringly of Lin: "The household, or any other scene she was in, tended to revolve around her."[69]

From 1932 until 1937, Liang, Lin and their colleagues conducted extensive field research, scouring northern Chinese provinces to identify, analyze, document, and sketch ancient temples and buildings wherever they could find them. In 1937, their discovery of a Tang Dynasty wooden temple in Shanxi Province dating to 857 was the high point of their field research careers. After 1937, the couple expanded their travels for the next five years to include southern and southwestern China. In all, their research teams cataloged and closely documented in excess of two thousand temples, pagodas, and other traditional structures across fifteen provinces.[70]

Liang's and Lin's research was the first of its kind in China and would later serve as an invaluable government aid in historical preservation. For Liang, their monumental information collection effort provided the raw material for his two major works: *History of Chinese Architecture* (中国建筑技术史, *Zhongguo jianzhushi*) and *Chinese Architecture, A Pictorial History* (manuscript completed 1946, in English).[71] While perhaps overly focused on the timber architecture system about which they had written in 1932 (to the detriment of other methods and styles among the differing peoples of China), Liang's books are regarded as foundational classics in their field.

The couple's private life during the war years was difficult, as it was for so many people fleeing the Japanese advances into China after 1937. They relocated first to Changsha (Hunan Province) with many of the Peking and Qinghua University students, then to Huangxuan (Yunnan Province), and finally to Kunming. Along the way, Lin Huiyin contracted pneumonia but slowly recovered.

When Japanese advances threatened again, they were forced at the end of 1940 to abandon the three-bedroom home they had managed to build in Kunming. This time, they settled in Lizhuang, a small, out-of-the-way village in southeastern Sichuan Province where Tongji University and the Society for the Study of Chinese Architecture had relocated. Lizhuang would be their wartime family home for the next six years, most of which Lin would spend bedridden because of a relapse of her tuberculosis. Even from her bed, she continued her research and writing, focusing on the Han Dynasty era.

Liang Sicheng meanwhile worked on his architectural history manuscripts and a history of Chinese sculpture. He also translated the Song-era *Yingzao Fashi* into modern Chinese and annotated the text with explanations. As if those projects were not enough, he served as vice-chairman of the Chinese Commission for the Preservation of Cultural Objects in War Areas, preparing maps to assist allied flight commanders in avoiding accidental bombings of important Chinese historical sites and relics. Liang's willingness to identify the numerous similar sites in Kyoto and Nara is said to have been instrumental in preserving both Japanese cities from American bombings at the close of World War II.

As much as they had already accomplished, even despite the war, they were far from finished with their life's work.

Mao Dun

On December 4, 1920, twelve writers (nine of them hailing from Zhejiang and Jiangsu Provinces) established China's first national society for New Literature, the Literary Research Association (文學研究會, *Wenxue yanjiu hui*). Number 9 on the 1924 Membership List[72] was Shen Dehong 沈德鴻, known to modern readers as Mao Dun 茅盾 (1896 – 1981), from Wuzhen Town, Jiaxing. Together with Lu Xun (Shaoxing) and Yu Dafu (Fuyang), they formed the northern Zhejiang triumvirate who cast a gigantic literary shadow across early modern Chinese fiction and beyond.

Mao Dun was a relative latecomer to literary authorship, only first taking up fiction in 1927, at the age of 31. His father, Shen Yongxi 沈永锡 (d. 1906) had taken charge of the boy's early education, succeeded when Mao Dun was ten years old by his mother, Chen Aizhu 陈爱珠, after her husband's death. Following his graduation from middle school in Hangzhou, Mao Dun attended Peking University's Preparatory College for three years until forced to leave for financial reasons. Fortunately, his background in literature and English language was sufficient to secure a position at the Commercial Press in Shanghai as a translator and editor.

After joining the Literary Research Association in 1920, he served for three years as editor of the society's highly respected *Short Story Monthly*, a magazine catering to serious literary works. Around the same time, he began to affiliate loosely with the Chinese Communist Party in Shanghai, working as a party liaison to the Guomindang, which he also joined in the interest of national unity. From 1921 to 1925, he supported the CCP as both a propagandist and labor movement activist.

Mao Dun joined Chiang Kai-shek's Northern Expedition in 1926, working in the Political Department. After Wuhan fell to the Nationalists, he was elevated to editor of the *National Daily* in that city. His political world fell apart in April 1927, however, when Chiang broke his relationship with the CCP and initiated a nationwide purge of its members. Angry and disillusioned, Mao Dun left Wuhan shortly afterward. He headed first to Jiangxi Province before finally returning quietly to Shanghai. Believing he was likely black-listed by the GMD, subject to arrest and unable to work openly, he chose for the first time to express his thoughts and feelings in the form of literary fiction.

Not surprisingly, he titled his first work *Disillusion* (幻滅, *Huanmie*), serialized in September - October 1927 in *Short Story Monthly* magazine. Also for the first time, Shen Dehong adopted the pseudonym "Mao Dun," meaning "contradiction." The contradiction arose from the modern human conflict between "the pursuit of personal liberation from economic insecurity, alienation, reduced social status, and the constrictions of traditional Chinese culture…in order to save one's individual self versus devoting oneself to active participation in revolutionary struggle in order to build a more just society"[73]

Mao Dun followed *Disillusion* in short order with two additional novellas, *Vacillation* (動搖, *Dongyao*) and *Pursuit* (追求, *Zhuiqiu*), serialized in *Short Story Monthly* during 1927 – 1928. His perception that the Northern Expedition had failed to create a revolutionary national transformation motivated the themes for these three loosely connected stories: revolutionary enthusiasm and expectations shattered by reality in *Disillusionment*, the doubts and insecurities of revolutionaries during their struggle (*Vacillation*), and how to respond to individual and collective despair and move forward in the aftermath of the failed revolution (*Pursuit*).

While lying low in Shanghai, Mao Dun secured rooms for his mother, his wife, and himself on the upper floor of a small house, only later to discover that Lu Xun had also moved there and was now his neighbor. In the summer of 1928, he left Shanghai for a two-year stay in Japan, during which time he is believed to have conducted a secret love affair with a married Chinese woman named Qin Dejun. Over the course of 1929, he successfully published a five-story collection titled *The Wild Roses* along with a novel, *Rainbow*. Mao had departed Shanghai still relatively unknown, but he returned as a writer already "acclaimed in China as the foremost novelist of his time."[74]

His three serialized novellas (*Disillusion*, *Vacillation*, and *Pursuit*) were re-published in 1930 as a trilogy, under the title *Eclipse* (蝕, *Shi*). Like Lu Xun in the 1920s, new works of fictional realism rushed out of Mao Dun like flood waters. In the period 1932 – 1933, he produced some of his greatest works: *The Lin Family Shop* (林家鋪子, *Linjia puzi*) and the rural trilogy *Spring Silkworms* (春蠶, *Chuncan*), *Autumn Harvest* (秋收, *Qiu shou*), and *Winter Ruins* (殘冬, *Candong*). In 1933, he published *Midnight* (子夜, *Ziye*), widely regarded as his crowning fictional achievement and the novel that made him internationally famous when it was translated into English and French.

Mao Dun's stories were generally sympathetic to peasants and small-shop owners but critical of capitalists and officious bureaucrats. *The Lin Family Shop*, for example, portrays a family's failed struggle to keep their small-town general merchandise store financially afloat despite suffering unpayable debts and uncollectable receivables. Bankers, wealthy private lenders, and officials from the Merchants Guild and the local Guomindang government are portrayed as greedy and heartless, ready to pounce on anyone over whom they can exert leverage. The story's GMD Commissioner seeks the Lin's daughter as a concubine in a clear attempt at extortion, and one of the Lin family's private lenders unwittingly causes her own five-year-old son's death in her mad rush to claim her share of the bankrupt store's assets.

Similarly, Old Tongbao in *Spring Silkworms* sees fortuitous signs in early spring for one of the family's best silkworm cocoon harvests ever. The family prays, attends to ancient superstitions, and borrows to purchase enough mulberry leaves to feed the bumper harvest of hungry silkworms. Just as the hard work, sleepless nights, and sacrificed meals yield a truly bountiful yield of fluffy white cocoons, Old Tongbao's family and their neighbors learn that all the silk spinning factories in the area are closed. Unknown to the villagers, the Great Depression has decimated the silk industry. By the time the family can find a distant silk factory willing to take their cocoons, they can only sell at a loss. Old Tongbao's son recognizes the larger dilemma, though: "He knew they would never 'get out from under' merely by relying on hard work."[75]

During the war years 1937 – 1945, Mao Dun founded a literary magazine in Wuhan, edited the *Literary Front* magazine, and continued his fiction writing with the wartime novels *Story of the First Stage of the War* (第一阶段的故事, *Diyi jieduande gushi*), the anti-Nationalist *Putrefaction*, (腐蚀, *Fushi*) and *Maple Leaves as Red as February Flowers* (霜叶红似二月花, *Shuangye hongsi eryuehua*). He visited the Soviet Union in 1946 before relocating for a time in Hong Kong as editor of another magazine, *Fiction Monthly*. It would not be long before he was back again on the mainland. The next time, it would be in Beijing.

Chapter 19

THE JAPANESE WAR IN ZHEJIANG

(1932 – 1945)

A Song on Watching the Tide at Qiantang[1]

Outside the 'Tide-Waiting Gate,' people are like ants,
When, after noon, a wild wind buffets the earth and rises.
The flowing waters of the Thrice-Twisted [Qiantang] River come
rolling, swelling,
A startled wave crashes into Heaven's Gate.
Heaven's Gate grows pale, clouds and wind transform,
Distant cliffsides, layer upon layer, disappear from sight.
At first you think it is merely some clouds emerging from the sea—
Then you start at seeing a bolt of silk cut across the river.
The silver sea surges and pours into whiteness of snowcapped mountains,
And roars like thunder drumming in the vault of bright blue sky.
A great high-masted barge is unceasingly tossed,
Armed with powerful crossbows and mighty bows—who would dare to shoot?
Amid the smoky azure of dusk, we descend the tower,
While residual ripples still flow without end.
To where have the white horse and chariot returned?—
A bend of blue river, ten thousand miles of autumn.

– Zhu Rouze (late 17th Century)

War Clouds Gather

The years following the Sino-Japanese War of 1895 – 1896 witnessed a steadily worsening relationship between China and Japan, characterized primarily by the latter's increasing aggressiveness toward the former. Where many young Chinese student-activists like

Lu Xun and Qiu Jin had looked to Japanese universities for nearby entrée to Western learning in the first decade of the 20th Century, the Meiji government (1868 – 1912) began eyeing China in terms of territorial expansion and desirable natural resources.

The decade of the 1910s witnessed Japanese incursions into Manchuria and the infamous Twenty-One Demands of 1915, capped by the Treaty of Versailles' territorial concessions of Chinese land to Japan. The 1920s saw further Japanese machinations in Manchuria, including support of warlord regimes. These indirect efforts for control finally ended in September 1931 with military occupation, precipitated by a blatantly staged and virtually harmless explosion near a railroad line on September 18, allegedly engineered by Chinese dissidents. The so-called Mukden Incident provided weak but sufficient cover for a *causus belli*. Japanese forces attacked and took control of Mukden (Shenyang) by the end of the following day.

Five months later, Heilongjiang, Jilin, and Liaoning provinces had fallen to the Japanese, who then declared the entire seized area to be the state of Manchukuo (满洲国, *Manzhou-guo*) on February 18, 1932. Adding further insult to the defeated Chinese government, Japan installed Puyi, the last emperor of the Qing Dynasty, as their puppet Kangde Emperor on March 19, 1932. Five years later, a Japanese soldier would describe without irony one of his first experiences after entering a primary school building near Hangzhou Bay at the beginning of the War of Resistance Against Japanese Aggression: "Opening out a map [in a book on Chinese history] I found that parts of China which were under the domination of foreign powers were clearly marked, and the whole thing entitled 'Map of Humiliation'. Manchukuo was shown as though it were a part of China."[2]

Even as military conflict raged in the far north, a harsh new battle unexpectedly broke out further south. On January 18, 1932, five Japanese Buddhist monks, members of the ultranationalist Nichiren sect,[3] were attacked by Chinese workers outside the Sanyou Towel Mill (三友实业社毛巾厂, *Sanyou shiyeshe maojin chang*). Two of the monks were badly injured and one was fatally beaten. Two days later, Japanese residents in Shanghai retaliated by setting fire to the mill. When police arrived to restore order and extinguish the fire, several were seriously injured and one was killed; some sources allege that two Chinese factory workers died in the fire as well.

The Shanghai GMD quickly organized a new Anti-Japanese and Protect Overseas Association which in turn declared a nationwide boycott of Japanese goods and services at their first meeting. Meanwhile, Japan reinforced its already substantial military and naval presence in the Shanghai area, ostensibly for the protection of its expatriate citizens who lived in the Hongkou (虹口) district of the International Settlement.[4] In response, the Chinese 19th Route Army under General Cai Tingkai 蔡廷锴 (1892 – 1968) prepared itself for battle while camped just outside of the city.

This bubbling pot boiled over on the night of January 28, 1932. Japanese carrier-based planes initiated unprovoked and seemingly indiscriminate aerial bombardment of the heavily populated district of Zhabei (闸北). "The rain of bombs, the thousands killed, the ruins and wounded and refugees..." resulting from "...the first

440

terror bombing of a civilian population…"[5] triggered a thirty-three-day armed conflict. The fighting began with Japanese invasion of Hongkou and spread across most of Shanghai outside of the International Settlement. Early British, French, and American attempts to negotiate a ceasefire were rejected outright by the Japanese, who simply inserted additional forces into the campaign through February.

The Chinese 19th Route Army, supplemented by the 5th Army, put up surprisingly stiff resistance that largely stymied the Japanese attempt to gain control of Shanghai. The bitter conflict continued until March 1, when the Japanese landed additional troops behind the Chinese lines at Taicang and forced their withdrawal on March 8. The League of Nations passed ceasefire resolutions in early March that were accepted by the Chinese but initially rejected by Japan. Temporary peace returned when the attackers agreed to withdraw all military from Shanghai beyond their normal garrison complement and the Chinese agreed to demilitarize an entire thirty-mile zone around the city.

Negotiations brokered by League representatives finally achieved a more permanent ceasefire agreement, sealed on May 5, 1932. The Japanese emerged victorious from the First Battle of Shanghai, but the Chinese military had proven itself a fearsome and determined opponent. More ominous was the Japanese Army's brutality and utter disregard for Chinese civilian lives.[6] Official estimates of Chinese military casualties in the 1932 Shanghai conflict were nearly 4,300 killed and over 9,800 wounded. Civilian casualties enumerated by the Shanghai Bureau of Social Affairs included 1,739 dead, 719 wounded, and 985 missing. The GMD government in Nanjing claimed total civilian casualties of about 13,000, of which over 6,000 were said to have been killed.[7]

Barely over a month's duration, the First Shanghai War (1932) has often been overlooked in light of events that came after. However, the January 28 Incident, as it is remembered to Chinese history, proved a dire portent of things to come.

Learning to Fly

In 1922, Guangdong Province established China's first Aviation Bureau, built the nation's first domestically-produced airplane, and created (in 1924) its first Aviation School. Throughout the 1920s, warlords and the Chinese Nationalists procured aircraft and flight training, primarily from France and Great Britain. Zhang Zuolin 張作霖 (1875 – 1928), the powerful warlord over Manchuria, employed airplanes during conflicts in 1923 – 1924; by 1925, he had amassed a fleet of one hundred airplanes divided into five squadrons. Chiang Kai-shek also made effective use of aircraft for reconnaissance and field support through the mid-1920s during his Northern Expedition.[8]

In March 1929, the Nationalist government created the National Aviation Administration to oversee formation of a unified Chinese Air Force under the command of General Zhang Huichang 張惠長 (1898 – 1980, also written as Chang Waijung or Chang Weichang).[9] Just five months earlier, Zhang had thrilled the Chinese media with a series of long-distance barnstorming flights in his American-made Ryan-Broughman plane, earning him the nickname "the Lindbergh of China." Hardly surprising, considering that he had already brazenly christened his new plane "the Spirit of Canton."

Western-manufactured aircraft poured into China between 1928 and early 1932, many sold as commercial planes to circumvent foreign bans on the sale of military equipment to either Japan or China. Most of those were converted upon delivery to military use. In 1929, the Nationalist government funded the purchase of sixty-two planes. More than thirty Vought-Corsair fighters arrived in Shanghai in 1930, and at least thirty Douglas bombers were delivered to China in 1930 -1931.[10] Despite these expenditures, Japanese planes in the 1932 Shanghai conflict had outnumbered and quickly dispatched the new, undermanned, and inadequately trained Chinese Air Force. From January to March 1932, Japan had ruled the skies over Shanghai, and the lesson was clear.

George C. Westervelt (1879 – 1956), manager of naval aircraft manufacturing for Curtiss-Wright, witnessed the first Japanese bombings of Shanghai from his hotel room. When the fighting ended, he delivered an integrated plan for upgrading China's aviation capabilities to Minister of Finance T.V. Soong (宋子文, Song Ziwen, 1894 – 1971). Westervelt's program called for China's acquisition of professional military and general aviation advice, dispatch of carefully selected Chinese flight candidates to an American aviation and technical support training school, construction of an airplane manufacturing facility, and expansion of China's incipient commercial air services. Soong largely agreed to Westervelt's plan but insisted that the aviation training take place in China, specifically in Hangzhou.

Senior American officials reacted negatively. The U.S. State Department summarily rejected the Soong/Westervelt program, preferring to maintain American neutrality in East Asia. General Douglas MacArthur declined military support as well, but he forwarded the project to the considerably more receptive, trade-driven Department of Commerce. Major Edward P. Howard (b. 1894), Commerce's trade commissioner in Shanghai, was tasked with developing the program specifics and staffing needs. His most significant decision: convincing Colonel John H. Jouett (1892 – 1968) to lead the training mission in Hangzhou.

After graduating from West Point in 1914, Jouett had flown balloons during World War I, commanded flight wings in France, organized flight training programs in the 1920s, and managed multiple airfields before retiring from military service in 1930.[11] Furthermore, his post-military position as head of aviation services for Standard Oil of New Jersey made him a noncontroversial civilian participant. He quickly set about recruiting a training school staff of nine flight instructors, along with four mechanics and a flight surgeon.

After arriving in Shanghai on July 8, 1932, Jouett and Howard personally presented T.V. Soong with three program options, ranging from three years' training of 150 pilots and minimal new facilities construction at a cost of $4.2 million to a $13.7 million program for training three hundred pilots, constructing a permanent training center, and providing two hundred hours of basic and advanced training for each student. Soong chose the most expensive option.[12]

Jouett and his American training staff arrived that same month at the proposed training school site, Jianqiao Airfield (笕桥机场, *Jianqiao jichang*), about seven miles northeast of Hangzhou city.[13] Finding little more than flimsy wooden barracks and dilapidated hangars housing a few obsolete aircraft, they set about converting this warlord-era relic into what would become the Central Aviation School (CAS).

By September, Jouett had reviewed two hundred Chinese candidates with flight experience for refresher courses and selected fifty of them. Seven of the fifty were retained as Chinese-speaking flight instructors for Jouett's planned "train the trainers" program.[14] On the 18th of the following month, eighty-eight fresh young cadets began their flight training based on the U.S. Army Air Corps program of four months each of primary, basic, and advanced training. Many of the cadets demonstrated their commitment by arriving at Jianqiao with their own copies of *We*, Charles Lindbergh's 1927 autobiography. "The Chinese make excellent fliers," Jouett would later declare. "They are resourceful and…are very much like our American flying cadets."[15]

Not everything went swimmingly, however. Jouett had virtually no control over the cadets offered to him; many were physically unqualified and had to be rejected out of hand. Too often, cultural traits such as deference to teachers caused the Chinese students to nod in agreement even when they failed utterly to understand or overcome language differences, a serious risk factor at five thousand feet.[16]

Politics intervened as well. Jouett's early successes redounded to T.V. Soong's credit, and a wary Chiang Kai-shek grew concerned with Soong's hold over CAS as an emerging new military power base. Chiang ordered the entire program relocated to Luoyang in Henan Province, but after a few weeks of operation interrupted by dust storms, the school was returned to Jianqiao, no longer under Soong's control. In 1933, Jouett had also refused Chiang's request for his American instructors to fly combat missions against Communist forces. The penalty for doing so would have meant loss of their American citizenship for any who might have participated.[17]

Despite these difficulties, Jouett's mission was highly successful. By the time the Americans' contract expired on June 1, 1935, over 300 cadets had graduated as qualified pilots,[18] with another 250 cadets already in the trainee pipeline.[19] In addition to multiple purchases of new Curtiss-Wright planes by the Nationalist government in Nanjing, the new Central Aircraft Manufacturing Company (CAMCO) at Jianqiao, with three hundred Chinese employees overseen by William D. Pawley (1896 – 1977), produced 127 Curtiss planes between its opening at Jianqiao in August 1934 and the end of 1936. The Nationalist Air Force grew to 645 aircraft by the start of 1937, with several aviation training schools and aircraft factories.[20]

Upon the Americans' departure, Chiang Kai-shek relocated the CAS once again to Luoyang and turned its operation over to the Italians. For several years they had courted him assiduously with promises of formal diplomatic recognition of the Republic of China and assurances of reduced costs for aircraft production and pilot training. This would prove to be a serious misjudgment by Chiang, reflected in the quality and quantity of not only the planes but also the aviators thus produced.

Among John Jouett's initial recruits as a CAS flight instructor was Christopher Mathewson, Jr. (1906 – 1950). Known as Christy, just like his renowned Baseball Hall of Fame father, the young man had graduated from Bucknell and attended flight school for the Army Air Corps. Patiently but eagerly awaiting the completion of his tour of service was his fiancée, Miss Margaret (Peggy) Phillips (1909 – 1933), just completing her own college education.

When Christy agreed to join the Jouett mission, he suggested to Peggy that she join him in China, where they could marry and live together until his three-year pilot training assignment ended. Adventurous by nature, Peggy agreed. On Thanksgiving Day 1932, she left her home in Philadelphia, accompanied by Christy's mother, Jane (1880 – 1967). On Christmas Eve, the couple were married in Hangzhou in a double ceremony with another of the Jouett instructors, Ellis Shannon (1908 – 1982).[21] Both couples then set out for two-week honeymoons in Shanghai.

On January 8, 1933, the Shannons boarded a train back to Jianqiao, but Christy had a special surprise for his new wife. T.V. Soong had made the use of his Sikorsky S-38 amphibious plane available to the Mathewsons as a wedding gift. Christy planned to take his bride on the ride of her lifetime over the Yangzi Delta countryside and on to Hangzhou, just 120 miles away.

The couple boarded the plane to the cheers and well wishes of family and friends. Less than a minute after take-off from Longhua 龙华Airfield on the banks of the Huangpu River, the crowd looked on in disbelief as the plane lost control, nosed down several times, and bounced along the river surface until it hit a mud flat and overturned. Peggy Phillips Mathewson was fatally crushed in the accident, having never regained consciousness. She was just 23 years old. Christy suffered two broken arms and a badly broken leg that ultimately had to be amputated. The Phillips family held long afterward that the accident was the result of Japanese sabotage directed at T.V. Soong.[22]

A more rigorous aeronautical assessment came from William Langhorne Bond (1893 – 1985), operations manager for China National Aviation Company (CNAC), who witnessed the events. According to Bond, the S-38 had flown into Shanghai with a full, eight-passenger load the day before, requiring appropriate settings of the stabilizer trim control to provide adequate tail lift. When Mathewson and his wife took off, the two-person load was too light for the previous day's trim setting; a simple adjustment to a trim control wheel would have corrected the problem. However, Christy was making his first solo flight in an S-38 and was insufficiently familiar with its handling under different conditions.

Subsequent flight tests by Bond and a formal hearing chaired by Jouett all indicated pilot error; no evidence of sabotage was found by the hearing committee. Interestingly, Captain Cecil G. Sellers of CNAC, a more experienced pilot, testified that he had been asked to fly the Mathewsons to Hangzhou but had been waved off at Longhua by Christy, who likely hoped to impress his new bride.[23]

Christy Mathewson, Jr. recovered the use of his arms and received a prosthetic leg, enabling him to walk again. He went on to enjoy a lengthy career with the Army Air Corps, serving with the Air Transport Command in WWII Europe and rising to lieutenant colonel before retiring in 1946. He twice remarried, but more tragedy awaited. On August 16, 1950, Christy was horribly burned in an explosion at his home near San Antonio. He died the following day, at age 43.[24]

The Chinese Tragedy of Shanghai

Fighting at the Marco Polo Bridge (卢沟桥, Lugouqiao) near Beijing on July 8, 1937—ostensibly over a missing Japanese soldier who, in fact, was never missing—is widely regarded as the opening salvo of what the Chinese came to call the War of Resistance Against Japanese Aggression (中国抗日战争, Zhongguo kangri zhanzheng). One month later, an incidental shooting at Shanghai's Hongqiao Airport on August 9 led to full-scale conflict four days later in several districts of the city. The following day, August 14, was one of both victory[25] and ignominy for the graduated pilots of Hangzhou's Central Aviation School. The names most associated with those two outcomes were Gao Zhihang and Izumo, respectively.

As active conflict began in Shanghai, the Japanese sent eighteen bombers to attack two airfields around Hangzhou. At the same time, Gao Zhihang 高志航 (1907 - 1937), a CAS graduate and commander of the China Air Force (CAF) 4th Pursuit Group, stood by at Jianqiao as a new fleet of Curtiss Hawk IIIs arrived and began refueling. When the warning for incoming Japanese planes sounded, Gao went immediately airborne in his own partially refueled plane, downing one bomber and badly damaging another before running out of fuel. Three other fliers from Gao's group managed to down two more bombers; total losses for Japan came to six bombers, with only one CAF Hawk lost. Gao could rightly claim the first Chinese kill of a Japanese bomber. Over the next three months, he would be shot in one arm but still make multiple additional kills, only to die in action later in Henan Province. To the present day, Gao Zhihang remains China's first national aviation hero.[26]

The same day of Gao's first successful kill, a fleet of five light bombers from Hangzhou Jianqiao took off for Shanghai. They were tasked with destroying Japanese cruisers that had shelled the city the day before from anchorages along the city's Huangpu River shoreline. The fliers' main objective was the Izumo, the lead Japanese cruiser. The weather in Shanghai that day was overcast with a low ceiling, producing strong winds and periodic rain squalls. The CAF bomber pilots had only been trained for high altitude bombing from 7,500 feet, but they chose to proceed rather than abort the mission. They flew in fast and low, but most of their bombs missed the Izumo and the other cruisers.

No serious damage was done to any of the Japanese ships, but three of the CAF bombs landed along Nanjing Road, the city's main commercial avenue. One detonated between the Cathay and Palace hotels where many civilians had sought shelter from the rain and wind; an estimated seven hundred people died instantly, with hundreds more injured. Two more bombs from a damaged CAF plane landed in the French Concession, not far from the Great World Amusement Center and a movie house, inflicting numerous more deaths and injuries. In all, the two accidental detonations resulted in more than three thousand civilians killed or injured.[27] The event is remembered in Chinese history as "Black Saturday."

Japanese retaliation against Jianqiao Airport came quickly. Even as CAF planes continued with their air defense of Shanghai, Japanese fighters and bombers struck the airfield, bombing and strafing the buildings and planes. Not until later did the Japanese discover that their bombs and machine gun fire were destroying mock aircraft made of paper and bamboo. The real planes sat hidden nearby among bamboo groves and mulberry trees. The CAF flyers reverted to using two undetected small airfields for their takeoffs and landings. Similarly, machinery from the airplane manufacturing plant had already been removed from the factory buildings and hidden among mulberry trees before the first Japanese bombers ever arrived.[28]

Despite the clever deception, Japanese air superiority inevitably obliterated Jianqiao. What aircraft and equipment could be saved were soon relocated to Nanjing. The Central Aviation School relocated and continued operation with French mechanics in Kunming, in southwestern Yunnan Province.[29] Spirited as the Chinese air defense might have been, it was no match in technology or numbers for the Japanese air strength.

Equally spirited was the Chinese army's defense of Shanghai. An invasion the Japanese had expected to take less than a week stretched to over three months, with nearly unimaginable losses on both sides.[30] In a massive flanking maneuver, the Japanese landed troops at Jinshanwei (金山衛) on the north bank of Hangzhou Bay on November 5, 1937. Fresh troops poured north toward Shanghai, forcing Chiang Kai-shek to pull his remaining forces back from the city on November 8, 1937.

Chinese troops had already begun pulling back from central Shanghai in late October, moving west behind other defensive lines in Jiangsu Province, in the general direction of the Nationalist capital at Nanjing. Troops in nearby towns also retreated behind those same defensive lines. Regardless, the Japanese moved aggressively westward and quickly pierced both Jiangsu defensive lines, reaching Nanjing by early December.

The rapid Japanese advance across Jiangsu took them through Suzhou, Wuxi, Changzhou, and Zhenjiang, leaving Huzhou and Hangzhou to the south of their march relatively untouched by military occupation. Jiaxing, however, was subjected to two months of occupation by the Japanese forces who landed at Hangzhou Bay on November 5. Over a thousand residents were killed and an estimated twenty percent of the city's homes were put to the torch; about eighty percent of Jiaxing's population evacuated.[31]

Hangzhou: The Conflict Arrives (Quietly, but Deadly)

The citizens and foreigners in Hangzhou watched the Japanese advance toward Nanjing warily. Business, schools, and life continued more or less normally but with an obvious dark cloud on the horizon. Wayland Academy boys' school staff began constructing

446

timber-covered dugouts on the school's campus grounds shortly after the first bombings at Jianqiao. At Hangzhou Christian College, students went on with their classes in September while the staff constructed sandbag dugouts on the campus hillside, secured gas masks, prepared first aid kits, and conducted air raid drills. Similar preparations were undertaken at the Union Girls' School inside the city.[32]

Local hospitals remained open but were now forced to contend with an influx of wounded soldiers. At the mission hospital in Huzhou, Dr. Fred Manget (1880 – 1979)[33] received Chinese soldiers who arrived in terrible shape. Despite their wounds and the loss of Shanghai, Manget detected a noticeable change in the soldiers, a growing sense of national pride. In his correspondence, Robert McMullen (1884 – 1962), Provost and Comptroller at Hangchow Christian College in 1937,[34] relayed Manget's observations during his visit to the Huzhou hospital in late October:

> He [Manget] expresses amazement at the change that has come over the soldiers of China. They are now terribly keen on fighting for their cause and bear their suffering for their country like martyrs. Japan has done something to China that has put backbone into them along with a large amount of patriotism.

Manget's conclusion, according to McMullen: "Japan hasn't a chance."[35]

In late September, war drew closer to Hangzhou as Japanese planes repeatedly bombed Jiaxing. Hangzhou had seen a few flyovers by then, most likely surveillance flights to observe the first-ever bridge over the Qiantang River,[36] scheduled to open on September 26, 1937. On September 30, one of the first Japanese bombing raids over Hangzhou targeted railroad yards, machine shops, and the electrical plant at Zhakou. The next day, no bombs were dropped, but the incoming planes poured machine gun fire in and around the bus station in the New Market area; local anti-aircraft fire was largely ineffectual.

In a circular letter dated October 6, 1937 and addressed to "Friends of Hangchow College," Robert McMullen expressed his concerns over the possibility of accidental bombing of the campus, with 530 students still in residence:

> We do not think the Japs will definitely try to bomb our buildings. It is much more likely that an attempt will be made to destroy the new [Qiantang River] bridge a short distance away The anti-aircraft guns stationed at each end of the bridge will cause them to fly high and their aim will not be too accurate.[37]

After a brief hiatus, partly weather-induced, multiple bombings resumed on October 13, this time focusing on the city railway station. The next day, Japanese planes attempted bombing runs on the new Qiantang River Bridge but were repulsed by a heavy barrage of Chinese anti-aircraft fire. Although he remained concerned about collateral damage or loss of life at Hangchow Christian College from conflict around the bridge, McMullen nevertheless commented with a degree of awed respect on the accuracy of Japanese bomber pilots: "At Zhakow no bomb fell more than fifty yards from the railroad and [machine] shops. At the city station all twelve fell in the station area."[38]

Despite these observations, McMullen commissioned a 40-by-60-foot American flag "to be placed in the center of the campus during an air raid and taken up when it is over." His letters also expressed biting criticism of the repeated Japanese bombing and strafing of civilians and refugees at train stations and on trains already in transit.[39]

By mid-November, the message was increasingly clear that Hangzhou was being "softened up" for assault. The *North China Herald* of November 17 reported multiple new Japanese landings along Hangzhou Bay, including forces put ashore at Zhapu, Haiyan, and Haining beginning on November 5. Pinghu, a county seat within Jiaxing Prefecture, fell to the new Japanese assault on November 19, with more than 1,500 civilian casualties from repeated aerial bombings during the preceding two weeks. Jiaxing fell the day before, and Huzhou was seized on November 25. Encirclement of Hangzhou from above the Qiantang River appeared inevitable.

As bombings increased in frequency (especially around Jiaxing), thousands of wounded Chinese soldiers poured into the city, and civilians by the tens of thousands evacuated, many headed south across the Qiantang River into Xiaoshan and beyond. As late as the mid-20th Century, Chinese people still followed the advice of an ancient adage: *Xiao nan bi xiang, da nan bi cheng* (小难避乡, 大难避城). "Small troubles, flee the countryside; big troubles, flee the city." McMullen conjectured that seventy-five percent of the population had abandoned Hangzhou by the end of November.[40] Few foreigners remained in the city as well; as early as mid-September, only about a dozen were still in residence, including several at the missionary hospital.[41]

Japanese targeting of Hangzhou continued to be relatively cautious, limited, and precise, almost as though they regarded the city as a Chinese version of Kyoto. Not so their treatment of Xiaoshan, the city across the river toward which so many soldiers and civilians had evacuated. Near midday on November 30, Japanese planes carpeted Xiaoshan with so many bombs that the city fell into ruins, a mixed mass of death and debris.

Government buildings, police stations, businesses, schools, hospitals, residences, and an ancient temple—all reduced to rubble. Dead bodies and unburied coffins lay scattered everywhere. "The people that remain are stunned, for the black shadow of fear haunts them, and they live in dread of a return visit of these terrible engines of death which ride in the wind."[42] The actions commonly known today as the Rape of Nanjing began on December 9, 1937, a little more than a week after the initial Japanese aerial decimation of Xiaoshan.

At 6:00 A.M. on December 22, Hangzhou's remaining residents were rudely awakened by several huge explosions. Eyes turned first toward the Qiantang River Bridge, the gleaming two-level, auto and railroad bridge that had only opened in September for rail and in November as the Qiantang's first-ever highway crossing. They saw that it stood intact, still crowded with fleeing refugees. The explosions had come from the city's $3.5 million electric plant (constructed in 1929 by MIT engineers) and its first-ever municipal water works (constructed in 1930) near the Qingtai Gate.[43] Both utility plants were now smoking ruins, demolished by the Nationalist Army as welcoming gifts for the oncoming Japanese occupiers.[44] Just the previous evening, Chinese forces had demolished the river wharf that had served for centuries as the (dis)embarkation spot for the ferry service between Hangzhou and Xiaoshan.

This macabre pre-Christmas gift-giving was still not yet ended. Early in the afternoon of December 23, the usual stream of outbound refugees fleeing on foot or in any conveyance they could manage, from cars to wheelbarrows, came to a sudden halt and the bridge emptied. Not long after, at 4:10 p.m., another massive explosion destroyed five of the bridge's sixteen support piers and damaged a sixth. Three years for construction, but less than three months in operation.[45] On the hills overlooking the river and bridge from a fair distance, more than four hundred windows in the campus buildings of Hangchow Christian College were shattered by the bridge detonation's blast.[46]

Governor Huang Shaohong's (黃紹竑, 1895 - 1966) car was the last vehicle to cross the bridge before its partial demolition. On only his fifth day in office in Hangzhou, he had been forced to dismantle, disable, or destroy much of the city's most vital infrastructure, including as many of its ten operating ironworks as he could manage in such a short time.[47] While the bridge demolition was far from total, the structure suffered enough damage to render it unusable for the time being.

The Japanese patched the destroyed roadway gap by September 1940 with a rickety, timber bridge that swayed perilously but allowed vehicles to move slowly and carefully across. Chinese guerrilla forces repeatedly harassed the repaired bridge during the war years. They attacked the damaged fifth and sixth piers a second time, and then demolished the fifth pier in March 1944 and the sixth pier in February 1945. By war's end, only the railroad bridge was serviceable.[48] Not until 1947 would the bridge be restored to normal use.

The morning after the bridge demolition, Christmas Eve Day of 1937, the Japanese Army began their occupation of Hangzhou with nary a shot fired. Chinese soldiers had quietly evacuated the city as the Japanese forces drew nearer, some heading south across the river to Xiaoshan while others headed west, upstream along the Qiantang and Fuyang rivers. The displaced Nationalist government ministries had already departed, heading southwestward. Zhejiang's provincial capital relocated as well, moving initially across the Qiantang to Jinhua. The physical city was thus temporarily preserved, its temples and historical venues and heritage elements mostly undisturbed, the beauties of West Lake momentarily unscarred and unblemished.

People still residing in Hangzhou were not so fortunate, however. For days after the occupation began, Western observers consistently remarked on the wanton rape and baldly indiscriminate killing of Chinese civilians, even when they were accompanied by Westerners. McMullen wrote bitterly and despairingly of the Japanese soldiers' seemingly endless capacity for rape: "It is doubtful there is a woman in or around Hangchow outside of a refugee camp or some such place of safety…who has not been raped once but many times."[49] Even months after the occupation, he repeatedly recorded further instances of rape, looting, and horrific civilian massacres reminiscent of Nanjing in the outlying areas of the city.

Edward Clayton (1887 – 1948), principal of the Wayland Academy since 1923, related a shocking event in which he was accompanied on a Hangzhou street by two young men who joined him for the ostensible protection afforded by being in the company of a foreigner. The threesome stopped on their walk momentarily, smiling at the sight of a Japanese soldier leading a small donkey piled high with plunder. Taking offense at their smiles, the soldier trained his rifle on the men and promptly shot dead the two Chinese men on Clayton's either side.[50]

As the initial looting and sexual assaults were slowly brought under a degree of control, relative peace in Hangzhou's urban center did not translate into pacification around the damaged Qiantang River Bridge area. Within three or four days of Hangzhou's occupation, the Japanese had positioned field guns in the riverside hills of Zhaku. Bombardments from across the river in Chinese-held Xioashan erupted for hours at a time, answered in kind by the new Japanese emplacements. Gunfire exchanges became routine, making passage along the river road fronting the Hangzhou Christian College campus particularly dangerous. With nearly everyone evacuated from the school, however, most at risk of harm were the nearly silent campus buildings.

Early signs of normal life began returning to Hangzhou in January. "While very few shops have opened up as of yet, there are many hucksters selling vegetables, salt, and meats on the streets….An effort is being made to establish a Chinese police force of a thousand."[51] Japanese soldier and war chronicler Ashihei Hino observed similarly: "It was almost beyond our comprehension that the Chinese should come and sell us vegetables or other things after we had been in occupation of the city for only a few days….turnips, radishes, and many other kinds were piled in their baskets."[52] Yet few if any shops opened other than several selling rationed rice; street markets made up nearly all the retail trade, mostly for vegetables and fish. As late as mid-June, Robert McMullen recorded that the situation had changed but little and that rice prices had increased substantially.[53]

Far from signaling military cowardice or surrender, the nondestructive occupation of Hangzhou had been accomplished by aggressive planning and negotiation begun jointly in November by Chinese civic leaders and resident foreign missionaries and diplomats. They presented their case to Japanese military representatives for establishing Hangzhou as an open city with clearly established encampments for fifteen thousand Chinese war refugees, mostly women, children, and the aged.[54] Such a peaceful turnover was hugely beneficial to Hangzhou, the city not having thus to suffer the devastations wreaked upon other cities in Jiangnan.

By the end of May 1938, the Japanese had installed a provisional government in Hangzhou, headed by Wang Ruikai 王瑞闓 (1873 – 1941) as the first Governor of Zhejiang for the Reformed Government of the Republic of China. The occupiers also appointed a former manager in the summer resort town of Moganshan as the city's mayor. While these appointments created a semblance of bureaucratic normalcy, they were exercised over a city largely devoid of Chinese citizens and whose designees were despised or ignored by those who still lived there. For example, Edward Clayton wrote of a conversation in which the provisional Mayor had explained with due foresight to a friend: "It is a duty of every patriotic citizen to try to kill me. I do not blame them." On February 7, 1944, the Japanese news agency reported the assassination of Hangzhou puppet Mayor Tan Shu-kuei, shot to death as he walked along a city street.[55]

Preserving Historical Heritage (文物, Wenwu)

Schools faced particular challenges in retreating and re-establishing operations ahead of the Japanese advance. Universities not only needed to shepherd their students and faculties to safety but also make decisions and arrangements with regard to administrative records, valuable library collections and journals, historical texts and cultural relics, expensive laboratory equipment, and irreplaceable research materials. Perhaps no university in 1937 China carried a heavier burden than Zhejiang University.

By 1937, only four original copies of the Qianlong Emperor's great encyclopedia, the *Complete Library of the Four Treasures* (四库全书, *Siku quanshu*), remained extant. Wenlan Hall on West Lake's Solitary Hill still held Hangzhou's version, the last remaining "southern copy"[56] As related earlier, the Wenlan Ge copy was not fully original, having been damaged and partly scattered during the Taiping occupation of Hangzhou in the 1860s. Restoration work begun by the Hangzhou brothers Ding Bing and Ding Shen had continued into the Republican era until a complete copy had been re-compiled under Qian Xun 钱恂 (1853 – 1927), founding director of the Zhejiang Library (and husband of travel writer Shan Shili).

From the moment of Shanghai's fall to the Japanese, Chen Xunci (陈训慈, 1901 - 1991), director of the Zhejiang University Library, had resolved to keep their priceless edition of *Siku quanshu* and other ancient books protected and out of enemy hands. The time had now arrived. Chen sought funding from the Ministry of Education for transportation of the historically invaluable library, but when his request was refused, he borrowed the necessary money and even sold his own property.[57]

Some 70,000 volumes "were packed in crates, boxes, burlap sacks, anything we had, and carried inland by car, boat, train or by the refugees themselves,"[58] beginning a thousand-mile, eight-year journey southwestward. The 230 boxes containing the collection followed the route taken by the University's staff and students, with stops first in Jiangxi Province, then Guangxi Province, and finally in the suburbs of Zunyi 遵义, Guizhou Province. There, the books were hidden in karst caves and cared for by two servants who rotated them into the sunlight twice a year to maintain their condition.[59]

Preserved in its entirety, the Wenlan Ge collection, including the *Siku quanshu*, was able to return to its Hangzhou home in 1946. In 1994, a note found among Japanese war archives in Kyoto reported that nine Japanese agents had traveled to Hangzhou in February, 1938, eager to seize the treasures of Wenlan Ge. They arrived too late.[60] The Wenlan Ge building still resides on Solitary Hill Island in West Lake, now part of the Zhejiang Provincial Museum complex. In 2015, the Hangzhou Publishing Group (杭州出版社, *Hangzhou chuban she*) produced three hundred reproductions of the *Wenlan ge*

He Who Rides the Tiger Is Afraid to Dismount, or The Dog that Caught the Car [61]

By April 1938, Western observers reported fewer than 100,000 people left in Hangchow, down from 500,000 to 600,000 a year earlier. One estimate put the out-migration in the Shanghai-Nanjing-Hangzhou triangle at sixteen million or more, adding: "During this spring only one fifth of those normally tilling the fields are at work."[62]

For the next two years, life in Hangzhou City under Japanese occupation settled into a pattern of wary accommodation between local military command and the remaining Chinese residents. A local government was established and a degree of order was restored inside the city walls. Commerce even returned as shops re-opened and farmers around the area brought fruits and vegetables to peddle on the streets. Most of the foreigners left in the city were focused on preserving their religious and educational institutions and providing safety and succor to Chinese refugees.

The surrounding countryside was an altogether different matter, as Hangzhou effectively became the Japanese base for a series of devastating combat operations on the opposite side of the Qiantang River. Xiaoshan suffered first and most. For more than six months, from the initial bombing on November 30, 1937, to mid-June 1938, Japanese military command directed sixty-eight air strikes against the city, killing over six hundred and wounding more than two thousand. Remarkably, these Japanese efforts to subdue resistance by aerial "shock and awe" seemed only to strengthen Chinese resolve in the countryside south of Hangzhou.

The year 1939[63] began with a spirited counterattack against the Japanese occupation in Zhejiang Province. On January 7, a three-pronged Chinese assault to reclaim Hangzhou began with forces advancing on Yuhang from the west, others crossing the Qiantang River about ten miles below Hangzhou to the southwest, and the third group crossing Hangzhou Bay at Haiyan to the east. Five days after the attacks began, Japanese artillery and air superiority had driven many of the Chinese troops back into the western hills. Even as the Japanese fortified Hangzhou and declared the area "pacified," intense guerrilla action kept the rural areas in a state that observers in Hangzhou described as "a virtual no-man's land."[64]

The Japanese military response began on March 21 with a heavily armed ground assault across the Qiantang River toward Fuyang, in what was assumed to be an offensive move into central or coastal Zhejiang Province. Warships shelled Ningbo and Wenzhou along the coast while Japanese airplanes bombed cities along the Zhejiang – Jiangxi (Zhegan 浙赣) rail line running southwesterly out of Hangzhou. Chinese reinforcements sought to stall the Japanese army advance while simultaneously launching a counterattack of their own, heading north toward Shanghai from Hangzhou Bay. Periodic fighting and aerial bombings continued without major victories on either side, but by the end of May,

Chinese forces claimed to have retaken Zhakou (just west outside of Hangzhou) and to be pressing Fuyang and Yuhang.

What had resolved into a stalemate situation accompanied by persistent guerilla warfare finally reached a new stage on the night of October 16, 1938, when Chinese army forces launched a direct attack on occupied Hangzhou, "killing numerous Japanese soldiers, destroying the [rebuilt] power plant and firing an ammunition dump and the headquarters of the Japanese puppet regime." During that same action, Chinese soldiers destroyed railroad tracks and blew up bridges between Hangzhou and Shanghai.[65] Reports followed within a week that the Japanese arranged loudspeakers along the Qiantang River in a futile (and somewhat bizarre) effort to broadcast calls for a cease fire. Chinese guerilla forces delivered their response in mid-December with a daring raid inside Hangzhou's city walls, killing about one hundred Japanese and burning a dozen or more government offices.

Having repeatedly pulverized Xiaoshan by air through the spring and summer of 1938, the inevitable land attack came amid heavy snowfall on the evening of January 21, 1940. By the next day, the city was in Japanese hands.[66] The occupiers vented two years of frustration on the entire county, "burn[ing] whatever they could: all the facilities of the Xiang Lake Normal School, an agricultural experimental farm and office, trees on the mountains, crops in the fields, even grass on the roadside."[67] The invaders reportedly launched a large balloon with a trailing banner declaring (in Chinese characters): "Those who resist will die; those who surrender will live."[68]

Holding Hangzhou and Xiaoshan opposite one another across the Qiantang River hardly meant control of Zhejiang Province, however. Most of the province south of the river, both southeastward toward Shaoxing and Ningbo and southwestward along the upper Qiantang – Fuyang River valley, had remained under control of Chinese military or guerilla forces since the war began.

This situation was strikingly illustrated in mid-to-late March 1939 when Zhou En-lai, dressed daringly in military uniform, traveled first to Jinhua and then by boat to Shaoxing, his ancestral native place and home to a number of living relatives. Zhou visited with local villagers, dined formally with Communist Party supporters, visited the memorial tomb of Yu the Great, and performed traditional grave-sweeping rituals on the advent of the Qingming Festival. According to Michael Dillon,[69] Zhou encouraged local resistance by recalling the persistence of King Goujian and the revolutionary spirits of Lu Xun and Qiu Jin.

In an effort to buffer and fortify their hold over the Shanghai-Nanjing-Hangzhou triangle, the Japanese command looked eastward from Xiaoshan toward the Zhejiang coast. With their new base at Xiaoshan, the Japanese could seize control of the Zhegan railway inland to the west and cut off the Chinese supply line originating from the Ningbo seaport to the east. When their advance toward Shaoxing in April 1940 was repelled by Chinese forces near Zhuji, they settled for fortifying Xiaoshan as a base for future military operations south of the Qiantang River and also as a command center from which to oversee and protect their efforts to rebuild the river bridge destroyed by Chinese troops in 1939.[70]

Japanese forces finally launched a new offensive south of Hangzhou in October 1940. They briefly occupied Shaoxing but were forced by Chinese counterattacks to abandon the city with heavy losses before month's end. Before departing, however, they "burned large sections of the city, including the business district, local government buildings, [and] telegraph, newspaper and bank buildings."[71]

Meanwhile, Japanese actions southwestward along the Qiantang River valley included bombing raids in Jinhua, site since late 1939 of the relocated Zhejiang Provincial government. The closing paragraph of the short *New York Times* report on the bombings declared somewhat matter-of-factly from a local Western missionary operation "that bubonic plague had broken out in [Jinhua], taking many lives."[72] Unknown to all, it was a warning message lost in the chaos and disease endemic to warfare. So easily overlooked: unthinkable as somehow deliberate, too horrifying even to imagine.

The long-anticipated Japanese coastal assault finally arrived in earnest in April 1941. Shaoxing was attacked on April 17 and fell two days later on the 19th, the same day Ningbo was lost to a coastal invasion. While the invaders consolidated their hold on those two prefectural capitals, further assaults were successfully completed southward along the Zhejiang coast, capturing Wenzhou and most of the coastal counties down to Fujian Province. While many refugees from Shaoxing and Ningbo fled southward into mountainous areas, others made a logical but fateful choice to head westward toward Jinhua and Quzhou.[73]

Despite their military successes, the Japanese were not truly gaining ground or strengthening their foothold in China because they simply could not control the mountainous countryside. In mid-May, for example, Chinese forces retook the town of Kuaiji (near Shaoxing) and claimed over 4,000 Japanese killed.[74] Offensives and counter-offensives continued in Zhejiang by both sides through the remainder of 1941, along with persistent deadly actions and demolitions taken by Chinese guerrilla bands. The Japanese invaders were increasingly looking in Zhejiang Province like the proverbial dog that chased and caught the car, struggling to hold on and at a loss for what to do next with what they had seized.

Throughout Chinese history, invaders like the Mongols, Manchus, and even the Taipings had succeeded when their tactical military victories had been accompanied by absorption of the defeated onto their side or into their armies—conscription by force, threat, loot, or personal conviction. The Japanese military's failure to pacify or persuade, to win hearts and minds, marked the invading force as penetrators but not occupiers, able to seize cities or terrorize villages but critically unable to control territories. They were now riding the tiger they had mounted in 1937 – 1939, but there no longer appeared to be a safe way to dismount.

The consequences were indeed consequential. Japanese forces operated throughout the

Zhejiang countryside at will during daylight hours, then retreated to their bases in larger cities and towns by evening. In the dark of night, Chinese guerrilla fighters roamed freely, ambushing vehicles and killing their occupants, conducting sabotage operations, attacking isolated guard stations and pillboxes, disrupting supply lines, seizing cargo, destroying supply depots, and infiltrating the cities with spies.[75]

In his memoir, Edward Clayton outlined with barely disguised admiration a series of such guerrilla activities. He described how these "patriot bands" ambushed Japanese military vehicles by weakening roads or cutting wide and deep traps into the roadway, overloading ferries so they would capsize, or setting warehouses afire. He reported further that the guerilla fighters disrupted Japanese transportation by sabotaging railroad tracks and relocating beacons or moving channel markers in the Yangzi River, causing boats to run aground.

In yet another anecdote, Clayton claimed with near glee to having asked one Hangzhou citizen why he worked every day posting Japanese propaganda across the city. "'You see,'" the man explained, "'I put them up in the afternoon and get paid for it. I earn my living that way. Then I tear them all down at night. That's my real job.'"[76] According to Clayton, the Japanese military leadership asserted that at least fifty thousand guerrilla fighters/saboteurs continuously occupied the Shanghai-Nanjing-Hangzhou triangle, with "…another 50,000 avoiding pitched battle but requiring the Japanese to garrison heavily every town they expect to hold."[77]

Chinese guerrilla fighters, regular soldiers, and activist, anti-Japanese civilians found further support for morale-building in the words of Yue Fei, their great patriot of the Song Dynasty. It was commonly believed, though likely not historically true, that Yue had written the following poem to the tune "The River Is Red" (滿江紅, Man jiang hong) :

> My hair stands on end in my helmet.
> I lean against the railing; the driving rain lets up.
> I lift my eyes, and roar long at Heaven.
> My breast is filled with violence.
> I am thirty but my deeds and name are as earth and dust.
> Eight thousand li of road—nothing but moon and clouds.
> Do not slacken! The hair of young men whitens with useless sorrow.
> The shame of [Nanjing] is not yet made white as snow.
> When will the minister's hatred come to an end?
> Let us drive our chariots through the Helan Pass.
> My bold aim is to eat the flesh of the nomads.
> Laughing I thirst for the blood of the Xiongnu.
> Wait until we can begin again,
> Recovering our old rivers and mountains,
> And paying homage again in the imperial court.[78]

The five characters comprising the penultimate line, 收拾旧山河 (*Shoushi jiu shanhe*), were taken to be Yue Fei's warrior motto, understood as declaring "Give us back our mountains and rivers!" These same five characters could often be found brushed graffiti-like onto building walls in Japanese occupied zones, inspiring all to emulate Yue's indomitable fighting spirit.

Despite their tenuous hold over Zhejiang territory west of Hangzhou and south of the Qiantang River, the Japanese remained an ever-present strike force that could—and did—ravage small towns and villages at will. Given any provocation, they could appear suddenly and in force, burning and looting homes, raping women and children, torturing and even massacring the residents.[79] They could inflict terror and spread death wherever they wished, but they could not command loyalty, achieve submission from the Chinese people, or take secure possession of the land.

Jimmy Doolittle's Second China Visit

As 1941 drew to a close, a dangerously unpredictable stasis reigned over Hangzhou and northern Zhejiang. Inside Hangzhou's city walls, an uneasy "new normal" had been established, with hospitals and refugee camps providing safe haven and medical care to refugees and orphans. The Japanese authorities might be running the city, but the fighting seemed to have moved on elsewhere.

All of this changed forever on December 7, when fate, by just one degree of separation, would unexpectedly link northern Zhejiang to a faraway Hawaiian naval base called Pearl Harbor. For the remaining Westerners in Hangzhou, most of them American and British, relationships with the local Japanese military authorities reset immediately after December 7, 1941. They were now non-military enemies of the occupying army. In relatively short order, many departed occupied China for home, while others were arrested and interned for the balance of the war.[80]

Pearl Harbor activated the American war machine and cast America into what to this point had been a studiously avoided Sino-Japanese conflict. The surprise attack in Hawaii also motivated thoughts of near-term retaliation that crystalized in an audacious, carrier-based bombing raid over Japan. Simple in concept but dangerously radical in execution, the plan called for sixteen B-25 long-distance bombers to lift off from an aircraft carrier (something never done before) positioned some five hundred miles off the Japanese coast, drop their payloads on military and industrial targets over several cities, and then head for airfields in Zhejiang. After refueling, they would fly on to Chongqing, now the temporary seat of the Nationalist government and headquarters for U.S. advisory operations under Lieutenant General Joseph Stilwell (1883 – 1946).

General Henry H. ("Hap") Arnold (1886 – 1950) chose as project officer for the planned raid Lieutenant Colonel James (Jimmy) Doolittle (1896 – 1993). Already famous as a flying ace, speed-record holder, stunt pilot, test pilot, degree-holding aeronautical engineer, and pioneering advocate of instrument flying, Doolittle also had passing familiarity with China. In 1933, the U.S. Department of Commerce had sent Doolittle to Shanghai as part of an aircraft trade mission. Boarding the latest Curtiss Hawk P-40 biplane, Doolittle astonished his audience, skimming Shanghai rooftops at two hundred miles per hour. The Nationalist government purchased seventy-two Hawk IIs after seeing Doolittle's performance.[81]

Such a complex bombing raid had never before been undertaken by the U.S. military. In addition to coordinating between the Army Air Force command and the U.S. Naval fleet command, countless hours were spent on tactical planning, target selection and identification, aircraft modification, crew selection, and short-runway takeoff training with planes never designed for that capability.

Planning for the China side of the mission was equally critical for the pilots' safety, and equally complicated. To begin with, General Stilwell deeply distrusted the ability of the Chinese officials surrounding Chiang Kai-shek to maintain the mission's secrecy. Stilwell himself was kept somewhat in the dark, as General Arnold refrained from providing Chongqing with many of the raid details.

To the extent that Chiang was provided a general sense of the planned raid, he expressed serious reservations. Concerned that three of the five landing fields identified by the Americans were unsuitable for landing B-25s,[82] he expressed even greater fear for the retaliation the Japanese might inflict once they discovered China's support role. Chiang was likely unaware that a U.S. State Department report of February 1942, the month before Doolittle's raid, had expressed nearly identical concerns regarding retaliatory Japanese treatment of captured Americans from the raid as well as any local village residents who assisted them. [83] They could not possibly have imagined the horrific consequences that would actually ensue.

Despite these reservations, the bombing raid over Japan took place on April 18, 1942. Eight of the sixteen B-25s headed for Tokyo, while the rest spread out to strike Yokohama, Nagoya, and Kobe. Aircraft and diesel motor factories, steel mills, electric power plants, gas storage tanks, naval stations and laboratories, and industrial warehouses—168 buildings in all—were damaged or destroyed. Japanese casualties from the bombing came to 87 dead and more than 150 seriously wounded.[84]

Contemporary American news media reported on the raid in mystified but patriotically exultant terms. How could such a raid have been executed—from the Aleutian Islands, or some mystery Asian island? From Shangri-la, as President Franklin D. Roosevelt jokingly suggested to reporters, or from Russia? Perhaps from an aircraft carrier? No one had a clue where the pilots and crews had come from, who they were, or where they went.[85] In fact, Jimmy Doolittle's name did not appear as the raid's leader until a month later, on May 21, the day he received the Congressional Medal of Honor from President Roosevelt and only one day after he had returned safely to the United States. [86]

Americans were electrified by a sweet mixture of retributive justice, collective uplift of the national psyche, and corresponding deflation of the Japanese national psyche. Never mind that the damage itself was relatively limited. The act was more important than the result, exposing Japan's vulnerability and putting Tokyo on notice that America had the ability, determination, and tactical imagination to strike back in ways the Japanese military brain trust had never conceived.

457

Even as Americans cheered the news, conditions on the ground in China were decidedly more serious. The American carrier fleet had been spotted by a Japanese scout boat sooner than expected, so Doolittle's bomber flight group had been forced to take off more than ten hours earlier and about 250 miles further from the Japanese coast than planned. Strong headwinds and rain storms had further stressed the attack fleet's fuel supplies, although favorable tailwinds on the way to China made up for some of the excess early usage. One of the planes headed for Russia after the raid and landed safely in Vladivostok.[87] The rest followed flight paths toward Hangzhou Bay and the airfield further inland at Quzhou, where they planned to refuel and then head for Chongqing.

By prearrangement with the Nationalist government in Chongqing, the Doolittle fliers' target landing fields were to be equipped with homing beacons. Two days before the Tokyo raid, however, the plane carrying the beacons to Quzhou crashed and the signaling devices were never delivered. Compounding the problems on the night of the American planes' arrival over Zhejiang, when the sound of their own approaching engines was mistaken for enemy aircraft, air raid sirens were sounded. All lights were turned off and signal flares doused. As a result, not one American plane landed at a Chinese airfield on April 18; all fifteen depleted their fuel in the night skies over China.

In most cases, the pilots and crews parachuted from their planes before the empty aircraft crashed to the ground: four crews in the Ningbo area or just off the Ningbo coast, six in central or south-central Zhejiang Province (including Doolittle's), and five further west in Jiangxi Province (three near Shangrao 上饶and two around Nanchang 南昌). In all, seventy-five Americans parachuted into China. Three died (two by drowning), four were imprisoned by the Japanese, three more were executed by Japanese captors in October 1942, and another died of malnutrition while a Japanese prisoner.

Most of the pilots and crew members ultimately made it safely to Chongqing, aided in virtually every case by local villagers (and occasionally, doctors) who discovered, patched, fed, hid, guided or transported the Americans to safety, away from Japanese soldiers who were frantically seeking them. Nearly every Raider had his own survival story that included life-saving assistance from rural villagers. One such story was related years later by Zhao Xiaobao from Nantian Island, south of Ningbo, where Captain Donald G. Smith and Crew #15 had ditched just off shore:

> "I heard some sound like thunder. We quickly realized it was an airplane. The Japanese were in the area, so everyone ran to the mountain [to hide]. After a while, nothing had happened so we returned home. In the pigsty I found four Americans crouched. We figured the Americans must have helped the Chinese." The couple gave the crew of plane #15 the leftovers of their wedding feast, as they were recently married.[88]

The Japanese Response

Back in Tokyo, the stunned military leadership may have been uncertain about the origins of the American attack, but they determined almost immediately where the

B-25s had headed after dropping their payloads. The Japanese reasoned that if those Zhejiang-area bases were close enough to land upon, they could equally be used to stage additional attacks on Japanese cities. The Japanese military command quickly resolved upon a plan to obliterate the air bases they did not already control, punish every Chinese city, town, village, and person who had in any way assisted the Americans, and wage a merciless campaign across Zhejiang Province as an object lesson on the price of assisting their enemies.

Coincidental or not, Chinese guerrilla forces executed a coordinated, multi-city attack on fifteen major Japanese-held cities on April 20, 1942, just two days after the Doolittle raid. Shanghai, Nanjing, Suzhou, Hangzhou, Ningbo, Nanchang, Wuhu, and Xiamen were all hit simultaneously: bombs exploded, fires set, railways and power plants badly damaged, factories destroyed, bridges blown up. In Hangzhou, a match factory was demolished and city bridges (including the Qiantang River bridge) were crippled. Fighting in Hangzhou city reportedly went on for two days.[89]

The Japanese command was already surprised and embarrassed by Doolittle's Tokyo raid and were immediately fearful of American use of eastern China as a launching ground for further aerial attacks. Two days later, they were humiliated by the Chinese fifteen-city assault, a signal to the world of the Japanese weakness in holding and controlling the lands they had ostensibly captured. On May 8, *The New York Times* made the latter message explicit. "Japan's Weakness Exposed by China" was the title to Harrison Forman's article, with a subtitle reading, "Guerrilla Raids in Big Cities Show Invaders Are Unable to Guard Communications."[90]

All true, but the Japanese military were furious and still riding the tiger. It was time to save face with a knockout blow, and Zhejiang Province was a primary target. In particular, the invaders viewed Jinhua as one of their most important objectives. Not only had the provincial government relocated there in 1939, but numerous businesses, banks, and factories had re-established themselves in that area.

In the early 1940s, Jinhua had become a crucial location on the communications, transportation, and supply lines to Nanchang and on to Changsha and interior China. Recognizing that Jinhua was such a target, the Zhejiang provincial government relocated again, first to Yongkang County (about forty miles further southeast of Jinhua), and then another fifty-five miles south to Songyang County, and ultimately (until 1945) to even more remote (and ninety-five percent mountainous) Yunhe County in Lishui Prefecture.[91]

Japanese troops already amassed in Hangzhou for a planned advance on Quzhou were now turned loose in mid-May 1942, as were similar forces in Nanchang: a 100,000-man revenge force, heavily equipped with artillery, supported by air power, and filled with patriotic rage. They planned their advance to follow the Zhegan railway line from both east and west. Claire Chennault (1893 – 1958) described this three-month campaign by the Japanese as a "bloody spear [driven] two hundred miles through the heart of East China."[92] Chennault's spear traced a straight southwesterly line between Hangzhou and

Nanchang (in Jiangxi Province), obliterating the airfields at Lishui, Yushan, Ji'an, and Quzhou, as well as any smaller airfields they could find.

Jinhua fell to the Japanese advance on May 29, 1942, as did the city of Lanxi. Quzhou followed on June 10, nearly every building and home in the city destroyed by intense Japanese bombardment. With Quzhou's downfall, a major Allied airfield was lost as well. Yet even as 80,000 Japanese troops advanced southwest toward Changsha in Jiangxi Province, Zhejiang guerrillas were active behind the lines near Jinhua once again, retaking Yiwu and Pujiang and threatening Dongyang.[93] Nevertheless, by July 9, Japanese forces had taken control of the entire length of the Zhegan railway line from Hangzhou to Nanchang.

Conflict raged through western Zhejiang in 1942, with city's taken and lost, then retaken and re-lost, the warp and weft of the blood-dyed cloth woven by war. In late July, Chinese forces retook Jiande and threatened Lanxi, reclaimed Jiangxi sections of the Zhegan Line in August, captured Lanxi and other towns at the beginning of September, then lost Lanxi again just a few days later. Action in 1943 followed much the same pattern, with devastating effects on the countryside and the residents who had remained there.

A report issued by the Church Committee on China Relief presented statistics on the Japanese assault against Quzhou and its surrounding area as collected by Reverend Bill Mitchell (United Church of Canada): 1,131 air raids, 10,246 people killed, 62,146 homes destroyed, over 7,500 cattle seized, thirty percent of crops burned. In Yushan, over two thousand were killed and most of the city burned to the ground.[94] Chennault wrote in his memoirs: "One sizable city was razed for no other reason than the sentiment displayed by its citizens in filling up Jap bomb craters on the nearby airfields."[95]

The Japanese advance was pure scorched-earth, reflecting the imperially sanctioned battlefield annihilation policy later known as "Loot All, Burn All, Kill All (三光政策, Sanguang zhengce). Anyone found or even suspected to have aided the Doolittle fliers or to have retained any memento of their presence was horribly murdered, often along with everyone in their village, which was then razed to the ground. In the countryside, the objective was death by famine if not by murder: farm animals seized or killed, crops burned, farm implements ruined or confiscated for their iron, homes torched, roads and bridges demolished.

In larger cities, rape, looting, burning, torture, and murder terrorized residents and left everything in charred ruins. Missionaries surveying the devastation in Nancheng County 南城县 (in Fuzhou 抚州, Jiangxi Province) summarized what they saw as the "Rape of Nancheng."[96] A deeply disturbed Chiang Kai-shek summarized the horrors in a cable to Washington:

> After they had been caught unaware by the falling of American bombs on Tokyo, Japanese troops attacked the coastal areas of China where many of the American fliers had landed. These Japanese troops slaughtered every man, woman, and child in those areas—let me repeat—these Japanese troops slaughtered every man, woman, and child in those areas.[97]

Chinese forces defending against this onslaught were simply overwhelmed, outgunned and lacking the air power of the Japanese forces. From the end of May into August 1942, they lost as many as fifty thousand men in a valiant but hopeless cause. Then, unexpectedly, the Japanese forces began withdrawing, allowing Chinese troops to reoccupy the lost territory and former residents their abandoned homes. They could not have known that the recent military strike had merely been the first phase of an even more terrifying campaign.

Since before the Sino-Japanese conflict began, Japan's biological warfare group, known as Unit 731 under the command of Major General Shiro Ishii 石井四郎 (1892 – 1959), had been developing, refining, and practicing its plague- and disease-spreading capabilities. In the fall of 1940, a new form of terror had quietly arrived in Zhejiang. On October 4, Japanese planes had flown over Quzhou and over Ningbo on October 27. Instead of dropping explosives, they had released peculiar bundles of rice, wheat, and wheat chaff designed to open while falling or upon impact with the ground.

Far from being humanitarian relief, each bundle was infested with thousands of bubonic-plague-carrying fleas. Plague deaths from this test strike numbered in the low hundreds, but they announced an entirely new weapon in the Japanese arsenal: war, plague, famine, and death. The Four Horsemen of the Apocalypse, mercilessly wrapped in air-dropped food packages.

Shiro Ishii arrived in the Zhejiang-Jiangxi area on August 24, 1942, and outlined his plan. Airplanes would drop packages containing plague-infested fleas and other diseased items, while on the ground, members of Unit 731 would follow the withdrawing Japanese soldiers to further infect the vacated areas, especially the airfield cities of Quzhou, Jinhua, and Yushan.[98]

"Cholera, typhoid, and paratyphoid bacteria were dropped into wells and reservoirs; plague-infested fleas and anthrax bacteria were spread throughout the rice fields. Contaminated sweet cakes and snacks were left for the children to pick up and eat."[99] Ishii expected waves of Chinese soldiers and civilians to return unwittingly to the now-contaminated zones, and indeed they did. At Chongshan village near Yiwu, one-third of the population died from bubonic plague; in Quzhou, an estimated fifty thousand people died in repeated plague outbreaks from 1942 through 1948.[100]

The unrestricted spread of pathogens also caused blowback among Japanese troops. Because their infantry units had not been informed of the biological warfare attack, some units inadvertently crossed over into hot zones. Soldiers infected with cholera, dysentery, and plague began appearing in sizable numbers at the Japanese Army Hospital in Hangzhou. As many as ten thousand were infected, and at least seventeen hundred died. Thousands of Japanese troops were still being treated for these diseases in the Hangzhou hospital as late as the summer of 1943.[101]

Chiang Kai-shek had been correct all along. The price paid by the Chinese people for Doolittle's air raid "victory" over Tokyo was death, destruction, and desolation over a

461

20,000-square-mile area of east-central China. An estimated 250,000 Chinese people, military and civilian, died as a direct result of the Japanese blitzkrieg through Zhejiang and Jiangxi in the summer of 1942, triggered in fair part by a thirty-second, wartime bombing run over Tokyo. As one Chinese journalist summarized the Japanese military assault and use of biological warfare: "The invaders made of a rich, flourishing country a human hell, a gruesome graveyard, where the only living thing we saw for miles was a skeleton-like dog who fled in terror before our approach."[102]

Memories persisted well after the war ended. A village southwest of Hangzhou identified as Congshan, victimized in August 1942 by bubonic plague, renamed a nearby, white-pago-da-topped hill in 1979 as "The Mountain of Remembering Our Hatred."[103] Based on extensive research and exploration of historical records, historians attending a 2002 International Symposium on the Crimes of Biological Warfare in Changde (Hunan Province) agreed upon an overall death count of 580,000 from Japanese biological warfare activities.[104]

The American flyers became popularly known as "Doolittle's Raiders," the subject of multiple books and several movies.[105] Western histories would mark their daring raid as a major psychological turning point in the Pacific War theater, while Chiang's warnings and the 250,000 dead Chinese soldiers and civilians would go largely unmentioned. Wayland Academy's Edward Clayton put it succinctly: "From the Chinese point of view, the Doolittle raid could be regarded only as a terrible fiasco."[106]

A Birch among the Bamboo

In 1893, William S. Sweet and his wife, Josephine, arrived as Southern Baptist missionaries in Hangzhou. Mr. Sweet founded Wayland Academy for boys, while Mrs. Sweet founded a girls' school and multiple churches and chapels in the city and outlying villages. As "Mother Sweet's" health weakened from age, a young American missionary named John Birch (1918 – 1945), newly arrived in Shanghai in July 1940, was asked to take over and continue her work. Philosophically deeply fundamentalist, Birch decided after a time to leave Hangzhou and pursue his mission away from the Japanese occupation. He headed southwest and resettled in the Free China area at Shangrao, in Jiangxi Province, from which he could proselytize throughout Jiangxi and southwestern Zhejiang.

In early April 1942, Birch decided to take his missionary work into the Qiantang River Valley toward the cities of Quzhou, Lanxi, and Jinhua. One day around mid-month, he stopped to eat at a small restaurant overlooking the Lan River outside of Lanxi. A Chinese officer approached his table and quietly informed him there were several Americans hiding in a boat nearby. Skeptical but curious, Birch stood alongside the boat and shouted, "Are there any Americans on this boat?" Jimmy Doolittle and his entire flight crew eagerly invited him inside.[107] They had parachuted to earth well north of Lanxi, either in the Tianmu Mountains or near the Zhejiang-Anhui border, and had been re-united by local Chinese officials aiding in their rescue.

Having previously volunteered for service by enlisting in the U.S. Army, Birch agreed to guide the five men to Lanxi. A boat from there would take them immediately to Quzhou, and then by air to Chongqing. Along the way to Lanxi, Birch spoke to Doolittle with a passion equal to his Christian beliefs about his interest in military service. Doolittle promised to recommend the young missionary to the American command in Chongqing. Sure enough, Birch soon received a telegram from General Joseph Stilwell's staff asking him to travel to Quzhou to locate and bury or assist medically any additional Doolittle Raid flyers he could find. He found about twenty more.[108]

Birch eventually met Colonel Claire Chennault, leader of the Flying Tigers, who recruited Birch into his military intelligence operation in July 1942 as a second lieutenant. With his language fluency, knowledge of Chinese customs, and ability to live comfortably on a modest Chinese diet, Birch soon became a crucial element in Chennault's efforts to collect actionable information and create an early warning network against Japanese air attacks. Three years later, Birch was shot and killed by local Chinese Communist militia near Xuzhou (in northern Jiangsu Province) after refusing to give up his firearm. Sadly, the date of this event was August 25, 1945, almost three weeks after the atomic bomb blast at Nagasaki and ten days after fighting with the Japanese had ended. He was buried on September 2, the day of Japan's formal surrender on the carrier *USS Missouri*.

By a strange twist of fate, Birch's final days in 1945 became a subject of renewed interest among American conservatives in the early 1950s, especially to a candy company executive named Robert Welch. It was Welch who wrote a polemical biography, *The Life of John Birch: In the Story of One American Boy, the Ordeal of His Age*. In December 1958, Welch announced the formation of the John Birch Society, which "rapidly became the most effectively managed and best financed grassroots conservative movement in the United States.....Perhaps as many as one hundred thousand Americans...joined the JBS at its height."[109]

The life story of a Christian missionary from Hangzhou who worked tirelessly to aid the Chinese nation in its defense against the Japanese invaders was posthumously co-opted by an American businessman as the namesake of one of America's best known, most ultra-conservative, and most virulently anti-Communist organizations. It was a regrettable besmirching of a young man's name and an undeserved ending to the story of a courageous life. As another John Birch biographer would write disparagingly, "The terms 'Bircher,' 'Birchite,' 'Birchitis,' 'Birchism,' and 'Welchism' entered the national vocabulary in the 1950s and 1960s to signify radicals, extremists, paranoiacs, and super patriots."[110] Jimmy Doolittle later opined with understatement on the co-optation of Birch's life story by American conservatives: "I feel sure he would not have approved."[111]

Cartoons in Wartime

Wearied by the incessant warlord conflicts of the 1920s, Feng Zikai had increasingly turned to his children and the innocence of childhood as his artistic inspiration. He initially focused on his own six children, but as they aged into adolescence, he broadened his attention to childhood in a more general sense. Then, in 1926, he received a letter from his former art teacher Li Shutong, now a Buddhist monk in Hangzhou with the adopted name Hongyi (演音). After visiting his former teacher, Feng asked Hongyi to conduct a ritual ceremony on his thirtieth birthday in which he and his sister (Feng Man) became lay Buddhists. His attitude toward daily affairs also underwent a change; at the still-young age of thirty, a distinct world-weariness crept into his drawings. In a self-portrait titled "An Old Man at Thirty," Feng even depicted his seated self as slouching, bespectacled, goateed, and balding.[112]

Into the 1930s, Feng Zikai developed a strong connection with Ma Yifu 马一浮 (1883 – 1967), a Shaoxing scholar of the Chinese classics living a reclusive life at West Lake. Swayed by the influence of Hongyi and Ma Yifu, Feng's work took on strong overtones of Buddhist philosophy, reflected in the titles of Feng's published collections in the 1930s: *Paintings on Impermanence* and the three-volume *Paintings for the Preservation of Life*. Although Feng retained his business connections to Shanghai, his growing revulsion with modernism led him in 1933 to design and build a new family home, a two-story affair he called Yuanyuan Hall, in his native town of Shimenwan (Jiaxing Prefecture). He also leased rooms at Tianjia Garden on the shores of West Lake, close to his children's school while simultaneously offering personal space for quiet contemplation, artistic work, and interaction with Hongyi and Ma Yifu. Such were their respective levels of personal interconnection, artistic talent, and classical scholarship that all three were welcomed as members of the elite Xiling Seal Engraving Society.

The years from 1932 to 1937 were immensely productive ones for Feng Zikai. His prolific output in this period included essays, paintings, translations, commentaries, and art histories, resulting in more than twenty books. When war arrived in Zhejiang in November 1937, Feng and his family of ten fled Yuanyuan Hall before it was destroyed by Japanese bombers, residing first in Guilin and finally in Chongqing. Returning to Shimenwan after 1945, Feng found Yuanyuan Hall in ruins. His books, many of his works, and cherished calligraphy from Hongyi and others were all lost to the fires of war.

"After our little boat moored at the wharf next to Nan'gao Bridge," Feng later wrote about returning to his devastated hometown, "I looked around and wondered whether we had somehow come to the wrong place. This was not the Shimenwan I knew; surely it was another town entirely." He could barely even find the place where his residence had been located. His reaction to his first return visit to West Lake eerily channeled that of Zhang Dai nearly three hundred years earlier: "It was as though everything had been inundated by a great flood; only a hundredth of what had once stood now remained. I hastened to quit this place, for although I had come in search of West Lake, what I saw made me realize that it is far better to savor the dreams of what once was."[113]

During the war years, Feng turned his artistic expression toward the horrors of the anti-Japanese war. His work was as much anti-war as anti-Japanese, sometimes containing a not-so-subtle undercurrent of his humanistic Buddhist convictions against the very existence of war. Thus, he depicted an armed soldier picking a flower ("War and Flower") or playing a musical instrument ("War and Music"), and he employed a flowering potted plant and a water can as national defense metaphors ("Let the Blood of the Martyrs Nourish the Flower of Freedom"). In one particularly gripping but hopeful cartoon,

"The Instinct for Life,"[114] Feng drew a few stone blocks in a plain stone wall, partially obscured by piled dirt or rubble, with a tiny, two-petal flower grasping at life as it grows out from one of the crevices between the stones.

In many of his cartoons, Feng Zikai focused compassionately on the suffering and depredations of war wreaked upon the lives of ordinary people rather than depicting the Japanese as inhuman invaders. Unlike the more violent and graphic work of other wartime cartoonists, Feng's *manhua* most often depicted the results of acts rather than the acts themselves. His artistic expressions of the war were deeply and personally felt, as in his "Bombs in Yishan." In a 1939 Japanese bombing raid of a bus station, Feng admitted to being "one of those frightened out of their wits." He added:

> Ever afterward I blanched at the sound of an iron wok lid being banged, or the hiss of steam from a kettle. I was such a bundle of nerves that when the old lady next door called her little boy Jinbao, I used to think she was shouting 'Jingbao!' (Air raid warning!).[115]

His cartoons could nevertheless be brutally nationalistic: encouraging resistance and determination, illustrating wartime horror, calling out traitorous behavior, and lamenting the ruins of battle. In one of Feng's sketches, a woman is decapitated by an exploding bomb as her infant breastfeeds. Feng's own poetry accompanies this simple *manhua*:

> In this aerial raid,
> On whom do the bombs drop?
> A baby is sucking at its mother's breast,
> But the loving mother's head has suddenly been severed.
> Blood and milk flow together.[116]

In another, a mother carries an infant child on her back even as the baby's head is severed from its body by a bomb blast.[117]

Feng Zikai's legitimization of *manhua* as an art form in the 1920s had motivated other practitioners of cartoon art, paving the way for their wartime participation with more explicitly patriotic, nationalistic, and anti-Japanese propaganda than Feng's. Not long after the Japanese conflict broke out in 1937, *manhua* artists quickly formed the Shanghai National Salvation Cartoon Association. Out of this larger association emerged a small group of artists who formed the National Salvation Cartoon Propaganda Corps (救亡漫画宣传队, *Jiuwang manhua xuanchuan dui*).

The leader of the Cartoon Propaganda Corps was the well-established cartoonist Ye Qianyu 叶浅予 (1907 – 1995), but among their number was an unheralded twenty-seven-year old cartoonist from Shaoxing named Zhang Leping 张乐平 (1910 – 1992). It was Zhang who (along with his work) would become a national treasure in the years following the war. This artistic group—along with Feng Zikai and the other *manhua* groups formed and operating throughout the war years—demonstrated that "cartoons, like spoken dramas, were more than an art form: they were an effective educational tool and a potent agent for political indoctrination."[118] And for patriotism, resistance, morale, and inspiration.

Yu Dafu and the Anti-Japanese Propaganda Campaign

During his four years in Japan, Yu Dafu had bonded with like-minded activists and intellectuals in Tokyo, and together they formed the Creation Society (創造社, Chuangzao she) in support of the modern vernacular literary movement. Following publication of the *Sinking* trilogy, he secured occasional university teaching positions while directing much of his time to writing and editing the Creation Society's magazine. In 1927, the already-married Yu Dafu met Wang Yingxia 王映霞 (1908 – 2000), the only child of a scholarly Hangzhou family. Yu was lovestruck and persistent in his entreaties until Wang finally yielded; they were married in 1927. That same year, Yu published *Nine Diaries* (*Riji jiu zhong*, 日記九種) describing his love affair with Wang Yingxia. The book broke Chinese sales records.

From 1932 – 1936, Yu, Wang, and their son Yu Fei 郁飞 (b. 1928) lived in Hangzhou. Yu Dafu wrote and published anti-Japanese war propaganda while Wang Yingxia took the Hangzhou social scene by storm. Believing they would be safer outside China, Yu left with his family for Singapore in 1938.[119] There he continued his anti-Japanese writing, monitored and translated Japanese propaganda broadcasts, and assumed editorship of the *Overseas China Weekly*, an anti-Japanese propaganda organ of the British Information Services Bureau. In the meantime, Yu's twelve-year marriage disintegrated, and Wang Yingxia returned to China.

The Japanese military overran Singapore on February 15, 1942, but Yu Dafu had already departed the island with colleagues, headed for Sumatra. Japanese advances in Java drove Yu to relocate to more and more remote villages. In September 1943, he met and married an Indonesian-born Chinese woman twenty-eight years his junior, Chen Lianyou 陈连有 (whom Yu renamed He Liyu 何丽有).

Because Yu feared the Japanese would recognize his identity as a vocal anti-Japanese propagandist, he adopted the alias Zhao Lian. His fluency in Japanese positioned him as a Chinese-Japanese translator, even working in that capacity for the local Japanese military headquarters. In 1944, the Japanese discovered his true identity but chose not to act on their information.

The Pacific War with Japan ended on August 14, 1945. Fifteen days later, in the midst of a meeting of overseas Chinese at his home, Yu answered a knock on his door and walked outside briefly with whomever had called. He was never seen again. Yu's young wife gave birth to their second child, this time a daughter, the very next day. Evidence suggests that Japanese military police likely assassinated Yu out of fear that he would be a witness against them in war crimes trials.

466

Chapter 20

ANOTHER RECOVERY,
AND A PEOPLE'S REPUBLIC

(1945 – 1976)

Seeing Someone Off on His Travels to Jiangnan[1]

Outside Yongjin Gate you'll be free of the red dust,
Nearby the city dressed in brocades you'll wear white duckweed flowerets.
Until you come to West Lake and see the colors of the hills,
Say what you will, you're not yet ripe to call yourself a poet.

– Chao Zhongzhi (c. 1090)

"Three Hairs" Lightens the Mood

Chinese forces had been aggressively advancing up the eastern coast against the Japanese occupiers in 1945, taking Fuzhou, Wenzhou, and Taizhou and threatening to retake Hangzhou and Shanghai when the war abruptly ended with the Japanese surrender announcement on August 15. After eight years of war, the Chinese people's sense of victory was tempered by the human dislocation and loss and the physical devastation of cities and countryside. Grief and despair undoubtedly mixed with anger at the Japanese aggressors, but the immediate challenge was repair and recovery, not recrimination. Many also sensed the growing threat of civil war between the GMD Nationalists and the rising Chinese Communist Party (CCP).

When the nation's mood most needed to be lightened and its spirits lifted, along came a series of cartoons perfectly suited to the moment. On May 12, 1946, the first episode in the comic serial *Sanmao Joins the Army* (三毛从军记, *Sanmao congjun ji*) appeared in Shanghai's *Shenbao* 申報. Newspaper readers immediately recognized the comic's main character, the little orphan boy Sanmao (三毛). He looked to be about ten years old, with arms and legs as thin as sticks, wearing short pants and a sleeveless shirt, barefooted or wearing shoes several sizes too big for his feet. Sanmao was well known for his small black eyes, big ears, button nose, and his famously oversized head, seemingly bald except for the three protruding hairs (三毛, *san mao*) that gave him his cartoon name. Readers also knew well the identity of Sanmao's cartoon artist, Zhang Leping.

Zhang Leping was born Zhang Shen in the smallest of Chinese villages in the Hai-yan district of Jiaxing, near the northern shores of Hangzhou Bay. The district was a farming area where almost everyone cultivated mulberry trees and grew silkworms. In his youth, he demonstrated talent and enthusiasm for drawing, fostered by his mother until she died when her son was only nine years old. At fourteen, Zhang's father apprenticed his son to a carpenter, but the young man continued his experimentation with illustration. Finally, at age 27, he settled into a struggling life in Shanghai, changed his given name to Leping, and created advertising art whenever he could find an interested client. He also conceived a street urchin character, "oppressed, weak, clever, and tough, with a strong instinct for survival."[2]

Zhang's orphan-boy character first appeared in the pages of pre-war Shanghai's *Xiaozhenbao* newspaper in November 1935. The initial strips were strictly comical and nonpolitical, focusing on the childlike misadventures of its main character. Yet those cartoons' focus on the hardships and abuses suffered by Shanghai's street orphans, however humorously presented, offered a sharp counterpoint to the sanitized strips of Mickey Mouse and Donald Duck also appearing in the Shanghai newspapers of the day. Between 1935 and 1937, Zhang produced over two hundred panels featuring Sanmao's gritty life.

When the Japanese conflict broke out in 1937, Zhang joined the Cartoon Propaganda Corps in Nanjing and published many of his works in the magazine *Resistance Cartoons*. Sanmao now only showed up occasionally in his wartime propaganda strips. In one series, Sanmao publicly denounces his father for avoiding military conscription by dressing as a woman. In another, he pulls the blanket off his sleeping father to remind him of the sufferings of Chinese soldiers in the field. In yet another sequence, the young orphan boy organizes a group of children to start a propaganda group of their own after his parents are ruthlessly killed by Japanese soldiers and his uncle has abandoned him to join the resistance.[3]

The relative infrequency of Sanmao's appearances during the war years did not signify lack of work on Zhang Leping's part. To the contrary, he produced visually terrifying cartoons illustrating Japanese soldiers gleefully bayonetting Chinese infants, accompanied by equally provocative captions: "Ah! A Chinese child!" (1938) and "This is how the enemy murders us!" (1939).[4] He also authored a series about a Chinese collaborator (*Biography of a Bastard*, 王八別傳 *Wangba biezhuan*) plagued by comedic misadventures in his persistent failed efforts to please the Japanese masters who despise him.

Most of Zhang's wartime works were unmistakably cartoon-like, composed with minimal detailing and emphatic in their use of caricature. He adopted a radically different style in December 1940, however, when he published a series of detailed and dramatically moving sketches in *Southeast Daily* (东南日报, *Dongnan Ribao*). Their collective title, "Zhuji after the Devastation," referred to the town of Zhuji, outside of Shaoxing, where extensive Japanese bombing had largely destroyed the city.

Zhang's sketches depicted the suffering of Zhuji's survivors, many of them women and children, in simple but realistic terms. These pictures rarely offered scenic background or locational context in order to direct the viewer's focus solely toward the human figures. Japanese soldiers never appeared in this series, only the continuing tragic consequences of the warfare they left behind.[5] Zhang's ironic choice of locale would have been doubly impactful for his Chinese readers. Zhuji was well known as the birthplace of the nation's greatest beauty, Xi Shi, and the site of Wang Xizhi's Orchid Pavilion, birthplace of its finest work of calligraphy.

When Sanmao returned with acclaim to the public scene in May 1946, his comic panels in *Shenbao* did not address postwar China. Rather, they looked backward with an angry edge to recount a story of the war just finished. Zhang's opening panels have the orphan child Sanmao attempting to enlist in the army and being summarily rejected for his size and age. Undeterred, Sanmao returns again to enroll, this time walking on stilts, his body hidden behind long pants and the rest covered by a man's jacket and hat. His outlandish scheme works, and he enters the Chinese army.

Little Sanmao's army experiences played out in serialized form for six months. The panels were entirely visual, devoid of dialog throughout and relying instead on slapstick humor and farce. Zhang depicted his character occasionally in battle, but more often among his comrades in the field or in their barracks, experiencing the daily life of a soldier in wartime. Sanmao's fellow soldiers were hardly heroic: "often lazy, fearful, and far from exemplary...signs of heroism and friendship between comrades rarely appear, while indifference, competition, and selfishness seem rampant in the Chinese army."[6] Zhang also highlighted the comfortable lifestyles and abuses of power by officers. In one strip from the series, Zhang lambastes army officers for their fixation on medals ("earned" with the lives of their troops) by having Sanmao create a medal out of paper and proudly displaying it before an officer who is showing off his own newly-awarded medallion.

Zhang's humorous but sarcastic postwar cartoons in *Sanmao Joins the Army* stood in sharp contrast with the heroic wartime images of Chinese soldiers published by the Cartoon Propaganda Corps during the conflict. They could be viewed as criticism of Chiang Kai-shek's ineffectual Nationalist government and military, but they also contained a reminder that the realities of war differ enormously from that of propaganda posters. By "transforming the Second Sino-Japanese conflict into a tragicomic spectacle,"[7] Sanmao's story represented a plea for avoidance of further conflict from a potential civil war between the GMD and the CCP.

The last panel of *Sanmao Joins the Army*, published on November 4, 1946, laid out two paths for his little hero. No longer a soldier, the orphan boy stands, undecided, facing two roads leading away from him in the shape of a "V," the wartime victory symbol. Both roads are lined with grave markers; one road leads away toward a rural life, the other toward big city urban life, although both are now in ruins. The restoration challenges will be the same for either, harsh and difficult.

After returning to post-war Shanghai and observing at first-hand the winter hardships of that city's actual war orphans, Zhang transformed his little war hero into one of those suffering street orphans. This new version of Sanmao remained comical, but with a strong air of pathos as he endured the indignities and hardships of street orphan life. The more emotionally engaged among his readers followed his stories as if they were real, sometimes sending letters or even gifts of money or clothes to ease the little boy's troubles. No matter how destitute, how cold and hungry, Sanmao carried on with an indomitable spirit and dreams of an unreachable better life. His experiences also pointed out the hypocrisies, cruelties, and indifference of modern life, whether they occurred intentionally, from ignorance, or from simple lack of awareness.

In one series of strips, for example, Sanmao sees a man advertising his children for sale on the street. The little orphan boy soon sits down beside them with a similar placard, advertising himself for one-seventh the asking price of the man's children. The man leaves his station, not wanting to compete with Sanmao on price (or perhaps shamed into changing his mind). Then Sanmao watches a fur-enwrapped woman exit a toy shop; the little girl at her side carries a new doll with a price tag seven times that for which Sanmao offered himself for sale.

Over the next two years, in the pages of Shanghai's *Dagong bao* 大公报 newspaper, Sanmao reached his highest level of acclaim yet. Collected in 1961 under the title *The Wandering Life of Sanmao* (三毛流浪记选集, *Sanmao liulangji xuan ji*),[8] this *manhua* series ran from 1947 to 1949. Over 250 strips were published through the civil war era that ended with the People's Liberation Army (PLA) entering Shanghai and the establishment in October 1949 of the People's Republic of China.

Hangzhou Is Liberated

The formal Japanese surrender on September 2, 1945 may have ended the anti-Japanese war, but it reopened the door to the Nationalist-Communist (GMD-CCP) conflict that had mostly simmered from 1937 – 1945. From June 1946 to early in 1950,[9] civil war raged through China. For much of the first three years, the conflict was largely confined to Manchuria and territory north of the Yangzi River. It was not until April 20, 1949, that PLA forces under the command of Marshal Chen Yi 陈毅 (1901 – 1972) crossed the traditional Yangzi River boundary separating North and South China and began their assault on Nanjing. Such by then was the deteriorated state of the Nationalist Army that their self-proclaimed capital fell within four days (April 24); the fabled city of Suzhou was under PLA control by April 27.

Six days later, on May 3, PLA troops marched into Hangzhou, not just unopposed but warmly and even raucously welcomed by the city's residents. As his parting gesture to Hangzhou, the fleeing GMD city mayor absconded one day earlier with fifteen thousand silver dollars. A few of the remaining city officials greeted the incoming Communist Party representatives, who in turn entered the local government offices. One of the new government's first visible acts involved flags: lowering the building's Republic of China emblem and raising in its place an unadorned red flag. Not until September 27 would the People's Republic have an official (five-star) national flag,[10] first flown at Tiananmen Square on October 1, 1949.

An imminent and more significant challenge for the national Communist Party concerned staffing the provincial and local government offices in Hangzhou. The former GMD officials had abandoned their posts, and local individuals who might have taken their place were merchants or members of the educated elite. The CCP had largely risen and advanced in North China, where unions leaders, workers, and rural peasants led the revolution, suffered the deaths and privations of the civil war, and assumed leadership and bureaucratic roles in the cities that fell under Communist Party control.

Hangzhou's long history of educational and cultural excellence hardly reflected the peasant or worker roots of the North, nor had the citizens of Hangzhou paid much of a wartime price during the post-1945 revolutionary years. Other than silk, textiles, and tea—not exactly smokestack operations—the city had little in the way of industry or unions from which to draw cadres for civil administration. At the advent of the PRC, Hangzhou's population was about 520,000, but only about 28,000 were laborers in factories or mills. Most of the city's factories were quite small, with just thirty-three having work forces in excess of one hundred employees.[11]

The CCP's solution for Hangzhou, domestic immigration of Party cadres, was simple in conception but fraught with potential complexity and misunderstandings. In late 1948, the Party announced a plan to recruit fifty thousand cadres for placement in official and administrative positions nationwide, with fifteen thousand of those individuals to come from Shandong Province. From among that cohort, the CCP assigned nearly 3,700 to Zhejiang Province, where they would occupy official positions from the town, city, and county level to the highest provincial levels. Zhejiang Province and its major cities were about to be put *en masse* under the control of individuals with no knowledge of local history, culture, cuisine, dialect, or traditions.

Initial CCP leadership of Zhejiang Province was granted to Tan Zhenlin 谭震林 (1902 -1983) and Tan Qilong 谭启龙 (1913 – 2003), responsible for military and civil affairs, respectively. Within a few months, the first level of transformation reached completion. Public and semi-public institutions—electric and water utilities, postal, transportation, and communication services, and factories, mines and warehouses—became CCP state enterprises. New PRC currency, the renminbi (RMB), replaced the former GMD currency; even the use of silver dollars was banned.

Within the first days, "all three public universities and twelve public high schools in Hangzhou changed hands....But most private schools remained untouched."[12] Political education and physical labor were added to many schools' curricula, as was

471

political study for faculties and staffs. For the time being, the still-private Hangzhou College of Science and the Humanities (formerly the Hangzhou Christian College) on the hilly western outskirts of Hangzhou continued to operate cautiously and with minimal change.

In 1951, the two schools (Qiushi Academy and Hangchow Presbyterian College) that had evolved and operated in parallel for fifty-four years finally intersected. The former Christian college sitting astride the western hills overlooking the Qiantang River was formally incorporated into Zhejiang University as the Zhijiang College (之江大学, Zhijiang daxue) campus.

Meanwhile, the Buddhist and Daoist temples sprinkled liberally about West Lake's surrounding hills were permitted to welcome adherents and host their traditional annual pilgrimages, although some of the lesser temples were closed. In November 1949, a story in the *Zhejiang Daily* reported that as many as two-thirds of the monks in the area before Liberation had since been transported back to their native places. Those who remained were now organized into work groups to perform manual labor.[13]

Although the Shandong cadres believed wholeheartedly in Mao Zedong's call for industrialization, their vision of smoke-belching factories failed utterly to coincide with the realities of Hangzhou and northern Zhejiang. The area lacked natural resources like coal and iron, and any effort to scale up major new industry could also threaten some of the nation's most productive agricultural land. Furthermore, industry could disrupt the common people's livelihood from sericulture, silk, and tea, jeopardize world-recognized export industries in silk textiles and tea, and perhaps even tarnish the natural beauty of the city's surroundings.

The "production over all else" mentality so infused the Shandong cadres' actions that they even threatened West Lake. Early CCP projects to build new roads around the lake, renovate or create new parks and gardens, and improve the lake's water quality appeared well-intentioned to provide badly needed employment to displaced workers and the city's poor. However, the motivation was not natural beauty or tourist enjoyment but productive resource use. The goal was to transform West Lake into a fish farm for carp and abalone. Work to improve the lake's water quality and depth in the 1950s was later described in terms of stocking fish in the lake "to increase the supply to the city."[14]

A balance between production/industrialization and cultural/environmental preservation would need to be struck. Meanwhile, modern Hangzhou's future, and perhaps West Lake's as well, hung in that balance.

Farewell, Leighton Stuart

On August 18, 1949, an article entitled "Farewell, Leighton Stuart" (别了司徒雷登, Biele, Situ Leideng) appeared in the Chinese press, distributed through the Xinhua News Agency.[15] The essay, a sarcastic, 2,500-word, anti-American diatribe, gained immediate national attention in China because its author was Mao Zedong 毛泽东 (1893 – 1976),

472

leader of the CCP and soon to be Chairman of the People's Republic of China. By any measure, Mao's essay was an international declaration of victory in the recently concluded Civil War (1945 – 1949) and a statement of intention that China would now be the sole master and determinant of its own future.

In his opening paragraphs, Mao excoriated U.S. policy in support of the defeated Chiang Kai-shek, describing the recent anti-Nationalist conflict as "the war to turn China into a U.S. colony…in which the United States of America supplies the money and guns and Chiang Kai-shek [supplies] the men to…slaughter the Chinese people." Mao taunted Secretary of State Dean Acheson (1893 – 1971), declaring that the Chinese people were unafraid. Even if blockaded by foreign powers for the next eight or ten years, Mao wrote, "by that time all of China's problems will have been solved." He chided Stuart for having to "take to the road, his briefcase under his arm," closing with this declaration: "Leighton Stuart has departed and the White Paper has arrived. Very good. Very good. Both events are worth celebrating."[16]

Those final lines referenced two recent developments in Chinese-American relations: American Ambassador John Leighton Stuart's departure from China on August 2, 1949, and the U.S. State Department's publication on August 5 of a thousand-page White Paper entitled *United States Relations with China*. The State Department's report surveyed American foreign policy with China dating from 1844, with particular focus on actions and events during the period from 1945 – 1949. The White Paper concluded, in short, that the Communist victory was a measure of the incompetence and lack of will exhibited by the Nationalists despite billions of dollars given them in U.S. financial aid.

To the politically aware in China, John Leighton Stuart (1876 – 1962) was America's official representative; to the more politically informed, Stuart was also the former president of Yenching College in Beijing, one of China's premier institutions of higher learning. But for many citizens of Hangzhou, the relationship ran much deeper and closer, encompassing two generations of the Stuart family.

John Leighton Stuart was born in Hangzhou, the eldest of the four sons[17] of American Presbyterian missionaries John Linton Stuart (1840 – 1913) and Mary Louise Stuart (1843 – 1925). The elder Stuart first arrived in Hangzhou in 1868 as an unmarried missionary and spent five years preaching in the streets, running a modest clinic, and itinerating through the Zhejiang countryside before deteriorating health forced him to return to the U.S. While recuperating from his illness in 1873, he met Mary Louise Horton, a young woman from Alabama who had recently lost her fiancé in naval military action.

In less than a year, the young couple were married and headed together for Hangzhou, where they took up residence in the Presbyterian compound near Wulin Gate. Despite giving birth to four boys in Hangzhou in just seven years and overseeing their care and early education, Mary Stuart committed herself to female education, opening one of the earliest girls' boarding schools in China,[18] the Hangzhou School for Girls.

Meanwhile, first born son Leighton Stuart was raised in Hangzhou, home-schooled but nevertheless intimately familiar with Chinese life, culture, and language. In his autobiography, he recalled his "excursions to the scenic spots of Hangchow, picnic lunches, hunting for wild strawberries, the hills ablaze with azaleas in the spring... surrounded with glamorous adventure."[19] When his parents returned to Mobile, Alabama, for their first furlough in 1887, Leighton and younger brother David Todd Stuart (1878 – 1909) were enrolled in local public schools and then private, college preparatory schools. Leighton graduated second in his class from Hampden-Sydney College in 1896 and married Aline Rodd (1879 – 1926) in November 1904. They sailed together to China right after their honeymoon, Leighton's return being his first in almost eighteen years.

Back again in Hangzhou, Leighton Stuart set out first to refresh and expand his atrophied command of the Chinese language. After four years of missionary field work in Hangzhou, he accepted a position as professor of New Testament Language and Literature at the newly-founded Presbyterian Union Theological Seminary in Nanjing. He remained at the Seminary from 1909 – 1919, teaching, writing, and observing at close hand the events and impacts of the 1911 Revolution and the efforts to establish the new Republic of China. In 1913, he traveled back to Hangzhou to bury his father, who passed away after forty-five years in Hangzhou. John Linton Stuart was laid to rest at Jiulisong 九里松 Cemetery near West Lake alongside his son David, who had also returned to Hangzhou after graduating from college but had died tragically from a gun accident four years earlier. Leighton would return again in 1925 to lay his mother to rest alongside her husband and son David.

In 1918, Stuart was approached as a candidate for the presidency of a new university being formed in Beijing by the union of four separate Christian colleges.[20] After several rounds of discussion, he accepted the position at what would be known as Yenching University (燕京大学, Yanjing daxue), a sophisticated allusion to Beijing's role as capital of the ancient Yan State from the 11th to 3rd Centuries BCE. As a condition of his recruitment, Stuart insisted that new, more expansive grounds be purchased for the campus and that he, as president, not be saddled with fund-raising responsibilities. The latter challenge fell to another long-time China missionary, an acquaintance of Leighton Stuart's named Henry W. Luce (1868 – 1941), whose son Henry Robinson Luce (1898 – 1967) would later found *Time* and *Life* magazines in America.

In 1927, Stuart voluntarily resigned as Yenching's Chancellor in accordance with new Nationalist government regulations that all Chinese universities must be headed by Chinese citizens. Wu Leichuan 吴雷川 (1870 - 1944) accepted the Chancellor position with Leighton Stuart as President. The next year, Yenching received a substantial grant from the estate of ALCOA co-founder Charles M. Hall (1863 – 1914) "to conduct and provide research, instruction and publication in the culture of China and/or elsewhere in Continental Asia and Japan."[21] From this generous funding, Stuart and William Hung (Hong Ye, 洪业, 1893 – 1980), Chairman of Yenching's History Department, arranged with Harvard University to create the prestigious Harvard-Yenching Institute, which continues to support education, research fellowships, workshops, and publications to the present day.

Leighton Stuart presided over Yenching University for twenty-two years. In the four years following the Japanese invasion of China in 1937, Stuart steadfastly remained at the Beijing campus and boldly refused Japanese demands to lower the American flag in favor of the Rising Sun. The day after the attack on Pearl Harbor in December 1941, he was arrested and held in an internment camp for the duration of the war.

In July 1946, George C. Marshall (1880 – 1959) approached Stuart with a request that he accept the American ambassadorial position in post-war Nanjing. Now age 70, Stuart reluctantly agreed. As he prepared to leave Hangzhou in October for his new diplomatic assignment in Beijing, city officials demonstrated the esteem in which he and the whole Stuart family were held by presenting him with a gold key to the city and designating him an honorary citizen of Hangzhou.[22]

Throughout his years in Nanjing and Beijing, Stuart had consistently supported Chiang Kai-shek and the Guomindang, perhaps seeing in them a future Christian China. He could still be a vocal critic of Nationalist corruption, and at times he openly voiced admiration for the Communists' concern with the welfare of the common people. Nevertheless, he repeatedly argued with Washington for stronger support of Chiang Kai-shek's regime or at least an accommodation and possible coalition government uniting the Nationalists with the CCP. Both Marshall and President Harry S. Truman (1884 – 1972) rejected any consideration of a coalition government.

As late as June 1949, Leighton Stuart still hoped to facilitate a rapprochement between the two sides, especially after receiving an intriguing invitation to visit Mao Zedong and Zhou Enlai in Beijing as an "old friend of many"[23] in the CCP. Stuart's hopes were quashed when the State Department rejected the plan, concerned that such a meeting would provoke a strong anti-communist backlash in the United States. Mao Zedong's "Farewell, Leighton Stuart" declared a harsh goodbye, at once personal to Stuart but equally a rejection of any Sino-American relationship, at least for the time being. Mao's essay effectively shut the door to all forms of American support or involvement in what was soon to be the new People's Republic of China.

Gordon Chang neatly summarized Stuart's Chinese life and career: "He possessed a sincere affection for the Chinese people, but Chinese politics continually challenged him."[24] Stuart's boyhood home in Hangzhou, originally built by his father, remains today as a modest museum to his family's memory, complete with a memorial bust honoring him for his contributions to the development of China in the first half of the 20th century. The Stuart residence is located at No. 3 Yesutang Lane, adjacent to the Tianshui Christian Church.[25] The residence and church are located on the original site of the land given to missionaries Ben Helm and M.H. Houston in 1873 in exchange for their *feng-shui*-disturbing residence on City God's Hill.[26]

Mao's Home Away from Home

By 1953, rapid industrialization reigned as the CCP's primary domestic focus, resulting in hundreds of new factories and mills, predominantly located in North China or far inland. Relatively little of this activity took place in Zhejiang, leaving Hangzhou's future direction still unresolved despite the Shandong cadres' fierce intentions to follow the central dictate to "replace consumption with production."[27] That same year, the PRC's First Five-Year Plan effectively doubled down on this strategy by prioritizing the development of heavy industry. Hangzhou was left even further out in the cold: of nearly seven hundred state-funded industrial enterprises identified in the formal plan, not one was slotted for Hangzhou.[28]

Local meetings to address the city's dilemma were organized, and a Russian urban planning expert, A.C. Maxim, was invited to participate. He doubtless saw what artists and scholars had seen in Hangzhou's natural setting and long cultural history: an ideal locale for cultural tourism and associated business and leisure activities, transforming Hangzhou into a "Geneva of the East." Of course, such a development framework meant minimizing industry and placing a premium on preservation and enhancement of both the natural environment and the traditional cultural elements already in place, including temples, pagodas, tomb sites, gardens, and specialized arts and crafts, as well as famous teahouses, performance venues, and medicine shops. Maxim argued for limited industrial development, strictly confined to areas well north of the city, with the city's population capped at around 800,000.

Maxim's proposal was hardly revolutionary. In many ways, it mirrored ideas at least as far back as the replacement of the Manchu Qiying with the New Business District in the 1910s. But now the times were different and the nation had changed. Maxim's urban plan was anathema to the Shandong cadres. They wanted to provide factory jobs to the working classes and wipe away the centuries-old stain of Hangzhou's reputation as "heaven on earth" for educated elites and wealthy and middle-class merchants. For those locally in political charge, the objective was simple: "Hangzhou would no longer belong to the rich and powerful but to working people."[29]

Resolution of this directional impasse began unexpectedly on December 27, 1953. On that day, Mao Zedong arrived for his first visit to Hangzhou since his brief sightseeing excursion with Xiao Yu in 1921. This time, however, his planned one-month stay at West Lake stretched into three months, until March 13, 1954. He took up residence at Liu Villa (刘庄, Liu zhuang) on West Lake,[30] built in 1905 by Liu Xuexun 劉學詢 (1874 – 1908). Liu's villa was renowned for its bamboo garden and its "Little Solitary Hill" (小孤山, Xiao Gushan), positioned opposite the former imperial Solitary Hill palace of Emperors Kangxi and Qianlong.

It was during this first extended visit to West Lake that Mao worked with his advisers to draft the Constitution for the People's Republic. In addition, his three-month hiatus from the political whirlwinds of Beijing gave Mao an arm's-length distance from which to observe, test political winds and individual loyalties, and contemplate plans and strategies. At the same time, he could enjoy the scenic views of West Lake and the area's culinary, cultural, and climatic pleasures. Mao's favorable viewpoint sealed the city's future: Hangzhou would assume a distinctly non-industrialized place in the national economy and serve a unique role in how the PRC presented itself to the world beyond.

Mao's actions in Hangzhou created an unexpected ancillary benefit for one of the city's important industries. Amid the initial rush among the northern cadres to eliminate all traces of 'feudal culture," questions had been raised regarding tea houses. But Mao enjoyed drinking tea and sometimes even consumed the well-soaked leaves. He also exhibited particular interest in the nearby tea plantations at the village of Meijiawu, famous for their production of one of the country's most esteemed varieties, Longjing ("Dragon Well"). Mao visited the village and took great interest in the local people who grew, harvested, and cured the tea leaves. His personal involvement, as well as Zhou En-lai's similar actions and preferences, helped preserve Hangzhou's tea industry not for its elitist elements but for its importance to farmers and working people.[31]

Like so many before him, Mao had fallen for West Lake's many charms. Besides the obvious pleasure of seasonal West Lake views, Mao enjoyed climbing the surrounding hills, visiting famous sites, taking photographs, and writing poetry. Always an avid swimmer, he occasionally left the villa to swim in the Qiantang River. He also traveled in the Zhejiang region. In September 1956, for example, he visited Haining to observe the Qiantang tidal bore and swim in the river. In April 1960, he traveled by train to Shaoxing and Ningbo, stopping to see several villages along the route.

Over the course of more than two decades, Mao would return dozens of times, over forty by most counts.[32] Some lasted only a few days, but most ran for at least one week, with at least nine stays of one to two months or more. Shortly after his first 1953 – 1954 visit, Hangzhou officials authorized modifications at Liu Villa to suit administrative and security needs as well as the Chairman's personal tastes and interests, such as a swimming pool on the grounds. Notably, a wholesale dredging of West Lake began after Mao's visit, one of the most comprehensive lake restorations in three centuries.[33]

On some occasions, Mao stayed at Wang Zhuang, a more secluded garden villa on West Lake's south shore, overlooked today by the rebuilt Leifeng Pagoda. Wang Villa 汪庄 was built in 1927 by Wang Zixin 汪自新 (1868 – 1941), a wealthy Shanghai tea merchant and avid *qin* collector who filled the villa's grounds with rockeries and tea trees.[34]

Mao Zedong's brief visit to Hangzhou in 1921 had been mere prelude to his ultimate love affair with Hangzhou and West Lake. He often referred fondly to his arrivals at West Lake as "being home,"[35] adding Hangzhou to Beijing and his birthplace of Shaoshan Village in Hunan Province. In the end, there was simply no denying Hangzhou's birthright. Following Mao's lead, the navy, air force, railway administration, and other government agencies constructed sanitoriums around or near West Lake for their senior officials and honored workers. A dozen or more centuries' worth of scholars, poets, and painters, followed in the 20th century by Republicans, Nationalists, Russian advisers, foreign visitors, and now Chinese Communist Party officials, all agreed: Hangzhou with West Lake was a special place and should be preserved as such.

Mao's commitment to the West Lake scenic area resulted in a near-immediate commitment to the lake's well-being.[36] A large-scale dredging effort, initiated in 1952 and lasting six years, salvaged the lake from devolving into marshland. Well over seven million cubic meters of sludge were removed, the most of any dredging in West Lake's long history. This clean-up restored the waters after the years of Japanese conflict and civil unrest, increasing the lake's average depth from less than two feet (0.55 meters) to just under six feet (1.8 meters). Another dredging from 1976 to 1982 collected nearly 200,000 more cubic meters of sludge, increasing further West Lake's full carrying capacity.

As impressive as this lake restoration was, an even more visible effort was taking place simultaneously in the surrounding hills. Years of war damage and deforestation had left the once-verdant hills barren of foliage and color. Under the new CCP administration, a citizen volunteer program reportedly planted nearly thirty million trees in the four thousand hectares (almost ten thousand acres) of the bare southern and western hills surrounding West Lake between 1950 and 1957.[37]

Attention was also directed toward the tourism-related elements of the West Lake area. Multiple projects were initiated to renovate Lingyin Temple and an array of other famous sites, replace lost and damaged Buddhist statuary, renovate many of the area's famous views, scenic sites, and villas, and implement improvements at the Meijiawu village's Longjing tea plantations that increased agricultural productivity by more than 350 percent. These efforts were motivated less for fostering traditional tourism and more for "serving the working people" and making West Lake "a place for the working people to enjoy."[38]

National Symbols, Monumental Design

While still waiting out the war in Lizhuang, Sichuan Province, Liang Sicheng proposed creating a post-war Architecture Department at Qinghua University, if only to plan for the nation's reconstruction. When he and Lin Huiyin finally returned to Beijing in July 1946, Liang was appointed dean of Qinghua's new School of Architecture with Lin, now reasonably recovered from her illness, an administrative adjunct. Within a year, the Architecture faculty would expand to include members of the Society for the Study of Chinese Architecture, of which Liang Sicheng was president.

From the autumn of 1946 into the summer of 1947, Liang traveled in America. Now an internationally recognized architectural historian, he lectured at Yale, studied post-war reconstruction, was awarded an honorary doctorate from Princeton, and accepted an invitation to the design commission for the new United Nations headquarters buildings in New York. Meanwhile, Lin Huiyin assisted with Qinghua's School of Architecture. As always, everyone who met Lin was smitten by her lightning-quick mind, sense of humor, and collegial manner. One colleague noted, "When the couple were together, Lin Huiyin, not Liang Sicheng, was the talker."[39]

Lin fell gravely ill once again in 1947, near enough to death that she wrote a poem to her sister:

To My Elder Sister[40]

When I am gone, with unfinished words,

Like tea leaves in the cup left by guests,
The moments to speak and to drink are both lost.
The host, the guest as well, fell silent.
And yet, no need to lament.
If a little sadness sets in, just turn your face to the window,
For the setting sun, before its death,
Always there would remain the evening light.

Liang Sicheng returned to Beijing in 1947, his health somewhat diminished as well. Nevertheless, the couple together in 1948 put the finishing touches on *An Index to the Cultural Relics and Ancient Architecture of the Nation*, a guide to China's architectural preservation in anticipation of the resolution of the Civil War and the arrival of the PLA in Beijing. A new nation would also need new symbols, and new symbols would need designs and designers.

With the establishment of the People's Republic in 1949, Lin Huiyin was accorded some of the highest honors of her life. She was invited to participate in the design of the new national flag and national emblem and given responsibility for design of the relief carvings for the famed Monument to the People's Heroes at Tiananmen Square. For the next six years, despite failing health and the loss of one of her kidneys, Lin remained utterly indefatigable. She helped establish a Qinghua University course in modern residential housing, served as advisor for two doctoral theses, participated as a member of Beijing's Urban Planning Committee and as a deputy to the first Beijing People's Congress, held an Executive Committee position for the Architectural Society of China, wrote a regular architecture column ("Our Capital") for *New Observer* magazine, and edited the *Journal of Architecture*.[41]

On April 1, 1955, Lin Huiyin passed away, probably from tuberculosis. She was only 50 years old. Liang Sicheng designed her tombstone with carvings similar to that of Lin's design for the Monument to the People's Heroes. He carried on for another seventeen years, involved both in the development of urban architecture concepts for modern Beijing as well as continuing his work on China's ancient architectural history. He died on January 9, 1972, regarded in history as the "Father of Modern Chinese Architecture."

Fair to say that Lin Huiyin was one of, if not the first, "Renaissance woman" of modern China: artist, poetess, essayist, cultural socialite, architecture scholar and historian, graphic designer, teacher, intellectual companion, wife, and mother.[42] Her accomplishments were all the more remarkable in light of her constant battle with tuberculosis and repeated upheavals in her family life due to their several wartime relocations. All this was achieved in a male-dominated field by a woman who was told in 1925 America that women could not be admitted to University of Pennsylvania's School of Architecture.

This modern daughter of Hangzhou is celebrated today at West Lake with, appropriately, a unique, unimposing, and almost hidden lakeside sculpture. The inscribed metallic structure—a life-size, full-length, silhouette profile—calls to mind traditional inscribed stone steles while cleverly integrating the view of West Lake through her outlined body. She would likely have declined the honor but heartily approved of the ingenious design.

Had she lived long enough, Lin Huiyin would no doubt also have reveled in the American career success of her niece, Maya Lin (1959 –),[43] internationally acclaimed for her designs of (among others) the Vietnam War Memorial in Washington, D.C. and the Civil Rights Memorial in Montgomery, Alabama.

Restoring the Great Waterway

The advent of the People's Republic prefigured major societal change, but it was hardly a wholesale repudiation of China's ancient traditions, culture, famous sites, or public works. In the swinging pendulum of political movements—traditional versus reformist, feudalistic versus communistic, religious versus secular, classical versus modern—there would be losses. But there would also be repurposing, adaptation, preservation, and restoration.

Among the PRC's earliest major restorations was one of China's greatest historical achievements, the *Da yunhe* 大运河, (literally, the Great Canal River), or as it is known to the West, the Grand Canal. That ancient waterborne lifeline, stretching 1,784 kilometers from Hangzhou to Beijing, had been victimized to near national irrelevance by the confluence of natural and man-made events with modern transport technology over the past century. Repeated flooding in the early 1850s had caused a drastic change of course in the Yellow River in 1855. When the river's flow suddenly shifted far northward from upper Jiangsu Province into Shandong Province, the waters cut across the Grand Canal and effectively separated it into two non-communicating sections.

The Taiping War caused further neglect and degradation of the southern section of the Canal through Jiangsu and Zhejiang Provinces. Maritime shipment of rice replaced canal barge shipment, so that by 1902, the Qing government had ended the centuries-old taxation via grain tribute and dismissed all the officials responsible for the Canal's management.[44] Disuse and neglect of the great inland waterway was only further reinforced by the development of railroad transport, the Japanese invasion of the 1930s and 1940s, the 1945 – 1949 Civil War, and the nascent commercial airline industry.

By 1949, the Grand Canal had not only decayed from silting and neglect, it posed serious dangers due to "unexploded ordnance from the bridges, locks and dykes, a legacy of the civil war….There were many reports in the Chinese press of explosions along the Grand Canal during 1949 and 1950, but by the end of 1950 most land mines and bombs had been cleared away."[45] From 1958 – 1961, Beijing instituted a plan to restore the full length of the Canal via dredging and construction of new locks and bridges, as well as straightening and shortening some sections. By one estimate, almost 160 million cubic meters[46] of dredged soil were excavated, nearly all by manual labor.

The plan this time was not to move rice or silks or convoluted Taihu rocks for garden decoration but coal, lime, bricks, gravel, and scrap iron…the building materials for reconstructing the nation. Although not an industrial center itself, Hangzhou nevertheless stood to benefit once again as the southern terminus of a transport network for materials heading northward.

Following A.C. Maxim's proposed plan for Hangzhou as a tourist city (seconded, explicitly or otherwise, by Mao Zedong), the old Japanese concession area to the north of Wulin Gate experienced a resurgence of light industrial development. Neither the Japanese nor other nations had invested in the 1890s foreign concession zone, although the Chinese-owned Tongyi Silk Reeling Factory was established there in the late 1890s. After 1951, however, light manufacturing moved into the Gongchen District and surrounding area: flax, silk and cotton weaving and dyeing, shipbuilding, paper and thermos bottle manufacturing, flour milling, and an automotive plant. Hangzhou's limited industrialization was thus able to take advantage of the revitalized Grand Canal while the factories remained more or less invisible to tourists.[47]

By 1974, the magazine *China Reconstructs* crowed over West Lake's natural restoration and tourism development (temple restorations, new lakeside parks, and new roads linking the lakes and surrounding hills) alongside its industrial development. Titled "Hangchow – Garden City," the article extolled the city's eighteen modern silk mills and its almost ten-times growth in raw silk production since Liberation in 1949. Proclaiming that fully one-third of the city's 700,000 population were now engaged in industrial work, the anonymous author asserted that no longer could the rest of the nation scorn Hangzhou's lack of production power. The old adage describing Hangzhou as simply "'West Lake plus scissors' is history,"[48] the magazine proudly declared.

A New "New Culture" in the Theater

In the cultural domain, the Communist Party government understood the need for both communication with and education of illiterate peasants and workers, particularly in light of the rapid-fire shifts from imperial rule to Republicanism to a communist society and the twin shocks of foreign invasion and civil war. Storytelling and performance had always been employed to communicate social mores and cautions, as more recently had vernacular writing and visual images from *manhua*, prints, and woodcuts. After 1949, these forms were all revived and put to use as instructional media, as were theatrical performances.

Through the late Republican and Nationalist years, Yue Opera (*Yueju*) had only grown in popularity in Zhejiang and Shanghai. The 1920s witnessed growing emphasis on strong female roles played on stage by males, especially the four renowned female impersonators of the era: Mei Lanfang 梅兰芳 (1894 – 1961), Shang Xiaoyun 尚小云 (1900 – 1976), Cheng Yanqiu 程砚秋 (1904 – 1958), and Xun Huisheng 荀慧生 (1900 – 1968). Female performers studied their impersonating counterparts and gradually assumed the same roles. All-female troupes emerged in early 1938, expanding rapidly in both number and popularity to dominate the Shanghai Yue Opera scene. As a consequence, male performers and all-male troupes gradually disappeared.

A theatrical style born out of Shaoxing peasant culture that preserved its working-class roots while winning over Shanghai audiences proved an ideal cultural vehicle for the new People's Republic. Attempts to reform Yue operas were complicated, partly due to their immense popularity, but also because they relied so heavily on well-established, traditional stories. Instead, cultural officials supplied *Yueju* with enhanced costuming

481

and more theatrical staging and orchestration. At the same time, they directed content reform toward class struggle messages and interpretations more in line with the CCP's mass education initiatives.

The resulting revitalization of Yue Opera was remarkably successful as Yueju performance troupes were consolidated and reorganized. A 1951 performance in Beijing of the Zhu Yingtai and Liang Shanbo (the Butterfly Lovers) story marked the first known instance of Yue Opera being performed in northern China. At a theatrical drama competition in Beijing the following year, thirty-seven opera troupes performed eighty-two plays (sixty-three of them traditional plays, the rest either revised or modern). The Yue Opera performance of the Butterfly Lovers story (*Liang Zhu*) was awarded first prizes for "script, performance, music, stage design, and best actor and actress."[49]

The earliest movie version of *Liang Zhu* had been produced in China in 1926. However, under the aegis of the CCP and possibly at the behest of Chairman Mao, the Shanghai Film Production Studio created a new, full-color, Yue Opera version in 1953.[50] Despite daunting technical challenges for China's still-nascent movie industry, Director Sang Hu's 桑弧 (born Li Peilin 李培林, 1916 - 2004) production was a cinematic *tour de force*. The movie won international festival awards in the next two years, and a live performance in Berlin received such acclaim from its audience, "the actresses had to answer twenty-eight curtain calls."[51]

At the June 1954 Geneva Conference, Zhou Enlai entertained journalists and a group of foreign dignitaries, including British Prime Minister Anthony Eden, with two showings of the Butterfly Lovers film (titled *Liang Shanbo and Zhu Yingtai*). Zhou had even arranged beforehand for those attending the film screening to receive English-language materials introducing the traditional story line as well as providing explanations of Yue Opera.[52]

Zhou's movie showing granted Yue Opera official imprimatur and increased interest in both the operatic genre and Hangzhou and Shaoxing as tourism venues. In the first two decades of the PRC, Yue Opera developed a national following, nearly as popular as Peking Opera. *Liang Zhu* received particular government support in the early 1950s, since its story line of free but chaste love matches perfectly aligned with one of the PRC's first legislative initiatives: the 1950 Marriage Law seeking to end "feudal" arranged marriages. *Yueju* troupes performed the play repeatedly, especially before rural audiences where traditions remained strong and illiteracy was common. One Yue Opera troupe is reported to have performed *Liang Zhu* eighty-two times in 1953 for over 120,000 total attendees.[53]

A subsequent full-color cinematic version from the Shaw Brothers studio in 1963, titled *The Love Eterne* in English, was a resounding national success. Several television series based on the Liang-Zhu story have also been produced and aired since the late 1990s. Notable as well is the instantly recognizable *Butterfly Lovers Violin Concerto*, created in 1958 by Chen Gang 陈钢 (b. 1935) and He Zhanhao 何占豪 (b. 1933). Inspired by the traditional story line, this concerto has become a modern classic of Chinese symphonic production and has been used as theme music in several films.

Further support for Yue Opera came in Xie Jin's 1964 film, *Two Stage Sisters* (*Wutai jiemei*), which follows the evolution of *Yueju* from rural Shaoxing to cosmopolitan Shanghai and its post-1949 adaptation to socially conscious themes. As Luo Hui points out, the film presents Shaoxing Opera "as a metaphor for a traditional China trying to cope with events of historical, political, and cultural import. The theatre troupe's trajectory from the 'feudal' countryside to the Shanghai entertainment arena, and finally to a stage politicized with revolutionary causes, functions as a microcosm of the struggles of the Chinese nation."[54]

New Culture Enters the New Era

Following establishment of the People's Republic, the Shaoxing/Jiaxing New Culture cohort of Mao Dun, Zhang Leping and Feng Zikai each maintained their relevance. Surprisingly, however, the inimitable Shaoxing native Lu Xun would surpass them all, despite having passed away in 1936.

For **Mao Dun**, the path forward after 1949 was more bureaucratic than literary. After the war years, his fictional output declined, but he continued to write journal articles and newspaper essays. In 1949, he was named Chairman of the Chinese Writers Union and then Minister of Culture, a government position he retained for fifteen years. During that period, he editing the *People's Literature* and *World Literature* journals and advocated for cultural exchanges. In 1978, the first of fifteen serialized installments of his memoirs appeared in publication, ignoring his early life and focusing almost entirely on his New Culture and formative Communist movement years (1916 to 1930).

Mao Dun passed away in 1981 at age 84. Although his memoirs—titled *The Road I Walked* (我走過的路, *Wo zouguo de lu*)—were never completed, he left behind an enormous oeuvre of "thirteen novels, more than a hundred short stories, a play, two studies of Chinese mythology, two studies of Western mythology, and [more than three hundred] articles and books on Western literature, thought, and literary theories" as well as compilations of traditional Chinese literature for secondary school education.[55] One of modern China's most prestigious literary prizes, the quadrennial Mao Dun Literature Prize for novels, was instituted by the China Writers Association in 1982, funded in part by 250,000 RMB from the writer himself in his last will.

Zhang Leping's popularity had only grown during the Civil War years (1945 – 1949) thanks to his San Mao *manhua*. He maintained his basic artistic style after 1949 and adapted his content to the needs of the new People's Republic. In 1949, Kunlun Film Studio in Shanghai produced the first cinematic version of San Mao, a black-and-white film titled *An Orphan in the Streets*. The film remains a classic children's movie, filled with slapstick worthy of Western television shows like *The Little Rascals* or *Dennis the Menace* and movies like *Home Alone*. As the amended version of the movie ends, San Mao and his orphan friends excitedly join in the celebratory parade marking the Liberation of 1949.[56]

In the early 1950s, having already replaced the Japanese invaders with the wealthy and uncaring Chinese elite as the orphan's prime antagonists, Zhang's work transformed yet again. San Mao gained weight, his arms and legs thickened with nourishment, and his head now appeared proportionate to his body size. He looked clean and cared for, wearing neat shirts, shorts and a belt, laced shoes with clean ankle socks, and the red scarf of a Young Pioneer around his neck. Even his three unruly hairs took on a somewhat more groomed look.

Zhang's *manhua* panels became hopeful and forward-looking, with titles like *Sanmao Greets Liberation, Sanmao Stands Up, Sanmao's Past and Present, Sanmao Loves Sports, San Mao Learns from Lei Feng,* and *Sanmao Loves Science.*[57] Of particular interest is *Sanmao's Past and Present,* which juxtaposed 1946 – 1947 Sanmao panels of hopeless deprivation with the more positive, post-1949 representations. Zhang continued producing San Mao comics into the 1980s in addition to serving as Chief Editor of *Manga World* magazine in Shanghai. In 1992, his *San Mao Joins the Army* was transformed into a film by director Zhang Jianya 张建亚 (1951 –).[58]

Zhang Leping died on September 27, 1992, at age 82, but his beloved orphan San Mao remains popular to the present day, the hero of a CCTV cartoon series (*Wanderings of Sanmao*) in 2010 and even a book in which he becomes a time-traveler. The Zhang Leping Memorial Hall in his hometown of Haining has celebrated his life and work since its opening in November 1995.[59]

Feng Zikai's work received a more mixed reception after 1949, as some saw his art as too traditional and lacking in social realism. The official government position on cartoons viewed them as valuable for public communication and education but demanded that they explicitly support CCP principles and objectives, including opposition to national enemies. Feng's aesthetics and philosophy did not lend themselves easily to such artistic themes, and his worries led him to withdraw more deeply into lay Buddhism.

Feng progressed somewhat warily with new work (no longer in simple black-and-white), preferring reclusion in Shanghai. However, he unexpectedly received qualified official support in 1954. In a *People's Daily* article titled "We Need Children's Cartoons," the influential art theoretician Wang Zhaowen 王朝闻 (1909–2004), held up Feng Zikai as a model for other cartoonists. While cautioning against merely copying Feng's style due to its "escapist, pessimistic mentality, and an old-fashioned humanism," Wang claimed to have enjoyed the artist's cartoons since his youth. He wrote of Feng's cartoons: "As long as they have a healthy content, cartoons in the style of Zikai can become a part of the new (socialist) realism in art.... We should all appreciate life with the sensibility of a child, in the manner of Zikai."[60]

Zhou Enlai provided further public support for Feng that same year and even commissioned publication of a compilation of Zikai's past work. With such official backing, Zikai was awarded prominent membership in the Chinese Artists' Association as well as Vice-Chairmanship of the Shanghai chapter. Regrettably, Feng was accused of rightist sentiments in 1958 and suffered persecution as a "reactionary academic authority" during the

1960s. He retreated into translation work, including the first complete Chinese translation of the Japanese classic, *The Tale of Genji*, only to have these criticized as well. Having long suffered from poor health, he succumbed to lung cancer in September 1975.

In the 1920s, Feng had made an unusual commitment to his mentor and teacher-turned-Buddhist monk Hongyi (formerly Li Shutong). Every tenth anniversary of Hongyi's birth (b. 1880), Feng promised to produce a matching number of Buddhist-themed drawings: fifty on Hongyi's 50th birthday, sixty on his 60th, continuing until in 1980 he reached one hundred drawings at the 100th anniversary. As he had originally done with the first group of Hongyi's drawings in 1930, he continued to call each decennial collection *Paintings for the Preservation of Life*. Feng completed the fifth series of ninety paintings in 1965 and the sixth and final series of one hundred paintings in 1971 (published in Hong Kong in 1979). Remaining true to his karmic commitment to Hongyi, Feng Zikai produced most of these six series despite his mentor's death in 1942.

In June 1978, the Shanghai Municipal Cultural Bureau officially exonerated Feng Zikai, followed the next year with a memorial reburial of his funerary urn at a martyrs' columbarium by the Shanghai Municipal Writers and Artists Association. In 1985, Feng's former home, Yuanyuan Hall in Shimenwan (Jiaxing), was reconstructed and opened to the public; the grounds had most recently been occupied by a fiberglass factory. Formal academic recognition came in 1997 when the Feng Zikai Research Institute was created at Hangzhou Normal College. To the present day, especially in Hangzhou, one can find replicas of Feng Zikai's classic drawings imprinted on a variety of decorative items, often marked by the artist's familiar "T.K." initials.[61]

Although **Lu Xun** had been instrumental in founding and leading the League of Left-Wing Writers in the 1930s, he largely abandoned fiction writing as well as teaching. With a "second wife," Xu Guangping, and a son, Zhou Haiying 周海婴 (1929 – 2011), to support, he derived most of his income from his essay writing and a monthly stipend from the Ministry of Education. When the Guomindang passed stricter censorship laws in 1931 that led to the execution of two dozen writers in Shanghai, Lu staunchly opposed the Nationalist government and grew closer to the Communist Party, although never formally becoming a Party member. He remained a prolific essayist through the early 1930s but fell ill seriously ill in March 1936. After a partial recovery at midyear, his condition worsened again at summer's end. He died on October 19 of that year, only 55 years of age.

As early as 1940, Mao Zedong adopted Lu Xun's legacy as the model cultural warrior for the new communist society:

> In the cultural battle front, Lu Xun was the representative of the large majority of the nation and the most correct, courageous, resolute, loyal, and sincere fighter against the enemy, indeed an unprecedented national hero. The direction of Lu Xun is the direction of the new Chinese culture.[62]

In the years after 1949, Mao Zedong's words of praise acted as a secular canonization of

Lu Xun and his works. Even through the difficult years from 1966 – 1976 when nearly all works of fiction were disregarded, Lu Xun's work continued to be readily available to the public and read by students. The celebrated modern novelist and Hangzhou native Yu Hua 余华 (1960 -) wrote tellingly of Lu Xun's status at that time:

> The assigned texts were confined to the works of just two authors: Lu Xun's stories and essays and Mao Zedong's poetry. In my first year of primary school I believed innocently that there was only one prose author in the world, Lu Xun, and only one poet, Mao Zedong….'Chairman Mao teaches us' and 'Mr. Lu Xun says' were the standard political tags punctuating speeches and articles throughout the land. There was something paradoxical about the use of that prefix, 'Mr.,' for during the Cultural Revolution this form of address was thoroughly debunked as a Bad Thing associated with feudalism and the bourgeoisie. Lu Xun alone was permitted to enjoy this feudal/bourgeois title.[63]

To the present day, "Mr." Lu Xun retains his premier place as modern China's greatest and most influential storyteller and essayist. No other 20th-Century Chinese writer has been more often and more closely studied, analyzed, interpreted, and critiqued, both domestically and internationally. His former residence in Shaoxing has been transformed into a museum, and there are additional Lu Xun museums in Shanghai and Beijing. Perhaps most remarkably, an entire Disney-like village was established in 2003 in the Keyan Scenic Area (柯岩风景区), about five miles northwest of Shaoxing City. Called Luzhen (鲁镇, Lu Town), after one of the author's fictional village settings, this makeshift town recalls the sites and scenes from Lu Xun's work and even has costumed characters from his stories walking the village streets.

For anyone wishing to understand the trajectory of China's past one hundred years, there is no more fascinating and informative place to begin than the short stories and novellas of Lu Xun and Mao Dun and the expressive *manhua* art of Feng Zikai and Zhang Leping.[64] The fact that they all were born and raised within fifty miles of one another and well within the cultural orbit of Hangzhou[65] seems hardly coincidental.

Ping Pong and a President

Mao Zedong's rather unceremonious send-off of John Leighton Stuart in 1949 effectively closed the door on Chinese-American relations in the early decades of the People's Republic. But no diplomatic door stays closed forever; it only needs a reason, an encouragement, or just a fortuitous coincidence to open once again. In 1971, the trigger event for reopening formal relations between the PRC and the USA may have come from the most inadvertent, unlikely, and genuinely human of circumstances: a missed bus.

After missing the team bus following a practice session at the 31st World Table Tennis Championship in Nagoya, Japan in 1971, team member Glenn Cowan (1952 – 2004) hesitantly boarded the bus of the Chinese national team. Cowan was studiously ignored by the Chinese players until world champion Zhuang Zedong 庄则栋 (1940 – 2013)[66]

came forward, shook Cowan's hand, and presented him with a silk embroidery depicting China's scenic Huangshan Mountains. The next day, Cowan returned the favor with a red, white, and blue T-shirt inscribed with a peace symbol and the title of the Beatles' song "Let It Be." Japanese press enthusiastically captured images of the Chinese and American player together and reported the American team's interest in visiting and playing in China.

The diplomatic door had opened with just enough pretext for a rapprochement. Mao Zedong learned of the exchange and decided to invite the American table tennis team to visit China for sightseeing and exhibition matches from April 11 – 17, 1971. "Ping-pong diplomacy," as it came to be called, led to a secret preparatory visit with Premier Zhou Enlai in Beijing by National Security Advisor Henry Kissinger (1923 –) in July and a second conference with Zhou in August. In between, on July 15, 1971, President Richard Nixon (1913 – 1994) announced to the world via live television his planned visit to the People's Republic.

President Nixon, his wife, and their diplomatic and security entourage, including Kissinger and Secretary of State William P. Rogers (1913 – 2001), arrived in Beijing on February 21, 1972. At Chairman Mao's request, Nixon and Kissinger met with him almost immediately upon arrival; their one-hour session would be their only meeting. The next several days included multiple discussions with Premier Zhou Enlai and other government officials, state dinners, and visits to the Great Wall and the Forbidden City.

With the hard work of diplomacy and media exposure accomplished, the Nixons and Premier Zhou left Beijing by plane on the morning of February 26 for a short but pre-arranged tourism experience before departing China. The choice for location was an easy one. By that afternoon, the Nixons were admiring the scenery of Hangzhou's West Lake and cruising the lake waters with Premier Zhou as their guide. According to Margaret MacMillan, "The Chinese had insisted on putting this, one of China's most beautiful cities, on the itinerary."[67]

At the northwest corner of West Lake, Zhou escorted the Nixons to view their state gift to the citizens of Hangzhou: two California redwood trees, planted in the Hangzhou Botanical Garden at the foot of Jade Spring Hill. At that evening's banquet dinner, President Nixon offered a toast to the host city. "I am sure that the proud citizens of this province would say that Peking is the head of China," he pronounced, "but Hangchow is the heart of China."[68]

Before he departed Hangzhou the next day for Shanghai and his return flight to America, Nixon was presented with a gift of Longjing (Dragon Well) Tea, the same tea he had shared with Chairman Mao during their meeting in Beijing. Once again, Mao Zedong and Zhou Enlai[69] had reaffirmed Hangzhou's place as one of the nation's premier scenic and tourism locales. *The New York Times* on the day of Nixon's visit sent the same message to the English-speaking world in a lengthy, photo-filled article filled with superlatives: "wide, tree-lined streets…air refreshingly clean…lush green wooded suburbs...picturesque mountains...resort for emperors," adding "...one can wander through scroll-like Song Dynasty gardens...[where] all contact with the modern world is lost."[70]

Less well known is the fact that, before Nixon's visit, Hangzhou had already been a favored diplomatic and tourism venue for foreigners welcomed to the People's Republic: a delegation of British Labour Party representatives, including former Prime Minister Clement Atlee (1883 – 1967), in 1954; Simone de Beauvoir (1908 – 1986) and Jean-Paul Sartre (1905 – 1980) in 1955; British artist Paul Hogarth (1917 – 2001) in 1956, an International Youth Delegation in 1956; and Pierre Elliott Trudeau (1919 – 2000) in 1960.[71]

Beauvoir expressed a rather derisive opinion of 1955 Hangzhou, apparently insufficiently Parisian for her taste. She described the city as "provincial and rather dreary" with monuments and sculpture "singularly lacking in any artistic value."[72] Her assessment may have met wider agreement than she would have expected, since a common folk description of the city went: "Beautiful West Lake, ragged city."[73] Yet all of this contrasted sharply with Seymour Topping's visit to Hangzhou sixteen years later, in 1971. Topping wrote, in part:

> The tree-lined streets are immaculate....Office buildings, shops and homes are neat and in a frugal manner extraordinarily well-maintained.... The factories, built since the Communist take-over, have been situated mainly in wooded suburbs with surrounding vegetation intensively cultivated as screening and to absorb fumes....Hangchow remains a leading vacation mecca but no longer only for well-to-do Chinese and foreigners....[T]he mainstream of visitors consists of ordinary people. Thousands are bused into Hangchow on organized tours. Family groups also travel here from nearby cities.[74]

More foreign visitors included Hangzhou in their itineraries after Nixon's trip, such as the group of Yale faculty members that included the university's eventual president, Bartlett Giamatti (1938 – 1989). He later described the city as "a place of almost incandescent beauty" with a "'soft, golden quality' to the light, 'almost as if you were in an Impressionist painting'."[75] Two memorable Western-made documentaries of that time also incorporated Hangzhou in their films: *Chung Kuo* by Michelangelo Antonioni (1912 – 2007) from his 1972 tour, and *The Other Half of the Sky* by Shirley Maclaine (1934 –) from her 1973 visit.

Richard Nixon would visit Hangzhou again in 1993 during his third trip to China, finding it remarkable how much the city had grown since 1972. In 1998, his younger brother, Edward Nixon (1930 – 2019), a frequent traveler to China, would closely retrace the late President's 1972 steps through Beijing, Hangzhou, and Shanghai. Stopping at the site of the celebratory redwood tree planting at West Lake, he noted that the trees were not thriving because of Hangzhou's persistently high humidity.[76] In 2016, eighteen years subsequent to Edward Nixon's tour, Hangzhou Botanical Garden director Yu Jinliang 余金良 reported that grafts from Nixon's trees had been more successfully cultivated in less humid areas of China.[77]

488

The Weather Man

In May 2014, a Chinese hydrographic survey ship, the *Zhu Kezhen*, began surveying the deep-sea floor of the Indian Ocean preparatory to an international search for the disappeared Malaysian Airlines flight MH370. Zhu Kezhen's 竺可桢 (1890 – 1974) connection to oceanographic and atmospheric research could hardly have been imagined a century earlier when, as a young man from Shangyu (Shaoxing), he entered Tangshan (Hebei) School of Railroads and Mines in 1909 to study civil engineering, or when he began his studies in agriculture at the University of Illinois in 1911.

The youngest of six children in a Shaoxing rice merchant's family, Zhu was educated in the Confucian tradition. His misfortune of coming into mid-adolescence just as the civil service examination system was abolished in 1905 was countered in 1910 when he qualified in a national examination for study at the University of Illinois under the Boxer Indemnity Scholarship program.[78] However, he soon recognized from his studies that American agricultural methods were not readily applicable to Chinese farming. Upon graduation from Illinois, Zhu therefore enrolled at Harvard University for graduate work in meteorology, seeking to apply his knowledge of Chinese history to the study of weather and climate in his native land. While working toward his doctorate (1918), he published multiple articles on meteorology in *Kexue (Science)*, a Chinese-language journal begun in 1915 by the Science Society of China.[79]

Returning to China with Harvard degree in hand, Zhu Kezhen took academic positions, first in Wuhan and then in 1920 with the newly-formed National Southeastern University (modern Southeast University 东南大学, Dongnan Daxue) in Nanjing. National Southeastern grew during the 1920s into one of China's premier science education and research institutions. Under Zhu's guidance as founding chairman, the Geoscience Department "trained China's first generation of meteorologists and geographers."[80] Through the 1920s, he published textbooks, conducted climate-based research, assisted creation of the Chinese Meteorological Society in 1924, and accepted Cai Yuanpei's invitation in 1928 to join the new Academia Sinica.

In 1928, Zhu Kezhen ascended to the heights of his field as head of Nanjing's Institute of Meteorology. Recognizing the need for a national network of weather observation and data collection stations, he oversaw the deployment of new, Chinese-manned weather outposts and the training of qualified observers. In doing so, he successfully eliminated foreigners from the nation's weather forecasting and data accumulation process.

In 1936, Zhu's life took a fateful turn when Chiang Kai-shek recruited him to the presidency of Hangzhou's National Chekiang (now Zhejiang) University. He soon stamped his imprint on the university by establishing new academic disciplines in history and geography, but the Japanese attacks in Jiangsu and Zhejiang came just a year later. It was Zhu Kezhen who oversaw Zhejiang University's organized withdrawal southwestward from Hangzhou to Zunyi City in Guizhou Province. His efforts saved students' and faculty lives, institutional records, and valuable equipment and materials, but at a tragic cost: his wife and second son died from illness in 1938.

At war's end, Zhu Kezhen not only restored Zhejiang University's operations in Hangzhou but continued to build its capabilities and reputation as one of China's premier educational institutions. As civil war came to an end in the late 1940s, Chiang Kai-shek appealed for Zhu to flee with the Nationalists to Taiwan. Zhu chose instead to resign the university presidency and went into hiding in Shanghai to avoid the possibility of being assassinated.

After Liberation and declaration of the People's Republic, the new government installed Zhu Kezhen in positions befitting a national leader in earth science studies. He was placed in charge of geosciences at the new Chinese Academy of Science, asked to supervise creation of the Institute of Oceanology in Qingdao as well as an Office of the History of Natural Sciences in Beijing, and given the chair for China's participation in 1954's International Geophysical Year project.[81] By the mid-1950s, Zhu was a senior member of the Chinese Academy of Sciences and president of both the Chinese Geographical and Chinese Meteorological Societies. Yet despite an already long and storied career, his single most famous work was yet to come.

After years of painstakingly detailed research drawn from centuries' worth of Chinese archaeological and historical records, including ancient oracle bones, personal accounts, diaries, journals, and local gazetteers, Zhu published "A Preliminary Study on the Climatic Fluctuations of the Last 5000 Years in China" in 1972. His paper traced mean temperature variations over historical time and provided foundational evidence for aligning historical events and dynastic changes with climatic changes.[82] Perhaps most remarkable, Zhu compared his data with that of historical European research data and drew conclusions about the global nature and pattern of climate fluctuations that prefigured present-day studies in global climate change.

"On the evening of 6 February 1974, Zhu made, as he had done every day for the last sixty years, an entry in his diary about the day's weather. A few hours later he died of pneumonia."[83] The reasons for naming a modern-day hydrographic survey ship in honor of "the Father of Chinese Meteorology" seem self-evident, and an honor well deserved.

Old Landscapes Anew

Vistas immense, panoramic, and monochromatic. Waters receding into a mist-filled distance. Mountains so unreal and imposing they feel alien and threatening, sparsely populated and with human figures and lodgings miniscule to the point of irrelevance. Locales not Nature copied, but Nature imagined and suffused with meaning. These are some of the characteristics of traditional Chinese landscape (山水, shanshui, literally "mountains and water") paintings.

As China entered the 1920s, the New Culture movement sought new forms of expression for literature (新文學, xinwenxue) that moved beyond traditional storytelling conventions. Such was also the case in painting, where a similar search looked for a modern national painting style (國畫, *guohua*). Merging the old and the new, the Chinese and the Western, all the while maintaining the essential Chinese character of the finished work, would require knowledge of classical painting styles and techniques as well as familiarity with Western ones. Many artists would contribute to the aesthetic goal, but one of its strongest proponents and practitioners was a Zhejiang native with strong connections to Hangzhou that continue to the present day.

Pan Tianshou 潘天寿 (1897 – 1971) was born to a scholarly family in Ninghai County of Ningbo Prefecture in the final years of the Qing dynasty. He demonstrated interest and ability in drawing, calligraphy, and seal carving from a young age and was said to have taught himself about painting by studying and copying from Wang Gai's *Mustard Seed Garden Painting Manual*. At age 18, Pan relocated to Hangzhou to enroll at the Zhejiang First Normal School where, like Feng Zikai, he fell under the teaching influence of Li Shutong (later, monk Hongyi). Li introduced his students to Japanese and Western art styles and techniques; his intense commitment to Buddhism heavily influenced Pan's pre-1949 work, just as it had with Feng Zikai.[84]

Following a series of art teaching positions in Zhejiang Province, Pan Tianshou instructed students in Shanghai between 1923 and 1928 at some of the most progressive and outward-looking art schools. In 1928, he was appointed head of the Chinese Painting Department at the newly-formed National Art Academy (国立艺术院, Guoli yishu yuan) in Hangzhou. This multidisciplinary art institution declared as its mission "the introduction of Western art, the reorganization of Chinese art, the synthesis of Chinese and Western art and the creation of an art for the epoch."[85] Pan held various educational positions during the war years (1937 – 1945) before returning to Hangzhou and the National Art Academy at war's end, focusing on education and his own painting work.

Over the years, Pan's art had concentrated on brush-and-ink works, specializing in the separate genres of landscapes and bird-and-flower painting. In the early 1950s, his artistic breakthrough arrived when he combined the two styles into a single work, simultaneously magnifying the foreground of the former and expanding the vistas of the latter. The effect was dramatic, providing entirely new perspectives and intimacies in classical landscapes while still preserving their Chinese essence. After 1949, Pan continued working and teaching and was placed in charge of the Hangzhou branch of the new National Art Research Office. He continued to advocate vigorously for national painting (*guohua*) founded on and adapted from traditional painting styles and genres.

Through the late 1950s and into the 1960s, Pan Tianshou continued his experimentation with ink painting despite the government's insistent focus on socially realist oil paintings. He found a way to produce works consistent with CCP dictates but in his characteristic new style, sometimes at the request of party officials and even as public displays. For example, two of his paintings, each four meters long, were commissioned for display at the Hangzhou Hotel,[86] followed in 1964 with another oversized painting, *The Brilliance of Auspicious Clouds*, for the same hotel.[87]

His work and his academic and public positions on *guohua* helped reinvigorate official interest, evidenced by the First National *Guohua* Exhibition in 1953. Pan was elected President of the Zhejiang Provincial Artists' Society in 1961 as well as Vice Chairman of the Chinese Artists Association. The following year, a formal exhibition of over ninety of his paintings was held at the Central Academy of Fine Art. After 1966, he suffered persecution and was personally denounced by Jiang Qing and the *Zhejiang Daily* before passing away in September 1971 at 75 years of age.

In 1977, Pan Tianshou was posthumously exonerated and honored with a memorial exhibition in Hangzhou. With the willing support of Pan's widow He Yin 何愔 (d. 1983)[88] and son Pan Gongkai, the artist's former residence near West Lake's eastern shore was renovated in 1981, restoring his studio and displaying some of his works. An expanded gallery was opened to the public in 1991 as the Pan Tianshou Memorial Museum,[89] now housing a wider range of his paintings thanks to a bequest of over one hundred works in He Yin's will. According to Claire Roberts' incisive summary, "Pan Tianshou is generally regarded as an innovative traditionalist, yet he may be more accurately regarded as a Chinese modernist—but one who pursued an indigenous form of modernism."[90] With talent, commitment, and persistence, Pan Tianshou helped bring China's premier classical painting genre into the 20th Century.

Three Men of Modern Social and Physical Science

Several of the most significant figures in modern Chinese science have hailed from the Hangzhou vicinity, a reminder of the area's long claim to academic excellence through the many centuries of the civil service examination system. Following are brief biographical recaps of three such individuals and their work.

Ma Yinchu 马寅初 (1882 – 1982) was born in Shengxian (present-day Shengzhou), Shaoxing Prefecture, home district of Yue Opera. He studied mining and metallurgy at Beiyang (now Tianjin) University before receiving government sponsorship for advanced studies at Yale (Economics) and a doctoral degree in 1914 from Columbia University (Economics and Philosophy). His doctoral thesis evaluated advanced methods for budgeting and financial control in New York City's municipal administration and was reportedly adapted as a college textbook.[91] Upon returning to China, he served as a professor of Economics at Peking University and Dean of Teaching. After two years as President of Zhejiang University from 1949 – 1951, he assumed the same position at Peking University for the following nine years.

Based on his years of national economics study and three separate investigations in 1955 of population growth in his home province,[92] Ma observed with increasing concern the growth trajectory taking place in the People's Republic in its early years. Given China's level of industrial and agricultural development in the 1950s, he viewed excessive population expansion as harmful to the nation's future. In June 1957, he formally presented what he called his "New Population Theory," in which he outlined "the detrimental effects of population growth on capital accumulation and thus on industrialization."[93] He therefore recommended a nationwide program of fertility control based heavily on delayed marriages, contraceptive practices, tax disincentives, and aggressive public education. Ma's theory was roundly rejected over the next two or three years, however, when State policy reverted back in favor of strong population growth. Ma was subjected to intense criticism for several years and academic exile for almost two decades.

Meanwhile, his growth projections proved correct. After a national population of 546.8 million in 1950 ballooned to 916.4 million by 1975 (and was on its way to exceed one billion in 1982), Ma Yinchu's plan was rejuvenated in 1979 and served as a foundational document for the resulting "One Child Policy" implemented that same year. He was fully exonerated in 1979 and, at age 97, granted the position of Honorary President of Beijing University, the position from which he was forced out in 1960. An article appearing in *Guangming Daily* on August 5, 1979, was titled "Erroneously Criticized One Person: Population Mistakenly Increased 300,000,000."[94] Ironically, the "father of family planning in China" himself sired five daughters and two sons. He remains honored today for his intellectual integrity and dedication to China's economic development, with a Memorial Hall in his name located several blocks from West Lake.[95]

Qian Sanqiang 钱三强 (1913 – 1992) was born in Shaoxing, the son of Qian Xuantong 钱玄同 (1887 – 1939), a nationally famous scholar, philologist, and advocate (with Lu Xun) for vernacular Chinese.[96] After he graduated from Qinghua University in 1936 with a degree in Physics, he traveled to Paris to study for his doctorate in nuclear physics at the Curie Lab. Qian Sanqiang was twice victorious in Paris, winning a scholarship from the French Academy of Sciences and meeting and marrying his Suzhounese wife and fellow nuclear scientist, He Zehui 何泽慧 (1914 – 2011). Both separately and together, Qian and He made significant discoveries in the area of nuclear fission while working at the Curie Lab.

The couple returned to China with their infant daughter in 1948 after Qian Sanqiang accepted a physics professorship at Qinghua University. He began working with the Academy of Sciences and advanced to the directorship of the Institute of Physics and then the Institute of Atomic Energy. After Qian joined the Chinese Communist Party in 1954, Premier Zhou Enlai invited him in January 1955 to brief Mao Zedong and other senior government officials about nuclear research and weapons development.[97] Not long after, the Politburo authorized establishment of China's nuclear weapons research program.

Under Qian's guidance, the Chinese detonated their first atomic bomb in October 1964 and conducted its initial hydrogen bomb tests just two years later. For his efforts, he was awarded honors with the Academy of Science and assumed the presidency of Zhejiang University in 1978. All the while, He Zehui continued her high-level work in nuclear fission and development of China's first cyclotron and nuclear reactor, resulting in her election to the Chinese Academy of Sciences in 1980. Their work was so instrumental in China's nuclear physics programs that Qian Sanqiang became known as "the father of the Chinese atomic bomb" and He Zehui dubbed "the Marie Curie of China."

Although **Qian Xuesen** 钱学森 (1911 – 2009) only lived in Hangzhou for the first three years of his life, he was nevertheless a true son of the city. His father Qian Jiazhi

钱家治 (1882 – 1969) was born into a family of successful silk merchants who traced their lineage directly back ten centuries to Qian Liu, the first king of Wuyue from the Five Dynasties and Ten Kingdoms period (907 – 960). Iris Chang assessed Qian's Hangzhou heritage this way:

> The city—or rather, his family's ancient heritage there—was to shape and define his life for years to come. These family legends…instilled in him a sense of pride and reminded him as he grew older—however depressed or tired he might have felt in the moment—that the history of one of China's greatest cities was entwined with the story of his ancestors. If nothing else, it was a reminder that the blood of kings flowed through his veins.[98]

After completing a science-oriented academic track in high school, Qian matriculated from the prestigious Jiaotong University in Shanghai with a first-in-his-class degree in railway engineering. His excellent score in a qualifying examination earned him a Boxer Indemnity scholarship in 1934 and a place in the aeronautical engineering program at Massachusetts Institute of Technology. Seeking a more theory-based curriculum, he transferred after just one year into the Theoretical Aeronautics program at California Institute of Technology (Caltech) under the leadership of Theodore von Karman (1881 – 1963).

Through the 1930s and 1940s, Qian conducted advanced research in aeronautics and published groundbreaking and seminal papers in his field. He also worked on projects for the U.S. War Department and became recognized as "the world's foremost expert on jet propulsion."[99] In late 1948, he was named the first director of the new Jet Propulsion Laboratory (JPL) at Caltech; the following year, he applied for American citizenship. Tragically, the Communist witch hunts of the McCarthy hearings led to questioning by the FBI in June 1950 and revocation of his security clearance. When Qian resigned from JPL and threatened to return to China, the U.S. government arrested and detained him for two weeks in September 1950.

Despite widespread support from the scientific community, political fearmongering prevailed. While deportation hearings and appeals were failing to achieve a resolution, Qian continued to teach and publish but was restricted from all classified work and materials. Finally, talks between the U.S. and China led to a large-scale exchange of prisoners and restricted personnel. Qian Xuesen was one of the ninety-four such individuals, all of them American-educated Chinese scientists. He and his family[100] departed by ship from Los Angeles on September 17, 1955. Zhou Enlai reportedly declared of the "prisoner" exchange that Qian's return alone "made the talks worthwhile," while Qian's American defense lawyer termed his loss "one of the tragedies of this century."[101]

Qian Xuesen's contributions to Chinese ballistics and rocketry after 1955 were incalculable. Aside from being a trusted scientific advisor to Chairman Mao, he was instrumental in developing China's first national scientific development plan. He helped organize a new missile design academy and "initiated and oversaw programs to develop some of China's earliest missiles, the first Chinese satellite, missile tracking and control telemetry systems, and the…Silkworm missile. And it was he who helped turn systems engineering into a science in China."[102]

His greatest successes with missile and satellite development were often noted with a tinge of irony in the American press. For example, *The New York Times* report on October 28, 1966, of China's successful test of a guided missile carrying a live nuclear device contained a sidebar in which the opening sentence described as "an irony of cold war history" that the "key Chinese scientist" Qian Xuesen was "trained, nurtured, encouraged, lionized, paid, and trusted for fifteen years in the United States."[103] He is honored in history as "the father of Chinese rocketry" and "the father of China's space program."

Although Qian was not a frequent visitor to Hangzhou because of his work in Beijing, his connection to his native city was exemplified by his interest in the evolving mid-1990s concept of the "Shan-shui City" in urban planning and architecture. Wu Liangyong 吴良镛 (1922 –) had first argued in 1986 – 1987[104] for integrating landscape (*shanshui*) and architecture in the city environment. In 1990, Qian Xuesen wrote to Wu Liangyong proposing the formal concept of a Shan-shui City "by integrating Shan-shui poems, traditional Chinese gardens and landscape paintings."[105] Such was Qian's stature and influence that his letter initiated more than a decade of urban planning discussions about how to integrate natural environmental elements into the urban landscape.[106] It is easy to imagine that Qian had his native Hangzhou in mind as the exemplar of the urban design concept he was promoting.

The Man—and Woman—Behind the Camera

In 1938, China had two separate armies loosely and warily linked together to resist the Japanese invasion: the forces of Chiang Kai-shek's Nationalist government and those of Mao Zedong's Communist Party. One day that summer in Yan'an, Mao stood arms akimbo before a large group of seated men. As he lectured them intensely on military tactics, a photographer attached to the Yan'an Film Studio took his first still photograph of the speaker. The photo was taken from Mao's side and slightly behind him, creating a profile view that barely identified its subject—a view perhaps intriguing for Western journalists and photographers but unusual in Chinese depictions of great leaders. Such was Xu Xiaobing's first photograph of Mao Zedong, one destined to become an iconic representation of the future Chairman of the PRC.

Xu Xiaobing 徐肖冰 (1916 – 2009), a native of Tongxiang (Jiaxing), had arrived in Shanxi Province the year before, having departed his work with two different Shanghai film studios known for their adaptation of Western cinematography to new Chinese films. For the next several years, Xu accompanied the Communist troops as a war photographer until, in 1942, he met a young Shanxi peasant woman, orphaned several years earlier, named Hou Bo 侯波 (1924 – 2017). By the next spring, they were married. As Hou Bo later described the wedding: "About ten friends gathered with us in our cave; we bought jujubes and dried buns, and we all sang together."[107]

While Xu Xiaobing traveled with the Communist troops during the war years, Hou Bo stayed in Jilin Province and began learning the photographic trade from her husband and from Japanese prisoners-of-war. The couple's wartime separation ended in Beijing in early 1949, at which time their new careers began. Xu Xiaobing, with Hou Bo assisting, was taking photos of a meeting between Mao Zedong and several foreign dignitaries when Mao approached Hou and asked about her life. Hearing of the young woman's peasant origins, Mao told her she would now be his official photographer, unexpectedly reversing the roles of husband and wife, teacher and apprentice.

Although Xu remained primarily a documentary filmmaker, the couple would live in Beijing at the central government compound of Zhongnanhai and share responsibilities as Mao's personal photographer for the next dozen years. Hou Bo also took photos of Zhou Enlai, Liu Shaoqi (刘少奇, 1898 – 1969), and other senior officials residing at Zhongnanhai. She would be the only woman and seemingly the most prolific from among Mao's small cohort of photographers, credited with more than four hundred of Mao's seven hundred-plus officially published portrait photos.[108]

Most famous of Hou Bo's photos of Mao Zedong came at Tiananmen Gate on October 1, 1949 ("Founding of the PRC"), during Mao's famous swim in the Yangzi River, and in 1959's "Chairman Mao at Work in an Airplane." Several of Hou's portrait photos of Mao were transformed into posters and banners that were famously spread across the nation.

Xu Xiaobing would go on to be named President of the Chinese Photographers' Association; Hou Bo would chair the China Women's Photography Association. Xu and Hou together completed a photographic tour of Xinjiang Province in the 1980s and a photographic record of the Three Gorges Dam development in the 1990s. In 1999, a traveling exhibition of their work was first displayed at Beijing's Museum of the Chinese Revolution in honor of the 50th anniversary of the founding of the PRC. Their lives and life's work were celebrated in a documentary by the French filmmaker Claude Hudelot (1942 – 2021) in 2003. Hudelot subsequently organized public exhibitions of their work in London and Paris in 2004.

In 1992, Xu Xiaobing's native city of Tongxiang built the Xu Xiaobing / Hou Bo Memorial Hall as an extension of the Tongxiang Art Museum in order to exhibit the couple's photographic works. In 2006, Xu Xiaobing was named an honorary member of the Chinese Federation of Literature and Art. In 2016, seven years after Xu's passing, 92-year-old Hou Bo received a lifetime achievement award at that year's International Photography Festival in Pingyao.[109]

Chapter 21

INTO THE NEW MILLENNIUM

(1986 – PRESENT)

Green mountains surround on all sides[1]
The still waters of the lake.
Pavilions and towers in hues of gold
And azure rise here and there.
One would say a landscape composed by a painter.
Only towards the east,
Where there are no hills,
Does the land open out,
And there sparkle, like fishes' scales,
The bright-colored tiles of a thousand roofs.

– Anonymous (13th Century)

A View from Above

Since the time Yang Su first erected walls around Hangzhou in the 590s, Hangzhou by the early 1980s had not grown significantly beyond those limits. Modest development northward toward the terminus of the Grand Canal was logistically essential, and limited suburban development resulted from both agricultural needs and the early 20th-Century advent of the rail line from Shanghai.

A satellite image[2] from as recently as 1984 (Figure 1, top) illustrates the restricted scale of this urban expansion. The outline of the original walled city is clearly still visible, showing growth on both sides of the small canal running north to Gongchen Bridge, the terminal port of the Grand Canal, and then wrapping around the south end of Banshan 半山 (Ban Mountain). This image also reveals modest suburban expansion southeast from the ancient city toward the Qiantang River, and a modest finger of development following the Qiantang River southwestward toward Zhakou.

The eastern shores of the Qiantang River remain underdeveloped, as does the river's entire south shore and the areas north and northwest of the hills bordering West Lake. To the northeast, Jianqiao Airport, former home of Colonel John Juett's flying school, stands isolated in the near countryside. Across the river to the southeast, a small version of Xiaoshan folds itself around the northern tip of Xiang Lake.

The modest level of Shaoxing's development in the same year of 1984 (Figure 2, top) is even more striking. With hills to the south and west and the zigzagging Qiantang to the north, Lu Xun's hometown and Zhou Enlai's native place stands alone, a small, *jiao*-sized[3] circle in a broad expanse of green. The Qiantang River continues at this time as a sort of riverine "great wall" separating the two sides of eastern Zhejiang. Only one bridge can be seen connecting the two regions anywhere from Hangzhou City to river's end at Hangzhou Bay.

These same satellite images from just thirty years later, in 2014, nearly defy belief. They show massive urbanization in every direction for both cities, and in Hangzhou's case, on both sides of the Qiantang River. Hangzhou's ancient city outline is barely discernable, and similarly for the now almost hidden airfield. At least five bridges can be seen crossing the river. Around Hangzhou, only the mountains around West Lake, the Xixi Wetlands area, and Banshan Mountain remain green and undeveloped.

Hangzhou's Development, 1984 - 2018

1984

2000

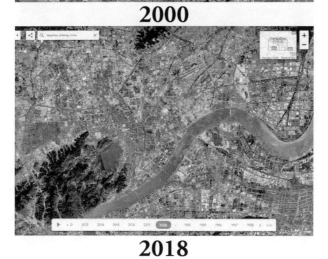

2018

Note: Satellite images for Hangzhou adapted from Google Earth
Engine, https://earthengine.google.com/timelapse/

Shaoxing's Development, 1984 - 2018

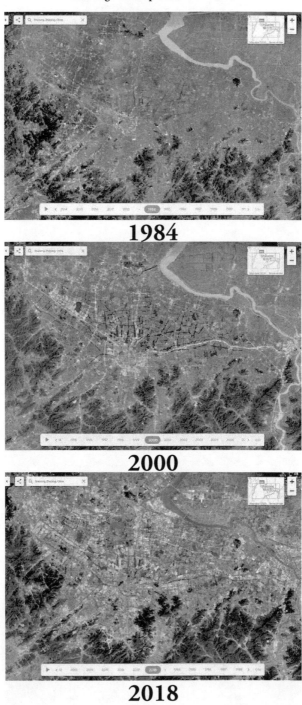

1984

2000

2018

Note: Satellite images for Shaoxing adapted from Google Earth
Engine, https://earthengine.google.com/timelapse/

The story of Hangzhou (and countless other cities in China) since Deng Xiaoping's 1978 call for opening up the country to a socialist market economy and foreign investment is one of economic and industrial development and urbanization on an unprecedented, almost unimaginable scale.

Setting the Stage

It was not until the late 1970s or early 1980s that the central and local governments conceded Zhejiang Province's lack of the natural resources necessary to develop heavy industry. Light industry, textiles, and assembly operations, along with consumer products, formed the economic base in those years, spurred in part by the evolution and rapid proliferation of rural TVEs (town and village enterprises - 乡镇企业, *xiangzhen qiye*). Combined with agricultural reforms from the household contract responsibility system, TVEs provided the foundation for rural industrialization and employment consistent with the region's needs and resource availability.

The majority of TVEs began as collective enterprises, operated primarily by communes and work brigades. In 1984, the central government formally identified them as TVEs and encouraged their formation alongside household-run firms. Their numbers multiplied explosively in Zhejiang and throughout the nation after 1984, growing from 1.65 million units in 1984 to nearly nineteen million by 1988.[4] Furthermore, town and village administrations began assuming collective ownership or management of these growing businesses. New TVEs "were allowed to develop agricultural, industrial, commercial, construction, transportation, and service industries simultaneously" as well as "introduce foreign and domestic connections to increase social supply."[5]

Not only was Zhejiang forming a suitable industrial base, but the rural labor force was evolving away from agricultural production and toward industrial production. In 1978, for example, ninety-two percent of the province's labor force was employed in agriculture; ten years later, that figure had already declined to around sixty-three percent.[6]

Problems of quality control, small scale, and poor management caused the growth of TVEs to slow and their value-added production to level off between 1988 and 1991. The following year, Deng Xiaoping made his famous "southern tour" (南巡, *nanxun*), visiting Zhuhai and Shenzhen in Guangdong Province, two of the original special economic zone (SEZ) cities established in August 1979. During his tour, Deng sought to reinvigorate the "Reforms and Opening-Up" program by opening the door to new forms of ownership and creating free-trade zones and high-tech industrial zones designed to attract foreign direct investment.

In the Hangzhou greater municipal area, and even within the urban district, the options for various forms of shareholder cooperative enterprises, limited liability companies, and even private entrepreneurships radically transformed the local industrial economy. The shift from TVEs and collective enterprises to these new, profit-sharing forms—and the growth of their industrial output—was dramatic, as shown in Table 21.1 below.

Year	# State-Owned Enterprises	# Collective-Owned Enterprises	# Other Types of Ownership	Gross Indust. Output Value (Billion RMB)
Whole Municipality				
1992	941	5,162	132	45.27
1997	760	3,250	970	91.47
2002	172	232	3,611	240.03
2004	134	241	5,252	414.91
Urban District Only				
1992	395	1,024	71	22.91
1997	372	951	410	49.97
2002	140	178	2520	202.52
2004	105	166	3,527	346.39

Table 21.1 Shift in Type of Industrial Enterprise Forms in
Hangzhou for Selected Years, 1992 – 2004[7]

Hangzhou's industrial composition also changed as its industrial base grew. From 1978 to 1990 to 2004, primary industry (mining, oil and gas, agriculture, fishing, forestry) as a share of Hangzhou's GDP shrank from 22.3% to 16.3%, and then to 5.5%. Meanwhile, the GDP share contributed by secondary industry (manufacturing and construction) declined modestly, from 59.9% to 50.7% and then rose in 2004 to 53%. Tertiary industry (finance, education, and health, hospitality, transportation, and personal services) grew from 18.1% to 33.0%, and then to 41.5%.[8]

In a nation that was experiencing dramatic economic growth nationwide between 1978 and 1995, no province experienced a greater average annual growth rate in per capita GDP than Zhejiang, at 12.8%. In the years from 1992 to 1997, Zhejiang Province enjoyed growth of 230 percent in per capita GDP, rising from 3,187 RMB to 10,515 RMB.[9]

As early as the mid-1980s, Hangzhou's built area also began expanding, extending axially along the highways, major roads, and rail lines.[10] Most of the city's physical growth during this time took place to the northeast and northwest, with some additional expansion to the southeast. Development and population pressures continued unabated, causing the city government in 1996 to annex three townships each from neighboring Yuhang and Xiaoshan counties, known today as the Xiasha 下沙区 and Binjiang 滨江区 Districts, respectively. The new city boundaries created modest geographic "wings" to the east and west and added new urban land across the Qiantang River, expanding Hangzhou's formal footprint by almost sixty percent, from 430 to 683 km^2 (166 to 264 mi^2).[11]

The newly merged land allowed the city to create new, national-level industrial and technological development zones: Hangzhou High-Tech Zone (HHTZ) north and northwest of West Lake, initiated in 1990; Xiaoshan Economic and Technological Development Zone (XETDZ) southeast across the Qiantang River, initiated in 1990; Zhijiang Tourism and Vacation Zone southwest along the Qiantang River, initiated in 1992; and Hangzhou Economic and Technological Development Zone (HEDTZ) east of the city, initiated in 1993. With this new wave of industrialization came an increasingly urbanized population, the need for more housing, and the outward growth of the city, away from the traditional core urban area.

In 2002, the management systems of the Hangzhou High-Tech Zone were integrated with those of the Binjiang District to create an expanded high-technology zone that quickly grew to host companies in such areas as "control chip design, sensor and terminal equipment manufacturing, network communication, information software development,... e-commerce, financial service[s]...network operation service[s] and big data platform[s]."[12] Binjiang became the corporate home to firms like Alibaba (e-commerce), NetEase (Internet, video game, and music streaming services), and H3C (cloud computing, big data, information security, and AI). As Deputy Mayor Ye Rong observed in a *Beijing Review* article about Hangzhou's tech-industry transformation, "We are striding from the West Lake era into the Qiantang River era."[13] Perhaps it was time to update the early 20th Century saying about West Lake by adding, "The river entered the city."

The city's built-up area grew correspondingly, from 319 km^2 in 1978 to over 569 km^2 in 2000, an increase of nearly eighty percent. Hangzhou city's urban district population (based on residence registration) nearly doubled during the same period, and it would more than double again by 2019. The entire municipal area population correspondingly expanded by nearly three million more people between 1978 and 2019, as shown in Table 21.2 below.

Year	Population, Urban District	Population, Whole Municipality
1951	731,000	3,048,900
1965	1,073,900	4,356,600
1978	1,160,600	5,055,500
2000	2,270,000	6,215,800
2010	3,652,400	6,891,200
2019	5,359,600	7,953,700

Table 21.2 Hangzhou Population, Urban District and Whole Municipality, Selected Years, 1951 – 2019[14]

In order to accommodate the city's continuing expansion and regional urbanization, the national government in 2001 approved Hangzhou's plan to annex the entirety of Yuhang and Xiaoshan districts into the city's official boundaries, more than quadrupling the size of Hangzhou City from 683 km^2 (264 mi^2) in 1996 to 3,068 km^2 (1,185 mi^2).[15] Above the Qiantang River, Hangzhou City now extended beyond Liangzhu and Pingyao as far as Baizhangzhen in the northwest, most of the way to Lin'an in the southwest, and to Renhe in the north and Yuhang in the east. South of the Qiantang, the urban area of the former Xiaoshan District ranged well south toward Zhuji and well east above Shaoxing, nearly reaching the Cao'e River.[16]

With these geographic expansions and new development zones came increased industrial output (GDP), additional domestic and foreign investment, growth in personal and household income, new housing development, and multiple urban sub-centers. The following data traces the enormous changes in GDP and annual disposable income over the years.

Year	Gross Domestic Product (Billions 2019 RMB)	Annual Disp. Income - Urban Residents (RMB)	Annual Disp. Income - Rural Residents (RMB)
1951	0.38		
1965	1.28		
1978	2.84		
1985	9.05	1,026	624
1990	18.96	1,985	1,171
2000	139.57	9,668	4,894
2010	604.96	30,035	13,186
2019	1,537.30	66,068	36,255

Table 21.3 Hangzhou Gross Domestic Product and Annual Disposable Income, Selected Years, 1951 – 2019[17]

New Millennium, New City

As the city grew and became increasingly polycentric after the year 2000, physical expansion, industrial development, and population growth demanded massive new infrastructure as well as cultural, educational, and environmental/ecological investment. These needs have been met by the Hangzhou city government through a host of major initiatives.

Major physical infrastructure

Among the more visible, large-scale infrastructure developments were transportation hubs and service lines, sports and exposition centers, and passenger traffic crossings over (and under) the Qiantang River:

- On December 30, 2000, flight services officially began at the new Hangzhou Xiaoshan International Airport, replacing the former Jianqiao Airport. Between 2013 and 2018, the total number of cities connected to Hangzhou by air grew from 103 to 183, with the international city connections (excluding Hong Kong, Macao, and Taiwan) nearly doubling, from twenty-seven to fifty-two.[18]
- In 2008, the new Hangzhou East Railway Station replaced the older, Japanese-designed Chongzhen Station.
- In 2010, service began on the Shanghai–Hangzhou High-Speed Railway.
- In 2012, Line 1 of the Hangzhou subway system began operation.
- In 2014–2015, Lines 2 and 4 of the Hangzhou Metro began operation.
- In 2016, the Hangzhou International Expo Center hosted the G20 Summit in the site's inaugural year of operation.
- In 2018, the new Hangzhou Sports Park Stadium (Olympic Sports Center) began operation for soccer games as well as tennis. The main stadium seats up to 80,000 visitors. Hangzhou will be the host city for the 2022 Asian Games, with events also scheduled to take place in Shaoxing, Huzhou, and Ningbo. Hangzhou will be only the third Chinese city to host the Asian Games, after Beijing (1990) and Guangzhou (2010).
- In 2019–2021, Metro Lines 5, 6, 7, 8, 9, and 16 commenced service. Line 5 is planned ultimately to connect with the western terminus of Line 1 of the Shaoxing Rail Transit system.
- In the mid-1990s, the original Qiantang River Bridge southwest of the city was the only such river crossing. By the year 2020, there were ten bridges (nine servicing greater Hangzhou and one, east of the Cao'e River outlet, directed more toward greater Shaoxing) and a tunnel crossing, not counting the Hangzhou Bay Bridge well to the east, linking Shanghai by roadway to Ningbo via Jiaxing.

Cultural infrastructure

In the cultural arena, the 1990s witnessed the opening of the National Tea Museum's Shuangfeng Pavilion (1991), the South Song Dynasty Guan Kiln Museum (1992), the China National Silk Museum (1992), and the Song Dynasty Town cultural amusement park along the Qiantang River (1997). These institutions were only a civic dry run, however, for the cultural expansion in the first two decades of the new millennium. Between 2000 and 2019, the number of public libraries grew from ten to sixteen. More remarkably, the number of museums went from nine to seventy-nine,[19] represented by the following partial list (in order by the year of their opening).

2001	Hangzhou Museum (reconstructed/re-opened 2012)
2002	West Lake Cultural Square (including the Zhejiang Provincial Museum, Zhejiang Museum of Natural History, and Zhejiang Museum of Science and Technology)
2003	West Lake Expo Museum
	Meijiawu Tea Museum

2005	West Lake Museum
2007	Beijing-Hangzhou Grand Canal Museum (new museum projected 2023)
2009	China Umbrella Museum
	China Fan Museum
	China Knives, Scissors and Swords Museum
	Xixi National Wetland Museum of China
2009	Hangzhou Philharmonic Orchestra inaugurated[20]
2011	Hangzhou Arts and Crafts Museum
2012	Hangzhou Cuisine Museum
2015	National Tea Museum, Longjing Pavilion
2016	China National Silk Museum (expanded)
2018	Liangzhu Culture Museum
	Zhejiang Natural Science Museum, Anji location
	China Museum of Design (China Academy of Art)
2019	New Xiaobaihua Yue Opera Theater
2020	Museum of Seawall Site of Hangzhou
2022	Zhijiang Cultural Center (including Zhejiang Literature Museum, Zhejiang Intangible Cultural Heritage Museum, and additional locations for Zhejiang Provincial Museum and Zhejiang Library)

In addition to the multiplicity of new public and private museums, Hangzhou's city government preserved important elements of the ancient walled city. Visitors can stroll along the sedate and car-free former Imperial Way, now known as Zhongshan Middle Road. The more frenetic night-market scene along Hefang Ancient Street presents Qing-era architecture containing a number of century-old businesses and shops, including traditional Chinese medicines, fans, scissors, celadon porcelains, teas, and stationery items.[21]

Hefang Street sits at the foot of Wushan (Wu Hill), site of the restored City God's Temple and its magnificent view over West Lake. Less well-known on Wushan are other preserved and restored sites from Hangzhou's history, including the Temple to Ruan Yuan, the Daoist Temple to Shennong (the God of Medicine), the Dongyue Temple, and the Wugong Temple to Wu Zixu, the Tide Immortal.

Nearby, at the base of Phoenix Hill, the city in 2001 began excavating the buried ruins of Deshou Palace at the site of the Southern Song imperial palace complex.[22] That effort provided the historical and architectural framework for a large-scale plan currently underway to preserve ancient ruins and restore elements of the former palace complex as part of a Southern Song Dynasty exhibition and educational program. Upon completion, the restored palace area, along with Song-era Five Willows Lane, Hefang Street, and Hu Xueyan's Qing-era former residence will form an integrated historical tourism area,[23] with Wushan's multiple sites also readily accessible.

Hangzhou's preservation and promotion of the city's cultural heritage, coupled with its thoughtful husbandry of the West Lake scenic area, have resulted in major increases in both domestic and international tourism in the past two decades, as seen in Table 21.4 below (measured in person-times).

Year	Total Visitors	International Visitors	Foreign Visitors
1995	21,480,000	441,000	249,000
2000	23,760,000	707,000	401,000
2010	65,810,000	2,757,000	1,879,000
2018	184,030,000	4,205,000	2,990,000

Table 21.4 Hangzhou Domestic and International Tourism, Selected Years, 1995 – 2018[24]

In 2019, the twelve highest sources of foreign visitors in the table above originated, in ranked order, from USA, Korea, Japan, Malaysia, Singapore, Australia, Germany, Canada, Britain, Thailand, India, and France.[25]

Education

While kindergarten, primary, secondary, and vocational education enrollment has grown along with population, Hangzhou takes particular pride in its higher education institutions and the opportunities they provide. From a base year of 2000, the number of senior high school students in 2019 has grown by 61.6% due to geographic expansion, domestic immigration/urbanization, and natural population growth. By comparison, the number of higher education institutions have doubled from twenty to forty since 1995 and the student population has multiplied by more than eight times in the same period. Even measured from the year 2000, the higher education population has more than quintupled (up 423.5%), from 122,400 to 518,300. One interesting measure of Hangzhou's academic elevation came with Zhejiang University's hosting of an astrophysics conference on string theory in which Stephen Hawking was a featured visiting speaker before three thousand students on August 15, 2002.

Zhejiang University (ZJU)—the school that began as the Qiushi Academy, transformed into the Zhejiang Higher Education Institute, and absorbed the original Hangzhou Christian College as the Zhijiang Campus—has become one of the nation's leading institutions of higher learning.[26] In 2020, ZJU announced enrollment of more than 60,000 students, of whom about 29,200 were undergraduates, 5,600 were international students, and nearly 13,500 were doctoral candidates. The University operates thirty-seven colleges across seven campuses,[27] offering over 140 undergraduate study programs and three hundred graduate study and research programs.

Numbers alone do not tell the story, however. In October 2009, the Ministry of Education announced formation of China's equivalent of the American Ivy League consortium. Labeled the C9 League, the government named Zhejiang University to membership in this new collaboration among the country's most elite educational institutions.[28] Creation of the C9 collegiate cohort was designed to foster student exchange, earned-credit transfers, and post-graduate research among its nine members.

In recent international rankings, Zhejiang University was rated 45th by the 2022 QS World University Rankings (fourth best among the C9 members), 75th by the Times Higher Education ratings for 2022 (fourth best among the C9), and 52nd in the 2021 Academic Ranking of World Universities (third best among the C9). In a table summarizing the C9 members' rankings in nine different surveys from 2021 or 2022, Zhejiang ranked third overall in average rating and even bested #2-ranked Peking University in four of those nine surveys.[29]

The former Zhejiang Provincial Secondary Normal School, founded in the years just prior to the 1911 Xinhai Revolution, continues its educational mission in 21st-Century Hangzhou under almost the same name: Zhejiang Normal University (ZNU). The product of consolidation of five colleges in the year 2000, Zhejiang Normal University now operates several campuses with twenty-three colleges and one affiliated hospital. ZNU offers more than seventy-five undergraduate majors and enrolls more than twenty thousand full-time students and over three thousand post-graduate degree candidates.[30]

Environmental / Ecological

Beyond its caretaking of the West Lake Scenic Area and the waters of the lake itself, the city of Hangzhou has worked to create a green-space environment for its residents. According to the city's annual statistical reports, the number of parks has increased almost fourfold, from 70 in 2000 to 260 in 2019. Park and scenic resort areas in that same timespan grew more than sixfold from 489 hectares (1,208 acres) to 3,208 hectares (7,927 acres), respectively. Reported public green area for the same period has increased tenfold, from 976 hectares (2,412 acres) in 2000 to 9,246 hectares (22,847acres) in 2019.[31]

Equally notable, Hangzhou has created two new wetlands and ecology parks. In 2005, the Xixi Wetlands Park opened to the public, located just northwest of West Lake. Four years later, the Xixi National Wetland Museum opened to the public, the first such institution in China. The Wetland Museum focuses on both study and maintenance of wetland areas as well as public education, with 360 exhibits and a hundred-foot tower from which visitors can overlook the surrounding marshes.[32] In 2010, the Jiangyangfan Ecological Park (江洋畈生态公园, Jiangyangfan shengtai gongyuan) opened on the opposite side of the Qiantang River, in the hills southwest of the Xiaoshan District.

Glorious West Lake

Through the later 1980s and much of the 1990s, the city of Hangzhou maintained a dual focus on the West Lake scenic area, with continuing restoration on the one hand

and strategic planning on the other. Restoration meant in part a new round of lake bed dredging from 1999 – 2003 that reinforced and improved upon the projects undertaken in 1952 - 1958 and 1976 - 1982. Most significant, the lake's storage capacity increased by another 53 percent, from 9.34 to 14.29 million cubic meters. In 1952, that figure had amounted to only 4.13 million cubic meters.[33] Increased conservation and pollution controls[34] combined with water renewal intake from the Qiantang River also improved the lake's water quality significantly.

On the planning front, the "2002 Master Plan for the West Lake Scenic Area" promised both environmental protection and improvement of the lake water as well as controlled and coordinated development of the surrounding area. Under this formal plan, West Lake would be expanded somewhat further westward toward the hill area. The north side of the lake would continue focusing on historical sites, while the south and east sides would be devoted to upscale business development. In addition, the area would become the host site for conferences and exhibitions, beginning with the return of the West Lake Expo, last held for its first and only time in 1929.

The Second West Lake Expo[35] took place over a three-week period, from October 20 – November 10, 2000. The exhibition reportedly drew 5.7 million visitors, with over 2,500 exhibitors and such special events as an International Tea Trade Fair, an International Design and Silk Fair, a Tourism Trade Fair, and a Contemporary Arts & Crafts Fair. Product displays promoted both international trade as well as domestic consumption, while the scenic venue opened Hangzhou to a wider audience as a premium resort and tourism destination.

Positive results from the 2000 Second West Lake Expo reinforced the plans of the Hangzhou Municipal Government and Municipal Party Committee for annual West Lake exhibitions. In 2006, Hangzhou hosted its Eighth West Lake Expo in parallel with the city's First World Leisure Expo, building on a branding campaign identifying Hangzhou as a world class "leisure city." The three-week program of 2000's Second West Lake Expo was expanded to 180 days and well over two hundred conferences, exhibitions, and special events, reaching an attendance of 20.4 million tourists and more than 27 million exhibition and conference visitors. With a theme of "Leisure changes people's life," the World Leisure Conference "promoted leisure life, led the leisure trend,…witnessed the arrival of 'the First Year of the Leisure Era' and enhanced people's living quality."[36]

In 2018, the city hosted the 20th China Hangzhou West Lake International Expo. In October 2019, the 21st Expo program featured a parade of floats on Hubin Road alongside West Lake and encompassed global leisure, creative arts, high-tech concepts, and cultural studies. Several foreign countries, including India, South Korea, and Malaysia displayed information and examples of their jewelry, wine, food, and tourism services.

Following adoption of the master development plan for West Lake in 2002, the Hangzhou city government undertook a number of cultural and tourism promotion programs. In 2003, for example, the new West Lake Expo Museum was joined by the launch of the nearby Xixi Wetlands Park northwest of the lake along with the Meijiawu Tea Village and Museum in the Longjing tea-growing area in the western hills. Two years later, the West Lake Museum opened to the public. In 2007, the program "Impressions West Lake" debuted on the lake's northern shore, opposite the Temple of Yue Fei. Designed by China's most famous movie director, Zhang Yimou 张艺谋 (1951 –),[37] with music written by Kitaro (Masanori Takahashi, 1953 –), "Impressions West Lake" presents an after-dark spectacle of traditional Chinese culture, featuring music, dance, and colorful lighting effects.

These restoration and development efforts were rewarded in 2011 when the West Lake Scenic Area was added to the UNESCO World Heritage list. Three years later in 2014, Hangzhou's reclamation, restoration, and historical/cultural enhancement projects at the Gongchenqiao terminal area helped achieve UNESCO World Heritage recognition for the entire length of the Grand Canal.

On September 3, 2016, the day before opening of the G20 Summit, President Xi Jinping welcomed U.S. President Barack Obama at the West Lake State Guesthouse for a private meeting. In this, the two leaders mirrored a similar event forty-four years prior, when Premier Zhou Enlai received President Richard Nixon on February 26, 1972, to finalize the formal communique that marked the return of normalization between their two countries. The State Guesthouse, formed in 1953 from three lake manor properties, is also the site where Mao Zedong first drafted the modern constitution of the People's Republic.

Ten New Views

As early as the Southern Song era, the concept of "Ten Views" was widely acknowledged as the hallmark of fine appreciation of West Lake's landscape. So popular were these guidelines for "visual consumption" of the Lake's scenery that they continued in a geographically expanded (but still highly localized) form even after "Lin'an, the imperial capital" reverted back to being "Hangzhou, the provincial capital." For a time, the list was called the "Ten Views of Qiantang (County)," but traditionalist Ming literati restored the cultural and geographic focus to West Lake and nearby sites. The "Ten Views" gradually crystallized into an accepted list, canonized by the Qing Emperors Kangxi and Qianlong in the 18th Century.

Despite Lu Xun's literary scorn of the "Ten Views," the idea of experiencing West Lake by appreciating its imperially blessed scenes had become inseparable from the lake's very existence. Qing-era pavilions and imperially inscribed steles had also transformed such ephemera as "Orioles Singing in the Willows" and "Autumn Moon over the Peaceful Lake" into concrete spaces with physical existence and historical significance not casually displaced.

In 1983, the central government classified Hangzhou as a "Famed Historical and Cultural Site" and a "National Key Scenic Tourism City," effectively mandating the preservation and enhancement of the ancient city area and surrounding West Lake environs. As had been recognized by creation of the "Ten Views of Qiantang" in the 13ᵗʰ Century, the traditional "Ten Views of West Lake" were inherently geographically circumscribed and, in some instances, physically ephemeral. As early as the 1590s, Li Ding 李鼎 had written, "Of what were previously called the Ten Views, half are no longer identifiable."[38] In the 20ᵗʰ Century, Li Yimeng 李一氓 (1903 – 1990) added a sterner assessment:

> Talking about the Ten Views and imagining the scenery of the past is fine, but actual touring should not follow these ten views. It is meaningless for people to think they are still the essence of the lake scenery.[39]

In 1984, *Hangzhou Daily* newspaper co-sponsored a public initiative to devise by popular vote a "New Ten Views of West Lake," an array of updated and more widely dispersed sites. The selected set of new scenes maintained much of the atmospheric flavor of the originals: time of day, season, weather conditions, and the like:

- Cloud-Sustained Path in a Bamboo Grove (雲棲竹徑),
- Misty Trees by Nine Streams (九溪煙樹),
- Dreams at Galloping Tiger Spring (虎跑夢泉),
- Yellow Dragon Cave Dressed in Green (黃龍吐翠),
- Sweet Osmanthus Rain at Manjuelong Village (滿隴桂雨),
- Clouds Scurrying over Jade Emperor Hill (玉皇飛雲),
- Inquiring about Tea at Dragon Well (龍井問茶),
- Precious Stone Hill Floating in Rosy Clouds (寶石流霞),
- Heavenly Wind over Wushan Hill (吳山天風), and
- Ruan (Yuan)'s Mound Encircled by Greenness (阮墩環碧).

The "New Ten Views" informed visitors about places of interest beyond the immediate boundaries of West Lake. In addition, several of the views highlighted elements of modern Hangzhou's tourism and branding efforts. For example, "Ruan's Mound Encircled by Greenness" featured the 1982 creation of the new tourist attraction on the mid-lake islet originally built from dredged silt by Ruan Yuan in 1800, while "Sweet Osmanthus Rain at Manjuelong Village" not only promoted rural culture but celebrated the 1984 designation of osmanthus as Hangzhou's city flower. "Inquiring about Tea at Dragon Well" was equally a promotion of Longjing Tea, the celebrated China brand enjoyed by Richard Nixon and Queen Elizabeth II. Appendix A provides a brief description of each of the traditional Ten Views of West Lake as well as each of the New Ten Views.

In August 2007, another noticeably less poetic "Ten Views of West Lake" was created in concert with that year's West Lake Expo. This list offered an itinerary somewhat more characteristic of the typical present-day tourist visiting the West Lake vicinity:

- Lingyin Temple (灵隐禅踪, Lingyin chan zong),
- Six Harmonies Pagoda (六和听涛, Liuhe ting tao),
- General Yue Fei's Temple and Tomb (岳墓栖霞, Yuemu xi xia)

- Hubin Park (湖滨晴雨, Hubin qingyu),
- Memorial Temple of Qian (钱祠表忠, Qianci biao zhong),
- Wansong Academy of Learning (万松书缘, Wansong shuyuan),
- Yang Causeway (杨堤景行, Yangdi jing xing),
- Clouds Touring Santai Mountain (三台云水, Santai yun shui),
- Meijiawu Tea Culture Village (梅坞春早, Meiwu chun zao),
- Dreams of North Street (北街梦寻, Beijie meng xun).

For present-day visitors, likely not steeped in the long literary traditions of West Lake, specific sites as tourism venues and photo opportunities have largely supplanted poetic views, deep historical contemplation, or cultural creation. However, their leisurely appreciation of West Lake's scenery and historicity is not so much lesser than simply different. As Duan Xiaolin summarized it, "In the twenty-first century, West Lake was discovered as a global tourist destination, and the lake was reinvented and redefined as both an international and a national symbol of 'Chineseness'."[40]

Aboard the "Silver Dragon"

One of Hangzhou's most groundbreaking new programs to promote the city and add culturally contemporary events to its tourism attractions recalls a daring tidal bore performance activity dating back to at least the 13th-Century Song Dynasty. Huzhou native Zhou Mi described the event in "Observing the Tidal Bore," from his *Recollections of Wu-lin*:

> There were several hundred youths of Wu who were expert at swimming. They had loosened their hair and had tattoos on their bodies. In their hands they held colored banners some twenty feet in size and raced against each other with the utmost exertion, swimming against the current, floating and sinking in the leviathan waves a myriad *jen* high. Their leaping bodies executed a hundred different movements without getting the tail of the banners even slightly wet—this was how they showed off their skill. Prominent commoners and high officials competed to bestow silver prizes.[41]

A more sober assessment comes from *Description of Lin'an in the Xianchun Reign* (咸淳临安志, *Xianchun Lin'an zhi*),[42] written by Qian Shuoyou 潜說友 (1216 – 1277) and published in 1274:

> At every mid-autumn full moon when the fury of the tide is [e]specially great, the people of Hang swim in the water with flags in their hands to meet Wu Zixu. This is the origin of the performance called "sporting the tide." Very often some are drowned.[43]

In November 2013, the Hangzhou city government put an altogether new and modern spin on the practices of those ancient wave-riders (弄潮兒, nongchao'er) by hosting the first-ever Qiantang Shoot Out.[44] The competition, usually held during the Mid-Autumn Festival, pitted eight professional surfers, working in pairs, in a scored competition as they ride the tidal bore up the Qiantang River. Unlike normal surfing contests,

512

the participants have only the one continuous wave on which to demonstrate their skills, even as the wave grows, recedes, or barrels as it advances. Teammates alternate rides, using jet skis to tow each other into the bore and begin rides that can last as long as twenty minutes.

First prize in the 2015 Shoot Out was $10,000. In that same year, Yang Xue joined Zhao Yuanhong as Team Hangzhou and became the first Chinese female ever to ride the tidal bore wave. By 2019, the Shoot Out had expanded to nine teams (eighteen surfers). Romain Laulhe and P.V. Laborde from the co-winning France Team enthusiastically summarized the experience as "insane," "an incredible week and a fantastic experience to surf the world's largest tidal bore."[45]

Final Rests

During the 1950s, the Communist Party government in Shaoxing transformed Qiu Jin's family residence into a historical museum, thanks in part to the support of Zhou Enlai. However, philosophical breaks in the Party's perception of historical revolutionaries sought for a time in the early 1960s to exclude Qiu Jin from their ranks because her actions had pre-dated the Party's existence.

The consequences for Qiu Jin's remains were dramatic, but the surrounding events ended up vaguely farcical and a bit macabre. In December 1964, her remains were once again disinterred from West Lake and reburied, this time at Jilong Mountain, more than fifty miles southwest in the hills of Tonglu County. This, her sixth burial, was effectively a symbolic banishment. Within months, official sentiment brought her remains back to West Lake for reburial, only to be returned once again to Jilong Mountain in the revolutionary mid-1960s for her eighth burial. In that instance, her West Lake tomb site was demolished.

Finally, in 1981, Qiu Jin's tomb was rebuilt once again near Xiling Bridge on Solitary Hill and her remains interred for the ninth and last time at that site. A white marble statue raised high on a pedestal looks over passersby into a distant future, her left arm poised defiantly akimbo as her right hand covers the hilt of a sword that touches the ground at her feet. She is curiously dressed, neither as a revolutionary nor in pre-revolutionary era style, nor cross-dressed in male clothing as was her wont. Rather, she is adorned with a two-piece dress and a short, shoulder-covering cloak in the ancient style of the Tang Dynasty. Sun Yat-sen's calligraphy on the face of the pedestal once again proclaims her "Female Hero" (巾幗英雄, Jinguo yingxiong).

Qiu Jin was not the only revolutionary martyr of her era whose West Lake tomb was relocated during the 1960s. Xu Xilin's tomb on Solitary Hill, along with those of fellow Xinhai Revolution martyrs Chen Boping 陈伯平 (1885 – 1907) and Ma Zonghan 马宗汉 (1884 – 1907) were also demolished and their remains moved to Jilong Mountain.

In 1981, their tombs were restored just west of West Lake on Longjing Road at the newly built Zhejiang 1911 Revolutionary Martyrs Shrine (浙江辛亥革命幕群, Zhejiang

513

Xinhai geming muqun). A plaza-like memorial walk leads to the three martyrs' tombs, with the plaza containing their statues and two groups of three others, all in white stone. Interestingly, a figure of Qiu Jin fronts one of the two groupings, standing erect with her hand on the hilt of a downward-pointing sword. In 1991, on the 80th anniversary of the Xinhai Revolution, a tall stele was added to this memorial tableau inscribed with Sun Yat-sen's phrase, "National spirit lives forever (国魂不死, *Guo hun bu si*).[46]

The story of Leighton Stuart's final resting place served as a somewhat bittersweet postscript to his life as well. He passed away in America in 1962 at the age of 86, but he also died an honorary citizen of Hangzhou. His last wishes included placement of his ashes alongside his wife Aline's in the cemetery at Yenching University. Aline Stuart died from chronic illness in 1926, age 48, on the very day the new campus was to be opened. She had been the first person buried in the new cemetery.

Philip Fugh (傅泾波, Fu Jingbo, 1900 – 1988),[47] Stuart's former private secretary, visited China twice in attempts to honor Stuart's wishes for his interment, but he failed to secure a definitive response. Regrettably, earlier construction of a campus dormitory had required disinterring Aline Stuart's remains in the Yenching cemetery and in the process, the location of Mrs. Stuart's grave site was lost.[48] Fugh tried again by letter to Deng Xiaoping in January 1986 and received approval in June of that year for Stuart's burial at the Lake House, his former residence at Yenching. Before the burial could be arranged, however, it was postponed due to political opposition. Fugh fell ill soon after and passed away in 1988. Stuart's remains were held in the U.S. for another thirty years by Fugh's family.

During a State visit to Peking University in 1998, U.S. President Bill Clinton (1946 –) appealed to the Party and University leaders to allow Stuart's remains to be buried on the campus. The request was approved for the second time, but new political tensions between the two countries caused another postponement. In 2006,[49] Philip Fugh's son, Major General John Fugh (1934 – 2010), appealed once more for Stuart's burial in China.[50] After repeated requests, John Leighton Stuart's ashes were finally permitted in 2008 to be returned to China, the land of his birth, and interred at Anxian Cemetery 安贤园, Banshan District of Hangzhou.

In his brief remarks at the burial on November 17, 2008, U.S. Ambassador to China Clark T. Randt, Jr. (1945 –) summarized the arc of John Leighton Stuart's days: "He was born in Hangzhou and today he comes back here, completing the journey of his life."[51]

Regional Growth and Development

Just as Hangzhou has urbanized and developed economically and culturally in the 21st Century, so have Shaoxing, Jiaxing, Huzhou, Jinhua, Yiwu, and many of the other cities and towns of northern Zhejiang. All show dramatic growth in their urban footprints between 1984 and 2019, with noticeable acceleration of that process after 1994 and especially since 2004.[52]

These growth patterns represent large-scale urbanization and are reflected in each city's population figures, as summarized in Table 21.5 for Shaoxing, Jiaxing, and Huzhou.

Year	Shaoxing	Jiaxing	Huzhou
1950	64,400	72,800	58,600
1976	188,400	136,900	138,200
1985	316,300	171,700	187,400
2000	1,124,300	440,300	543,500
2010	1,702,500	749,300	741,200
2015	2,082,400	973,900	856,400
2020	2,540,000	1,259,800	988,400
2021	2,633,100	1,318,400	1,015,500

Table 21.5 Population Figures for Shaoxing, Jiaxing, and Huzhou, Selected Years, 1950 – 2021[53]

Each of these cities is a modern and vibrant hub of commercial and light industrial enterprise, yet each has also maintained a firm grip on its historical and cultural traditions. In some cases, that has meant rehabilitating, preserving, or even reconstructing sites that had been lost to war or neglect. In other instances, new museums have been created to celebrate and educate locals and visitors alike about each city's past and its role in creating the present.

In Shaoxing, for example, the former residences of Lu Xun, Qiu Jin, and Cai Yuanpei are now museums, as is the ancestral home of Zhou Enlai. Shen Garden is an urban oasis filled with reminders of the famous love of Lu You and Tang Wan. New museums, such as the China Shaoxing Rice Wine Museum and the Yue Opera Museum, have been built and/or expanded to recognize these important elements of the city's history, while Wang Xizhi's famous Preface at Orchid Pavilion and Lu Xun's short stories are remembered by suburban locations at Lanting and Keqiao District, respectively. Similarly, new museums and memorials honor the ancient legends of Yu the Great (at Kuaiji Mountain), the Yue beauty Xi Shi (at Zhuji), and even the filial daughter Cao'e (at Shangyu).

The temple renovation for Da Yu's tomb was accompanied by the addition of a massive bronze bell and tripod, a stone table for sacrificial offerings, and various implements for ritual ceremonies. These enhancements, along with commemorative calligraphy supplied by Jiang Zemin 江泽民 (1926 –), were undertaken in preparation for a four-day ceremonial heritage celebration and conference on Da Yu that began on April 18, 1995. Segments of the two-hour ceremony with ritual offerings, bell ringing, and music were even broadcast on national television. Among the invited guests were Yu's reputed descendant clan, surnamed Si (姒), most of whom were living close by Kuaiji Mountain in Yuling Village (窝陵村, Yulingcun).[54] The annual remembrance has continued since 1995 and, in 2007, was raised to national ceremonial status and included in China's National Intangible Cultural Heritage list.[55]

Amidst their growth and modernization, Jiaxing and Huzhou have also preserved their history in much the same manner. In Jiaxing, visitors can enjoy the South Lake Revolutionary Hall and the former residences of Mao Dun, Feng Zikai (at Shimenwan), Zhang Leping (at Haiyan), and Xu Zhimo (at Hainan). In Huzhou's case, the China Huzhou Writing Brush (湖笔, *Hubi*) Museum offers insight into the nation's most important writing instruments through the ages, while historically-minded visitors can tour the Lu Yu Tea Culture Museum and the former residence/museums of Yuan-era painter Zhao Mengfu and calligrapher Wu Changshuo. In the suburbs of both cities, ancient water towns like Xitang, Wuzhen, and Nanxun recall life and architecture from the days of the Ming and Qing emperors.

While these cities have developed and grown more or less organically from their traditional economic foundations, two more cities in the greater Hangzhou region—Quzhou and Yiwu—have evolved in rather unique ways that deserve mention.

Confucius' Second Home

Few Chinese people of any era are as well-known outside of China as the great philosopher Confucius (551 – 479 BCE), but not many Westerners are aware of his family name, Kong 孔. Confucius was born Kong Qiu 孔丘 in Qufu, located about halfway between Beijing and Shanghai in eastern coastal Shandong Province.[56] The wisdom of his teachings was acknowledged in his own lifetime, resulting in his family home being consecrated as a temple just two years after his death. His former home became a pilgrimage and devotional site and was eventually subsumed into a magnificent temple complex that was subjected, in turn, to multiple reconstructions due mostly to fires.

The Confucius Temple at Qufu was first visited by an emperor in the Han Dynasty. For centuries afterward, emperors or their representatives would travel to Qufu to worship and offer sacrifices. However, an historical break occurred during the Song Dynasty that divided the Kong family lineage. As the Jurchen Jin advanced into northern China in 1127 and captured Emperors Huizong and Qinzong, the newly enthroned Emperor Gaozong commanded Kong Duanyou, 48th-generation descendant of Confucius, to leave Qufu for the south. The first emperor of the Southern Song wanted to ensure that the Kong family would be safely able to fulfill their ceremonial obligations to their great ancestor and hence to the State.

In 1136, Kong Duanyou, his brothers, and numerous members of the Kong family clan resettled in Quzhou, about 140 miles southwest of Hangzhou. When Kong Duanyou died without a male heir, his title as Duke Yansheng was passed to one of his nephews. At around the same time, the Jin ruler in the north appointed that nephew's brother, who had remained behind in Qufu, as Duke Yansheng.

This circumstance of two individuals and locales competing for leadership of the Kong clan persisted through the end of the Southern Song Dynasty. Yuan Emperor Shizu (Khubilai Khan) attempted a resolution by ordering the Duke Yansheng in Quzhou to return to Qufu. That individual, a 53rd-generation descendant of Confucius, declined the Emperor's order in favor of remaining at the place where his more recent ancestors were now buried. The Emperor had little choice at that point but to rescind the Quzhou Duke's title and recognize that of the Qufu Duke as the legitimate title-holder. The Quzhou Kongs were consequently reduced to commoner status.

During the Ming Dynasty, the northern Kongs continued as the primary lineage and celebrants of rituals and ceremonies. However, the southern lineage was granted official recognition as well. The court even awarded them income-generating land and tax exemptions to ensure continuity in the family line. Thanks to this financial support, the Quzhou Kongs rebuilt their family temple in 1520, the original having been destroyed in the Mongol conflict three hundred years prior, Until the early 20th Century, the title of Duke Yansheng was passed down through the northern (Qufu) Kong lineage, while the new title of "Erudite of the Five Classics in the Imperial Academy,"[57] bestowed during the Ming era, was passed from generation to generation in the southern (Quzhou) lineage.[58]

Through the years from the Republican era until the 1980s, the Kong family in Quzhou was reduced in official status, and their clan temple[59] and homestead were converted to public property. In the early 1980s, the complex was returned to the city of Quzhou, albeit in seriously deteriorated condition. Renovation work began in the mid-1980s, and the rejuvenated temple and Kong Mansion were opened to the public in 1988. However, one important element of the Confucian Family Temple was still missing: its 75th-generation clan leader, Kong Xiangkai 孔祥楷 (1938 – 2021).

As it turned out, Kong Xiangkai had departed from Quzhou in the 1950s, studying mining in northeastern China. A career in engineering led to his directorship at a mining company and a senior position in Shenyang at the College of Metal Industry as well as membership in the Communist Party. All the while, he had held in secret the Confucian title passed to him in the 1940s by his uncle: "Official for Offering the Exalted First Teacher of Culture of the Southern Lineage."[60] As the 1980s drew to a close, Quzhou city officials asked Kong Xiangkai to return to his native city, assume his ancestral role, and help restore the Confucian Family Temple as an important historical, cultural, and educational tourism site.

In 1994, the Confucian complex at Qufu was enrolled in the UNESCO World Heritage list as "Temple and Cemetery of Confucius and the Kong Family Mansion in Qufu." In 2004, the renamed Temple of Southern Confucianism in Quzhou sponsored its first International Confucian Cultural Festival. In September of the following year, ten famous Confucian temples organized to perform simultaneous offering rituals, televised live by CCTV from six of the temple sites, including Qufu and Quzhou. Several televised documentaries were produced in the succeeding years, bringing national recognition to the story of the dual lineages of Confucius' descendants.

The City of a Million Small Things

The ascent of Hangzhou as a domestic and international travel, tourism, and business locale has undoubtedly aided the development of the more remote cities along the western reaches of the Qiantang/Fuyang River basin. Cities like Quzhou offered unique cultural attractions, while others developed national brand identities for local product specialties such as Jinhua for its hams (*Jinhua huotui*). The city of Yiwu 义乌, located about sixty miles due south of Hangzhou and administratively part of Jinhua, developed a distinct path of its own and has evolved a truly unique position in modern global commerce.

Yiwu's history is as old as Hangzhou's, beginning in the Han Dynasty as Wuchang County and renamed Yiwu County early in the Tang Dynasty. In an area not gifted with abundant and fertile agricultural land, the people of Yiwu learned centuries ago that they needed fertilizer to make their cultivated plots more productive. Their solution to the problem became famously known as "sugar for chicken feathers" (鸡毛换糖, *jimao huan tang*). Yiwu people traveled their region as walking traders (行商, *xing shang*), twisting pellet (rattle) drums between their hands and shouldering long poles with bamboo baskets hanging from either side. They traded in personal services and small commodities (and brown sugar candies, 红糖 *hongtang*) for the aforementioned chicken feathers, which made for excellent fertilizer as well as salable brooms and dusters for trade.[61]

Yiwu's long history in barter trade led to its emergence as a wholesale market town in the 1700s. After suffering the ravages of the Taiping Rebellion in the 1860s and the Japanese invasion (1937 – 1945), the town resumed its life in relative obscurity. However, the townspeople's trading mentality came to the fore once again after Deng Xiaoping announced the economic reforms of 1978. No one could have imagined where this would lead.

By most accounts, the legendary birth of modern Yiwu began with a disgruntled woman who sold shoelaces and buttons on the city streets to support her four children. After having her wares confiscated by police for the "umpteenth" time, Feng Aiqian 冯爱倩 stormed into Mayor Xie Gaohua's 谢高华 (1931 – 2019) office in April 1982. Why, she asked, could she not be permitted to sell such small items so her children could eat? After further consideration, the Mayor decided to allow Ms. Feng and others to proceed in a designated location, even though the legality of such private business was not yet clear at the time.[62]

When the new open air street market quickly grew to over seven hundred outdoor stalls, the former "walking traders" became "sitting traders" (坐商, *zuo shang*).[63] In 1992, the number of stalls had grown to 16,000; by 2004, 42,000; and by 2014, 65,000.[64] They traded in small, inexpensive commodity goods: toys, ornaments, handicrafts, clocks, suitcases, electrical appliances, buttons and zippers, rain gear and umbrellas, plastic flowers, cosmetics, sports caps, eyeglasses, religious paraphernalia, and the like.

What started in 1982 as a government-organized street market transformed in 1995 into the first China Yiwu International Commodities Fair,[65] finally relocated indoors. By 2006 or 2007, the "Yiwu Fair" was the third largest trade fair in China, exceeded only by the annual exhibitions in Guangzhou (the "Canton Fair") and Shanghai.

Today, Yiwu is host to the year-round International Trade Mart, a colossal, multi-building complex of forty-six million square feet. The wholesale market houses more than 60,000 booths for over 100,000 suppliers of more than 400,000 kinds of products, welcoming an average of 40,000 visitors every day.[66] Commodity City, as it is sometimes called, stands today as the world's largest wholesale market for small commodities. As one example meaningful to Westerners, Yiwu is said to be the source for seventy percent of the world's supply of Christmas decorations and ornaments.[67]

The nature and structure of Yiwu's commodity trade also lent itself to the development of specialized industrial clusters in which a number of local firms participate in the vertically integrated production of similar products. As just one example, Yiwu grew since 1995 into the world capital of socks production, home in 2009 to over 1,400 socks firms, nine hundred registered trademarks, and the world's four largest socks manufacturers. Nearly all of these businesses evolved out of small family workshops and in their essence remain family or clan enterprises.[68]

The success of these commodities markets utterly transformed the city and surrounding area. Once a poor and remote farming community, Yiwu is now a light manufacturing and logistics hub, with much of its commodities supply manufactured nearby in businesses that did not exist in 1982 and on land that once needed chicken feathers to grow crops. The modern city of Yiwu occupies more than one hundred square kilometers of built-up (urbanized) land, compared to less than three square kilometers in 1982, and its population of about 1.9 million includes almost 1.2 million non-local residents.[69] The city's growth, light-industrial development, urbanization, and wealth (it ranked 14th highest GDP among the 2,100 counties in China in 2016)[70] all began with the persistence of Feng Aiqian and the foresight of Xie Gaohua.

Stories of towns like Yiwu and individuals like Alibaba's Jack Ma hardly seem anomalous in the Hangzhou region. Another Yiwu-like "entrepreneurial miracle" arose just east of Huzhou City in Zhili Town in the early 1980s from similarly modest (if not subsistence-level) beginnings. The town's itinerant traders carrying small commodities and children's clothing items up and down what became known as Shoulder Pole Street blossomed by the mid-1990s into Children's Wear City.[71] By 2017, Zhili Town manufacturers and distributors accounted for fully one-half of China's domestic market in children's wear. In 2018, Zhili was reported as home to over 13,000 manufacturers of children's clothing and accessories.[72]

Modern Architecture, Modernizing Tradition

In a country with five thousand years of history and culture, modernization often clashes with tradition, whether through urban renewal of older neighborhoods or simply erecting towering new glass and steel structures whose modernist elements bear minimal connection to their older surroundings. Two examples of recent public development that demonstrate the positive efforts of Hangzhou to integrate local heritage with modern urban architectural design are particularly worthy of notice. In both instances, these two structures portray an absolute sense of current design and construction technology combined with captivating visual appearance that equally celebrates the city's traditional culture

Although not visible from West Lake, the first building is situated sufficiently nearby to share in the lake's ethereal aura and indeed contribute some aura of its own. Conceived in 2008 by the Taiwanese architect[73] Li Zuyuan 李祖原 (b. 1938) and first opened in 2019, the exterior design of the Xiaobaihua Yue Opera House immediately calls to mind the most celebrated of Yue operas, *Liang Shenbo and Zhu Yintai*, commonly referred to as "The Butterfly Lovers."[74] The new theater is multi-purpose, with a 900-seat grand theater, a smaller theater for more intimate Yue Opera performances, and a third space intended for experimental theater performances.[75]

From its spectacular, butterfly-shaped entranceway to the negative-space butterfly field carved out of the building's side to the "world's largest butterfly" hovering low over its roof, the Opera House is dramatically modern in appearance and yet unmistakably hearkens to an opera dating back to the Ming Dynasty. Viewed from above and looking east over the hills bordering West Lake on its north, the "butterfly theater" pairs with the needle-like Baochu Pagoda rising in the near distance. Furthermore, the building's celebration of the Butterfly Lovers on the northwest side of West Lake complements the Wansong Academy on the southeast side of the lake.

The second building of note in this discussion is the Hangzhou Sports Park across the Qiantang River in Binjiang District. This open-air soccer stadium and companion, retractable-roofed tennis center will host competitive events for the 2022 Asian Games and Paralympic Games. These two structures were designed to appear as blooming lotus flowers ("Big Lotus" and "Little Lotus"), with exterior materials presenting the visually softening texture of silk fabric.[76] Together, these two sports centers represent clearly modern design and Frank Gehry-like application of advanced materials while referencing the long-honored, symbolic beauty of lotus flowers and their much-loved presence not far away at West Lake.

Modern Hangzhou has its share of dramatic, skyscraping glass and steel, but the Yue Opera Theater and the Hangzhou Sports Park buildings demonstrate a city administration dedicated not just to modernizing but integrating and celebrating the city's rich historical and cultural traditions in uniquely attractive and memorable ways.

Conclusion

Hangzhou in the present era remains the stellar center of Zhejiang Province, as befits a former capital of the empire. The city has been and continues to be a shining jewel of the Chinese nation, witnessed by its repeated selection for global and regional international events such as the 2016 G20 and the 2022 Asian Games.

Since the dawn of the new millennium, Hangzhou has grown explosively, urbanized dramatically, industrialized smartly, and preserved wisely. A once wealthy and highly cultured city, nearly obliterated by wars in the 1860s and 1930s, has drawn upon its civic genes and natural surroundings to restore its place as the metaphorical Chinese "heaven on earth." In September 2021, *The Economist* magazine's Intelligence Unit ranked Hangzhou first among all Chinese cities as having the greatest near-to-intermediate-term economic growth potential.[77]

Gone are the days when long-robed literati wandered the lake shores, composing poetic lines while strolling the Bai or Su embankments or floating on the quiet wavelets while sipping fine wine or tea. As one modern commentator has noted, "Over the centuries, West Lake has been transformed from a natural landscape that inspired the production of knowledge into a human-made lake that embodies idealized nature and cultural memories."[78]

Although the deep poetic and historical familiarity of those literati who speak to us from the past may not be common today, West Lake persists as one of China's most loved tourist destinations for its natural beauty as well as its historical aura. One does not have to spout poetry to enjoy the scenic elegance, nor does one have to come armed with encyclopedic historical or literary knowledge to take away new appreciation for Hangzhou's (and China's) rich past and West Lake's place in the city's promising future. As ICOMOS (International Council on Monuments and Sites) summarized the West Lake environment in its review for UNESCO of Hangzhou's application for listing the lake area as a World Heritage site:

> [The] West Lake landscape…can be said to be an exceptional testimony to the very specific cultural tradition of improving landscapes to create…a perfect fusion between people and nature, a tradition that has continued its relevance to the present day.[79]

One hopes far into the future as well.

Appendix A

"Ten Views of West Lake"

In past years I have seen the painting of this lake, but I did not believe that such a lake could exist under heaven. Today I went across the lake, (I feel that) the painters were not skilled enough (to fully depict the beautiful scenery).[1]
— *A visiting Japanese ambassador to West Lake during the reign of Emperor Zhengde (1506 – 1521)*

One of the most accessible yet comprehensive sources for detailed histories, descriptions, architectural plans and elevations, aerial and topographic maps, and photographs of West Lake is the *2011 Nomination File* for inscription of West Lake Cultural Landscape of Hangzhou into the UNESCO World Heritage List. Information regarding all Ten Views sites can be found in several sections, especially PDF pages 63 – 165, 467 – 476, and 511 – 527. This 1,342-page document is readily accessible for online viewing or downloading as a PDF file at https://whc.unesco.org/en/list/1334/documents/.

West Lake achieved its World Heritage List honor on June 24, 2011, at the 35th session of the World Heritage Committee. It was the 41st World Heritage List site to be added from China.[2]

The Traditional "Ten Views of West Lake"

1. Spring Dawn at the Su Causeway (苏堤春晓, *Sudi chunxiao*)

Regarded by many as the most enchanting of the Ten Views, spring sunrise reveals this long walkway blanketed by pink and red peach blossoms and weeping willow catkins. The placid water, golden sunrise, and the colorful mix of blossoms and pillowy white catkins combine with the sounds of birds chirping in the trees and the fragrance of the peach blossoms to create a captivating, multi-sensory experience. Along the way, visitors will cross six stone-arch bridges (from south to north): Yingbo (映波桥), Suolan (锁澜桥), Wangshan (望山桥), Yadi (压堤桥), Dongpu (东浦桥), and Kuahong (跨虹桥).

Built under the governorship of Su Shi in 1090, the causeway is 2.8 kilometers (about 1.7 miles) in length, running south to north, lakeshore to lakeshore, dividing the Outer Lake to its east from the Inner Lake to its west. Kangxi's inscribed stele from 1699 is located just south of the Yadi Bridge; the reverse side of this stele contains a poem written by his grandson, the Qianlong Emperor. The narrow sides of the imperial stele display poems written by Qianlong in 1757 and 1762. In the late 1920s or early 1930s, the six bridges underwent major restoration and the causeway was paved for the first time with asphalt; it has since been repaved several times to maintain its appearance. During the period from 1937 – 1942, the Japanese occupiers planted cherry blossom trees along the causeway, but these were removed after the war to restore the traditional foliage.

2. Summer Breeze Stirring Lotuses at Quyuan Garden (曲院风荷, *Quyuan fenghe*)

Quyuan Garden is located at the northwestern corner of West Lake. The site originated in the Southern Song Dynasty as the location of the imperial winery. Because the first character in the garden's name, 曲 (*qu*), is often translated in its modern (simplified) form as "crooked," the garden is called the Crooked Garden. However, the traditional *qu* character 麴 meant "yeast," as in brewer's yeast, so some translations of this view read as " Lotus Breeze in the Brewing Courtyard."

The brewery no longer exists, but in its time, summer visitors marveled at the fragrant mixture of the brewing wine combined with the scent of lotus flowers blossoming in the nearby lake. West Lake wanderers could admire the beautiful pink and white lotus flowers along the shore while inhaling the intoxicating flower-and-wine bouquet. As the lake silted up over time, the small garden and pavilion became somewhat separated from the lake.

In honor of the Kangxi Emperor's visit in 1699, the site of the lotus flowers at Quyuan Garden was quickly restored with new flower plantings, garden construction, and a stele pavilion. At that time, the 曲 (*qu*) character was modified to mean crooked or winding. The Kangxi Emperor's inscribed stone stele is located just west of the north end of Su Causeway. The stele identifies the names of three officials who copied Kangxi's original inscription for the engraving. It also contains three poems written in 1757 and 1762 by the Qianlong Emperor.

A 1980s project expanded the area into a wooded park with gardens and a lakeshore view over plentiful lotus flowers. As the viewer takes in the beauty and fragrance of the lotus flowers, he or she is called upon to contemplate their symbolism, representing noble character and alluding to the ability of purity, transcendence, and enlightenment to arise from the muddy waters of the human condition.

3. Autumn Moon over the Peaceful Lake (平湖秋月, *Pinghu qiuyue*)

Just as the most magnificent tidal bore occurs at new and full moons in August due to the orbits and alignments of the Sun, Moon, and Earth, so too was the autumn moon regarded by the literati as the most beautiful to view. This temporal preference may also have been enhanced by the heavy summer atmosphere of Jiangnan, where humid nights created a misty pallor to ring the visible moon.

On such nights, when the lake was calm and the moon its visibly largest, people would gather at Solitary Island, just south of the western end of the Bai Causeway. There they could listen to the quite lapping of wavelets against the dike, view the moon and clouds reflected in the water, and admire the hills above the opposite shore, bathed in moonlight. Whether viewed from a pavilion, a terrace, or a teahouse, the full moon on such a night could inspire shared appreciation and poetic sentiments that might result in written verse.

Although visitors often enjoyed this scene from a boat on the lake, the Kangxi Emperor designated this garden location at the island's southeast corner as the formal viewing site during his 1699 visit. That same year, the Pavilion for Imperial Calligraphy was constructed with a viewing platform. The Moon Wave Pavilion and the stele pavilion were also built at that time. The combination of pavilions and viewing areas thus established a fixed location for this famous West Lake site.

Unlike the steles at some other Ten Views sites that share calligraphy by both Kangxi and his grandson Qianlong, the Autumn Moon stele contains the same four-character Kangxi inscription from 1699 (平湖秋月, *Pinghu qiuyue*, reproduced in 1980) on both front and back.

4. Lingering Snow on Broken Bridge (断桥残雪, *Duanqiao canxue*)

The arched bridge on Bai Causeway is the place in the fictional *Legend of the White Snake* where handsome young Xu Xian first met and fell in love with Bai Suzhen, the white snake who had transformed into a beautiful maiden. Consequently, this view is considered the most romantic of the Ten Views sites. Hangzhou people like to think of Broken Bridge as an enchanted place for love relationships to bloom.

The name Broken Bridge (断桥, Duanqiao) arose from a visual illusion. On the rare occasions where enough snow has fallen to coat the bridge in a layer of fine white flakes, the sun gradually melts the snow on one side of the bridge faster than the other. From a distance, the bridge appears as though broken in half, snow-covered white on one side and bare, dark stone on the other. The Broken Bridge segment of the causeway is 8.8 meters (about 29 feet) in length. The Bai Causeway's gradual but shallow rise to and descent from the central arch[3] give it a striking elegance that is best appreciated from a distance or from above on Baoshi Shan (宝石山) to the north.

First built in the Tang Dynasty, Bai Causeway served for centuries as the sole means of land access to Solitary Hill at the embankment's western end. The stele pavilion was added in 1702, three years after the Kangxi Emperor's visit and written inscription. The Kangxi Emperor's calligraphy appears on both sides of the engraved stele. In 1929, an east-facing waterside viewing pavilion was added to the site.

5. Leifeng Pagoda in the Sunset (雷峰夕照, *Leifeng xizhao*)

Leifeng (雷峰, Thunder Peak) Pagoda was first built atop the lakeside Xizhao (夕照, Sunset Glow) Hill in 975 to the height of seven stories by Wuyue King Qian Chu. After suffering damage in the 1120s at the end of the Northern Song era, the pagoda was restored to five stories during the Southern Song. In the mid-1500s, Leifeng's wooden flying eaves and balconies were lost to fires set by pirate raiders. Afterwards, the pagoda's bare, fire-reddened brick shell was all that remained standing on the south shore of West Lake. Leifeng's squat, flat-topped shell offered a unique architectural counterpoise to the tapering, needle-like shell of the Baochu Pagoda on the lake's opposite shore.

Emperors Kangxi and Qianlong both visited the ruins and left inscriptions that were then inscribed on stone steles (in 1699 and 1751, respectively). From 2000 – 2002, a new, seven-story exterior was built to restore the pagoda's appearance and protect the remains of the original inner core. At that time, both Emperors' stele inscriptions were also restored from original rubbings.

In the evenings, visitors on West Lake's eastern shore near the city wall could take in a spectacular view: sun setting behind the western hills and beneath a multi-colored sky, southern hills slowly being enveloped in shadow, the lake waters reflecting the sunset's colors, and the Leifeng Pagoda radiating in the spreading evening glow and also reflecting in the water. As with the Broken Bridge, the romance of Leifeng Pagoda was only enhanced by its connection to the *Legend of White Snake* story, beneath which it was said that Monk Fahai imprisoned White Snake and her goddess-friend Green Snake for eternity.

6. Twin Peaks Piercing the Clouds (双峰插云, *Liangfeng chayun*)

Among the western hills sheltering West Lake rise two peaks that, though modest in height, nevertheless stand taller than those around them. Northern Peak (北高峰, Beigaofeng), whose name matches its relative location, reaches a height of 355 meters (about 1,165 feet), while its taller directional companion, Southern Peak (南高峰, Nangaofeng) stands about one hundred meters shorter (256.9 meters, or 840 feet).

On mornings of low-hanging clouds that shroud the lower hills behind a screen of fog or mist, the two disembodied peaks can sometimes remain visible, appearing to pierce the clouds and creating a visual illusion that suggests a greater altitude than they actually have. Similarly, during the days of spring or autumn rains, the two peaks can repeatedly appear and disappear among the drifting clouds as they wreath the hills.

In the Southern Song Dynasty era, both peaks were capped with pagodas that amplified the sense of "piercing the clouds." The Northern Peak pagoda was built around 750 during the Tang Dynasty, and its southern version in around 940. Both pagodas rose seven stories above their mountain peaks. Conflict damage and fires due to lightning caused the twin pagodas to deteriorate over the centuries until both were lost in the Qing Dynasty.

In ancient days, poets often claimed that days of mist and fine rain displayed West Lake at its most beautiful. The Twin Peaks can of course be viewed in sunshine and clear weather as well. Lake-view aficionados say that the best location for admiring the Northern and Southern Peaks is at Hongchun Bridge (洪春桥) on Lingyin Road, not far from viewing the lotus flowers at Quyuan Garden. The imperial stele pavilion for the Twin Peaks view is located just north of the Hongchung Bridge.

7. Orioles Singing in the Willows (柳浪闻莺, *Liulang wen ying*)

The Southern Song imperial Jujing Garden along the southeastern shore of West Lake during the Southern Song Dynasty[4] was later celebrated by Ming and Qing Dynasty literati visitors for its numerous weeping willow trees. With the willows' long hanging branches mimicking the quiet waves of the lake water as they swayed gently in the spring breeze and with orioles flitting and warbling among the trees, the scene was consecrated as one of West Lake's Ten Views. As one Ming poet wrote, "The singing of the orioles never stops in the forest; also [from] somewhere in the forest the pleasure boats over the lake comes more music."[5]

This scenic area was restored in 1699 and renovated again in the late 1950s as a people's park, adding pavilions and bridges as well as a variety of willow species from around China and from overseas. In the present day, the park is sometimes used for public entertainments and holiday shows. The Orioles Singing in the Willows site and accompanying stele pavilion are located along West Lake's eastern shore, opposite the western end of Hefang Street and in front of the Temple of Wuyue King Qian. The stele, restored in 1980, contains the Kangxi Emperor's script on both front and back

8. Fish Viewing at Flower Cove (花港观鱼, *Huagang guanyu*)

During the Southern Song era (1127 – 1279), when Lin'an (Hangzhou) was the temporary imperial capital, a palace eunuch named Lu Yunsheng 廬庐允升 (c. 1224 – 1264) built a private villa and garden for himself. He chose a magnificent location on the southwestern shore of West Lake, at the foot of Flower Hill (花家山, Huajia shan). The garden was originally named Lu Garden, but over time it became known as Flower Harbor because a stream from the hill flowed into the garden pond and allowed many flowers to grow there.

In the Qing Dynasty, the Kangxi Emperor directed the garden to be rebuilt to include a fish pond and a Taihu stone rockery. At that time, he wrote the four characters in the above title (花港观鱼) for the name of this view. The same four characters are inscribed on a stone stele still on display beneath a pavilion alongside the fish pond; the current stele was created in 1980 from a rubbing of the original.

An interesting anecdote about the stele inscription[6] tells why Kangxi recorded the traditional character 魚 (*yu*) for " fish" with just three dots (short strokes) on the bottom instead of the normal four. After doing so, he explained that the Chinese radical ⺣ (the subject indicator for fire) at the bottom of the *yu* character consists of four dots, but the water radical 氵 has only three (on the left of the radical). The Emperor wanted to wish the fish a happy life in the water, and not the fate of being boiled or cooked with fire.[7]

The fish pond and stele pavilion were badly damaged during the Taiping occupation in 1861 but were restored in 1869 during Hangzhou's post-war recovery. In the late 1950s, the garden was renovated and expanded into a fifty-acre park. The new park included pavilions, rockeries, and numerous fresh plantings as well as a peony garden and an amply filled goldfish pond. New walking bridges enable visitors to watch the goldfish swarming the waters before them.

9. Three Pools Mirroring the Moon (三潭印月, *Santan yinyue*)

At the height of the Mid-Autumn Festival, when the full moon shines its brightest, lit candles are placed in the windows of three stone pagodas, each about two meters tall and set equilaterally some sixty-two meters apart from one another in the lake waters. Seen from a boat on West Lake or from the nearby Lesser Yingzhou Isle (also known as Three Pools Mirroring the Moon), the reflections from the illuminated pagodas join with that of the moon to create the classic symbol of West Lake and one of its most widely cherished views. In fact, this Ten Views scene has been celebrated in the modern era by its illustration on the reverse side of China's one-renminbi note.

The three pagodas were originally installed in West Lake by then-Governor Su Shi in 1089 after completion of the major dredging project that resulted in construction of the original Su Causeway. They were intended to demarcate a "no planting" zone, but the moon-shaped light shining through the pagodas' openings added scenic interest to the moonlight already reflected from the lake waters. The pagodas deteriorated during the Yuan period but were restored in the Ming era (in 1607) and substantially renovated in 1699 during the reign of Qing Emperor Kangxi.

In 1607, during the waning years of the Ming Dynasty, Lesser Yingzhou was built up as a garden island from the silt and sludge excavated during a dredging authorized by the Wanli Emperor. The garden was constructed in the four-square-grid shape of the Chinese character for field or farm, 田 (*tian*), built within a fully encircling ring causeway nearly one kilometer in circumference. Because the garden layout includes pools of lake water with north-south and east-west paths crisscrossing through a smaller island in the center, the saying developed of "an island within the lake and a lake within the island."[8]

In 1727, during the Qing Dynasty, several pavilions were constructed around Lesser Yingzhou, adding to the first pavilion (1699) built to house the Kangxi Emperor's inscribed, four-character stele for the Three Pools view.[9] Zigzag bridges, corridors, halls, and a "nine-lion" rockery provide further architectural interest while willows, maples, cotton roses (hibiscus), lotus flowers, and goldfish swimming in the pool waters add natural flora and fauna to the scene. In the post-Taiping period of the later 1800s, Minister of War

Peng Yulin 彭玉麟 (1816 – 1890) built his Tuixing Retreat 退省庵 on the island and added multiple new structures, some of which have been preserved to the present day.

10. Evening Bell from Nanping Hill (南屏晚钟, *Nanping wanzhong*)

Jingci Temple (built in 954) sits at the foot of Nanping Shan, a low-rise (100-meter) hill that stretches across much of the south end of West Lake. Late in the afternoon, as the sun begins to set behind the lake's western hills, a massive bronze bell rings out the day's approaching end. The sound reverberates across the lake as the bell's tolling rebounds off the hills on the northern shore. Coming as it does from a Buddhist temple, the bell's sound calls on everyone to contemplate the day's events and the smallness of human lives amid Nature's breadth and timelessness.

Among the Ten Views, Evening Bell at Nanping Hill is a solid candidate for "most poetic." The Northern Song painter Zhang Zeduan 张择端 (1085 – 1145) may well have been the first to identify or name this West Lake view by virtue of his *Painting of Evening Bell Ringing at Nanping Hill*. The massive bronze bell, nearly ten feet tall and weighing more than ten tons, is inscribed with the 67,000 characters of the Lotus Sutra. It is said that each strike of the bell generates a note that can be heard for up to two minutes.[10]

In modern times, Hangzhou citizens and visitors come to Jingci Temple on Chinese New Year's Eve to hear the ceremonial ringing of the bell 108 times in hopes of an auspicious new year. The temple bell is also rung ritually twice every day during the monks' morning and evening recitations. For a small donation, visitors can also strike the bell for good luck.

A replica of Kangxi's original Ten View stele was constructed from an original rubbing and installed near the temple gate in 2002. Second only to Lingyin Temple in local prominence, Jingci Temple is also known for its life-releasing (放生, *fangsheng*) pool where Buddhist adherents can show compassion for living creatures by releasing captive animals such as fish or turtles.

The "New Ten Views of West Lake" (1984)

The "New Ten Views of West Lake," inspired in 1984 by readers of the *Hangzhou Daily* newspaper, increased awareness of tourism and viewing opportunities beyond the original Ten Views. They also expanded the geographic range and variety of tourism venues beyond the immediate confines of West Lake. Note that the new list and brief commentaries that follow conserve the traditional convention of naming West Lake views with exactly four characters.

1. Cloud-Dwelling Bamboo Path (云栖竹径, *Yunqi zhujing*)

Yunqi Bamboo Trail is located at the foot of Wuyun Mountain on the southwest side of West Lake. The name derived from a legend that five colorful clouds gathered here when the King of Wuyue built a temple in the year 967. The altitude and dense bamboo forest are said to form misty clouds of condensation on early mornings. During the reign of Qing Emperor Yongzheng, this area of winding bamboo trails was included as one of eighteen famous scenes at West Lake. The park area contains several pavilions, including a stele pavilion at the entrance identifying it as the Yunqi Bamboo Path.

2. Nine Streams in Misty Forest (九溪烟树, Jiuxi yanshu)

Nine Streams is a pleasant walking trail in the western hills of West Lake. Nine shallow creeks merge into a single Y-shaped stream in a wooded area as they flow southward into the Qiantang River. It is said that each creek begins with two sources, one to the west at Shizi Hill 狮子山and one to the east at Yangmei Ridge 杨梅岭, so locals sometimes refer to this site as Nine Streams and Eighteen Streams (九溪十八涧, Jiuxi shiba jian) or simply Jiuxi 18.

The 5.5-kilometer, paved walking path takes the traveler through a portion of the Longjing tea-growing area and offers the opportunity to enjoy both the tea plantation scenery as well as tea-tasting. The reference to misty forest comes from the predictable rise of mists after rain. This West Lake View is recent in origin and is very popular in spring and fall. It is also a favorite locale for wedding photography. Visitors say it is a delightful place for children to enjoy the creek water.

3. Dreaming at Running Tiger Spring at Hupao (虎跑梦泉, *Hupao mengquan*)

According to ancient legend, a Tang Dynasty monk named Xingkong 性空resided at a temple on Daci shan 大慈山 ("Great Compassion Hill") in Hangzhou's western hills. Due to an extended drought, Xingkong had reached a decision to leave Daci Temple in search of a more habitable place. One night before he left, however, he dreamed that two wild tigers would open a fountain near the temple. The next day, a pair of mighty tigers arrived, ran around in circles, and dug a pit from which spring water poured out. The monks built a well on the spot, known afterwards as Running Tiger Spring (虎跑泉, Hupao quan).

As tea drinking matured into an aesthetic cultural art, water quality and taste grew in importance and selectivity. By most traditional accounts, the waters of Running Tiger Spring are among the three best in China for brewing tea, especially nearby Longjing (龙井, Dragon Well) tea. The spring water is unusually low in mineral content and is said to taste pure and sweet. It also has a remarkably high surface tension, such that coins gently dropped one-by-one into a full cup can raise the water level to as much as three millimeters above the rim without spilling a drop.

Hupao (or Dinghui) Temple is located about three miles southwest of West Lake at the foot of Daci Hill. Statues in the temple area celebrate the dreaming monk Xingkong and his mystical tigers as well as the spring waters they reputedly brought forth from the mountain. In addition, Hupao is home to a stupa and memorial building in honor of Li Shutong (Monk Hongyi), who entered the Buddhist monkhood at Hupao Temple at age 38 in 1918. Li is remembered for his own artistry (painter, poet, musician, calligrapher, dramatist) and as a teacher and influencer of such famous painters as Feng Zikai and Pan Tianshou. "Mad Monk" Ji Gong is also said to be buried at Tiger Spring.

4. Yellow Dragon Cave Dressed in Green (黄龙吐翠, *Huanglong tucui*)

Yellow Dragon Cave, located well into the northern hills of West Lake, is substantially more than a cave mouth, although that is one of its attractions. Once the site of the Zen Huguo Renwang Temple 护国仁王禅寺 (built in 1245), the area is now something of an ancient culture park celebrating the Buddhist concept of 缘 (*yuan*), signifying pre-destined fate (karma) and extended to include "good luck" or "good fortune."

The origin of the cave name arises from multiple different legends concerning the appearance of one or a pair of dragons and the spring water that resulted from their presence. "Yellow Dragon Cave Dressed in Green" refers to a modest cave opening topped by a golden dragon head out of which pours spring water. "Dressed in green" refers to the lush bamboo forest surrounding this mountain cave.

In the present day, this popular site is better known for its tea houses and performance venues featuring classical Yue Opera scenes focusing on love and marriage. Statues of six children located near a pair of small ponds represent six kinds of good luck: wealth, education, love, marriage, career, and family.[11] Reception, sales, and wait staff dress in Song Dynasty costumes, adding to an atmosphere of traditional culture celebration.

5. Sweet Osmanthus Rain at Manjuelong Village (滿陇桂雨, *Manlong guiyu*)

Manjuelong 满觉陇 Village rests among the hills and valleys southwest of West Lake, not far from the Southern Peak of Twin Peaks Piercing the Clouds. In times past, monks from Yuanxing Temple planted osmanthus in this area. In the year 1065, Yuanxing was renamed as Manjue Temple, signifying "achieving enlightenment."

As these trees flourished in the rainy hills, so too for centuries did the trade in their flowers among the villagers who lived there. They planted thousands of osmanthus everywhere around their homes and into the hills, tending the trees and harvesting the sweet-smelling autumn flowers. In more recent times, the ubiquity of these fragrant trees with their yellow, orange, and creamy white flowers transformed the village into a "must see" autumn tourist destination. Rain or shine, visitors take in the fragrance, admire the natural flower-carpeted grounds, and even partake in local dishes that incorporate the flowers into their presentation. In September and October, Hangzhou celebrates its official city flower with the West Lake Osmanthus Festival.

6. Clouds Scurrying over Jade Emperor Hill (玉皇飛云, **Yuhuang fei yun**)

Rising almost eight hundred feet high and standing about midway between West Lake and the Qiantang River, Jade Emperor Hill (玉皇山, Yuhuang shan) is the focal point of this New West Lake View. The name "Jade Emperor" refers to the deity to whom a Daoist temple on the hill was dedicated during the Five Dynasties era (907 – 960) of the Wuyue State. Various Buddhist and Daoist temples were located on Jade Emperor Hill over the centuries.

Since earlier times, observers noted that the hill seemed always to be shrouded in mists or topped by swiftly moving clouds which magnified the mountain's feeling of majesty. In the modern era, the hill is capped by the Seven-Star Pavilion, alluding to the seven iron cauldrons positioned around the pavilion structure. In ancient times, seven such vats were arranged in the shape of the Big Dipper constellation, since the heavenly waters contained therein would surely help ward off fires in Hangzhou.

Visitors can ascend the hill by a paved, four-kilometer roadway that wraps itself twice around the mountain, or they can ascend on foot along a marked pathway. On the ascent, they can view the ancient Purple Source Cave. They can also look down southward at the Qiantang River as well as the Eight Trigram Field where it is believed the Southern Song Emperors made seasonal agricultural sacrifices.

7. Inquiring about Tea at Dragon Well (龙井问茶, *Longjing wen cha*)

While most tourists are guided to Meijiawu Village (梅家坞忖, Meijiawucun) as the center of Longjing (Dragon Well) Tea culture, the focus of this New Ten View entry is Lion's Peak (狮峰, Shifeng), a mile or two northeast of Meijiawu. In the Lion's Peak area, visitors will discover the tea villages of Longjing (龙井忖, Longjingcun) and Wengjia Mountain Village (翁家山村, Wengjiashancun). All these areas in Hangzhou's western hills cultivate fine Longjing varietals, but Lion's Peak and Dragon Well are regarded as the top of the line.[12]

In ancient times, local people believed that Dragon Well was connected to the ocean and that a dragon lived deep beneath, hence the name. Widely rated as the finest tea-brewing spring water in the nation, Dragon Well water is the perfect complement to the teas grown in the plantations of West Lake's western hills. The best time to inquire (and taste) Longjing tea is in early April, when the first spring leaves have matured just enough to be gently harvested. The area has plentiful opportunities for hiking, scenic viewing, exploring tea cultivation and culture, and visiting teahouses to taste and enjoy the local products.

8. Precious Stone Hill Floating in Rosy Clouds (宝石流霞, *Baoshi liu xia*)

Baochu ta 保俶塔 (Protecting Chu Pagoda) rises thin and needle-like over the northeastern shore of West Lake, perched atop Baoshi shan 宝石山 (Precious Stone Hill). The pagoda was built in 963 as a prayer offering for the safe return of Wuyue King Qian Chu when he was called north by the court of the newly installed (Northern) Song Emperor. The offering apparently proved efficacious, since Qian Chu returned to Hangzhou unharmed after his diplomatic mission.

The original octagonal structure stood nine-stories, built of stone and brick with wooden eaves and balconies. Today's restored pagoda stands with only its tapering, inner stone core intact, topped by an iron finial (replaced in 1997). The present structure, restored in 1932, contains just seven stories and ascends to a height of forty-five meters (about 148 feet).

Baochu Pagoda is admired for its slender appearance, particularly against colorful morning and evening skies. Added to its luster are the sparkling stones that cover the hill as visitors ascend the long stone stairways to the hilltop.

9. Heavenly Wind over Wushan Hill (吴山天风, **Wushan tianfeng**)

Wushan 吴山 (Wu Hill) rises over the southern end of the ancient walled city of Hangzhou. Consisting of ten or more peaks, Wushan's most easily notable feature is the renovated City God's Temple that soars above the hill and overlooks West Lake. In earlier times, the Temple's presence caused the hill often to be called City God's Hill (城隍山, Chenghuang shan).

Wushan covers a large area and provides ample opportunities to wander and discover. The hill is covered in a variety of trees: pine, camphor, sweet gum, and gingko to name several. It also features pavilions, memorial temples and shrines, caves, and a rock formation at which it is said that perceptive viewers can make out representations of all twelve Chinese Zodiac animals. Ancient Hefang market street runs east-to-west near the northern foot of Wushan.

10. Ruan (Yuan)'s Mound Encircled by Greenness (阮墩环碧, *Ruan dun huan bi*)

The newest artificial island in West Lake, known as Ruan Gong Dun (阮公墩, "Lord Ruan's Pier"), was constructed in 1800 from silt dredged from the lake bottom. For more than a century and a half, the island remained a wildlife refuge because the land was not solid enough to support buildings.

Finally, in 1982, another thousand tons of soil was added to the island as part of a West Lake tourism development project. New construction on the enhanced island included bamboo halls, pavilions, fishing terrace, and paved lanes along with a range of willows, bamboos, camphors, roses, and osmanthus. Visitors began calling it a Fairy Island, alluding to the mythical island of Penglai, ancient home of the Eight Immortals. The island is accessible only by boat ride on West Lake.

Appendix B

Selected Historical/Cultural Places to Visit

West Lake Vicinity

The following list of sites at or adjacent to West Lake begin with Baoshi Hill at the lake's northeast corner and proceed more or less counterclockwise around its perimeter. Sites in the western hills are listed in the next grouping, "West of West Lake."

Northern Hills Area

Baochu Pagoda - Rising needle-like from the eastern end of Baoshi shan (Precious Stone Hill), Baochu Pagoda soars alone above the forested hills bordering West Lake on the north. The pagoda was constructed in the 960s as a nine-story prayer offering for the safe return of King Qian Chu after he was summoned north to meet with the founding emperor of the Song Dynasty. It has been reconstructed on several occasions, but after its latest restoration in 1932, the height was reduced to seven stories. The brick structure is octagonal and tapered from an unusually small base, so that in earlier times Baochu Pagoda was imagined as a slender young beauty and the stumpy brick core of Leifeng Pagoda across the lake was compared to an aged monk.

Papou Temple – West of the pagoda on Baoshi Hill, Papou (Daoist) Temple was dedicated to Ge Hong (281 – 341), who manufactured immortality pills in a hut where the temple now stands. The current temple is a Ming-era restoration.

Yellow Dragon Cave – One of West Lake's "Ten New Views," "Yellow Dragon Dressed in Green" (黄龙吐翠, *Huanglong tucui*) is a garden with bamboo groves and a pavilion, along with a small cave opening and a spring which pours out from a dragon mouth sculpture. The garden is located on Baoshi Hill.

Manao Temple – Although Manao Temple was established in 946 during the Wuyue State era, it was not located at West Lake's northern hills until 1152. The Qianlong Emperor is said to have visited Manao Temple on three occasions during his Southern Tour stays in Hangzhou. In modern times, the temple is no longer an active religious institution.

Bai Causeway – The first and most famous of the water-crossing embankments at West Lake, access to Bai Causeway begins from the northeastern shore area. The first (and shorter) bridge is Duanqiao (断桥, Broken Bridge), one of the original Ten Views of West Lake for its winter appearance when partially snow-covered. The second and longer bridge is called Jindaiqiao (锦带桥), Brocade Belt Bridge, so named for its long, slender, and low-slung design. The western terminus of Bai Causeway is Solitary Hill (Gushan).

Solitary Hill (Gushan) and Nearby

"Autumn Moon over Peaceful Lake" – A pavilion and inscribed stone stele mark the imperially designated location for this "Ten Views of West Lake" site. In addition to moon viewing, the southeastern end of Solitary Hill offers a good spot for taking ground-level photos of West Lake.

Zhejiang Museum – Formerly known as West Lake Museum from its construction in 1929 for the first West Lake Exposition, Zhejiang Museum exhibits a number of artifacts from the Liangzhu, Hemudu, and several other Neolithic Cultures found on the northern outskirts of Hangzhou. The Museum also houses artifacts from the 10th-Century Wuyue (Five Dynasties and Ten Kingdoms) period as well as paintings and calligraphic works. There are additional halls for celadon objects, coins, and handicrafts. A second Zhejiang Museum building was opened in late 2009 at the West Lake Cultural Square, near Wulin Square.

Wenlan Hall – Renovated after the Taiping Rebellion, Wenlan Hall was the library facility built in the 18th Century to house one of the three "southern copies" of the Qianlong Emperor's *Four Treasuries*. It is now part of the Zhejiang Provincial Museum complex.

Former Residence of Yu Yue – Located on Solitary Hill island, the late Qing scholar Yu Yue's residence was also the site of his personal library and the location where he often taught students between 1862 and 1908.

Xiling Seal Art Society – The gardens, halls, and shop for the Xiling Seal Art Society provide a garden-like place to rest and enjoy West Lake's history and scenery while learning more about seals and seal carving.

Tombs and Memorial Statues – Scattered across Solitary Island are a modest array of tomb sites, memorial statues and pavilions, and reminders of the former "temporary" imperial palace for the Kangxi and Qianlong Emperors' Southern Inspection Tours:

-   **Lin Bu's Tomb** – Burial site of the hermit-like literatus who claimed winter plum trees as his wife and pet cranes as his children.
-   **Lady Huixin's Tomb** – Honored burial site for the Manchu woman whose suicide after failing financially to sustain a new girls' school captivated the nation in the early 1900s and propelled the school of her vision into existence.
-   **Zhongshan Memorial Pavilion** – A pavilion built to honor Dr. Sun Yat-sen, first president in 1911 of the Republic of China and a patron of West Lake.
-   **Lu Xun Statue** – A bronze statue honors the extraordinary literary impact of Zhou Shouren (Lu Xun), a native of Shaoxing.
-   **Imperial Relics** – A pavilion and some architectural and garden relics from the Qing-era temporary imperial palace can be seen higher up on Solitary Hill.

Xiling Bridge Tombs – Three individuals are remembered and celebrated at or near the western exit from Solitary Island:

-   Revolutionary hero **Qiu Jin**'s pedestaled white statue marks the site of her final resting place at Xiling Bridge, just as she had wished before her death.
-   Fifth-Century poetess **Su Xiaoxiao**'s yellow-domed tomb beneath the Mucai 慕才 ("Admired Talent") pavilion also fulfills her poetic wish for eternal rest at Xiling Bridge. Unfortunately, she was never able to marry or be joined by the handsome object of her poetic love wish.
-   **Wu Song**, the fictional, tiger-killing hero from the classic novel, *Water Margin*, enjoys an elaborate tomb site with paved walkway in an area just northwest of Su Xiaoxiao's tomb.

Along Beishan Road (north side of lake)

West Lake Expo Museum – Located at No. 40, Beishan Road, in what was originally the Industrial Exposition Building in 1929, the West Lake Expo Museum offers an historic tour of early 20th-Century Hangzhou and communicates the flavor of the East/West, Chinese/Art Deco fusion adopted for the First Expo's architectural style.

Yue Fei's Tomb and Temple – Arguably one of West Lake's main tourist attractions (along with Leifeng Pagoda and Lingyin Temple), Yue Fei's temple complex is noteworthy for his tomb and that of his son Yue Yun, as well as for the caged, kneeling metal sculptures of Qin Hui, his wife, and two compatriots who helped engineer Yue's execution. The temple building and tomb that honor one of the Chinese nation's great patriots is located across Beishan Street, not far from the north end of Su Causeway.

Along Su Causeway

Flower Cove - Formerly the location of a court eunuch's private villa in the 13th Century, Flower Cove offers flowers, rockeries, and a famous fish pond. Marked by one of the Kangxi Emperor's inscribed stone steles, this site is marked as "Fish Viewing at Flower Cove" (花港观鱼, *Huagang guanyu*), one of the original Ten Views of West Lake.

Lin Huiyin Monument (in Huagang Park) – Unlike the usual sculpted stone and metal statuary typical of monuments to individuals, Lin Huiyin's metallic, two-dimensional, full-body profile honors China's modern poetess and first woman architect in a quiet and subdued manner perfectly suited to both her persona and the genteel beauty of West Lake. This is an excellent spot for some shaded rest, quiet lake viewing, and thoughtful contemplation.

Impressions West Lake – Conceived and produced by the acclaimed director Zhang Yimou, Impressions West Lake offers a spectacular nighttime presentation of Chinese music and dance using light, water, and West Lake itself as staging elements. The performance stage is actually set three centimeters below the lake's surface, making possible some extraordinary visual effects.

Quyuan Garden – Quyuan Garden, the former site of the Song Dynasty imperial brewery, is located near the northern end of Su Causeway. The park and lotus garden are reminiscent of the days when the summer breeze melded the fragrance of lotus flowers and brewer's yeast into a mixture that pleased multiple senses and earned it a place among the famous Ten Views of West Lake, "Summer Breeze Stirring Lotuses at Quyuan Garden" (曲院风荷, *Quyuan fenghe*).

West Lake's Southern and Eastern Shores

Leifeng Pagoda – Perhaps the most famous and most visited site at West Lake, the rebuilt Leifeng Pagoda soars over the southern shore. No visit to West Lake is complete without ascending this Hangzhou landmark, admiring the lake views, and enjoying the carved displays retelling the story of White Snake (Bai Suzhen) and her lover, Xu Xian.

Jingci Temple – Located across Nanshan Road from Leifeng Pagoda and readily visible from the pagoda's upper level walkways, Jingci Temple is second only to Lingyin Temple among Hangzhou's Buddhist monasteries. Jingci was once the residence of the beloved Mad Monk Ji Gong and the site of one of Ji Gong's legendary magical skills, drawing timber from a water well.

Zhejiang Art Museum – Located at 138 Nanshan Road, the museum offers a range of Chinese paintings and works of art in a modern, architecturally attractive setting.

King Qian's Temple – For all the fame granted to Bai Juyi and Su Shi (Su Dongpo) for their poetry and lake-crossing dikes, no two individuals in Hangzhou's history left a greater mark on West Lake's scenery and the city's welfare than Wuyue King Qian Liu (r. 923 – 932) and his grandson, King Qian Chu (r. 948 – 978). Constructing the Leifeng, Baochu, and Liuhe Pagodas, strengthening the seawalls against the raging tidal bore, promoting Buddhist religious practice, and protecting Hangzhou from harm during an era of political instability, these two kings are well remembered to this day by the citizens of Hangzhou. The King Qian memorial temple honors the reign's founder, King Qian Liu, and his four sons or grandsons who successfully guided Jiangnan's ship of state to safe harbor during sixty perilous years of dynastic uncertainty.

Pan Tianshou Memorial Hall – Pan Tianshou's former residence has expanded into a museum celebrating his life with works donated by his wife at the time of her death. The address is 212 Nanshan Road.

Map of Hangzhou City – Engraved in granite on the palisade along West Lake's eastern shore is a detailed, inscribed map of Hangzhou as it looked in 1892, replicated from a 1:400 scaled map produced by the Zhejiang Territorial Mapping Bureau at that time. The map is topographic and shows the city walls, the Wushan hills, the Imperial Way, and the inner-walled Manchu garrison.

West of West Lake (the Western Hills)

Lingyin Temple – Along with Yue Fei's tomb and Leifeng Pagoda, Lingyin Temple is the third of West Lake's "absolute must-see" sites. Not to be missed are the seemingly countless Buddhist statues and carvings that populate the nearby cliffsides as visitors progress along the creek-side path toward the temple grounds. At the temple itself, view the two ancient stone pagodas (similar to the White Pagoda near the Qiantang River), the main temple halls, the memorial hall to Mad Monk Ji Gong, and the Hall of Five Hundred Arhats (holy men).

Three Tianzhu Temples – Tianzhu Mountain 天竺山 hosts three richly historic Buddhist temples, named **Faxi Temple (法喜寺), Fajing Temple (法净寺) and Fajing Temple (法镜寺)** but colloquially known, respectively, as the Upper (上, Shang), Middle (中, Zhong), and Lower (下, Xia) Tianzhu Temples (天竺寺). They are located on a southwest-to-northeast line along Meiling North Road, running slightly to the east of the Lingyin Road to Lingyin Temple. Lower Tianzhu, founded in 330 CE, is the oldest of the three temples and is Hangzhou's only nunnery. Middle Tianzhu has operated since 597 CE, while Upper Tianzhu (Faxi Temple) is the largest of the three and the newest (yet still over one thousand years old).

Feilai Peak – The Peak Flown from Afar was so named by the Monk Huili in the 4th Century CE because its shape reminded him of a familiar mountain from his homeland in India. Situated alongside Lingyin Temple, Feilai Peak is renowned for its multiple caves and grottoes filled with more than three hundred Buddha statues and carvings dating back to the 10th to 14th Centuries.

Xinhai Revolutionary Martyrs Memorial and Tombs – Located southwest of West Lake along Longjing Road, the Xinhai Revolutionary Martyrs' Cemetery and Tombs (辛亥革命烈士墓群, Xinhai geming lieshi mu qun) contains the burial sites of heroes of the 1911 anti-Qing revolution that instituted the Republic of China: Xu Xilin, Chen Boping, and Ma Zonghan. The site includes a memorial plaza with statues of revolutionary martyrs, including that of Qiu Jin.

Yu Qian's Tomb – The memorial temple and tomb of Hangzhou native Yu Qian are located on Santaishan Road, southwest of West Lake. Yu is celebrated for his heroic defense of Beijing against the Mongols in 1449, for which he (like Yue Fei) was unfairly executed as a traitor.

China National Tea Museum – Located at 88 Longjing Road, a little north of the Revolutionary Martyrs' Tombs, the National Tea Museum offers extensive, English-friendly exhibits on the history and culture of tea production and tea drinking. Nicely situated among surrounding hills, the Tea Museum provides an educational introduction to the tea-producing villages and hills further west.

Longjing Village and Dragon Well Spring – Longjing Village and Dragon Well Spring are located southwest on Longjing Road on Phoenix Mountain (凤凰山, Fenghuangshan). Dragon Well Spring is situated east of picturesque Longjing Village, surrounded by tea plantations that give the hills a terraced appearance. Longjing Teahouse sits nearby, offering Longjing Tea brewed with the local spring water. An older Longjing Well, since closed, is also a few hundred meters away.

Hugong Temple - Site of Emperor Kangxi's famous Eighteen Emperor's Tea Trees (the fenced-off Imperial Tea Garden), Hugong Temple 胡公庙 is located on Shifeng Mountain, west of Longjing Village along Longjing West Road.

Meijiawu Tea Cultural Village – Brought to greater public notice by former premier Zhou Enlai, Meijiawu Tea Plantation and Meijiawu Tea Village (梅家坞茶村 (Meijiawu cha cun) on Meiling Road have become the cultural and tourist center of Hangzhou's Longjing Tea industry. Visitors can experience all aspects of tea production, from planting and harvesting tea leaves from the surrounding plantations to its dry-heat processing and, of course, tea drinking appreciation in one of the many local teahouses.

"Nine Streams in Misty Forest" – One of the New Ten Views of West Lake, Nine Creeks in Misty Forest is a favorite, three-mile nature trail for families with children. The nature trail runs north-south through the western hills and provides opportunities to enjoy seasonal woodland colors, Longjing tea plantations, and the year-round creeks, pools, and waterfalls.

Hupao Temple ("Dreaming of Tiger Spring") – Yet another of the New Ten Views in West Lake's western hills, Hupao Temple celebrates the spring-water legend of Monk Xingkong with its statues of the dreaming monk and the wild tigers who revealed the spring. The temple buildings include a teahouse, a hall of five hundred holy men (arhats), an exhibition hall relating the story of Running Tiger Spring, and a memorial hall for Mad Monk Ji Gong. Hupao Temple is also the tomb and stupa site of Monk Hongyi (Li Shutong), teacher of Feng Zikai. The temple is located at 39 Hupao Road.

Hangzhou Zoo – Located off Hupao Road in the forested western hills of West Lake (north of Liuhe Pagoda and the White Pagoda Park), the Hangzhou Zoo covers about fifty acres and includes a full range of species, from giant pandas and South China tigers to Asian elephants and lots of monkeys. Many of the buildings are constructed in Chinese style, including the classic Jiangnan architectural standard of white walls with black tile roofs.

Xiaobaihua Yue Opera Theater – Opened to the public in 2019, the new Yue Opera Theater is instantly recognizable by its giant, butterfly-shaped entrance and the "world's largest butterfly" hovering horizontally over the roof. The theater is located at the north foot of Beigao (Northern) Peak, at No. 59 Shuguang Road. Lingyin Temple is located on the hill's south side.

Hangzhou Ancient City Area

This section begins with sites of interest located within the boundaries of the ancient city walls, followed by sites in Hangzhou's northern and southern suburbs.

Wu Hill (Wushan) – Although City God's Temple is the most obvious and easily seen attraction on Wushan, the well-forested hills provide for pleasant walks, photogenic views over West Lake, and opportunities for wandering some less-traveled paths and enjoying less-seen sites. Ascending Wushan on Liangdaoshan from its intersection with Hefang Street, one encounters:

- **Hangzhou Museum** – Opened in 2001 as the Hangzhou History Museum, the present Hangzhou Museum (upgraded in 2012) offers exhibitions related to various cultural elements of Hangzhou, including jades and ceramics, paintings, seals, books, and calligraphy, and coins and postage stamps. Many of the ancient relics were unearthed by archaeological excavations in the ancient city and surrounding area and date back to Neolithic times and the Warring States period.
-- **City God's Temple** – Chenghuang Miao, Hangzhou's City God's Pavilion, is located at the nicely shaded peak of Wu Hill. The temple building rises seven stories above the peak, granting visitors panoramic, camera-worthy views of West Lake to the north, Leifeng Pagoda and the hills to the west, and Hangzhou City to the east. The temple is dedicated to Zhou Xin, designated the

City God in 1405 during the early years of the Ming Dynasty.

- **Twelve Zodiac Animals Stone** – An interesting diversion on Wushan is the in-ground rock configuration in which some claim to see images of all twelve of the Chinese Zodiac animals. In 1728, Governor Li Wei built a pavilion alongside the rocks for people to rest and employ their creative imagination to identify each of the zodiac animal figures.
- **Ruan Yuan Temple** – A former nunnery was transformed in 1880 into a memorial temple dedicated to Ruan Yuan 阮元 (1764 – 1849), Education Commissioner and then Governor of Zhejiang. It was Ruan whose West Lake dredging project resulted in the creation of Master Ruan's Island, the most recent (in 1800) man-made island constructed on West Lake.
- **Stone Memorial to Guan Hanqing** – Regarded as one of the Yuan Dynasty's greatest playwrights, Guan Hanqing 关汉卿 (1209 - 1301) visited Hangzhou after Lin'an's fall to the Mongols and wrote of the city's scenic beauty. A prolific dramatist and song writer, Guan melded storytelling and singing into the early dramatic form known as *zaju* 杂剧, out of which evolved the later dramatic and operatic forms such as Yue Opera, Peking Opera, and Kunqu Opera.
- **Shennong Daoist Temple** – A temple dating from the Song Dynasty dedicated to the God of Medicine.
- **Zhongxing Dongyue Temple** - Dedicated to Dongyue 东岳, the revered Daoist god of Mount Tai in distant Shandong Province, Dongyue Temple was first constructed in the Song Dynasty and rebuilt in the Ming era. The hall displays a colorful relief carving of Dongyue astride his heavenly cloud, complete with longevity symbols and elixirs. One of the columns for the main hall is made of stone carved in the design of a spiraling dragon. The grounds contain two impressively ancient Mongolian catalpa trees leaning toward one another.
- **Wugong Temple of Wu Zixu** – A well-maintained temple honoring Wu Zixu, military advisor to Wu King Fuchai during the Warring States period who was acclaimed God of the Tides after the King ordered his death by suicide. Multiple displays in the temple halls illustrate Wu Zixu's involvement in the famous conflict between the Wu and Yue States in the 6th Century BCE.
- **Wansong Academy** – Wansong ("Myriad Pines") Academy (万松书院, Wansong shuyuan) was the site of one of Zhejiang's premier educational institutions in the Ming Dynasty era. Founded in 1498, the academy was named in allusion to a line in Bai Juyi's poem "Return at Evening" in which the poet described a long, moonlit beach and a hillside blanketed by thousands of pine trees. The location serves today primarily as a peaceful memorial commemorating the Academy's rich intellectual history along with the romance story of Zhu Yingtai and Liang Shanbo, the legendary "Butterfly Lovers." It is located at 81 Wansongling Road, on the southern side of the Wushan Mountain range.

Hefang Street – Also called Qinghefang Street for its Qing Dynasty architecture and its stores dating to that era, Hefang Street occupies Hangzhou's centuries-old market area at the foot of Wushan, near the site of the former Song Dynasty imperial palaces. In the modern era, car-free Hefang Street is a popular night market that celebrates the city's history and some of its oldest trades: pharmacies for Chinese medicinal herbs and shops featuring fans, umbrellas, teas, and ceramics. For more modern tastes, there are also restaurants, teahouses, bubble tea shops, and a kitschy giant, gold-colored, big-bellied Maitreya Buddha statue to welcome visitors at the street's western end.

Hu Qingyu Pharmacy and Museum – Founded in the late 1800s by the millionaire banker Hu Xueyan, Hu Qingyu Tang pharmacy opened in 1874 to nearly instant success and national fame for its promise of quality, fair prices, and customer service. The ground floor of the building still operates as a retailer of Chinese traditional medicines and as part of the overall Museum of Traditional Chinese Medicine (TCM). The rest of the Museum includes exhibitions on the history of TCM and preparation of TCM medicines as well as TCM health care and diet advisory clinics. Just look for the building emblazoned with its name in the largest Chinese characters imaginable.

Hu Xueyan Former Residence – Built in 1872 and occupying a huge lot of prime Hangzhou city real estate just south and east of Hefang Street, Hu Xueyan's former residence is truly a "must see," especially for anyone who has never visited a Suzhou or Yangzhou garden residence. The residence buildings illustrate the best of late Qing design and décor, including such westernizing elements as stained glass, large mirrors, and a basement, while the exterior grounds feature the most extravagant aspects of Jiangnan garden design. Hu Xueyan's residence represents the "modern mindset" of late Qing culture, executed by a merchant who could afford the best of everything in his time.

Hangzhou Confucius Temple – Located at No. 8 Fuxue Lane near Laodong Road, Hangzhou Confucius Temple (杭州孔庙, Hangzhou kongmiao) was the site of the Lin'an Prefectural School, built during the first years of the Southern Song Dynasty. In the modern era, the Confucius Temple serves primarily as a library of inscribed stones, preserving hundreds of engraved steles with historical records, imperial inscriptions, astronomical maps, water conservancy records, and copies of calligraphy from such masters as Wang Xizhi, Su Shi, Mi Fu, and Zhu Yunming.

Phoenix Mosque – Located north from Wushan along the old Imperial Way, now called Zhongshan Middle Road, is the Phoenix Mosque. Originally constructed during the Tang Dynasty (618 – 907) but largely destroyed during the Song Dynasty, the mosque was rebuilt with the financial support of Ala al-Din in 1281 and enlarged during the Ming Dynasty. Phoenix Mosque is regarded as one of the four major ancient houses of Islamic worship in China.[1] About half the size now than it was in earlier times, the mosque houses historically valuable steles documenting its own history along with nearly two dozen tombstones from the Yuan-era Moslem community's cemetery discovered during excavations near West Lake.

Cathedral of Our Lady of the Immaculate Conception – Referred to locally as simply "the Catholic Church" (天主堂, Tianzhu tang), Martino Martini's and Prospero Intorcetta's Romanesque church was constructed in 1659 and continues operation to the present day. It is located near the Tianshui Qiao (天水桥, Heavenly Water Bridge) at 415 Zhongshan North Road. Major restoration work over the summer of 2009 included refurbishment of the cathedral and installation of a new set of stained-glass windows.

Tianshui Christian Church - Slightly north of the Cathedral on Yesutang Long (耶稣堂弄, Church of Jesus Lane) is the Tianshui Christian Church, founded on that site in 1860 by M.H. Houston and Ben Helm after they gave up their chapel's first location on Wushan Hill. Tianshui Christian Church was largely built by John Linton Stuart, father of John Leighton Stuart.

Former Residence John Leighton Stuart – This two-story residence, built by Christian missionary John Linton Stuart and childhood home of John Leighton Stuart, is located alongside the Tianshui Christian Church.

Ma Yinchu Memorial Hall – Native of Shaoxing, former president of Zhejiang University and Peking University, and proponent of population controls in China that led to the "One-Child Policy," Ma Yingfu's memorial hall is located at 210 Qingchun Road, Xiacheng District, Hangzhou, several blocks east of the former site of Qiantang Gate.

Former Residence of Yu Dafu – Known as Fengyu Maolu 风雨茅庐 (Humble Shelter from the Elements), Yu Dafu designed and built this residence in 1936 for his wife Wang Yingxia. Prior to the Japanese occupation, Yu's home contained a library numbering over 9,000 volumes, all lost to the war. The residence is located at No. 63 Guanchang Lane.

Zhejiang Museum of Natural History – Established at the Wulin Cultural Square in 1984, the Zhejiang Museum of Natural History maintains over 200,000 natural science specimens focused on paleontology, geology, and ecology. A second, larger branch of the Museum opened northwest of Hangzhou in late 2018 at 1 Meiyuan Road, near the Zhongnan Baicao (Botanical) Garden, Anji County (Huzhou Prefecture).

Seawall Museum – The Museum of Seawall Site of Hangzhou is located at 109 Jiumu Road. Opened in January 2020, the museum was built on the site of an archaeological excavation and illustrates with models and other visuals the various ways (such as stone-filled gabions and overlapping, "fish-scale" walls) government officials of past centuries attempted to shelter the city and populace from the Qiantang River tidal bore.

City Walls Museum – Hangzhou's City Walls Museum, the Guchengqiang 古城墙Exhibition Hall, is located at the former site of the Qingchun Gate (庆春门).

One of the eastern wall gates of the Southern Song era, Qingchunmen was also known as Dongqingmen东青门 Gate. The City Walls Museum gives visitors a sense of what it was like to live in a city surrounded by massive stone walls 20 – 30 feet high.

Greater Hangzhou - South

China National Silk Museum – Founded in 1992 and since renovated and expanded, the China National Silk Museum presents the history and technology of Chinese silk in a gorgeous natural and architectural setting. Located on Yuhuangshan (Jade Phoenix Hill) Road about halfway between Leifeng Temple and Eight Trigrams field, this complex is both an English-friendly museum and an educational center for sericulture and silk production and use from ancient times to the modern era.[2]

Eight Trigrams Field – The cultivated octagonal field of the *bagua* 八卦, the eight trigrams of the *I Ching (Book of Changes)*, offers one of Hangzhou's most unusual and memorable sites. Located on the south side of Jade Phoenix Hill, not far from the Qiantang River, this multi-colored plot of about one-third acre (14,350 square feet) is divided into eight wedge-shaped sections around a central *yin-yang* symbol. Each section was traditionally planted with a different grain or crop: wheat, barley, rice, millet, soybean, red bean, and the like. In modern times, Eight Trigrams is both a brilliant, multi-colored agricultural garden as well as a reminder of the Southern Song Dynasty times when the Emperor came to this field each year to offer sacrifices for a plentiful harvest.

Southern Song Dynasty Guan Kiln Museum – Located on Nanfu Road just east of Eight Trigrams Field, the Southern Song Kiln Museum stands on the site of an ancient kiln for producing pottery and porcelains. Opened in 1992 and expanded in 2002, the Kiln Museum contains exhibits of ancient works of fine porcelain and ceramics, some of them the results of archaeological excavation in the Hangzhou area. One section of the Museum also preserves elements of the original kiln structure dating back to the 1100s and 1200s.

Fengshan Water Gate - Located near the junction of Zhongshan South Road and Zhonghe South Road, the Fengshan Water Gate across the Zhonghe River is the only remaining relic of Hangzhou's ancient city walls and gates. Classified as a National Cultural Heritage site in 2006 following its renovation in 1983 (and again in 2010), the parallel twin arched entrances are now also elements of the UNESCO World Heritage Grand Canal network. Fengshan Gate thereby joined Panmen Gate in Suzhou as the only two such water gates to be so recognized and incorporated into the Grand Canal's World Heritage network.

Zhakou White Pagoda – White Pagoda Park (白塔公园, Baita gongyuan) is located below the southern base of Phoenix (Fenghuang) Hill. Built as a navigation marker during the Wuyue Era (907 – 960) at the confluence of the Grand Canal

543

with the Qiantang River, the ancient White Pagoda features an octagonal design with scriptural engravings and Buddha and Bodhisattva figures, with mountain and wave carvings on the base to symbolize "Nine Mountains and Eight Seas." White Pagoda Park celebrates some of the earliest guide maps known to China and also serves as an "outdoor museum" for Hangzhou's first rail line, the 16-kilometer Jiangshu line running along the eastern city wall from the Grand Canal terminus at Gongchen Bridge to the Zhakou river port.

Liuhe Pagoda – The thirteen-story Six Harmonies Pagoda rises majestically over the northern banks of the Qiantang River, just west of the double-decker Qiantang River Bridge. Built in around 970 by Wuyue King Qianchu, the original seven-story stone pagoda was built as a navigational aid and also with the metaphysical intent of calming the tidal waters. A climb to the pagoda's highest floor provides a great view of the river, bridge, and the surrounding hills. Along the way up or down through the pagoda, visitors can enjoy the pagoda's decorative interior work.

Zhijiang Campus, Zhejiang University – The Zhijiang Campus of Zhejiang University, located southwest of the city along the Qiantang River on Zhijiang Road (a little beyond the Liuhe Pagoda), is the site of the former Hangzhou Christian College and still preserves many of its early 20th-Century buildings.

Song Dynasty Town – Song Dynasty Town is located along Zhijiang Road beyond the Zhijiang Campus, near the great southeastern turn of the Qiantang River toward its junction with the Fuchun and Puyang Rivers. Built in 1997 after the style of Zhang Zeduan's painting "Along the River during the Qingming Festival," the town is a replica and theme park representing the early history, culture, and daily life of Lin'an, as Hangzhou was called during its 150 years as the imperial capital of China. Song Dynasty Town offers multiple types of cultural and children's performance as well as seasonal folk activities and two haunted houses with connections to Southern Song Dynasty mystery/horror tales.

Tidal Bore Sculptures – Binjiang District features two oversized metal sculptures along the southern bank of the Qiantang River, both related to myths of taming the waters of the tidal bore. One statue features a mounted King Qian Liu shooting arrows at the tidal bore wave in opposition to Wu Zixu, the presumed water god driving the bore upriver. The second sculpture represents an even more foundational myth about the dragon beneath the river, as sometimes depicted in the legend of the famous Dragon Well (龙井, Longjing) in West Lake's western hills.

Greater Hangzhou - North

Xixi Wetland Park and Museum – Located opposite the "back side" of the northern hills above West Lake, Xixi National Wetland Park (西溪国家湿地公园, Xixi guojia shidi gongyuan) was first opened to the public in 2005. Covering four square miles, Xixi is unusually large for an urban wetlands district and is distinctive for its integration of urban, agricultural, environmental, and historical/cultural elements. Once a retreat area for Buddhist nunneries and literati recluses (and conjectured as the site of Hangzhou's first-ever performance of Shaoxing Yue Opera), it is now a place for ecological education, Nature appreciation, and even bird-watching. The Xixi Wetland Museum was the first such institution in China when it was founded in 2009. In addition to its wetlands-related exhibitions, the Museum also has a hundred-foot-high observation tower from which to view the entire park. The Wetland Park is located off of Tianmushan Road.[3]

Jesuit Cemetery – The protected remnants of this Jesuit cemetery founded in the 17th Century celebrate the lives of Martino Martini, Prospero Intorcetta, and other Christians who not only brought their religion to China but helped educate the Europeans of their time about the history, culture, and geography of China. The cemetery is located on Xixi Road at the foot of Beigao Peak (北高峰, Beigao feng), just south of the Xixi Wetlands area and next to the Xihu Brewery. An inscribed archway (牌楼, *pailou*) opens onto a memorial walkway (神道, *shendao*, "spirit walk") leading to the crypt. Access needs to be arranged in advance, best accomplished through the Cathedral of the Immaculate Conception.

Gongchen Bridge and Qiaoxi Historical Block – The area around the three-arched Gongchen Bridge served in the Ming and Qing Dynasties as an inland domestic port for Grand Canal transport to and from Hangzhou. The area has been revitalized in the past few decades for a mix of residential, light industrial, and historical/cultural uses. Aside from viewing or taking a boat ride on the Grand Canal, there are several cultural museums in the area immediately west of the bridge that celebrate manufactured products for which the city has long been famous:

- China Fan Museum
- China Umbrella Museum
- Knife, Scissors and Sword Museum
- Museum of Applied Arts
- Handicraft Dynamic Exhibition Museum

In addition, the China Grand Canal Museum is located nearby on the opposite side of the Gongchen Bridge.

Liangzhu Museum – Located in Liangzhu Town, about 15 miles northwest of Hangzhou, the Liangzhu Museum provides an attractively modern, highly informative, and English-friendly view of the Neolithic Liangzhu culture and the archaeological field work and research that revolutionized China's understanding of the birth and development of its ancient civilizations and cultures.

Liangzhu Archaeological Excavation at Pingyao Town – Liangzhu and nearby Pingyao were among the first towns where relics of the Liangzhu culture were systematically discovered and identified.

Hangzhou Regional Cities and Sites

Shaoxing

Lu Xun Village – Arguably the most visited of Shaoxing's historical tourist sites, Lu Xun Village is a museum and park complex that celebrates his life from childhood to his death. The village includes his restored childhood home, the room in which he studied as a youth, a pictorial exhibition that traces the events of his life, and a flower-filled garden where he wandered as a youth.

Shen Garden – Located just a short distance southeast of Lu Xun Village, Shen Garden is remembered for the famed romantic encounter of Lu You and Tan Yang, childhood sweethearts who married only to be forced by Lu's mother into a divorce. The result of this encounter were two poems referred to together as "The Phoenix Hairpin," the first written by Lu You on the garden wall and the second written similarly, in response, by Tan Yang. The garden area is attractive in its own right and offers interesting Song Dynasty historical perspective with its Lu You Memorial Hall.

Qiu Jin Former Residence – Located at No. 35 Hechangtang Road (west of Jiefang South Road), Qiu Jin's former residence not only illustrates late 19th-Century urban residential life but also contains an extensive display of period photographs of Qiu Jin and the people with whom she associated.

Qiu Jin Martyr's Monument – The site of Qiu Jin's execution in 1907 is marked by a monument located at the intersection of Fushan Street and Jiefang North Road, east of Fushan Hill. At the base of the monument is a white stone statue of Qiu Jin.

Calligraphy Sage Historic Site – While Lu Xun Village attracts the largest crowds, another area to its north is also rich in local and national history. Referred to by the entrance sign as the Calligraphy Sage Historic Village, this nearly one-square-kilometer neighborhood boasts the former residences of the great calligraphy master Wang Xizhi and the father of modern Chinese education, Cai Yuanpei. Strolling through an area of quiet, narrow lanes, bridge-spanning canals, and traditional Chinese residences and shops of old Shaoxing, visitors encounter the reputed Ink Pond where Wang Xizhi is said to have washed so many brushes that the water turned black, an exhibition hall of Wang Xizhi's calligraphy, Shaoxing wine shops, and the former residence of Cai Yuanpei with a picture-filled exhibition hall. The area is contained within the space bordered by Zhongxing Road on the east, Jiefang Road on the west, Huancheng Road on the north, and Shengli Road on the south. It is north of Lu Xun Village tourism area; head north on Jiefang Road from the Qiu Jin Martyr's Monument.

Greater Shaoxing

Yu the Great Temple and Tomb at Kuaiji Mountain – Located a short way south of Shaoxing's city area at Kuaiji Mountain 会稽山, Yu the Great's Mausoleum and Temple is a fascinating historical site. In 2020, the long memorial walkway, tomb, and temple were joined by a new memorial hall.[4] Despite the summer heat, the staircase climb up the hill to the colossal Da Yu statue that towers over the mountain is well worth the effort.

Lanting Pavilion Scenic Area – Heading southwest of Shaoxing City for about fourteen kilometers (about 8.5 miles) on Highway S308, visitors will find Lanting Town 兰亭镇 and the Lanting Scenic Spot, host to what is represented as the site that inspired Wang Xizhi's famous preface to twenty-six poems written by his guests on a single spring outing at Lanting (Orchid) Pavilion. Regardless whether the current site is historically precise, the rural mountain atmosphere, running brook, and restored pavilion create an atmosphere where the legendary events can be easily imagined.

Lu Xun Village – Keyan Resort, northwest of Shaoxing City following Highway G104, features a theme park called Luzhen (Lu Town), modeled on the fictional setting of the same name in Lu Xun's story "Kong Yiji," published in *New Youth* magazine in April 1919. Lu Xun set several of his subsequent stories in Luzhen. The modern version of the town includes statues, named shops from various of his stories, and individual persons dressed and performing as fictional characters from Lu's stories.[5]

Jiaxing

South Lake – The main attractions at Jiaxing's South Lake begin with the Mid-Lake Island. The island features the Pavilion of Mist and Rain, fronted by gingko trees whose leaves turn brilliant yellow in Fall. Anchored in the waters nearby is the Red Boat, constructed in the manner of the lake boat upon which the early leaders of the communist movement completed their work of founding the Chinese Communist Party in 1921.[6]

Revolutionary Memorial Hall – Positioned on the Mid-Lake Island from 1959 – 1990, the Revolutionary Memorial Hall was relocated in 1991 to South Lake's eastern shore. The hall serves as a museum dedicated to the founding of the Chinese Communist Party.

Wuzhen Water Town – Located in the Tongxiang City area of Jiaxing Prefecture, Wuzhen is one of Jiangnan's premier water towns. With over six thousand years of history, the village of Wuzhen deftly illustrates the canal town lifestyle, from its classically white-walled, black-tile-roofed residences to its arched bridges and traditional shops. For a unique cultural learning experience, visit the Chinese Foot

547

Binding Culture Museum or the blue calico cloth dyeing houses, a product for which Wuzhen is also famous. Curiously for such a traditional town, Wuzhen hosted the first World Internet Conference in 2014 and every such annual conference since, welcoming such visitors as Xi Jinping and Alibaba's Jack Ma in 2015 and Apple's Steve Cook in 2017.[7]

Mao Dun's Former Residence – Renovated and opened to the public in 1985, the Mao Dun Museum incorporates both his family residence as well as the former school (Lizhi Shuyuan) where he received his early education.

Xitang Water Town – Dating back to the Warring States period (770 – 476 BCE) and marking the boundary between the Wu and Yue States, Xitang is a classic Jiangnan water town. The quiet village contains residences and buildings dating from both the Ming and Qing Dynasties and is criss-crossed with canals and ancient bridges. Although Xitang is famous among Chinese people for its kilometer-long covered walkway, Westerners may know Xitang better as the location where Tom Cruise filmed portions of *Mission Impossible III*. Regardless, Xitang is an excellent example of the centuries-old atmosphere of Jiangnan, where canals were at least as important as roads for transportation and commerce and where residences backing onto canals was the norm.

Haining Tidal Bore Viewing – Since the time of the Kangxi and Qianlong Emperors in the 17th and 18th Centuries, Haining has been considered the premier locale for viewing the Qiantang River tidal bore. In modern times, this practice has crystallized into the annual Tidal Bore Watching Festival, celebrated on the eighteenth day of the eighth lunar month in Yanguan Town's Tide Viewing Park (观潮胜地公园, *Guanchao Shengdi Gongyuan*). Visitors to Haining's Yanguan Town also take in the Ming/Qing Culture Street as well as the renowned Chen Family Residence so often visited by Qianlong.

Xu Zhimo's Former Residence – Built by Xu Zhimo's father in 1926 for his newly-wedded son and bride, this Republican-era residence was a modern mansion in its time. It was said that Xu Zhimo did much of the decorative design himself and referred to this home as his "love nest." The house is now the Xu Zhimo Museum, located at 38 Ganhe Street, Xiashi Town, Haining.

Huzhou

Brush Museum – The China Hubi (Huzhou Writing Brush) Museum (中国湖笔博物馆) celebrates the premier tools of Chinese calligraphy: the Huzhou brush, Hui ink, Xuan paper, and the Duan ink slab. Opened in 2010 on Lianhuazhuang Road, Wuxing District, the museum traces the history of ink brush development, demonstrates the production process, and displays the calligraphy of past masters and famous practitioners of the art, including works by Zhao Mengfu of the Yuan Dynasty.[8]

Zhao Mengfu – The former residence and garden of Zhao Mengfu has been transformed into a museum and opened to the public in 2001. It is located along with the Brush Museum at the Lianhuazhuang Park area, 258 Lianhuazhuang Road. Zhao and his wife Guan Daosheng are buried at their country home in Dongsheng Village 东升村, due south of Huzhou and northeast of Deqing Town, east of Dongtiao Brook.

Nanxun Water Town – Located east of Huzhou and bordering Suzhou Prefecture, Nanxun water town was a silk center populated by a number of wealthy families with their large residences and ornate gardens. In addition to its historical museum, Nanxun preserves the mansion residences of the Liu and Zhang families, including that of Zhang Jingjiang. Some of these buildings demonstrate elements of both Chinese and Western design and décor. Shanlian Town in Nanxun District is also home to the Shuangyi Hubi Factory, renowned manufacturers of the finest ink brushes in China.

Moganshan – One of China's most famous summer mountain resort areas, first developed by heat-escaping Westerners in the late 19th Century, Moganshan is only thirty-five miles northwest of Hangzhou and about twenty-five miles southwest of Huzhou in Deqing County. Moganshan is famous for its clear air, scenic hills, lush bamboo forests, and numerous vacation villas and resorts. The area is rich in late-Qing and early modern history, reflected in the style of many of the area's older villas. The name Mogan is said to derive from the renowned sword-making husband and wife Moye and Ganjiang, who fashioned swords of extraordinary quality and strength there for the King of Wu during the time of the Wu-Yue conflict (see Chapter 2).

Other

Anji Bamboo Forest – About forty miles northwest of Hangzhou is the natural environment of Anji Bamboo Forest, at 230 square miles one of the largest such forests in the world. The forest contains about forty different species of bamboo, while the Anji Bamboo Expo Park museum and exhibition presents nearly four hundred species. The forest also features a Panda Garden and a tower from which one can look down over what is called the "Sea of Bamboo." Anji Bamboo Forest achieved a new level of international fame and awareness after it served as the film site for the bamboo forest fighting scenes in Ang Lee's *Crouching Tiger, Hidden Dragon*. Anji White Tea (安吉白茶, *Anji bai cha*) is one of China's fine teas and is often priced higher than Dragon Well Tea, due in part to its relative scarcity.

Kuahuqiao Museum – The boat-shaped Kuahuqiao Museum is located at the site of the original archaeological excavations on the shore of Xiang Lake in Xiaoshan. Opened in 2009, the museum exhibits artifacts from the 8,000-year-old Kuahuqiao Culture, explains discoveries about the lives of those ancient people, and preserves the excavation site.

Jinhua Hams and Flowers – At ninety miles distance southwest from Hangzhou, Jinhua is a historical city famous for its city flower, the camellia, and especially beloved for its ancient art of producing cured ham. Unavailable for export outside of China, Jinhua's dry-cured hams are the product of over one thousand years of processing experience. Visitors to Jinhua can learn about the locally produced hams at the Chinese Ham Exhibition Hall.[9] A new China Camellia Museum also opened in Spring 2021 at the Camellia Culture Park.

Yiwu and Hengdian World Studios – Yiwu, about seventy miles south of Hangzhou, offers an "off the beaten track" trip to see the modern world center of small commodities. Just a few miles further southwest of Yiwu, however, visitors can see China's cinematic answer to Hollywood, the Hengdian World Studios. Visitors to Hengdian can tour a number of different thematic film production studios and sets with such names as Ming and Qing Palace Area, Chinese Cultural Garden, Buddhist Temple, Hong Kong Street, Riverside Scene, and Fantasy Valley.

Quzhou Confucius Temple – Rather more distant (120 miles) southwest of Hangzhou, Quzhou is home to the southern branch of the Kong family clan, the descendants of the philosopher known as Kongzi, or as Confucius in the West. The temple was first constructed in around 1255 at the direction of Emperor Lizong as a religious home for the southern branch of the Kong clan who departed Shandong Province to escape the Jurchen Jin invaders. The temple buildings have undergone multiple renovations and rebuilding over the centuries, the most recent at Xinqiao Street in 2005.

END NOTES

Epigram

1. Bai Juyi, from Sun Xiaoxing (1994), p. 26.
2. Tang Wei (2010), p. 94.
3. Yang (2011), p. 25. This line was written for Nixon by speech writer Raymond Price – see Footnote No. 95, p. 42.

Introduction

1. There are a number of translations for this sentiment from Su Shi. This one is from Grimes (1983), p. 28.
2. Marco Polo (1993), p. 185.
3. Shanghai first became the center of a new Shanghai County in 1291 when five villages were consolidated into one administrative unit. Through the Ming and Qing eras, Shanghai remained a sub-unit of Songjiang Prefecture. Songjiang remained part of Jiangsu Province until 1958 when it was ceded to Shanghai Municipality.
4. See, for example, Xu Lin, "Most Popular Domestic and Overseas Destinations in 2019," *Chinadaily.com.cn* (January 28, 2019), accessed at http://www.chinadaily.com.cn/a/201901/28/WS5c4e9c-5ca3106c65c34e6da6.html, or Fan Junmei, "Top 10 Tourism Cities on Chinese Mainland," *China.org.cn* (July 18, 2017), accessed at http://www.china.org.cn/top10/2017-07/18/content_41228041_3.htm.
5. The official Chinese name for the Yangzi River is Changjiang, meaning "long river." The Yangzi divides Jiangsu Province into two parts. North of the river is the Subei; south of the river, the Sunan. The Sunan, along with Shanghai and the plains area of Zhejiang Province north of the Qiantang River are generally regarded as Jiangnan.
6. Zhejiang ranks 25th in size, constituting just 1.06% of China's land mass and exceeding in size only Ninxia, a handful of stand-alone city municipalities (Beijing, Tianjin, Shanghai, Chongqing, and Chengdu) and the islands of Hong Kong, Macao, and Hainan.
7. "Zhejiang Among Top 10 Chinese Provincial Regions with Strongest GDP in 2020," *Zhejiang China* website, accessed at http://www.ezhejiang.gov.cn/2021-02/10/c_589414_2.htm.
8. See "Zhejiang's GDP Up 3.6% in 2020, *China.org.cn* (January 26, 2021), accessed at https://www.chinadaily.com.cn/a/202101/26/WS600fbb2aa31024ad0baa5327.html for Zhejiang Province data, and "List of U.S. States and Territories by GDP," accessed at https://en.wikipedia.org/wiki/List_of_U.S._states_and_territories_by_GDP for ranked listing by State.
9. From https://en.wikipedia.org/wiki/List_of_Chinese_prefecture-level_cities_by_GDP , using the 2020 annual average exchange rate of 6.8974 RMB = $1 US.

10. See "List of U.S. States and Territories by GDP," accessed at https://en.wikipedia.org/wiki/List_of_U.S._states_and_territories_by_GDP for ranked listing by State.

11. For example, on the "36 West Lakes," see Martin Williams, "China Weekend Break: Huizhou Lake District's Rich History and Idyllic Walks Make for a Relaxing Trip," *South China Morning Post* (December 1, 2018), accessed at https://www.scmp.com/lifestyle/travel-leisure/article/2175760/china-weekend-break-huizhou-lake-districts-rich-history-and. Williams identifies Huizhou's West Lake (Guangdong Province) and Yingzhou's West Lake (Anhui Province) as being the other two of China's three famous West Lakes.

Author's Note

1. Leys (1977), p. 95.

Chapter 1

1. Fang Qin (2008), pp. 114 – 115. Qianlong identified his imperial river boat by its Chinese name, *Jiang shan chuan*, "River and Mountain Boat."

2. Fuxi's sister Nüwa was said to be the inventor of marriage and musical instruments.

3. Marshall (2001), p. 145. Also Goddard (1948), p. 94.

4. Cui Maoxin and Song Dongyang (2011) identify the mountain as Maoshan, p. 123.

5. See Doar (2007), accessed at http://www.chinaheritagequarterly.org/articles.php?searchterm=009_deluge.inc&issue=009.

6. Confirmation bias is the tendency to search for, interpret, prefer, and recall information that aligns with and supports one's already existing beliefs and values and to discount or reject information conflicting with those beliefs.

7. Zhou Ying (2007), p. 22, identifies Liangzhu sites northwest of Hangzhou at or near Gudang, Jianqiao, Sandun, Cangqian, Yuhang, Jingshan, Pingyao, Liangzhu, Renhe, and Chongxian.

8. For a map and list of specific sites and descriptions (in dual Chinese and English) in each region, see Zhou Ying (2007), pp. 217 – 227.

9. Qin Ling (2013), p. 577. See also the "Description" section of the UNESCO World Heritage tentative list submission for the Liangzhu Neolithic Cultural Site, accessed at http://whc.unesco.org/en/tentativelists/5805/.

10. Wang Mi (2018), p. 20.

11. Sun Guoping (2013), p. 560.

12. The past 75-plus years of Yangzi Delta archaeology has revealed an extensive geographic and temporal web of ancient cultures and sites far too complex for discussion here. A good starting point for deeper, non-technical exploration are the articles in Part VII, "The Lower Yangzi River Region" of Underhill (2013), pp. 535 – 596.

13. For more on the Kuahuqiao Culture, see Innes, et. al. (2010), or Jiang Leping (2013), pp. 537 – 554.

14. Wang Mi (2018), p. 74.

15. Yang Xiaoneng (1999), p. 117.

16. Sun Zhixin (1993), p. 14.

17. Zhou Ying (2007), pp. 7, 15.

18. Xu Zhuoyun (2012), Chapter 1.

19. Zhou Ying (2017), p. 27.

20. Ibid., p. 27. Zhou cites Wang Zunguo, "Searching for the Source of Chinese Civilization and Liangzhu Culture," in *Messages on Liangzhuology*, 2002; and Su Bingqi, "The Historical Status of the Liangzhu Culture: In Memory of the 60th Anniversary of the Discovery of the Liangzhu Sites," in Committee of Cultural and Historical Data under Yuhang CPPCC, *Dawn of Civilization:*

Liangzhu Culture (Hangzhou: Zhejiang People's Press, 1996).

21. Lu Yan, "Traces of Time," *Beijing Review*, Vol. 65, No. 29 (July 21, 2022), p. 17.

22. Zhang Haiwei, et. al. (2021).

23. See, for example, Berry (2015), which describes the River Severn bore in Bristol, UK, that experiences tidal bores about fifty times out of each year's 730 tides.

24. For detailed discussion of the geomorphology of Hangzhou Bay, see Chen Jiyu (1990), pp. 559 – 572.

25. Kahler (1905), p. 7. G.T. Moule (1921) noted that changes in Hangzhou Bay's sand deposits could prevent the bore from performing for years at a time, citing non-occurrences from 1841 to 1845 as one such instance.

26. "Zhou Mi 周密 (1232 – 1298)," in Mair (1994), pp. 623 – 624.

27. Barmé (2011B).

28. George F. Fitch, "A Visit to the Hangchow Bore," *The Chinese Recorder and Missionary Journal*, Volume XXIV, No. 11 (November, 1894), p. 524.

29. Kahler (1905), pp. 22 – 23. See also Scidmore (1900); Edmunds (1908); and Moore (1888) and Moore (1893).

30. Discussion of West Lake's natural geologic development derived from the West Lake Museum website, accessed at http://www.westlakemuseum.com/index.php/bwggk/bwgjj-en.

31. Duan Xiaolin (2020), p. 5.

32. Holledge (1981), p. 13.

33. A half-submerged golden ox statue can be seen today in a southeastern corner of West Lake in recognition of this long-lasting myth story.

Chapter 2

1. Birch (1995), p. 67.

2. The Wu capital city built by King Helü was only first called Suzhou in 589, and not permanently called by that name until after 1368.

3. Zuiji is believed to have marked the border between the Wu and Yue states.

4. Cohen (2009), p. 29, citing the account given by Sima Qian 司马迁 (145 – 86 BCE) in the *Shiji* 史记, *The Records of the Grand Historian*, written around 90 BCE.

5. Milburn (2010), p. 13.

6. Sima Qian (2007), p. 35.

7. Although the ancient sources concur that the decisive battle occurred at a place called Fujiao, there is little certainty about where Fujiao was located. Some sources place it a little southwest of modern Suzhou, thus supporting the notion that Goujian invaded well into Wu before being driven back. Other sources place Fujiao a little northwest of modern Shaoxing, suggesting that Fuchai actually attacked Yue before Goujian was able to organize his assault on Wu. See, for example, Daniels (2013), p. 60, Footnote No. 75, for a brief discussion which also leaves the question unresolved. In the end, all agree that Goujian retreated to Kuaiji Mountain in ignominious defeat.

8. Cohen (2009), pp. 5 – 7.

9. This event is regarded as marking the founding of Shaoxing. The city was also known as Shanyin 山阴 during the Qin and Han dynasties, after which the name reverted back to Kuaiji, then Yuezhou, and finally Shaoxing in 1132.

10. Milburn (2007), pp. 127 – 128.

11. In Chinese tradition, Xi Shi is ranked as the greatest of the Four Great Beauties of China (四大美人, *Si da meiren*): Xi Shi 西施, Wang Zhaojun 王昭君, Diaochan 貂蝉, and Yang Guifei 楊貴妃.

12. A Chinese idiom celebrates the effect on Nature of the Four Great Beauties: "Fishes sink (before Xi Shi), and birds fall from the sky (before Wang Zhaojun), the moon hides (before Diao-

chan), and flowers are embarrassed (before Yang Guifei)," (沉鱼落雁,闭月羞花, *Chenyu luoyan, biyue xiuhua*).

13. Milburn (2013), pp. 31 – 32, citing Li Bai's lines from "Crow Roosting Song" (乌棲曲, "Wuqi qu").

14. Ibid., p. 32, citing Li Bai's lines from "A Panegyric on the King of Wu's Half-drunken Favorite" (口號吳王美人半醉, "Kouhao wuwang meiren banzui").

15. Sima Qian (2007), p. 39.

16. The meeting was convened in Huangchi, located in modern Fengqiu County, Henan Province.

17. Milburn (2010), pp. 31 – 32.

18. Henry (2007), pp. 11 – 16.

19. The earliest known written accounts specific to Wu and Yue, the *Spring and Autumn Annals of Wu and Yue* (吳越春秋, *Wuyue chunqiu*), and the accounts collected in the *Yuejue shu* 越絕書, both date to the Eastern Han Dynasty era (25 – 220 CE).

20. Milburn (2013), p. 23. Milburn outlines how various elements of the stories of Xi Shi and Zheng Dan—their three years of training, their use in distracting Fuchai from his duties, Xi Shi's peasant life as a silk-washing maiden, and her relationship with Fan Li—were added to their earliest mentions in the *Yuejue shu*.

21. Cohen (2009), p. 27.

22. Milburn (2007), p. 131, Footnote No. 82.

23. Johnson (1981), p. 259.

24. Cohen (2009), p. 27. See also "Qiantang River Tidal Bore - the Most Spectacular Tide in the World," accessed at https://www.chinadiscovery.com/zhejiang/hangzhou/qiantang-river-tid-al-bore.html.

25. Johnson (1980), p. 473.

26. Ibid., pp. 477 – 478.

Chapter 3

1. Graham (1990), p. 13.

2. His birth name was Ying Zheng 嬴政.

3. Ye Han (2017), pp. 82 – 83. The temple was destroyed around the end of the Yuan Dynasty, circa 1368.

4. An Eastern Han official named Ban Gu 班固 (32 – 92 CE) and his sister Ban Zhao 班昭 (49 – c. 120 CE) completed a history of the Western Han (220 BCE – 9 CE) begun by their father, Ban Biao 班彪 (3 – 54 CE). Ban Biao had undertaken his work as a continuation of Sima Qian's 司马迁 (c. 145 – c. 86 BCE) famous historical work, *Records of the Grand Historian* (史记, *Siji*). Zhu Maichen's biography is contained in Volume 64.

5. Translated *Han shu* version of the Zhu Maichen story and quoted text from Stenberg (2009), p. 8.

6. Ibid., pp. 9 – 18. Stenberg notes the existence of at least eight dramatic adaptations.

7. A.C. Moule (1923), p. 173, or Needham (1971), p. 320.

8. Hua Xin's project is noted in Hangzhou's UNESCO World Cultural Heritage application, Section 2.b-2-1, "Evolution of the Natural Components for the West Lake Cultural Landscape," and also represented by a display in the new Museum of the Seawall Site of Hangzhou. See Wu Huixin (2020), accessed at https://www.shine.cn/feature/art-culture/2003265092/.

9. Shangyu is a district just east of Shaoxing. The Shun (now Cao E) River passes through Shangyu and enters Hangzhou Bay just at the first bend where the Qiantang River "funnel" begins to form. Cao Xu presumably stood near the junction of the Shun and Qiantang rivers.

10. Chan (2012), pp. 43 – 45.

11. Gilbert Chen (2016), pp. 92 – 94. Chen presents a detailed dissertation on the nature and content of the forty-two images.

12. Han Emperor Huandi reigned for twenty-two years (146 – 168 CE), Lingdi twenty-one years (168 – 189), and Xiandi thirty-one years (189 – 220). This sequence ignores the four-month reign of the poisoned, thirteen-year-old Emperor Shao.

13. The conflict among these three states formed the basis for the classic Chinese historical novel, *Romance of the Three Kingdoms*.

14. The year 326 was the founding year of Lingyin Temple in the nearby hills.

15. Geil (1911), p. 2.

16. Minford and Lau (2000), p. 479.

17. The Four Books are: *Great Learning, Doctrine of the Mean, The Analects*, and *Mencius*. The Five Classics are *Classic of Poetry, Book of Documents, Book of Rites, Book of Changes (I Ching)*, and *Spring and Autumn Annals*.

18. See, for example, Hearn (2008), p. 5.

19. Excerpts from Minford and Lau (2000), p. 479.

20. See, for example, Qian Zhongshu (1998), p. 94.

21. Leys (1989), p. 8. Accessed at http://www.chinaheritagequarterly.org/articles.php?search-term=014_chineseattitude.inc&issue=014.

22. Such was the fame of *Lanting xu* and the notoriety of He Yanzhi's story that the very scene depicting Xiao Yi stealing the scroll from Monk Biancai became the subject of multiple paintings. See, for example, Weidner (2006), pp. 399 – 417.

23. Ledderose (1979), p. 20. See pp. 12 – 27 for extended discussion of the fate of *Lanting Xu* and Tang Emperor Taizong's crucial role in collecting well over two thousand scrolls and pieces of Wang Xizhi's calligraphy, thereby elevating Wang's status as Chinese history's premier calligrapher.

24. Lu Hui-Wen (2017), pp. 213 – 217, discusses the Song-Ming passion among *Lanting xu* collectors and the consequent proliferation of copies and forgeries.

25. Xu Lanjun (2016), p. 112. See "Introduction" in Idema (2010) for a more comprehensive discussion of the story's origins and evolution.

26. Figures for number of temples in Hangzhuo from Duan (2014), p. 115 (Footnote No. 263) and p. 117. Duan's Southern Song figure is 971 Buddhist monasteries. She later (p. 138) states that the number of monks in Southern Song "reached 200,000."

27. Shahar (1992), p. 200.

28. Both poems from Barnstone and Chou (2005), p. 85.

29. Rexroth and Ling Chung (1972), p. 12.

30. Faxian (1886), pp. 1 – 2, 111 – 114, accessed at https://archive.org/details/recordofbuddhist00fahsuoft.

Chapter 4

1. Cheung (2011), p. 205.

2. Lewis (2009), p. 249.

3. Paludan (1998), p. 86.

4. As in Fuzhou in Fujian Province or Guangzhou in Guangdong Province.

5. Emperor Wendi's new capital of Daxing was similarly divided into 108 wards. In Buddhist belief, humans experience 108 different feelings, the multiplicative product of six senses (touch, taste, smell, hearing, sight, and consciousness), three experiences of those senses (painful, neutral, or pleasurable), two sources (internal or external), and three spheres of temporal occurrence (past, present, or future); 6 x 3 x 2 x 3 = 108. Other common examples of 108 in Buddhist practice are 108 beads on the rosary, 108 steps at many temples, and 108 ringings of cast iron temple bells to herald the New Year.

6. Interesting perspective on the full history of the Grand Canal can be found in the *UNESCO World Heritage Nomination Document*, Section 2.b History and Development, pp. 319 – 459, downloadable at https://whc.unesco.org/en/list/1443/documents/.

7. Xiong (2006), pp. 29 – 32.

8. Ibid., pp. 19 – 20.

9. Yangdi imprisoned Yang Liang until his death the following year.

10. Xiong (2006), pp. 34 – 35.

11. Ibid., pp. 35 – 36.

12. The Xiling Canal was built in 307 CE. See Tang Wei (2013), pp. 395 – 400.

13. Extended to Ningbo during the Southern Song Dynasty. Canal segment lengths are from Xiong (2006), pp. 86 – 93, especially p. 92.

14. In 2013, two tombs discovered the previous year at a residential construction site in the Hanjiang District of Yangzhou City were determined to be the tombs of Emperor Sui Yangdi and Empress Xiao. See Shu Jiaping (2015), pp. 73 – 79.

15. Duan (2020), pp. 52 – 55. The Six Wells were named, respectively from north to south, Small Square Well (小方井, Xiaofang jing), White Turtle Well (白龟井, Baigui jing), Prime Minister Well (相国井, Xiangguo jing), Square Well (方井, Fang jing), Golden Ox Well (金牛井, Jinniu jing), and West Well (西井, Xi jing). Written records from the Ming Dynasty era indicate that some of these wells still remained in use more than eight hundred years later.

16. For a more extensive presentation on the multicultural history of tea, see Benn (2015); Hinsch (2015); Martin (2007); MacFarlan and MacFarlane (2004); or Rose (2010).

17. While the Shennong story is pleasantly mythical, recent archaeological discoveries at the Hemudu Culture site of Tianloushan (between Ningbo and Yuyao) in 2004 uncovered multiple preserved tea plant (*camellia sinensis*) roots, arranged in rows that suggest deliberate planting. Radiocarbon testing dates the roots to 3400 – 3500 BCE. See Steven D. Owyoung, "Tianloushan: Tea in the Neolithic Era," accessed at http://www.tsiosophy.com/2013/06/tianluoshan-tea-in-the-neolithic-era-3/.

18. Hinsch (2015), p. 14 or Benn (2015), p. 27.

19. Reid (2012), p. 37.

20. As described by Lu Yu himself in his *Classic of Tea*, the *Cha Jing*.

21. Monk Zhiji is commonly known by his more popular name, Mad Monk Jigong.

22. Lu Yu, "The Autobiography of Imperial Instructor Lu," in Mair (1994), p. 700.

23. The original manuscript of Lu Yu's *Classic of Tea* is no longer extant; the earliest known copies date to the Ming Dynasty era (1368 – 1644).

24. Reid (2012), p. 41.

25. Written by Pi Rixui in the preface to his various poems on tea, dating to 853 – 855, fifty years after Lu Yu's death. See Benn (2015), p. 99.

26. Ibid., pp. 14 – 15. These famous lines are actually part of a longer poem by Lu Tong with the title, "Written in Haste to Thank Censor Meng for His Gift of New Tea." The five immediately preceding lines read: "By what chance has [this gift of tea cakes] reached the hut of this mountain hermit? / My brushwood gate is closed, keeping out worldly visitors; / I don my gauze cap, and in solitude I brew and taste. / Clouds of emerald that even the wind cannot disperse, / White flowery froth radiantly congeals on the surface of the bowl." See Benn (2015), p. 91.

27. Penglai is the mystical home of the Eight Immortals in Chinese mythology.

28. Accessed at http://www.tsiosophy.com/2014/04/tea-pagoda-poem/. Also found at Benn (2015), p. 71, in a less aesthetically engaging form.

29. Martin (2007), pp. 98 – 99.

30. Zanini (2004), pp. 134 – 136.

31. Bai Juyi is celebrated in Suzhou for ordering construction of the famous Shantang Canal connecting the city at Chang Gate with Tiger Hill, the city's landmark historical location and tomb site of Suzhou's founder, King Helü.

32. As An Lushan's forces approached Chang'an in July 756, Emperor Xuanzong secretly abandoned the capital for Chengdu, taking with him his family members along with Yang Guifei

and her family. The soldiers escorting the party grew increasingly angry over the circumstances, blaming Yang Guifei's brother for An Lushan's military successes. They seized and killed all of Yang Guifei's family members in the procession and informed the Emperor they would advance no further unless Yang Guifei was also executed. After first refusing, Xuanzong relented, and his concubine was strangled or hanged with a silk cord.

33. Barnstone and Chou (2005), pp. 171 – 174.

34. Waley (1949), p. 147.

35. Ibid., p. 148.

36. Ibid., p. 156.

37. Wang Huiming (1982), p. 50.

38. Bai Juyi (2012), p. 123.

39. Mair (1994), p. 304.

40. Durand (1960), Table 2: "China: Recorded Population Statistics, A.D. 606 – 845," p. 223.

41. Ouyang Xiu (2004), pp. 561 – 562. See also Clark (2009), pp. 140 – 141.

42. Ouyang Xiu (2004), p. 562.

43. Needham (1971), pp. 321 – 322.

44. Barmé (2011B). An intimidating metal sculpture of a mounted Qian Liu the Archer stands on the south shores of the Qiantang River.

45. Clark (2009), pp. 173 – 174.

46. Qian Liu was believed to have had as many as one hundred children, a substantial candidate pool from which to draw.

47. Worthy (1978), p. 27.

48. Ibid., p. 29.

49. In around 960, Hongchu dropped the *hong* character in his name to observe the traditional name taboo of sharing a character with the imperial family. In Qian Chu's case, the *hong* character in his name matched that of Zhao Hongyin 趙弘殷, father of the first emperor of the Song Dynasty, Taizu.

50. About the ceramics from Wuyue, see Ruan Pinger (1994) and Lai Suk-Yee (1994).

51. Albert Welter contends that Wuyue leaders adapted Chan (Zen) Buddhist doctrinal traditions in an effort to revive the past glories of the collapsed Tang Dynasty, arguing that Buddhism in Wuyue "was linked to social and political stability" and that Buddhism in turn "served as the strongest cornerstone of Wuyue cultural policy." See Welter (2016), pp. 230 – 237, especially pp. 233 – 234.

52. Tiantai is a school of Mahayana Buddhism centered around Tiantai Mountain near Taizhou, Zhejiang Province, known especially for its elevation of the 68,000-character Lotus Sutra as the highest form of Buddhist teaching. Tiantai is also considered the earliest Buddhist school of Chinese (i.e., non-Indian) origin.

53. The temple was originally named Huiri Yongming Temple (慧日永明院); it was renamed Jingci Temple during the Southern Song Dynasty era.

54. Haichao Temple was built near the Qiantang River during the reign of the Wanli Emperor 萬曆帝 (r. 1572 – 1620) and destroyed during the Taiping Rebellion. The temple was rebuilt near the end of the Qing Dynasty but lost to a lightning-induced fire in 1944. For a time, the temple site was used by the Hangzhou Rubber Factory with only one old temple building still standing. Plans began in 2012 to restore Haichao Temple, and the restoration project began officially in 2019. See "Hangzhou 'Four Jungles' - Haichao Temple" (August 10, 2021) accessed at https://min.news/en/buddhism/8220423b44aa024fbf8f3b6ae07ddde3.html.

55. Chinese sources assert that the fire was caused by fireworks stored in the hall in preparation for the 1929 West Lake Expo. See for example, in Chinese, 少年宫的前世居然是杭州一座千年古寺？从昭庆寺飞出去的金色蝴蝶, "The Previous Life of the Children's Palace Was Actually a Thousand-Year-Old Temple in Hangzhou? Golden Butterfly Flying Out from Zhaoqing Temple," *Urban Secrets* (April 4, 2020), accessed at https://translate.google.com/translate?hl=en&sl=zh-CN&u=https://

56. The Children's Palace was built on the former site of Zhaoqing Temple in 1963.

57. In the era of its construction, Leifeng Pagoda was commonly referred to as Huangfei Pagoda.

58. See discussion in Eugene Y. Wang (2003), pp. 492 – 493.

59. Ibid., p. 491.

60. Huang Shih-shan Susan (2011), p. 138. Huang also notes that similar scrolls were discovered in Huzhou in 1917, dating to 956, and in Shaoxing in 1971, dating to 965. As with the Hangzhou scrolls, they, too, indicate that Qian Chu commissioned 84,000 copies of the sutra. Yen-Shou (904 – 975), the Buddhist abbot at Lingyin Temple during the Wuyue era, also had multiple different sutras and illustrations printed, their combined quantity totaling 400,000 or more copies. See Tsien Tsuen-Hsuin (1985), p. 158.

61. The entrance plaque to White Pagoda Park states that the White Pagoda "was first built during [sic] 948 and 978 as a navigation mark on the Qiantang River."

62. Worthy (1978), p. 32.

63. Ibid., p. 32.

64. Ye (2017), p. 27, Footnote No. 48.

Chapter 5

1. Graham (1990), p. 23. With this poem, Su Shi immortalized the linkage between 西湖and 西施, between West Lake (Xihu) and the great Yue beauty, Xi Shi.

2. Egan (2008), p. 309. The original Chinese consists of eight lines of seven characters each.

3. Bi Sheng 毕昇 (990 – 1051) invented Chinese movable type during the first century of the Northern Song Dynasty, somewhere around the year 1041 (four hundred years before Johannes Gutenberg). Although he was a native of Hubei Province, he is believed to have followed his parents to Hangzhou in his youth and apprenticed with publishers in that city for a number of years.

4. Thanks to a series of canals that connected it to Hangzhou (about 85 miles to its northwest), Ningbo after the Sui Dynasty effectively became the maritime terminus of the Grand Canal. The city was also one of the first five treaty ports opened to Westerners in 1842. For an extended introduction to the history of Ningbo and its surrounding area, see Shiba (1977), pp. 391 – 439.

5. See Borgen (2007), pp. 386 – 388, for a more detailed account of Jojin's earlier years and monkhood.

6. Saichō also visited Shaoxing in 805 to learn more about another school of Buddhism called Vajrayana (Esoteric). He and a fellow traveling monk named Kūkai are often credited as the first persons to introduce tea to Japan.

7. Harui (2018), p. 43.

8. Ibid., pp. 50 – 51. Another translation of Jojin's night market observations can be found in Borgen (1987), pp. 9 – 10.

9. Borgen (2007), pp. 400 – 401.

10. Lin Yutang (1947), pp. 148 – 149.

11. Crow Terrace was the name of the prison where Su Shi was held. For more detailed discussion of the case, see Hartman (1990), pp. 15 – 44, and Wang Yugen (2011), pp. 29 – 65.

12. Lin Yutang (1947), pp. 201 – 202.

13. Ibid., p. 287.

14. Ibid., pp. 305 – 306.

15. Duan (2020), p. 57.

16. The small mid-lake island alongside the three pagodas, once known as Lesser Yingzhou Isle, was built up from dredged silt in around 1607; Su Shi's three pagodas preceded the island's existence by more than five hundred years. The island today is commonly referred to by the name of the famous view with which it is associated, "Three Pools Mirroring the Moon."

17. Lin Yutang (1947), p. 301 for quote, pp. 303 – 305 for details on building repairs, hospital construction, and famine relief.

18. Leung Angela Ki Che (1987), p. 136, Footnote No. 9.

19. Tang Wei (2009), p. 198.

20. Zuo Ya (2018), p. 27.

21. Ibid., pp. 62 – 72 for an extended discussion of Shen Gua's work in the astronomical observation domain.

22. Ibid., pp. 59 – 62.

23. Holzman (1958), pp. 265 – 266.

24. Pregadio (1997), pp. 894 – 895.

25. Sivin (1977), p. 35. Reprinted from *The Dictionary of Scientific Biography, Vol. 12* (New York: Scribner, 1975). Sivin provides an extended and scholarly discussion of Shen Gua's natural science work and writings in the context of Song Dynasty politics and common understandings of nature and knowledge in that era.

26. Holzman (1958), p. 277.

27. Shen Gua's 11th Century term 石油 *shiyou* ("oil of rocks") remarkably prefigured the German mineralogist George Bauer (1494 – 1555) who, in 1546, first combined the Greek words *petra* (rock) and *oleum* (oil) to create the modern word "petroleum."

28. See "Shen Gua's Tomb" (沈括墓, Shen Gua mu), accessed (in Chinese) at https://web.archive.org/web/20140502074744/http://www.yhwt.com/newsshow.aspx?artid=3169.

29. Shen Gua (2011), p.5. See also JPL Small-Body Database Browser entry, accessed at https://ssd.jpl.nasa.gov/sbdb.cgi?sstr=2027#content.

30. Fraser and Haber (1986), pp. 226 – 227.

31. Sivin (1977), pp. 35 and 51.

32. Needham (1969), p. 27.

33. Bianjing/Kaifeng had an inner palace wall, an older city wall, and, in 956, a newer city wall that encircled additional area after the city had grown substantially beyond its earlier walls. See Hargett (1988/89), pp. 15 – 16.

34. Keswick (1978), p. 53. See p. 55 for the name "Impregnable Mountain" and Hargett (1988/89), p. 5, for the name "Northeast Marchmount."

35. Hargett (1988/89), pp. 18, 20. In addition to Hargett's article, information about Huizong's fantastical park can be found in Ebrey (2014), pp. 273 – 283.

36. Levine (2009), p. 625.

37. Kao Yu-kung (1966), p. 213.

38. Levine (2009), pp. 624 – 625.

39. Kao Yu-kung (1966), p. 214.

40. Ibid., p. 215.

41. The Sixteen Prefectures of Yan and Yun bordered the Great Wall (on both sides) and stretched from modern Tianjin and Beijing into northern sections of Hebei and Shanxi Provinces.

42. See Ebrey (2014), pp. 401 – 406, for a more detailed discussion of the Song and Jin efforts to take Yanjing from the Khitan Liao.

43. Ibid., p. 431.

44. Ibid., pp. 437 – 438.

45. Ibid., pp. 454 – 458.

46. Ibid., pp. 460, 471.

Chapter 6

1. Graham (1990), p. 39.
2. Mote (1999), pp. 295 – 296.

3. Wright (1977), pp. 63, 66.

4. Phoenix Mountain[4] (Fenghuangshan) is one of several linked hills together known as Wu Mountain (Wushan).

5. Ridgway (2017), p. 238.

6. The steady flow of northern migration into the south since at least the An Lushan Rebellion era, particularly among the wealthy and the educated elite, certainly would have favored such tighter linkages.

7. Schoppa (1989), p. 5. Viewing the autumnal tidal bores too casually or closely continued to be dangerous into the modern era. Chinese newspaper accounts of unexpectedly high tidal surges have reported the occurrence of more than seventy deaths between 1998 and 2007, twelve deaths in 2007, two deaths and two missing in 2010, twenty injured but no deaths in 2011, one death and four missing in 2015, and one death in 2019.

8. The Heavens were conceived of as circular, the Earth as square.

9. Xie Jing (2016), p. 186.

10. Ibid., p. 187.

11. Ibid., p. 186, citing a Song writer named Nai Deweng 耐得翁.

12. The names of the land gates, starting on the northeastern corner of the wall and proceeding clockwise, were Genshanmen 艮山门, Dongqingmen 东青门, Chongxinmen 崇新门, Xinkaimen 新开门, Bao'anmen 保安门, Houchaomen 侯潮门, Bianmen 便门, Jiahuimen 嘉会门, Qianhumen 钱湖门, Qingbomen 清波门, Fengyumen 丰豫门, Qiantangmen 钱塘门, and Yuhangmen 余杭门. The five water gates were Nanshuimen 南水门 (South Water Gate), Beishuimen 北水门 (North Water Gate), Bao'anshuimen 保安水门, Tianzongshuimen 天宗水门, and Yuhangshuimen 余杭水门.

13. Schoppa (1989), p. 17.

14. The Empress Dowager was Empress Meng 昭慈圣献皇后, widow of Emperor Zhezong 宋哲宗 (r. 1085 - 1100). Zhezong was Emperor Huizong's brother and Emperor Gaozong's uncle.

15. Near Shangjiang Village, Gaobu Town.

16. Southern Song Emperors Gaozong, Xiaozong, Guangzong, Ningzong, Lizong, and Duzong were buried at Baoshan Mountain in addition to Northern Song Emperor Huizong. The area is maintained today under control of the Shaoxing Cultural Relics Protection Department.

17. Ridgway, "A City of Substance," pp. 236, 247.

18. Although the content of *Rhapsody on Land and People* parallels that typically found in local gazetteers, Wang's work preceded the first Kuaiji gazetteer by nearly five decades.

19. Ridgway (2017), p. 241; textual quote p. 235.

20. This marvelous phrase, so perfectly descriptive of Li Qingzhao, is the title of Wei Djao's (2010) book about the poetess, *A Blossom Like No Other: Li Qingzhao*.

21. *Ci* is a form of lyric poetry in which verses of variable line length must conform to one of a large set of predefined tone, rhythm, and rhyme arrangements referred to as "tunes."

22. Zhao Tingzhi 赵挺之 (1040 – 1107, *jinshi* 1070).

23. Peterson (2000), pp. 262 – 263. Translation from Rexroth and Ling Chung (1979), p. 27.

24. Ho Chao, Lucy (1968), pp. 23 – 24.

25. The tune reference in Chinese, 声声慢 "Shengsheng man," could also be translated as "Each Note, Slowly," a fitting title for a work of such deeply felt sorrow and loss.

26. Peterson (2000), p. 267. Translation from Rexroth and Chung (1979), p. 27. I have chosen this particular translation for its powerful brevity and its preservation of the stark and radical opening word repetition that parallels Li Qingzhao's own character repetition in the Chinese. For alternative translations, see Hu Pin-ching (1966), pp. 37 – 38; Wang Jiaosheng (1989), pp. 108 – 109; Li Qingzhao (2019), pp. 142 – 145; or Egan (2013), p. 353, which presents English and Chinese versions side by side.

27. Wei Djao (2010), pp. 52 – 54.

28. Van Gulik (1974), p. 242.

29. Peterson (2000), pp. 268.

30. Wang Jiaosheng (1989), p. xii.

31. The treaty terms offered by the Jin included return of Henan Province to the Song along with the body of the deceased Emperor Huizong on condition of submitting to vassal-state status and payment of substantial tribute every year. In addition, the Southern Han Dynasty would have to renounce the name Song in favor of a new reign name: Jiangnan. See Wills (2012), pp. 176 – 177. Gaozong accepted these humiliating terms but the Jin broke the treaty themselves in 1140.

32. Chang Shaowen (1980), p. 55.

33. For example, see the story of Fan Chengda's embassy to the Jin court in the 1160s on Emperor Xiaozong's behalf in Koss (2015), pp. 87 – 88.

34. Fuller (1990), p. 243.

35. Barnstone and Chou (2005), p. 271.

36. Ibid., p. 273.

37. A modern-era Yue Opera simply titled *Lu You and Tang Wan* celebrates the couple's unrequited love story. See "*Lu You & Tang Wan* Won One Million Award by Provincial Government," 12/31/2003, accessed at https://web.archive.org/web/20090223115623/http://english.zjcnt.com/culture_news/view.php?article_id=274&article_type=2, and "A Classic Love Story Mesmerizes Beijing Audiences," 2/24/2014, accessed at http://english.cntv.cn/program/cultureexpress/20140224/104177.shtml.

38. See Watson (2007) for a translation and treatment of Lu You's travel diary.

39. Watson (1973), p. xiii; Mair (2001), p. 360; Barnstone and Chou Ping (2005), p. 269; Fuller (2013), p. 287; or Mote (1999), p. 370.

40. Barnstone and Chou Ping (2005), p. 272.

41. Fuller (2013), pp. 286 – 287.

42. Ji Gong's Wikipedia entry lists nineteen films between 1939 and 2010 and seventeen television series between 1984 and 2011.

43. Sources vary on Li Xiuyuan's dates, from 1130 to 1148 for his birth and typically either 1207 or 1209 for his death.

44. "Legend of a Mad Buddhist Monk," *ShanghaiDaily.com*, May 21, 2017, accessed at http://www.shanghaidaily.com/sunday/now-and-then/legend-of-a-mad-buddhist-monk/shdaily.shtml.

45. Guo Xiaoting (2014). A charming Ji Gong story can also be found in Cass (2008), pp. 86 – 93.

46. See, for example, Wu Yong, "The Merry Monk of Hangzhou." *Chinadaily.com.cn*, January 27, at https://global.chinadaily.com.cn/a/201201/27/ws5a2f3b1aa3108bc8c6721f82.html.

47. Chan Kar Yue (2005), p. 39. According to Chan, Wei Zhonggong recorded 337 of Zhu's *shi*-poems and 32 of her *ci*-poems.

48. Ibid., pp. 49, 68.

49. Ibid. p. 54.

50. Goedde (2013), p. 177.

51. Chan Kar Yue (2005), p. 71 for "Self-Reproving," pp. 59 – 60 for "Moved by Hearing Farmers' Words in Bitter Heat." Another selection of Zhu Shuzhen's poems is presented in Chang and Saussy (1999), pp. 100 – 106.

52. Van Bibber-Orr (2013), p. 4.

53. Ridgway (2020), p. 271, Footnote No. 70, citing Wu Songdi, *Nan Song Renkou Shi* 南宋人口史 (Shanghai: Shanghai guji chubanshe, 2008), p. 146.

54. Gernet (1970), pp. 29 – 30. Records report the presence of 104,669 households in 1170; the household figure for the 1240s was 111,336, and for 1270, 186,330. It has been standard practice to assume 4.5 – 5.0 persons per household for pre-modern Chinese cities.

55. Other estimates of Southern Song Lin'an's population range higher. Lin Zhengqiu estimated Lin'an's 1265 – 1274 population at 1.25 million; see Gao (2004), p. 269, Footnote No. 84. Hartwell

estimated Lin'an's 1225 population at 200,000 households and a regional population of more than 391,000 households (almost two million people) by 1225; see Hartwell (1982), pp. 392 – 393.

56. Unless otherwise indicated, the following physical description of Song Lin'an is adapted from Gernet (1970), pp. 30 – 55. Gernet's study of late Song Hangzhou remains a classic in its field.

57. Ibid., pp. 34 – 35.

58. Ibid., pp. 36 – 37.

59. A.C. Moule (1920), p. 208. Moule used the pinyin *t'a fang* for "warehouse"; a more current choice would be 库房 *kufang*.

60. Gernet (1970), p. 44.

61. Duan Xiaolin (2020), pp. 61 – 64. Duan (2014), p. 68, identifies six dredging projects in the Southern Song, taking place in 1139, 1148, 1173, 1189, 1247, and 1268. She notes as well that the lake "ran out of water" in 1247 due to "a serious drought."

62. Liu Gang (2010), p. 151.

63. See McDermott (2006) for an informative history of Chinese book publishing, production, distribution, and collection.

Chapter 7

1. Laurence Bergreen (2007), p. 223. Xie Ao 谢翱 , Song loyalist poet, describes the ruins of the abandoned Southern Song palace at Hangzhou's Phoenix Hill.

2. Charles A. Peterson astutely termed it "schadenfreude." See Peterson (1978), p. 205.

3. For an extensive treatment of Xi Xia and Jin and the Mongol conquest of those two states, see Mote (1999), pp. 168 – 288.

4. Fan Cheng-Hua (2003), pp. 54 – 56, 59 - 60. Fang's article provides useful background as to how and why the Lü family's wide-ranging military influence developed.

5. Davis (1996), p. 43.

6. Franke (1962), p. 223.

7. Marco Polo referred to Bayan 伯顏as "Baiyan Hundred Eyes," apparently confusing Bayan 伯顏 with Baiyan 百眼, the latter translated as 'hundred eyes.'

8. Lorge (2005), pp. 84 – 86.

9. Credit to Waterson (2013), p. 97, for noting this parallel. It is hard not to believe that some members of the Lü clan would have seen the connection.

10. Ibid., p. 105.

11. Khubilai had already begun building his empire's capital at Dadu (present-day Beijing) in 1267.

12. Cleaves (1956), p 248, cited in Lane (2018), p. 29.

13. The remnant Song government fled Fuzhou for Guangzhou in 1277 to escape the pursuing Mongols and relocated eight different times in 1278. Boy-emperor Duanzong died in May after a cyclone struck their fleet; his younger brother, Emperor Bingdi, died by suicidal drowning in the final naval battle off Yashan Island in March 1279. It is said that over 100,000 Song soldiers, courtiers, and consorts followed Bingdi in committing suicide at Yashan.

14. Yi Xu, van Leeuwen, and van Zanden (2018), "Table 5: Comparison Between Numbers of Inhabitants of Seven Cities in the Lower Yangtze Delta in 1205 and 1290," p. 339.

15. Hua Kaiqi, p. 5. See also DeRachewiltz, et.al. (1993), p. 561.

16. The mausoleums of Southern Song emperors Gaozong, Xiaozong, Guangzong, Ningzong, Lizong, and Duzong were all located near Baoshan Mountain, Shaoxing district. Also buried nearby were Northern Song Emperor Huizong and several empresses and high-ranking officials. The mausoleums and tombs are now officially recognized cultural relics, provincially protected since 1961 and nationally protected since 1989. See, for example, http://en.chinaculture.org/focus/focus/cities/2010-08/11/content_390534.htm.

17. Jay (1991), pp. 150 – 151.

18. The temple names and their Buddhist School affiliations were Baoguo 報國 (Chan or Zen), Xingyuan 興元 (Tiantai), Banruo 般若 (Baiyun), Xianling 仙林 (Cien), and Zunsheng 尊胜 (Tibetan).

19. Hua Kaiqi, pp. 13 – 15. See also Joo (2015), p 66. Joo, p. 55, describes the intention as 'subjugating the unruly dead."

20. Joo (2015), p. 57, Footnote No. 10. Joo notes on pp. 58 – 59 that Zhu Yuanzhang, founder in 1368 of the Ming Dynasty as Emperor Hongwu, ordered that the bones of the Southern Song emperors be exhumed from their sacrilegious burial at the White Pagoda site and relocated for proper burial at Jubao Mountain in Nanjing.

21. Jay-Preston, (1983), p. 57.

22. Zhou Mi (2002), p. 3. Weitz cites Su Shi from his "On Wang Shen's Hall of Precious Paintings."

23. For example, his book contains the world's earliest known reference to the game of dominoes (in Chinese, 骨牌 gupai). The modern casino game paigow (牌九, pái jiǔ) uses domino tiles, and even mahjong tiles are called 麻将牌, majiangpai.

24. Zhao's paternal lineage traced through the brother of Emperor Xiaozong and thus descended from Emperor Taizu. His maternal lineage ran from the granddaughter of Emperor Huizong.

25. Zhao had previously declined an invitation to the Hanlin Academy four years earlier, in 1282. See Hearn (1996), p. 273.

26. McCausland (2011), pp. 14, 39, and 339.

27. Fong (1996), p. 273.

28. Only Qian Xuan 钱选 (c. 1235 – before 1307) among the "Eight Talents of Wuxing" refused to serve the Yuan, having spurned his Confucian learning and destroyed his examination manuscripts in order to support himself solely from his paintings. On Qian Xuan, see Watt (2011), pp. 186 – 187.

29. Barnstone and Chou Ping (2005), pp. 290 – 291.

30. Lane (2018), p. 32.

31. George Lane speculated that General Bayan's youth spent in Persian Turkestan followed by ten years in Iran from age 18 may have fostered connections upon which he relied to populate Hangzhou with a pool of Moslem administrators and specialists to help manage the city. See Lane (2016), p. 240.

32. Lane (2018), p. 41, translated from a 1670 stele by Liu Zhi, a Chinese Muslim. The stele is retained at the Phoenix Mosque.

33. Alessandra Cappelletti, (2022), n.p. Open access (Springer Link) - downloadable at https://doi.org/10.1007/s11562-022-00509-2

34. Lane (2018), pp. 51 – 52, 101, 136.

35. In 1623, a Nestorian stele originally inscribed in Chinese and Syriac, dated 781, was unearthed in the area of Xi'an. The stele text describes the history of the Nestorian Church in China from the year 638 to the time of its inscription 150 years later. The stone is preserved today in the Beilin (Forest of Steles) Museum in Xi'an. A complete translation of the stele can be found at https://sourcebooks.fordham.edu/eastasia/781nestorian.asp.

36. Sturton (1945), pp. 82 – 84. At the time of his investigation, Dr. Sturton was President of Hangzhou's Guangji Hospital.

37. Like Marco Polo, Ibn Battuta dictated his travel report in the last years of his life. Scholars have long questioned the veracity of his works and asserted that parts appear to have been copied from the work of other travelers. Even if plagiarized, however, his reports would simply reflect the observations of contemporary travelers of that time.

38. Ibn Battuta (2004), p. 30.

39. Polo's identification of Lin'an or Hangzhou as "Kinsay" indicates that he adopted the formal Southern Song view of that city as 行在xingzai, the "temporary residence" of the imperial capital.

40. Polo stated that the name "Kinsay" signified "Heaven" and Suzhou's name, "Suju," signified "Earth." In this, he clearly confused the meaning of an ancient Chinese adage he must have heard, that "Above us are the heavens, but here on earth, we have Suzhou and Hangzhou" (想有天堂下有苏杭" *Xiang you tian tang, xia you su hang*").

41. Analysis from A.C. Moule (1937), p. 107. Chapter 60 reference and quote for Yangzhou on pages 301 - 302 of *Travels of Marco Polo, the Venetian* (London: Henry G. Bohn, 1854), a revised version of William Marsden's 1818 translation, edited by Thomas Wright. Wright's appears to be the version cited in Moule's paper.

42. Needham asserts that Polo could only have seen at most 347 bridges in the Hangzhou area, with just 117 of them inside the city walls. See Needham (1971), p. 148.

43. Polo (1993), pp. 185 – 192.

44. Ibid., p. 189.

45. Ibid., p. 205.

46. Hobart, (1959), p. 67.

47. Odoric of Pordenone (2002), pp. 129 – 130.

48. Ibid., p. 130.

49. Benincampi (2017), pp. 128 – 129. The gravestones were engraved with images of the Madonna and Child, Saint Catherine, and a scene depicting resurrection at the Last Judgment.

50. Polo (1993), p. 213, Footnote No. 12.

51. By Chen Jiru (陈继儒, 1558 – 1639). See Li Chu-Tsing (1987), p. 16.

52. Hearn (1996), p. 274.

53. The Que and Huabuzhu Mountains are located outside of Jinan, where Zhao Mengfu had served as Vice-Governor.

54. Li Chu-tsing (1965), pp. 58 – 59. McCausland phrases the revolution this way: "Zhao's work reinvented figure painting as an art about the self, through meaningful dialogue with a canon of old master sources, in order to shape dialogue about the contemporary role of the individual in society and the state….[I]t adopted the visual language of the past to make more blatant statements about selfhood, ethics, and values…." McCausland (2011), p. 116.

55. Hearn (1996), p. 280. McCausland (2011), p. 51, also states: "Zhao developed colophon writing far beyond its Song mandate to authenticate an ancient work, into a place for critical commentary juxtaposed with the artifact itself."

56. Hearn (1996), p. 279.

57. Stanley-Baker (1995), p. 82, citing 14th-Century writer Sun Zuo.

58. Hearn (1996), p. 320.

59. Chang (2009), pp. 33, 36. Chang notes that the handscroll is extant at the University of Pennsylvania Museum.

60. Weidner (1990A), p. 14.

61. The *Thousand Character Classic* contains 1,000 distinct Chinese characters, with no repetitions. It was used for centuries as a school primer for learning to read. Because the *Classic* was arranged in 250 lines of four characters each, rhymed in four-line stanzas, children could memorize and sing it in its entirety, loosely akin to the considerably more abbreviated English ABC song.

62. Lee and Wiles (2014), p. 96.

63. Adapted by the author from the translation in Rexroth and Ling Chung (1972), p. 53. For other nice translations, see Purtle (2011), pp. 297 – 298, or Barnstone and Chou Ping (2005), pp. 295 – 296. Barnstone and Chou also includes a translation of Zhao Mengfu's "concubine request" poem.

64. Marco Polo marveled at the speed and efficiency of the Mongol postal network that was first built to communicate with their Persian empire.

65. See Mote (1999), pp. 489 – 494, for a detailed discussion of the Mongol-imposed social ranking system and the privileges associated within it for the *semuren* who populated the Yuan gov-

ernment's official ranks. "People of varied categories" is Mote's translation of 色目人, *semuren*.

66. See Liu Ai-Lian (2011), pp. 4 – 15 for a biographical summary of Yang Weizhen.

67. Waterson (2013), p. 155.

68. Ibid., p. 158. By Waterson's estimate, this genocidal proposal would have eradicated ninety percent of China's Han population.

69. Ibid., p. 160. Waterson asserts that China in the Yuan Dynasty experienced "ninety-two floods, eighty-six droughts, sixty-one locust epidemics, fifty-six earthquakes, forty-two typhoons and twenty extensive epidemics including…the Black Death."

Chapter 8

1. Yang Ye (1999), p. 47.

2. Crow (1913), p. 105.

3. For the 1359 siege of Shaoxing, see Franke (1974), pp. 188 – 192. Hu Dahai was a Hui Muslim of mixed Persian-Chinese descent from Anhui Province.

4. Brook (2010), p. 37.

5. Sivin (1977), p. 31. Here Sivin is referring to the Tang Dynasty era, but Zhu's goals in part were to restore Chinese life to that of idealized earlier times.

6. Brook (1998), p. 19.

7. Zang Jian (2003), pp. 129 – 130.

8. For more detailed discussion, see Liu Yunsheng (2020), pp. 63 – 65.

9. See "First Family of Southern China: Pujiang," accessed at http://travelzhejiang.com/prefectures/jinhua/pujiang/first-family-of-southern-china/.

10. Liang Ye (2019), pp. 80 – 81. For a more recent update on Pujiang's and the Zheng clan's continuing fame, see Wu Huixin (2014).

11. For a nicely annotated map in English, see Map 13, "Hangzhou during the Qing Dynasty," in Wang Liping (1999), p. 109. For a satellite image overlay with gate labels (in Chinese), see "1368 – 1912 Hangzhou City Wall and Gates, Zhejiang Province, China," Regional Religious System Project Maps, The University of Arizona, accessed at https://rrs.arizona.edu/project/1368-1912-hangzhou-city-wall-and-gates-zhejiang-province-china/ .

12. The song, in Chinese: 武林门外鱼担儿，艮山门外丝篮儿，凤山门外跑马儿，清泰门外盐担儿，望江门外菜担儿，候潮门外酒坛儿，清波门外柴担儿，涌金门外划船儿，钱塘门外香篮儿，庆春门外粪担儿.The gate sequence in the song is Wulin, Genshan, Fengshan, Qingtai, Wangjiang, Houchao, Qingbo, Yongjin, Qiantang, Qingchun.

13. After a fire in the Forbidden City in 1562, a complete copy of the *Yongle Dadian* was produced. The original encyclopedia was lost in a fire at the Wenyuan Hall near the end of the Ming, although some (see Mote (1999), p. 601) suggest it was buried in its entirety with the Jiajing Emperor in 1567. The copy had been stored at the Yuanmingyuan Summer Palace in Beijing, but most of it was either burned or stolen when the British and French sacked the European-style palace in 1860. Only a small number of original volumes survive today.

14. The *Four Books* are *Great Learning, Doctrine of the Mean, Analects*, and *Mencius. The Five Classics* are the *Classic of Poetry, Book of Documents, Book of Rites, Book of Changes (I Ching)*, and the *Spring and Autumn Annals.*

15. Yongle's immediate successor, the sickly and gout-ridden Emperor Hongxi, held the throne for less than a year before dying.

16. Wen C. Fong (1996A), p. 173.

17. Ma Yuan was born in Hangzhou into a three-generation lineage of Imperial Academy painters; his son Ma Lin was also an accomplished painter. Xia Gui, whose work has generally been regarded as surpassing Ma Yuan's, was also born in or near Hangzhou, although little detail is known of his life. For more detail on their extant work, see Cahill (1996), pp. 183 – 194.

18. The Ma-Xia style of the Southern Song Academy strongly influenced landscape painters in Japan during the 14th – 16th Centuries. See Sullivan (1961), p. 151.

19. Metropolitan Museum of Art, "Returning Home through the Snow," accessed at https://www.metmuseum.org/art/collection/search/44699.

20. Cheung (2011) presents an extended discussion on the *Sidian*, pp. 71 – 78. In 1488, the Hongzhi Emperor affirmed City God temples as an acceptable part of this group even though they were not originally so designated in the *Sidian* (p. 72).

21. Ibid., p. 73. Quoted text in Cheung is cited from Romeyn Taylor, "Official Religion in the Ming," in Denis Twitchett and Frederick W. Mote, *The Cambridge History of China, Volume 8: The Ming Dynasty, 1368 – 1644*, Part 2 (Cambridge: Cambridge University Press, 1988), p. 880.

22. Yu Qian's tomb and memorial temple are located beyond the southwest corner of West Lake, off Santaishan Road.

23. Cheung (2011), p. 235.

24. Ibid., p. 243. Cheung reports 7,000 laborers for 152 working days, or 1,064,000 man-days.

25. Ibid., p. 244.

26. Something like a combination special investigator and judicial auditor.

27. Thornton (1996), pp. 22 – 25, makes the case that this supernatural incident was simply contrived as a political move by provincial-level authorities of the new dynasty in concert with the temple monks.

28. Feuchtwang (1977), pp. 601 – 602.

29. Cheung (2011), p. 183.

30. Ibid., p. 188.

31. Goodrich (1976), p. 435.

32. Mote and Twitchett (1988), pp. 490 – 491.

33. Most historians of the period have concluded that typical pirate bands of the peak (1550s) period consisted of about thirty percent Japanese and seventy percent Chinese, South Asian, and Western (mostly Portuguese) members.

34. So Kwan-wai (1975), pp. 53 – 54.

35. Goodrich (1976), pp. 373 – 374, describes those among the rest as "three chiefs, sixteen white barbarians, forty-six black barbarians,…and twenty-nine barbarian women."

36. Fitzpatrick (1979), pp. 19 – 26.

37. Ibid., pp. 29 – 32.

38. Ibid., pp. 46 – 47.

39. Schoppa (1989), pp. 75 – 76. Some of the most intense fighting to drive the pirates out of Zhejiang in 1555 occurred in and around Xiaoshan and near Xiang Lake (pp. 76 – 77).

40. Hu Jintao 胡锦涛 (1942 –) is a direct lineal descendant of Hu Zongxian.

41. See Hucker (1971), pp. 13 – 27 for an extended discussion of Hu Zongxian's campaign against Xu Hai.

42. Lim (2017), pp. 34 – 35. See also Lorge (2017), pp. 59 – 71, and Swope (2017), pp. 167 – 173, for discussions of Qi Jiguang's military tactics.

43. "10 of 31 Children Rescued from Chinese Pirate Band," *The New York Times*, September 29, 1935. The village is identified as Peihsiang, but the Peixiang Village in Jinhua Prefecture, Pan'an County, Huzhai Town appears too far distant from the sea to have been the incident site. A more likely location might be Beichanxiang on Zhoushan Island.

44. Meskill (1965), p. 88.

45. Brook (2010), p. 121.

46. Brook (1998), pp. 72 – 73.

47. VanderVen (2012), p. 20.

48. Hu Ying (2016), p. 108.

49. The history of Zhang Xiaoquan scissors dates back 400 years. See Sudworth (2013), , ac-

cessed at https://www.bbc.com/news/business-22160739.

50. See "Huzhou Factory Produces Prestigious Writing Brushes," *Chinadaily.com.cn*, (August 8, 2017) accessed at http://www.chinadaily.com.cn/a/201708/08/ws59bb583ca310d4d9ab7e2d79.html and "Huzhou Writing Brush Still Contributes to Its Hometown's Economy," *Chinadaily.com.cn*, (June 18, 2020), accessed at https://www.chinadaily.com.cn/a/202006/18/ws5eeb233ca310834817253fdb.html.

51. There are museums in their respective cities for each of these products, including a National Silk Museum at West Lake.

52. Cheung, *A Socio-Cultural History of Sites in Ming Hangzhou*, p. 64, Footnote No. 202.

53. See Ridgway, "City in a Garden," pp. 255 – 270 for details on Yang's and Guo's hundred-poem collection.

54. Ridgway's terminology in "City in a Garden," pp. 239 – 240.

55. Ibid., pp. 274 – 275. Ridgway also points out (p. 273) that only twenty-three of Dong Sigao's one hundred sites match those on Yang's and Guo's list from two centuries earlier. He suggests this lack of overlap is indicative of the changes around West Lake resulting from its role as imperial capital during the Southern Song era as well as adaptation to and support of steadily growing tourism over the intervening two centuries.

56. Ibid., p. 276.

57. Cheung (2011), p. 61.

58. No archaeological evidence has yet been found to support the existence of Da Yu or any person of comparable, if perhaps less god-like, achievement.

59. Pietz (2015), p. 26. Tregear (1965), pp. 218 – 219, puts the figures for the past 2,500 years at 1,593 floods and 26 river course changes.

60. Dodgen (2001), p. 16.

61. Ge Jianxiong and Hu Yunsheng (2021), p. 147.

62. Ibid., p. 148.

63. For a more current view of this reservoir release practice on the Yellow River, see JoAnna Klein, "A New Formula to Help Tame China's Yellow River," *The New York Times* (June 2, 2017).

64. Ruth Mostern presents the case that by merely routing the Yellow River silt away from the Grand Canal, Pan's actions had longer-term and unforeseen adverse consequences: flood crises, increased delta accretion that eventually created a silt backwash that worsened the situation, and permanent damage to the agricultural productivity of the Huai River floodplain. See Mostern (2016), pp. 141 – 143.

65. Needham (1971), p. 319.

66. Mostern (2016), p. 141.

67. Dodgen (2001), p. 20.

68. Paludan (1998), p. 181.

69. Clunas (1991), p. 18.

70. Hardie 2004), p. 138.

71. Ibid., pp. 137 – 138. Zhang Lian's son, Zhang Ran 张然 (1621 – 1696), would continue his father's legacy, later designing some of the famous imperial garden rockeries in Qing-era Beijing.

72. Patrick Hanan states that Wang Ruqian was also known as "Mr. West Lake" for "the various improvements he had made in the lake at his own expense." See Hanan (1988), p. 217, Footnote No. 41.

73. Smith (2009), pp. 110 – 111.

74. Stuart (1990), p. 167, quote on p. 170.

75. Fung (1997), pp. 15 – 17.

76. Ko (1994), pp. 92 – 93.

77. Berg (2006), p. 314.

78. Yangzhou and Suzhou were long regarded as prime sources for "skinny mares," as young girls sold into concubinage were called. The term dates back at least as far as one of Bai Juyi's Tang Dynasty poems.

79. Ko (1994), p. 92.

80. Brook (2010), p. 196.

81. Scholars have long debated whether Xue Susu was born in Jiaxing or Suzhou.

82. Lin Yanqing (2014), "Xu Yuan," in Lee and Wiles (2014), p. 516.

83. Hanan (1981), p. 144.

84. Ling Mengchu's grandfather, Ling Yueyan (凌约言) was a *juren* and high judicial official, and his father, Ling Dizhi 凌迪知, was a *jinshi* (1556) and, after retirement from official life, a book publisher.

85. Feng Menglong's was not the first such collection of vernacular short stories. In around 1550, Hangzhou native Hong Pian 洪楩 compiled a rather less formally curated collection called *Sixty Stories* (六十家小说, *Liushijia xiaoshuo*). See Hanan (1981), pp. 56 – 58.

86. Ibid., p. 149.

87. Altenburger (2009), pp. 22 – 23. See also Scott (1973), pp. 162 – 170.

88. Hsia, Ronnie Po-Chia (2010), pp. 88 – 89.

89. *Hanyu pinyin* is the modern-day system for converting Chinese characters into their English-letter equivalents.

90. Li was ranked eighth by the examiners out of 262 candidates in 1598 and ranked fifth in the follow-on imperial examination of top finishers. See Yu Liu (2011), p. 436.

91. In Chinese cosmologic tradition, Earth was regarded as square and the heavens as round.

92. An allusion to "The Letter of Paul the Apostle to the Galatians" in *The New Testament*. Galatians 2:9 reads in part, "...Recognizing the grace that had been given to me, James and [Peter] and John, who were reputed to be pillars, gave to me and Barnabas the right hand of fellowship...." From the *New American Standard Bible* (La Habra, CA: The Lockman Foundation, 1995).

93. Engelfriet (1988), p. 133.

94. Standaert (1988), p. 53.

95. G.E. Moule (1889), p. 83.

96. Brockey (2008), p. 68.

97. Ibid., p. 71.

98. This discovery would first be made in a 1972 paper by Shaoxing native Wu Kezhen, based in part on his years of detailed research through ancient records.

99. Hong Chengchou, perhaps the only Ming military commander to have defeated Li Zicheng decisively in battle (at Chengdu in 1638), went over to the side of the Manchus sometime after they captured him near Jinzhou, Liaoning Province, in 1642. Mote's view is that Hong's defection from the Ming was the result of persistent indecision and micromanagement from the Chongzhen Emperor and his court. See Mote (1999), pp. 804 – 805.

100. The 1642 conquest of Kaifang is remembered for the incredibly callous decisions by both Li Zicheng and the opposing Ming commanders to breach the nearby dikes of the Yellow River in an attempt to flood one another out. In doing so, they flooded the city and killed as many as 300,000 of its citizens and up to a million people in total.

101. Parallels with the commoner background and rise of Zhu Yuanzhang, founder of the Ming dynasty, would certainly not have gone unnoticed among Li Zicheng and his advisors.

Chapter 9

1. "Glow of Sunset upon Thunder Peak" is from a set of poems written by Ming poet and essayist Zhang Dai. Each poem celebrates one of the famous "Ten Views of West Lake." This poem was translated by Duncan Campbell (2011A) in his "Ten Scenes of West Lake: Poems by Zhang Dai 張岱," accessed at http://www.chinaheritagequarterly.org/features.php?searchterm=028_poems.inc&issue=028.

2. The character 明 *ming* for the name of the Ming Dynasty meant "Bright," while the character 清 *qing* for the Qing Dynasty meant "Clear" or "Pure."

3. Dorgon was the fourteenth-born son of Nurhaci.

4. Barnhart (1993), p. 81.

5. Mote (1999), p. 818.

6. Ibid., p. 869. Mote presents an extended discussion of the curious Manchu-Mongol relationship on pp. 868 – 876.

7. Wakeman (1985) , p. 562. An English translation of Wang Xiuchu's "A Record of Ten Days in Yangzhou" can be found in Backhouse and Bland (1914), pp. 188 – 208, or in Struve (1993), pp. 28 – 48.

8. Only tonsured monks were exempted from the queue.

9. For example, see Dennerline (1981).

10. Jiaxing story and quote from Wakeman (1985), pp. 651 – 652.

11. A market town in Suzhou Prefecture, located thirty-three miles northeast of the prefectural capital.

12. Wakeman (1925), p. 652.

13. Schoppa (1989), p. 91.

14. Ko (1994), p. 92.

15. Ten *mu* 亩 is 1.65 acres, or about 72,600 square feet.

16. Smith (1992), p. 60.

17. Li Wai-yee (2012), p. 317, citing Cao Shujuan, *Liubian zhong de shuxie: Qi Biaojia yu yushan yuanlin lunshu*流变中的书寫:祁彪佳與寓山园林论述 (Taipei: Liren Shuju, 2006), pp. 11, 153 – 272.

18. Campbell (2004), p. 262.

19. Wakeman (1925), p. 649 and Footnote No. 185, p. 649.

20. Goodrich (1976), p. 1423.

21. Ko (1994), p. 129.

22. Yi Lidu (2011), p. 33.

23. Cahill (1982), pp. 108 – 109.

24. Burkus-Chasson (2002), p. 330, Footnote No. 1.

25. Liu Shi-yee (2008), p. 174.

26. Kafalas (2007), p. 53. Jonathan Spence (2007) offers another translation, pp. 272 – 273.

27. Spence (2007), p. 219.

28. Kafalas (2007), pp. 10 – 11, quoting from Zhang Dai's preface to his *Dream Reminiscences of Tao'an* (*Tao'an mengyi*).

29. Broken Bridge is a single-arch bridge near the eastern end of the Bai Causeway at West Lake. The name is generally believed to result from the appearance of the snow-covered bridge when the sun warms one side but not the shaded sign, causing the bridge to appear broken when viewed from the nearby northern hills.

30. Spence (2007), pp. 250 – 251.

31. Kafalas (2007), pp. 88 – 90. Another full translation can be found in Pollard (2000), pp. 86 – 88.

32. The Three Eternals were Virtue (立德, *lide*), Word (立功, *ligong*), and Deed (立言, *liyan*).

33. Campbell (2012), pp. 5 – 9.

34. Mote (1973), pp. 50-51. See also Leys (1989) for his similar discussion of the "parallel phenomena of spiritual preservation and material destruction that can be observed in the history of Chinese culture."

35. Both Lu Xun and his brother Zhou Zuoren would reference Zhang Dai's *Dream Reminiscences of Tao'an* in their early 20th Century essays. See Kafalas (2007), pp. 200 – 207.

36. Dennerline (1981), p. 267.

37. See, for example, Yim (2009), p. 10.

38. Schmidt (2008), pp. 167 – 168.

39. There is some uncertainty as to Liu Rushi's birthplace. Some historians have contended that she was born in Suzhou.

40. An active Ming loyalist, Chen Zilong would ultimately commit suicide by drowning in 1647.

41. Cass (1999), p. 40.

42. Ibid., p. 43.

43. A market town in Suzhou Prefecture, located about thirty miles north of the prefectural capital.

44. Campbell (2014), p. 69, citing in translation the Liu Rushi biography written by Niu Xiu 钮琇 (1644 – 1704).

45. Berg (2007), p. 285.

46. Hsiung Ping-chen (2007), pp. 99 – 102.

47. The following discussion draws heavily from Wang Liping's (2011) succinct but informative survey of West Lake's history, accessed at http://www.chinaheritagequarterly.org/features.php?Searchterm=028_kangxi.inc&issue=028 .

48. Ibid., n.p.

49. Barmé (2011), accessed at http://www.chinaheritagequarterly.org/features.php?searchterm=028_chrono.inc&issue=028 .

50. Campbell (2011), accessed at http://www.chinaheritagequarterly.org/features.php?searchterm=028_ming.inc&issue=028 .

51. For 217 lakes in the Song era, see Schoppa (1989), p. 6. For Ming Dynasty and modern era figures and quote, see Osborne (1998), pp. 208 – 209.

52. See Schoppa (1989), pp. 237 – 239.

53. Lake Heart Pavilion (湖心亭, Huxin ting) is an island pavilion built on West Lake.

54. Wang Liping (2011), n.p.

Chapter 10

1. A.C. Moule (1957), p. 34. Wei's poem was addressed to Abbot Shan-chin at the Tao Guang Temple 韬光寺, in memory of a sunrise visit on October 17, 1724.

2. Wakeman (1985), p. 476.

3. Crossley (1990), p. 49, asserts "more than 106."

4. In the early 1600s, Nurhaci organized the Manchu military into the Eight Banner system as a way to militarize various tribes and groups of Mongols as well as Han Chinese who had been accepted into Manchu society. The Eight Banners were identified by flags of four different colors—Yellow, White, Red, and Blue—and either Plain (square and borderless) or Bordered. Han Chinese who surrendered or were captured in conflicts with Manchu forces were formed into a separate, Manchu-commanded force known as the Green Standard Army.

5. Figures from Elliott (2001), p. 110 and Table 2.1 "Approximate Area of Eight Banner Garrisons," p. 111. Estimates of the size of Hangzhou's garrison vary substantially, from 240 acres in Crossley (1990), p. 65, to 1,150 acres (7,000 mu) in Wang Liping (1999), p. 109. The latter figure seems overstated. The ancient wall is described as having a perimeter of 36 li, or about 12 miles, yielding an interior area of perhaps 8 square miles (5,120 acres). A garrison occupying 1,150 acres (1.8 square miles) would have consumed more than 20% of the land inside the walled city.

6. Crossley (1990), pp. 65 – 67.

7. Elliott (2001), p. 110.

8. In Chinese history, Shunzhi's reign is marked from his ascendency to the throne in Beijing in 1644.

9. Chang Chia-Feng (2002), p. 181.

10. Mann (1994), pp. 20 – 21.

11. A more complete rendition of this gendered saying goes: "A man with virtue is a man of

talent, a woman without talent is a woman of virtue" (男子有德便是才,女子无才便是德, *Nanzi youde bianshi cai, nüzi wucai bianshi de*).

12. It was commonly reported of Huang Yuanjie's moral virtue that she was sought as a concubine by Zhang Pu (1602 – 1641), the well-respected founder of the Ming Restoration Society, but she rejected his offer on the grounds that she was already promised in marriage to another.

13. Huang Yuanjie wrote poetically of the challenges of providing for her family (from Idema and Grant (2004), p. 455):

Who, traveling far from home, can bear the rain and the wind?
My bitter longing for home communicates with the drifting cloud.
All alone I ascend the dilapidated tower and fancy myself in heaven,
I laugh at myself for being afraid of seeing my sorrowful face in the mirror.
The branches are cold, the blossoms freezing, the orioles want to fly away,
My bags empty, the tip of my brush worn to a nub—it's hard to write well.
But what I most hate is that although the spring has long gone, I am still around,
In a corner of the room insects chirp, blaming me for being so damned poor!

14. Ko (1994), p. 118.

15. Lee and Stefanowska (1998), pp. 82 – 85.

16. Ko (1994), p. 122.

17. Her father Shangzuo (*jinshi* 1601) was Minister of Works in Nanjing in 1627.

18. For more detail, see Hardie (2007), pp. 48 – 50.

19. Ellen Widmer (1989), p. 10, citing Deng Hanyi, 1672. See also Footnote No. 25, p. 10.

20. Ko (1994), p. 238.

21. Berg (2013), p. 8.

22. Ko (1994), p. 130.

23. Idema and Grant (2004), p. 439.

24. Ko (1994), p. 133.

25. Wang Duanshu resolutely rejected an offer of a position as a teacher of women at Emperor Shunzhi's Court.

26. Ko (1994), pp. 133 – 134 and Widmer, "Wang Duanshu," in Chang and Saussy (1999), p. 363.

27. Apparently not one to shy away from self-promotion, Wang exercised her authorial privilege to include sixty-three of her own poems in the anthology. She also authored a companion work, 名媛文緯 *Mingyuan wenwei*, an anthology of women's prose.

28. Idema and Grant (2004), pp. 447 – 448.

29. Qin and Jin were states in the northwest, Qi and Yen in the northeast; hence, indecision or caprice.

30. The cuckoo bird with the impossible task was called the Jingwei bird, a reference that will famously recur later in the writings of Qiu Jin.

31. Barr (2005), p. 5. Mote (1999) takes a more lenient but accusatory view that many of the disparagements were the result of editorial carelessness, a conclusion that only renders the court's response all the more horrific.

32. Hummel (2018), p. 206.

33. Ibid., pp. 205 – 206. See also Waley-Cohen (2000), p. 120.

34. Jiading, Songjiang, Taicang, Kunshan, and others.

35. For further details on the Rebellion of the Three Feudatories, see Mote (1999), pp. 844 – 848; in Hummel (2018), "Keng ching-chung 耿精忠," pp. 415 – 416; and Spence (1991), pp. 49 – 53.

36. Kangxi still needed to address the removal of rebel descendants of Koxinga (Zheng Chenggong) from Taiwan and solidify control over his northern and western borders.

37. Michael Chang (2007), p. 73, including Footnote No. 6.

38. Ibid., p. 1, citing Gao Jin in the *Nanxun shengdian* (*Great Canon of the Southern Tours*).

39. Hearn (1990), "Table 1. Itinerary of the Kangxi Emperor's Second Tour of the South," pp. 20 – 22. Kangxi also spent nine days in Suzhou and its vicinity (five days in Suzhou on his way south and four more on his return trip north).

40. Ibid., pp. 45 – 46.

41. Campbell (2011B), n.p.

42. Hearn (1990), "Table 2. Extant Scrolls from *The Kangxi Southern Inspection Tour*," p. 66, and "Table 3. Approximate Number of Figures Depicted in *The Kangxi Southern Inspection Tour*," p. 179.

43. Ibid., p. 55.

44. Chinese scroll paintings like Hui's would be unrolled slowly from right to left. The act of unrolling yields a sense of physical movement through the scenery along the Emperor's travel route.

45. Scroll IX is held at the Palace Museum in Beijing. It can be viewed online in full detail at https://translate.google.com/translate?Hl=en&sl=zhcn&u=https://zh.wikipedia.org/zhhans/file:wang_hui_and_others._emperor_kangxi_touring_the_south._9th_handscroll_of_a_set._1691-98_palace_mus._beijing.jpg&prev=search&pto=aue . The location of Scroll VIII depicting Kangxi's route segment from Suzhou past Jiaxing to the northern outskirts of Hangzhou remains regrettably unknown, but Wang Hui's paper and ink draft version is still extant.

46. See, for example, Hearn (1990), pp. 132 – 133.

47. Kangxi's Southern Inspection Tours were fraught with political concerns that they were financially wasteful junkets, perceptions that the Emperor strove repeatedly to deflect in the poems he wrote while traveling. Michael Chang (2007) provides extensive, book-length treatment of this and other issues for both Kangxi's and Qianlong's Southern Tours.

48. Wang Liping (2011), n.p.

49. Ibid., n.p. In a footnote, Wang cites as her source Li Wei 李卫, *Xihu zhi* 西湖志 (Hang-zhou: Zhejiang shuju, 1870), *juan* 5, p. 20a.

50. Spence (1966), pp. 130 – 131.

51. The earliest extant list of Ten Scenes at West Lake is found in Zhu Mu's 祝穆 (d. 1255) *Topographical Guide to Touring Sites of Scenic Beauty* (方与胜览, *Fangyu shenglan*).

52. For an extended discussion of the editorial approach in the 1734 *Gazetteer of West Lake* and how it differed from earlier, more sightseeing-oriented books, see Altenburger (2017), pp. 118 – 131.

53. Kile (2013), p. 53.

54. Ibid., p. 57. Other sources state that Li Yu purchased the two young girls.

55. Ibid., from unnumbered "Abstract" page.

56. Chang Chun-shu and Shelley Hsueh-lun Chang (1992), p. 69.

57. Pollard (2000), translated from Li Yu, p. 97.

58. Zhou Lüjing 周履靖 (c. 1542 – c. 1633) from Jiaxing is said to have published China's first multi-genre painting manuals sometime before 1579, *Huilin* 绘林(*Forest of Paintings*) and *Huasou* 画薮 (*Grove of Paintings*). See Park (2011), p. 5.

59. Chang and Chang (1992), p. 95.

60. For an informative online discussion of *The Mustard Seed Garden Manual of Painting*, see "Chinese Literature: *Jieziyuan huapu* 芥子園畫譜 *The Painting Book of the Mustard Seed Garden*" at the *Chinaknowledge* website, accessed at http://www.chinaknowledge.de/Literature/Science/jieziyuanhuapu.html. An English-language version of the book was published in 1956 by Sze Mai-mai and Michael J. Hiscox under the name *The Tao of Painting: A Study of the Ritual Disposition of Chinese Painting* (New York: Pantheon Press, 1956) and since republished by Princeton University Press as *The Mustard Seed Garden Manual of Painting*.

61. Translated in Patrick Hanan's oft-referenced version as the Latin-sounding name Vesperus.

62. Hanan (1988), p. 76.

63. Huc (1857), p. 341.

64. Ibid., pp. 342 – 343.

65. Demarchi and Scartezzini (1996), p. 19.

66. The pressure on so many scholars and officials to withdraw from official life and disavow service to the new dynasty may have facilitated Martini's ability to find unemployed literati willing to work with him on translations.

67. Martini had written most of a second volume to carry his historical account forward through the Ming Dynasty, but that manuscript was lost.

68. Xu Mingde (1996), p. 28.

69. According to David Mungello, the book was republished more than twenty times between 1654 and 1706 in French, German, English, Italian, Dutch, Portuguese, Spanish, Swedish, and Danish. Hsia asserts that the book was reprinted twenty-two times in the first twenty years after its introduction. See Mungello (1985), p. 110, and Hsia (1998), p. 29.

70. Mungello (1994), pp. 28 – 29.

71. In 1687, for example, the French journal *Le Petit Messager* described the Church of the Immaculate Conception: "Its shape is so harmonious that words fail to describe it." From Liu Jiantang (1996) p. 337.

72. Mungello (1994), pp. 28 – 30. The Cathedral of the Immaculate Conception is now also called "The Catholic Church" (天主堂, Tianzhu tang). It continues as an active religious institution at its original site and (renovated) building. The church is located at 415 Zhongshan Road North (中山北路415号), near today's Wulin Square.

73. The Wei Kuangguo [Martino Martini] Missionary Memorial Park 卫匡国传教士纪念园, as it is identified on Google Maps, is located at 549 Xixi Road, Xihu District. It is easily accessible by public bus but requires an appointment to be admitted by the caretaker, best arranged at the Cathedral of the Immaculate Conception. For Google Maps location, use this link: https://www.google.com/maps/place/wei+kuangguo+missionary+memorial+park/@30.2613993,120.1023477,20.9z/data=!4m9!1m2!2m1!1z6kw_5rmw5zwk6yws5y6cioilv-a6qui3rw!3m5!1s0x0:0xef1af72782b5889d!8m2!3d30.261489!4d120.102572!15schnopb_muzbllatphzlljoig6kw_5rqq6levkgegbxvzzxvt]

74. For Couplet, see Heyndrickx (1990).

75. Liu Jiantang (1996), p. 331. Prospero Intorcetta witnessed these events and described them in his writings.

76. Rev. George E. Moule visited the cemetery in 1890 and described it similarly, adding of the setting at that time: "The situation is beautiful; a quiet valley guarded by lofty hills; their Western and Northern slopes clothed with wood." See G.E. Moule (1890), pp. 509 – 510. Moule wrote that during his visit to the site, he noted funerary urns identified as containing the remains of Nicolaus Trigault and Emmanual Diaz, both of whom had formerly headed the Jesuit mission in Hangzhou. The cemetery was badly damaged during the troubles of the 1960s and was restored in a smaller but still parklike space in 1985. The gated cemetery today contains statues and biographical information for both Martino Martini and Prospero Intorcetta. The underground crypt contains a dozen funeral urns, two of which are respectively labeled for those two celebrated Jesuits. The cemetery is protected today as a Provincial Historical Site.

77. These incidents are related in some detail in Mungello (1994), pp. 60 – 61.

78. Treutlein (1941), p. 442, Footnote No. 23.

79. Mungello (1994), pp. 62 – 66.

80. The Cathedral of the Immaculate Conception was occupied by the Taiping rebels in the 1860s and placed under French Catholic control after the conflict ended. In the 1960s, the church buildings were converted into residences, but they were returned to Catholic religious use again in 1982 and underwent major renovation in 2009. In 2018, the pastor was Father Paul Zheng.

81. A famous 1930 painting of an Iowa farmer and his daughter by Grant Wood.

82. Francesca Bray states that "'Promoting Agriculture' (劝农, *Quannong*) was one of the principal responsibilities of government in imperial China." See Bray (2007), p. 523.

83. Hammers (2011), p. 2. Hammers contends (pp. 4 – 7) that Lou Shou's scrolls offered a

"commentary on the momentous developments within the civil service and their impact on Song society" (p. 4), referring to the changing relationship between the Emperor and the people due to a professionalized bureaucratic class growing between them.

84. During the Ming era, copies of the scrolls made their way to Japan and Korea, where they were widely received as the inspiration for new versions more closely attuned to each country's rural economy. See Bray (2007), p. 527.

85. The two added panels for rice cultivation portrayed the emergence of the first rice shoots and a post-harvest thanksgiving sacrifice to the gods. For silk production, Jiao omitted three images but added two, one for dyeing and the other for finished clothing.

86. Golas (2015), pp. 149 – 150.

87. Philip Hu (2000), pp. 74 – 75.

88. Bray (2007), p. 524.

89. The revised title signified that these images were Kangxi's updated and approved version and included his poems in addition to Lou Shou's original verses.

90. Golas (2015), p. 150; Bray (2007), pp. 521, 530; and Hammers (2011), p. 247, Footnote No. 2.

91. Golas (2015), pp. 152 – 154, contends that Jiao Bingzhen also took many of the hard edges off of the original work, depicting peasant life as far less onerous and with far fewer hardships than Lou Shou had conveyed in his work. The Kangxi Emperor no doubt approved of Jiao's idealization of the peasant life in his reign era. For another interesting comparison of the Lou Shou and Jiao Bingzhen images, see Laufer (1912), pp. 102 – 106.

92. Excerpted from Berg (2013), pp. 225 – 226.

93. Ibid., p. 227.

94. Berg (2007A), p. 84.

95. Ibid., p. 77, or Wang Yanning (2013), p. 108.

96. Clunas (2013), p. 472.

97. Laing (1990), p. 95. Laing's source is Yü Chien-Hua, *The Biographical Dictionary of Chinese Artists* (Shanghai, 1981).

98. "Chen Shu," in Hummel (2018), p. 58.

99. Ibid., p. 58.

100. "Qian Chenqun," in Hummel (2018), pp. 477 – 478.

101. Weidner (1988), pp. 117 – 120.

102. Weidner (1990), p. 129.

103. "Chen Shu," in Hummel (2018), p. 58.

104. See, for example, what appears to be an archived page from the Beijing Palace Museum website at https://web.archive.org/web/20140513161725/http://www.dpm.org.cn/www_oldweb/English/E/e9/14-01.htm.

105. Weidner (1990), p. 149.

106. An entirely separate communication channel from the long-established palace memorial and postal system that continued to operate in its traditional manner. An excellent source for more information on Kangxi's private memorial system can be found in Spence (1966).

107. Mote (1999), p. 885.

108. Hummel (2018), p. 551, claims that as early as age 8, Lü was able to write proper essays.

109. Ibid., p. 551.

110. Spence (2001). Quote on p. 78, information on Zeng's and Zhang's arrests, pp. 83 – 84.

111. Ibid., p. 105.

112. The period from 1683 – 1799 is commonly referred to by historians as the "High Qing."

113. See interactive animation model of John Burn-Murdoch of the *Financial Times*, "Ranking the World's Most Populous Cities, over 500 Years of History," at https://www.visualcapitalist.com/worlds-most-populous-cities-500-years-history/. Data for years prior to 1900 are drawn from

NASA Earth Data's "Historical Urban Population, 3700 BC to 2000."

114. Lillian M. Li (1981), p. 4.

115. Ibid., pp. 41 – 42.

116. Ibid., p. 44.

117. Widmer (1996), p. 93.

118. Chow Kai-wing (2004), p. 80.

119. DuHalde (1741), pp. 193 – 194.

120. Anderson (1795), p. 256.

121. Barrow (1804), pp. 527 – 528.

122. Fortune (1847), p. 36.

123. Barrow (1804), p. 524.

124. Smith (1859), p. 127.

125. Fortune (1847), p. 35.

126. Cole (1986), p. 7.

127. Ibid., pp. 177 – 178.

128. Ibid., p. 179.

129. Franck (1925), p. 37.

130. Cole (1986), p. 75.

131. Figures from Elman (1994), p. 117.

132. Li Chen (2012), pp. 22 – 24. Li's article provides an exhaustive discussion of the legal specialist profession in Qing Dynasty China.

133. Ho Ping-ti (1962), Table 35, "Prefectures of Unusual Academic Success in Ming Times," p. 246. By Ho's accounting for the Ming era, Ningbo produced 598 *jinshi* (8th most), Jiaxing 528 (9th most), and Hangzhou 520 (11th most).

134. Jiaxing had 476 *jinshi* during the Qing era (7th most) and Huzhou had 421 (8th most). See Ho (1962), Table 36, "Prefectures of Unusual Academic Success in Ch'ing Times," p. 247.

135. Cole (1980), p. 319.

136. Ibid., p. 318. Cole's "vertical administrative clique" is what today would be called *guanxi* 关系 in China and "networking" in the Western world, although the Chinese conception of *guanxi* is far more culturally complex and ingrained with elements of trust and reciprocity than the more superficial Western notion of networking.

137. Cole (1986), p. 132.

138. Ibid., p. 10.

139. Watt (1977), p. 364. Watt's essay provides an exhaustive introductory discussion of the structure, operation, staffing, layout, and management of local government offices in the Qing Dynasty era.

140. Cole (1986), p. 10.

Chapter 11

1. Schmidt (2003), p. 500.

2. The Kangxi Emperor's full name was Aisin Gioro Hongli爱新觉罗弘历. Aisin Gioro was the Manchu family name of all the Qing Dynasty emperors.

3. Chang, Michael G. (2007), p. 307.

4. Elliott (2009), pp. 78 – 79.

5. In Chinese culture, a person's 60th birthday was particularly auspicious as marking the completion of one full life cycle through the five elements (Wood, Fire, Earth, Metal, and Water) and, within each element, the twelve years corresponding to the Chinese Zodiac (Rat, Ox, Tiger, Rabbit, Dragon, Snake, Horse, Sheep, Monkey, Rooster, Dog, and Pig).

6. Chang, Michael G. (2007), p. 100.

7. Ibid., p. 173.

8. The Extending Propitious Omens Temple (延祥觀, Yanxiang guan).

9. Dong Sigao had outlined this briefly in poem No. 30 on Solitary Hill in his "One Hundred Poems on West Lake," discussed earlier in Chapter 8. See Ridgway (2020), pp. 276 – 277.

10. Around the beginning of the Republican era in 1911, the temple was converted into an imperial garden and shrine. The temporary palace, long since destroyed, remains only as architectural relics. In 1927, that portion of Gushan was renamed Zhongshan Park in honor of Sun Zhongshan (Sun Yat-sen).

11. Adapted from Chang, Michael G. (2007), p. 352. The reference to disaster in Line 3 concerns local flooding in the year prior to Qianlong's visit.

12. Hearn (1988), p. 103. Hearn's paper provides a helpful comparison between the Kangxi and Qianlong Southern Inspection Tour scrolls. David Hockney and Philip Haas provide close-up views and revealing video analysis of how Xu Yang's painting differed from Wang Hui's in artistically significant ways in their forty-six-minute DVD, *A Day on the Grand Canal with the Emperor of China, or Surface Is Illusion but so Is Depth* (New York: The Metropolitan Museum of Art, 1988).

13. For a list of the locations and measured lengths of all twenty-four Southern Inspection Tour scrolls, see the chart on the Columbia University website http://projects.mcah.columbia.edu/nanxuntu/html/scrolls/locations.htm.

14. For a detailed treatment of the history of the Hangzhou Bay seawalls and Qianlong's political motivations for his direct involvement, see Fang Qin (2008).

15. Chang, Michael G. (2007), p. 372 – 373.

16. Fang Qin (2008), pp. 112 – 146.

17. Chen family history from "Chen Shiguan," in Hummel (2018), pp. 55 – 56.

18. Hummel attributes fatherhood to Chen Xian but identifies him in Chinese as 陳詵 (Chen Shen), while the less authoritative Wikipedia entry for the Yongzheng Emperor claims, without a source reference, Chen Shiguan.

19. Fang Qin (2008), p. 133, states that it was the Emperor Qianlong himself who gave the garden its name. Previously, the family had referred to it as the "Corner Garden" for being located in a corner of their property.

20. Doar (2007B).

21. Benn (2015), p. 174.

22. Jiang Yuanxin (2019), p. 107. Jiang points out (pp. 107 – 108) that the Zhejiang gazetteer from just a few decades earlier had listed several famous Zhejiang teas as local products but made no mention of any Longjing area teas.

23. For more information on the tea-for-horses trade and the Imperial Tea and Horse Agency, see Smith (1991).

24. Translation courtesy of Zheng Hanqi.

25. Zhou En-lai and Richard Nixon shared Longjing tea together in 1962 Hangzhou, and Longjing was presented as a gift to Queen Elizabeth II during her State visit in 1986. It was also a favorite tea of Chairman Mao Zedong.

26. Yang Jianxin (2010), p. 27.

27. Ibid., p. 27.

28. Wakeman (1985), pp. 1096 – 1097.

29. Ibid., pp. 1097 – 1098.

30. Guy (1987), p. 36.

31. Ibid., p. 90.

32. Ibid., p. 1. A number of online sources use the figure 3,461.

33. Goodrich (1966), pp. 108 – 109.

34. Guy (1987), pp. 166 – 171.

35. Goodrich (1966), pp. 34 – 35. The Index listed 2,855 titles to be eradicated and another

400 – 500 to be "corrected."

36. Hummel (2018), p. 518.

37. Wei, Betty Peh-t'i (2006), p. 68, Footnote No. 33.

38. Ruan Yuan also compiled the oldest extant collection of more than 300 biographies of scientists, titled *Biographies of Astronomers* (畴人传, *Chouren zhuan*). His work included Western figures such as Ptolemy, Euclid, Archimedes, Wallis, Fermat, and Newton. It also punctured a tradition that only government officials and Confucian scholars merited such biographical memorializations.

39. The island is also sometimes identified by the mixed Chinese/English name, "Ruangong's Islet."

40. Wei, Betty Peh-t'i (2006), p. 70.

41. Schmidt (2008), p. 133.

42. From the 1740s until his death in 1764, Cao Xueqin 曹雪芹 (1715 - 1764) wrote the classic novel *Dream of the Red Chamber* (红楼梦, *Hong lou meng*) that included the fictional Prospect Garden (大观园, Daguan yuan).

43. Waley (1956), p. 100. Sui Yuan would survive in the family's possession until the Taiping occupation of Nanjing in 1853. A number of Yuan Mei's descendants committed suicide upon the Taipings' arrival. By the time the city was retaken from the Taipings, the garden was in ruins, converted into urban rice paddies by flattening the manmade hills and filling in the ponds. The family's collection of books, paintings, and other cultural treasures was lost or destroyed as well. According to Schmidt (2003), p. 122, "The only physical features [of Harmony Garden] that survive to this day are some ponds on the campus of Nanjing Normal University."

44. Yuan Mei had at least six concubines during his lifetime—Misses Tao, Fang, Lu, Chung, Jin, and Zhong—and at least one more he gave away after she was scarred by smallpox. In fact, it was Miss Chung who gave Yuan his first surviving son in 1778, at the grandfatherly age of 62. Yuan named him Achi 阿迟, meaning "Late One."

45. Riegel (2010), pp. 96 – 97. Riegel suggests that Yuan Mei's "elegant gathering" of four male literati at his Harmony Garden in 1765, including having afterward commissioned a portrait of the occasion, might have informed his thoughts about his 1790 gathering of women disciples in Hangzhou.

46. Meng Liuxi (2007), p. 71.

47. Chen, Janet C. (2016), pp. 2 – 5. Chen (pp. 17 – 18, 22) notes that the portrait was not factually accurate in its roster of attendees at the 1790 gathering but was intended instead to demonstrate Yuan Mei's support for women's education and literary/artistic creations. See also Riegel (2010), p. 107.

48. Mann (1992), p. 55.

49. *Tanci* 弹词 is a form of narrative involving both storytelling and ballad singing, mixing both prose and verse. Singing is usually accompanied by playing a stringed instrument called a pipa. *Tanci* and its related form, *pingtan*, have long been popular entertainment forms throughout Jiangnan.

50. Meng Lijun, 孟丽君 translates as "Beautiful Gentleman," telegraphing a significant element of the story line.

51. Suzhou native Gao Qi was a highly accomplished poet in the waning years of the Yuan Dynasty. Despite his efforts to remain politically unaffiliated in the dynastic succession, he was implicated by association and subsequently cut in half at the waist in one of Zhu Yuanzhong's zealous purges for having written a congratulatory poem to Wei Guan 魏观 (1305-1374), the first Ming Prefect of Suzhou. Zhu believed that Wei's popularity posed a threat to his rule of the nascent Ming Dynasty. See also Koss (2015), pp. 119 – 125.

52. According to a famous legend, Xie Daoyun's uncle challenged Xie and her brothers, sisters, and cousins to see who could best describe falling snow in a poetic image. Xie Daoyun easily bested all her competition by comparing the snow to white willow catkins.

53. Volpp (2001), p. 243.

54. Ibid., p. 240.

55. Ibid., p. 241. According to the legend, Qu Yuan ultimately committed suicide by drowning.

56. Ibid., p. 241.

57. Crossley (1990), pp. 67 – 68.

58. Ibid., pp. 72, 77.

59. Ibid., p. 85, from Lao She, *Huang huo*, [*Anxiety and Disaster*] (Hong Kong: Weitong, 1972), p. 274.

60. For a measured, contrarian view of the usual historical assessment of Qianlong's actions, see James Carter, "Lord Macartney, China, and the Convenient Lies of History," *Supchina.com* (September 9, 2020), accessed at https://supchina.com/2020/09/09/lord-macartney-china-and-the-convenient-lies-of-history/. For Lord George Macartney's summary political assessment of 1793 China and its future, see Macartney (1807), p. 398, accessed at https://archive.org/details/someaccountofpub02barr/page/398/mode/2up?Q=old%2c+crazy%2c+first-rate. For the translated contents of Qianlong's written response to Macartney, see Backhouse and Bland (1914), pp. 322 – 331.

61. As the Japanese army would discover and use in their 1937 assault on Shanghai.

62. Crossley (1990), *Orphan Warriors*, p. 103.

63. For more details on the skirmishes of 1841 and early 1842 and the imperial strategy of that moment, see Elleman and Paine (2019), pp. 140 -145.

64. According to Waley (1958), p. 167, the attack was planned in the Tiger year (1842), in the Tiger month (March), on the Tiger day (the 10th), at the Tiger hour (3:00 – 5:00 a.m.), all mirroring a legendary "Four Tigers" conquest attack attributed to the founding of the Sui Dynasty in 589.

65. The following details of the Chinese counter-attack on Zhenhai, Ningbo, and Zhoushan from Waley (1958), pp. 158 – 178, drawn in great part from Bei Qingqiao's book of 120 poems about his Opium War experiences, 咄咄吟 (*Duo-duo yin*), translated by Waley as *Songs of Oh Dear, Oh Dear!* and in more modern times as *The Cry*.

66. Waley (1958), p. 170 for monkeys, pp. 177 – 178 for smallpox. Waley's account of these Opium War incidents, drawn largely from first-hand Chinese accounts, makes for remarkable reading about the state of the Qing military in the mid-19th-Century.

67. Hall and Bernard (1847), p. 377.

68. Ibid., p. 380.

69. Ibid., p. 383.

70. Ibid., p. 384.

71. Ibid., pp. 387 – 388.

72. Ibid., p. 385.

73. The British battle fleet also threatened to attack Yangzhou but were paid 500,000 taels of silver by the Yangzhou salt administration and salt merchants to bypass the city. See Li Xue (2018), p. 67.

74. The five 1842 Nanjing Treaty ports opened by the Treaty of Nanjing were Canton, Xiamen, Fuzhou, Ningbo, and Shanghai. The Nanjing agreement became the first in a series of what in Chinese history are known as the "unequal treaties." The Nanjing Treaty also marked the beginning of the period now called the "hundred years of humiliation."

75. Hall and Bernard (1847), p. 283.

Chapter 12

1. Graham (1990), p. 61.

2. Jen Yu-wen (1973), p. 118.

3. Built in the 15th Century and often listed as one of the Seven Wonders of the World, the Porcelain Pagoda was celebrated in the 1878 poem *Keramos* by Henry Wadsworth Longfellow.

4. Jen (1973), p. 370.

5. For details, see Spence (1997).

6. Giquel (1985), p. 5.

7. See Spence (1997), pp. 66 – 109, for details about the origins of the Taiping crusade.

8. Curwen (1977), p. 88.

9. Platt (2012), pp. 64 – 65. Platt describes these discussions taking place before the Qing siege was broken. Jen (1973), p. 378, places the same events as happening after the siege ended. Both present essentially the same conclusion.

10. Curwen (1977), p. 230, Footnote No. 45.

11. Jen (1973), p. 371 and Crossley (1990), p. 130.

12. Meyer-Fong (2013), p. 115. Meyer-Fong cites the source as the memoir of Anhui native Xu Feng'en.

13. Curwen (1977), p. 112.

14. Platt (2012), pp. 93 – 94.

15. Modern Anhui Province.

16. Platt (2012), p. 205.

17. Even with a 20,000-man reinforcement headed by Hong Rengan, the Taipings failed to break Zeng Guofan's siege of Anqing, thanks in major part to the fearsome defensive work of a cavalry unit led by the Manchu commander Duolonga. Anqing finally fell on September 3, ending a gruesome period of starvation that culminated with the sale of human meat in Anqing's city markets. Platt (2012), p. 215, reports that despite the horrific suffering of the civilian residents, Zeng's soldiers nevertheless slaughtered all the survivors they could find.

18. Some records estimate that Hangzhou's population had swollen from 600,000 to well over two million as the Taipings approached the area.

19. Jen (1973), p. 441.

20. Meyer-Fong (2013), p. 106.

21. Ibid., pp. 178-179, 191 – 194.

22. Zhang's short-lived Martyr's Garden, built near the site of his mother's death, was a small and macabre memorial. It included buildings with names like "Martyr" and "Corridor of Bitter Tears." See Meyer-Fong (2013), pp. 185 – 186.

23. Jen (1973), p. 442.

24. Ibid., p. 438.

25. What must have seemed to Ward as an honorific may have been tinged with a touch of Chinese irony or sarcasm. In the final years of the Northern Song, General Guo Yaoshi 郭藥師 led a mixed Chinese/barbarian army by the same name as he switched allegiances in 1122 from the Khitan Liao to the Song, and in 1125 from the Song to the Jin as he surrendered to the Jurchens the city that is now Beijing.

26. As much as the British troop transport assistance was provided as a self-protective measure for the defense of Shanghai, it was hardly without commercial benefit. For three round trips ferrying Li's new army down the Yangzi, Mackenzie, Richardson exacted an outlandish fee of 180,000 taels of silver, much to the displeasure and disgust of Zeng Guofan. See Platt (2012), pp. 270 – 271.

27. Ward had discovered that shallow-draft steamships provided the most effective means in canal-laced eastern Jiangsu for moving heavy artillery rapidly and positioning it to fire, largely uncontested, from outside Taiping-held walled cities.

28. See Koss (2015), pp. 259 – 271, for an extended description of Li and Gordon's collaboration to retake southern Jiangsu Province from Shanghai to Nanjing.

29. Cantlie and Jones (1912), p. 248. Hart would later write optimistically, and presciently, that "the China of the year 2000 will be very different from the China of 1900!" See Preston (2001), pp. 346 – 347.

30. Leibo estimates about fifty Western instructors, fifty Filipinos, and "a few hundred" Chinese. See Giquel (1985), p. 20.

31. Leibo (1985), p. 37.

32. Wilson (1868), p. 116.

33. Ibid., pp. 115 – 116, and Giquel (1985), p. 34.

34. Chen Qitian (1938), pp. 6 – 7.

35. Boulger (1885), p. 353.

36. Backhouse and Bland (1911), pp. 508 – 509.

37. Bales (1937), p. 150.

38. Platt (2012), p. 307.

39. Minturn (1858), pp. 54 – 55.

40. Williams (1883), p. 621.

41. Zuo Zongtang had argued for months with Zeng Guofan about diverting forces from the latter's siege of Nanjing in order to secure Guangde against a rebel consolidation that could even spawn a relaunch of the rebellion. Zeng refused, probably focusing on the honors and awards that would accrue from retaking Nanjing and eliminating the Taiping Heavenly King. Subsequent events proved Zuo correct in his strategic assessment of Guangde's significance.

42. Williams (1883), p. 621.

43. Leibo (1985), p. 58, citing Giquel's journal entry of August 26, 1864.

44. *The London and China Telegraph*, Vol. VII, No. 161 (January 12, 1865), p. 24. See also Clarke and Gregory (1982), pp. 412 – 416.

45. *The London and China Telegraph*, Vol. VII, No. 161 (January 12, 1865), p. 25.

46. For Jennifer 8. Lee, see Lee (2008) and YouTube video at https://www.ted.com/talks/jennifer_8_lee_the_hunt_for_general_tso?language=en#t-239314. For Fuchsia Dunlop, see Dunlop (2006). See also Matt Soniak, "Who Was General Tso?" (August 4, 2011), accessed at https://www.mentalfloss.com/article/28421/who-was-general-tso.

47. Liu Haiming (2015), p. 99.

48. Dunlop (2006), p. 171.

49. Liu Haiming (2015), p. 99.

50. Lee, YouTube video at 3:33, accessed at https://www.ted.com/talks/jennifer_8_lee_the_hunt_for_general_tso?language=en#t-239314.

Chapter 13

1. Two poems by Zhu Shuzhen. Adapted from Goedde (2013), "Zhu Shuzhen," pp. 186 – 187.

2. Although all such estimates are speculative, most estimates of deaths from the rebellion range from twenty to thirty million, with twenty million the most commonly cited figure.

3. Zhang Daye (2013), p. 93.

4. Meyer-Fong (2013), p. 126.

5. Cloud (1906), p. 8. Frederick Douglass Cloud served as a consular officer in China in the early 1900s, including a stint in Hangzhou which led him to write his "City of Heaven" guidebook.

6. Meyer-Fong (2013), pp. 124, 131.

7. Ibid., p. 196.

8. Meyer-Fong (2014), pp. 86 – 88.

9. Ho Ping-ti (1959), p. 154.

10. Ibid., pp. 155 – 156.

11. Ibid., p. 158.

12. Von Richtofen (1903), p. 75.

13. Ibid., p. 76.

14. He Yimin (2008), p. 272.

15. Ho Ping-ti (1959), Table 40, p. 241.

16. He Yimin (2008), p. 273. Estimates of Shanghai's population in the 1840s range from

200,000 – 300,000, about the size of second-tier cities like Songjiang, Jiaxing, or Huzhou.

17. Lyon (1936), p. 7.

18. A.E. Moule (1891A), p. 3.

19. Lyon (1895), p. 82.

20. Griffiths (2004), p. 62.

21. A.E. Moule (1891A), p. 104.

22. Geil (1911), p. 38.

23. DeGruche (1930), pp. 16 – 17.

24. Bird (1895), p. 37.

25. Husbands and families publishing the poetry collections of their female family members became increasingly common and socially accepted in the late imperial era. Nearly four thousand such published collections by women writers were catalogued in one study by the scholar Hu Wen-kai 胡文楷 (1901 – 1988). See Grace Fong (2014), p. 126.

26. Rankin (1986), pp. 107 – 108.

27. The five garrison gates were Hongzhen in the northeast section, Chengqian (in the north-west), Pinghai and Yangzhai (on the eastern wall), and Yanling (north wall). The garrison covered the area bounded in today's Hangzhou by Changsheng Road on the north, Kaiyuan Road on the south, Zhongshan Central Road on the east, and West Lake on the west.

28. Meyer-Fong (2013), p. 205.

29. Crossley (1990), pp. 147 – 148.

30. Lyon (1895), p. 7.

31. Oliver (1974), p. 85.

32. Kahler (1895), p. 53. Kahler's visit took place in 1894, indicating that this damage still remained visible thirty years after the end of the war.

33. Crossley (1990), p. 152.

34. Hummel (2018), pp. 101 – 103.

35. Bird (1895), p. 34.

36. Silkworm eggs were smuggled into Japan in 199 CE.

37. The microsporidium was *Nosema bombycis*, the virus was infectious flacherie, and the fungus was *Beauveria bassiana*.

38. Li (1981), p. 42, Table 4. Similarly for Suzhou, the number of looms fell from 650 – 700 to around 245 in 1870, after the war ended.

39. Yeh Wen-hsin (1996), p. 58. Some sources modify the "four elephants" epithet to say "seventy-two *golden* dogs." For the past decade, Huzhou's city government has converted this high-society putdown into praise for social consciousness by selecting a major local enterprise to receive its annual "New Elephant Award." See, for example, https://www.giantkone.com/en/site/newsdetails/379 .

40. Li (1981), p. 106. Across the Qiantang River, cotton production from Xioashan east to Yuyao slowly expanded and paralleled the trade expansion in silk. In the final decades of the 19th century, cotton exports to Shanghai, Japan, and Fujian Province dominated the commercial trade flow through the ports at Ningbo and exceeded even that of tea exports. See Rankin (1986), p. 66.

41. Li (1981), p. 82.

42. Widmer (2006), p. 221. Natasha Jennifer Chow (2012), p. 28, lists nine *Honglou meng* sequels by name, published respectively in 1796, 1798, 1799, 1805, 1814, 1819, 1820, 1824, and 1843, each produced before *Honglou meng ying* in 1877.

43. The missing manuscript section to one of Gu Taiqing's two published poetry collections, discovered in Japan by Zhao Botao 赵伯陶, included a poem in which Gu mentions her occasional efforts to complete the sequel.

44. Widmer (2006), p. 191.

45. Shen Shanbao (沈善宝, 1808–1862) was already a well-established poet in Hangzhou's

female literary circles when her husband Wu Lingyun's 武凌云 official position in Beijing required her to relocate to the capital in 1837. There she connected with the Xu sisters and was introduced to their Beijing network of Hangzhou natives as well as Gu Taiqing. In addition to her own poems, Shen Shanbao is best remembered for her compilation *Remarks on Poetry by Notable Women* (名媛 诗话, *Mingyuan shihua*), a collection of poetry by more than 600 Qing-era women authors that Shen compiled and edited between 1845 and 1855. For more on Shen Shanbao, see Fong (2008), pp. 142 – 157.

46. Huang Qiaole (2004), p. 36.

47. Widmer (2006), p. 193. Note that Shen Shanbao passed away the following year (1862).

48. Natasha Jennifer Chow (2012), p. 67. Chow's thesis paper offers a detailed and well-sourced comparison of Gu Taiqing's *Honglou meng ying* sequel with Cao Yueqin's original novel.

49. Zhou's father-in-law, Yan Tingyu 严廷钰, had passed away in Yunnan Province in 1852.

50. Yu Zhang (2013), p. 40.

51. Ibid., pp. 45 – 46.

52. Ibid., p. 97.

53. An 1876 article in the *North China Herald* stated that Hu's uncle was a Hangzhou money changer or lender and that his nephew took over his uncle's small business. See Stanley (1961), p. 8.

54. Ibid., pp. 12 – 13.

55. A. E. Moule (1891), p. 40.

56. Stanley (1961), p. 18. One tael equaled roughly 1.2 – 1.3 ounces of silver.

57. In 1876, violent summer thunderstorms in Italy, France and Spain had resulted in the death of more than half of that year's silkworm crop, leading foreign silk merchants to turn to Chinese suppliers and bid up the price of silk by over 50%. See Nelson Chang and Laurence Chang (2010), p. 35.

58. Stanley (1961), p. 73.

59. Edward Young (1874), p. 434.

60. Stanley (1961), p. 80.

61. See, for example (in Chinese), "胡雪岩故居见闻：富丽堂皇、金碧辉煌，现当年富豪妻妾成群的奢华 (Rich Wives and Concubines Lived in Luxury)," October 17, 2006, accessed at http://baijiahao.baidu.com/s?id=1580400922108201809&wfr=spider&for=pc.

62. The building address is No. 18 Yuanbao Street, at Zhonghe S. Road, a little east of the Hangzhou Drum Tower.

63. See Yi Xu, et. al. (2018), pp. 330 – 331.

64. Rankin (1986), p. 7.

65. Ibid., p. 3.

Chapter 14

1. Lee Hui-shu (2001), p. 19. Translated from Xihu Laoren's *Fansheng lu, Records of Splendor*, during the reign of Emperor Ningzong (r. 1194 – 1224).

2. Smith (1859), p. 127. For an interesting historical view of 19th-Century Westerners and their hunting parties in Jiangnan, see Wade (1895).

3. A.E. Moule (1891A), p. 47.

4. Joseph Edkins, "Protestant Missions in China: To H.E. Sir Rutherford Alcock, K.C.B., H.M. Envoy Extraordinary and Minister Plenipotentiary, Peking," *The Chinese Recorder and Missionary Journal*, Volume II, No. 4 (September 1869), p. 104.

5. In his written response in 1792 to the entreaties of the British envoy George Lord Macartney for a British trade relationship with imperial China, the Kangxi Emperor declared: "As your Ambassador can see for himself, we possess all things. I set no value on your country's manufactures." Translation from Backhouse and Bland (1914), p. 325.

6. Nevius (1869), p. 153.

7. Griffiths (2004), p. 30.

8. Cited from the Royal Scottish Geographical Society in Gammie (1935), pp. 151 – 152. Main's obituary notice in the *British Medical Journal*, Vol. 2, No. 3844 (September 8, 1934), p. 495, can be found online at https://www.ncbi.nlm.nih.gov/pmc/articles/PMC2445124/?page=1.

9. Gammie (1935), *Duncan Main of Hangchow*, p. 154.

10. Ibid., pp. 45 – 46.

11. DeGruche (1930), p. 38.

12. Fang Xiaoping (2009), p. 3.

13. Bird (1895), pp. 42 – 46.

14. Gammie (1935), *Duncan Main of Hangchow*, p. 68.

15. Fang Xiaoping (2009), pp. 2 – 3.

16. "The Crisis in China," *The British Medical Journal*, Vol 1, No. 3465 (June 4, 1927), pp. 1014.

17. Campany (2002), p. 144. Apricots were domesticated in China as early as 2000 BCE and later migrated through the Middle East to Europe in the 1st Century CE.

18. Elwin (1909), pp. 70 – 71.

19. Bond (2019), p. 448.

20. Ibid., p. 447.

21. Yifang School is located on the site of today's Changsha Tianjiabing Experimental Middle School 长沙市田家炳实验中学; see Bond (2019), p. 461. Louise Barnes's decision to remain in England in 1913 as Zeng Baosun's college-years guardian—in the capacity she had promised to the Zeng family—required her to resign as Principal of the Mary Vaughan School in 1913.

22. A.E. Moule (1891A), p. 138.

23. Cohen (1963), p.181.

24. Lyon, "Historical Sketch of the Hangchow Station," pp. 87 – 88.

25. "Missionary News," *The Chinese Recorder and Missionary Journal*, Volume V, No. 4 (July – August 1874), p. 223.

26. Lyon (1895), p. 86.

27. A rather fascinating collection of diplomatic, missionary, and Hangzhou officials' correspondence on this issue and its resolution can be found online in *Papers Relating to the Foreign Relations of the United States, Transmitted to Congress* (Washington: Government Printing Office, 1874), pp. 232 – 246, using the link https://books.google.com/books?id=1ThGAQAAMAAJ&pg=PA233&lpg=PA233&dq=Inslee+Hangchow&source=bl&ots=Cwncrze6iu&sig=Z6aMB8aU1zJ0zCTdx-1hHarsChUA&hl=en&sa=X&ved=0CDUQ6AEwCGoVChMI6MC546K5yAIVgRk-Ch33H-wEY#v=onepage&q=Inslee%20Hangchow&f=false .

28. From "Missionary News," *The Chinese Recorder and Missionary Journal*, Volume V, No. 4 (July – August 1874), p. 223.

29. Church legend has J. Hudson Taylor walking alone on the beach in Brighton, England when he received the epiphanous, Saul of Tarsus-like inspiration to found a mission whose sole strategy was to establish Christian outposts in every Chinese province. Hence the name he chose for his organization: China Inland Mission.

30. Broomhall (1915), pp. 56 – 57. Aside from the Taylor family, Miss Blatchley, Miss Desgraz, Mr. and Mrs. Rudland, Mr. Duncan, and Mr. Reid.

31. Austin (2007), p. 131. Footnote 57, p. 131, cites the *Times* (London) of May 10, 1869, p. 6.

32. From "Missionary Intelligence," *The Chinese Recorder and Missionary Journal*, Volume II, No. 2 (July 1869), p. 56.

33. For Meadows and Douthwaite (Huzhou), see "Missionary News," *The Chinese Recorder and Missionary Journal*, Volume V, No. 6 (November – December 1874), pp. 374 – 375. For Dodd (Jiaxing), see Lyon, "Historical Sketch of the Hangchow Station," pp. 88 – 89.

34. Rev. G.W. Painter, "A Peculiar Superstition," in "Collectanea," *The Chinese Recorder and Missionary Journal*, Volume XXII, No. 8 (August, 1891), pp. 358 – 360.

Chapter 15

1. Graham (1990), p. 15.
2. "Tso Tsung-t'ang," in Leung (1992), p. 430. Zeng Guofan had reportedly attempted a similar steamer-building project in Anqing, but the results were described as "a failure." See Chen, *Tso Tsung T'ang*, p. 11.
3. Zhao Suisheng (2004), p. 17.
4. Translated treaty text quoted herein retrieved from https://china.usc.edu/treaty-shimonoseki-1895 (USC US-China Institute) on August 1, 2020.
5. Rivers (1903), pp. 86 – 87.
6. Peattie (1989), pp. 174 – 175.
7. Remick (2014), pp. 58 – 59.
8. Peattie (1989), Table 6.1 "Population Distribution of Japanese Nationals in Selected Cities in Mainland China, 1935," p. 170.
9. Rankin (1986), p. 73.
10. Wang Liping (1999), p. 112.
11. Rankin (1986), p. 178.
12. Jiang Menglin 1947), p. 40. Jiang Menglin would have been 11 years old when the school was founded. In the present day, Zhongxi Xuetang continues to operate as Shaoxing No. 1 High School on Zhanqian Avenue. The school's history can be found in detail, in Chinese, at http://www.sxyz.net/bnxs/bnxs1.
13. Wu Jiangzhong (2005), p. 17. Dai Lianbin (2014), p. 27, states that Guyue Cangshulou was "the first public library in modern China." The library continues as a branch operation in modern Shaoxing on Shengli Avenue.
14. Mary Backus Rankin identified at least ten gentry/merchant-sponsored public schools with reformist perspectives in the immediate Hangzhou district, plus five in the Huzhou area, four in the Jiaxing district, and six in the Shaoxing prefectural area. See Rankin (1986), Table 12, p. 175.
15. Ruth Hayhoe (2007), p. 45.
16. *The Hangchow Presbyterian College, Hangchow, China: Introspect, Retrospect, Prospect* (1911), p. 5.
17. Day (1955), pp. 11 – 12.
18. Mike Ives, "Overlooked No More: Yamei Kin, the Chinese Doctor Who Introduced Tofu to the West," *The New York Times* (October 17, 2018). Shurtleff and Aoyagi (2016) provide a detailed, downloadable bio-bibliography of Jin Yunmei.
19. See Elliott (2001) for a comprehensive treatment of Manchu life in the Qing Dynasty.
20. Hu Wei (2017), p. 36.
21. Quoted text translated from the *Shenbao* newspaper article, "Lady Hui Xing Sacrificed Herself for Women's Education," December 30, 1905, cited in Hu Wei (2017), p. 33. *Shenbao*'s article cites her date of death as November 25, 1905 (Hu Wei, pp. 26 - 27). Joan Judge (2008) places her date of death as December 21. Similarly, *Shenbao*'s story relates Huixing cutting flesh from her arm in June 1904, in front of "famous local people," while Judge puts that event on the day of the school's opening, which *Shenbao* puts at September 16, 1904.
22. Geil (1911) provides what appears to be a full translation of Huixing's final letter on pp. 26 – 27.
23. Hu Wei (2017), *Beyond Life and Death Images of Exceptional Women and Chinese Modernity*, p. 56.
24. Ibid., pp. 60 – 61.

25. Ibid., p. 73.

26. Cong Xiaoping (2008), p. 120.

27. Ibid., pp. 133, 137, and 139.

28. Ibid., p. 116.

29. Yuan Xing (2019), p. 143.

30. Hu Ying (2005), p. 144.

31. Joan Judge (2001), p. 780.

32. Widmer (2007), p. 24. It is worth noting that Shan's *Travels of 1903* was written in classical Chinese (see p. 32) rather than vernacular language, suggesting that her intended audience was *guixiu* like herself.

33. Qian Xun's preface tacitly reflects the long-standing Confucian tradition, still influential in 1904, that women could only publish their writing with their husband's consent and (usually) direct involvement.

34. Yuan Xing (2019), p. 139.

35. Hu Ying (2005), p. 149.

36. See Brezzi (2016), pp. 175 – 189 for an extended discussion of Shan's interactions with Western art in Italy.

37. Hu Ying (2005), p. 151.

38. Information about Sidney Gamble's life drawn exclusively from "Introduction," in Reed (2018).

39. George F. Fitch (1860 – 1924) arrived in China in 1879 and served as the editor of the *Chinese Recorder and Missionary Journal*.

40. *How Chinese Families Live in Peking* (1933), *Ting Hsien: A North China Rural Community* (1954), *South China Villages* (1963), *North China Villages: Social, Political and Economic Activities Before 1933* (1963), and *Chinese Village Plays* (1970). Gamble visited Hangzhou on each of his four China visits between 1908 and 1932.

41. Sidney Gamble's archives are housed at Duke University. Portions of the photo archives are accessible online at https://repository.duke.edu/dc/gamble.

42. "Hangchow Colloquial Paper," *The Chinese Recorder and Missionary Journal*, Volume XXXII, No. 9 (September, 1901), pp. 459 – 460. A postscript to the article by Rev. J.H. Judson adds, "The starting of such a paper is an index of the thoughts and desires of these young men and of a great number throughout China."

43. Laitinen (1990), pp. 80 – 82.

44. Shimada (1990), pp. 18 – 19.

45. Zou Rong was a co-defendant in the *Subao* case, one of the six arrested by police. He and Zhang Binglin were the only ones to face trial, with Zou receiving a sentence of two years in prison. He became ill while serving his sentence and died in April 1905, just 20 years old. Zhang Binglin wrote the preface to Zou's *The Revolutionary Army*.

46. Y.C. Wang (1965), p. 87.

47. For a comprehensive study of railroad development in early 20th-Century China, see Kent (1907). For deeper exploration of the railroad rights movement, see Barry (1909), pp. 541 – 558; Chi (1973), pp. 85 – 106; Min Tu-ki (1989); Rankin (2002), pp. 315 – 361; and Sun E-Tu Zen (1951), pp. 136 – 150.

48. See Kent (1907), pp. 9 – 15, for more information on the creation, brief operation, and early demolition of Jiangnan's first railroad line, from Shanghai to nearby Wusong district.

49. A joint venture formed by Jardine, Matheson and the Hong Kong and Shanghai Banking Corporation.

50. Chi (1973), p. 88.

51. Fu Shulan (2015), p. 367.

52. Chi (1973), p. 103. See also He Shan (2013), pp. 2 - 3 and He Shan (2017), pp. 87 – 88.

53. Min Tu-ki (1989), pp. 186 – 189.

54. In what was one of Hangzhou's first opportunities for urban modernization, the new City Station project was accompanied by construction of park land and the city's first automobile road. See Fu Shulan (2015), p. 368.

55. Qiu Jin adopted for herself a number of chivalrous names in her too-short life, but none better exemplifies her spirit and the cause closest to her heart than Jin Xiong 竞雄, "Competes with Men."

56. A more extensive discussion of Qiu Jin's life can be found in Rankin (1975), pp. 39 – 66, or in Hu Ying (2016), especially Chapter 3, pp. 96 – 173.

57. Edwards (2016), p. 45.

58. Mei Yubing (2012), pp. 38 – 41; Wang Lingzhen (2004), pp. 42 – 43.

59. Judge (2001), pp. 770. By 1907, there would be almost one hundred Chinese women studying in Japan, increasing to 126 in 1908, and 149 in 1909 (p. 783). By comparison, the number of male Chinese students in Japan rose from two hundred in 1898 to thirteen thousand in 1906 (p. 770).

60. Spence (1981), p. 52.

61. Yan Haiping (2006), p. 41.

62. Rankin (1975), p. 50.

63. Jinghu 鉴湖 (Mirror Lake) was one of the largest and most visited lakes in the Shaoxing area during the Tang and Song Dynasties. The lake was man-made in the year 140 CE and became famous for its mirror-like surface and its role in brewing Shaoxing wine. Tang poet Li Bai wrote: "Jinghu Lake is bright as moonlight, and the pale skin of Shaoxing ladies is like snow." The lake no longer existed after the Song, having been lost to sedimentation and persistent land reclamation for cultivation. In modern times, it is maintained as an urban wetland park.

64. Qiu Jin's lasting notoriety for cross-dressing as a man reflected in part a growing trend among Shanghai theater actresses in the 1890s and into the new century. According to Chou Hui-ling (1997), p. 139, "By the early 1900s, cross-dressing had become a fashionable practice among Shanghai actresses. They walked brazenly on Shanghai streets wearing men's clothing of both Chinese and Western styles."

65. Hu Ying (2016), p. 108.

66. For more commentary on *The Tale of Heroic Sons and Daughters*, see Epstein (2001), pp. 271 – 302, Chiu Suet Ying (2000), pp. 29 – 48, or Hamm (1998), pp. 328 – 355. Thirteenth Sister (Shisanmei) would later be the popular heroine in Chinese operas, movies, television series, and even comic books; see Hamm (1998), p. 334.

67. For further discussion of *Jingwei Shi*, see Wu Qingyun (1995), pp. 153 – 155 and Yan Haiping (2006), pp. 61 – 66.

68. Yan Haiping (2006), p. 65.

69. Dooling and Torgeson (1998), pp. 43 – 44.

70. This plot was reportedly conceived by Cai Yuanpei's younger brother.

71. Rankin (1976), pp. 164 – 165.

72. Rankin (1970), pp. 182 – 183.

73. Edwards (2016), p. 49.

74. Chang and Saussy (1999), pp. 656 – 657.

75. Hu Ying (2007), p. 139, Footnote No. 2.

76. *Report of Hangchow Station, 1907 – 1908*, p. 20: "There is unrest among the Chinese, a feeling after something better."

77. Wikipedia alone lists 15 uprisings.

78. DeGruche (1930), p. 90.

79. Day (1955), pp. 28 – 29.

80. Rhoads (2000), p. 200.

81. DeGruche (1930), p. 91.

82. Chen Wenxi (2017), p. 84.

83. This discussion of Hangzhou's revolutionary overthrow in November 1911 drawn largely from Schoppa (1982), pp. 145 – 151.

84. The Nationalist Guomindang government formally adopted the Gregorian calendar nationwide, effective January 1, 1929.

85. Puyi, the last Chinese emperor, was born Aisin Gioro Puyi 愛新覺羅溥儀.

Chapter 16

1. Excerpt from "Ten Miles of Lotus Flowers" by Liu Yong 柳永 (Qiqing 耆卿), in Liu Gang (2010), pp. 142 – 143.

2. Credit to Duan Xiaolin for crystallizing this transformation. She cites several other supporting factors such as improved water transportation systems and mobility. See Duan Xiaolin (2014), pp. 1, 9-11, 16.

3. Ibid., pp. 28 – 29, for a 13th-Century (Southern Song era) poem imagining Lin Bu, Bai Juyi, and Su Shi conversing together about West Lake.

4. Hobart (1959), p. 73.

5. Fu Shulan (2015), "Shan-shui Myth and History," pp. 368 – 371.

6. Fu Shulan (2009), p. 369.

7. Fu Shulan (2015), p. 380.

8. Chen Wenxi (2017), pp. 81 – 82.

9. Opening the city to West Lake meant demolishing its three western gates: Qingbo, Yongjing, and Qiantang.

10. Wang Liping (1999), p. 114.

11. Fu Shulan (2015), p. 377 and map (Figure 6), p. 375.

12. Wang Liping (1999), pp. 115 – 116.

13. Rhoads (2000), p. 263.

14. See, for example, He Shan (2017), pp. 87 – 89.

15. Wang Liping (1999), p. 117.

16. For "little Hangzhou," see Johnson (1993), p. 155 (151 – 181). For "little Suzhou," see Wakeman (1985), p. 633.

17. Wang Liping (1999), p. 117.

18. Ibid., p. 120.

19. Ibid., pp. 119 – 120.

20. Ibid., p. 120.

21. Russell, (1998), p. 359.

22. Edwards (2016), p. 49 and Mair (2013), pp. 198 – 199.

23. Rankin (1970), pp 187 – 190. Note the reference to "Tides of Zhejiang." Zhang's *hao* 号 (art name) was Xiaofan, with Fan written 帆, the character for "sail."

24. Qiu Jin's memorial stele is located in modern Shaoxing at the intersection of Jiefang North Road and Fushan Cross Street.

25. For a detailed study of the relationships among Qiu Jin, Xu Zihua, and Wu Zhiying, see Hu Ying (2016). Qiu Jin and Wu Zhiying met and bonded in 1903 when their husbands were both minor officials in Beijing. They became close friends in 1905 – 1906 in Huzhou, where they both worked at the Xunxi Girls' School.

26. Hu Ying (2004), p. 124.

27. Hu Ying (2007), p. 145.

28. In the earlier Wade-Giles *pinyin*, romanized as Kuomintang or KMT.

29. Bergère (1998), p. 259.

30. Fenby (2004), pp. 31 – 32, or Glick and Hong Sheng-hwa (1947), p. 238.

31. Chen's son Chen Lifu 陈立夫 (1900 – 2001) would serve Chiang Kai-shek as the Generalissimo's private secretary in the late 1920s and serve the Nationalist Government as Minister of Education from 1938 – 1944.

32. Chang and Chang (2010), pp. 156 – 157.

33. Ibid., pp. 161 – 166. In 1907, Zhang and his friend Li Shizeng also founded the first company to market tofu (*le fromage Chinoise*) and bean curd products in Europe, even building the first European factory of its kind in 1909.

34. Ibid., pp. 136 – 137.

35. Ibid., p. 141.

36. Ibid., p. 196.

37. Yao Hui died in a freak accident in New York City in 1918, killed by a falling tree branch in Riverside Park.

38. Hallet Abend, "Invalid Real Ruler of Nanking Regime: Chang Ching-Kiang, although a Cripple, Holds Sway Over the Inner Circle," *The New York Times* (August 8, 1928).

39. Zhang was particularly displeased with Chiang's opportunistic separation and poor public treatment of Chen Jieru in favor of Soong Meiling. Chen Jieru was not only his wife Zhu Yimin's close friend but also a favorite of Zhu's and Zhang's daughters.

40. Zhang's wife Zhu Yimin lived out her life in Riverdale (New York City) and died in 1991. Her ashes were scattered in the Gulf of Mexico in accordance with her wishes. Chang and Chang (2010), *The Zhangs from Nanxun*, pp. 265 – 266.

41. Lawrence (2014), p. 5.

42. The former residence of Hu Xueyan 胡雪岩 in Hangzhou City illustrates elements of the late Qing literati lifestyle in an upscale, Suzhou-style garden residence.

43. Details on Ding Jing's life and work are summarized from Lau Chak Kwong (2006), especially pp. 6 – 7, 16, 28 – 37, and 45 – 46.

44. The other popular style, using similar Han-era characters but employing more rounded and fluid character presentation, is known as the Anhui (Province) School.

45. See Yeh Ch'iu-yuan (1940), reproduced at *China Heritage Quarterly*, No. 29 (March 2012). Along with Ding Jing, the other seven are Jiang Ren (蔣仁, 1742-1795), Huang Yi (黃易, 1744-1801), Xi Gang (奚岡, 1746-1803), Zhao Zhichen (趙之琛, 1781-1806), Qian Song (錢松, ?-1860), Chen Hongshou (陳鴻壽, 1768-1822), and Chen Yuzhong (陳豫鐘, 1762-1806).

46. The year 1913 was the final year of the 26th 60-year cycle (a traditional Chinese calendar practice) since the Orchard Pavilion gathering of 353 CE.

47. See, for example, Lawrence (2014), pp. 49 – 53, for discussion of the Society's work to purchase and protect its most significant relic, an inscribed stele discovered in Yuyao in 1852, known as the San Lao Stele and dating to the Eastern Han Dynasty (25 – 220 CE).

48. Shen Kuyi (2010), p. 78.

49. Sullivan (1996), p. 14.

50. Shen Kuyi (2010), pp. 81 – 82.

51. The Wu Changshuo Memorial Hall in Lujiazui, Pudong District, Shanghai celebrates the artist's works and that of other artists he influenced. See Yang Zhenqi, "Leisurely Lujiazui," *Global Times*, 9/10/2013, accessed at http://www.globaltimes.cn/content/810115.shtml.

52. Day (1955), p. 27.

53. Ibid., p. 38.

54. Cai Yuanpei and Chang Qiyu founded the Girls' Patriotic School in 1901.

55. Duiker (1977), pp. 11 – 12.

56. Leung (1992), p. 421.

57. Weston (2004), pp. 118 – 122.

58. *Papers Relating to Pacific and Far Eastern Affairs Prepared for the Use of the American Del-*

egation to the Conference on the Limitation of Armament, Washington, 1921 – 1922 (Washington, D.C.: Government Printing Office, 1922), p. 283.

59. Wood and Arnander (2016), pp. 73 – 76 and p. 95. Some sources claim numbers as high as 200,000 Chinese laborers in Europe; see, for example, Chow Tse-tsung (1967), p. 37.

60. The Diligent Work and Frugal Study program was established by Zhang Jingjiang and Li Shizeng to assist Chinese students in France with language acquisition and moral development. No smoking, gambling, or alcohol was allowed. The participation of Chinese laborers in WWI is one of the lesser-known stories of that conflict. Post-war beneficiaries of the program included Zhou Enlai and Deng Xiaoping in the early 1920s. See Cao Siqi, "Diligent Work-Frugal Study Movement Marks 100th Anniversary in France," Global Times, 3/24/2019, accessed at http://www.globaltimes.cn/content/1143254.shtml.

61. A possible motivation for this decision was Woodrow Wilson's desire to secure Japan's agreement to join the new League of Nations.

62. Yeh Wen-hsin (1994), pp. 909 – 910.

63. Weston (2004), p. 197. Deng Chunlan, from Gansu Province, was featured in the October 1919 issue of Young China magazine, which included Deng's own article on women's rights and education.

64. Ibid., p. 200.

Chapter 17

1. Lee Hui-shu (2001) , p. 32, translated from Wu Zimu's 吴自牧 discussion of the Southern Song-era Ten Scenes of West Lake and the lake's changing seasonal atmosphere in Mengliang lu (Dream-like Memories of the Capital).

2. See Dudbridge (2004). According to the legend, Miaoshan revealed herself to be the goddess Guanyin. A Guanyin/Miaoshan cult developed at the Upper Tianzhu Monastery at West Lake.

3. See Fong (2014), pp. 137 – 140.

4. Yeh Wen-hsin (1994), p. 919. For more detailed biographical background on Shi Cuntong's family, early home life in Jinhua, and later career, see Yeh Wen-hsin (1996), pp. 133 – 135, 150.

5. See, for example, Wang Xiaoping (2019), p. 57.

6. As compared to the use of the literati written language known as wenhua (文化).

7. Schwarcz (1986), pp. 108 – 109.

8. Sullivan (1996), p. 33.

9. The short preface to the story, presented by the literatus narrator to whom the diary has been given for medical research, is written in wenhua, the language of the educated elite. The diary entries are written in vernacular language (baihua).

10. In the classics, commentaries were written between the lines.

11. Not long after "Diary of a Madman" appeared, Wu Yu published an essay titled "Cannibalism and Confucian Ethics" (吃人與禮教, "Chiren yu lijiao").

12. Lu Xun is undoubtedly the most written-about author in modern Chinese history, and perhaps the most complex. As it is impossible to do justice to his life, his life's work, and the many ways they have influenced Chinese culture and been interpreted since his passing, the following are recommended as beginning sources for further exploration: Eileen J. Cheng (2013); Eva Shan Chou (2012); Huang Sung-K'ang (1992); or Spence (1981).

13. The servant sent to deliver the bribe foolishly demanded a receipt, forcing the official to open the package in front of others present in the room.

14. Wang Ping (2012), p 34. The adage in Chinese is 十年树木，百年树人, Shi nian shu mu, bai nian shu ren.

15. Huang Sung-K'ang (1992), p. 32. Quote from Lu Hsun, Na Han (Battle Cries), a special

series compiled by the Memorial Committee of Lu Hsun (Peking: People's Press, 1953), p. 3.

16. Eva Shan Chou (2002), pp. 1042 – 1064, presents a strong, evidence-based argument that it took up to five years (until 1923) for Chinese readers and writers to fully appreciate the literary awakening inaugurated by Lu Xun's "Diary of a Madman."

17. Lu Xun's setting for the story is the fictional town Weizhuang 未庄, translatable as "Not Yet Village." Many of his stories are set in S__ (referring to Shaoxing), or in another fictional town called Luzhen. About 15 miles southwest of Shaoxing today, there is a tourist town called Luzhen that celebrates and even mimics the characters from Lu Xun's works.

18. Although literally an allusion to the folk music of the ancient State of Chu (Sichuan), "Xia li ba ren" became an idiomatic expression for 'not elegant' or "lowbrow," as opposed to Yangchun baixue 阳春白雪, songs of the elite of the State of Chu, meaning "highbrow." Lu Xun used the pseudonym Ba Ren to suggest that the author of "Ah Q" is not a highbrow storyteller, more of a folk or popular culture person.

19. By one analysis, Lu Xun adopted or made use of more than 140 pseudonyms in his lifetime. See Wang Ping (2012), p. 29.

20. Lu Xun quote in Foster (2001), pp. 155 – 156.

21. Hangzhou University, known in Chinese as Zhijiang Daxue 之江大学 and now part of Zhejiang University.

22. C.T. Hsia (1961), pp. 102 – 103.

23. Ibid., pp. 102 – 103. For a detailed study of nationalism expressed in "Sinking," see Denton (1992), pp. 107 – 123.

24. Lau and Goldblatt (2007), p. 55.

25. Eva Yin-I Chen (2003), p. 570.

26. Barmé (2002), pp. 88 – 89.

27. Harbsmeier (1984), p. 17.

28. Barmé (2002), pp. 73 – 74.

29. Ibid., pp. 105 – 109.

30. Siu Wang-Ngai (1997), p. 19.

31. Jiang Jin (2009), p. 3.

32. Ibid., p. 7.

33. Scholars of the Ming and Qing eras asserted Shi's origins in the Hangzhou vicinity, but there is little modern evidence so far to support this claim.

34. Song Jiang in *Water Margin* is believed to be a fictionalized version of an actual historical figure of the same name from the Northern Song Dynasty era (960 – 1127). The *History of Song* and the *Biography of Emperor Huizong* both identify a rebel named Song Jiang as active in around 1120.

35. Shi Nai'an's original version is believed to have been 70 chapters, but extended versions developed later by other writers resulted in works containing either 100 or 120 chapters.

36. Muzhou Prefecture existed until 1121 and is now part of Hangzhou Prefecture. The main city in the area is Jiande, southwest of Hangzhou and north northwest of Jinhua.

37. See, for example, "Is the Real Wu Song Buried in the Tomb of Wu Song? What is the Funeral? Has the Grave Been Verified? Why Can the Tomb of Wu Song Survive Today?" 武松墓 里面埋的是真的武松吗？有何陪葬？是否开坟验证过？为啥武松墓能留存至今？ (March 23, 2016), accessed at https://www.zhihu.com/question/40520173 via Google Translate, or "Yayu Bookstore Gossip about Water Margin No. 24: Is the Tomb of Wusong in the West Lake True or Not?" 雅雨书屋闲话水浒之二十四：西湖武松墓是真是假？ (February 21, 2019), accessed at https://www.sohu.com/a/295345087_772510 via Google Translate. Both articles include a marvelous vintage photo of Wu Song's tomb site; the first article above also includes a vintage photo of Mao Zedong at West Lake.

38. Shi Nai'an (2006). For "A Tiger-Fighter Is Hard to Find," see Ha Jin (2000), pp. 54 – 70.

Chapter 18

1. Graham (1990), p. 49.
2. Preserved today as a museum on Xingye Road as the site of the First National Congress of the Communist Party of China.
3. Short (2000), pp. 120 – 121.
4. Xiao Yu (1959), p. 198. Despite Xiao's clear disagreements with Mao on numerous issues, there seems no reason to dispute the factual details concerning their 1921 travels to Jiaxing and Hangzhou.
5. Chang Jung (2005), p. 26.
6. Academia Sinica continues in operation today in Taipei.
7. "Dr. Tsai Yuan-Pei, Chinese Educator," *The New York Times* (March 6, 1940), p. 23.
8. As much as 25% of the Beida faculty in the 1920s hailed from Zhejiang. See Weston (2004), pp. 235 – 236.
9. Keenan (1974), pp. 226 – 227.
10. Ibid., pp. 228 – 229. *New Education* ceased publication after October 1925, when the May Thirtieth Movement prioritized nationalism over "social reconstruction through individual development" (p. 236).
11. Day (1955), p. 56.
12. Schoppa (1995), p. 143.
13. Qianlong's imperial residence in Hangzhou was built on West Lake's Solitary Hill (Gushan), directly opposite Leifeng Pagoda.
14. Huang Yuan-Chuan (2005), p. 5.
15. Feng Menglong's story appeared in his *Jinshi tongyan* 警世通言 (*Stories to Caution the World*, 1624). In some versions of the story, the Green Snake is blue or takes the form of a carp. The monk Fahai is sometimes said to have been a minor god as well, his true form being that of a turtle.
16. Mount Emei 峨眉山 (10,187 feet) is located in Sichuan Province. It is one of the "Four Sacred Buddhist Mountains in China." The other three are Mount Wutai 五台山 (10,033 feet) in Shanxi Province, Mount Jiuhua 九华山 (4,400 feet) in Anhui Province, and Mount Pütuo 普陀山 (932 feet) on Zhoushan Island, Zhejiang Province.
17. Eugene Y. Wang (2003), p. 502.
18. Joo (2015), "The Literary Imagination of the White Pagoda and Dynastic Change in Early Ming Hangzhou," pp. 56 – 57, 69 – 70.
19. Lu Xun (1980), "The Collapse of Leifeng Pagoda" and "More Thoughts on the Collapse of Leifeng Pagoda."
20. Fang Qin, pp. 157 – 158. The cited examples are extracted from the longer list provided in Fang's dissertation.
21. Duan Xiaolin (2020), p. 170.
22. Lu Xun (1980), "More Thoughts on the Collapse of Leifeng Pagoda."
23. David Der-wei Wang (2010), p. xvi.
24. 10,000 figure cited from "Revolt in Shanghai Nipped in the Bud," *The New York Times* (October 18, 1926), p. 7.
25. Jordan (1976), pp. 88 – 92; data on battle results, p. 92.
26. Ibid., pp. 95 – 96.
27. Ibid., pp. 103 – 105.
28. Day (1955), p. 58.
29. "Hangchow Citizens Turned on Looters," *The New York Times* (February 28, 1927).
30. Ibid.
31. Jordan (1976), p. 104.
32. Ibid., p. 104.

33. Around three hundred Communist Party members were arrested and executed that day in Shanghai, but others went missing. Death counts from April 12, 1927 and the days immediately following range from three hundred to as many as 10,000. Death counts over the full three years of the purge are often cited at more than 300,000. Two unintended consequences for Chiang Kai-shek were driving many of the CCP's early leaders together into Jiangxi Province for safety, including Mao Zedong, and also transforming the communist movement from an educated urban one to a mass movement of the people.

34. Fitch (1918).

35. Fitch (1922), p. 1.

36. Bratter (1925), p. 22.

37. Lin Yutang (2007), p. 638.

38. "The Grand Occasion of the First West Lake Expo," accessed at https://en.xh-expo.com/pages/history.html.

39. From 1927 – 1928, the school was briefly known as Third National Sun Yat-sen [Zhongshan] University. See Wan Yinmei (2008), p. 80.

40. "Hangchow School Closes: Board in America, Despite Faculty, Refused Nationalist Terms," *The New York Times* (July 9, 1928).

41. Day (1955), pp. 81 – 82.

42. Jin Jiayi (2015), p. 1. Jin offers an insightful and compelling analysis of Hobart's work, with particular focus on *Oil for the Lamps of China*.

43. For more on Pearl Buck's life in China, see Hilary Spurling, *Pearl in China: Journey to the Good Earth* (New York: Simon & Schuster, 2010) or the historical fiction *Pearl of China: A Novel* by Anchee Min (New York: Bloomsbury, 2010).

44. Hobart (1959), p. 62.

45. Mary Nourse would serve for a time as principal of Wayland Academy before moving on to Nanjing in 1915 as a co-founder and instructor at Jinling College, China's first women's college.

46. Jin Jiayi (2015), p. 2.

47. "Alice Tisdale Hobart, 85, Dies; Wrote 'Oil for Lamps of China'," *The New York Times* (March 15, 1967), p. 47.

48. See Hu Ying (2019), for an excellent and detailed treatment of Qiu Canzhi's methods of dealing with filiality, her mother's fame, and her mother's nearly lifelong absence.

49. Jing Xiong (竞雄, "Competes with Men") was one of the many names Qiu Jin adopted in her lifetime. Qiu Jin's "sworn sister" Xu Zihua ran the school for ten years before turning it over to Wang Canzhi. See Lee and Stefanowska (1998), p. 256.

50. Hu Ying (2007), "Qiu Jin's Nine Burials," p. 162.

51. Wang Ziyu 王子余 (1874 – 1944) was an acquaintance of both Qiu Jin and Xu Xilin and was politically sympathetic to their cause as a member of the Revolutionary Alliance.

52. Hu Ying (2019), pp. 210 – 212.

53. Some sources describe Qiu Canzhi as an aviatrix or suggest in vague terms that she was a pilot, possibly the first such woman in China. Hu Ying (2019), p. 236, Footnote No. 59, states from her research that "Canzhi…made no claim to having piloted a plane." She regarded herself rather as an "aviation scholar" (p. 231).

54. Hu Ying (2016), pp. 98 – 99, Footnote No. 2.

55. Cheng (2013), p. 85.

56. Gal Gvili (2019), p. 13.

57. An excellent source on Lin Huiyin's Liang Sicheng/Xu Zhimo story can be found in the multi-part video series, "Liang Sicheng and Lin Huiyin," from *Journeys in Time*, produced by CCTV and available on YouTube in English. An excellent first-hand Western source is Fairbank (1994).

58. Fairbank (1994), p. 17. Fairbank records (p. 18) from conversations with Liang Sicheng that it was Lin Huiyin who persuaded him to enter with her into the study of architecture.

59. Russell was in China at the time and had already been expelled from Cambridge, unbeknown to Xu Zhimo.

60. Batt and Zitner (2016), pp. 95 – 96.

61. Xu and Zhang had entered into an arranged marriage in 1915. Zhang ultimately returned to China, where she co-founded the Shanghai Women's Commercial and Savings Bank in 1924 and a clothing company specializing in Western-style women's wear. See, for example, Yao Minji, "Shanghai Women's Bank a First for 'Ladies'," accessed at *Shanghaidaily.com* (October 26, 2013), http://www.shanghaidaily.com/feature/art-and-culture/shanghai-womens-bank-a-first-for-ladies/shdaily.shtml.

62. Liang and Lin were married in Ottawa, where the husband of Sicheng's "Elder Sister" was the Chinese Consul General.

63. Paraphrased from CCTV series, "Liang Sicheng and Lin Huiyin." When Lin Changmin wrote to Xu Zhimo pressing him sternly to forego his romantic pursuit of his daughter Huiyin, Xu wrote in reply: "I shall search for my soul's companion in the sea of humanity: if I find her, it is my fortune; if not, it is my fate." See Fairbank (1994), p. 20.

64. See, for example, "New Opera Turns Spotlight on Legendary Lin Huiyin," *Chinaculture.org* (June 16, 2017), accessed at https://www.chinadaily.com.cn/culture/2017-05/16/content_29367787.htm. The article also mentions the Chinese TV drama of their love story, *You Are an April Day*, first broadcast in 2000.

65. Lau and Goldblatt (2007), pp. 499 – 500.

66. As evidence of how pivotal *Yingzao fashi* was to Lin and Liang, they named their first son Congjie in 1932, in honor of Li Jie. Interestingly as well, the *Yingzao fashi* also contained instructions for creating an artificial flowing stream for drinking parties, along the lines of that memorialized in Wang Xizhi's famous preface, *Lanting xu*, for the Orchid Pavilion gathering in 353. See Park (2011), p. 35.

67. Song Weijie (2014), p. 77

68. Ibid., p. 62.

69. Ibid., p. 80.

70. Zhu Tao (2012), p. 30.

71. Manuscripts completed in 1944 in Chinese and 1946 in English, respectively, but first published in 1985 and 1984, respectively. See Li Shiqiao (2002), p. 36.

72. Hockx (1998), pp. 73, 78.

73. Berninghausen (1977), pp. 250 - 251. Mao Dun originally used the characters 矛盾, but his fellow writer Ye Shengtao 叶圣陶 (1894 – 1988) later altered it with the grass element 艹 (*cao*) to transform it into a recognized Chinese surname. Berninghausen likens the adjustment to changing "contradiction" to "kontradiction." Note that Mao Dun's *mao* character 茅 is not the same as that of Mao Zedong 毛泽东.

74. C.T. Hsia (1961), p. 141.

75. Mao Dun (1979), p. 29.

Chapter 19

1. Chang and Saussy (1999), pp. 394 – 395. Zhu Rouze was the daughter-in-law of Chai Jingyi, one of the original Banana Garden Five poets. "Tide-Waiting Gate" may be a tide-viewing spot as well as the legendary location where Qian Liu ordered his soldiers to shoot 3,000 arrows into the tide to block its flow. "Heaven's Gate" refers to a metaphorical gate formed by two mountains (Kanshan and Zheshan) between which the tidal bore flowed (the "south passage") until 1695, after which the flow shifted north of Zheshan (the "north passage"). The "white horse and chariot" allude to the legend of Wu Zixu as the god of the tides, returning to exact revenge.

2. Ashihei Hino (1939A), p. 74.

3. Followers of the Nichiren sect professed belief that Japan had a divine right to rule Asia. Some have suggested that their presence was part of a deliberate Japanese effort to provoke a conflict.

4. See Mo Yajun (2004), for extended discussion of Japanese settlement in Hongkou and Tokyo's motivations for protecting their presence in Shanghai.

5. Tuchman (1971), p. 168.

6. See, for example, Lu Suping (2019), p. 8.

7. Jordan (2001), pp. 186 – 190 for military casualties, pp. 192 – 193 for civilian casualties.

8. Boyne (2002) p. 125.

9. Eighteen-year-old Zhang Huichang (also written as Chang Waijung or Chang Wei-chang) received his initial flight training at the Curtiss Flying School in New York in 1917. For an extended discussion of Zhang's aviation career and celebrity, see O'Keefe (2013), pp. 135 – 160.

10. Xu Guangqiu (1997), pp. 156 – 158.

11. "John H. Jouett, Adviser to Chiang," *The New York Times* (October 22, 1968).

12. Leary (1969), p. 454.

13. Jianqiao Airfield continues military-only flight operations to the present day under the name Hangzhou Air Base.

14. Leary (1969), pp. 455 – 456.

15. "John H. Jouett, Adviser to Chiang," *The New York Times* (October 22, 1968).

16. Lance (2014), p. 21.

17. Ibid., p. 22.

18. Ding Yan, a descendant of Ding Bing and Ding Shen, was one of the cadet pilots trained by Jouett's CAS at Jianqiao. See "Museum Glorifies Pilots' Youth and Passion in War" 每页都刻写着青春热血的飞鹰 (June 6, 2019), accessed at *In Zhejiang* website, http://inzj.zjol.com.cn/zhejiangfocus/cd/201906/t20190621_10385598.shtml.

19. Leary (1969), p. 461.

20. Xu Guangqiu (1997), pp. 165 – 166.

21. Ellis Shannon would go on to a long post-war career as a test pilot and would be the first person ever to fly a delta-wing jet. See https://www.thisdayinaviation.com/tag/ellis-d-shannon. Another CAS flight instructor, W.C. Kent, would be killed by Japanese fighter planes over Kunming (Yunnan Province) on October 29, 1940 while flying for China National Aviation Corporation.

22. Welsh (2012), pp. 111-112.

23. Bond (2001), pp. 91 – 95.

24. "Mathewson's Son Is Fatally Burned," *The New York Times* (August 17, 1950).

25. In 1939, Chiang Kai-shek proclaimed August 14 as Air Force Day, a national holiday and an effort to boost morale in wartime China.

26. Bergin (2012), p. 18.

27. Wakeman (1995), pp. 280 – 281.

28. Clayton (1944), p. 171. See also the fascinating story of the Songjiang (Shanghai) rail bridge deception, p. 178.

29. "Chinese Aviators Train at Kunming," *The New York Times* (March 29, 1938).

30. McMullen (2017), p. 92, remarked tongue-in-cheek on the strength of the Chinese defense of Shanghai in a letter dated October 14, 1937: "It has now been nine weeks since the Japs were going to run over the Chinese around Shanghai. They are still 'running' at the rate of a mile per week! It will take several days at this rate to get to Szechuen [Sichuan Province]."

31. Schoppa (2011), p. 15.

32. See Clayton (1944), p. 172 for Wayland; McMullen (2017), pp. 61, 65, 67, and 71 for Hangchow Christian College. Much of the following detail is drawn from the invaluable series of letters written by McMullen between September 1937 and August 1938 and published with extensive annotation in 2017 as *War and Occupation in China*.

33. Atlanta native Fred Manget founded the Methodist Hospital in Huzhou in 1924 and re-

mained in charge until 1941. He was later credited by Robert Scott, author of the book *God Is My Co-Pilot*, with providing the inspiration for his book's famous title. See Richard Goldstein, "Robert Scott, War-Hero Author, Dies at 97," *The New York Times* (February 28, 2006).

34. During the beginning months of Japanese occupation of Hangzhou, Robert McMullen remained in residence at Hangchow Christian College to safeguard the campus physical plant and any Chinese who remained at or affiliated with the school. With his wife Emma Moffett, McMullen began his religious work in 1911 China at the Hangzhou mission of John Leighton Stuart and oversaw construction of the Union Girls' School in 1915 – 1916.

35. McMullen (2017), p. 111.

36. Designed by Mao Yisheng 茅以升 (1896 – 1989). He was born in Zhenjiang, graduated with a civil engineering degree from Jiaotong University (Chengdu), a Master's Degree from Cornell, and first-ever Doctoral Degree from Carnegie-Mellon University. He is considered the Father of Chinese Bridge Engineering. The bridge was situated about three miles west (upstream) of the traditional free-ferry river crossing.

37. McMullen (2017), p. 87.

38. Ibid., pp. 91 – 92; also, pp. 95 and 99.

39. Ibid., pp. 113, 117 – 118 for the American flag, p. 102 for the bombing and strafing of civilian trains and their passengers. The large flag, and three smaller, 15-by-30-foot ones, were never used while the school was in operation, since the Chinese students strongly opposed the display of American flags on Chinese soil (pp. 131 – 132). McMullen used it later, after the Japanese occupation, to protect the campus and himself from Chinese fire from across the river in Xiaoshan (p. 173).

40. Ibid., p. 119, Footnote No. 215 for Japanese landings at Hangzhou Bay, p. 141 for population departures from Hangzhou.

41. Ibid., pp. 56 – 57.

42. Hsü Shuhsi (1939), p. 75.

43. The municipal water works was built near its fresh water source, the Tiesha River 贴纱河, which ran parallel to the city's eastern wall. See "City Water for Hangchow," *The New York Times* (September 28, 1930). The same location and water sourcing remain in use today.

44. The Japanese occupiers restored the electric service using conscripted labor, but the wartime power plant only generated about two thousand kilowatts, well short of its pre-demolition level of fifteen thousand. See Schoppa (2011), p. 242.

45. McMullen (2017), p. 156.

46. Clayton (1944), p. 184, and McMullen (2017), pp. 155 – 156.

47. Schoppa (2011), pp. 216 – 217.

48. Ibid., pp. 244 – 245.

49. McMullen (2017), p. 168.

50. Clayton (1944), p. 202. Clayton was the principal of Wayland Academy beginning in 1923.

51. McMullen (2017), p. 163.

52. Ashihei Hino (1939), p. 12.

53. McMullen (2017), pp. 257 – 258.

54. Much of the credit for Hangzhou's non-destructive takeover goes to the Hangzhou branch of the International Red Cross established by a committee of local Chinese and foreign representatives, including a Bank of China vice president, the Chinese president of the YMCA, and the president of the Hangzhou Chamber of Commerce. They chose Robert McMullen to chair their new organization.

55. Clayton (1944), p. 239. News report from "Puppet Chinese Slain," *The New York Times* (February 14, 1944).

56. The Yangzhou and Zhenjiang copies were destroyed by Taiping rebels in the 1850s.

57. Janie Chang, "The Risky Journey that Saved One of China's Greatest Literary Treasures," *TIME.com*, June 15, 2020, accessed at https://time.com/5852229/saving-chinese-encyclopedia/.

58. Hsieh Chiao-Min and Jean Kan Hsieh (2009), p. ix.

59. Ibid., p. x, Footnote No. 2.

60. Ibid., p. x, Footnote No. 1.

61. "He who rides the tiger is afraid to dismount" (骑虎难下, *Qihu nan xia*) is a Chinese idiom meaning that it may be easier to continue a risky or dangerous endeavor than end it. "The dog that caught the car" is an American idiom referring to the tendency for some dogs to chase passing cars despite the impossibility of actually catching one or knowing what to do with it if they somehow succeeded. This idiom refers to accomplishing a very difficult task but not knowing what to do next after having achieved the first objective.

62. H.B.P. (1938), p. 82.

63. Wartime events from 1939 compiled from published reporting by *The New York Times* (unless otherwise noted) on January 8, 11, 12, and 15; February 7 and 12; March 2, 21, 22, 23, and 25; April 1 and 8; May 25; October 17 and 26; and December 16 and 20.

64. "Japan Intensifies Shantung Mop-Up," *The New York Times* (February 7, 1939).

65. "Chinese Soldiers Attack Hangchow," *The New York Times* (October 17, 1939).

66. Schoppa (2011), p. 22.

67. Ibid., p. 22.

68. "Japanese Halt Push South of Hangchow," *The New York Times* (January 26, 1940).

69. Dillon (2020), in Chapter 10.

70. "Chinese Report Foe Halted in Suiyuan," *The New York Times* (February 2, 1940).

71. "Chinese at Tatang in Kwangsi Clean-up," *The New York Times* (November 2, 1940.

72. "Fighting Is Reported in Northwest China," *The New York Times* (December 11, 1940).] Early Japanese experiments and trial runs with biological warfare delivery mechanisms from Ningbo to Jinhua would not be discovered until after the war's end.

73. Schoppa (2011), pp. 25 – 26.

74. "Chekiang Victory Claimed," *The New York Times* (May 22, 1941).

75. See, for example, Harrison Forman, "Japan's Weakness Exposed by China," *The New York Times* (May 8, 1942).

76. Clayton (1944), p. 238.

77. Ibid., pp. 229 – 233. A Japanese military spokesman in November 1938 doubled Clayton's estimate, putting it at 200,000 "guerillas, bandits and irregulars." F. Tillman Durdin, "200,000 Guerrillas Are Near Shanghai," *The New York Times* (November 20, 1938).

78. Wills (2012), pp. 172 – 173. "The shame of Jingkang (Nanjing)" refers to the Jurchen sacking of Kaifeng; Xiongnu were nomadic peoples from lands to the north and west of China.

79. See, for example, Schoppa (2011), pp. 2 – 5, for the story of the massacre at Qiaosi Village (Qiaosizhen 乔司镇), about five miles northeast of Hangzhou and just east of Jianqiao Airfield, beginning on February 18, 1938.

80. McMullen was interned at Shanghai in January 1943, repatriated in September 1943, and arrived in New York on December 2. Sturton was arrested on November 11, 1942, interned at Shanghai until June 1945, then near Beijing until being released on August 19, 1945. Clayton was repatriated in 1942 but died on November 17, 1946, before he could make his planned return to China and his principal's position at Wayland Academy, which he had held since 1923.

81. Pomfret (2016), pp. 217 – 218.

82. Chiang Kai-shek believed Quzhou 衢州 (in Zhejiang Province) and Guilin 桂林 (in the more distant Guangxi Zhuang Autonomous Region) were adequate, but opposed use of airfields at Lishui 丽水 (in Zhejiang), Yushan 玉山 (in Jiangxi Province), and Ji'an 吉安 (also in Jiangxi Province) unless they were first personally inspected and approved by the Americans.

83. Scott (2015), p. 306.

84. Ibid., pp. 308 – 309. At the time, the Japanese acknowledged 114 fatalities according to the BBC. See "Japan Said to Admit 114 Deaths in Air Raid," *The New York Times* (April 26, 1942).

85. Hanson W. Baldwin, "Mystery in Tokyo Raid," *The New York Times* (April 21, 1942).

86. W.H. Lawrence, "Airman Decorated," *The New York Times* (May 20, 1942).

87. The crew was seized and interned in Russia for the balance of the war.

88. Wheeler (2016), p. 30. An excellent, detailed information source on the Doolittle Raiders and each individual crew and crewman can be found at the website, *Children of the Doolittle Raiders Presents* [sic] *the Doolittle Raiders Legacy: 80 Men / 16 Airplanes / 1 Mission* at https://www.childrenofthedoolittleraiders.com/.

89. "China's Guerrillas Attack 15 Cities," *The New York Times* (May 5, 1942).

90. Forman, "Japan's Weakness Exposed by China." See also, Harrison Forman, "Chinese Say Japan Fights Air Menace," *The New York Times* (May 22, 1942), in which Forman links this campaign to both Doolittle and the April 20 guerrilla raids on fifteen Japanese-held cities which "appear to have goaded the Japanese to retaliate."

91. Schoppa (2011), pp. 138 – 139, 150 – 158.

92. Scott (2015), p. 383.

93. "Kiangsi Air Base Neared by Enemy," *The New York Times* (June 13, 1942).

94. Scott (2015), p. 385.

95. Glines (1988), pp. 150 – 151.

96. Scott (2015), p. 382.

97. Hoyt (2001), p. 95.

98. Williams and Wallace (1989), p. 69.

99. Peter Li (2003), pp. 294 – 295.

100. Barenblatt (2004), p. 159 for Chongshan, p. 174 for Quzhou. An interesting 2016 follow-up to the Doolittle rescues and the horrific Japanese retaliation around Quzhou can be found at Wheeler (2016), pp. 29 – 38.

101. Williams and Wallace (1989), pp. 69 – 70.

102. Scott (2015A), accessed at https://www.smithsonianmag.com/history/untold-story-vengeful-japanese-attack-doolittle-raid-180955001/.

103. Patrick E. Tyler, "Germ War, A Current World Threat, Is a Remembered Nightmare in China," *The New York Times* (February 4, 1997). Unclear if this village is located in Quzhou or Jinhua Prefecture.

104. Lockwood (2009), p. 127, or Barenblatt (2004), p. 173.

105. For Doolittle Raid books, of which there are many, see in this bibliography Lawson (1943), Glines (1988), Doolittle (1992), or Scott (2015). Michel Paradis (2020) provides an interesting book about closure, at least on the American side. Related movies include *Thirty Seconds over Tokyo* (1944), *Pearl Harbor* (2001), *The Hidden Soldier*, a.k.a. *In Harm's Way* and as *The Chinese Widow* (2017), and *Midway* (2019).

106. Clayton (1944), p. 271.

107. Lautz (2016), pp. 81 – 84.

108. Glines (1964), pp. 322 – 327; Lautz (2016), pp. 84 – 85.

109. Lautz (2016), p. 229.

110. Ibid., p. 239.

111. Doolittle (1992), p. 258.

112. Barmé (2002), p. 168.

113. Schoppa (2011), pp. 85 – 86.

114. See illustrations in Hung Chang-tai (1990), pp. 149, 146, 142, 146, respectively.

115. Lau and Goldblatt (2007), p. 649.

116. Hung Chang-tai (1990), p. 55. Cartoon appeared in *The China Weekly Review* 88.6 (April 8, 1939). Feng claimed that he had actually witnessed this event in Jiaxing in 1937.

117. Both cartoons illustrated in Hung Chang-tai (1990), pp. 57 and 59.

118. Hung Chang-tai (1994), p. 94.

119. Information on the last years of Yu Dafu's life in Singapore and Sumatra from Wong Yoon-Wah (1988), pp. 11 – 26 and in Wong Yoon-Wah (2002), pp. 83 – 100.

Chapter 20

1. Graham (1990), p. 31.

2. Rosen, et. al. (2009), p. 122.

3. Titles, in sequence: "San Mao's Father," "Taken by Strategy," and "Sanmao Escapes from the Enemies' Bayonets." All three strips published in *Resistance Cartoons*, respectively, in Issue 3 (February 1938), Issue 6 (March 1938), and Issue 10 (May 1938). Citations and descriptions from Pozzi (2014), pp. 117 – 121. Accessed at http://cross-currents.berkeley.edu/e-journal/issue-13.

4. Ibid., pp. 107 – 109.

5. Ibid., pp. 103, 123 – 127. This sketch series ran in December 1940 and January 1941.

6. Pozzi (2018), p. 46.

7. Ibid., p. 47.

8. Also known as *An Orphan on the Streets* or simply *The Story of San Mao*.

9. Fighting continued after October 1, 1949. Chengdu (Sichuan Province) did not fall until December, and Hainan and Zhoushan Islands were taken by the PLA in April and May 1950, respectively.

10. The ultimate flag design was a modified version of a design submitted in a national competition by a Wenzhou (Zhejiang Province) citizen named Zeng Liansong 曾联松 (1917 – 1999).

11. The population figures reported by the new CCP government from an official, early-1950 census were 120,799 households and 520,730 residents. See Gao (2004), p. 138. Factory and worker data from p. 34. Gao's book offers a comprehensive English-language study of Hangzhou's transition from the Nationalist regime to the CCP government.

12. Ibid., p. 113.

13. "The Monks in Lingyin Temple Are Changing," *Zhejiang Daily* (November 21, 1949), cited in Gao (2004), p. 227.

14. "Hangchow – Garden City," *China Reconstructs*, Vol. 23, No. 3 (March 1974), p. 21.

15. "Farewell, Leighton Stuart" was the second in a series of five editorial essays Mao published through Xinhua News Agency criticizing the U.S. State Department's White Paper.

16. Translation of "Farewell, Leighton Stuart" from *China Heritage Annual 2017: Nanking*, accessed at http://chinaheritage.net/annual/2017/republic/the-long-farewell/farewell-leighton-stuart/

17. John Leighton Stuart's brothers were David Todd Stuart (1878 - 1909), Warren Horton Stuart (1879 – 1961), and Robert Kirland Stuart (1883 – 1890). See Shaw (1992), pp. 12 – 13.

18. Hao Ping (2018), p. 6, describes Mary Stuart's girls' school as the second such opened anywhere in China. Leighton Stuart (1954), p. 14, wrote likewise, but Shaw (1992), p. 24 cites Stuart describing it as "the third oldest girls' school in China."

19. Stuart (1954), *Fifty Years in China*, pp. 14 – 15. Stuart's Hangzhou girls' school is also said to have been the first in China to include physical education in its curriculum.

20. Hweiwen University (1890), North China Union College, North China Union Women's College (1907), and a School of Theology (already formed from three existing seminaries).

21. From "History of the Harvard-Yenching Institute," accessed at https://www.harvard-yenching.org/history-of-the-harvard-yenching-institute/.

22. Gao (2004), p. 127.

23. Shaw (1982), p. 80.

24. Gordon H. Chang (2015), p. 191.

25. See, for example, "Hidden Life of a US Diplomat," *Shanghai Daily* (December 21, 2009), p. B3. Accessed at https://archive.shine.cn/city-specials/hangzhou/hidden-life-of-a-us-

diplomat/shdaily.shtml .

26. Shi Hengtan, "The Spiritual Heritage of Tianshui Church in Hangzhou," *China Christian Daily* (November 29, 2019), accessed at http://chinachristiandaily.com/news/category/2019-11-29/the-spiritual-heritage-of-tianshui-church-in-hangzhou_8685 .

27. A *People's Daily* article on March 17, 1949, "Transform the Consumptive City into the Productive City," announced this rapid industrialization policy.

28. Gao (2004), pp. 217 – 218.

29. Ibid., pp. 220 – 221.

30. Located at No. 18 Yanggong Causeway, now called the West Lake State Guesthouse, opened in 1973, renovated in 2012 and 2016.

31. Gao (2004), pp. 155 – 156.

32. An interesting chronology of thirty-four of Mao's visits to Hangzhou can be found at Wang Huai (2011) and Wang Huai (2012).

33. "Hangchow – Garden City," *China Reconstructs*, pp. 20 – 21.

34. Wang Zixin was the scion of a tea merchant father who began a famous network of teahouses and tea brands under the name Wang Yutai (汪裕泰). Wang Villa today is the Zhejiang Xizi Hotel, located at 37 Nanshan Road, opened in 1979.

35. Gao (2004), p. 223, and Barmé (2011A).

36. Data on West Lake dredging and reforestation of the surrounding hills from West Lake Museum website, accessed at http://www.westlakemuseum.com/index.php/bwggk/bwgjj-en.

37. "Hangchow – Garden City," *China Reconstructs*, p. 20.

38. Ibid., pp. 20 - 24.

39. Cited in CCTV News video documentary, *Journeys in Time: Liang Sicheng and Lin Huiyin, Part 10c.*, at 1:24.

40. Cited in CCTV9 documentary series, *Liang & Lin, Part 6: Glory*, at 28:18.

41. Lee and Stefanowska (2003), pp. 340 – 341.

42. Liang Shicheng and Lin Huiyin had two children, Liang Zaibing 梁再冰 (1929 –) and Liang Congjie 梁從誡 (1932 – 2010).

43. Maya Lin (1959 –) is the daughter of Lin Huan 林桓 (1915 – 1989), who was a half-brother to Lin Huiyin by their common father, Lin Changmin. Maya Lin was born in Athens, Ohio, four years after Lin Huiyin's death from tuberculosis.

44. Bishop and Roberts (1997), p. 27.

45. Doar (2007A).

46. Ibid., n.p.

47. Tsai Shu-wei (2020), pp. 49 – 58.

48. "Hangchow – Garden City," *China Reconstructs*, p. 25.

49. Xu Lanjun (2016), p. 109.

50. Ibid., p. 112.

51. Jiang Jin (2009), p. 105.

52. Gao (2004), p. 236; Xu Lanjun (2016), pp. 117 – 119.

53. Xu Lanjun (2016), p. 110.

54. Luo Hui (2008), p. 126.

55. Chen Yu-Shih (1986), p. 12.

56. The original *manhua* series ended with "A Big Uproar," in which San Mao is absorbed into a large and boisterous crowd at a crossroads. The GMD banned the film and, after liberation, the CCP appended the parade scene (as occurred in Shanghai on July 6, 1949) and also created a political and artistic counterpoint of Communist Party acceptance of the orphans. This contrasts with the movie's earlier scene where San Mao is ejected from a GMD Boy Scout parade. See David Der-wei Wang (2017), pp. 411 – 412.

57. "Sanmao, China's Favorite Son, Turns 70," *Chinadaily.com* (July 28, 2005), accessed at

http://www.chinadaily.com.cn/english/doc/2005-07/28/content_464182_4.htm. Some fascinating historical examples of Zhang's cartoon panels that cross-mix Sanmao with the 1960s-era model citizen Lei Feng can be seen at https://mauracunningham.org/2013/03/05/sanmao-learns-from-lei-feng/.

58. For an interesting discussion of how the 1992 movie differs from the 1946 serial, see Pozzi (2018), pp. 49 – 54.

59. See "Zhang Leping Memorial Hall," accessed at http://english.haiyan.gov.cn/art/2010/12/23/art_866_29447.html .

60. Harbsmeier (1984), pp. 37 – 38.

61. Many of Feng Zikai's works were signed with the Western alphabetic initials "TK" for Tsi-Kai, the older Wade-Giles romanization of Zikai.

62. C.T. Hsia (1961), p. 29, citing Mao Zedong's "*The New Democracy,*" published in January 1949 in the first issue of *Chinese Culture* magazine.

63. Yu Hua (2011), pp. 98 – 99.

64. See Spence (1981), for an excellent English-language introduction to the entire Chinese revolutionary era.

65. All four are less than forty miles from Hangzhou.

66. Jonathan Dehart (2013), accessed at https://thediplomat.com/2013/02/the-legacy-of-ping-pong-diplomat-zhuang-zedong/. See also Martin Douglas, "Zhuang Zedong, Skilled in China Foreign Relations and Ping-Pong, Dies at 72," *The New York Times* (February 11, 2013).

67. MacMillan (2007), p. 300.

68. Yang (2011), p. 25.

69. Although his grandfather had moved Zhou's branch of the clan to Huai'an in northern Jiangsu Province, his family still regarded Shaoxing as their ancestral home.

70. Audrey R. Topping, "Hangchow a Resort with the Best Tea in China," *The New York Times* (February 26, 1972).

71. For British Labour Party, see Gale (1955). For Hogarth, see Hogarth (1956). For DeBeauvoir, see DeBeauvoir (1958). For the International Youth Delegation, see Michael Croft (1958). For Trudeau, see Hébert and Trudeau (1968).

72. DeBeauvoir (1958), pp. 457 – 458.

73. He Shan (2017), p. 5.

74. Seymour Topping, "Industry Fails to Blight Chinese 'Paradise'," *The New York Times* (May 25, 1971).

75. Fred Ferretti, "A Year's Worth of Travel Wishes," *The New York Times* (December 29, 1985).

76. Humes and Ryals (2009), p. 3.

77. Mike Peters, "Botanical Garden – A Colorful Treat," *chinadaily.com.cn* (September 5, 2016), accessed at https://www.chinadaily.com.cn/travel/2016-09/05/content_26698166.htm.

78. An American scholarship program (1909 – 1929) funded from $17 million in excess indemnities paid by the Qing government for damages associated with the 1900 Boxer Rebellion. Other recipients included Lin Huiyin, Liang Shicheng, Hu Shih, and Qian Xuesen.

79. Founded in 1914 by Chinese students at Cornell University.

80. Wang Zuoyue (2008), p. 402.

81. Ibid., p. 404.

82. Hsieh Chiao-Min (1976), pp. 254 – 255. See Hsieh's article for a more detailed discussion of Zhu's analysis.

83. Wang Zuoyue (2008), p. 405.

84. Roberts (1998), pp. 70 – 71.

85. Ibid., p. 74.

86. *Flowers in Yangdang Mountains in My Memory* and *Landscape Radiating Beauty*. See Kim (2017), p. 147.

87. Ibid., pp. 150 – 151.

88. He Yin was the sister of He Tianxing, "Father of the Liangzhu Culture."

89. Address is 212 Nanshan Road, Hangzhou.

90. Roberts (1998), p. 96.

91. Jackson (2012), p. 48.

92. You Yuwen, "Ma Yinchu and His Theory of Population," *China Reconstructs*, Vol. 28, No. 12 (December 1979), pp. 28 – 30.

93. Greenhalgh (2008), p. 57. Only a month or so earlier, Mao Zedong had announced his support for State management of births and active population control.

94. Tien H. Yuan (1981), pp. 688, 701. Islam, et. al. (2011), rephrases the situation more colloquially: "We lost one Ma Yinchu but we gained an extra 300 million people," p. 29.

95. Ma Yinchu Memorial Hall, 210 Qingchun Road, Xiacheng District, Hangzhou.

96. Qian Xuantong was born in Huzhou.

97. Nicholas D. Kristof, "Qian Sanqiang, Chinese Physicist on Atom Bomb Team, Dies at 79," *The New York Times* (July 3, 1992).

98. Iris Chang (1995), p. 2.

99. Ibid., p. 106.

100. In 1947, Qian married Jiang Ying 蒋英 (1919 – 2012), an accomplished opera singer from Haining whom Qian knew from youth as an "adopted sister." They had two American-born children, a son (Yucon) and a daughter (Yung-jen).

101. Iris Chang (1995), p. 190 for Zhou Enlai, and p. 198 for Qian's deportation lawyer Grant B. Cooper.

102. Ibid., pp. 210 – 211.

103. "Key Chinese Scientist: Tsien Hsue-Shen," *The New York Times* (October 28, 1966), p. 18. The sidebar article incorrectly identifies Qian as having been born in Shanghai.

104. As part of a study of city planning for Guilin.

105. Chen Yulin (2010), p. 1.

106. Ma Yansong of MAD Architects presented a *Shanshui* city exhibition for new urban development in Guiyang, China in June 2013 along with a book titled *Shanshui City*. See, for example, https://www.dezeen.com/2013/06/11/shanshui-city-exhibition-by-ma-yansong/.

107. Description of the wedding event from Hou Bo's reminiscence, from Yang Guang, "Through Her Own Lens to Mao," *Chinadaily.com.cn* (February 5, 2010), accessed at http://www. chinadaily.com.cn/cndy/2010-02/05/content_9431509.htm.

108. Ibid.

109. "Chairman Mao's Photographer Wins Life Achievement Award in Pingyao International Photography Festival," *Chinadaily.com.cn* (September 22, 2016), accessed at https://www.chinadaily.com.cn/culture/2016-09/22/content_26867114.htm.

Chapter 21

1. Gernet (1970), p. 23. The source Gernet listed somewhat cryptically in dated *pinyin* as "*Kuei hsin tsa chih*, Hsü B, §82." Although he describes this poem as "clumsy enough when compared to the eloquence of a scholar, but perhaps sufficiently evocative," this work of the 13th Century still seems a remarkably apt description of Hangzhou today as seen from West Lake.

2. A fascinating and easy-to-use time-lapse tool from Google Earthengine, accessed at https://earthengine.google.com/timelapse/.

3. The Chinese *jiao* coin is one-tenth of a *yuan* in value. Not only is it the monetary equivalent of a U.S. dime, both coins are approximately the same physical size.

4. Chen Xiao (2020). See also Figure 1, "Number of China's TVEs (1978 – 2010)," accessed online at http://www.cikd.org/english/detail?leafid=217&docid=1611.

5. Ibid.

6. Keith Forster (1998), p. 148.

7. Gu Xiaofen, et. al. (2006), Table 4-01, "Number of Industrial Enterprises in Main Years," p. 141, and Table 4-02, "Gross Industrial Output Value in Main Years," pp. 142 – 143.

8. Ibid., unpaginated first page of color introductory exhibits.

9. Skinner, et. al. (2001), pp. 331 – 332.

10. See, for example, He Shan (2013), p. 9, "Figure 5. Hangzhou Urban Footprint and Rail Developments between 1949 and 1990s," or the same diagram presented as Figure 3.59 in He Shan (2017), p. 125.

11. Hangzhou city's area in 1970 was only sixty-five square kilometers, and only thirteen square kilometers in 1950. See Dennis Wei Yehua (2015), Table 12, "Growth of Population and Land Areas in Hangzhou City, 1950 – 2009," p. 31.

12. "Introduction to the High-Tech Zone (Binjiang)," Hangzhou High-Tech Zone website, accessed at http://www.hhtz.gov.cn/art/2022/1/25/art_1487272_20481188.html via http://www.hhtz.gov.cn/col/col1487272/index.html.

13. Fu Yongwei, et. al. (2020), Table 1-19, "The Total Population of the City at the End of the Year (Household Registration)," pp. 57 – 58.

14. Ding Ying and Wang Hairong, "Limited Space, Unlimited Growth," *Beijing Review*, Vol. 61, No. 49 (December 6, 2018), p. 13.

15. By way of comparison, New York City had a 2020 population of 8.8 million and a land area of 778 square kilometers (300.5 square miles).

16. He Shan (2013), "Figure 4. Municipal Boundary Expansion and Population Increase of Hangzhou," p. 8. This diagram, sourced from the Hangzhou Planning Bureau, gives an excellent perspective on the magnitude and direction of Hangzhou City's physical growth.

17. Fu Yongwei, et. al. (2020). For GDP data, Table 1-05, "Gross Domestic Product and Its Indices (1978 – 2019)," p. 30, and Table 1-19, "Main Indicators Since the Founding of PRC: The City's GDP," p. 53, for 1951 and 1965 figures. For annual disposable income data, Table 1-04, "Major Indicators of National Economy (Main Years)," pp. 28 – 29.

18. Ibid., Table 6-05, "Length of Transportation Routes (2013 – 2019)," p. 240.

19. Ibid., Table 12-08, "Number of Culture Institutions (2002 – 2019)," p. 383.

20. The Hangzhou Philharmonic Orchestra performed for the G20 Summit in 2016.

21. More details on Qinghefang ancient street are available at the *Travel China Guide* website, accessed at https://www.travelchinaguide.com/attraction/zhejiang/hangzhou/qinghefang-ancient-street.htm.

22. See Wu Huixin, "Restoring the Glory of Ancient Song Dynasty" (January 11, 2021), at https://www.shine.cn/feature/art-culture/2101113025/ or "Grand Plan to Rebuild Ancient Palace," *Shanghaidaily.com* (September 13, 2010), accessed at https://archive.shine.cn/city-specials/hangzhou/grand-plan-to-rebuild-ancient-palace/shdaily.shtml.

23. Sun Peifang (2021), p. 154.

24. Fu, et. al. (2020), Table 9-14, "Statistics on Tourism (1995 – 2019)," and Table 9-15, "Number of International Tourists (1978 – 2019)," pp. 331 – 332, measured in person-times. Note that "International Visitors" includes tourist visits from Hong Kong, Macao, and Taiwan; "Foreign Visitors" excludes them.

25. Ibid., Table 9-17, "Number of International Tourists by Country or Territory (2018 – 2019)," p. 334.

26. In 1998, the government created the consolidated, present-day Zhejiang University by combining the former Zhejiang University, Hangzhou University, Zhejiang Agricultural University, and the Zhejiang Medical University.

27. Zijingang, Yuquan, Xixi, Huajiachi and Zhijiang in Hangzhou along with campuses at Haining and Zhoushan Island.

28. The other eight members of the C9 are the Beijing, Qinghua, Fudan (Shanghai), Nanjing, Shanghai Jiaotong, and Xi'an Jiaotong Universities, the Harbin Institute of Technology, and the University of Science and Technology of China in Hefei, Anhui Province.

29. From Wikipedia entry for the C9 League as of October 2021, accessed at https://en.wikipedia.org/wiki/c9_league.

30. From Hangzhou Normal University website, accessed at https://www.hznu.edu.cn/xxgk/xxjj/.

31. Fu, et. al. (2020), *Hangzhou Statistical Yearbook, 2020*, Table 11-04, "Urban Forestation (2012 – 2019)," p. 368. Year 2000 data from Tu Xingeng, et. al. (2010), Table 11-04, "Urban Forestation in Main Years," p. 314.

32. Ma Zhenhuan, "Xixi Wetland Museum Helps Expand China's Environmental Knowledge," *chinadaily.com* (May 2, 2020), accessed at https://www.chinadaily.com.cn/a/202005/02/ws5eacc1aba310a8b2411532b1.html.

33. Data on West Lake dredging and reforestation of the surrounding hills from West Lake Museum website, accessed at http://www.westlakemuseum.com/index.php/bwggk/bwgjj-en.

34. Increased conservation and pollution controls were formally promulgated in the 1998 "Regulations of Hangzhou Municipality on Protection and Management of West Lake Water Area."

35. The 1929 West Lake Expo was renamed the First West Lake Expo.

36. West Lake International Expo website, accessed at https://web.archive.org/web/20150407065906/http://en.xh-expo.com/pages/history01.html.

37. Hangzhou was actually Zhang Yimou's third site-specific installation of an Impressions program. The first two were located in Yangshuo (Guangxi Province, debuted 2004) and in Lijiang (Yunnan Province, debuted 2006).

38. Duan Xiaolin (2020), p. 169.

39. Ibid., p. 170.

40. Ibid., pp. 190 - 191.

41. Strassberg (1994), p. 255.

42. Xianchun 咸淳 was the reign name of the Duzong Emperor 宋度宗 (r. 1264 – 1274).

43. A.C. Moule (1923), p. 153.

44. Interest in the potential of tidal bore surfing may well have been prompted by several earlier illegal surfing escapades by Westerners, including two surfers, one French and one Brazilian, who teamed up for a continuous, 17-kilometer, one-hour-and-ten-minute ride on October 24, 2007. See https://cathayseas.wordpress.com/2007/11/12/surfing-the-longest-wave-in-the-world/.

45. "France and South Africa Share Victory at 2019 Silver Dragon Shootout," *Surfer Today* (September 18, 2019), accessed at https://www.surfertoday.com/surfing/france-and-south-africa-share-victory-at-2019-silver-dragon-shootout.

46. Hamilton (2011), p. 151.

47. Philip Fugh was of Manchu descent. In 1984, his son John Fugh (傅履仁, Fu Luren, 1934 – 2010) was the first Chinese-American to be made a general in the United States Army. He retired in 1993 with the rank of Major General.

48. Hao Ping (2018), p. 167.

49. During then-Vice Party Secretary of Zhejiang Province Xi Jinping's visit to the United States.

50. Zhang Yu, "China-Born US Diplomat Recognized Decades after Chairman Mao Labeled Him an Imperialist," *Global Times* (September 27, 2016). Accessed at https://www.globaltimes.cn/content/1008641.shtml.

51. Hao Ping (2018), pp. 167 – 168. Stuart's parents and a younger brother were each buried in Hangzhou.

52. Yearly satellite images for each city from 1984 – 2020 taken from Google Earthengine,

accessed at https://earthengine.google.com/timelapse/.

53. From "World Population Review," accessed at https://www.crunchbase.com/organization/world-population-review.

54. Michael Leibold (2008), pp. 363 – 364, 375.

55. See "The Ritual Ceremony for Great Yu," accessed at http://en.tourzj.com/zhejiang-tradition/ritual-ceremony-great-yu.html or "Memorial Ceremony in Honor of Yu the Great Held," *chinadaily.com* (April 21, 2021), accessed at http://www.ezhejiang.gov.cn/shaoxing/2021-04/21/c_612980.htm. This event now takes place every year on April 20.

56. Confucius is commonly known in China by the name Kongzi 孔子, short for Kong Fuzi 孔夫子, "Master Kong." The Latinized name "Confucius" originated with the Jesuit missionaries in 16th-Century China.

57. Wang-Riese (2014), p. 188. Much of the Quzhou Confucian Temple story herein is drawn from Wang-Riese's 2014 essay.

58. Dr. Arthur W. Douthwaite (1880) reported on the presence in Quzhou of "about 100 families of the descendants of Confucius" and an ancestral hall.

59. The Quzhou Confucian Temple was first built in 1253 at the order of Song Emperor Lizong 宋理宗 (r. 1224 – 1264).

60. Wang-Riese (2014), p. 189.

61. Rui Huaichuan (2018), pp. S14 – S30. Accessed at https://www.tandfonline.com/doi/full/10.1080/02757206.2018.1516654 . Rui dates the "sugar for chicken feathers" traders back to the 16th Century.

62. For a more extended discussion of Yiwu's trading history and the early develop of its markets, see Jacobs (2016), pp. 53 – 65. Jacobs presents excerpts of his interview with Xie Gaohua on pp. 128 – 132.

63. Rui Huaichuan (2018), "Yiwu."

64. Belguidoum and Pliez (2015), p. 3 of 17. Accessed at https://journals.openedition.org/articulo/2863.

65. In 1995, it was called the China Fair of Famous and Outstanding Commodities, then renamed the China Small Commodities Fair in 1996 before adopting its current name, usually abbreviated to "the Yiwu Fair." See Mu Guo (2010), pp. 91 – 115, for the evolution of the Yiwu fairs from 1995 to 2007.

66. Benazir Wehelie, "No Shortage of Color in 'Commodity City," *CNN.com* (March 2, 2015). Accessed at https://edition.cnn.com/2015/03/01/world/cnnphotos-commodity-city/index.html.

67. Helen Roxburgh, "Welcome to Yiwu: China's Testing Ground for a Multicultural City," *theguardian.com* (March 23, 2017). Accessed at https://www.theguardian.com/cities/2017/mar/23/welcome-yiwu-china-testing-ground-multicultural-city .

68. Wang Jinmin (2010), pp. 101 – 105.

69. Yiwu, China City Government website, accessed at http://www.yw.gov.cn/art/2021/1/21/art_1229142411_50636241.html . The city website also indicates that Brooklyn, New York is a rather unexpected member of Yiwu's cohort of thirty-two sister cities.

70. Rui Huaichuan (2018), p. 14.

71. Zhang Xiao, "Small Town, Big Dream," *China Today*, Vol. 68, No. 2 (February 2019), p. 47.

72. Wen Qing, "From Rags to Riches," *Beijing Review*, Vol. 61, No. 36 (September 6, 2018), accessed at https://www.bjreview.com/Current_Issue/2018/202102/t20210204_800235119.html.

73. Li Zuyuan is also known as Chu-yuan Lee or C.Y. Lee. He was the lead architect for the Taipei 101 skyscraper.

74. See photo and short news story at "Xiaobaihua Yue Opera Theater," *ezhejiang.gov.cn* (March 11, 2021), accessed at http://www.ezhejiang.gov.cn/2021-03/11/c_601887.htm . Xiaobaihua 小白

花 ("Hundred little flowers") refers to the name of the all-female Yue Opera troupe (小白花越剧团, Xiaobaihua Yueju tuan) begun in Zhejiang with the 1983 revival of Yue Opera. Twenty-eight young women were selected from among thousands of applicants for intensive training by the still-living elder generation of performers.

75. Yue Opera has remained immensely popular in Shanghai into the new millennium, as evidenced in part in Sheila Melvin, "Into the Stronghold of Shaoxing Opera," *The New York Times* (September 4, 1999), accessed at https://www.nytimes.com/1999/09/04/style/IHT-into-the-stronghold-of-shaoxing-opera.html.

76. See photo of "Big Lotus" at Michael Houston, "Hangzhou 2022 Organisers Launch Asian Games Channel," *Inside The Games* website (June 2, 2020), accessed at https://www.insidethegames.biz/articles/1094892/hangzhou-2022-asian-games-channel, or at "A City Blossoms," NBBJ Architects website, accessed at http://www.nbbj.com/work/hangzhou-stadium/. Aerial photo of both stadiums available at https://mobile.twitter.com,/19thagofficial/status/1505887727169912834/photo/1.

77. Woo (2021). Their survey also listed Jiaxing as a prospective high performer.

78. Duan Xiaolin (2020), p. 183.

79. International Council on Monuments and Sites (ICOMOS) (2011), p. 147.

Appendix A

1. Duan (2014), p. 164, Footnote No. 387.

2. "West Lake Inscribed on World Heritage List," *Chinadaily.com* (June 27, 2011), accessed at https://www.chinadaily.com.cn/life/2011-06/27/content_12787804.htm.

3. The causeway's full length is 987 meters, or about 3,240 feet.

4. Built during the reign of Song Emperor Xiaozong (1162 – 1189).

5. Liu Jue, "Top 10 Scenes of West Lake," *The World of Chinese* website (April 29, 2017), accessed at https://www.theworldofchinese.com/2017/04/top-10-scenes-of-west-lake/. Liu cites Ming poet Wan Dafu 万达甫 as the author of this sentiment.

6. "Viewing Fish At Flower Harbor," *Travel China Guide* website, accessed at https://www.travelchinaguide.com/attraction/zhejiang/hangzhou/red-carp-pond.htm.

7. A radical is something like a group prefix or indicator. Examples of the fire radical in Chinese characters include 煮 (*zhu*, to cook), 燃 (*ran*, to ignite), and 阻燃 (*zuran*, fire resistant)]; examples of the water radical include 河 (*he*, river), 江 (*jiang*, river), 湖 (*hu*, lake), 浪 (*lang*, wave) and 潮 (*chao*, tide).

8. One could argue that the center island on Lesser Yingzhou is "an island within a lake within an island within a lake."

9. The stele was reconstructed in 1979 from a rubbing taken from the original.

10. As a modest demonstration of the modern adage "nothing is sacred," see the interesting social-scientific analysis of the Jingci Temple bell ringing at Ge Jian, et.al. (2013), downloadable PDF available at https://link.springer.com/article/10.1631/jzus.a1200159.

11. A variant of *wufu*, the five blessings represented by five bats on the slate-roof eves of many old-style residences.

12. Longjing teas are divided in four groups, related to the local tea plantation areas at which they are grown in the hills west of Hangzhou: *shi* 狮 (lion) from Shifeng (Lion's Peak), *long* 龙 (dragon) from Longjing (Dragon Well), *yun* 云 (cloud) from Yunqi (Cloud Dwelling), and *hu* 虎 (tiger) from Hupao (Tiger Spring).

Appendix B

1. The other three famous mosques are located in Yangzhou, Quanzhou, and Guangzhou.

2. For more information, see the Silk Museum website at www.chinasilkmuseum.com.

3.	See Ma Zhenhuan, "Xixi Wetland Museum Helps Expand China's Environmental Knowledge," *Chinadaily.com.cn* (May 2, 2020), accessed at https://www.chinadaily.com.cn/a/202005/02/WS5eacc1aba310a8b2411532b1.html.

4.	"Memorial Hall of Yu the Great," *Chinadaily.com.cn* (November 18, 2020), accessed at http://www.ezhejiang.gov.cn/2020-11/18/c_565292.htm.

5.	Denton (2005), pp. 55 – 58.

6.	For Jiaxing's South Lake, see Ma Zhenhuan, "The Small Red Boat that Rode the Wave of History," *chinadaily.com.cn* (May 20, 2021), accessed at https://www.chinadaily.com.cn/a/202105/20/WS60a5b44da31024ad0bac0283.html.

7.	For updated information as of 2021, see the World Internet Conference website (with English language option) at http://www.wuzhenwic.org/.

8.	See "Huzhou Writing Brush Museum," *Chinadaily.com.cn* (November 2, 2021), accessed at http://www.ezhejiang.gov.cn/2021-11/02/c_676550.htm.

9.	For an introduction to Jinhua hams and their production, see Clarissa Wei, "This Chinese City Has Been Producing Ham for More Than 1,000 Years," at the *Vice* website (February 5, 2016), accessed at https://www.vice.com/en/article/vvqy98/this-chinese-city-has-been-producing-ham-for-more-than-1000-years.

BIBLIOGRAPHY

_____ (1911). *The Hangchow Presbyterian College, Hangchow, China: Introspect, Retrospect, Prospect*. Omaha NE: Franklin Publishing.

_____. "Liang Sicheng and Lin Huiyin," in *Journeys in Time*, CCTV program series.

_____ (1922). *Papers Relating to Pacific and Far Eastern Affairs Prepared for the Use of the American Delegation to the Conference on the Limitation of Armament, Washington, 1921 – 1922*. Washington, D.C.: Government Printing Office.

_____ (1958). *The West Lake Companion*. Beijing: Foreign Languages Press.

Altenburger, Roland (2017). "Layered Landscape: Textual and Cartographic Representations of Hangzhou's West Lake, 16th – 18th Centuries," in Zhuang Yue and Andrea M. Riemenschnitter, *Entangled Landscapes: Early Modern China and Europe*. Singapore: NUS Press, pp. 115 – 143.

_____ (2009). *The Sword or the Needle: The Female Knight-errant (xia) in Traditional Chinese Narrative*. Bern: Peter Lang.

Anderson, Aeneas (1795). *A Narrative of the British Embassy to China, in the Years 1792, 1793, and 1794*. Basil: J.J. Tourneisen.

Austin, Alvyn (2007). *China's Millions: The China Inland Mission and Late Qing Society, 1832 – 1905*. Grand Rapids MI: William B. Eerdmans.

Backhouse, Edmund and J.O.P. Bland (1914). *Annals & Memoirs of the Court of Peking*. London: William Heinemann.

_____ (1911). *China Under the Empress Dowager, Being the History of the Life and Times of Tzu Hsi*. Philadelphia: J.B. Lippincott.

Bai Juyi (2012). *Waiting for the Moon: Poems of Bo Juyi*. (Arthur Waley, Trans.). Mount Jackson VA: Axios Press.

Bales, William L. (1937). *Tso Tsung-t'ang, Soldier and Statesman of Old China*. Shanghai: Kelly & Walsh.

Bao Shixing (2000). "Qian Xuesen and Shan-shui City." *Urban Studies*, Issue 6, pp. 15 – 20.

Barenblatt, Daniel (2004). *A Plague upon Humanity: The Hidden History of Japan's Biological Warfare Program*. New York: HarperCollins.

Barmé, Geremie R. (2002). *An Artistic Exile: A Life of Feng Zikai (1898 – 1975)*. Berkeley: University of California Press.

_____ (2011). "A Chronology of West Lake and Hangzhou." *China Heritage Quarterly*, No. 28 (December).

_____. (2011A) "Mao Zedong's West Lake: The Revolutionary Retreats Liu Villa 劉庄 and Wang Villa 汪庄." *China Heritage Quarterly*, No. 28 (December).

_____. (2011B) "The Tide of Revolution." *China Heritage Quarterly*, No. 28 (December).

Barnhart, Richard M. (1993). *Li Kung-lin's Classic of Filial Piety*. New York: The Metropolitan

Museum of Art.

Barnstone, Tony and Chou Ping (2005). *The Anchor Book of Chinese Poetry: From Ancient to Contemporary, the Full 3000-Year Tradition.* New York: Anchor Books.

Barr, Allan H. (2005). "The Ming History Inquisition in Personal Memoir and Public Memory." *Chinese Literature: Essays, Articles, Reviews (CLEAR)*, Vol. 27 (December), pp. 5 – 32.

Barrow, John (1804). *Travels in China, Containing Descriptions, Observations, and Comparisons Made and Collected in the Course of a Short Residence at the Imperial Palace of Yuen-Min-Yuen, and on a Subsequent Journey through the Country from Pekin to Canton.* London: T. Cadell and W. Davies.

Barry, Arthur J. (1909). "Railway Development in China." *Journal of the Royal Society of Arts*, Vol. 57, No. 2948 (May 21), pp. 541 – 558.

Batt, Herbert and Sheldon Zitner (2016). *The Flowering of Modern Chinese Poetry: An Anthology of Verse from the Republican Period.* Montreal: McGill-Queen's University Press.

Beauvoir, Simone de (1958). *The Long March: An Account of Modern China.* Cleveland: World Publishing.

Belguidoum, Saïd and Olivier Pliez (2015). "Yiwu: The Creation of a Global Market Town in China." *Articulo: Journal of Urban Research*, Vol. 12.

Benincampi, Iacopo (2017). "China and Europe: Hangzhou and the Spread of Architecture *Chinoiserie* in the 18th Century," in Dai Xiaoling, Anna Irene Del Monaco, Yu Wenbo, *Hangzhou from Song Dynasty Capital to the Challenge of Cultural Capital in Contemporary China.* Rome: Edizioni Nuova Cultura, pp. 127 – 137.

Benn, James A. (2015). *Tea in China: A Religious and Cultural History.* Honolulu: University of Hawai'i Press.

Berg, Daria. (2009). "Cultural Discourse on Xue Susu, A Courtesan in Late Ming China." *International Journal of Asian Studies*, Vol. 6, No. 2, pp. 171 – 200.

_____ (2007). "Female Self-Fashioning in Late Imperial China: How the Gentlewoman and the Courtesan Edited Her Story and Rewrote Hi/story" in Berg, Daria, *Reading China: Fiction, History and the Dynamics of Discourse. Essays in Honour of Professor Glen Dudbridge.* Leiden: Brill, pp. 238 – 89.

_____ (2006). "Miss Emotion: Women, Books and Culture in Seventeenth-Century Jiangnan," in Santangelo, Paolo and Donatella Guida, *Love, Hatred and Other Passions: Questions and Themes on Emotions in Chinese Civilization.* Leiden: E.J. Brill, pp. 314 – 330.

_____ (2007B). "Negotiating Gentility: The Banana Garden Poetry Club in Seventeenth-Century Jiangnan," in Berg, Daria and Chloë Starr (2007A), pp. 73 – 94.

_____ (2013). *Women and the Literary World in Early Modern China, 1580 – 1700.* Abingdon, Oxon, UK: Routledge.

Berg, Daria and Chloë Starr (2007A). *The Quest for Gentility in China: Negotiations Beyond Gender and Class.* Abingdon, Oxon, UK: Routledge.

Bergère, Marie-Claire (1998). *Sun Yat-sen.* (Janet Lloyd, Trans.). Stanford: Stanford University Press.

Bergin, Bob (2012). "High Aviation Ideals." *Aviation History*, Vol. 23, No. 1 (September), pp. 18 – 19.

Bergreen, Laurence (2007). *Marco Polo: From Venice to Xanadu.* New York: Alfred A. Knopf.

Berninghausen, John (1977). "The Central Contradiction in Mao Dun's Earliest Fiction," in Goldman, Merle, *Modern Chinese Literature in the May Fourth Era.* Cambridge: Harvard East Asian Series 89, Harvard University Press, pp. 233 – 259.

Berry, Michael (2015). "Chasing the Silver Dragon." *Physics World* (July).

Bieler, Stacey (2011). "Zeng Baosun: Embracing Chinese Ideals and Christian Education," in Hamrin, Carol Lee and Stacy Bieler, *Salt and Light (Vol. 3): More Lives of Faith that Shaped Modern China.* Eugene OR: Pickwick, pp. 93 - 115.

Birch, Cyril (1995). *Scenes for Mandarins: The Elite Theater of the Ming*. New York: Columbia University Press.

Bird, Isabella L. (1895). *The Yangtze Valley and Beyond: An Account of Journeys in China, Chiefly in the Province of Sze Chuan and Among the Man-tze of the Somo Territory*. London: Virago.

Bishop, Kevin and Annabel Roberts (1997). *China's Imperial Way: Retracing an Historical Trade and Communications Route from Beijing to Hong Kong*. Hong Kong: Guidebook.

Bond, Jennifer (2019). "'The One for the Many': Zeng Baosun, Louise Barnes and the Yifang School for Girls at Changsha, 1893 – 1927." *Studies in Church History*, Vol. 55 (June), pp. 441 – 462.

Bond, W. Langhorne (2001). *Wings for an Embattled China*. Bethlehem PA: Lehigh University Press.

Bonta, Steve (2003). "Soldier-Missionary." *The New American*. (October 20), pp. 31 – 34.

Bordahl, Vibeke (2007). "The Man-Hunting Tiger from 'Wu Song Fights the Tiger' in Chinese Traditions," *Asian Folklore Studies*, Vol. 66, pp. 141 – 163.

Borgen, Robert (2007). "Jojin's Travels from Center to Center (with Some Periphery in between)," in Adolphson, Mikael S., Edward Kamens, and Stacie Matsumoto, *Heian Japan, Centers and Peripheries*. Honolulu: University of Hawai'i Press, pp, 385 – 413.

_____ (1987). "*San Tendai Godai san ki* as a Source for the Study of Sung History." *Bulletin of Sung-Yuan Studies*, No. 19, pp. 1 – 16.

Boulger, Demetrius C. (1885) *Central Asian Questions: Essays on Afghanistan, China, and Central Asia*. London: T.F. Unwin.

Boyne, Walter J. (Ed.) (2002)). *Air Warfare: An International Encyclopedia, Volume One, A – L*. Santa Barbara CA: ABC Clio.

Bratter, H.M. (1925). "The Jeweled Waters of Hangchow." *Travel*, Vol 45, No. 5 (September), pp. 22 – 25.

Bray, Francesca (2007). "Agricultural Illustrations: Blueprint or Icon?" in Bray, Francesca, Vera Dorofeeva-Lichtmann, and Georges Metallie, *Graphics and Text in the Production of Technical Knowledge in China: The Warp and the Weft* (Sinica Leidensia, Vol. 79). Leiden: Brill, pp. 521 – 567.

Brezzi, Alessandra (2016). "Some Artistic Descriptions and Ethical Dilemmas in Shan Shili's Travel Notes on Italy (1909)." *International Communication of Chinese Culture*, Vol. 3, No. 1, pp. 175 – 189.

Brockey, Matthew (2008). *Journey to the East: The Jesuit Mission to China, 1579 – 1724*. Cambridge: Belknap Press of Harvard University Press.

Brook, Timothy (1998). *The Confusions of Pleasure: Commerce and Culture in Ming China*. Berkeley: University of California Press.

_____ (2010). *The Troubled Empire: China in the Yuan and Ming Dynasties*. Cambridge: Harvard University Press.

Broomhall, Marshall (1915). *The Jubilee Story of the China Inland Mission*. London: Morgan & Scott.

Burkus-Chasson, Anne (2002). "Between Representations: The Historical and the Visionary in Chen Hongshou's *Yaji*." *The Art Bulletin*, Vol. 84, No. 2 (June), pp. 315 – 333.

Cahill, James (1982). *The Compelling Image: Nature and Style in Seventeenth-Century Painting*. Cambridge: Harvard University Press.

_____ (1996). "The Imperial Painting Academy," in Fong, Wen C. (1996), pp. 159 – 199.

Campany, Robert F. (2002). *To Live as Long as Heaven and Earth: A Translation and Study of Ge Hong's Traditions of Divine Transcendents*. Berkeley: University of California Press.

Campbell, Duncan (2004). "The Cultivation of Exile: Qi Biaojia and His Allegory Mountain," pp. 255 – 269 in Hanne, Michael, *Creativity in Exile*. Amsterdam NY: Rodopi.

_____ (2012). "Mortal Ancestors, Immortal Images: Zhang Dai's Biographical Portraits." *POR-*

TAL Journal of Multidisciplinary International Studies, Vol. 9, No. 3 (November), pp. 1 – 26.

_____ (2014). "Reflections on the Tower of the Crimson Clouds and the History of the Private Library in Late-Imperial China," *East Asian History*, No. 38 (February), pp. 63 – 74.

_____ (2011). "Searching for the Ming: Zhang Dai Introduced and Translated by Duncan Campbell," *China Heritage Quarterly* No. 28, (December).

_____ (2011A). "Ten Scenes of West Lake: Poems by Zhang Dai 張岱." *China Heritage Quarterly*, No. 28 (December).

_____ (2011B). "The Ten Scenes of West Lake, *Xihu Shi Jing*." *China Heritage Quarterly*, No. 28 (December).

Cantlie, James and C. Sheridan Jones (1912). *Sun Yat Sen and the Awakening of China*. New York: Fleming H. Revell.

Cappelletti, Alessandra (2022). "Losing Centrality and Socialization of Islam in Suzhou Memories, Identities, and Positionality Around the City Mosques." *Contemporary Islam* (December 8).

Cass, Victoria (1999). *Dangerous Women: Warriors, Grannies, and Geishas of the Ming*. Lanham MD: Rowman & Littlefield.

_____ (2008). *In the Realm of the Gods: Lands, Myths, and Legends of China*. South San Francisco: Long River Press.

Chan Kar Yue (2005). *Ambivalence in Poetry: Zhu Shuzhen of the Song Dynasty*. Doctoral Dissertation: The University of Edinburgh.

Chan, Timothy Wai Keung (2012). *Considering the End: Mortality in Early Medieval Chinese Poetic Representation*. Leiden: Brill.

Chang Chia-feng (2002). "Disease and Its Impact on Politics, Diplomacy, and the Military: The Case of Smallpox and the Manchus (1613–1795)." *Journal of the History of Medicine and Allied Sciences*, Vol. 57, No. 2 (April), pp. 177 – 197.

Chang Chun-shu and Shelley Hsueh-lun Chang (1992). *Crisis and Transformation in Seventeenth-Century China: Society, Culture, and Modernity in Li Yü's World*. Ann Arbor: University of Michigan Press.

Chang, Gordon H. (2015) *Fateful Ties: A History of America's Preoccupation with China*. Cambridge: Harvard University Press.

Chang, Iris (1995). *Thread of the Silkworm*. New York: Basic Books.

Chang, Janie (2020). "The Risky Journey that Saved One of China's Greatest Literary Treasures." *TIME.com* (June 15).

Chang, Joseph (2009). "From the Clear and Distant Landscape of Wuxing to the Humble Hermit of Clouds and Woods." *Ars Orientalis*, Vol. 37, pp. 32 – 47.

Chang Jui-te (1993). "Technology Transfer in Modern China: The Case of Railway Enterprise (1876 – 1937)." *Modern Asian Studies*, Vol. 27, No. 2, pp. 281 – 296.

Chang Jung (2005). *Mao: The Unknown Story*. New York: Knopf.

Chang, Kang-I Sun and Haun Saussy (1999). *Women Writers of Traditional China: An Anthology of Poetry and Criticism*. Stanford: Stanford University Press.

Chang, Michael G. (2007). *A Court on Horseback: Imperial Touring and the Construction of Qing Rule, 1680 – 1785*. Cambridge: Harvard University Press.

Chang, Nelson and Laurence Chang (2010). *The Zhangs from Nanxun: A One Hundred and Fifty Year Chronicle of a Chinese Family*. Palo Alto CA: CF Press.

Chang Shaowen (1980). "Tomb of Yue Fei, Song Dynasty Hero," *China Reconstructs*, Vol. 29, No. 3 (March), pp. 55 – 57.

Charbonnier, Jean (2007). *Christians in China: A.D. 600 to 2000*. San Francisco: St. Ignatius Press.

Chen, Eva Yin-I (2003). "Shame and Narcissistic Self in Yu Da-fu's *Sinking*." *Canadian Review of Comparative Literature* (September-December), pp. 566 – 585.

Chen, Gilbert (2016). "A Confucian Iconography of Cao E (Maiden Cao): Narrative Illustrations of a Female Deity in Late Imperial China." *Nan Nü*, Vol. 18 (2016), pp. 84 – 114.

Chen, Janet C. (2016). *Representing Talented Women in Eighteenth-Century Chinese Painting: Thirteen Female Disciples Seeking Instruction at the Lake Pavilion*. Doctoral Dissertation: University of Kansas.

Chen Jiyu, et. al. (1990). "Geomorphological Development and Sedimentation in Qiantang Estuary and Hangzhou Bay." *Journal of Coastal Research*, Vol. 6, No. 3 (Summer), pp. 559 – 572.

Chen Qitian (1938). *Tso Tsung T'ang: Pioneer Promoter of the Modern Dockyard and the Woolen Mill in China*. Beijing: Yenching University.

Chen Wenxi (2017). *Chinese Local Elites and Institutional Changes: The Local Self-Government in Jiaxing, 1905 – 1914*. MA Thesis, Universiteit Leiden.

Chen Xiao (2020). "The Evolution of China's Township and Village Enterprises," Center for International Knowledge on Development, China (October 27).

Chen Xing (2011). "Drinking by West Lake: Feng Zikai and Zheng Zhenduo." *China Heritage Quarterly*, No. 28 (December).

Chen Yulin (2010). "Shan-Shui City: A Chinese Spatial Planning Tradition and Its Implications on Urban Sustainability." Paper presented at 46th ISOCARP Congress, Nairobi, Kenya (September 19 – 23).

Chen Yu-Shih (1986). *Realism and Allegory in the Early Fiction of Mao Tun*. Bloomington: Indiana University Press.

Cheng, Eileen J. (2013). *Literary Remains: Death, Trauma, and Lu Xun's Refusal to Mourn*. Honolulu: University of Hawai'i Press.

Cheung, Desmond H. H. (2011). *A Socio-Cultural History of Sites in Ming Hangzhou*. Doctoral Dissertation, University of British Columbia.

Chi, Madeleine (1973). "Shanghai-Hangchow-Ningpo Railway Loan: A Case Study of the Rights Recovery Movement." *Modern Asian Studies*, Vol. 7, No. 1, pp. 85 – 106.

Chiu Suet Ying (2000). "*Ernü yingxiong zhuan*: An Integrative Reflection of Manchu and Han Cultures." *Siksaha: A Journal of Manchu Studies*, Vol 7, pp. 29 – 48.

Chou, Eva Shan (2002). "Learning to Read Lu Xun, 1918 – 1923: The Emergence of a Readership." *The China Quarterly*, No. 172 (December), pp. 1042 – 1064.

_____ (2007). "'A Story about Hair': A Curious Mirror of Lu Xun's Pre-Republican Years." *The Journal of Asian Studies*, Vol. 66, No. 2, pp. 421 – 459.

Chou Hui-ling (1997). "Striking Their Own Poses: The History of Cross-Dressing on the Chinese Stage." *The Drama Review*, Vol. 41, No. 2 (Summer), pp. 130 – 152.

Chow Kai-wing (2004). *Publishing, Culture, and Power in Early Modern China*. Stanford: Stanford University Press.

Chow, Natasha Jennifer (2012). *Sequels to Honglou Meng: How Gu Taiqing Continues the Story in Honglou Meng Ying*. M.A. Thesis, University of British Columbia (Vancouver).

Chow, Tse-tsung [Zhou Cezong] (1967). *The May Fourth Movement: Intellectual Revolution in Modern China*. Cambridge: Harvard University Press.

Clark, Hugh R. (2009). "The Southern Kingdoms between the T'ang and the Sung, 907 – 979," in Twitchett, Dennis and Paul Jakov Smith, *The Cambridge History of China: Vol. 5, Part One, The Sung Dynasty and Its Precursors, 907 – 1279* (Cambridge: Cambridge University Press.

Clarke, Prescott and J.S. Gregory (1982). *Western Reports on the Taiping: A Selection of Documents*. Honolulu: University of Hawai'i Press.

Clayton, Edward H. (1944). *Heaven Below*. New York: Prentice Hall, 1944.

Cleaves, Francis Woodman (1956). "The Biography of Bayan of the Barin in the Yuan Shih." *Harvard Journal of Asiatic Studies*, Vol. 19, No. 3 – 4, pp. 185 – 303.

Cloud, Frederick Douglass (1906). *Hangchow: The "City of Heaven."* Shanghai: Presbyterian Mission Press.

Clunas, Craig (2013). "The Family Style: Art as Lineage in the Ming and Qing," in Silbergeld, Jerome and Dora C.Y. Ching, *The Family Model in Chinese Art and Culture*. Princeton NJ: Kin-may Tang Center for East Asian Art, pp. 459 – 474.

_____ (1991). *Superfluous Things: Material Culture and Social Status in Early Modern China.* Cambridge: Polity Press.

Cohen, Paul A. (1963). *China and Christianity: The Missionary Movement and the Growth of Chinese Antiforeignism, 1860 – 1870.* Cambridge: Harvard University Press.

_____ (2009). *Speaking to History: The Story of King Goujian in Twentieth-Century China.* Berkeley: University of California Press.

Cole, James (1986). *Shaohsing: Competition and Cooperation in Nineteenth-Century China.* Tucson: University of Arizona Press.

_____ (1980). "The Shaoxing Connection: A Vertical Administrative Clique in Late Qing China." *Modern China*, Vol. 6 (July), pp. 317 – 326.

Cong Xiaoping (2008). "From 'Cainü' to 'Nü Jiaoxi': Female Normal Schools and the Transformation of Women's Education in the Late Qing Period, 1895 – 1911," in Qian Nanxiu, Grace S. Fong, and Richard J. Smith, *Different Worlds of Discourse: Transformations of Gender and Genre in Late Qing and Early Republican China.* Leiden: Brill, pp. 115 – 144.

Croft, Michael (1958). *Red Carpet to China.* London: Longmans, Green.

Crossley, Pamela Kyle (1990). *Orphan Warriors: Three Manchu Generations and the End of the Qing World.* Princeton: Princeton University Press.

Crow, Carl (1913). *The Traveler's Handbook for China.* San Francisco: San Francisco News Co.

Cui Maoxin and Song Dongyang (2011). *Myths Stories.* Beijing: China Intercontinental Press.

Curwen, C.A. (1977). *Taiping Rebel: The Deposition of Li Hsiu-ch'eng* [Li Xiucheng]. Cambridge: Cambridge University Press.

Dai Lianbin (2014). "China's Bibliographic Tradition and the History of the Book." *Book History,* Vol 17, pp. 1 – 50.

Dai Xiaoling, Anna Irene Del Monaco, Yu Wenbo (2017). *Hangzhou from Song Dynasty Capital to the Challenge of Cultural Capital in Contemporary China.* Rome: Edizioni Nuova Cultura. [*L'architettura della citta, The Journal of the Scientific Society Ludovico Quaroni*]

Daniels, Benjamin (2013). *"Yuewang Goujian Shijia": An Annotated Translation.* M.A. Thesis, University of Arizona.

Davis, Richard L. (1996). *Wind Against the Mountain: The Crisis of Politics and Culture in Thirteenth-Century China.* Cambridge: Council on East Asian Studies, Harvard University Press.

Day, Clarence Burton (1955). *Hangchow University: A Brief History.* New York: United Board for Christian Colleges in China.

De Beauvoir, Simone (1958). *The Long March: An Account of Modern China.* Cleveland: World Publishing.

De Gruche, Kingston (1930). *Dr. D. Duncan Main of Hangchow, Who Is Known in China as Dr. Apricot of Heaven Below.* London: Marshall, Morgan & Scott.

De Hart, Jonathan (2013). "The Legacy of Ping-Pong Diplomat Zhuang Zedong." *The Diplomat,* February 13.

De Rachewiltz, Igor, et.al. (Eds.) (1993). *In the Service of the Khan: Eminent Personalities of the Early Mongol-Yuan Period.* Wiesbaden: Harrassowitz.

Demarchi, Franco and Riccardo Scartezzini (1996). *Martino Martini: A Humanist and Scientist in Seventeenth Century China.* Trento IT: Universita degli studi di Trento.

Dennerline, Jerry (1981). *The Chia-ting Loyalists: Confucian Leadership and Social Change in Seventeenth-Century China.* New Haven: Yale University Press.

Denton, Kirk A. (1992). "The Distant Shore: Nationalism in Yu Dafu's 'Sinking'." *Chinese Literature: Essays, Articles, Reviews (CLEAR)*, Vol. 14 (December), pp. 107 – 123.

_____ (2005). "Museums, Memorial Sites and Exhibitionary Culture in the People's Republic of China," in Hockx, Michel and Julia Strauss, *Culture in the Contemporary PRC.* Cambridge: Cambridge University Press, pp. 43 – 64.

Dillon, Michael (2020). *Zhou Enlai: The Enigma Behind Chairman Mao.* London: I.B. Tauris, 2020.

Doar, Bruce Gordon (2007). "Chinese Myths of the Deluge." *China Heritage Quarterly*, No. 9 (March).

_____ (2007A). "Heritage of the Grand Canal." *China Heritage Quarterly*, No. 9 (March).

_____ (2007B). "The Southern Expeditions of Emperors Kangxi and Qianlong of the Grand Canal." *China Heritage Quarterly*, No. 9 (March).

Dodgen, Randall A. (2001). *Controlling the Dragon: Confucian Engineers and the Yellow River in Late Imperial China.* Honolulu: University of Hawai'i Press.

Dooling, Amy D. and Kristina M. Torgeson (1998). *Writing Women in Modern China: An Anthology of Women's Literature from the Early Twentieth Century.* New York: Columbia University Press.

Doolittle, James (1992). *I Could Never Be So Lucky Again.* New York: Bantam Books.

Douthwaite, Dr. A.W. (1880). "A Journey Up the Ts'ien-t'ang River from Hangchow to Its Source." *The Chinese Recorder and Missionary Journal*, Volume XI, No. 1 (January – February), pp. 32 – 40.

Duan Xiaolin (2020). *The Rise of West Lake: A Cultural Landmark in the Song Dynasty.* Seattle: University of Washington Press.

_____ (2014). *Scenic Beauty Outside the City: Tourism around Hangzhou's West Lake in the Southern Song (1127 – 1276).* Doctoral Dissertation, University of Washington.

Dudbridge, Glen (2004). *The Legend of Miao-shan.* Oxford: Oxford University Press.

DuHalde, Jean-Baptiste (1741). *The General History of China: Containing a Geographical, Historical, Chronological, Political and Physical Description of the Empire of China, Chinese-Tartary, Corea, and Thibet (3rd Edition).* London: J. Watts.

Duiker, William J. (1977) *Ts'ai Yüan-p'ei: Educator of Modern China.* University Park PA: Pennsylvania State University Press.

Dunlop, Fuchsia (2006). "The Strange Tale of General Tso's Chicken," in Hosking, Richard, *Authenticity in the Kitchen: Proceedings of the Oxford Symposium on Food and Cookery 2005.* Blackawton, Devon UK: Prospect Books, pp. 165 – 177.

Durand, John D. (1960) "The Population Statistics of China, A.D. 2 – 1953." *Population Studies*, Vol. 13, No. 3 (March), pp. 209 – 256.

Ebrey, Patricia Buckley (2014). *Emperor Huizong.* Cambridge: Harvard University Press.

Edmunds, Charles Keyser (1908). "A Visit to the Hangchow Bore." *Popular Science Monthly*, Vol. 72 (February).

Edwards, Louise (2016). *Women Warriors and Wartime Spies of China.* Cambridge: Cambridge University Press.

Egan, Ronald C. (2013). *The Burden of Female Talent: The Poet Li Qingzhao and Her History in China.* Cambridge: Harvard-Yenching Institute Monograph Series (90).

_____ (2008). "Shi Poetry: Ancient and Recent Styles," in Cai Zong-qi, *How to Read Chinese Poetry: A Guided Anthology.* New York: Columbia University Press, pp. 308 – 328.

_____ (1994). *Word, Image, and Deed in the Life of Su Shi.* Cambridge: Harvard University Press.

Elleman, Bruce A. and S.C.M. Paine (2019). *Modern China: Continuity and Change, 1644 to the Present (2nd Edition).* Lanham MD: Rowman & Littlefield.

Elliott, Mark C. (2009). *Emperor Qianlong: Son of Heaven, Man of the World.* New York: Longman.

_____ (2001). *The Manchu Way: The Eight Banners and Ethnic Identity in Late Imperial China.* Stanford: Stanford University Press.

Elman, Benjamin A. (1994). "Changes in Confucian Civil Service Examinations from the Ming to the Ch'ing Dynasty," in Elman, Benjamin and Alexander Woodside, *Education and Society in Late Imperial China, 1600 – 1900.* Berkeley: University of California Press, pp. 111 – 149.

Elvin, Mark and Liu Ts'ui-jung (1998). *Sediments of Time: Environment and Society in Chinese History.* Cambridge: Cambridge University Press.

Elwin, Arthur (1909). *A Short Sketch of the Life of Mary Vaughan of Hangchow.* Oxford: [Arthur Elwin].

Engelfriet, Peter M. (1998) *Euclid in China: The Genesis of the First Chinese Translation of Euclid's Elements in 1607 & Its Reception up to 1723*. Leiden: Brill.

Epstein, Maram (2001). *Competing Discourses: Orthodoxy, Authenticity, and Engendered Meanings in Late Imperial Chinese Fiction*. Cambridge: Harvard University Press.

Evans, John C. (1992). *Tea in China: The History of China's National Drink*. New York: Greenwood Press.

Fairbank, Wilma (1994). *Liang and Lin: Partners in Exploring China's Architectural Past*. Philadelphia: University of Pennsylvania Press.

Fan Cheng-Hua (2003). "Military Families and the Southern Song Court – the Lü Case." *Journal of Song-Yuan Studies*, No. 33, pp. 49 – 70.

Fan Hong and J.A. Mangan (2001), "A Martyr for Modernity: Qiu Jin, Feminist, Warrior and Revolutionary," in Fan Hong, *Freeing the Female Body: Inspirational Icons*. London: Frank Cass.

Fang Qin (2008). *Creating Local Landscape: Tidal Bores and Seawalls at Haining (1720s – 1830s)*. Doctoral Dissertation, University of Minnesota.

Fang Xiaoping (2009). "Dedicated to a Medical Career in the 'Heaven Below': David Duncan Main's Correspondence, 1914 – 1926." Rockefeller Archive Center Research Reports Online.

Farman, Michael (2013). *Jade Mirror: Women Poets of China*. Buffalo NY: White Pine Press.

Farquhar, Mary Ann (1995). "Sanmao: Classic Cartoons and Chinese Popular Culture" in Lent, John A., *Asian Popular Culture*. Boulder: Westview Press.

Faxian (1886). *A Record of Buddhistic Kingdoms; Being an Account by the Chinese Monk Fa-Hien of His Travels in India and Ceylon, A.D. 399 – 414, in Search of the Buddhist Books of Discipline*. (James Legge, Trans.). Oxford: Clarendon Press.

Feinerman, James V. and R. Kent Guy (2000). *The Limits of Rule of Law in China*. Seattle: University of Washington Press.

Fenby, Jonathon (2004). *Chiang Kai-Shek: China's Generalissimo and the Nation He Lost*. New York: Carroll & Graf.

Feuchtwang, Stephen (1977). "School-Temple and City God," in Skinner (1977), pp. 581 – 608.

Fitch, Robert F. (1918). *Hangchow Itineraries*. Shanghai: Kelly & Walsh.

_____ (1922). *Hangchow Itineraries*. Shanghai: Kelly & Walsh.

Fitzpatrick, Merrilyn (1979). "Building Town Walls in Seven Districts of Northern Chekiang, 1553 -1556." *Papers on Far Eastern History*, Vol 17 (March), pp. 15 – 51.

Fong, Grace S. (2008). *Herself an Author: Gender, Agency, and Writing in Late Imperial China*. Honolulu: University of Hawai'i Press.

_____ (2014). "The Life and Afterlife of Ling Zhiyuan (1831 – 1852) and Her Poetry Collection." *Journal of Chinese Literature and Culture*, Vol. 1, No. 1-2 (November), pp. 125 – 154.

Fong, Wen C. (1996). *Possessing the Past: Treasures from the National Palace Museum, Taipei*. New York: Metropolitan Museum of Art.

_____ (1996A). "The Scholar-Official as Artist," in Fong, Wen C., (1996), pp. 147 – 157.

Forster, Keith (1998). "The Political Economy of Post-Mao Zhejiang: Rapid Growth and Hesitant Reform," in Cheung, Peter T.Y., Chung Jae Ho, and Lin Zhimin, *Provincial Strategies of Economic Reform in Post-Mao China: Leadership, Politics, and Implementation*. Armonk NY: M.E. Sharpe.

Fortune, Robert (1847). *Three Years' Wanderings in the Northern Provinces of China*. London: John Murray.

Foster, Paul B. (2001). "The Ironic Inflation of Chinese National Character: Lu Xun's International Reputation, Romain Rolland's Critique of 'The True Story of Ah Q,' and the Nobel Prize." *Modern Chinese Literature and Culture*, Vol. 13, No. 1 (Spring), pp. 140 – 168.

Franck, Harry A. (1925). *Roving through Southern China*. New York: The Century Co.

Franke, Herbert (1962). "Chia Ssu-Tao (1213 – 1275): A 'Bad Last Minister'?", in Wright, Arthur F. and Denis Twitchett, *Confucian Personalities*. Stanford: Stanford University Press, pp. 217 –

234.

_____ (1974). "Siege and Defense of Towns in Medieval China," in Kierman, Frank A. and John K. Fairbank, *Chinese Ways of Warfare*. Cambridge: Harvard University Press, pp. 151 – 201.

Fraser, Julius Thomas and Francis C. Haber (1986). *Time, Science, and Society in China and the West*. Amherst: University of Massachusetts Press.

Fu Shulan (2009). "Revival of Shan-shui Idea as a Sustainable Urban Form – A Case Study on Hangzhou." 4th International Conference of the International Forum on Urbanism, Amsterdam.

_____. (2015) "Shan-shui Myth and History: The Locally Planned Process of Combining the Ancient City and West Lake in Hangzhou, 1896 – 1927. *Planning Perspectives*, Vol. 31, pp. 363 – 390.

Fu Yongwei, Huan Jinyuan, and Ye Feixia (2020). *Hangzhou Statistical Yearbook, 2020*. Beijing: China Statistics Press.

Fuller, Michael A. (2013). *Drifting Among Rivers and Lakes: Southern Song Dynasty Poetry and the Problem of Literary History*. Cambridge: Harvard-Yenching Institute Monograph Series (86).

_____ (1990). *The Road to East Slope: The Development of Su Shi's Poetic Voice*. Stanford: Stanford University Press.

Fung, Stanislaus (1997). "The Imaginary Garden of Liu Shilong." *Terra Nova: Nature and Culture*, Vol. 2, No. 4 (Fall), pp. 15 – 21.

Gale, George Stafford (1955). *No Flies in China*. New York: Morrow.

Galik, Marian (1969). *Mao Tun and Modern Chinese Literary Criticism*. Wiesbaden: F. Steiner.

Gammie, Alexander (1935). *Duncan Main of Hangchow*. London: Pickering & Inglis.

Gao, James Zheng (2004). *The Communist Takeover of Hangzhou: The Transformation of City and Cadre, 1949 - 1954*. Honolulu: University of Hawaii Press.

Ge Jian, Guo Min, and Yue Miao (2013). "Soundscape of the West Lake Scenic Area with Profound Cultural Background: A Case Study of Evening Bell Ringing in Jingci Temple, China." *Journal of Zhejiang University – Science A (Applied Physics and Engineering)*, Vol. 14, No. 3, pp 219 – 229.

Ge Jianxiong and Hu Yunsheng (2021). *A Historical Survey of the Yellow River and the River Civilizations*. Singapore: Springer Nature.

Geil, William Edgar (1911). *Eighteen Capitals of China*. Philadelphia: J.B. Lippincott.

Gernet, Jacques (1970). *Daily Life in China: On the Eve of the Mongol Invasion 1250 – 1276*. Stanford: Stanford University Press.

Giles, Lionel (1917). *Ch'iu Chin: A Chinese Heroine*. London: East & West.

_____ (1913). "The Life of Ch'iu Chin." *T'oung Pao*, Vol. 14, No. 2, pp. 211 – 226.

Giquel, Prosper (1985). *A Journal of the Chinese Civil War, 1864*. (Steven A. Leibo and Debbie Weston, Trans.). Honolulu: University of Hawai'i Press.

Glick, Carl and Hong Sheng-hwa (1947). *Swords of Silence: Chinese Secret Societies—Past and Present*. New York: McGraw-Hill.

Glines, Carroll V. (1988). *The Doolittle Raid: America's Daring First Strike Against Japan*. New York: Orion Books.

_____ (1964). *Doolittle's Tokyo Raiders*. Princeton: Van Nostrand.

Goddard, Francis W. (1948). *Called to Cathay*. New York: Baptist Literature Bureau.

Goedde, Emily (2013). "Zhu Shuzhen," in Farman, Michael, *Jade Mirror: Women Poets of China*. Buffalo NY: White Pine Press, pp. 164 – 189.

Golas, Peter J. (2015). *Picturing Technology in China from Earliest Times to the Nineteenth Century*. Hong Kong: Hong Kong University Press.

Goodrich, L. Carrington (1976). *Dictionary of Ming Biography, 1368 – 1644*. New York: Columbia University Press.

_____ (1966). *The Literary Inquisition of Ch'ien-lung*. New York: American Council of Learned Societies, 1935. Reprinted—New York: Paragon.

Graham, Angus C. (1990). *Poems of the West Lake*. London: Wellsweep.

Green, Rev. D.D. (1869). "Early History of Hang-chow and Its Surroundings." *The Chinese Recorder and Missionary Journal*, Vol. 2, No. 6 (November), pp. 156 – 162, and Vol. 2, No. 7 (December), pp. 177 – 183.

Green, John (1905). "A Holiday on the West Lake, Hangchow." *The Far East*, pp. 16 – 37.

Greenhalgh, Susan (2008). *Just One Child: Science and Policy in Deng's China*. Berkeley: University of California Press.

Griffiths, Valerie (2004). *Not Less than Everything: The Courageous Women Who Carried the Christian Gospel to China*. Oxford UK: Monarch Books.

Grimes, Sara (1983). *West Lake Reflections: A Guide to Hangzhou*. Zhejiang: People's Publishing House.

Gu Xiaofen (2006). *Hangzhou Statistical Yearbook, 2005*. Beijing: China Statistics Press.

Guo Xiaoting (2014). *Adventures of the Mad Monk Ji Gong*. Tokyo: Tuttle Publishing.

Guy, R. Kent (1987). *The Emperor's Four Treasures: Scholars and the State in the Late Ch'ien-lung Era*. Cambridge: Council on East Asian Studies, Harvard University Press.

Gvili, Gal (2019). "Gender and Superstition in Modern Chinese Literature." *Religions*, Vol. 10, No. 10.

Ha Jin (2000). *The Bridegroom: Stories*. New York: Pantheon.

Hall, W.H. and W.D. Bernard (1847). *The Nemesis in China*. London: Henry Colburn.

Hamilton, Robyn (2011). "The Legacy of Qiu Jin (1875 – 1907): A Variety of Forms and Voices of Remembrance," *Proceedings of the 19th New Zealand Asian Studies Society International Conference*. Massey University, Palmerston North, New Zealand.

Hamm, John Christopher (1998). "Reading the Swordswoman's Tale: Shisanmei and 'Ernü yingxiong zhuan'." *T'oung Pao*, Vol 84, Fasc. 4/5, pp. 328 – 355.

Hammers, Roslyn Lee (2011). *Pictures of Tilling and Weaving: Art, Labor, and Technology in Song and Yuan China*. Hong Kong: Hong Kong University Press.

Hanan, Patrick (1981). *The Chinese Vernacular Story*. Cambridge: Harvard University Press.

_____ (1988). *The Invention of Li Yu*. Cambridge: Harvard University Press.

Hanson, Paul (1993). *Lin He-Jing: Recluse-Poet of Orphan Mountain*. Waldron Island: Brooding Heron Press.

Hao Ping (2018). *John Leighton Stuart's Missionary-Educator's Career in China*. (Hao Tianhu, Trans.). London: Routledge.

Harbsmeier, Christoph (1984). *The Cartoonist Feng Zikai: Social Realism with a Buddhist Face*. Oslo: Universitetsforlaget.

Hardie, Alison (2004). "The Life of a Seventeenth-Century Chinese Garden Designer: 'The Biography of Zhang Nanyuan,' by Wu Weiye (1609 – 71)." *Garden History*, Vol. 32, No. 1 (Spring), pp. 137 – 140.

_____ (2007). "Washing the *Wutong* Tree: Garden Culture as an Expression of Women's Gentility in the Late Ming," in Berg, Daria and Chloë Starr (2007A), pp. 45 – 57.

Hargett, James M. (2013) "Guaiji? Guiji? Huiji? Kauiji? Some Remarks on an Ancient Chinese Place-Name. *Sino-Platonic Papers*, No. 234 (March).

_____ (1988/89). "Huizong's Magic Marchmount: The Genyue Pleasure Park." *Monumenta Serica*, Vol. 38, pp. 1 – 48.

_____ (1988). "The Pleasure Parks of Kaifeng and Lin'an During the Sung Dynasty (960 – 1279)," in *Proceedings of International Symposium on Sung History*. Taipei: Chinese Culture University, June 24 – 26, 1988.

Harris, Sheldon H. (2002). *Factories of Death: Japanese Biological Warfare, 1932 – 1945, and the American Cover-up*. New York: Routledge.

Hartman, Charles (1990). "Poetry and Politics in 1079: The Crow Terrace Poetry Case of Su Shih." *Chinese Literature: Essays, Articles, Reviews (CLEAR)*, Vol. 12 (December), pp. 15 – 44.

Hartwell, Robert M. (1982). "Demographic, Political, and Social Transformations of China, 750 – 1550." *Harvard Journal of Asiatic Studies*, Vol. 42, No. 2 (December), pp. 365 – 442.

Harui, Kimberly Ann (2018). *Jōjin's Travels in Northern Song China: Performances of Place in the Travel Diary* A Record of a Pilgrimage to Tiantai and Wutai Mountains. Doctoral Dissertation: Arizona State University.

Hayhoe, Ruth (2007). *Portraits of Influential Chinese Educators*. Dordrecht, The Netherlands: Springer.

H.B.P. (1938). "War in China Ushers in Mass Migration Movement," *Far Eastern Survey*, Vol. 7, No. 7 (April 6).

He Shan (2017). *Chinese Urbanisation Powered by High-Speed Rail: Challenges for Hyper Densities and Diversities*. Doctoral Dissertation, University of Western Australia.

_____ (2013). "From 'Insertion' to 'Incorporation': The Hangzhou Example of the Transformation of the Railway in Chinese Urban Life." Frontiers of Planning – Evolving and Declining Models of City Planning Practice, 49th ISOCARP Congress.

_____ (2003). *Urbanisation of China: A History of Power*. Diploma of Architecture Dissertation, University of Cambridge.

He Yimin (2008). "The Decline of Traditional Industrial and Commercial Cities in Modern China: Exemplified with Suzhou, Hangzhou and Yangzhou." *Frontiers of History in China*, Vol. 3, No. 2 (June), pp. 263 – 292.

Hearn, Maxwell K. (1996A). "The Artist as Hero," in Fong, Wen C. (1996), pp. 299 - 323.

_____ (1988) "Document and Portrait: The Southern Tour Paintings of Kangxi and Qianlong," in Chou Ju-hsi and Claudia Brown, *Chinese Painting Under the Qianlong Emperor: The Symposium Papers in Two Volumes, Phoebus* 6, No. 1, pp. 91 – 131, 183 – 189.

_____ (2008). *How to Read Chinese Paintings*. New Haven: Yale University Press.

_____ (1990). *The Kangxi Southern Inspection Tour: A Narrative Program by Wang Hui*. Doctoral Dissertation, Princeton University.

_____ (1996). "Reunification and Revival," in Fong, Wen C. (1996), pp. 269 - 297.

Hébert, Jacques and Pierre Elliott Trudeau (1968). *Two Innocents in Red China*. (I.M. Owen, Trans.). Toronto: Oxford University Press.

Henry, Eric (2007). "The Submerged History of Yue." *Sino-Platonic Papers*, No. 176 (May), pp. 1 – 38.

Heyndrickx, Jerome (1990). *Philippe Couplet, S.J. (1623 – 1693): The Man Who Brought China to Europe*. Nettetal: Steyler-Verlag.

Hino, Ashihei (1939). *Flower and Soldiers*. (Lewis Bush, Trans.). Tokyo: Kenkyusha.

_____ (1939A). *Mud and Soldiers*. (Lewis Bush, Trans.). Tokyo: Kenkyusha.

Hinsch, Bret (2015). *The Rise of Tea Culture in China: The Invention of the Individual*. Lanham MD: Rowman & Littlefield.

Ho, Lucy Chao (1968). *More Gracile than Yellow Flowers: The Life and Works of Li Ch'ing-chao*. Hong Kong: Mayfair Press.

Ho Ping-ti (He Bingdi) (1962). *The Ladder of Success in Imperial China: Aspects of Social Mobility, 1368 – 1911*. New York: Columbia University Press.

Hobart, Alice Tisdale (1959). *Gusty's Child*. New York: Longmans, Green.

Hockx, Michel (1998). "The Literary Association (Wenxue yanjiu hui, 1920 – 1947) and the Literary Field of Early Republican China." *The China Quarterly*, No. 153 (March), pp. 49 – 81.

Hogarth, Paul (1956). *Looking at China, with the Journal of the Artist*. London: Lawrence & Wishart.

Holledge, Simon (1981). *Hangzhou and the West Lake*. Chicago: Rand McNally.

Holzman, Donald (1958). "Shen Kua and His Meng-ch'i pi-t'an." *T'oung Pao*, Vol. 46, pp. 260 – 292.

Hoyt, Edwin P. (2001). *Warlord: Tojo Against the World*. New York: Cooper Square Press.

Hsia, Adrian (1998). *Chinesia: The European Construction of China in the Literature of the 17th and 18th Centuries*. Tübingen, Germany: Niemeyer.

Hsia, C.T. (1961). *A History of Modern Chinese Fiction, 1917 – 1957*. New Haven and London: Yale University Press.

Hsia, Ronnie Po-Chia (2010). *A Jesuit in the Forbidden City: Matteo Ricci, 1552 – 1610*. Oxford: Oxford University Press.

Hsieh Chiao-Min (1976). "Chu K'o-chen and China's Climatic Changes." *The Geographical Journal*, Vol. 142, No. 2 (July), pp. 248-256.

_____ and Jean Kan Hsieh (2009). *Race the Rising Sun: A Chinese University's Exodus during the Second World War*. Lanham MD: Hamilton Books.

Hsiung Ping-chen (2007). "Female Gentility in Transition and Transmission: Mother-Daughter Ties in Ming/Qing China," in Berg, Daria and Chloë Starr (2007A), pp. 97 – 116.

Hsü Shuhsi (1939). *A Digest of Japanese War Conduct*. Shanghai: Kelly & Walsh.

Hu, Philip (2000). *Visible Traces: Rare Books and Special Collections from the National Library of China*. New York: Queens Borough Public Library.

Hu Pin-ching (1966). *Li Ch'ing-chao*. New York: Twayne.

Hu Wei (2017). *Beyond Life and Death Images of Exceptional Women and Chinese Modernity*. Doctoral Dissertation, University of South Carolina.

Hu Ying (2016). *Burying Autumn: Poetry, Friendship, and Loss*. Leiden: Brill.

_____ (2019). "Haunting, (In)Visibility, Filiality: Qiu Canzhi (1901 – 67) and Her Works of Mourning," *The Journal of Chinese Literature and Culture*, Vol. 6, No. 1 (April), pp. 205 – 238.

_____ (2007). "Qiu Jin's Nine Burials: The Making of Historical Monuments and Public Memory." *Modern Chinese Literature and Culture*, Vol. 19, No. 1 (Spring), pp. 138 – 191.

_____ (2005). "'Would that I Were Marco Polo': The Travel Writing of Shan Shili (1856 – 1943)," in Fogel, Joshua A. *Traditions of East Asian Travel*. New York: Berghahn, pp. 144 – 159.

_____ (2004). "Writing Qiu Jin's Life: Wu Zhiying and Her Family Learning." *Late Imperial China*, Vol. 25, No. 2 (December), pp. 119 – 160.

Hua Kaiqi. "Investment for the Karma and the Khan: Remolding Sacred Landscape under Yang Lianzhenjia in Early Yuan Hangzhou (1277 – 1292)." Unpublished research paper, University of Hawai'i at Manoa.

Huang Qiaole (2004). *Writing from within a Woman's Community: Gu Taiqing (1799 – 1877) and Her Poetry*. M.A. Thesis, McGill University.

Huang, Shih-shan Susan (2011). "Early Buddhist Illustrated Prints in Hangzhou," in Chia, Lucille and Hilde de Weerdt, *Knowledge and Text Production in an Age of Print: China, 900 – 1400*. Leiden: Brill, pp. 135 – 166.

Huang Sung-K'ang (1992). *Lu Hsun and the New Culture Movement of Modern China*. Westport CT: Hyperion Press.

Huang Yuan-Chuan (2005). "Preface," in Ge Siming, *From the Legend of Lady White Snake: The Hidden Treasures in the Leifeng Pagoda*. Taipei: Guoli Lishi Bowuguan.

Huc, M. L'Abbé (1857). *Christianity in China, Tartary, and Thibet, Vol. I & 2*. London: Longman, Brown, Green, Longmans, & Roberts.

Hucker, Charles O. (1971) "Hu Tsung-hsien's Campaign Against Hsu Hai, 1556," in *Two Studies on Ming History*. Ann Arbor MI: University of Michigan, pp. 1 – 40.

Humes, James C. and Jarvis D. Ryals (2009). *"Only Nixon": His Trip to China Revisited and Restudied*. Lanham MD: University Press of America.

Hummel, Arthur W. (2018). *Eminent Chinese of the Qing Period (Revised Edition)*. Great Barrington MA: Berkshire Publishing.

Hung Chang-tai (1990). "War and Peace in Feng Zikai's Wartime Cartoons." *Modern China*, Vol.

16, No. 1, pp. 39 – 93.

_____ (1994). *War and Popular Culture: Resistance in Modern China, 1937 – 1945*. Berkeley: University of California Press.

Ibn Battuta (2004). *The Travels of Ibn Battuta: in the Near East, Asia, and Africa, 1325 – 1354*. (Rev. Samuel Lee, Trans.). Mineola NY: Dover Publications.

Idema, Wilt L. (2010). *The Butterfly Lovers: The Legend of Liang Shanbo and Zhu Yingtai: Four Versions, with Related Texts*. Indianapolis: Hackett Publishing.

_____ and Beata Grant (2004). *The Red Brush: Writing Women of Imperial China*. Cambridge: Harvard East Asian Monographs.

Innes, James B., et. al. (2010). "Environmental History, Palaeoecology and Human Activity at the Early Neolithic Forager/Cultivator Site at Kuahuqiao, Hangzhou, Eastern China." Durham Research Online, Durham University.

International Council on Monuments and Sites (ICOMOS) (2011), "West Lake of Hangzhou (China), No. 1334," in *ICOMOS 2011 Evaluations of Nominations of Cultural and Mixed Properties to the World Heritage List WHC-11/35.COM/INF.8B1*. Paris: Secretariat ICOMOS International, pp. 140 – 154.

Islam, Mohammad Mainul, et. al. (2011) "Review of Ma Yinchu on Chinese Population." *Society & Change*, Vol. 5, No. 2 (April – June), pp. 28 – 38.

Jackson, Richard L. (2012) "Ma Yinchu: From Yale to Architect of Chinese Population Policy." *American Journal of Chinese Studies*, Vol. 19, No. 1 (April), pp. 47-54.

Jacobs, Mark D. (2016). *Yiwu, China: A Study of the World's Largest Small Commodities Market*. Paramus NY: Homa and Sekey Books.

Jay, Jennifer W. (1991) *A Change in Dynasties: Loyalism in Thirteenth Century China* (Studies on East Asia, 18). Bellingham, WA: Western Washington University.

Jay-Preston, Jennifer (1983). "The Life and Loyalism of Chou Mi (1232 – 1298) and His Circle of Friends." *Papers on Far Eastern History*, No. 28 (September), pp. 49 – 105.

Jen Yu-wen (1973). *The Taiping Revolutionary Movement*. New Haven: Yale University Press.

Jiang Jin (2009). *Women Playing Men: Yue Opera and Social Change in Twentieth-Century Shanghai*. Seattle: University of Washington Press.

Jiang Leping (2013). "The Kuahuqiao Site and Culture," in Underhill (2013), pp. 537 – 554.

Jiang Menglin (Chiang Monlin) (1947). *Tides from the West: A Chinese Autobiography*. New Haven: Yale University Press.

Jiang Yuanxin (2019). *More than just a Drink: Tea Consumption, Material Culture, and "Sensory Turn" in Early Modern China*. Doctoral Dissertation: University of Minnesota.

Jin Jiayi (2015). *Sentiment, Orientalism, and American Women Writers in Republican China*. Master's Thesis, University of Hong Kong.

Johnson, David 1981. "Epic and History in Early China: The Matter of Wu Tzu-hsu." *Journal of Asian Studies*, Vol. 40, No. 2 (February), pp. 255 – 271.

_____ (1980). "The Wu Tzu-hsü Pien-wen and Its Sources: Part II." *Harvard Journal of Asiatic Studies*, Vol. 40, No. 2 (December), pp. 465 – 505.

Johnson, Linda Cooke (1993). "Shanghai: An Emerging Jiangnan Port, 1683 – 1840," in Linda Cooke Johnson, *Cities of Jiangnan in Late Imperial China* (Albany: State University of New York Press), pp. 151 – 181.

Joo, Fumiko (2015). "The Literary Imagination of the White Pagoda and Dynastic Change in Early Ming Hangzhou." *Frontiers of Literary Studies in China*, Vol. 9, No. 1, pp. 54 – 74.

Jordan, Donald A. (2001) *China's Trial by Fire: The Shanghai War of 1932*. Ann Arbor: University of Michigan Press.

_____ (1976). *The Northern Expedition: China's National Revolution of 1926 – 1928*. Honolulu: University Press of Hawai'i.

Judge, Joan (2008). *The Precious Raft of History: The Past, the West, and the Woman Question in Chi-

na. Stanford: Stanford University Press.

_____ (2001). "Talent, Virtue, and the Nation: Chinese Nationalisms and Female Subjectivities in the Early Twentieth Century." *The American Historical Review*, Vol. 106, No. 3 (June), pp. 765 – 803.

Kafalas, Philip A. (2007) *In Limpid Dream: Nostalgia and Zhang Dai's Reminiscences of the Ming*. Norwalk CT: East Bridge.

Kahler, William R. (1905) *The Hangchow Bore, and How to Get to It (2nd Edition)*. Shanghai: Union Office.

_____ (1895). *My Holidays in China: An Account of Three Houseboat Tours, from Shanghai to Hangchow and Back Via Ningpo; from Shanghai to Le Yang Via Soochow and the Tai Hu; and from Kiukiang to Wuhu*. Shanghai: The Temperance Union.

Kao Yu-kung (1966). "Source Materials on the Fang La Rebellion." *Harvard Journal of Asiatic Studies*, Vol. 26, pp. 211 – 240.

_____ (1963). "A Study of the Fang La Rebellion." *Harvard Journal of Asiatic Studies*, Vol. 24, pp. 17 – 63.

Keenan, Barry C. (1974) "Educational Reform and Politics in Early Republican China." *The Journal of Asian Studies*, Vol. 33, No. 2 (February), pp. 225 – 237.

Kent, Percy H. H. (1907) *Railway Enterprise in China: An Account of Its Origin and Development*. London: Edward Arnold.

Keswick, Maggie (1978). *The Chinese Garden: History, Art and Architecture*. New York: Rizzoli International Publications.

Kile, Sarah E. (2013) *Toward an Extraordinary Everyday: Li Yu's (1611 – 1680) Vision, Writing, and Practice*. Doctoral Dissertation, Columbia University.

Kim, Mina (2017). "The Embodiment of Time and Space: Political Expression of Pan Tianshou." *American Journal of Chinese Studies*, Vol. 24, No. 2 (October), pp. 141 – 151.

Ko, Dorothy (1994). *Teachers of the Inner Chambers: Women and Culture in Seventeenth-Century China*. Stanford: Stanford University Press.

Koss, Stephen L. (2015). *Beautiful Su: A Social and Cultural History of Suzhou, China*. San Francisco: China Books.

Lai Suk-Yee (1994). "Yue Ware: A Continuation of Tang Gold and Silver Wares," in Ho Chuimei, *New Light on Chinese Yue and Longquan Wares: Archaeological Ceramics Found in Eastern and Southern Asia, A.D. 800 – 1400*. Hong Kong: University of Hong Kong Press, pp. 21 – 29.

Laing, Ellen Johnston (1990). "Women Painters in Traditional China," in Weidner, Marsha (Ed.), *Flowering in the Shadows: Women in the History of Chinese and Japanese Painting*. Honolulu: University of Hawai'i Press, pp. 81 – 101.

Laitinen, Kauko (1990). *Chinese Nationalism in the Late Qing Dynasty: Zhang Binglin as an Anti-Manchu Propagandist*. London: Curzon Press.

Lam, Joseph S. C., et. al. (2017) *Senses of the City: Perceptions of Hangzhou and Southern Song China, 1127 – 1279*. Hong Kong: The Chinese University Press.

Lance, John Alexander (2014). *Icarus in China: Western Aviation and the Chinese Air Force, 1931 – 1941*. MA Thesis, Western Carolina University.

Lane, George A. (2016). "The Phoenix Mosque of Hangzhou," in De Nicola, Bruno and Charles Melville, *The Mongols' Middle East: Continuity and Transformation in Ilkhanid Iran*. Leiden: Brill, pp. 237 – 276.

_____ (2018). *The Phoenix Mosque and the Persians of Medieval Hangzhou*. London: Gingko Library.

Lau Chak Kwong (2006). *Ding Jing (1695 – 1765) and the Foundation of the Xiling Identity in Hangzhou*. Doctoral Dissertation, University of California, Santa Barbara.

Lau, Joseph S.M. and Howard Goldblatt (2007). *The Columbia Anthology of Modern Chinese Literature*. New York: Columbia University Press.

Laufer, Berthold (1912). "The Discovery of a Lost Book." *T'oung Pao*, Second Series, Vol. 13, No. 1, pp. 97 – 106.

Lautz, Terry (2016). *John Birch: A Life*. Oxford UK: Oxford University Press.

Lawrence, Elizabeth (2014). *The Chinese Seal in the Making, 1904 – 1937*. Doctoral Dissertation, Columbia University.

Lawson, Ted W. (1943) *Thirty Seconds over Tokyo*. New York: Random House.

Leary, William M., Jr. (1969) "Wings for China: The Jouett Mission, 1932 – 1935." *Pacific Historical Review*, Vol. 38, No. 4 (November), pp. 447 – 462.

Ledderose, Lothar (1979). *Mi Fu and the Classical Tradition of Chinese Calligraphy*. Princeton: Princeton University Press.

Lee Hui-shu (2001). *Exquisite Moments: West Lake and Southern Song Art*. New York: China Institute in America.

Lee, Jennifer 8. (2008). *The Fortune Cookie Chronicles: Adventures in the World of Chinese Food*. New York: Twelve/Hachette.

Lee, Lily and A.D. Stefanowska (1998) *Biographical Dictionary of Chinese Women: The Qing Period, 1644 – 1911*. Armonk NY: M.E. Sharpe.

_____ and Sue Wiles (2014). *Biographical Dictionary of Chinese Women: Tang Through Ming, 618 – 1644*. Armonk NY: M.E. Sharpe.

_____ and A.D. Stefanowska (2003). *Biographical Dictionary of Chinese Women: The Twentieth Century, 1912 – 2000*. Armonk NY: M.E. Sharpe.

Leibo, Steven A. (1985). *Transferring Technology to China: Prosper Giquel and the Self-Strengthening Movement*. Berkeley: University of California.

Leibold, Michael (2008). "Da Yu, A Modern Hero? Myth and Mythology in the People's Republic of China," in Kuhn, Dieter and Helga Stahl, *Perceptions of Antiquity in Chinese Civilization*. Heidelberg: Wurzburger Sinologische Schriften, pp. 361 - 375.

Leung, Angela Ki Che (1987). "Organized Medicine in Ming-Qing China: State and Private Medical Institutions in the Lower Yangzi Region." *Late Imperial China*, Vol. 8, No. 1 (June), pp. 134 – 166.

Leung, Edwin Pak-wah (1992). *Historical Dictionary of Revolutionary China, 1839 – 1976*. New York: Greenwood Press.

Levine, Ari Daniel (2009). "The Reigns of Hui-tsung (1100 – 26) and Ch'in-tsung (1126 – 27) and the Fall of the Northern Sung," in Twitchett, Denis C. and Paul Jakov Smith, *The Cambridge History of China, Vol. 5, Part I: The Sung Dynasty and Its Precursors, 907 – 1279*. New York: Cambridge University Press, pp. 556 – 643.

Lewis, Mark Edward (2009). *China between Empires: The Northern and Southern Dynasties*. Cambridge: Harvard University Press.

Leys, Simon (1989) (Ryckmans, Pierre). "Chinese Attitudes Towards the Past." *Papers on Far Eastern History*, Vol. 39 (March), pp. 1 – 16.

_____ (1977). *Chinese Shadows*. New York: Viking Press.

Li Chen (2012). "Legal Specialists and Judicial Administration in Late Imperial China, 1651 – 1911." *Late Imperial China*, Vol. 33, No. 1 (June), pp. 1 – 54.

Li Chu-Tsing (1987). "The Artistic Theories of the Literati," in Li Chu-Tsing and James C.Y. Watt, *The Chinese Scholar's Studio: Artistic Life in the Late Ming Period*. New York: The Asia Society Galleries.

_____ (1965). "*The Autumn Colors on the Ch'iao and Hua Mountains*: A Landscape by Chao Meng-fu." *Artibus Artae Supplementum*, 21. Ascona, Switzerland: Artibus Asiae.

Li, Lillian M. (1981) *China's Silk Trade: Traditional Industry in the Modern World, 1842 – 1937*. Cambridge: Harvard East Asian Monographs No. 97, Harvard University Press.

Li, Peter (Ed.) (2003). *Japanese War Crimes: The Search for Justice*. New Brunswick NJ: Transaction Publishers.

Li Qingzhao (2019). *The Works of Li Qingzhao*. (Ronald Egan, Trans.). Boston: Walter de Gruyter.

Li Shiqiao (2002). "Writing a Modern Chinese Architectural History: Liang Sicheng and Liang Qichao." *Journal of Architectural Education*, Vol. 56, No. 1 (September), pp. 35 – 45.

Li Wai-yee (2012). "Gardens and Illusions from Late Ming to Early Qing." *Harvard Journal of Asian Studies*, Vol. 72, No. 2, pp. 295 – 336.

Li Xue (2018). *Making Local China: A Case Study of Yangzhou, 1853 – 1928*. Zurich: Lit Verlag GmbH.

Liang Ye (2019). "The Practice and Innovations of Socialist Consultative Democracy," in Fang Ning, Chen Huaxing, and Yun Jie, *Chinese Dream and Practice in Zhejiang – Politics*. Singapore: Springer Nature, pp. 73 – 98.

Lim, Ivy Maria (2017). "Qi Jiguang and Hu Zongxian's Anti-wokou Campaign," in Sim (2017), pp. 23 – 41.

Lin Yutang (1947). *The Gay Genius: The Life and Times of Su Tungpo*. New York: J. Day.

_____ (2007). "The Monks of Hangzhou," (Nancy E. Chapman and King-fai Tam, Trans.), in Lau, Joseph S.M. and Howard Goldblatt. *The Columbia Anthology of Modern Chinese Literature*. New York: Columbia University Press, pp. 637 – 640.

Liu Ai-lian (2011). *Yang Weizhen (1296 – 1370) and the Social Art of Painting Inscriptions*. Doctoral Dissertation, University of Kansas.

Liu Gang (2010). *The Poetics of Miscellaneousness: The Literary Design of Liu Yiqing's Qiantang Yishi and the Historiography of the Southern Song*. Doctoral Dissertation: University of Michigan.

Liu Haiming (2015). *From Canton Restaurant to Panda Express: A History of Chinese Food in the United States*. New Brunswick NJ: Rutgers University Press.

Liu Jiantang (1996), "Martino Martini in Confucian China," in Demarchi, Franco and Riccardo Scartezzini, *Martino Martini: A Humanist and Scientist in Seventeenth Century China*. Trento IT: Universita degli studi di Trento, pp. 331 – 342.

Liu Shi-yee (2008). "The World's a Stage: The Theatricality of Chen Hongshou's Figure Painting." *Ars Orientalis*, Vol. 35, pp. 155 – 191.

Liu Yong, et. al. (2011) "Spatial Determinants of Urban Land Conversion in Large Chinese Cities: A Case of Hangzhou." *Environment & Planning B: Planning & Design*, Vol. 38, No. 4 (July), pp. 706 – 725.

Liu Yunsheng (2020). *The History of the Contractual Thoughts in Ancient China*. (Sun Lin, Duan Jing, Trans.). Singapore: Springer Law Press China.

Lockwood, Jeffrey A. (2009) *Six-Legged Soldiers: Using Insects as Weapons of War*. Oxford UK: Oxford University Press.

Lorge, Peter (2017). "The Martial Arts in Qi Jiguang's Military Training," in Sim (2017), pp. 59 – 71.

_____ (2005). *War, Politics, and Society in Early Modern China, 900 – 1795*. New York: Routledge.

Lu Hui-Wen (2017). "A Forgery and the Pursuit of the Authentic Wang Xizhi," in Ebrey, Patricia Buckley and Shih-Shan Susan Huang, *Visual and Material Cultures in Middle Period China*. Leiden: Brill, 2017, pp. 193 – 225.

Lu Suping (2019), *The 1937 – 1938 Japanese Atrocities*. Singapore, Springer Nature.

Lu Xun (1980). "The Collapse of Leifeng Pagoda" and "More Thoughts on the Collapse of Leifeng Pagoda," (Yang Xianyi and Gladys Yang, Trans.), in *Lu Xun, Selected Works* (4 Vols.). Beijing: Foreign Language Press.

Lu Yu (2009). *The Classic of Tea*. (Jiang Yi and Jiang Xin, Trans.). Changsha: Hunan People's Publishing House.

Luo Hui (2008). "Theatricality and Cultural Critique in Chinese Cinema." *Asian Theater Journal*, Vol. 25, No. 1 (Spring), pp. 122 – 137.

Lyon, David Nelson (1895). "Historical Sketch of the Hangchow Station," in *Jubilee Papers of the*

Central China Presbyterian Mission, 1844 – 1894. Shanghai: American Presbyterian Mission Press, pp. 78 - 97.

_____ (1936). *Hangchow Journal of 1870.* Pebble Beach CA.

Macartney, (Lord) George (1807). *Some Account of the Public Life, and a Selection from the Unpublished Writings of the Earl of Macartney,* Vol. II. London, T. Cadell and W. Davies.

MacFarlane, Alan and Iris MacFarlane (2004). *The Empire of Tea: The Remarkable History of the Plant that Took Over the World.* Woodstock NY: Overlook Press.

MacMillan, Margaret (2007). *Nixon and Mao: The Week that Changed the World.* New York: Random House.

Mair, Victor H. (1994). *The Columbia Anthology of Traditional Chinese Literature.* New York: Columbia University Press.

_____ (2001). *The Columbia History of Chinese Literature.* New York: Columbia University Press.

_____ (2013), Chen Sanping, and Frances Wood. *Chinese Lives: The People Who Made a Civilization.* London: Thames & Hudson.

Mann, Susan (1994). "The Education of Daughters in the Mid-Ch'ing Period," in Elman, Benjamin and Alexander Woodside, *Education and Society in Late Imperial China, 1600 – 1900.* Berkeley: University of California Press, pp. 19 – 49.

_____ (1992) . "'Fuxue' (Women's Learning) by Zhang Xuecheng (1738 – 1801): China's First History of Women's Culture." *Late Imperial China,* Vol 13, No. 1 (June), pp. 40 – 62.

Mao Dun (1979). *Spring Silkworms and Other Stories.* Beijing: Foreign Languages Press.

Marshall, S.J. (2001). *The Mandate of Heaven: Hidden History in the I Ching.* New York: Columbia University Press.

Martin, Laura C. (2007). *Tea: The Drink that Changed the World.* Tokyo: Tuttle.

McCausland, Shane (2011). *Zhao Mengfu: Calligraphy and Painting for Khubilai's China.* Hong Kong: Hong Kong University Press.

McDermott, Joseph P. (2006). *A Social History of the Chinese Book: Books and Literati Culture in Late Imperial China.* Hong Kong: Hong Kong University Press.

McMullen, R. J. (2017). *War and Occupation in China: The Letters of an American Missionary from Hangzhou, 1937 – 1938.* Bethlehem PA: Lehigh University Press.

Mei Yubing (2012). *A Fragrant Path of Thorns: Chinese Women in the Past Century.* Beijing: New Star Press.

Meng Liuxi (2007). *Poetry as Power: Yuan Mei's Female Disciple Qu Bingyun (1767 – 1810).* Plymouth, UK: Lexington Books.

Merrill, James M. (1964). *Target Tokyo: the Halsey-Doolittle Raid.* Chicago: Rand McNally.

Meskill, John (1965). *Ch'oe Pu's Diary: A Record of Drifting Across the Sea.* Tucson: University of Arizona Press.

Meyer-Fong, Tobie (2014). "Civil War, Revolutionary Heritage, and the Chinese Garden." *Cross-Currents: East Asian History and Culture Review,* E-Journal No. 13 (December), pp. 75 – 98.

_____ (2013). *What Remains: Coming to Terms with Civil War in 19th Century China.* Stanford: Stanford University Press.

Milburn, Olivia (2010). *The Glory of Yue: An Annotated Translation of the* Yuejue shu. Leiden: Brill.

_____ (2013). "The Silent Beauty: Changing Portrayals of Xi Shi, from *Zhiguai* and Poetry to Ming Fiction and Drama." *Asia Major,* Vol. 26, No. 1, pp. 23 – 53.

_____ (2007). "A Virtual City: The 'Record of the Lands of Yue' and the Founding of Shaoxing." *Oriens Extremus,* Vol. 46, pp. 117 – 146.

Min Tu-ki (1989). *National Polity and Local Power: The Transformation of Late Imperial China.* Cambridge: Harvard University Press, pp. 181 – 189

Minford, John and Joseph S.M. Lau (2000). *Classical Chinese Literature: An Anthology of Transla-*

tions. New York: Columbia University Press.

Minturn, Robert B., Jr. (1858). *From New York to Delhi*. London: Longman, Brown, Green, Longmans, and Roberts.

Mo Yajun (2004). *"Little Japan" in Hongkou: The Japanese Community in Shanghai, 1895 – 1932*. Master's Thesis, The Chinese University of Hong Kong.

Moore, Commander W. Usborne (1888). "Report on the Bore of the Tsien-Tang Kiang." London: Hydrographic Office, Admiralty.

_____ (1893). "Further Report on the Bore of the Tsien-Tang Kiang." London: Hydrographic Office, Admiralty.

Mostern, Ruth (2016). "Sediment and State in Imperial China: The Yellow River Watershed as an Earth System and a World System." *Nature and Culture*, Vol. 11, No. 2 (Summer), pp. 121 – 147.

Mote, Frederick W. (1999). *Imperial China, 900 – 1800*. Cambridge: Harvard University Press.

_____ (1973). "A Millennium of Chinese Urban History: Form, Time, and Space Concepts in Soochow," *Rice University Studies*, Vol. 59, No. 4, pp. 35-65.

_____ and Denis Twitchett (1988). *The Cambridge History of China, Vol. 7: The Ming Dynasty, 1368 – 1644, Part 1*. Cambridge: Cambridge University Press.

Moule, A.C. (1923). "The Bore on the Ch'ien-T'ang River in China." *T'oung Pao*, Second Series, Vol. 22, No. 3 (July), pp. 135 – 188.

_____ (1920). "The Fire-Proof Warehouses of Lin-an." *New China Review*, Vol. 2, No. 2 (April), pp. 207 – 210.

_____ (1937). "Marco Polo's Description of Quinsai." *T'oung Pao*, Vol. 33, No. 2, pp. 105 – 128.

_____ (1957). *Quinsai, with Other Notes on Marco Polo*. Cambridge: Cambridge University Press.

Moule, Arthur E. (1891). *New China and Old: Personal Recollections and Observations of Thirty Years*. London: Seeley.

_____ (1891A). *The Story of the Cheh-Kiang Mission of the Church Missionary Society (4th Edition)*. London: Church Missionary Society.

Moule, G.E. (1889). "Early Chinese Testimony to Matteo Ricci." *The Chinese Recorder and Missionary Journal*, Vol. 20, No. 2 (February), pp. 81 – 83.

_____ (1907). *Notes on Hangchow, Past and Present (2nd Edition)*. Private Printing.

_____ (1890). "A Roman Catholic Cemetery near Hangzhou." *The Chinese Recorder and Missionary Journal*, Vol. 21, No. 11 (November), pp. 509 – 512.

Moule, G.T. (1921). "The Hangchow Bore." *New China Review*, Vol. 3 (August), pp. 289 – 301.

Mu Guo (2010), "The Yiwu Market Model of China's Exhibition Economy," *Provincial China*, Vol. 2, No. 1 (September), pp. 91 – 115

Mungello, David E. (1985). *Curious Land: Jesuit Accommodation and the Origins of Sinology*. Honolulu: University of Hawai'i Press.

_____ (1994). *The Forgotten Christians of Hangzhou*. Honolulu: University of Hawai'i Press.

Needham, Joseph (1969). *The Grand Titration: Science and Society in East and West*. London: Allen & Unwin.

_____ (1971). *Science & Civilization in China, Volume 4: Physics and Physical Technology, Part III: Civil Engineering and Nautics*. Cambridge: Cambridge University Press.

Nevius, Helen S.C. (1869). *Our Life in China*. New York: Robert Carter.

Odoric of Pordenone (2002). *The Travels of Friar Odoric*. (Henry Yule, Trans.). Grand Rapids MI: Wm. B. Eerdmans.

O'Keefe, Amy (2013). "Stars in the Nation's Skies: The Ascent and Trajectory of the Chinese Aviation Celebrity in the Prewar Decade," in Pickowicz, Paul G., Shen Kuiyi, and Zhang Yingjin, Liangyou: *Kaleidoscopic Modernity and the Shanghai Global Metropolis, 1926 – 1945*. Leiden:

Brill, pp. 135 – 160.

Oliver, Jay Charles (1974). *Memoirs: "Lest We Forget."* Self-Published.

Osborne, Anne (1998). "Economic and Ecological Interactions in the Lower Yangzi Region under the Qing," in Elvin, Mark and Liu Ts'ui-jung, *Sediments of Time: Environment and Society in Chinese History*. Cambridge: Cambridge University Press, pp. 203 – 234.

Ouyang Xiu (2004) (Richard L. Davis, Trans.). *Historical Records of the Five Dynasties*. New York: Columbia University Press.

Owyoung, Steven D. (2000). "The Connoisseurship of Tea: A Translation and Commentary on the '*P'in-ch'a*' Section of the *Record of Superlative Things* by Wen Chen-heng (1585 – 1645). *Kaikodo Journal* (Spring), pp. 25 – 50.

Paludan, Ann (1998). *Chronicle of the Chinese Emperors: The Reign-by-Reign Record of the Rulers of Imperial China*. London: Thames & Hudson.

Paradis, Michel (2020). *Last Mission to Tokyo*. New York: Simon & Schuster.

Park, J.P. (2011). "The Art of Being Artistic: Painting Manuals of Late Ming China (1550 – 1644) and the Negotiation of Taste." *Artibus Asiae*, Vol. 71, No. 3, pp. 5 – 54.

Peattie, Mark R. (1989). "Japanese Treaty Port Settlements in China, 1895 – 1937," in Duus, Peter, Ramon H. Myers, and Mark R. Peattie, *The Japanese Informal Empire in China, 1895 – 1937*. Princeton: Princeton University Press, pp. 166 – 209.

Peterson, Barbara Bennett (2000). *Notable Women of China: Shang Dynasty to the Early Twentieth Century*. Armonk: M.E. Sharpe.

Peterson, Charles A. (1978). "Old Illusions and New Realities: Sung Foreign Policy, 1217 – 1234," in Rossabi, Morris, *China Among Equals: The Middle Kingdom and Its Neighbors, 10th – 14th Centuries*. Berkeley: University of California Press, pp. 204 – 240.

Pietz, David A. (2015). *The Yellow River: The Problem of Water in Modern China*. Cambridge: Harvard University Press.

Pinger, Ruan (1994). "Yue Ware: The Distribution of Manufacturing Sites and Markets," in Ho Chuimei, *New Light on Chinese Yue and Longquan Wares: Archaeological Ceramics Found in Eastern and Southern Asia, A.D. 800 – 1400*. Hong Kong: University of Hong Kong Press, pp. 3 – 20.

Platt, Stephen R. (2012). *Autumn in the Heavenly Kingdom: China, the West, and the Epic Story of the Taiping Civil War*. New York: Knopf.

Pollard, David (2000). *The Chinese Essay*. New York: Columbia University Press.

Polo, Marco (1903) (Henry Yule, Trans., Henri Cordier (Ed.). *Book of Ser Marco Polo, the Venetian Concerning the Kingdoms and Marvels of the East, Volume 2*. New York: Charles Scribner's Sons.

_____ (1993). (Henry Yule, Trans., Henri Cordier (Ed.). *The Travels of Marco Polo: The Complete Yule-Cordier Edition, Volume II*. Mineola NY: Dover.

Pomfret, John (2016). *The Beautiful Country and the Middle Kingdom: America and China, 1776 to the Present*. New York: Henry Holt.

Pozzi, Laura (2014). "'Chinese Children Rise Up!': Representations of Children in the Work of the Cartoon Propaganda Corps during the Second Sino-Japanese War." *Cross-Currents: East Asian History and Culture Review*, E-Journal No. 13 (December), pp. 99 – 133.

_____ (2018). "Humor, War and Politics in *San Mao Joins the Army*: A Comparison Between the Comic Strips (1946) and the Film (1992)," in Tam King-fai and Sharon R. Wesoky, *Not Just a Laughing Matter: Interdisciplinary Approaches to Political Humor in China*. Singapore: Springer Nature, pp. 39 – 56.

Pregadio, Fabrizio (1997). "Shen Gua," in Selin, Helaine. *Encyclopaedia of the History of Science, Technology, and Medicine in Non-Western Cultures*. Dordrecht, The Netherlands: Kluwer Academic Publishers, pp. 894 – 895.

Preston, Diana (2001). *The Boxer Rebellion: The Dramatic Story of China's War on Foreigners that*

Shook the World in the Summer of 1900. New York: Berkley Publishing.

Purtle, Jennifer (2018). "Guan Daosheng and the Idea of a Great Woman Artist." *Orientations*, Vol. 49, No. 2 (March/April), pp. 1 – 9.

_____ (2011). "The Icon of the Woman Artist: Guan Daosheng (1262 – 1319) and the Power of Painting at the Ming Court c. 1500," in Brown, Rebecca M. and Deborah S. Hutton, *A Companion to Asian Art and Architecture.* Chichester, West Sussex, UK: Wiley-Blackwell, pp. 290 - 317.

Qian Zhongshu (1998), (Ronald Egan, Trans.). *Limited Views: Essays on Ideas and Letters.* Cambridge: Harvard University Press.

Qin Ling (2013). "The Liangzhu Culture," in Underhill (2013), pp. 574 – 596.

Rankin, Mary Backus (1970). *Early Chinese Revolutionaries: Radical Intellectuals in Shanghai and Chekiang, 1902 – 1911.* Cambridge: Harvard University Press.

_____ (1986). *Elite Activism and Political Transformation in China: Zhejiang Province, 1865 – 1911.* Stanford: Stanford University Press.

_____ (1975). "The Emergence of Women at the End of the Ch'ing: The Case of Ch'iu Chin," in Wolf, Margery and Roxane Witke, *Women in Chinese Society.* Stanford: Stanford University Press, pp. 39 – 66.

_____ (1976). "Local Reform Currents in Chekiang before 1900," in Cohen, Paul and John Schrecker, *Reform in Nineteenth Century China.* Cambridge: Harvard University Press, pp. 221 – 230.

_____ (2002). "Nationalistic Contestation and Mobilization Politics: Practice and Rhetoric of Railway-Rights Recovery at the End of the Qing." *Modern China*, Vol 28, No. 3 (July), pp. 315 – 361.

Reed, Frances Miriam (2018). *China 1908: Sidney D. Gamble & Brother Clarence Discover China.* CreateSpace.

Reid, Daniel (2012). *The Art and Alchemy of Chinese Tea.* London: Singing Dragon.

Remick, Elizabeth J. (2014). *Regulating Prostitution in China: Gender and Local Statebuilding, 1900 – 1937.* Stanford: Stanford University Press.

Rexroth, Kenneth (1971). *One Hundred Poems from the Chinese.* New York: New Directions.

_____ and Ling Chung (1979). *Li Ch'ing Chao: Complete Poems.* New York: New Directions.

_____ and Ling Chung (1972). *The Orchid Boat: Women Poets of China.* New York: McGraw-Hill.

Rhoads, Edward J.M. (2000) *Manchus & Han: Ethnic Relations and Political Power in Late Qing and Early Republican China, 1861 – 1928.* Seattle: University of Washington Press.

Ridgway, Benjamin (2020). "The City as a Garden: The Emergence of the Geo-poetic Collection in Dong Sigao's 'One Hundred Poems on West Lake'." *Journal of Song-Yuan Studies*, Vol. 49, pp. 239 – 294.

_____ (2017). "A City of Substance: Regional Custom and the Political Landscape of Shaoxing in a Southern Song Rhapsody," in Lam, Joseph S. C., et. al., *Senses of the City: Perceptions of Hangzhou and Southern Song China, 1127 – 1279.* Hong Kong: The Chinese University Press, pp. 235 – 254.

Riegel, Jeffrey (2010). "Yuan Mei (1716 – 1798) and a Different 'Elegant Gathering.'" *Chinese Literature: Essays, Articles, Reviews (CLEAR)*, Vol. 32 (December), pp. 95 – 112.

Rivers, William A. (1903) (Pseudonym, Paul King) *Anglo-Chinese Sketches.* Shanghai: Kelly & Walsh.

Roberts, Claire (1998). "Tradition and Modernity: The Life and Art of Pan Tianshou (1897 – 1971), *East Asian History* 15/16 (June /December), pp. 67 – 96.

Rose, Sarah (2010). *For All the Tea in China: How England Stole the World's Favorite Drink and Changed History.* New York: Viking.

Rosen, Barbara, Norman Bock, Jen Ching-lan, et. al. (2009). "The Wandering Life of Sanmao." *Children's Literature*, Vol. 15, pp. 120 – 138.

Rossabi, Morris (1978). *China Among Equals: The Middle Kingdom and Its Neighbors, 10th – 14th Centuries*. Berkeley: University of California Press.

Roxburgh, Helen (2017). "Welcome to Yiwu: China's Testing Ground for a Multicultural City." *Theguardian.com*, March 23.

Ruan Pinger (1994). "Yue Ware: The Distribution of Manufacturing Sites and Markets," in Ho Chuimei, *New Light on Chinese Yue and Longquan Wares: Archaeological Ceramics Found in Eastern and Southern Asia, A.D. 800 – 1400*. Hong Kong: University of Hong Kong Press, pp. 3 – 20.

Rui Huaichuan (2018). "Yiwu: Historical Transformation and Contributing Factors." *History and Anthropology*, Vol. 29, Sup.1, pp. S14 – S30.

Russell, Bertrand (1998). *Autobiography*. London: Routledge.

Schmidt, J.D. (2003). *Harmony Garden: The Life, Literary Criticism, and Poetry of Yuan Mei*. London: Routledge.

_____ (2008). "Yuan Mei (1716 – 98) on Women." *Late Imperial China*, Vol. 29, No. 2 (December), pp. 129 – 185.

Schoppa, R. Keith (1995). *Blood Road: The Mystery of Shen Dingyi in Revolutionary China*. Berkeley: University of California Press.

_____ (1982). *Chinese Elites and Political Change: Zhejiang Province in the Early Twentieth Century*. Cambridge: Harvard University Press.

_____ (2011). *In a Sea of Bitterness*. Cambridge: Harvard University Press.

_____ (1989). *Xiang Lake: Nine Centuries of Chinese Life*. New Haven: Yale University Press.

Schwarcz, Vera (1986). *The Chinese Enlightenment: Intellectuals and the Legacy of the May Fourth Movement of 1919*. Berkeley: University of California Press.

Scidmore, Eliza Ruhamah (1900). "The Greatest Wonder in the Chinese World: The Marvelous Bore of Hang-chau." *The Century Magazine*, Vol. LIX, No. 6 (April), pp. 852 – 859.

Scott, James M. (2015). *Target Tokyo: Jimmy Doolittle and the Raid that Avenged Pearl Harbor*. New York: W.W. Norton.

_____ (2015A). "The Untold Story of the Vengeful Japanese Attack after the Doolittle Raid." *Smithsonianmag.com* (April 15).

Scott, John (1973). *The Lecherous Academician and Other Tales by Master Ling Mengchu*. London: Rapp and Whiting.

Shahar, Meir (1992). "The Lingyin Si Monkey Disciples and the Origins of Sun Wukong." *Harvard Journal of Asiatic Studies*, Vol. 52, No. 1 (June), p. 193.

Shao Jianchun and Wu Hongyun (2020). "A Study on the Monk Official Yang Lianzhenjia in the Yuan Dynasty." 3rd International Conference on Interdisciplinary Social Sciences & Humanities (SOSHU).

Shaw, Yu-ming (1992). *An American Missionary in China: John Leighton Stuart and Chinese-American Relations*. Cambridge: Council on East Asian Studies, Harvard University (Harvard East Asian Monographs – 158).

_____ (1982). "John Leighton Stuart and U.S. – Chinese Communist Rapprochement in 1949: Was There Another 'Lost Chance in China'?" *The China Quarterly*, No. 89 (March), pp. 74 – 96).

Shen Gua (2011). *Brush Talks from Dream Brook*. (Wang Hong and Zhao Zheng, Trans.). Reading UK: Paths International.

Shen Kuyi (2010). "Wu Changshuo: The Last Scholar-Official Painter," in Yang Xiaoneng, *Tracing the Past Drawing the Future: Master Ink Painters in Twentieth-Century China*. Milan IT: 5 Continents Editions, pp. 73 – 83.

Shi Hengtan (2019) (Charlie Li, Trans.). "The Spiritual Heritage of Tianshui Church in Hangzhou." *China Christian Daily* (November 29).

Shi Nai'an (2006). *All Men Are Brothers*. (Pearl Buck, Trans.). Chicago: Moyer Bell.

Shi Yafeng (1994). "Professor Zhu Kezhen Opening Up a Path for Research on Climatic Change in China." *Chinese Geographical Science*, Vol. 4, No. 2, pp. 186 – 192.

Shiba, Yoshinobu (1977). "Ningpo and Its Hinterland," in Skinner (1977), pp. 391 – 439.

Shimada Kenji (1990). *Pioneer of the Chinese Revolution: Zhang Binglin and Confucianism*. Stanford: Stanford University Press.

Short, Philip (2000). *Mao: A Life*. New York: Henry Holt.

Shu Jiaping (2015) (Lee Yun Kuen, Trans.). "The Tomb of Emperor Sui Yangdi at Caozhuang in Yangzhou City, Jiangsu." *Chinese Archaeology*, Vol. 15, pp. 73 – 79.

Shurtleff, William and Akiko Aoyagi (2016). *Biography of Yamei Kin M.D. (1864 – 1934), (Also Known as 金韻梅 Jin Yunmei), the First Chinese Woman to Take a Medical Degree in the United States*. Lafayette CA: Soyinfo Center.

Sim, Y.H. Teddy (2017). *The Maritime Defense of China: Ming General Qi Jiguang and Beyond*. Singapore: Springer Nature.

Sima Qian (2007) (Yang Xianyi and Gladys Yang, Trans.). *Selections from Records of the Historian*. Beijing: Foreign Languages Press.

Siu Wang-Ngai (1997). *Chinese Opera: Images and Stories*. Vancouver BC: University of British Columbia Press.

Sivin, Nathan (1977). "Shen Kua: A Preliminary Assessment of His Scientific Thought and Achievements." *Sung Studies Newsletter*, No. 13, pp. 31 – 56. Reprinted from *The Dictionary of Scientific Biography, Vol. 12*. New York: Scribner, 1975.

Skinner, G. William (1977). *The City in Late Imperial China*. Stanford: Stanford University Press.

Skinner, Mark W., Richard G. Kuhn, and Alun E. Joseph. "Agricultural Land Protection in China: A Case Study of Local Governance in Zhejiang Province." *Land Use Policy*, Vol. 18 (2001), pp. 329 – 340.

Smith, George (1859). "Journal of a Visit to Ningpo and Hangchow, and the Adjacent Parts of Che Keang." *The Church Missionary Intelligencer*, Vol. 9 (May, June), pp. 97 – 112, 121 – 131.

Smith, Joanna Handlin (2009). *The Art of Doing Good: Charity in Late Ming China*. Berkeley: University of California Press.

_____ (1992). "Gardens in Ch'i Piao-chia's Social World: Wealth and Values in Late-Ming Kiangnan," *The Journal of Asian Studies*, Vol. 51, No. 1 (February), pp. 55 – 81.

Smith, Paul (1991). *Taxing Heaven's Storehouse: Horses, Bureaucrats, and the Destruction of the Sichuan Tea Industry, 1074 – 1224*. Cambridge: Harvard University Press.

So Kwan-wai (1975). *Japanese Piracy in Ming China during the Sixteenth Century*. East Lansing: Michigan State University Press.

Song Weijie (2014). "The Aesthetics versus the Political: Lin Huiyin and Modern Beijing." *Chinese Literature: Essays, Articles, Reviews (CLEAR)*, Vol. 36 (December), pp. 61 – 94.

Spence, Jonathan D. (1981). *The Gate of Heavenly Peace: The Chinese and Their Revolution, 1895 – 1980*. New York: Viking, 1981.

_____ (1997). *God's Chinese Son: The Taiping Heavenly Kingdom of Hong Xiuquan*. New York: W.W. Norton.

_____ (2007). *Return to Dragon Mountain: Memories of a Late Ming Man*. New York: Viking Penguin.

_____ (1991). *The Search for Modern China*. New York: W.W. Norton.

_____ (2001). *Treason by the Book*. New York: Penguin Group.

_____ (1966). *Ts'ao Yin and the K'ang-hsi Emperor, Bondservant and Master*. New Haven: Yale University Press.

Standaert, N. (1988). *Yang Tingyun, Confucian and Christian in Late Ming China*. Leiden: Brill.

Stanley, C. John. (1961). *Late Ch'ing Finance: Hu Kuang-yung as an Innovator*. Harvard East Asian

Monographs #12. Chinese Economic and Political Studies V. Cambridge: East Asian Research Center, Harvard University.

Stanley-Baker, Joan (1995). *Old Masters Repainted: Wu Zhen, 1280 – 1354: Prime Objects and Accretions*. Hong Kong: Hong Kong University Press.

State Administration of Cultural Heritage of People's Republic of China (2009). *Cultural Heritage Nominated by People's Republic of China, West Lake Cultural Landscape of Hangzhou*. (December).

Stenberg, Joshua Sidney (2009). *The Warrior Maiden and the Divorcée: The Universal Past Tense of the Traditional Chinese Theatre*. M.A. Thesis, University of British Columbia.

Strassberg, Richard E. (1994). *Inscribed Landscapes: Travel Writing from Imperial China*. Berkeley: University of California Press.

Struve, Lynn (1993). *Voices from the Ming-Qing Cataclysm: China in Tigers' Jaws*. New Haven: Yale University Press. .

Stuart, Jan (1990). "Ming Dynasty Gardens Reconstructed in Words and Images." *Journal of Garden History*, Vol. 10, No. 3, pp. 162 – 172.

Stuart, John Leighton (1954). *Fifty Years in China: The Memoirs of John Leighton Stuart, Missionary and Ambassador*. New York: Random House.

Sturton, Stephen D. (1945). "The Site of the Nestorian Monastery in Hangchow." *The Asiatic Review*, pp. 82 – 85.

Sudworth, John (2013). "The Scissor-maker that Has Cut through Chinese History," *BBC News* (April 22).

Sullivan, Michael (1996). *Art and Artists of Twentieth-century China*. Berkeley: University of California Press.

_____ (1961). *An Introduction to Chinese Art*. Berkeley: University of California Press.

Sun, E-Tu Zen (1951). "The Shanghai-Hangchow-Ningpo Railway Loan of 1908." *The Far Eastern Quarterly*, Vol. 10, No. 2 (February), pp. 136 – 150.

Sun Guoping (2013). "Recent Research on the Hemudu Culture and the Tianluoshan Site," in Underhill (2013), pp. 555 – 573.

Sun Peifang (2021). "Heritage Conservation and New Plan of the Deshou Palace Block." *Art and Design Review*, Vol. 9 (May), pp. 148 – 155.

Sun Xiaoxing (1994). "The City Should Be Rich in the Pleasures of Wild Nature – A Traditional Aesthetic Concept of China for Urban Planning. *Ekistics*, Vol. 61, No. 364/365 (January/April).

Sun Zhixin (1993). "The Liangzhu Culture: Its Discovery and Its Jades." *Early China*, Vol. 18, pp. 1 – 40.

Swope, Kenneth M. (2017). "Cutting Dwarf Pirates Down to Size: Amphibious Warfare in 16th-Century East Asia," in Sim (2017), pp. 163 – 186.

Tang Wei (2013). *The Grand Canal: World Heritage Convention, Cultural Heritage Nominated by People's Republic of China*. Beijing: State Administration of Cultural Heritage of People's Republic of China.

_____ (2009). *West Lake Cultural Landscape of Hangzhou: World Heritage Convention, Cultural Heritage Nominated by People's Republic of China*. Beijing: State Administration of Cultural Heritage of People's Republic of China.

Thornton, Suzanna (1996). "Provinces, City Gods and Salt Merchants: Provincial Identity in Ming and Qing Dynasty Hangzhou," in Liu Tao Tao and David Faure, *Unity and Diversity Local Cultures and Identities in China*. Hong Kong: Hong Kong University Press, pp. 15 - 35

Tien H. Yuan (1981). "Demography in China: From Zero to Now." *Population Index*, Vol. 47, No. 4 (Winter), pp. 683 – 710.

Tregear, Thomas R. (1965). *A Geography of China*. London: University of London Press.

Treutlein, Theodore E. (1941). "Jesuit Missions in China during the Last Years of K'ang Hsi," *Pa-*

cific Historical Review, Vol. 10, No. 4 (December), pp. 435 – 446.

Tsai Shu-wei (2020). *Heritage Modernity: Heritagization of the Grand Canal and Everyday Life in Hangzhou, China*. Doctoral Dissertation, University of California, Berkeley.

Tsien Tsuen-Hsuin (1985). "Part I: Paper and Printing," in Needham, Joseph, *Science and Civilisation in China, Volume 5: Chemistry and Chemical Technology*. Cambridge: Cambridge University Press.

Tu Xingeng, et. al. (2010). *Hangzhou Statistical Yearbook, 2010*. Beijing: China Statistics Press.

Tuchman, Barbara (1971). *Stillwell and the American Experience in China, 1911 – 45*. New York: Macmillan.

Twitchett, Denis and John K. Fairbank (2009).. *The Cambridge History of China: Vol. 5, Part One, The Sung Dynasty and Its Precursors, 907 – 1279*. Cambridge: Cambridge University Press.

Underhill, Anne P. (2013). *A Companion to Chinese Archaeology*. Hoboken NJ: Wiley.

UNESCO World Heritage Nomination Document [Grand Canal].

Van Bibber-Orr, Edwin (2013). *A Feminine Canon: Li Qingzhao and Zhu Shuzhen*. Doctoral Dissertation, Yale University.

VanderVen, Elizabeth R. (2012). *A School in Every Village: Educational Reform in a Northeast China County, 1904 – 31*. Vancouver: University of British Columbia Press.

Van Gulik, R.H. (1974). *Sexual Life in Ancient China: A Preliminary Survey of Chinese Sex and Society from 1500 B.C. till 1644 A.D.* in *Sinica Leidensia, Vol. LVII*. Leiden: Brill.

Volpp, Sophie (2001). "Drinking Wine and Reading 'Encountering Sorrow': A Reflection in Disguise, by Wu Zao (1799 – 1862)," in Mann, Susan and Yu-Yin Cheng. *Under Confucian Eyes: Writings on Gender in Chinese History*. Berkeley: University of California Press, p. 239 – 250.

Von Richtofen, Ferdinand, Freiherr (1903). *Baron Richtofen's Letters, 1870 - 1872*. Shanghai: North China Herald.

Wade, Henling T. (Ed.) (1895). *With Boat and Gun in the Yangtze Valley*. Shanghai: *Shanghai Mercury* Office.

Wakeman, Frederic (Jr.) (1985). *The Great Enterprise: The Manchu Reconstruction of Imperial Order in Seventeenth Century China*. Berkeley: University of California Press.

_____ (1995). *Policing Shanghai, 1927 – 1937*. Berkeley: University of California Press.

Waley, Arthur (1949). *The Life and Times of Po Chü-i, 772 – 846 A.D.* London: George Allen & Unwin.

_____ (1958). *The Opium War through Chinese Eyes*. London: Allen & Unwin.

_____ (1956). *Yuan Mei, Eighteenth Century Chinese Poet*. London: Allen & Unwin.

Waley-Cohen, Joanna (2000). "Collective Responsibility in Qing Criminal Law," in Turner, Karen G, James V. Feinerman, and R. Kent Guy, *The Limits of Rule of Law in China*. Seattle: University of Washington Press, pp. 112 – 131.

Wan Yinmei (2008). *Managing Post-Merger Integration: A Case Study of a Merger in Chinese Higher Education*. Doctoral Dissertation, University of Michigan.

Wang, David Der-wei (2010). "Introduction," in Chang, Eileen, *The Fall of the Pagoda*. Hong Kong: Hong Kong University Press.

_____ (2017). *A New Literary History of Modern China*. Cambridge: Belknap Press.

Wang, Eugene Y. (2003). "Tope and Topos: The Leifeng Pagoda and the Discourse of the Demonic" in Zeitlin, Judith T., Lydia H. Liu, and Ellen Widmer, *Writing and Materiality in China: Essays in Honor of Patrick Hanan*. Harvard-Yenching Monograph Series, 58. Cambridge: Harvard University Asia Center), pp. 488 – 552.

Wang Huai (2011). "Mao Zedong at West Lake, A Chronology, Part I: 1953 – 59." (Geremie R. Barmé, Trans.). *China Heritage Quarterly*, No. 28 (December).

_____ (2012). "Mao Zedong at West Lake, A Chronology, Part II: 1960 – 76." (Geremie R. Barmé, Trans.). *China Heritage Quarterly*, No. 29 (March).

Wang Huiming (1982). *Folk Tales of the West Lake*. Beijing: Foreign Languages Press.

Wang Jiaosheng (1989). "The Complete *Ci*-poems of Li Qingzhao: A New English Translation." *Sino-Platonic Papers*, No. 13 (October).

Wang Jinmin (2010). "Social Networks, Innovation and the Development of Industrial Clusters in China," in Yao Shujie, et. al., *Sustainable Reform and Development in Post-Olympic China*. London: Routledge, pp. 97 – 107.

Wang Lingzhen (2004). *Personal Matters: Women's Autobiographical Practice in Twentieth-Century China*. Stanford: Stanford University Press.

Wang Liping (2011). "Emperor Kangxi's Southern Tours and the Qing Restoration of West Lake." *China Heritage Quarterly*, No. 28 (December).

_____ (1999). "Tourism and Spatial Change in Hangzhou, 1911 – 1927," pp. 107 – 120 in Esherick, Joseph W., *Remaking the Chinese City: Modernity and National Identity, 1900 – 1950*. Honolulu: University of Hawai'i Press.

Wang Mi (2018). *Resource and Social Identity: Jade Usage in the Neolithic Liangzhu Culture, China, and the Modern Display and Uses of Liangzhu Jade Artifacts*. M.A. Thesis, Boston University.

Wang Ping (2012). "From Luzhen to Sendai: Locality and Metonym in Lu Xun's Pseudonyms." *Provincial China*, Vol. 4, No. 1, pp. 27 – 67.

Wang-Riese, Xiaobing (2014). "Globalization vs. Localization: Remaking the Cult of Confucius in Contemporary Quzhou," in Jansen, Thomas, Thoralf Klein, and Christian Meyer, *Globalization and the Making of Religious Modernity in China: Transnational Religions, Local Agents, and the Study of Religion, 1800 – Present*. Leiden: Brill, pp. 182 – 207.

Wang Xiaoping (2019). *Contending for the "Chinese Modern": The Writing of Fiction in the Great Transformative Epoch of Modern China, 1937 – 1949*. Leiden: Brill.

Wang, Y.C. (1965). "The *Su-Pao* Case: A Study of Foreign Pressure, Intellectual Fermentation, and Dynastic Decline." *Monumenta Serica*, No. 24, pp. 84 – 129.

Wang Yanning (2013). *Reverie and Reality: Poetry on Travel by Late Imperial Chinese Women*. Lanham MD: Lexington.

Wang Yugen (2011). "The Limits of Poetry as Means of Social Criticism: The 1079 Literary Inquisition against Su Shi Revisited." *Journal of Song-Yuan Studies*, Vol, 41, pp. 29 – 65.

Wang Zuoyue (2008). "Zhu Kezhen," in Koertge, Noretta, *New Dictionary of Scientific Biography*. Detroit: Charles Scribner's Sons, pp. 402 – 405.

Waterson, James (2013). *Defending Heaven: China's Mongol Wars, 1209 – 1370*. London: Frontline Books.

Watson, Burton (1973). *The Old Man Who Does as He Pleases: Selections from the Poetry and Prose of Lu Yu*. New York: Columbia University Press.

Watson, Philip (2007). *Grand Canal, Great River: The Travel Diary of a Twelfth-Century Chinese Poet*. London: Francis Lincoln.

Watt, James C.Y. (2011). *The World of Khubilai Khan: Chinese Art in the Yuan Dynasty*. New York: Metropolitan Museum of Art.

Watt, John R. (1977). "The Yamen and Urban Administration," in Skinner (1977), pp. 353 – 390.

Wei, Betty Peh-t'i (2006). *Ruan Yuan, 1764 – 1849: The Life and Work of a Major Scholar-Official in Nineteenth-Century China before the Opium War*. Hong Kong: Hong Kong University Press.

Wei Djao (2010). *A Blossom Like No Other: Li Qingzhao*. Toronto: Ginger Post.

Wei, Yehua Dennis (2015). *Urban Land Expansion and Structural Change in Shanghai, Suzhou, and Hangzhou*. Cambridge MA: Lincoln Institute of Land Policy.

Weidner, Marsha (1990). "The Conventional Success of Ch'en Shu," in Weidner, Marsha, *Flowering in the Shadows: Women in the History of Chinese and Japanese Painting*. Honolulu: University of Hawai'i Press, pp. 123 – 156.

_____ (1990A). "Introduction: Images and Realities," in Weidner, Marsha, *Flowering in the Shadows: Women in the History of Chinese and Japanese Painting*. Honolulu: University of Hawaii Press, pp. 1 – 25.

_____ (2006). "Picturing Monks as Connoisseurs and Monasteries as Sites of Aesthetic Engagement," in *Zurich Studies in the History of Art, Georges-Bloch Annual 13/14*. Zurich: University of Zurich, pp. 399 – 417.

_____ (1988). *Views from the Jade Terrace: Chinese Women Artists, 1300 – 1912*. Indianapolis: Indianapolis Museum of Art.

Welsh, Mary Sue (2012). *One Woman in a Hundred: Edna Phillips and the Philadelphia Orchestra*. Champaign: University of Illinois Press.

Welter, Albert (2016). "Confucian Monks and Buddhist Junzi: Zanning's Topical Compendium of the Buddhist Clergy and the Politics of Buddhist Accommodation at the Song Court," in Jülch, Thomas, *The Middle Kingdom and the Dharma Wheel: Aspects of the Relationship between the Buddhist Samgha and the State in Chinese History*. Leiden: Brill, pp. 222 - 277.

Weston, Timothy B. (2004). *The Power of Position: Beijing University, Intellectuals, and Chinese Political Culture, 1898 – 1929*. Berkeley: University of California Press.

Wheeler, C.E. (2016). "Letter from Quzhou: When Thunder Comes." *Brush Talks*, Vol 1, No. 1 (Winter/Spring), pp. 29 – 38.

White, E. Aldersey (1932). *A Woman Pioneer in China: The Life of Mary Ann Aldersey*. London: The Livingstone Press.

Widmer, Ellen (2006). *The Beauty and the Book: Women and Fiction in Nineteenth-Century China*. Cambridge: Harvard University Press.

_____ (1989). "The Epistolary World of Female Talent in Seventeenth-Century China." *Late Imperial China*, Vol. 10, No. 2 (December), pp. 1 – 43.

_____ (2006A). "Foreign Travel through a Woman's Eyes: Shan Shili's 'Guimao luxing ji' in Local and Global Perspective." *The Journal of Asian Studies*, Vol. 65, No. 4 (November), pp. 763 – 791.

_____ (2007). "Gentility in Transition: Travels, Novels, and the New *Guixiu*," in Berg, Daria and Chloë Starr (2007A), pp. 21 – 44.

_____ (1996). "The Huanduzhai of Hangzhou and Suzhou: A Study in Seventeenth-Century Publishing." *Harvard Journal of Asiatic Studies*, Vol. 56, No. 1 (June), pp. 77 – 122.

_____ (1992). "Xiaoqing's Literary Legacy and the Place of the Woman Writer." *Late Imperial China*, Vol. 13, pp. 111 – 155.

Williams, Peter and David Wallace (1989). *Unit 731*. London: Hodder & Stoughton.

Williams, Samuel Wells (1883). *The Middle Kingdom: A Survey of the Geography, Government, Literature, Social Life, Arts and History of the Chinese Empire and Its Inhabitants (Vol. 2)*. New York: Charles Scribner's Sons.

Wills, John E., Jr. (2012). *Mountain of Fame: Portraits in Chinese History*. Princeton: Princeton University Press.

Wilson, Andrew (1868). *The 'Ever-Victorious Army': A History of the Chinese Campaign Under Lt.-Col. C.G. Gordon, CBRE, and of the Suppression of the Tai-Ping Rebellion*. Edinburgh: William Blackwood and Sons.

Wong Yoon-Wah (1988). *Essays on Chinese Literature: A Comparative Approach*. Singapore: Singapore University Press.

_____ (2002). *Post-Colonial Chinese Literatures in Singapore and Malaysia*. Singapore: National University of Singapore.

Woo, Ryan (2021). "Hangzhou Tops EIU Chart of Chinese Cities with Most Economic Potential," *Reuters*, September 8.

Wood, Frances and Christopher Arnander (2016). *Betrayed Ally: China in the Great War*. South Yorkshire: Pen & Sword Military.

Worthy, Edmund H. (1978). "Diplomacy for Survival: Domestic and Foreign Relations of Wu Yüeh, 907 – 978, in Rossabi, Morris, *China Among Equals: The Middle Kingdom and Its Neighbors, 10th – 14th Centuries* (Berkeley: University of California Press), pp. 17 – 44.

Wright, Arthur F. (1977). "The Cosmology of the Chinese City," in Skinner (1977), pp. 33 – 74.

Wu Huixin (2014). "Ancient Villages a Reminder of the Old Ways." *ShanghaiDaily.com* (April 9). Accessed at https://archive.shine.cn/city-specials/hangzhou/Ancient-villages-a-reminder-of-the-old-ways/shdaily.shtml .

_____ (2020). "Seawall Museum Shows How Hangzhou Turned the Tides" (March 26), at https://www.shine.cn/feature/art-culture/2003265092/.

Wu Jiangzhong (2005). *The Library of the 21st Century*. San Francisco: Long River Press.

Wu Qingyun (1995). *Female Rule in Chinese and English Literary Utopias*. Syracuse NY: Syracuse University Press.

Xiao Yu [Siao-Yu] (1959). *Mao Tse-Tung and I Were Beggars*. Syracuse: Syracuse University Press.

Xie Jing (2016). "Disembodied Historicity: Southern Song Imperial Street in Hangzhou." *Journal of the Society of Architectural Historians*, Vol. 75, No. 2 (June), pp. 182 – 200.

Xiong, Victor Cunrui (2006). *Emperor Yang of the Sui Dynasty: His Life, Times, and Legacy*. Albany NY: State University of New York Press.

Xu Guangqiu (1997). "Americans and Chinese Nationalist Military Aviation, 1929 – 1949." *Journal of Asian History*, Vol. 31, No. 2, pp. 155 – 180.

Xu Lanjun (2016). "The Lure of Sadness: The Fever of 'Yueju' and 'The Butterfly Lovers' in the Early PRC." *Asian Theatre Journal*, Vol 33, No. 1 (Spring), pp. 104 – 129.

Xu Mingde (1996). "The Outstanding Contribution of the Italian Sinologist Martino Martini to Cultural Exchanges between China and the West," in Demarchi, Franco and Riccardo Scartezzini, *Martino Martini: A Humanist and Scientist in Seventeenth Century China*. Trento IT: Universita degli studi di Trento, pp. 23 – 38.

Xu Zhuoyun (Hsu Cho-yun) (2012). *China: A New Cultural History*. New York: Columbia University Press.

Yan Haiping (2006). *Chinese Women Writers and the Feminist Imagination, 1905 – 1948*. Abingdon, Oxon UK: Routledge.

Yang Jianxin (2010). "The Great Invention with Everlasting Immortal Masterpieces," pp. 25 – 34 in Allen, Susan M., et. al., *The History and Cultural Heritage of Chinese Calligraphy, Printing, and Library Work*. Berlin: De Gruyter Saur.

Yang, Michelle Murray (2011). "President Nixon's Speeches and Toasts During His 1972 Trip to China: A Study in Diplomatic Rhetoric." *Rhetoric and Public Affairs*, Vol. 14, No. 1, pp. 1 – 44.

Yang Xiaoneng (1999). *The Golden Age of Chinese Archaeology: Celebrated Discoveries from the People's Republic of China*. Washington D.C.: National Gallery of Art.

Yang Ye (1999). *Vignettes from the Late Ming: A Hsiao-p'in Anthology*. Seattle: University of Washington Press.

Ye Han (2017). *From Hangzhou to Lin'an: History, Space, and the Experience of Urban Living in Narratives from Song Dynasty China*. Doctoral Dissertation: Arizona State University.

Yeh Ch'iu-yuan (2012). "The Lore of Chinese Seals." *T'ien Hsia Monthly*, Vol. 10, No. 1 (January 1940), reproduced at *China Heritage Quarterly*, No. 29 (March).

Yeh Wen-hsin (1994). "Middle County Radicalism: The May Fourth Movement in Hangzhou." *China Quarterly*, No. 140 (December), pp. 903 – 925.

_____ (1996). *Provincial Passages: Culture, Space, and the Origins of Chinese Communism*. Berkeley: University of California Press.

Yi Lidu (2011). "'He Wore Flowers in His Hair': Understanding a Late Ming through His Mid-Ming Subject." *Ming Studies*, Vol. 64 (September), pp. 33 - 45.

Yi Xu, Bas van Leeuwen, Jan Luiten van Zanden (2018). "Urbanization in China, ca. 1100 – 1900." *Frontiers of Economics in China*, Vol. 13, No. 3, pp. 322 – 368.

Yim, Lawrence C.H. (2009). *The Poet-Historian Qian Qianyi*. New York: Routledge.

You Yuwen (1979). "Ma Yinchu and His Theory of Population," *China Reconstructs*, Vol. 28, No.

12 (December), pp. 28 – 30.

Young, Edward (1874). "The Silk Trade: Exports of Raw Silk from China and Japan for tthe Silk Season, Say from June 1 to May 31, Shanghai," in *Monthly Reports on the Commerce and Navigation of the United States for the Year Ended June 30, 1874* (Washington: Government Printing Office).

Yu Hua (2011). *China in Ten Words*. New York: Pantheon Books.

Yu Liu (2011). "The Spiritual Journey of an Independent Thinker: The Conversion of Li Zhizao to Catholicism.' *Journal of World History*, Vol. 22, No. 3 (September), pp. 433 – 453.

Yu Zhang (2013). *The Female Rewriting of Grand History: The* Tanci *Fiction* Jing Zhong Zhuan. Doctoral Dissertation, University of Oregon.

Yuan Xing (2019). "Wandering between the Inner and the Outer: Travel, Identity and Educational Arguments of the Gentry Women in Late Qing China: A Case Study on Zeng Yi (1852 – 1927) and Shan Shili (1863 – 1945)." *Journal Asiatique*, Vol. 307, No. 1, pp. 135 – 148.

Zang Jian (2003). "Women and the Transmission of Confucian Culture in Song China," in Ko, Dorothy, JaHyun Kim Haboush, and Joan R. Piggott, *Women and Confucian Cultures in Premodern China, Korea, and Japan*. Berkeley: University of California Press, pp. 123 – 141.

Zanini, Livio (2004). "'The Brush-Rest and the Tea Stove.' Xu Cishu's Biography." *Ming Qing Yanjiu*, 2002, pp. 123 – 152.

Zhang Daye (2013). *The World of a Tiny Insect: A Memoir of the Taiping Rebellion and Its Aftermath.* (Tian Xiaofei, Trans.). Seattle: University of Washington Press.

Zhang Haiwei, et. al. (2021) "Collapse of the Liangzhu and Other Neolithic Cultures in the Lower Yangtze Region in Response to Climate Change." *Science Advances*, Vol. 7 (November 24).

Zhao Suisheng (2004). *A Nation-State by Construction: Dynamics of Modern Chinese Nationalism*. Stanford: Stanford University Press.

Zhou Mi (2002) (Ankeney Weitz, Trans.). *Zhou Mi's Record of Clouds and Mist Passing Before One's Eyes: An Annotated Translation*. Leiden, The Netherlands: Brill.

Zhou Ying (2007). *The Dawn of the Oriental Civilization: Liangzhu Site and Liangzhu Culture*. Beijing: China Intercontinental Press.

Zhu Tao (2012). "To Search High and Low: Liang Sicheng, Lin Huiyin, and China's Architectural Historiography, 1932 – 1946." *Scapegoat*, No. 3 (Conference Paper, April 13-14).

Zuo Ya (2018). *Shen Gua's Empiricism*. Harvard Yenching Institute Monograph, Series 113. Cambridge: Harvard University Asia Center.

INDEX

Shanghai, 11, 12, 20, 27, 31, 36, 77, 178, 184, 214, 262, 282, 288, 322, 325, 328, 332, 334, 337, 339, 342-343, 350, 393, 394-395, 410-411, 415, 418, 419, 423-425, 426, 429, 430, 436-437, 467-468, 470, 484-486, 490, 491, 494, 495, 497, 505, 518, 551n3, 551n5, 551n6, 578n74, 579n26, 579n28, 580n16, 581n40, 585n48, 585n49, 586n64, 588n51, 592n33, 593n61, 594n4, 594n30, 596n77, 596n80, 599n56, 601n103, 603n28, 605n75
CPC formation in, 415-416
Early Christianity in, 186, 188
Japanese conflict in, 440-442, 444-446, 447, 451-453, 455-456, 459, 462, 464-465
and Nixon visit, 10, 487, 488
pirate attacks at, 167
railway rights recovery movement, 352-355, 384-386
revolutionary movement in, 351-352, 356, 359, 363, 364, 389-391, 397-398, 400, 403, 405
in Taiping conflict, 291, 293, 296-297, 299-303, 305, 309, 310, 317, 320
Yue Opera and *pingtan* in, 281, 412-414, 481-483
Shangyu (see Shaoxing)
Shannon, Ellis, 444
Shaohao, 25
Shaoxing, 15, 17, 19, 20, 21, 27-28, 34, 111-112, 135, 149, 152-153, 158, 158, 178, 184-185, 211, 213-217, 225, 230-232, 236-240, 245-246, 283, 287, 333-334, 344-347, 392, 401, 405-407, 411, 418-419, 486, 489, 492, 493, 535, 542
government clerks from, 264-266, 558n60. 558n6, 560n16, 562n16, 584n12, 584n13, 584n14, 586n63, 587n24, 590n17, 600n60
Japanese conflict in, 453-454, 469
as Kuaiji/Shangyu, 36, 39, 41, 43, 48-49, 50, 52-53, 56-57, 105, 108, 109, 5553n7, 553n9, 554n9
Lu You and Tang Wan, 116-119
modern development of, 391, 498, 500, 504, 505, 513, 514-515, 546-547
origin of modern name, 105
piracy in, 165, 168-169

revolutionary movement in, 326, 349, 355, 358-361, 387, 397, 430, 432, 513
Taiping conflict in, 293, 298, 303-304, 309, 314, 316-317
tinfoil spirit money from, 264
yellow wine from, 171, 261, 263-264
and Yu the Great (Da Yu), 25-26, 237-240, 263, 269-270
and Yue Opera, 412-414, 481-483, 545, 605n75
as Yuezhou, 65, 75-77, 78, 92, 105, 108, 553n9
Shen Baozhen, 342
Shen Defu, 181
Shen Dehong (see Mao Dun)
Shen Garden, 16, 117-119, 515, 546
Shen Gua, 15, 92-96, 559n25, 559n27, 559n29
Shen Que, 187-188
Shen Shanbao, 323-324, 581n45, 582n47
Shen Zhou, 92, 159, 255
Shennong, 24, 67, 506, 540, 556n17
Shengxian (Shengzhou), town of, 413, 492
Shenyang, 189, 237, 267, 275, 433, 440, 517
Shi Cuntong, 402-404
Shi Kefa, 210
Shi Nai'an, 414
Shi Xingeng, 26, 27
Shigeko, Hattori, 356
Shimonoseki, Treaty of, 342, 343
Sidian (Sacrificial Statutes), 160, 162, 566n20
Siku quanshu (Four Treasuries), 275-277, 320, 451-452
Silk, 40, 99, 101, 256, 261-262, 263, 505, 506, 509, 543, 567n51
Hu Xueyan bankruptcy, 328
in Neolithic cultures, 27
Pictures of Tilling and Weaving, 18, 250-252, 574n85
production of, 25, 86, 170-171, 225, 260, 321-322, 328, 343, 438, 471-472, 481, 549, 581n40, 582n57
sericulture of, 25, 171
Sima Qian, 218, 554n4
Siren, Osvald, 418
Smith, George, 262
Solitary Hill (Gushan), 60, 73, 85, 180, 269, 276, 277, 320, 388, 392, 393, 416, 430, 451, 476, 513, 524, 534, 535, 576n9, 576n10, 591n13

644

Acknowledgments

I am first of all deeply indebted to the hundreds of individuals who have performed the difficult work of accessing, translating, and analyzing historical records and primary source documents to provide the materials needed for a book such as this. Some are giants in the broad field of Chinese history: Timothy Brook, Craig Clunas, John Fairbanks, Jacques Gernet, Luther Carrington Goodrich, Arthur Hummel, Frederick Mote, Joseph Needham, Jonathan Spence, Arthur Waley, and Arthur Wright.

Others have focused on specific areas of study. Too many to name in their entirety, I nevertheless note with gratitude Geremie Barmé, Daria Berg, Ann Burkus-Chasson, James Cahill, Duncan Campbell, Paul Cohen, James Cole, Duan Xiaolin, Grace S. Fong, Keith Forster, Maxwell Hearn, Hu Ying, Lily Xiaohong Lee, Stephen Platt, Mary Backus Rankin, Keith Schoppa, Joanna Handlin Smith, Wang Liping, Marsha Weidner, and Ellen Widmer. My research took almost eight years, but without the benefit of their wide-ranging work and the insight and inspiration their work provided, this book would have been inconceivable. I have strived to the greatest extent possible to recognize their contributions, and everyone else's, by careful footnoting and provision of a lengthy bibliography, but this hardly seems thanks enough.

Well beyond the information-supplying wonders of a judiciously used Internet, I am beholden to the extraordinary research facilities available in my adopted hometown of New York City. The resources of the Research Branch of the New York Public Library (NYPL) in Midtown Manhattan are second to none, as is their institutional dedication to research support even under the dark cloud of a pandemic. Through NYPL's MaRLi program, I am equally indebted to the library network of Columbia University, especially the amazing stacks of the C.V. Starr East Asian Library and the Avery Architectural and Fine Arts Library. MaRLi also allowed me to wander the stacks and access the special collections at the Union Theological Seminary, another source of materials I would never otherwise have discovered. Many thanks as well to the NYPL Library for the Performing Arts and the Thomas J. Watson Library at the Metropolitan Museum of Art.

Additionally, I would like to express my gratitude to Chris Robyn at China Books for his original suggestion to pair my first book about Suzhou with a second one about Hangzhou. His patient shepherding of this one has been greatly appreciated.

Finally, but hardly least, I want to thank my wife Li Ping, without whom neither of my books would ever have been written. Her willingness to be my personal travel organizer, tour guide, interpreter, occasional translator, co-photographer, and general go-to explainer of Chinese language and culture are quietly hidden between the lines of every sentence of this book.

Made in the USA
Middletown, DE
28 October 2023

41378079R10387